Apocalypse in Rome

In memory of John D'Arms

Contents

Illustrations

Maps

Tables

Preface and Acknowledgments

Many statues adorn the Capitoline Hill in Rome: gods and demigods, heroes legendary and forgotten. But only two historical figures stand out from the stone and brick to carry on the ancient tradition of commemoration in bronze. The first dominates the center of Michelangelo's grand plan for the hill and its piazza: the emperor Marcus Aurelius, long mistaken by medieval Romans for Constantine the Great. The other stands down the grand stair, and a little to the periphery: that of the fourteenth-century Roman Cola di Rienzo. Rienzo's place there is not accidental, for in the minds of modern Romans, and Italians, he both symbolizes the rebirth of the dreams of united Italy so massively spelled out by the power and authority of Marcus Aurelius and to an extent, he rises as a counterpoise and interrogation mark to that very imperial power. The commoner Rienzo too, like Emperor Marcus, gazes out over their city, arm outstretched; but while the equestrian emperor's gesture is one of unifying power and command, the tribune's is one of exhortation: to community, and to the unity achieved by the joint goodwill and effort of his equals.

I first encountered Cola di Rienzo when I was an undergraduate at Fordham University, amid the social, political, and cultural changes of 1968, in a class on Renaissance and Reformation history taught by John C. Olin. I had come upon Cola through a circuitous route. In the Peasant's Revolt in Germany there appeared to be deep-rooted religious motivations that found their origins perhaps among the visionaries of medieval Italy, including Rienzo. This interest continued into graduate school at Columbia University, where I completed a master's thesis in 1970 under the supervision of Robert Somerville, investigating parallels between early concepts of the Renaissance and late medieval ideas of reform and renewal. I had the opportunity to pursue this theme in a graduate seminar conducted by Louis Pascoe, S.J., in 1972. A doctoral dissertation in 1977 under John Mundy on the Italian Spiritual Franciscan leader Angelo Clareno, several articles on Clareno and other Italian Joachites, and several books that sometimes touched on the medieval practice and ideas of peace and justice eventually brought me back to Rienzo. In 1986, I completed a revised edition of Mario Cozenza's *Francesco Petrarca and the Revolution of Cola di Rienzo* for Italica Press. Other projects and interests intervened over the succeeding decade; but my fascination reemerged in the late 1990s to synthesize all these research interests into this contextual biography.

This contextualization has, I hope, allowed me to examine and usefully synthesize many of the current trends in the study of Roman and Italian urban culture in the fourteenth century. At the same time, I have looked at all the available sources for Rienzo, his Rome, and its dealings with Avignon. With fellow medievalist, publisher, and life companion, Dr. Eileen Gardiner, I have discussed my ideas for this book at length, and during campaigns from 1998 to 2000 I had the pleasure with her of visiting Avignon and all the places in Lazio, southern Tuscany, and the Abruzzi described in the following pages. Many returns to Rome since my fellowship at the American Academy in 1978 and the ongoing hospitality of the Academy have allowed us to know and to feel the many layers of history beneath and around Rome's gently undulating streets and hills. For this, my thanks to successive Directors, including Joseph Connors, Caroline Bruzelius, and Lester K. Little, to Administrative Director Pina Pasquantonio and Library Director Christina Huemer, and to Norm Robertson for his extensive knowledge of the topography of northwestern Lazio.

My thanks are due to the libraries of Fordham and Columbia Universities and the collections of the New York Public Library, especially the Humanities Center. I owe a great debt to both the personal inspiration and the prior work of Robert Brentano in and on Rome, to the work of Richard Krautheimer, and the numerous publications of the Ecole Française de Rome. Their influences are apparent throughout this book. Although I have newly translated all selections of the *Anonimo romano*'s life of Cola di Rienzo presented here, John Wright's 1975 translation of that work has been an inestimable help. Dr. Carmen Bambach of the Metropolitan Museum of Art provided invaluable advice at a crucial stage of this project.

Eileen Gardiner of Italica Press, Amy Schwarz of the Frick Collection in New York, Benjamin G. Kohl of Vassar College, and Ronald G. Witt of Duke University read the manuscript and made fruitful and important suggestions for change. My participation in the April 2002 conference on the Cultures of Papal Avignon, sponsored by the Center for Medieval Studies of the University of Minnesota, Minneapolis, helped me focus many of the observations on Cola's *buono stato*. Stan Holwitz, my editor at the University of California Press, reacted with enthusiasm to my proposal for this book and guided its conceptualization and its eventual form. Rachel Berchten, senior editor, and Susan Ecklund and Kristen Cashman, manuscript editors, have provided clear and essential guidance in bringing this book to press.

Finally, it was John D'Arms who, as Director of the American Academy in Rome, guaranteed that my fellowship there would inspire a lifelong love of the city and of the scholars, artists, and other members of the Roman community who people it. Eileen Gardiner and I had the great privilege, joy, and challenge to work with John again at the American Council of Learned Societies for the past several years. He again invited us to participate in a vibrant and welcoming scholarly community, and for all that my thanks and fondest memories in dedicating this book to him.

New York City
May 2002

Abbreviations

AMA	Emmerson, R. E., and Bernard McGinn, eds. *The Apocalypse in the Middle Ages*. Ithaca, N.Y.: Cornell University Press, 1992.
AR	Anonimo romano. *Vita di Cola di Rienzo. Cronica.* Ed. Giuseppe Porta. Milan: Adelphi, 1979.
ASRSP	*Archivio della Società Romana di Storia Patria.*
Baluze	Etienne Baluze and Guillaume Mollat, eds. *Vitae paparum avenionensium*. Paris: Letouzey et Ané, 1914–22, 1960–61.
BBCR	Cola di Rienzo. *Die Briefwechsel des Cola di Rienzo*. Ed. Konrad Burdach and Paul Piur. *Vom Mittelalter zur Reformation*. Vol. 2.1–5. Berlin: Weidmann, 1913–29.
BFLT	Bynum, Caroline Walker, and Paul Freeman, eds. *Last Things: Death and the Apocalypse in the Middle Ages*. Philadelphia: University of Pennsylvania Press, 2000.
BISIMEAM	*Bullettino dell'Istituto storico italiano per il medioevo e Archivio Muratoriano.*
BLSSH	Brezzi, Paolo, and Egmont Lee, eds. *Sources of Social History: Private Acts of the Late Middle Ages*. Toronto: Pontifical Institute of Medieval Studies, 1984.
Brentano	Brentano, Robert. *Rome before Avignon: A Social History of Thirteenth-Century Rome*. New York: Basic Books, 1974.

CFP — Cammarosano, Paolo, ed. *Le forme della propaganda politica nel Due e nel Trecento*. Collection de l'Ecole française de Rome 201. Rome: EFR, 1994.

CLC — Clement VI. *Lettres closes, patentes et curiales intéressant les pays autres que la France (1342–1352)*. Ed. Eugène Déprez and Guillaume Mollat. Bibliotheque des Ecoles françaises d'Athenes et de Rome, ser. 3.3. Paris: A. Fontemoing, 1901, 1960–61.

CRCR — Cosenza, Mario, ed. and trans. *The Revolution of Cola di Rienzo*. 3d ed. rev. Ed. Ronald G. Musto. New York: Italica Press, 1996.

DBI — *Dizionario Biografico degli Italiani*. Rome: Istituto della Enciclopedia Italiana, 1961–.

DHP — *Dictionnaire historique de la Papauté*. Ed. Philippe Boutry and Philippe Levillain. Paris: Fayard, 1994.

DKPSP — Duncalf, Frederic, and August C. Krey. "The Coronation of Cola di Rienzo." In *Parallel Source Problems in Medieval History*, 177–237. New York: Harper and Row, 1912.

D'Onofrio 1 — D'Onofrio, Cesare, ed. *Visitiamo Roma mille anni fa. La città dei Mirabilia*. Rome: Romana Società Editrice, 1988.

D'Onofrio 2 — D'Onofrio, Cesare, ed. *Visitiamo Roma nel Quattrocento. La città degli Umanisti*. Rome: Romana Società Editrice, 1989.

Eisenbichler — Eisenbichler, Konrad, ed. *Crossing the Boundaries: Christian Piety and the Arts in Italian Medieval and Renaissance Confraternities*. Kalamazoo, Mich.: Medieval Institute, 1990.

Fam. — Petrarch, Francesco. *Rerum familiarium libri*. Various editions as cited.

Gabrielli — Gabrielli, Annibale, ed. *Epistolario di Cola di Rienzo*. Istituto storico italiano per il Medioevo. Fonti per la storia d'Italia 6. Rome: Forzani e Compagnia, 1890.

Gregorovius — Gregorovius, Ferdinand. *History of the City of Rome in the Middle Ages*. Trans. Annie Hamilton. 8 vols. in 13. London: G. Bell and Sons, 1903–12. Reprint, New York: AMS, 1967. Reprint and CD-ROM, New York: Italica Press, 2000–.

HBD	Horrox, Rosemary, ed. *The Black Death*. Mancheser Medieval Sources. Manchester: Manchester University Press, 1994.
Marvels	*The Marvels of Rome. Mirabilia Urbis Romae*. Ed. and trans. Francis Morgan Nichols. 2d ed. Ed. Eileen Gardiner. New York: Italica Press, 1986.
Papencordt	Papencordt, Felix. *Cola di Rienzo und sein Zeit*. Appendices. Hamburg: A. Perthes, 1841.
PLFM	Petrarch, Francesco. *Letters on Familiar Matters. Rerum familiarium libri*. Ed. Aldo S. Bernardo. 3 vols. Albany: SUNY Press; Baltimore: Johns Hopkins University Press, 1975–85.
RIS	Muratori, Ludovico Antonio, ed. *Rerum Italicarum Scriptores*. 25 vols. Milan: RIS, 1723–51. *Rerum Italicarum Scriptores*. 5th ed. Ed. Giosus Carducci and Vittorio Fiorini. Bologna: N. Zanichelli, 1931–39. *Rerum Italicarum Scriptores. Indexes*. Ed. Carlo Cipolla. Hildesheim, N.Y., 1977.
RRA	*Roma Anno 1300*. Ed. Angiola Maria Romanini. Rome: Bretschneider, 1983.
Seibt	Seibt, Gustav. *Anonimo romano. Scrivere la storia alle soglie del Rinascimento*. Trans. Cristina Colotto and Roberto Delle Donne. Rev. ed. Rome: Viella, 2000.
Theiner	Theiner, Augustin, ed. *Codex diplomaticus dominii temporalis S. Sedis: Receuil de documents pour servir à l'histoire du gouvernment temporal des états du Saint Siège*. 3 vols. Rome: Vatican Press, 1861–62.
TPPO	*Les textes prophetiques et la prophétie en Occident (XIIe–XVIe siècles)*. Mélanges de l'Ecole française de Rome. Moyen Age. 102(2): 1990.
VCT	Valentini, Roberto, and Giuseppe Zucchetti, eds. *Codice topografico della città di Roma*. Fonti per la Storia d'Italia. 4 vols. Rome: Tipografia del Senato, 1940–53.
Villani	Villani, Giovanni. *Cronica, con le continuazioni di Matteo e Filippo*. Turin: Einaudi, 1979.
Wilkins	Wilkins, Ernest Hatch. *Life of Petrarch*. Chicago: University of Chicago Press, 1963.

Wright   Wright, John, ed. and trans. *The Life of Cola di Rienzo*.
                Toronto: Pontifical Institute of Medieval Studies, 1975.

Zacour   Zacour, Norman, ed. *Petrarch's Book without a Name:
                A Translation of the* Liber Sine Nomine. Toronto:
                Pontifical Institute, 1973.

Cola di Rienzo

In Rome on May 20, 1347, Cola di Rienzo, a young visionary with a gift
for oratory, the former ambassador of the Roman commune to the pope
in Avignon, the friend of Petrarch, and now papal notary in Rome, overthrew the rule of the corrupt and lawless barons, and in the name of the
pope and the people of Rome reestablished the Roman republic. Cola's
new government, the *buono stato,* was soon to restore peace, prosperity,
and justice to the city and its countryside, revive the reputation of Rome's
ancient grandeur, and briefly make Rome the new center of diplomacy and
political life. Rome became the New Jerusalem of the Apocalypse, and
the world turned its eyes to the magical city and to its wondrous ruler in
rapt attention. The kings of England and France, the German emperor,
even the pope and, it was reported, the sultan of Egypt, looked to Rome
in awe and expectation.

This book is the story of Cola di Rienzo, of his rise to power, his coronation as tribune, his startling victories over the barons, his unexpected
fall, his years of hidden wandering among the apocalyptic heretics of Italy's
Abruzzi Mountains, his sudden appearance at the court of Emperor
Charles IV in Prague, and his return, under arrest, to Avignon, there to
stand trial as a heretic for his betrayal of the pope and the Roman church.
The story then traces Cola's return to power in Rome and his death on
the Capitoline near where the statue of him now stands. More than this,
however, this book is a history of Rome in the fourteenth century, and
of the life and hopes of its people for the dawning of a new age of peace,
liberty, and enlightenment. It attempts to place Cola di Rienzo into the

context of the medieval Italian city-states, to shed some light on the ideologies and the reform movements that shaped medieval Rome, and to help explain the deeply religious currents of the time and place that formed Cola's and his age's ideals of government, peace, justice, and rebirth.

Who was Cola di Rienzo? Every age has created its own image of the Roman tribune. Shortly after Cola's death in 1354, the Roman people declared May 20 to be a communal holiday to commemorate their dead tribune, to be celebrated by a mass of the Holy Spirit in the church of the Aracoeli on the Capitoline. The enactment was enshrined in the Statutes of Rome of 1363. It did not take long for such memory to transform itself into myth. The legend immediately grew up that Cola had been the ally of a hidden claimant to the French throne: Giannino di Guccio, son of Louis X of France (1314–16). Switched at birth by the Capetian's nursemaid, Giannino was discovered living in Siena. He came to Rome supposedly, in 1354, put forth his claim to the French throne, and was immediately recognized by the famous tribune and senator. Several letters purportedly written by Rienzo backing Giannino's claims have been part of the corpus of his letters since about 1527 and were finally discredited only in the 1920s. What is important, however, is the fact that Cola's legend was already strong enough in the early sixteenth century to lend itself to such obvious chivalric fiction.

Nearly two centuries earlier, sometime between 1358 and July 1359, there was completed but never published a *Vita* of Cola di Rienzo within a larger *Cronica* that set out to record the events of Europe, focusing on Rome and its district between 1327 and 1357/58. Cola's story was only one—the major—part (chapters 18 and 26–27) of this larger history. As such it has often been edited separately as the *Vita* and divided into four books. Though some attempt has been made to name its author, no firm identity has been generally accepted. This Anonimo romano was probably born in Rome to an upper-middle-class family between 1318 and 1320, in the *rione* Regola, and was thus a close neighbor of Rienzo's.[1] He was living in Rome in 1334 and began his medical studies at the University of Bologna in 1338/39. Internal evidence tells us that he returned to Rome in the mid-1340s and practiced medicine. Like Cola, he was no humanist but a trained professional with a good foundation in the Latin letters of his time. The Anonimo romano was also a naturalist imbued with the available corpus of Latin classics and Greek sciences. Sometime in the 1350s he moved to Tivoli, where he died around October 1360.

Whoever he was, and as sharp as his observations were, he was no political insider. Although he faithfully reported events in Rome with keen judgment and a reporter's sense of personality and drama, he relied on secondhand accounts for events away from Lazio—for French affairs and for Cola's stays in Avignon or Prague, for example—and for many of the central events that took place in Rome itself. While he used some of the best sources of the time, including the *Chronicle* of Martin of Troppau, the Mirabilian descriptions of Rome, medieval reinterpretations of ancient historians found in the *Liber ystoriorum,* and at least some of Cola's own official letters, his viewpoint was that of the public witness, not the personal intimate or the confidant of Cola or other key men. Despite the author's genius, recently fully analyzed by Gustav Seibt,[2] he lacked access to some of the most important documents for Rienzo's life and events in Rome in the 1340s and 1350s: the secret letters of the popes and their legates. While he cannot be blamed for this—most of these letters were only edited and published beginning in the 1860s—the Anonimo romano thus had to construct much of the causality so crucial to Cola's rise to power and his sudden overthrow, both of which, I shall argue, were heavily dependent on papal actions behind the scenes.

The anonymous Roman historian thus had to rely on both the psychological interpretations and the historical conventions available to him in the mid–fourteenth century, and most of these were derived from his classical sources: Livy, Sallust, Lucan, Valerius Maximus, Cicero, and the minor Roman historians. Seibt has also argued for the contemporary influences of Rolandino da Padova and against any direct traces of the Villani chronicles. Thus the Anonimo romano's basic interpretation of Cola di Rienzo: a plebeian skilled in oratory, imbued with classical learning, and devoted to the rebirth and reform of the city of Rome who ended in tragic failure because of personal vices befitting a debauched Roman emperor or eastern tyrant. Just as Rome rose again from its ruinous condition through the efforts and virtues of one man in imitation of its ancient heroes, so, too, did it sink back into degradation because of his shortcomings. Economic conditions; the physical traumas of climatic change, plague, earthquake, and depopulation; social dislocation; and the motives of the popes in Avignon were all invisible to the Anonimo romano, as they would have been to any historian before the late nineteenth century. But whatever his failings, the Anonimo romano was a brilliant storyteller and a great historian; and the starkly dramatic trajectory of Cola's rise and fall were to set the stage for all later interpretations. Even in the twentieth century, those writers who sought to tell a different version of the story could do so only by consciously ignoring the evidence and arguments that the Anonimo romano offered.

The Anonimo romano set out to write a vivid and convincing history of his times. To reach his audience he therefore wrote in the vernacular Italian of Rome called Romanesco and so created a masterpiece of fourteenth-century Italian literature. The Anonimo romano's autograph survived as a unique manuscript for over 150 years, and by the early sixteenth century the *Cronica* was widely read and existed in several copies. The earliest surviving ones date from shortly after 1527. Niccolò Machiavelli used a copy in writing his *History of Florence* of 1527. For the author of *The Prince*, Rienzo was a good example of the constant tension between *Virtù* and the wheel of *Fortuna,* a tension that pits the resources of the individual against the accumulated weight of circumstances and structures. In book I, chapter 6, of his *History,* Machiavelli records how Cola "restored" Rome "to its ancient form" and inspired the ancient provinces of Italy who, "seeing Rome arise to new life, again raised their heads." Cola was an early, if flawed, agent of both Italian unity and the Renaissance, who was unable to carry through successfully what he had begun. "Niccolò, notwithstanding his great reputation, lost all energy in the very beginning of his enterprise; . . . as if oppressed with the weight of so vast an undertaking."

Cola's *Vita* was first published in 1624 at Bracciano by Andrea Fei. The story of the Roman tribune proved so successful in print that it received a second edition in 1631. The work was attributed to Tomaso Fortifiocca, a Roman notary and enemy of Rienzo; but this attribution was soon disproven. The Fei editions of the Anonimo romano remained available to the interested scholar into the eighteenth century. Thus, in 1733, the French Jesuit Jean Antoine du Cerceau used a French translation of the *Vita* to paint a rather unattractive picture of Rienzo in his *Conjuration de Nicholas Gabrini, dit de Rienzi, Tyran de Rome* (Paris, 1733). The Jesuit's work well served the monarchist and papal interests of the time. Among Napoleon's possessions in his coach during the retreat from Moscow in 1812 was a fifth edition of Cerceau's *Rienzi.*

The Enlightenment

For the great historian of the Italian Enlightenment, Ludovico Antonio Muratori, Cola's life offered the opportunity to publish yet another important primary source for the history of Italy, a source that provided much valuable information not only on Rome but also on the era of the Avignon papacy. Building a wide circle of collaborators throughout Italy,

Muratori had set out in his encyclopedic, multivolume works to provide a complete universal history of the Italian people, as in the *Annali d'Italia* (1738–49). His *Antiquitates Italicae Medii Aevi* (1738–42) presented a social history of Italian money, trade, banking, health care, warfare, law, institutions, literature, and other topics. Muratori rounded out his monumental approach by launching a series of editions of Italian historical sources: the *Rerum Italicarum Scriptores ab anno aerae christianae 500 ad 1500* (RIS, 1723–51). In volume 3 of the RIS, published in 1740, Muratori issued a complete edition of all the surviving chapters of the Anonimo romano as the *Fragmenta Historiae romanae ab Anno 1327 usque ad Annum 1354*, including the *Vita* of Cola di Rienzo. Muratori presented the original Romanesco text, along with a Latin translation for use by the international scholarly community. By setting the *Vita* within the context of the Latin *Fragmenta*, Muratori furthered the Enlightenment task of the RIS of placing the individual within the broader context of the social, economic, and structural foundations of Italian history and thus making him more amenable to rational study and analysis. His edition of Cola's *Vita* within the *Fragmenta Historiae romanae* thus also sparked an new international look at Rienzo.

In the next generation Edward Gibbon (1737–94) conceived his *History of the Decline and Fall of the Roman Empire* (1776–88) in Rome itself "while musing amid the ruins of the Capitol." His book was to become the single most important—and most debated—work on the medieval history of Rome. Gibbon's view of Rome, a city of "poverty and debasement," would surprise few modern historians. Thus Gibbon (3, c.70) saw Rienzo, like Petrarch, as a harbinger of a new age of enlightenment about to dawn after a thirteen-hundred-year hiatus. But the tribune was a "patriot" and a "modern Brutus" who was worthy of praise only as far as he remained the perfect Enlightenment gentleman, applying the lessons of the ancients to the rational ordering of society. Gibbon used Muratori's editions both of the *Chronicle* of the Villani and of the *Fragmenta* and therefore mirrors the basic plot outline of the Anonimo romano. Thus Cola's learning and skill in the classics, so hard-earned in this time of ignorance, would be both his glory and the cause of his "untimely end." Gibbon had nothing but praise in his narration of Cola's rise to power. "Never perhaps has the energy and effect of a single mind been more remarkably felt than in the sudden, though transient, reformation of Rome by the tribune Rienzi." Cola's unexpected success led him to plan the eventual reunification of all of the peninsula as a great "Italian republic" that might have healed its civil wounds and "closed the Alps against the bar-

barians of the North." But Gibbon equally heaped scorn on the tribune when he is most a man of his own time and place. Cola was given to sumptuous clothing, great spectacle, harsh justice, and extravagant generosity; but he also lacked the "cool and commanding reason" that would have tempered these qualities. At the same time Cola's extravagant behavior "betrayed the meanness of his birth and degraded the importance of his office." Cola's decline was caused as much by his personal wantonness as by his inability to quell the revolt of the barons. "In the camp Rienzi appeared to less advantage than in the rostrum," and he brought the campaign against them to nothing. Gibbon shows little interest in his account for the role of the papacy in these events; but this is completely consistent with his indifference to most religious motivation or structures except to scoff at their absurd superstitions. At the same time he lacked most of the papal letters concerning the overthrow of Cola's government, letters that would be edited only in the 1860s. Thus he, too, was bound by the Anonimo romano's outline. In the end, however, his judgment on Cola di Rienzo is a generous one: "Posterity will compare the virtues and failings of this extraordinary man; but in a long period of anarchy and servitude, the name of Rienzi had often been celebrated as the deliverer of his country, and the last of the Roman patriots."

Romanticism

In the hands of the great romantic writers, Rienzo was to become the personification of their reaction against the rationalism and scientific determinism of the Enlightenment. They thus embraced the religious, mystical culture of the "Age of Faith" and the emergence of the common folk and their aspirations for national and local identity against the empires and elites of the ancien régime. For these poets, painters, dramatists, and novelists, the Sturm und Drang of individual emotions reflected the deep, untamed forces that control the physical world: the avalanche, the storm at sea, and the volcano that were to become emblems of romantic painting and fiction. The national hero, especially one who grew organically out of the "Folk" itself, thus personified these natural and local forces. As such Rienzo's birth, rise, very brief rule, and tragic death made him the ideal romantic hero. Cola makes his first romantic appearance in 1818 in the fourth and last canto of the epic poem *Childe Harold's Pilgrimage* by George Gordon, Lord Byron (1788–1824). Most of the fourth canto is a poetic meditation on the decline and desolate state of ancient Rome, itself now the perfect object of romantic elegy. In the midst of this decay and darkness, however, the image of Rienzo shines out as an isolated beacon of hope and light.

Writing in 1835, the prolific writer and Reform member of Parliament Edward Bulwer-Lytton (1803–73) noted that his own plan for Rienzo's biography had to be interrupted by his travel to Naples to complete the manuscript of his other well-known Italian epic: *The Last Days of Pompeii*. The two novels bear much in common: the romantic penchant for intricate plot, great sweeps of historic events that match his main characters in the emotional life that swells up from them. The Roman mob and the volcano of Vesuvius are themselves personifications of romantic nature whose force few can resist, but against whose inexorable tides true heroes can show steadfast resolution, even in the face of inevitable, tragic death. As one might expect, personal revenge mixes easily with two central love relationships, and a few more fictional characters round out an almost Shakespearean ensemble. The great romance ends amid the collapse of the Senators' Palace into smoke and flames on the last page.

Bulwer-Lytton was clearly writing in the wake of the popular stage tragedy *Rienzi* (1828) by Mary Russell Mitford (1787–1855). Here, as in her *Foscari,* Italy is the land of intrigues and dark vendettas, of high emotion and noble idealism. But as the novelist takes pains to make plain, his work is based fully upon the historical facts and the known sources, again, almost solely the Anonimo romano, with additions from Villani and other chroniclers. As Bulwer-Lytton notes in his preface to the 1848 edition, he had written "a work illustrative of the exertions of a Roman, in advance of his time, for the political freedom of a country, and of those struggles between contending principals of which Italy was the most stirring field in the Middle Ages." Thus Cola looks forward to the progress, enlightenment, and political reform of the novelist's own day. *Rienzi* enjoyed great popularity in the succeeding decade, so much so that it was translated almost immediately into Italian, and though banned in the Papal States, it provided some of the inspiration for the great republican revolt of 1848–49.

Between the first and second editions of Bulwer-Lytton's novel, the German composer Richard Wagner (1813–83) decided to set to music the story of the doomed tribune. Using the high emotional mode of French grand opera but taking as his sources Bulwer-Lytton's fiction and Miss Mitford's stage play, he completed the libretto in 1838 and the music in 1840. Wagner's *Rienzi: Der Letzte der Tribunen* premiered in Dresden on October 20, 1842. The opera strips Bulwer-Lytton's novel of much of its historical context and most of its characters and complexity, reducing it to an immense romantic tableau of heroism, loyalty, treachery, and fate. Rienzi remains throughout a grand and tragic superman, a leader who devotes his life to the peace and unity of Italy, and who watches in grandeur as the long processions of Roman soldiery parades below him. He urges his soldiers to martial valor and to their *Kampf*. Victory and death are the only choices, the Roman women sing. Rienzi brings victory to Roman arms, but finally, he is defeated not on the field of battle but by the treachery of those closest to him, by the church and by the frenzied people themselves. In the last scene the Roman mob attacks the Senators' Palace, as Rienzi and his ever-faithful sister Irene (a fabrication of Bulwer-Lytton's made almost incestuous by Wagner) embrace upon the balcony, engulfed in flames. The building—and the hopes of a new Roman *Reich*—collapse into ashes and arias all around them.

Risorgimento and Nationalism

Romantic idealism was also clearly evident beneath the grand scientific history of the German Ferdinand Gregorovius (1821–91), who began to write his magisterial *History of the City of Rome in the Middle Ages* in 1854. He, like Gibbon, had been deeply moved by contemplating the ruins of Rome; but unlike Gibbon, who saw the decayed results of medieval superstition and barbarity in the toppled temples and grand imperial buildings of the Forum, Gregorovius saw these very same, now romanticized, ruins as the birthplace of a new European civilization that arose from them. Like Gibbon, Gregorovius turned contemplation into a magnificent work spanning a thousand years, and taking eight volumes in thirteen parts in its masterful English translation by Annie Hamilton. But unlike Gibbon, Gregorovius was swept up in a passion that infused his life with new meaning as well as new work, and he set about composing his narrative of the birth and flowering of Roman freedom. He had grown up in the generation after the French Revolution, and his youth had been molded by the ideals of the anti-imperialist nationalisms of Germany and of the great revolutions of 1848. Yet he also shared the deep humanist culture of the north, with its classicism and faith in reason, progress, and idealism. Caught by the failure of the liberal revolutions in Germany and Poland, Gregorovius decided to travel south to Italy to finish a work on the emperor Hadrian, which was published in 1851.

In Italy, and in Rome, he witnessed firsthand the reaction under Pope

Pius IX (1846–78), who had used French and Austrian troops to put down the revolts of the Papal States in the 1830s, and who still ruled through an authoritarian, reactionary, and clerical bureaucracy. Gregorovius came to Rome in 1852 in the wake of Garibaldi's ill-fated revolt of 1849 and the return of Pius IX in 1850 to the battered city, again thanks to French troops. Pius had instituted a reign of terror against dissidents, where most of the "rights of man" were piously discarded. Gregorovius thus conceived his grand history as a saga of the rise of freedom and human rights against tyranny and authoritarianism, of nationalism against empire and religious superstition. As Gregorovius wrote at the conclusion of his last volume, he lived to see the final triumph of the republic against Pius IX with the liberation of Rome and its incorporation into the new kingdom of Italy in 1870. Pius put Gregorovius's *History* on the *Index of Prohibited Books* in 1874.

Thus, for Gregorovius the history of the medieval Roman commune became a great metaphor for his own age: a long, uneven struggle, full of triumphs and defeats for freedom, that reached its apogee with the revolutionary career of Cola di Rienzo. Rienzo emerges from Gregorovius's pages as a liberal hero of Italian unity, freedom, and civil rights; and the *History* remains the single most important narrative to date of medieval Rome and of the political career of Cola di Rienzo. Gregorovius had access to much of the papal correspondence concerning the tribune and the city; he was thus able to compose a much more nuanced and complex narrative, giving due attention to the papal role in Rienzo's downfall. Yet the central image of the tribune remains that drawn by the Anonimo romano, and in the end Gregorovius sees Rienzo's abdication and eventual fall as the result of personal failings.

With Gregorovius the classicism and rationalism of the nineteenth century finally merged with the grand themes of the romantic era, just as the reform spirit of the Enlightenment had merged with the age of revolution to finally, in 1870, bring about the triumph of the Italian Risorgimento: the reunification of the peninsula into a single and modern state. This event gave immense impetus to a generation of historians who now looked to the history of the medieval city-states as the foundations for their modern freedoms and political institutions. Gregorovius's *History* was immediately recognized for its contribution to the new Italy as the city of Rome granted its author Roman citizenship and commissioned an Italian translation of the work.

Gregorovius's landmark was soon joined by another major contribution to the study of Cola di Rienzo. In 1885 a manuscript arrived at the

Vatican Archives from a private collection in Prague that had been known to, and used by, only a few earlier scholars, such as Felix Papencordt. This was the collection of the letters of Cola di Rienzo. While in Prague, Rienzo had maintained a regular correspondence with the imperial chancellor Johann von Neumarkt, a German literary figure and correspondent of Petrarch's. These letters, and then others that the tribune had probably brought with him as letter forms, were soon collected into the *Liber diversas continens formulas* to make the basis of a new collection of the letter-writing art—the *ars dictaminis*—for the imperial German chancellery. The collection contained nearly two-thirds of Cola's extant letters when, sometime before 1500, they passed into the possession of Gaspare Schlick, then imperial chancellor and friend of the famous Italian humanist Aeneas Silvius Piccolomini, Pope Pius II (1458–64). The manuscript remained in the hands of Schlick's heirs in Prague until its return to Italy in 1885. In 1890 the discovery formed the basis of the first edition of Rienzo's letters by Annibale Gabrielli as the *Epistolario di Cola di Rienzo,* volume 6 of the new series *Fonti per la storia d'Italia* by the Istituto Storico Italiano per il Medioevo. Cola di Rienzo's own voice had at last been rediscovered, and it was immediately put into the service of the Risorgimento and new Italian state.

This same impetus conceived the statue of Cola di Rienzo now on the Capitoline (see frontispiece). Cast in bronze in 1887 by Girolamo Masini, the image of the tribune is diminutive in scale, almost self-effacing in its relationship to its own surrounding space. The statue rests on a "postmodern" base, almost as high as the figure itself and composed of a lovely—and intentionally haphazard—assemblage of *spolia:* bits and pieces of ancient and medieval architectural elements. The impression of the base speaks richly of the statue's romantic historicism: its conscious revival of one who himself had launched a very self-conscious revival of the city's great past. But the figure lacks classical balance and instead combines inner spiritual possession with practiced rhetorical gesture and pure romantic force. Rienzo's face is nearly hidden by a long-hooded cloak that makes him look more like one of Horace Walpole's monks than the reviver of the ancient republic. The mystery of the hooded figure lends it great emotional power, hiding Rienzo's eyes while at the same time accentuating the effect of his arm, outstretched, thrusting out toward the heart of the modern city in a forceful oratorical gesture. His gesture reaches out not toward the Capitoline but over the medieval city and directly at the Vatican, a fitting accusation and rejection for the new Italian state that had finally, only a decade earlier, managed to overthrow the papacy and shut it into its own small preserve across the Tiber. Nor was this orientation coincidence or the artist's personal whim. With the grand new boulevards laid out in the expansion of housing and government buildings that overwhelmed the Vatican *prati* after the Risorgimento, the main boulevard uniting the Piazza del Risorgimento—placed just outside the walls of the Vatican near where visitors now enter the Vatican Museums—and the Piazza del Popolo across the river was named via Cola di Rienzo; while Piazza Cola di Rienzo marks the grand space where it intersects the main boulevard that stretches between Piazza Cavour and Piazza Mazzini.

The spirit of the Risorgimento was to continue to inspire Italian and French writers for the next two generations. Sympathetic biographies appeared in France from Jacques Zeller (1874) and Emmanuel Rodocanachi (1888). Rienzo, as both romantic subject in literature and opera and the nationalist hero, also traveled across the Atlantic and entered the popular imagination. "Rienzi" was the name of Union general Philip Sheridan's favorite warhorse, the steed that carried him into battle nineteen times, most significantly to victory in the Shenandoah Valley Campaign of 1864. On the death of the horse, then named "Winchester" after Sheridan's famous victory, the Union general had Rienzi stuffed. The horse remained on display, behind glass at the Smithsonian in Washington, an equine hero of the democracy, freedom, and national unity his namesake represented for the late nineteenth century.

More serious American interest in Rienzo, coupled with the Italian American search for identity in the new Italian nationalism, led Renaissance historian Mario Cosenza (1880–1966) to undertake a careful study of the relationship between the high ideals of Italian culture, as exemplified by Francesco Petrarch, and the yearning of Italians for a new unified state, born in liberty and exemplified in the life of Cola di Rienzo. The result was published in 1913 as *Francesco Petrarca and the Revolution of Cola di Rienzo*. Petrarch, "the first modern man of letters," was also "the first real Italian patriot," and the story of his friendship with Rienzo traces less a full biography or critical study of the Roman tribune than the relationship of idealism and action. As Cosenza explained (vii–x), "The contents of the volume breathe forth . . . an atmosphere of Rome and of Italy, and the poet battles and preaches and sings with . . . inspiration for the political liberty of the capital of the Caesars and for the re-establishment of the ancient *imperium*." To balance out the account of the Anonimo romano, Cosenza brought together for the first time all the available sources for Petrarch's relationship with Rienzo, including papal and private correspondence and translated excerpts from Gabrielle's edition of Cola's letters.

This search for cultural identity and the synthesis of Enlightenment scholarship and romantic nationalism also had its effect in Germany. Here a search for the reform, apocalyptic, and mystical roots of the German Reformation and thus supposedly of the German national consciousness combined to produce the most exhaustive and comprehensive view of Rienzo yet in the work of Konrad Burdach and his student Paul Piur. Burdach's *Vom Mittelalter zur Reformation, Forshungen zur Geschichte der deutschen Bildung* was published in six volumes from 1912 to 1939 and thus bridges the period from the late romantic to the beginning of World War II. Volume 2 of the work, *Die Briefwechsel des Cola di Rienzo*, took up five parts in six physical tomes and was published between 1913 and 1929. Burdach theorized that the changes in the German language between the fourteenth century and the Reformation reflected a deep transformation of the German soul that ultimately had its roots in the mystical and apocalyptic thought that arose in Italy with the age of Francis of Assisi and reached its apogee in the Renaissance thought of Dante, Petrarch, and Cola di Rienzo, "the three great renewers of world culture" and the "three great pioneers of humanism."

Of the three, he argued, Cola was the most important, the man who took the imagery and thus the deep transformative thought of rebirth and renewal that had been developed in Italy and brought it with him to Germany when he arrived at the imperial court of Charles IV in Prague. From there such early German humanists as Johann von Neumarkt and Ackermann aus Böhmen used the new vocabulary of renewal and planted the seeds first for the linguistic renovation of the German language and then of the German soul that was to find its ultimate flowering in the Reformation. It was a heady and complex thesis, laid out in parts 1 and 2 of the *Briefwechsel* and entitled *Rienzo und die geistige Wandlung seiner Zeit*.

Students of the late Middle Ages and of the Renaissance were openly dumfounded by the thesis that made the Renaissance the result of words and intellectual transmission alone and Cola di Rienzo the apogee of that movement; yet Burdach was adamant in his insistence that this renewal of European, and thus world, culture had nothing to do with economic, social, or purely political structures. At the same time, however, Burdach and his student Piur, whose biography *Cola di Rienzo* appeared in 1931, remain the best and most informed of all scholars dealing with the tribune. Their editions of the texts and discussions of sources and manuscripts, their textual, historical notes and other apparatus offer the most comprehensive collection of materials, which go well beyond the scope found in the Anonimo romano. Their materials are still unsurpassed and form the basis for any scholarly study.

Fascism

In Italy both a romantic fascination with the great leader who would bring freedom to his people and usher in a new age, and also some sort of natural affinity with the orator who overwhelmed all obstacles to take and use power form a major element in the rise of Fascism in the twentieth century. In 1913 Gabriele D'Annunzio (1863–1938) published his *Vite di uomini illustri et di uomini oscuri: La vita di Cola di Rienzo*. His biography was something of a watershed; for almost any subject that the eminent Italian man of letters touched was bound to become the focus of literary attention. In addition to being Italy's preeminent poet, novelist, and playwright, D'Annunzio believed that the ideal writer is also the man of action, and he therefore played a leading role in urging Italy to join World War I. In the struggle he distinguished himself in many acts of military daring, and after the war's end, in 1919, he actually led a force that conquered Fiume and set him up as its dictator. An extreme nationalist who believed in the power of the will, D'Annunzio himself was later to embrace Mussolini and Fascism. From his overheated pen Cola di Rienzo emerges as the perfect bridge between the ideals of romanticism and those of Fascism, as a man of the people whose "face was turned to the future," open to the visionary power of Fra Venturino da Bergamo and his disciples. Yet Rienzo quickly overreached his status, and his reign turned to a "buffoonery" of one reaching hopelessly above his station in life and beset by vacillation. A man more suited to the cloister than the battlefield, in the end Cola proved himself a cowardly demagogue, unable to match the true nobility of the barons as men of action.

D'Annunzio's biography fit well the mood of the new Italy, longing to find its place in the modern world and seeking to do it quickly through decisive leadership and action. Many of these strains came together in the 1920s to produce Benito Mussolini as Italy's *Duce*. Sometime after World War II, Aldo Parini, an elderly Socialist, related the following story in Barzini's *The Italians* (133–34). Just before the outbreak of the war, Parini asked for a meeting with *Il Duce*. The two had been Socialist comrades before Fascism, and Parini had a favor to ask: that his old friend Benito now help some of their former Socialist comrades who, in their old age, had come upon hard times under the Fascist regime. Parini asked Mussolini to find some discreet and unofficial channel that would embarrass no one. The dictator immediately agreed to the request, for old time's sake. The two then went on to reminisce about their past and their comrades, and Mussolini began to brag about the accomplishments of his Fascist regime, gently upbraiding his old friend for not converting to the new political faith. Parini politely refused Mussolini's requests, realizing that the dictator would have then and there arranged for his comfortable old age if he agreed. But true to his youthful ideals, Parini finally blurted out, "This regime of yours, I am afraid, will end badly. Such things always do. Benito, you'll die like Cola di Rienzo." At these worlds Mussolini feigned horror, but then, extending his hands to Parini, he jokingly remarked, "I wear no rings, you see. It will not happen to me." Both men, like most Italians, knew the reference from Cola's life well. In April 1945, with Fascism collapsing all around him, Mussolini attempted to escape to Switzerland disguised as a German soldier. He was discovered with his mistress, Claretta Petacci, in a German truck and then shot with her by the Partisans. Their two bodies were brought back to Milan and hung—exposed and upside down—outside a gas station. Parini's prophecy had come true.

Adolf Hitler, too, was obsessed by the achievement and the ultimate fate of the Roman tribune; and he found his connection to Rienzo not through biography but through the music of Richard Wagner. After the war, August Kubizek, Hitler's teenage friend in Linz, Austria, reconstructed his own experience of Hitler's fascination with the tribune. It all started, according to Kubizek, the first time the fifteen-year-old Hitler attended Wagner's *Rienzi*. Emerging from the opera house, Hitler took Kubizek on a long climb on the Freinberg mountain outside the town. As Kubizek later recounted, "My friend, his hands thrust into his coat pockets, silent and withdrawn, strode through the streets and out of the city [to the mountainside]. Never before and never again have I heard Adolf Hitler speak as he did in that hour, and we stood there alone under the stars. . . . It was a state of complete ecstasy and rapture, in which he transferred the character of Rienzi . . . with visionary power to the plan of his own ambitions." Many years later, in 1939, at Bayreuth, Kubizek approached the führer and reminded him of that night. According to Kubizek, Hitler used the opportunity to add to his own legend for prophecy, telling his hostess, Winifred Wagner, "in that hour, it began." Despite Hitler's own propensity for mythmaking and Kubizek's fanciful memory, *Rienzi,* like so much of Wagner's work, did play a major part in Hitler's and the Nazis' symbolism and ceremonial. Rienzi represented the conquering folk hero who would bring his people "out of servitude" through struggle *(Kampf)*, military conquest, and bloodshed. Wagner's overture to the opera, the only portion of the *Rienzi* most Americans still hear, was the musical theme for Nazi Party rallies in Nuremberg. Hitler owned a Wagner manuscript of *Rienzi,* and as the war worsened, he refused to give it to the Bayreuth archives for safekeeping. At the end, in his burning bunker in Berlin, betrayed by everyone except his beloved, the Führer died amid the flames and wreckage of his new *Reich,* just like Wagner's Rienzi at the Capitoline, and with Wagner's manuscript still in his possession.[3]

After the War

In the wake of such catastrophes, it was not surprising that with the postwar revulsion at the effects of mass propaganda and the cult of the great hero, several British writers saw Rienzo as a protofascist. Iris Origo, in her *Tribune of Rome: A Biography of Cola di Rienzi* (1938), had already approached the man with a great deal of caution. Not so Victor Fleischer, whose *Rienzo: The Rise and Fall of a Dictator* (1948) unabashedly attempts to portray the fourteenth-century reformer as a medieval Hitler. Cola di Rienzo was a "cringing" and cowardly plebeian, who used his great skills as an orator and an actor to vent his hatred upon the world. Whatever religious or cultural elements Rienzo revealed were the result of his inclination "to seek and to perceive secret connections and symbolic meanings" in everything. After ruthlessly rising to the top through his putsch and claiming that he had been "elected" and that everything had been done "lawfully," this self-deluded egotist converted every shred of loyalty to the community and the idea of Rome to his own personal aggrandizement. His rise was marked by deception, manipulation, and the outright using of one ally after another. His fall came quickly, however, as the hollowness of his regime and his own penchant for interfering with his generals and the management of government business led to disaster. Just before the end, "His face was distorted into the mask of a fearful ruler, in his evil, rolling eyes was hidden the cowardice of a man who considers himself hated by all." Rienzo "had lied to his friends, and betrayed the men who had helped him, enchanted by his speeches, to win rulership; deceived and cheated the Pope, the pious hermits of the mountains, and the emperor in Prague" (210–16). Out of his hatred for the Colonna, Cola di Rienzo ultimately "betrayed everyone and everything." In France the judgment of François Ganshof was popularized in his influential *The*

Middle Ages: A History of International Relations (1953): "At Rome in 1347, Cola di Rienzo, a demagogue whose mind was possessed of mysticism and half-digested historical visions, imposed his dictatorship. Petrarch, with great lyrical imagination but with poor political sense, acclaimed this coup d'état as a glorious return to republican Rome, as the tyrant himself had claimed" (248). Ganshof sees the entire episode as a "harlequinade."

In Italy the study of Cola di Rienzo never really diminished, despite the regime or the political mood. Editions of Cola's *Vita* appeared with regularity in Italy in 1928 (A. M. Ghiselberti), 1943 (F. Cusin), 1957 (A. Frugoni), 1979 (G. Porta), 1980 (F. Mazzei), 1982 (U. Reale), and two in 1991 (U. Reale and E. Mazzali). Porta's edition, however, placed the study of Rienzo's life on a new scholarly plane, presenting a critical edition of the entire *Cronica* of the Anonimo romano, with excellent text and linguistic and historical notes. The chronicle has already appeared in full-text versions on several Italian Web sites. Porta's work was paralleled and followed up by numerous, more specialized, studies of the Romanesco dialect, of Italian literature in the fourteenth century, and of the life and work of the Anonimo romano himself, including those of Giuseppe Castellani (1920), Gianfranco Contini (1940), Lucio Felici (1977), Gian Mario Anselmi (1980 and 1984), Mario Sanfilippo (1980), Giuliano Tanturli (1980), Mario Pozzi (1982), Maurizio Dardano (1983), Pietro Trifone (1986), Arrigo Castellani (1987), Gianfranco Folena (1991), and Giuseppe Billanovich (1995). These works take for granted Rienzo's place in the history of Italian political ideals and reform movements, but on the whole they substitute the great passions of romanticism and Risorgimento with the careful study of texts and the rhetorical strategies of the medieval author. In that sense, they thus reveal a subtle turning away from politics, the hero worship of the Fascist years, and the disaster of the war.

As the image of postwar Italy gradually loosened itself from the grip of Fascist memory and humiliation and gave way to the Italian "miracle" in the 1960s, Italians themselves could afford to look at their past in the same way that many viewed their postwar present: with the ironic, somewhat bemused tolerance with which they viewed the corrupt, hypocritical, but highly successful government of the Christian Democrats. Thus for Luigi Barzini's *The Italians,* written and first published in 1964 for an English-speaking audience, Rienzo lost the dictatorial tarnish of the war decades and emerged as a postwar, post-Catholic, postideological master of the Italian political game. Barzini's Rienzo was "the greatest orator of his times," a poor man whom opportunity brought to the highest levels of power and who managed to use the media of oratory and painting to attract a large following from the disenfranchised and adventurous who

supported his new, if hollow, republic of words. But working-class ambition and public relations "chicanery" could not prevail for long against
the real centers of power in Rome: the barons and the papacy. Cola's house
of cards overthrown once, he returned to Rome much changed, and his
personal vices were soon his undoing. But in the light of posterity, Cola
did possess one great talent: an intuitive understanding of a people's political aspirations. He was "Italian," that is, "he spoke eloquently, wore
handsome clothes, invented flags. . . . The facade and the reality, for him
too, were one and the same thing (132)."

But other trends of the 1960s took a far more serious view of the short-
lived Roman republic. Combining much of Marxist historical analysis with
Western political and social progressivism, the 1960s produced many works
of radical history and the history of revolutionary movements. Among
these Michel Mollat and Philippe Wolff's *Popular Revolutions of the Late
Middle Ages* surveyed fourteenth-century Europe and saw one after another peasant and working-class revolution as motivated by the inherent
inequalities of the class and economic structures set into motion by a dying feudal and nascent capitalist society. But how to place Cola di Rienzo
into their panorama of "revolts against poverty," where such obvious "economic and social causes" seemed to take a backseat to Cola's clearly enun-
ciated religious, political, and cultural motives? Rienzo, it seems, was somewhat an exception to the masses of "lower-class" men and women who
pursued bread and shelter with furrowed brow and bent shoulder. Rienzo
was an "adventurer." As Mollat and Wolff declare, "There was in fact, in
Rienzi, as in many adventurers, a mixture of sincerity with a spirit of in-
trigue, of violence and evasiveness, of idealism and pragmatism, of boor-
ishness and culture." Rienzo was alternately both the traitor to his working-class origins and the ineffectual bourgeois intellectual so disdained by
sixties Marxists. If Rienzo showed any religious motivation, this was because "he handled the weapon of social provocation with the consummate
art of the actor and the demagogue." Ultimately Rienzo fell from a combination of his own "nervous depression" and the fact that "in the long
run the multitude grew tired of the tribune's mania for discoursing on ancient history. The gaudy ceremonies had also to be paid for" (98–104).

After Ideology

In Great Britain the late 1970s through the 1990s saw a reaction against
"revolutionary" studies and the rejection of any explicitly "popular" ideologies. Many historians now seemed to treat with suspicion any grand

narratives, political slogans, or grandiose symbols, and any movements for political change from the "bottom up." Some, in fact, have revealed a decided preference for history from the "top down." In addition, under the influence of the *Annales* and other social-scientific schools of history writing, few, if any, historians were willing to treat the biography of any individual figure with serious attention, given the weight then being placed upon more abstract and universal social and economic trends. What few comments there were in narrative histories or political analyses were derisive. Thus Peter Partner, in *The Lands of St. Peter* (1972), could dismiss Rienzo as "the Roman equivalent of a London Cockney" who soon became a tyrant. But this "fat little lawyer" was too much for the true Roman elites to bear, and once challenged by the barons, "Cola's nerve broke at once," and his tribunate was over. John Larner's survey, *Italy in the Age of Dante and Petrarch* (1980), again stresses Cola's working-class origins but adds that he was "endowed with a limitless faculty for fantasy and self-delusion." Cola's Pentecost revolution was backed by mercenaries, according to Larner, and then proceeded to the "high comedy" of his dubbing as knight, his coronation, and the Roman Synod. After exile and prison, Cola emerged "with a paunch 'like a satrap of Asia' and a new fondness for the bottle," while "his grasp on events was soon overtaken." Larner's final judgment on Rienzo was as harsh as it was disdainful: "The future of Italy lay not with men such as this." Diana Wood, in her *Clement VI* (1989), judges Rienzo from the point of view of the elites in Avignon as "the son of a washerwoman and an innkeeper" who, once in power, "became increasingly autocratic," revealed imperial aspirations, and fell from power "partly as a result of his cowardice." In his *Medieval Rome* (1994), art historian Paul Hetherington could label Cola a "major demagogue"; and George Holmes, writing his grand synthesis in *The Oxford History of Italy* (1997), emphasizes the shift away from "popular" movements by arguing that Cola's regime fell due largely to lack of support from any elites.

Class and politics aside, perhaps the most serious study of Rienzo in the past decade has been that of Gustav Seibt, whose *Anonimo romano: Geschichtsschreibung in Rom an der Schwelle zur Renaissance* (1992; Italian edition 2000) focuses on Rienzo's contemporary biographer and offers a comprehensive review of the historiography. While avoiding more tendentious elements of deconstruction, Seibt focuses on rhetorical strategies but still manages to analyze the *Vita* and its sources in the context of their time and place.

In North America few serious studies of Rienzo had emerged since Cosenza's edition of 1913 (reedited by the present writer in 1986 and again in 1996). Most historical *interpretation* of Rienzo in the United States after World War II has been shaped by the late Paul Oskar Kristeller.[4] A professor of philosophy at Columbia University and the leading scholar of the origins and nature of Renaissance humanism, Kristeller fled Nazi Germany in the 1930s but had been deeply influenced by Burdach's theory of the spiritual and apocalyptic origins of the Renaissance. By the 1950s, however, Kristeller had rejected "Burdach's attempts to derive the concept of the Renaissance from religious or mystical traditions" and instead delved deeper into the origins of humanism in the school culture of the Italian rhetoricians. Kristeller's change of heart and his emphasis on the professional origins of Renaissance thought were to have a profound influence on almost all subsequent American scholars of the early Renaissance. Part and parcel with this rejection of Burdach, however, remained a hesitance among Renaissance historians to study Rienzo in any serious way.

In 1961 Ernest Hatch Wilkins published his *Life of Petrarch*. Wilkins was thoroughly familiar with the sources for the period, and while his chief subject was the great poet and humanist, Cola di Rienzo played an important part in his narrative: he was "the most spectacular figure of the fourteenth century." Wilkins's attention and his assessment went some small way toward rehabilitating the Roman for the next generation. In 1975 there appeared the English translation of Ghisalberti's 1928 edition of the *Vita* by John Wright as *The Life of Cola di Rienzo*. Wright provides both an elegant translation and a solid introduction to Rienzo and the sources while going far to reintroduce the importance of the religious and civic trends that were so fundamental to Cola's life and career. Wright frames his edition without any apparent ideology; and while following the basic schema of the Anonimo romano, his ultimate judgment is a positive one, and one that reveals a close study and appreciation of the personality and mind of the tribune. Rienzo "had no permanent effect whatever on the political development of Italy or Rome. He had become a figure of heroic legend and romantic history: a perfectly appropriate fate, and one which, we can imagine, would have pleased him immensely" (20). Also in 1975, too late to benefit from Wright's work, William Melczer examined the divergent political paths of Petrarch and Rienzo, providing the best analysis to date of the contrast between Petrarch's "elegiac political ideal" for Rome's revival and Cola's own "dialectic grasp of the necessity for a dynamic correlation between political thought and political reality," a capacity that "makes [Rienzo's] greatness and accounts for his modernity." In 1991 Donald R. Kelley recapitulated the consensus among Anglo-American historians, introducing Rienzo through Bulwer-Lytton's fiction and summarizing him as "self-educated, visionary, supremely ambitious, and undoubtedly neurotic in more ways than one." Kelley did, however, move discussion forward by observing that Rienzo's "mad scheme" synthesized the revival of ancient Rome with Franciscan Spiritual ideas of renewal, "thus combining mysticism with classicism, religious fanaticism with political humanism." Kelley also contrasts Rienzo with Petrarch and finds the latter's option for the "contemplative life" the inspiration for humanist "methods of historical criticism." On the whole, however, in the United States, as in Great Britain and France, individual biography and the analysis of intellectual history were already becoming outmoded forms of history writing. It would really take another decade before the letter-form, the memoir, and the biography were again recognized as the legitimate province of the historian.

More recently Cola di Rienzo has been the subject of a doctoral thesis by art historian Amy Schwarz. Her "Images and Illusions of Power in Trecento Art: Cola di Rienzo and the Ancient Roman Republic" (1994) used the Anonimo romano's descriptions of the great political and religious paintings commissioned by Rienzo in preparation for his 1347 revolution as the basis for an analysis of the common visual language of the fourteenth century in Italy. While the paintings no longer exist, Schwarz provided analogous examples of political, apocalyptic, and *infamante* genres to demonstrate Cola's use of political metaphor as a basis for political power. Schwarz's serious treatment of the tribune seeks to place him squarely within the context of his time and place without resort to any of the ideologies or historical fashions that have so made him a projection for each successive generation's obsessions and predispositions. Thomas Giangreco approached Rienzo in his dissertation, "Reform, Renewal, and Renaissance: The Thought of Cola di Rienzo in Its Historical Context" (1997), but he offered a conventional retelling that relies almost solely on Wright's translation of the Anonimo romano and borrows Gerhard Ladner's interpretive framework of reform. Giangreco followed this up with an article in 1996 analyzing Cola's Joachimism that relied largely on findings from our own second edition of *Petrarch and the Revolution of Cola di Rienzo* (1986). In 1998 Amanda Collins thoughtfully analyzed Cola's rediscovery of the *Lex de imperio* of Vespasian.

Rienzo in His Own Time and Place

Using new research on fourteenth-century Italian religious life, on Rome's debt to its classical past, and on Roman social and economic structures of the later Middle Ages, this book will attempt to understand Cola di Rienzo in his own time and place and in the terms that he and his contemporaries saw him and his work for the revival of Rome. Thus the Cola who emerges from the following pages will, I hope, be placed into the context of a physical, cultural, and social world that is decidedly not our own. His actions and words—and those of his contemporaries—may seem foreign to modern eyes and ears, less resonant of the history and traumas of the twentieth century, and his motivations, both stated and unstated, more perplexing to attempts at analysis using familiar political, social, or psychological models. His story, however, and that of Rome in his time, makes an endlessly fascinating tale.

CHAPTER I

Birth, Youth, and Society

The myths surrounding Cola di Rienzo began with Cola himself.

In 1312 Rome was a bleeding corpse without a head. Following the deadly attack on Boniface VIII at Anagni in 1303, the papal court had fled Rome and in 1305 finally relocated to Avignon in southern France, where it was to remain until 1377. With it went the bureaucracy and all its attendant services, the diplomatic corps, the heads of the religious orders, and large portions of the noble Roman and Italian families who made up the cardinalate and the pope's Curia. Rome's population had reached a peak of about 1.5 million in the second century C.E.; had dropped to 800,000 by the time of Constantine the Great c. 325, and to 500,000 by 450. In the Middle Ages it had fallen precipitously, and at the height of papal power in the later Middle Ages, it had reached 80,000. But by 1310, with the papacy in France, the population of Rome has been estimated at between 18,000 and 30,000. Most Romans huddled within the bend of the Tiber marked by the triangle of the Mausoleum of Augustus at the north, Castel Sant'Angelo to the west (fig. 1), and the Tiber Island to the south, the area called the *abitato* (map 1). The Vatican Borgo, stretching from St. Peter's to the river, retained its boundaries set by the walls of Leo IV (847–55). The remaining 1,215 hectares (almost 4.7 square miles) within the ancient Aurelian Wall lay nearly empty.[1] This *disabitato* remained a dangerous waste of forest, vineyard, and garden, interrupted only by the irregular masses of Rome's fortified monasteries and the fortress-towers of its barons, by hamlets scattered around the major churches and the militarized hulks of Rome's vast ruins.[2] By 1340 approximately twenty-three

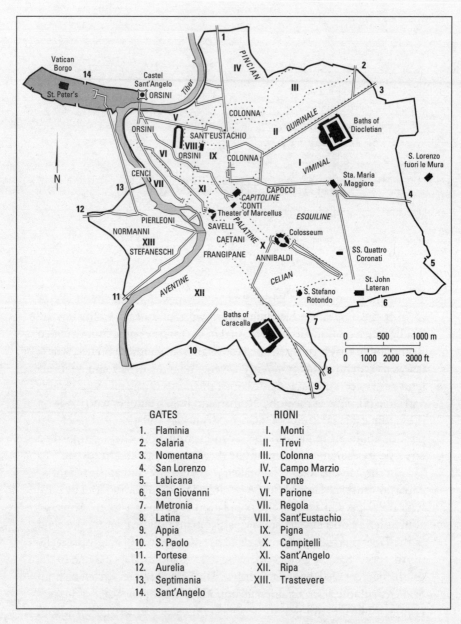

GATES

1. Flaminia
2. Salaria
3. Nomentana
4. San Lorenzo
5. Labicana
6. San Giovanni
7. Metronia
8. Latina
9. Appia
10. S. Paolo
11. Portese
12. Aurelia
13. Septimania
14. Sant'Angelo

RIONI

I. Monti
II. Trevi
III. Colonna
IV. Campo Marzio
V. Ponte
VI. Parione
VII. Regola
VIII. Sant'Eustachio
IX. Pigna
X. Campitelli
XI. Sant'Angelo
XII. Ripa
XIII. Trastevere

MAP I. Rome in the fourteenth century, showing gates, *rioni,* and major baronial families. Copyright Italica Press.

cities in northern and central Italy had populations over 20,000, but Rome lagged sadly behind other Italian and European capitals:[3] Venice with 120,000 on about 525 hectares; Padua with 30,000 on about 506 hectares; a vertical Genoa with 70,000 on 110 hectares; Florence with 95,000 on 630 hectares. Naples boasted 100,000 citizens on about 200 hectares just before 1350, while Paris counted 200,000 on 440 hectares. Constantinople, the largest city in the West, had a population of close to 1 million.

In May 1312 Emperor Henry VII (1309–13) was laying siege to the city of Rome, trying to seize and hold it long enough to be crowned emperor in St. Peter's and to quell opposition to German imperial claims on Italy. But Robert the Wise, king of Naples and chief ally of the pope and his Guelph Party, had dispatched his brother, John of Gravina, with a contingent of Neapolitan troops to seize the Ponte Molle on Rome's northern approach and to block the emperor's entry. While Henry's army forced its way across the bridge and entered Rome, it found more than half of the city occupied by the Neapolitans, reinforced by troops from the Guelph cities of Florence, Lucca, and Siena and elsewhere in Tuscany. The Roman nobility, long divided among themselves, broke into civil war, mostly ranged around the opposing pro-imperial Colonna and pro-papal Orsini families. The Borgo, the *abitato,* and the Tiber bridges were held by anti-imperial forces. Factional fighting was so fierce in the streets and roads of Rome, especially those leading to St. Peter's, that the emperor was forced to fight his way across the city street by street, and building by building, penetrating the *abitato* only as far as the Pantheon, Santa Sabina on the Aventine, and the Torre delle Milizie. Henry therefore crossed the *disabitato* to take his crown from unwilling papal legates at the Lateran on June 29, 1312.

But according to a letter written in July 1350 by Cola di Rienzo to Henry's grandson, Emperor Charles IV, Henry still wanted to see St. Peter's basilica, the traditional site of coronations for all his predecessors since Charlemagne:

But since he could do nothing else because of the barricades, he took only one companion, a native of Lazio who knew the hidden ways of the City. Disguised as a pilgrim, secretly crossing through the barricades and the roadblocks, he visited the precincts of St. Peter and the place of coronation, just as he wanted. But he was unable to return so secretly. The alarm rose up that the emperor, in disguise, was crossing through the territory of his rivals. Suddenly, the gates of all the roads in front of him were seized, guarded and closed, and a public crier was sent through the Guelph section of the city, shouting loudly that if anyone could recognize the emperor—who was secretly passing through the barricades that day—and could capture and turn him over to the Captain of the People, he would receive a large reward, in gold.

The emperor and the Latin heard the criers buzzing all around them, and so they passed through an out-of-the-way street, which is called the Ripa, since it is on the banks of the Tiber River, where my house still stands. Turning back from the barricades close by my house, away from the roadblocks and checkpoints, pretending they wanted a drink, they went into my house, which was a public tavern. Once inside they asked for room and board for a nice quiet night. Since her husband was then away, attending to some business, my mother cordially received and put up the gentlemen. The emperor hid out there, pretending to be sick, for ten days, according to some people, and for fifteen days, according to others. However long it was, my mother was completely unsuspecting and full of concern and care. If you want to know more about this brief encounter, you can get a statement from those who lived nearby—if any of them are still alive—as I think they are.

But, meanwhile, while the Latin was going out to buy provisions, my mother, who was a young woman and quite attractive—as I mentioned—served this lord freely, no less perhaps than their beloveds ministered to holy David and the just Abraham. Finally, once the streets were clear, the emperor, along with the Latin, secretly retreated to the Aventine Hill, where he was staying in Rome. A few days later, with his entire army, he left Rome and hastened toward Lombardy. Finally, in the month of August, on the 16th, I believe, [August 24 is correct] he died at Buonconvento [near Siena], as is well known.

And since there is no secret that is not revealed, after the emperor's absence and departure from the city, that same Latin revealed in my house, as he did in many other places, that the lord emperor himself had hidden in my tavern for many days. When this news about so great a lord became known to my mother, who before that—and I believe this—was truly ignorant of the fact, just as young women will, she confided to one of her woman friends that she believed that the emperor had made her pregnant. Now, that friend told the secret to another friend—in confidence as women do—so that she would keep the whole affair a secret. And so, from day to day, as it was whispered from ear to ear, the affair was kept a very big secret.

Finally, near death, my mother revealed it to the priest, as she should have. But back in those days, on account of his wife's infirmity, Lorenzo, as my father was called, made arrangements to have me, still an infant, raised by one of his male relatives in Anagni, a day's journey from the City. There I remained, a peasant among peasants, until my twentieth year. Finally, returning to Rome upon Lorenzo's death, I was then apprised of these facts both by the priest, as well as by a woman friend of mine, and also by quite a few secret sharers. (Letter 50, BBCR 2.3:198–213, at ll. 121–75)

Parcival, Boccaccio's or Sermini's tales, Robin Hood, and Bulwer-Lytton himself come to mind in Cola's marvelous account of his origins and birth, the earliest we possess.[4] What are we to make of this amazing tale? Cola was, after all, attempting to persuade one emperor that he was the bastard offspring of another—in fact Charles's own natural uncle—in order to be released from prison. But details ring true. The tribune knows his city and the neighborhood, or *contrada,* around Sant'Angelo in Pescheria well. He paints a vivid picture of this district and its social context: the narrow alleys and small courtyards, the cries of heralds and the sounds of crowds echoing down Rome's undulating streets by night, the life of a tavern, the gossip network of a densely packed neighborhood, the stuff of Italian *beffa* and *commedia;* and yet also the closely knit social fabric of a pulsing urban organism.

We also know the date that Cola thought most likely for his own birth: if the emperor died on August 24 and had left Rome a few days earlier, Cola was presumably conceived no later than late July 1312, and therefore was born no later than April 1313. He must have felt some shame about his origins, no matter how exalted their circumstances in his fictions or public memory: in a letter to the archbishop of Prague, dated no later than August 15, 1350, Cola compares his future political legitimacy under the emperor to his "hidden and adulterous" conception in his mother's bed, and his future true home as the church, and not in the tavern where he was born.

Cola's contemporary biographer, the Anonimo romano, recounts the publicly known facts: "Cola di Rienzo was of humble lineage: his father was a tavern keeper. He was named Lorenzo. His mother was named Matalena, and she earned her living by doing laundry and carrying water. Cola was born in the Regola, one of the city's thirteen *rioni,* or regions. His house was beside the river, among the mills, on the street leading to the Regola, behind San Tommaso, below the temple of the Jews" (AR XVIII, ll. 1–7, Porta, 143).[5]

For the fourteenth century these very few details spoke chapters: the region or *rione* of Rome, the parish, his parents' occupations, and the location of his home would have stood out like road signs, signifiers of family, social status, and economic class. Italians in the 1350s would have been able to pick up from these scanty references, as much as from a man's or woman's clothing, who and what Cola was.

On July 29/30, 1347, at the height of Cola's revolution, Ildebrandino Conti, bishop of Padua, wrote a letter to his vicar, Leonardo de San Sepulcro, from Valmontone on the via Appia south of Rome. He tells his vicar that Cola "was a man of the people, not wealthy." "Nicolaus Laurentii, the son of a miller," so Pope Clement VI refers to the former tribune in

November 1348. He confuses the occupation, but he knows the neighborhood from reputation.

Cola's house, the tavern of Rienzi, stood in the *rione* Regola, directly on the river, among the mills in fact, behind a church of San Tomasso, probably the parish church of San Tomasso dei Cenci or "in Capite Molarum," St. Thomas of the Mill Run. The church of San Tomasso still exists, tucked within the circuit of the Monte dei Cenci, opposite the remnants of the *torre* of the Cenci palace. Between the Monte and the Lungotevere the street drops off sharply before rising again to meet the embankment and the modern office and apartment buildings that line it. The parish of San Tomasso lay under what is now the area bounded by the via Arenula as it begins at the Ponte Garibaldi and includes the Palazzo and via Cenci. Another parish, Sta. Maria in Capite Molarum, sometimes called *iuxta flumen,* or "next to the river," extended between the Ponte Fabricio and San Tomasso parish, over the area that Rome's present chief synagogue, built in 1904, now covers. Both churches had the name *"in capite molarum"* from at least the twelfth century; and before the embankments were built, a second island—perhaps only a large sandbar— upstream and east of the Tiber Island, may have lain just across a narrow channel from both the *abitato* and the island, the perfect location for mill runs. Such mills that ground the wheat for Rome's bread had been in place along the Tiber since Roman times and were rebuilt there by Belisarius during the Gothic siege. A drawing from the Codex Escurialensis from about 1495 shows several of these wooden floating mills, complete with sheds, waterwheels, and pontoons, berthed between the shore of the Regola and the Tiber Island just upstream of the Ponte Fabricio (Giudeo) (fig. 2).

Before the great high embankments and wide boulevard of the Lungotevere finally channeled the Tiber's floodwaters in the 1880s, the Regola, or *arenula,* was literally the sandy bank where the Tiber bend deposited much of the river's long-traveling silt and where fishermen and millers mingled with the crews and passengers of riverboats up from the coast. Giovanni Cavallini's *Polistoria* (c. 1345) testifies to these well-known origins of the name *arenula,* its broad swatch of sandy beach still prominent in late-nineteenth-century photographs. Until the creation of the Lungotevere Cenci, the riverbank was lined with a solid wall of buildings, many as high as seven or eight stories, rising directly up from the walls on the river across from the Tiber Island. The overall effect was much like that of the Oltrarno in Florence today.

This "sandy shore" was accessed by a narrow gate below the Monte dei

Cenci and the church of San Tomasso, where via della Fiumara, which ran parallel to the river behind the row of houses fronting the Tiber, met via Cenci, and then continued west along via dei Vaccinari. Here, where small boats coming upriver could find a comfortable berth, and where the walls opened to give access to the *abitato,* was the natural place for a tavern. The location was also convenient both for merchants buying and selling in the neighboring cloth district, still marked today by via dei Botteghe Oscure, and for pilgrims traveling along via Papalis from the Lateran to St. Peter's. Access to both the riverfront road and the river reinforces the evidence from the Anonimo romano to point to the truth of Cola's claim that his parents' *domus* was right here on the river. Ironically, the entire neighborhood was destroyed in the act of creating the capital of the new Italian republic. Cola's birthplace now lies somewhere along the Lungotevere dei Cenci between via Beatrice Cenci and via del Progresso, perhaps beneath the Lungotevere, perhaps beneath the huge modernist apartment and office block to its north.

The Anonimo romano and Cola himself described his parents' *domus* as a *taverna.* In the fourteenth century in Rome, the places providing hospitality went by several names: *albergo, hospitium, osteria, hosteria, ostelleria.* By the fifteenth century, perhaps earlier, the *taverna* was defined as "a place where people drink and eat in exchange for payment to their owners." A *taverniere* could also provide lodging. While historians have given us good analyses of the types and locations of inns in the late fifteenth and sixteenth centuries, for the fourteenth century we have little information on the total number of inns in the *abitato.*[6] A Venetian Senate document of October 13, 1347 (K1175) reports that Venice once had 24 taverns but at that date had only 13. According to the chronicler Bonvesin della Riva, in 1288 Milan had 150 *alberghi.* Rome, the traveler's city par excellence, and in 1300 the destination for most of Europe's pilgrims, must have had a similarly large number; and their economic impact on the life of the city was proportionately great.

The hospitality industry was central to Rome's economy; but where did a taverner rank in Rome's social hierarchy, and what kind of income could he earn? We know that between the years 1300 and 1350, the yearly wages of a skilled artisan in Italy averaged 18 florins. By 1271 this Florentine gold coin was worth £1 s.9, or d. 348. We also know that a Roman innkeeper could earn 6 to 13 denarii per guest per night during the 1350 Jubilee; he might charge half this amount during regular seasons. In 1350 Buccio di Ranallo was outraged when he expected to be sharing a straw-mattressed bed with two or three more guests but found instead five, six, or even seven in his room. Little wonder, then, that Cola's father might earn a considerable income over the course of a year, perhaps 9 to 10 florins per year for each customer lodged on a given night, and with guests sometimes lodged five to seven per room, a popular five-room inn might bring in as much as 350 florins a year. Overhead, though considerable, was not overwhelming. In the 1370s, for example, in the *rione* Sant'Angelo, Cola's neighborhood, the rent on a large house that could be used for an inn was 20 to 30 florins a year; while that for a good-sized shop, with living space above, usually came to about 10 florins. Capital investment could be minimal. On July 15, 1395, the Aretine hotel owner Nofri di Giunta recorded his inventory of "4 beds filled with straw, 2 blankets, 4 feather pillows, 1 mattress," as well as "3 pairs of sheets, 1 azure-red blanket, 2 bedspreads." Lorenzo the taverner could therefore earn profit and a decent living for himself and his family.

To protect their rights, regulate trade, and guarantee status, Rome's innkeepers had formed their own guild, the *universitas* of *osti* and *tavernieri*, by the second half of the fourteenth century. In Rome, statutes regulating taverns date from the fifteenth century, but they represent a reform of statutes that probably originated in the fourteenth. These contain three chapters dealing with taverns and are evidence of their importance to the city's society and economy. They deal with opening and closing days and hours, prohibitions against bearing arms, weights and measures, and outdoor signage. Similar Venetian regulations of 1347 also prohibited nobles from managing, owning, or investing in taverns, a clear sign of their economic attractiveness.

Cola's father served a socioeconomic mix in keeping with the working-class nature of his busy commercial neighborhood: laborers, artisans, servants, small merchants, couriers, pilgrims, even the local priest, every workaday type except for public officials, who, at least in Siena, were prohibited from entering them. Social life consisted of activities confined to the public room where meals were served. In the mid–sixteenth century Montaigne recorded the types of entertainments provided by Italian inns: conversation across social class and occupation, singing, dancing, and some mild forms of gaming. Thus the inn formed a social nexus that made for easy interchange of news and opinion and so offered fertile ground for "transgressive ideology" of every sort to develop.

Cola's neighborhood stretched along the riverfront and included parts of three *rioni*: Regola, where he was born; Sant'Angelo, the commercial hub of the riverfront; and Ripa, the port farther down the Tiber bend. This urban scene has come vividly to life in Robert Brentano's use of the cartularies of the notary Antonio di Lorenzo Stefanelli de Scambiis, who worked around the fish market and church of Sant'Angelo in Pescheria. The cartulary dates from 1363 and portrays a vibrant neighborhood of brisk mercantile activity and a mix of classes and occupations.[7] Ensconced in their noble pile of the Theater of Marcellus, on the "Monte Savelli," the Savelli were the prominent family of the *contrada* and of the *rione* Ripa. Their predecessors in wealth and power, the Pierleoni, were also still important in the area. While we will look at Rome's barons in another chapter, we must not imagine these noble families as only knights and vassals. They also gained wealth as property owners, cattle dealers, vegetable sellers, and canons in the local churches. Sant'Angelo was, first and foremost, a *rione* dominated by the fishmongers and their families, leasing the ancient stones on which to sell their fish from the canons of Sant'Angelo in Pescheria, the focus of a fish market around and beneath its ancient arcade that gave the church its nickname, "Sant'Angelo *in foro Piscium*" (fig. 3).

We do not know where Cola's parents came from.[8] His father, Lorenzo, or "Rienzo" in Romanesco, had a common enough name. Following a standard form of surname only just then developing, Cola, the shortened form of Nicola, would then have been the equivalent of "Nickie, Larry's son." The form of his name reinforced what we already know of his decidedly non-noble roots. We also know that Cola had siblings. The Anonimo romano tells us that at least one brother was murdered. In a letter to the archbishop of Prague dated August 1350, Cola remarks that his sister and his mother-in-law were being held captive in a monastery. How many other brothers and sisters might Cola have had? There is no way of telling, but as in any preindustrial society, even today, a couple's children tended to be many. Tuscan evidence from 1427 indicates that, on the average, men tended to be a good deal older (thirty-eight) than their wives (twenty-six); male children outnumbered females by as high as 116 to 100 (158/100 for the rich). Of children who survived their first year, only 50 percent seem to have survived to age twenty-one. The number of children who survived their fathers could range from 1.7 in Sicily to 4.8 in Quercy in France.

But Cola's youth was not spent, with brothers and sisters, amid the crowded streets and alleys of Rome but in Anagni in Lazio, about 66 kilometers southeast of Rome at the beginning of the Apennine range called the Monti Ernici.[9] The ancient city had been a bishopric since about 487; it formed part of the Patrimony of St. Peter; and it had some geographic importance on the road to the kingdom of Naples. Along with other cities of the Lands of St. Peter, including Viterbo, Perugia, Orvieto, Rieti, and Tivoli, it was often the residence of the popes, the Curia, and their attendant administrators, attorneys, notaries, bankers and merchants, craftspeople, and servants. By 1300 it was a stronghold of the family of Benedetto Caetani, Pope Boniface VIII, and a focus of the Caetani's rapid acquisition of lands south of Rome, much to the detriment of their Colonna rivals.

The city became infamous throughout Christendom in the fall of 1303 with the "Crime of Anagni" during which Guillaume de Nogaret, the chancellor of Philip IV of France, attacked the papal city in response to Boniface's threat to excommunicate the king. He did so with the aid of Sciarra Colonna and a contingent of Colonna vassals. On September 7, 1303, amid anti-French rioting by the residents and looting led by the French and Colonna forces, Sciarra and Nogaret physically seized and beat the elderly Boniface, leading to the pope's death on October 12 and the eventual flight of the papacy from Rome to southern France.

If his story is true, Cola di Rienzo arrived in Anagni sometime after 1313. It was not unusual for children, even infants, of comfortable Roman families to be sent out to the countryside for nursing. We do not know where Cola lived in Anagni with his father's relatives. The Anonimo romano notes that Cola "had an uncle named Janni Varvieri. He was a barber [barbiere]," and Cola later knighted him. But we cannot be certain whether "Johnny the Barber" was a brother of Cola's father, Lorenzo, or of his mother, Matalena, or of where he lived. Since Cola says that he remained in Anagni until his twentieth year, he must have received at least his grammar-school education there, perhaps at the city's cathedral school.

The city's chief attraction then, as today, was this cathedral, one of the most important Romanesque buildings in Lazio. Built between 1077 and 1104 by Bishop Pietro da Salerno upon the remains of the Roman acropolis, by the end of the thirteenth century the cathedral had become the center of the Caetani's public display. Here they endowed their own burial chapel, and here in 1295 Boniface VIII had erected a portrait statue of himself. Cola thus had ample opportunity to gaze upon this portrait in its niche high on the church's exterior and to ponder the public meaning of Boniface's life and his martyr's death at the hands of the Colonna. But inside the cathedral, past its many ancient architectural fragments and inscriptions, and beneath its Cosmatesque pavement, lies a work of art that must have had even more impact. In the chapel of St. Magnus, the bishop of Trani martyred here in 250 and patron saint of Anagni, one of the most important cycles of medieval Italian fresco presents scenes of ancient pagan figures and Old Testament history, along with a nearly complete depiction of the unfolding visions of the Apocalypse (fig. 4).

Beyond the crypt, down a narrow passage, lies the Oratory of St. Thomas à Beckett, dedicated by Pope Alexander III in 1173 to that other loyal churchman martyred by an unjust king and his baronial henchmen. This overall visual education was unmistakable: Anagni and its people, since 1303 reduced to poverty and political backwardness, had been deprived of their native son and continued to be oppressed by the lawlessness of its barons. Pope Boniface, St. Thomas, and St. Magnus were all slain for their loyalty to the church. Like the martyrs beneath the altar in St. John's Apocalypse, they must suffer, perhaps even die, if the condition of the Christian people was to be renewed. But what kind of renewal should this be? And who would be its agents?

CHAPTER 2

Education, Profession, and Family

From his youth he [Cola] was nourished on the milk of
eloquence: a good grammarian, the best of rhetoricians, and
a good student of the Classical authors. My, what a fast and
voluminous reader he was. He loved to peruse Livy, Seneca,
Cicero, and Valerius Maximus. He delighted in recounting the
magnificent tales of Julius Caesar. . . . He was a handsome man
with a wonderful laughter always on his lips. He was a notary.

Anonimo romano, XVIII, ll. 7–22, Porta, 143

Cola di Rienzo never told us who his teachers were, or the subjects that
he took in school, or who paid for his classes and masters, or for his books.[1]
He never told us how he became a notary, or where he went to learn his
profession. But where the documents are missing, the historian may be
able to piece together from the context of Cola's time and place, and with
a reasonable chance of accuracy and success, the kind of school he most
likely attended, the subjects that he took, and how he obtained the elements of his profession and trade, even perhaps the books he read.

How did a young man like Cola get any education at all? While our
evidence for Rome and its district, including Anagni, is plentiful for the
later Renaissance, the fourteenth century is still largely undocumented.
By 1300 most church-sponsored schools—monastic or cathedral—had
seen a decline in both their numbers and their influence. At the same time,
however, many communal and independent schools begin to appear in
documents throughout Italy. This also coincides with the movement of

many clergy into the public sphere as household tutors and neighborhood masters, some even as masters hired by the communes. These lay schools were generally known as "grammar" schools.

We do know that by the mid–sixteenth century Rome had more grammar schools than either Venice or Florence, and that Rome's communal authorities made greater efforts than those of most cities to certify and inspect schools. The commune's schools were set up, like those of many other Italian cities, on a *rione* or *contrada* system. In Rome the *maestri di rioni* were paid by the commune through the university. Boniface VIII had established the *studium Urbis,* University of Rome, in 1303, and he might have also set up the system of *maestri di rioni* at that time. No evidence for this exists until 1458, although in 1283 a Maestro Giacomo, *doctor grammatice,* does appear in a notarial document. Further, we do know that the commune required poor students to be taught for free, and that the *maestri* were compensated for this public service by being allowed to charge their private students. But we do not know how far back this practice goes: no records exist until the mid-to-late sixteenth century. Again, Rome was a cosmopolitan city in which many people, not only merchants and princes, wrote and discussed many subjects. By the thirteenth century a *studium* had been organized within the papal Curia itself; and the Curia contained men of great learning, book collectors, patrons, and many scholars from disparate origins employed in the Curia and in Rome's many ecclesiastical institutions.

By the end of the fifteenth century, some form of education seems to have been available to most male urban dwellers of some status. By then practically all sons, and some few of the daughters, of nobles and wealthy merchants attended Latin school, as did the sons of professionals— lawyers, physicians, notaries, high-level civil servants, professors, and teachers. Almost all the sons of master craftsmen and major shopkeepers also attended some form of schooling—grammar schools, and from the later thirteenth century *abbaco,* or business schools—while fewer of the sons of petty artisans, shopkeepers, and industrial workers gained access to a rudimentary literacy and facility with commercial math, geometry, and bookkeeping. The motives for these *popoli minuti* in seeking schooling were not, by and large, the social mobility of later centuries but advancement in their trade and the acquisition of social skills, moral education, and the ability to read for pleasure saints' lives, works of popular spirituality, chivalric romances, *novelle,* and travel literature then being written in, or translated into, their vernacular languages, whether Venetian, Tuscan, Neapolitan, or Romanesco. We know from notaries' memoirs and the documents they prepared that the social origins of members of Cola's profession were diverse: they were often the children of innkeepers, shopkeepers, artisans, bakers, smiths, papermakers, butchers, and fishmongers; and although they rarely entered a higher class, they could leave their children very well off, with extensive properties and the ability to rise even higher.

Fourteenth-century Italian schoolchildren followed a normative curriculum of reading medieval authors and a few ancient poetic classics (or portions of them). This curriculum constituted the bulk of the "liberal" art inherited from ancient Roman practice referred to as the *ars grammatica*. First came basic grammar: the alphabet, words, phrases, sentences. The next step of Cola's education probably involved "reading the Psalter," which was also used to teach the alphabet, syllabication, groups of prayers, and often psalms. Students learned to read and write using such standard texts as the *Donatus,* so called after the *Ars minor* of the fourth-century grammarian Donatus. As a talented student, young Rienzo then would have proceeded to the more sophisticated grammars, including the *Doctrinale,* the most famous textbook of the Middle Ages, written around 1199 by Alexander de Villedieu.

Finally, the *ars grammatica* exposed well-advanced students like Cola to the Latin classics that had survived into the fourteenth century, including Virgil *(Aeneid, Eclogues, Georgics),* Ovid *(Ars amatoria, Metamorphoses, Fasti, Tristia,* and *Epistolae ex Ponto),* Statius *(Thebiad),* Lucan *(Pharsalia),* and Boethius *(De consolatione philosophiae).* Like today's "course packs," such texts were often gathered together in manuscripts in commercial *scriptoria,* workshops set up to copy manuscripts and produce textbooks on demand. In general, this medieval curriculum was intended to prepare students first to write and speak correctly for business, public affairs, and the courts of princes and prelates using rules based on examples of good Latin. Only secondarily was it intended as a preparation for the actual study of literature or the creation of new forms. The purpose of education remained the practical needs of communal culture: commerce and its record keeping, participation in urban democracy, and the relations of the city to its neighbors.

Along with these needs went the development of the *ars dictaminis,*[2] the art of letter writing, which formed the next level of proficiency after students had gained a command of the rules and methods of good grammar. Aside from the rhetorical devices used in sermons and in forms of poetry, the art of letter writing was one of the few elements of the classical rhetorical tradition retained in the Middle Ages. In Italy at least it grew in response to the need for court and communal secretaries and notaries to compose formal letters for kings, emperors, bishops, and city councils according to strict formulae, taking into account the status and power of the person or institution addressed. In Cola's time the sources for this art of letter writing were Cicero's *De inventione,* the pseudo-Ciceronian *Rhetorica ad Herennium,* and Julius Victor. It was not until Pier Paolo Vergerio's identification of the classical panegyric, judicial and deliberative speeches, and six-part oration defending Bartolomeo Cremisone (1390–92) that classical rhetoric forms and styles were again used in oratory. The sermon continued to be the model for even civic orations until then.

By the time Cola had mastered his basic letters, then spent years imitating good grammatical style, and then reading the available Latin classics, he was ready either to become a grammar-school master himself or to pursue higher learning, most likely in one of the three major disciplines: theology, law, or medicine. By that time he had also reached his late teens or early twenties. When he was about twenty, around the year 1333, Cola tells us, he returned to Rome. His decision may well have been based on the death of his father and his need to take up direction of what had now become his *domus,* the tavern by the Tiber. But it could also have been the outcome of his desire to continue his education and to enter a profession. Rome and its university could provide the perfect means to this end.[3] On April 20, 1303, Boniface VIII had issued the bull *In supremae,* creating a *studium generale* intended to serve all social elements of the city and all of Rome's professional and administrative classes. By the 1320s we have documentation for faculties of medicine, arts, and law at this university. On September 26, 1347, Cola di Rienzo himself sent his emissary, Giovanni del Giudice, to Clement VI to obtain the confirmation of the existing seat of grammar and logic. Some scholars also assert that a notarial faculty, granting degrees in the *ars dictaminis* and *ars notarie,* must have existed in Rome. This makes some sense, considering the prominent role played by notaries in both the papal administration and the economic and legal life of the city. If this is so, it also explains how and where Cola di Rienzo obtained the higher education that made him a notary and brought him into Rome's professional class. But the lack of evidence makes any definite statements impossible.

Quite unlike today's "notary public" in the United States, who acts almost solely as a witness to a variety of preprinted forms for business and banking, the medieval notary was the descendant and continuator of the ancient Roman profession of *tabellio,* the scrivener who, using a tablet, drew up such written instruments as contracts, letters, and wills, and is so recorded in the *Digest* of Emperor Justinian (527–565).[4] The ancient Roman *notarius,* on the other hand, was a shorthand writer, a stenographer, and hence a secretary or clerk. Form books for *tabelliones* already existed in the eighth century; by the ninth and tenth centuries, the emergence of the trading cities of Italy and the importance of written contracts increased people's reliance on the notary's knowledge of the exact legal formulae that insured their validity.

The evolution of the notary's profession took a unique turn in Rome, given the presence of the papal court and the long survival of Roman and Byzantine legal institutions and traditions there. From the twelfth century on, all candidates for the notariat were being granted their investiture, or license, by the papacy. The candidate had to undergo an examination, regularly conducted by cardinals, into his moral character and his knowledge of the rudiments of legal theory. Then he was invested with the symbols of his trade, a pen and ink, just as a knight was invested with his sword and spurs. As late as the early thirteenth century, Honorius III is recorded as personally traveling to Lazio's cathedral towns to perform these investitures. Only in the mid–thirteenth century did the popes delegate this authority, but they did so under strict limitations regarding the number of notaries to be invested and the length of the delegated authority. In the late thirteenth century, under Boniface VIII for the first time, a bishop, that of Anagni, was delegated authority to conduct these investitures. Soon thereafter, however, with the withdrawal of the popes and their Curia from Rome, the papal notariat fell into decline; and most notaries in Rome or Lazio who sought a public authority wider than that of their own commune favored investiture from an imperial authority, usually from a "count palatine" who by the fourteenth century could well be a non-noble lawyer.

This process of public investiture and authority was not unique to Rome or Lazio. By 1250 in most Italian communes, strict laws governed notaries' education, their public licensing, their fees, and the preservation of their protocol form books. In 1334 in Florence, for example, the successful candidate for notary was required to pass three exams before a board of six notaries: the first in Latin grammar and in the forms of contracts, and then a second and third public examination before the consuls of the notarial guild to test his knowledge of law and his ability to translate Latin documents into Italian. After serving a six-month apprenticeship with a senior notary and passing examinations given by the local notaries' guild, the young man was then adopted into the profession. In the *Statuta urbis,* the Roman statute book of the early fourteenth century, no fewer than forty-five sections detail the duties of various notarial officials both in private practice and attached to government bodies.

Communal regulation was necessary, for the notary was responsible for formulating and recording the very core of communal life: its good laws. While ancient *tabelli* used only four basic instruments, at the University of Bologna between 1200 and 1250, there issued forth a score of formularies for the notarial profession. By 1255, however, the *Summa totius artis notarie* of Rolandino Passagieri of Bologna (d. 1300, himself the son of an innkeeper) had become the standard work, most probably because it most consciously and successfully fit the new business and commercial climate of the age. At the same time, the growth of the notariat provided an essential element in the revival of Roman law, of new government and communal life. Hence the notary, aligned with the new legal science since the eleventh century, was used to documenting all kinds of private acts and communal statutes. Notaries were required to know the precise forms of legal instruments for wills, codicils, matrimonial agreements, dowries, emancipations, divisions of patrimonies, business partnerships, leases, and all kinds of commercial arrangements. In Lazio by the thirteenth century, notarial testimony validated even agreements between bishops and their cathedral chapters, agreements that continued to rely solely upon the affixation of the bishop's seal in the rest of Europe. In Italy the notary alone was viewed as guaranteeing the basic components of what medievals saw as a good law: *munimina, authentica, monumenta publica,* or *carte legales.*

Upon earning his license, Cola would have set himself up in a small shop, with enough room for a desk and chairs, a shelf of books and writing materials, perhaps with a storage room behind for his archives, perhaps even in a chamber in his family *domus,* the tavern. He might then visit clients or the parties about to enter into a contract, or the two parties would come to his office and present succinct notes of the salient points of their intended contract or other agreement on a note sheet, or *scheda.* Working from their rough outline, Cola would then create a *dicta,* the preliminary form of the definitive act. While in the tradition of the very influential Bolognese school these were called *rogationes* and usually appeared as notes on the back side of the actual contracts, in Rome the notary would create the *dicta* as an intermediary form to the final document: the *mundum.* Then, after the parties involved had received their copies of the *mundum,* the *dicta* were usually kept by the notary himself.

Cola di Rienzo, following Roman practice, probably put these on left-over pieces of parchment.

These notarial *dicta* thus also provided the basis for subsequent versions. Years later, for purposes of record or to resolve subsequent disputes, the parties or their heirs could then ask the notary or his successor either for a newly composed public record based on the *dicta* or for a copy of the *dicta* themselves. Between 1220 and 1240, Rome and Lazio saw the beginnings of regular copybooks, or registers, variously named *quaterni protocollorum, libri rogorum, libri actorum,* or *cartularia dictorum.* At first these were just long rolls, stitched together, with the notary's sign overlapping the seams to guarantee authenticity. In Lazio the earliest example comes from Anagni in 1240. Cartularies, the book or "codex" form of notarial records, probably came into use in the late thirteenth or early fourteenth century and point to the social and economic need to have the rights of the contracting parties well established and easily searchable. The codex enabled Roman notaries to create useful *fondi* of records; this made the notary not simply an expediter of instruments but a depository of record and hence even more important to Rome's commercial and administrative culture. Such record keeping also helped to reinforce the hereditary nature of this developing profession, for the *fondi* thus accumulated would become personal and inheritable family property. The practice was a mixed blessing. As Isa Lori Sanfilippo has noted, the treatment of such records as private property often resulted in their dispersal or destruction, despite repeated legislation on the part of commune and pope. No complete series of notarial records survives for Rome before the 1360s.[5]

The *public* office of the notary would bring Cola di Rienzo and his skills into quite another world. In an earlier era when Latin literacy had still been the province of the clergy, and vernacular literacy and skill in business mathematics that of the merchant, many in feudal society, and even in the government of the new urban communes of Italy—the most literate part of Europe—lacked basic literacy or sufficient training in the *ars grammatica,* or especially the *ars dictaminis,* to trust to their own skills in framing laws, statutes, or public decrees. While the balance of literacy had shifted to the laity—lawyers, notaries, physicians, grammar-school teachers—by the thirteenth century, notaries still accompanied many a podesta and judge in their duties and rounds, quoted them the law, and drew up official documents for their governments. By the fourteenth century most of these duties had been assumed by trained lawyers, and podestas were themselves often civil lawyers. Nevertheless, the notary's duties offered great possibilities for advancement in an increasingly so-phisticated political and cultural era.

With the thirteenth century, as individual notaries became over-whelmed by the number of public documents and diplomatic letters re-quired by their communes, town governments began to imitate papal and royal courts and to create their own chancelleries. By the late thirteenth century the chancellery had become a common feature of the Italian com-mune. The chief notary of a commune was often entitled "chancellor" and supervised the *notaro dettatore* (chancery), as well as the notaries who served the priors, consuls, podesta, captain of the people, *gonfaloniere* (standard-bearer) of justice, and the guilds. By 1327 Modena employed 51 notaries in its government; in 1381 Perugia employed 108.

Since the twelfth century the *ars dictaminis* had laid out the proper forms to be used when addressing, petitioning, or commanding a par-ticular audience. While the *dictatores,* or teachers of *ars dictaminis,* relied on ancient models, in antiquity the private letter was deemed best if it imitated simple conversation. But the medieval letter followed the rules of oratory, and the blur between public and private authority and indi-viduals made the private letter a thing of public concern. Thus those who could frame such letters properly and eloquently could become impor-tant public figures. It is no coincidence that by the mid–fourteenth cen-tury many notaries found themselves not only rising through the ranks of communal governments as secretaries, vicars, and legal advisers to the various departments but also emerging in the highest levels of town gov-ernments as orators, ambassadors, and chancellors of important cities. Coluccio Salutati and Leonardo Bruni of Florence are two of the best-known Renaissance chancellors.

Given the relatively small class of literate professionals and the high death rate in all classes, once Cola had passed the age of highest life risk, his path to advancement in the growing economies and administrations of the Italian city-states was predictable and smooth. While many young pro-fessionals seem to have postponed marriage and then family from a deep-rooted sense of social and economic necessity, Cola di Rienzo appears to have been married and to have had children when he was still in his twen-ties.[6] This does not mean that up until then he had lived like a celibate. Cola himself admits in his August 1350 letter to the archbishop of Prague that he had spent much of his youth in the "sin of fornication." He was a handsome young man, charismatic, well educated, and eloquent, clearly with good prospects for advancement. Even with the papal court in far-off Avignon, Rome continued its long-term obsession with property and its exchange, with the arrangement of dowries and marriage alliances among its great families, its work of government and diplomacy. Cola had returned to Rome from Anagni by the year 1333, when he was about twenty. He probably spent the next few years establishing himself, either as an assistant in a larger firm or on his own. He had apparently inherited his parents' tavern, which he referred to as his *domus,* and thus his earnings may well have gone to providing him with modest savings enough to marry soon after his return. Judging from the fact that immediately after his victory at the battle of Porta San Lorenzo in November 1347 he had had his son Lorenzo dubbed a knight, we can assume, with reservations, that the boy was already an adolescent. This would mean that Cola may have been married around 1334.

According to Cola, his wife's name was Livia. It was a cultured name, not that of a saint or a shopkeeper but of the wife of Emperor Augustus himself. But because of possible scribal errors in transcribing Cola's correspondence, it could be easy to mistake a series of strokes that looked like "Liina" either as the aristocratic "Livia" or as "Luna," a far more plebeian name. The possibility exists, of course, that once Cola had become Tribunus Augustus, he bestowed this grand name upon his wife himself. But we know from the Anonimo romano that she was "very young and beautiful" even at the time of Cola's rule in 1347. Cola's father-in-law was a Roman named Francesco, so identified in a letter Cola sent to the abbot of Sant'Alessio in Rome in 1350. We also know that Cola's own notary and his chancellor was an in-law, Cecco, or Francesco, Mancini, whose son Conte was also a member of Cola's government. The documents of the time also speak of a *Iohannes Francisci de Mancinis imperiali auctoritate notarius et nunc protonotarii dicti domini Tribuni,* "Giovanni, the son of Francesco Mancini, imperial notary and now protonotary of the said lord Tribune." But the Anonimo romano simply refers to Francesco's son as "Conte" and as Cola's *nepote,* "nephew." Some historians have identified Francesco as Cola's father-in-law and Livia's father, but there is little evidence to confirm this with any certainty. Whatever their relationship to Cola, however, it is probable that the Mancini were of the same class of rising professionals as Rienzo himself. Given Cola's own sense of style and the beauty of the diplomatic and other letters that survive from his reign, it is clear that he would not have been satisfied with anyone but the best available notary to represent both Rome and his new government. Cecco must therefore have been a well-regarded professional and representative of the circles within which Cola moved.

Livia therefore belonged to a class of Romans for whom the naming of their children after classical figures was not improbable; and a young beautiful woman with so evocative a name would not long have escaped the notice of the young Rienzo. The Anonimo romano, not one for sparing the overreaching and pretentious, never makes the slightest disparaging remark about Cola's wife but instead relates how not only Rome's barons but also Queen Giovanna of Naples herself courted her favor. Livia seems to have handled this attention, and her very public role, with a good deal of unfaulted grace, underscoring her solid professional family background. Whatever the status of Livia's family, however, it certainly was not wealthy. In a letter to Pope Clement VI dated October 11, 1347, Cola mocks the rumors then being circulated around Rome that he had grown richer than Boniface VIII and the emperor Charles IV, "a remarkable accomplishment and marvelous to think about," he writes, "that I [did this] with only 40 florins from my wife's dowry and my notary's profession combined!" Livia had brought to the young marriage enough funds to pay the rent on a house in the center of the *abitato* for about a year, the equivalent of a skilled artisan's wages for about two years: good and modest savings for humble people with humble goals, but a risky start for a handsome young couple with good backgrounds, solid professional status, and high ambitions. But start they did; and quite soon they had a family.

Cola and Livia had at least two sons: the Lorienzo whom Cola had dubbed a knight in 1347 was, according to the Anonimo romano, "one of Cola's sons." Cola also refers to "my son" in a letter to the abbot of Sant'Alessio in Rome in August 1350 and to "my son the knight" in a letter to the archbishop of Prague from about the same time. In the same letter Cola offers to act as the emperor's agent in taking back Rome. As surety for his good faith, he promises to give as a hostage "my one son the knight." But in a letter to Emperor Charles IV just a few weeks earlier, Cola had also noted that he had wanted to name one of his *sons* Boethius. Then, in 1351, Cola wrote a letter to Cardinal Gui de Boulogne from Raudnitz in Bohemia, in which he told him that for his pains in defending the people of Rome against tyrants, he had been forced into hiding, "living on poor alms with my wife, my daughters and sons, with my little nephews and my cousin." The contemporary *Chronicon Estense* reports another version of Cola's offer to the emperor, that if Cola had not established himself as lord of Rome within the space of twelve months, the emperor could then hang his *two* sons whom he had given as surety of his promise. In his letter to Fra Michele of Monte Sant'Angelo written in Raudnitz, Bohemia, on September 28, 1350, Cola himself refers to his two sons and two daughters. What is the truth in all these various accounts? Most probably the pride of a paterfamilias in his eldest male child, the one old enough to have shared his parents' rise to prominence and to have himself participated in his father's most famous victory. Lorienzo would remain his father's constant pride and concern, even during Cola's years of exile, and even when Livia and his other children seem to have slipped away from his conscious thoughts or his public letters.

The overall picture we get of Cola di Rienzo and his family is thus quite different, for example, from that of Cristofano di Gano, a notary of Siena born in about 1346, who recorded all the minutiae of his children's lives just as he had taken care of his account book and his steadily growing properties. On the face value of these few fragments from the surviving sources, Cola appears indifferent to the names, number, and sometimes even the fate of his children. Cristofano and most of his professional colleagues sought all the solid security and reputation that long years of quiet family life, steady work, and advancement could bring them. But Cola di Rienzo sought something more than the time, place, and position could offer, something transcending the overcrowded, formulaic, and uninspired boundaries of his profession. Looking beyond the form book and the standard works of the medieval curriculum, he sought inspiration from other, more ancient, sources.

CHAPTER 3

Reviving Antiquity

> Every day Cola di Rienzo used to examine and meditate upon
> the marble engravings that lie around Rome. No one else
> but he knew how to read the ancient epitaphs. He used to
> translate all the ancient writings. He would interpret these
> marble figures exactly. My, how often would he say, "Where
> have those good Romans gone? Where is their high justice?
> If only I could have lived in these people's time."
>
> Anonimo romano, XVIII, ll. 13–20, Porta, 143

For his anonymous Roman biographer, Cola di Rienzo's first, and greatest, claim to fame and to the enduring memory of his fellow citizens was
precisely his ability to answer these questions in fresh and new ways: to
decipher the long-lost meaning of the ruins of Rome that lay all about
them and to make the ancient Romans come alive again. And yet these
hopes for Rome's rebirth were not new with Cola, nor with the early stir-
rings of Renaissance humanism in late medieval Italy. For the story of
Rome's revival and reform is actually the history of Rome in the Middle
Ages. Medieval writers, thinkers, and politicians spoke in terms of two
great ideas: reform and renewal: *reformatio* and *renovatio*.[1] In antiquity,
as in the Middle Ages, the notion held sway that the present age was one
of decline: materially, morally, and culturally, from some golden age, some
paradisal garden, the original form or ideal from which the present reality had fallen. Society and individuals could return to the pristine state
of the golden age, or of the state of humanity before the fall, only by some

45

re-formation, a moral and political reshaping that would return individuals and societies *ad fontes,* to the original sources, or fonts, of purity. Thus for Christians, the fallen state of humanity was re-formed by the birth, suffering, and death of Christ, and thus again, the ideal purity of the life of Christ, the apostles, and the disciples of the "primitive church" before the corruption and worldliness that ensued after the Donation of Constantine could be regained by a moral re-form. Medieval political theorists and the emperors from Charlemagne on also spoke of a "renewal" of the Roman Empire, a *renovatio imperii.*

Yet as Augustine had written, no matter what the results of human efforts, true perfection would be achieved only though divine grace: the last, great intervention of the divine in human history. It was only in the apocalyptic events of the last days, when Babylon, the symbol of earthly (i.e., Roman) rule, would be toppled and destroyed, and the New Jerusalem would descend from the heavens. Then, as St. John's Revelation makes clear, the elect will see "a new heaven and a new earth" that would replace the tumbled ruins of the old one built by human hands (Apoc. 21).

A long millennium had intervened between the conversion and purported baptism of the emperor Constantine in the porphyry font in the Lateran baptistery. Throughout that long, middle age of decline and shadow—as Petrarch would dub it—succeeding generations of the Roman people, popes, and emperors had initiated, or claimed to have initiated, artistic, ideological, or political movements to return the city and its people to its splendor and glory. In Rome the mute stones themselves speak, and have spoken, of two millennia of such renewal and reform: by the fourteenth century its ancient monuments, its newly built Christian basilicas and churches, its converted temples, its myriad inscriptions, its *spolia*—displaced and reused columns, capitals, altars, sarcophagi, and arches—had left a chorus of reminiscence, of quotation, of newly whispered aspirations to grandeur, of the promise of rebirth in a new age.

If only the past could be revived: if a new life could be breathed once again into the ancient stones that had escaped the lime burner's kiln.[2] As column, capital, and broken inscription were placed into the wall or floor or altar stone of some new Christian church, there to recall the spiritual authority and worldly power of the city's sacred origins, so, too, were the words of its pontiffs, emperors, consuls, and senators recalled from their ancient sources to live again as the flesh and blood of a revived church, empire, or communal republic. And for medieval political thinkers and politicians all these strains—republican, imperial, and papal—could coexist on more than one level. Nor were these the only sacred cornerstones in Rome. The twelfth-century *Mirabilia Urbis Romae* (I.1) recounts a remarkable foundation story that antecedes even Romulus and Remus, even Aeneas and his Trojans, and includes Noah, Hercules, Saturn, Jupiter, Roma and Silvius, the Trojans and the children of Aeneas. Romulus and Remus had a long heritage that included not only pagan gods and mythological characters but also Old Testament figures, a legacy of sacred and profane that had its remote origins in the destruction of old worlds by flood and fire. The towers of both Babylon and Troy provided the seeds of the new city: Rome.

The city itself was a literal treasure trove of another type. "The blood of martyrs is seed," wrote Tertullian in the third century; and the bones of the saints and martyrs, who had suffered and died in its still mighty amphitheater and circuses, its marketplaces, even its sewers, gave Rome an immense reservoir of spiritual power as its early Christian emperors and empresses made the city a reliquary of Jesus' life that rivaled Jerusalem itself. Here rested the veil of Veronica kept in St. Peter's basilica, fragments of the True Cross and of the soil of Calvary unearthed by Constantine's own mother, the empress Helena; here, too, were the column of Christ's flagellation and the chains that bound both St. Peter and St. Paul in their Roman prisons. As for Christ, so, too, for his martyrs: one's proximity to their graves and to their relics brought a kind of surrogate proximity to the suffering and death of Jesus himself. Through the religious devotion to the martyrs, Christians could thus also return to the spiritual power of the primitive church. Rome became, more than it had ever been for the pagan world, a magnet of religious force, one of those special places on the earth that are the axis points of connection between heaven and earth, between the sacred and profane. Like Jerusalem itself, where Jesus had actually lived, suffered, and died, Rome thus became a passageway to the eternal, a gateway through which to return to the state of grace and renewal.

Rome's political history during the Middle Ages was also one long evocation of past imperial glory,[3] whether manifested in the great basilicas built by the popes of the fifth century to recall Constantine's churches, or in the self-conscious classicism of the Crescentii family, who ruled the city in the tenth century and built the now-truncated tower that stands behind the Theater of Marcellus, or in the great cultural revival known as the Twelfth-Century Renaissance, which saw a new wave of church building and the revival of classical models in the visual arts and architecture.

In 1143 the Romans rose up against Pope Innocent II, seized the Capitoline, and reestablished the Roman Senate. Several of the stated purposes of the revolt were "to rebuild the Capitol, to renew the dignity of the Senate, to reform the order of knights." From 1143 the city began to mint its own, new silver coinage emblazoned with the ancient "SPQR," the Senate and the People of Rome. The communal movement gained spiritual and intellectual form with the arrival of the radical reformer Arnold of Brescia, later executed by Emperor Frederick I at the instigation of the papacy. But just as Rome was both spiritual and secular *caput mundi,* so, too, the revolution of 1143 combined secular and religious reform and renewal. Rome's history was thus punctuated from time to time, like a folded banner pierced by an arrow, by figures whose careers combine the political and religious aspirations of the Romans themselves; as Arnold of Brescia was for the twelfth century, so Cola di Rienzo was for the fourteenth.

The papacy itself also laid claim to the ancient imperial capital. If Constantine served as symbol of the secular ruler who could call church councils and grant vast lands and powers to the pope, he also provided the model for papal attempts to build a new Christian capital that would reflect Rome's role as spiritual *caput mundi.*[4] In the twelfth century popes therefore went back to the artistic legacy of the Roman Christian empire and began building first a series of great basilicas, and then smaller chapels and local churches that incorporated the stylistic elements and programs—columns, capitals, entablatures, inscriptions, bits of bas relief and sculpture—that summoned ancient Rome back to life.

By 1100 the new basilica of San Clemente was rising in clear imitation of Constantine's great basilicas of the fourth century. The pattern is repeated again in SS. Quattro Coronati, completed in 1116, as it would be in the 1120s at Sta. Maria in Trastevere, and by a host of other twelfth-century churches: S. Giovanni Crisogono, San Lorenzo fuori le Mura, SS. Giovanni e Paolo, S. Giorgio in Velabro, S. Lorenzo in Lucina, all using a vocabulary of trabeated colonnades, narthexes, Cosmatesque pavements, Ionic capitols, apse mosaics with the Christ and/or the Virgin as central figures. Even as late as 1250, when the Franciscans began building their new Roman church atop the ancient arx of the Capitoline, they chose not the Gothic preaching-hall plan used so successfully for San Francisco in Assisi in 1228, or in San Francesco in Bologna in 1236, but the classic Roman basilican style employing spoliated columns, Cosmatesque pavement, and a flat ceiling. After all, did not their church of Sta. Maria in Aracoeli (fig. 5) enshrine the very spot where the first Roman emperor,

Augustus, had received the vision of the Virgin and Child to prophesy the coming of a new age?

To show their alliance with the urban commune, the Franciscans had chosen this site next to the Senators' Palace, the seat of civil government (fig. 6). Perhaps, also deliberately, they chose not to compete with that government by erecting that proud new feature of the Roman Revival style, a campanile, to rival that on the Senate building itself. But elsewhere, all over Rome, there arose from the new churches bell towers singing the praises of a revived Rome and raising a pointed reminder of the power of the spirit, and of the church, against the soaring towers of the barons. Such, in fact, was the very impression, of mixed awe and joy, upon first seeing Rome from Monte Mario circa 1230, recorded by Master Gregory in his *Narration of the Marvels of Rome.*

By the mid–thirteenth century the "fashion of antiquity" had swept and still held Rome. Just after Gregory wrote, in 1246 the Rome of Pope Innocent IV gained a new fresco cycle for the Oratory of San Silvestro in SS. Quattro Coronati. Here, as a clear rejoinder to the imperial claims of Frederick II, the pope chose to have depicted the legendary scenes that form the backdrop to the *Donation of Constantine.* One scene repeats the story told in the *Mirabilia:* "The same emperor, after he became a Christian and built these churches, also gave to the Blessed Silvester a *Phrygium* [tiara], and white horses, and all the *imperialia* pertaining to the dignity of the Roman Empire. Then he went away to Byzantium. The pope, decorated with these gifts, went forth with Constantine as far as the Roman Arch, where they embraced and kissed each other, and so parted" (II.8, *Marvels,* p. 30).

With the reign of Nicholas III (1277–80), Rome began to undergo yet another great artistic revival that was to last until 1303, as the papal capital had come to attract and employ the most illustrious of Europe's artists to reimage the city: Cimabue, Giotto, Arnolfo di Cambio, Pietro Cavallini, Jacopo Torriti, and Filippo Rusuti were among the most renowned of the artists employed to recast the city in imitation of its ancient glory. The expense lavished on such projects cannot be underestimated. In St. Peter's alone, Cardinal Jacopo Stefaneschi, a member of the Caetani clan of Boniface VIII, donated 8,000 gold ducats for work by Giotto: 2,200 for Giotto's Navicella mosaic in the atrium of St. Peter's, 800 for his altarpiece, and 5,000 for his paintings in the apse. The scale, richness, beauty, and consistent classical dignity of these projects were multiplied manyfold throughout the city and by the year 1300 showed the world that Rome was indeed its restored capital.

By 1100 Roman domestic architecture already seems to have felt this spirit of renewal. Roman secular architecture had long made a habit of incorporating the same ancient elements into the fabric of new building, or of actually remodeling and reusing ancient theaters, temples, and vaultings, just as the Colonna had done in the Temple of Serapis (fig. 7), the Orsini in the Theater of Pompey, or the Frangipani and Annibaldi in the Colosseum. The Casa dei Crescenzi, the Torre dei Margani on the piazza named after it, and the house just opposite the Ponte Sant'Angelo on via S. Celso 60/61 are excellent examples of the style.

In yet another tangible form, republican renewal and the summoning of ancient precedent went hand in hand with a revival of another antique Roman art form: public lettering to promulgate laws, to commemorate great victories, to dedicate monuments, temples, and triumphal arches, and finally to wish eternal rest and peace to the deceased on the flanks of their sarcophagi. Here again such ancient monuments as Trajan's column or the Arch of Constantine (fig. 8) provided the model for new forms of public lettering that broke from the bookish forms of the Gothic scripts long used on Rome's tombs and churches. The new forms of public communication coincided with the new civil life of the twelfth century's political revival.

Roman history and the Jewish, Christian, pagan, and imperial roots of Rome came together at the episcopal palace and cathedral of the bishops of Rome, St. John Lateran (fig. 9). By the year 1300 and the first Jubilee, the Lateran had become the focus of all the spiritual and political forces and aspirations of Western Christendom. While St. Peter's and the Vatican enjoyed first place among Latin churches as the site of the first bishop's martyrdom and cult, thus underpinning the spiritual supremacy of the bishop of Rome, the Lateran had, from the start, been associated with the pope's inheritance of imperial authority. By the late thirteenth century the Donation of Constantine had become the leitmotif of the Lateran complex; its imperial connections and traditions were underscored by legend and the assemblage there of a series of potent symbols that resonated with all the facets of Rome's past.

As Benedict's *Marvels of Rome* relates:

During the days of Pope Sylvester, Constantine Augustus built the Lateran Basilica, which he adorned beautifully. He put there the Ark of the Covenant, which Titus had carried from Jerusalem with many thousands of Jews, and the Golden Candlestick of Seven Lamps with vessels of oil. In the ark are these things: the golden emeralds, the mice of gold, the Tablets of the Covenant, the Rod of Aaron, manna, the barley loaves, the golden urn, the coat without seam, the reed and garment of Saint John the Baptist, and the tongs that Saint John the Evangelist was shorn with. Moreover he also put in the basilica a ciborium with pillars of porphyry. And he set there four pillars of gilded brass, which the consuls of old had brought to the Capitoline from the Campo Marzio and set in the Temple of Jupiter. (II.8, *Marvels,* p. 29)

The legend survived through the Middle Ages. In 1291 Pope Nicholas IV confirmed that the bronze columns had also come directly from Solomon's Temple, brought by Titus's legions after the destruction of Jerusalem. Furthermore, each of them contained earth from the site of Christ's death on Calvary. A century after Benedict's *Mirabilia,* Master Gregory's *Narration of the Marvels of Rome* confirms the story of the four bronze columns but combines it with another of the medieval Lateran's great treasures:

There is another bronze statue in front of the papal palace: an immense horse, with a rider whom the pilgrims call Theoderic, although the Roman people say he is Constantine, and the cardinals and clerks of the Roman curia call him Marcus or Quintus Quirinus. In ages past this memorial, made with extraordinary skill, stood on four bronze columns in front of the altar of Jupiter on the Capitoline, but blessed Gregory [the Great, pope] took down the horse and rider, and placed the four columns in the church of St. John Lateran. The horse and rider were set up outside the papal palace by the Roman people. (c. 4, Osborne, trans., p. 19)

The equestrian statue actually represents Emperor Marcus Aurelius and was moved from the Lateran to its present site on the Capitoline in 1538 by order of Pope Paul III in keeping with Michelangelo's master plan in anticipation of the triumphal entry of Emperor Charles V into Rome. In the Middle Ages the rider was most commonly identified as Emperor Constantine. Whether or not one ascribes the collection at the Lateran to a high aesthetic sense developed at the papal Curia and occasionally shared by highly cultured visitors to the city, at the Lateran the popes had, in fact, systematically brought together a collection of some of Rome's most beautiful, and potent, political symbols, housing them for public view in the cathedral's porch.

Here, too, were the popes' three other great prizes. The first consisted of the bronze fragments—the head and hand—of a colossal statue, perhaps of Constantine, now also in the Capitoline Museums. The second was the bronze she-wolf now restored to its place on the Capitoline and reunited with a Romulus and Remus. The symbol of Rome's birth, it was called the *mater Romanorum* in the Middle Ages and was the very image of the earthly origins of the city. Beneath it judicial sentences were pronounced and punishment meted out as late as 1438. The papacy's display of the she-wolf on the porch of the Lateran would thus bring Constantine's donation to the papacy back to its very foundations. The third other great prize was a bronze tablet described as follows by Master Gregory, himself no mean antiquarian: "In front of it [the Lateran portico] there is a bronze tablet, called the tablet 'prohibiting sin,' on which are written the principal statutes of the law. On this tablet I read much, but understood little, for they were aphorisms, and the reader has to supply most of the words" (c. 33, Osborne, trans., p. 36).

A thirteenth-century Bolognese jurist, Odofredo, well skilled in law and in late medieval book hands—but not in ancient inscriptions—also failed to decipher the clean, v-cut Roman capitals and concluded that they must be the early Roman Law of the Twelve Tables. The tablet was actually the *lex de imperio Vespasiani,* a bronze inscription enumerating the rights and powers transferred from the Senate and People of Rome to the emperor Vespasian in December 69 C.E. It remained in the Lateran until 1576, when it, too, was brought to the Capitoline; it now hangs in the Capitoline Museums. The text was a perfect match for the pope's two other political symbols: for here he possessed the bronze she-wolf who gave birth to Rome and the bronze tablet granting power and authority from the Senate and People to the emperor, and then the bronze statue believed to be the very emperor who had donated this power and authority to the pope himself upon his departure for Byzantium. Thus the Lateran was a political powerhouse: a showcase of the secular power granted the popes and confirmed not only by the magical treasures of the Temple of Solomon—the king who was also a religious leader—but also by the most precious treasures of the Roman Empire. Such symbols held enormous strength in the Middle Ages—both on a popular level of magic power and for those who knew their deepest meanings and could unravel them to bolster their own claims to spiritual authority and political power.

While the public defeat and humiliation of Boniface VIII by the French king and the exile of the papacy to distant Avignon did much to destroy the effective power of these symbols within Rome, their authority lingered on in the minds of the learned and unlearned. As late as March 1337, Francesco Petrarch (1304–74) (fig. 10) described a visit he had taken to Rome to see his good friend, the Dominican Giovanni Colonna di San Vito, a member of the minor Gallicano branch of the Colonna family and the author of *De viris illustribus* (c. 1335) and the *Mare Historiarum* (c. 1340). The letter (*Fam.* II.14) is a vivid document of the effect of Rome's magical power over the medieval imagination: "In truth Rome was greater, and greater are its ruins than I imagined. I no longer wonder that the whole world was conquered by this city but that I was conquered so late" (PLFM 1:113).[5]

Although the sources are mute about Cola's early life and education, Petrarch himself never hesitated to make his private life a public matter. In this he consciously imitated the model of his ancient hero, Cicero, whose "private" letters were written to maintain and perpetuate a public persona. Thus Petrarch's *Familiares,* his letters to friends, are in effect a public legacy, and they and other sources tell us much about his life, thoughts, and attitudes, and in this help establish a new level of letter writing that surpasses the handbooks and formulae of the medieval notaries. His European fame in later life and his wide circle of friends and admirers also led to intense interest in almost every aspect of his life. Petrarch was born on June 20, 1304, in Arezzo in eastern Tuscany. His father, like his grandfather and even his great-grandfather, was a notary; and like many members of the urban middle class, the family still had no surname. Pietro, Francesco's father, was called by a nickname, "Petracco," or "Petraccolo"; and, like Dante Alighieri, an acquaintance, he was a political exile from Florence. In 1312 the family moved to Avignon, and Petracco settled his family in nearby Carpentras.

Francesco Petracchi, or di Petracco, was expected to follow in his father's footsteps, perhaps to rise a little higher, and so he studied law both at the University of Montpellier and then, back in Italy, at the University of Bologna. In 1325, on his father's death, Francesco returned to Avignon, already determined to forge a career as a lyric poet and scholar. He had inherited his father's love of classical learning, especially of Cicero; but in April 1327 he began something new: his famous series of Italian sonnets in honor of a still-unknown woman, whom he called Laura, the wife of another man. These courtly poems of unrequited love, written in the language of Dante but set in a new form that would forever after be termed "Petrarchan," brought him instant fame throughout Italy and Europe.

Petrarch's distaste for legal practice was so strong, his contempt for the medical profession so deep-rooted, and his love for poetry and literature so all-consuming that he decided to enter the lower orders of the only other profession suitable for a young man of his class and education: the clergy. In the spring of 1330, therefore, he was invited to spend the summer at the estate of the bishop of Lombez, the Roman Giacomo Colonna, and from that time his deep friendship and loyalty to that Roman family were solidified. Later that year, Giacomo's brother, Cardinal Giovanni

Colonna, invited Francesco into his service as a household chaplain. In 1333 Petrarch took the first of his literary journeys, this time to northern Europe, along the way stopping into monastic libraries in search of manuscripts of the ancient classics, thus establishing a pattern for humanist scholars ever since. By that time he had also begun his works on both Christian and pagan classics: his editions of Virgil and Livy earned him a solid reputation for scholarship and a new understanding of the classical past, both Christian and pagan. In December 1336 Bishop Giacomo Colonna invited Petrarch to Rome for the first time, and from then his romance with the city and its history remained constant.

By the 1340s Petrarch's reputation as Europe's preeminent love poet and student of the classics had led him to conceive a major propaganda coup not only for himself but also for the reawakening of classical civilization after its long decline in what he called the present "middle age." "For who can doubt that Rome would rise again instantly if she began to know herself," he wrote in November 1341 to Fra Giovanni Colonna. Petrarch knew that back in 1315 Albertino Musato had received the crown of poet laureate in his native Padua, an early center of humanist revival of ancient cultural practices. Dante himself had made known his desire for the laurel and had been offered it by Bologna; but he refused, awaiting the nod from his native Florence, which never came. From late 1339 or early 1340, Petrarch, now calling himself by the more Latin "Petrarca," had begun campaigning for his own crown. He efforts paid off quickly. As he told Giacomo Colonna from Avignon on February 16, 1341 (*Fam.* IV.6):

And when I in my insignificance was eagerly implored by two of the greatest cities, Rome and Paris, one the capital of the world and queen of cities, the other [Paris] the mother of studies of our time, after consideration and thanks primarily to your great brother who above all others served as my advisor and counselor, I determined finally to receive it nowhere else than in Rome on the ashes of ancient poets and in their dwelling. So on this very day I have begun my journey. It will require more time than usual for I must first go to the king, visiting Naples, and only then take the road to Rome. (PLFM 1:192)

Petrarch had established contacts with the court of Naples, where King Robert of Anjou (1278–1343) and his consort, Queen Sancia of Majorca (1286–1345), had made the city a center of learning, open intellectual discussion, and religious dissent. Naples was at that time the most powerful capital in Italy, and perhaps the wealthiest in Europe. Robert, known as "the Wise," had already earned a widespread reputation for learning and support of the arts. As papal vicar in Italy he was the official "protector" of the neighboring Papal States, a position he took quite literally, often—as in 1312—intervening in the affairs of Rome. In the fall of 1340 Petrarch arrived in Naples; there he met the venerable king, who held lengthy discussions with the poet on the classics and the various legends associated with Virgil's presence in and around Naples. It was decided that the king himself would perform the crowning ceremony on the Capitoline in Rome the following spring. The king's age and failing health, however, forced him to name Giovanni Barrili as his representative in Rome; but he did present Petrarch with some of his own robes—as was the ancient custom for the coronation. The ceremony took place on the Capitoline, in the assembly hall or Sala Senatorio on the *primo piano* of the Senators' Palace (see fig. 6). The room survives to this day, much altered, in what is now the Sala di Giulio Cesare. The day had more than ordinary significance for the revival of an ancient pagan custom, for in 1341, April 8 was also Easter Sunday: the feast of the Resurrection of Jesus from the dead and his victory over the old age of sin and corruption. The significance of the day in this capital of the world, both pagan and Christian, could thus not be lost on any of the Romans present.

After the sounding of trumpets and the hushing of the assembled audience of barons and people, Petrarch prefaced the ceremony with an oration of his own, in which he asked for the crown. Orso degli Anguillara, along with Giordano Orsini one of the two papally appointed senators then in office, gave a lengthy Latin oration. At its conclusion Orso asked for, and received, the Romans' approbation of the coronation. He then crowned the poet and granted him a diploma, the *Privilegium lauree domini Francisci Petrarche,* in wording borrowed from the formula for granting teaching licenses at the University of Rome but that also conferred on Petrarch full rights of Roman citizenship. Next the head of Rome's most powerful clan, and of Petrarch's protectors, Stefano Colonna il Vecchio, rose and offered his own concluding *laudatio* to the poet. The assembly then followed Roman custom but reversed the direction of more recent, papal, processions and wound its way from the Capitoline, across the *abitato* and Ponte Sant'Angelo to St. Peter's. There, as the true son of both classical and Christian Rome, Petrarch laid his newly won crown upon the main altar.

A few days later Petrarch wrote to King Robert (*Fam.* IV.7):

Recently you obliged the abandoned Muses with new kindness by solemnly consecrating to them this talent of mine, however small. To this end you decorated the city of Rome and the decaying palace of the Capitoline with unexpected joy and unusual foliage. . . . This custom of the laurel crown, which has not only been interrupted for so many centuries, but here actually condemned to oblivion as a variety of cares and problems grew in the republic, has been renewed in our own age through your leadership and my involvement. (PLFM 1:193–95)

Petrarch spent the next few days after his coronation in the city strolling around its ruins with his friend Giovanni Colonna. In his letter to Giovanni dated November 30, 1341 (*Fam.* VI.2), he created a romantic picture of their wanderings together across a landscape both pagan and Christian, both the city of history and surviving ruin and the ideal city of the imagination. Petrarch's letter can be seen as perhaps the last flowering of Mirabilian Rome, of a city where ruined baths evoke ancient palaces and converted temples evoke the lives of emperors and martyrs. Yet Petrarch also sees the Rome of literary evocation and classical allusion, the world of humanism:

We used to wander together in that great city . . . and at each step there was present something which would excite our tongue and mind. . . . But where shall I end? Can I really describe everything in this short letter? Indeed, if I could, it would not be proper; you know all these things not because you are a Roman citizen but because since your youth you have been intensely curious especially about such information. For today who are more ignorant about Roman affairs than the Roman citizens? Sadly do I say that nowhere is Rome less known than in Rome. I do not deplore only the ignorance involved . . . but the disappearance and exile of many virtues. For who can doubt that Rome would rise again instantly if she began to know herself? (PLFM 1:290–95)

We do not know who filled the Senate chamber that day of Petrarch's coronation, or whether or not a young notary, back in Rome from Anagni since at least 1333, was part of the audience. And yet it seems likely that Cola di Rienzo attended. He was, after all, a young professional whose business had by then probably brought him into at least the fringes of Rome's cultural and political elite.

Just over a year after Petrarch's coronation, in May 1342, and with the cooperation of Petrarch himself, the Roman people sent a delegation to the newly elected Pope Clement VI to acclaim the Roman bishop, as was their custom and right, and to plead with the pope to return to his see in Rome. The Romans, suffering both from economic depression with the loss of the papal court and from constant civil war between the forces allied with the rival Colonna and Orsini clans, also requested that the pope follow the model of Boniface VIII and declare a new Jubilee, not at the turning of the century but for its fiftieth year, in 1350. The embassy numbered fifteen citizens, of all classes, and was headed by Stefano Colonna the Younger, along with Francesco di Vico, son of the Prefect of the City, and Lello di Pietro di Stefano dei Cosecchi. Petrarch's hand in the embassy was clear: he was then a Roman citizen, and at Stefano Colonna's urging he composed a metrical letter from his residence in Avignon, urging the pope to return to Rome and revive its ancient glories. Clement refused to move the papacy from the safety of Avignon and named two new senators: Bertoldo Orsini and Stefano Colonna the Younger.

Their rule did not last for long, however. In November or December 1342 the Roman people finally came to the end of their patience with the feuding barons, overthrew the senators, and established a revived communal government: that of the Thirteen Good Men. They did all this in the name of their overlord, the pope, recruited members from among the merchant and craft guilds, and appointed a new embassy to Avignon to bring the news to Clement VI. As we have already seen, such diplomatic missions were often entrusted by Italian city-states to prominent and skilled notaries; and this mission was entrusted to one who had already established himself as the leading advocate of Rome's revival within the city: the twenty-nine-year-old Cola di Rienzo. The embassy reached Avignon in late 1342 or January 1343, and there, on the banks of the Rhone River, Cola di Rienzo emerged fully into history for the first time.

CHAPTER 4

The Popes at Avignon

It happened that a brother of his was killed and he did not avenge his death. Cola could not help him. He thought for a long time about how to avenge his brother's death. He thought for a long time about how to set right the badly governed City of Rome. Through his hard work he went to Avignon as ambassador to Pope Clement on behalf of the Thirteen Good Men of Rome.

Anonimo romano, XVIII, ll. 22–29, Porta, 143–44

This passage reveals a key technique of the Anonimo romano: the highly vivid, compact, almost pictorial phrase to convey a wealth of information and the elements of an underlying psychological drama.[1]

The Anonimo romano deliberately juxtaposed these sentences in this order: the murder of Cola's brother (by unnamed assailants), Cola's thoughts of revenge, his analysis of Rome's bad government, and his rise to prominence in the city, culminating in his appointment as chief ambassador to Avignon. In so doing, Cola's biographer lays out for the reader—from a completely external series of descriptives—a profound choice between private revenge and Cola's determination to reform the civil life of Rome, the conflict between the private man and the public figure, between personal vendetta and public duty. Out of the trauma of his brother's death and the psychic crisis that ensued, the young Rienzo apparently went through a long process of pondering the meaning of these same, haphazardly joined facts. In a few terse phrases, the Anonimo romano has traced the young man's growth from adolescence to maturity: to the realization that the attempt to bring about a more just society would require long commitment and hard work that surpassed personal or even family interest.

Cola, the Anonimo romano tells us, was handsome and affable; he had gained a reputation as an excellent speaker and skilled scholar. A relief long in the Palazzo Barberini, the only purported portrait of Rienzo based on a contemporary view, shows him as Roman tribune, perhaps in 1347, when he must have been about thirty-four (fig. 11). He poses in profile, as any worthy royal or imperial portrait head ought, his close-cropped hair set in Roman Augustan style, perhaps a bit longer and curlier behind. Like Augustus, he is clean-shaven, a good reason to date the portrait to 1347, as we shall see. A laurel wreath crowns his head. Beneath his high forehead, a nose somewhat less imperial, because flatter, but still elegant, ends in a flaring nostril. His mouth is slightly open, not too large or too small, his parted lips thin on top and more full below, perhaps poised with his ever-ready smile, eager to give voice to wit or deeper learning. His chin is firm and strong, while his jawbone, though strong beneath, seems a bit obscured by cheeks just a bit too full. His ear is strong and well in proportion to a handsome, energetic face, his neck firm and strong enough to support so worthy a head. Perhaps the most telling features of Cola's portrait, however, are his eyes: sharp and strong, set beneath a straight and not-too-thick brow, but showing signs of all-too-human lines and wrinkles. Crow's-feet, clear and prominent, dash back from his lids, the artist giving the effect of winged eyes reminiscent of Gianbattista Alberti's own portrait medal: the emblem of far-searching and seeing, of wisdom. Cola's portrait is the image of an ordinary man thrust into a great role: strong enough to perform it, yet burdened and worn down enough by the task to show it.

In late November or December 1342 the Thirteen Good Men dispatched Rienzo's delegation to the court of the new pope in Avignon. How did this relatively obscure city of medium size and power, on the confluence of the Rhone and Durance Rivers in northern Provence, come by the mid–fourteenth century to be the capital of the popes, and thus of Christendom?[2] Avignon was not as large, ancient, or powerful as Arles to the south, or Marseilles on the coast, or Lyons farther up the river. Nor had it been the seat of ancient church councils like Arles, or of more recent ones like Lyons. Unlike the relatively tiny Saint-Gilles-du-Garde across the Rhone, or Saint-Maxime farther south in Provence, it did not attract pilgrims to its shrines. It could not boast the relics of many saints or martyrs; it lay far off the major pilgrim routes to Santiago de Compostela in Spain or to Rome itself. It did boast a famous bridge, that of Saint-Bénézet, the Pont d'Avignon of the children's song; but that could hardly claim the decades of loyal residence the Roman pontiffs gave it.

With Italy still in turmoil following the deaths of Boniface VIII in October 1303 and of his successor, Benedict XI, in July 1304, the deadlocked conclave of cardinals sitting at Perugia finally elected a compromise candidate, Bertrand de Got, the archbishop of Bordeaux, as Clement V on June 5, 1305. Bertrand decided to negotiate a settlement of the coming English-French war from the convenience of Lyons, and to prepare for a church council there that would handle the charges against Boniface VIII, still pressed by Philip of France, and settle the guilt of the Knights Templars charged with heresy and treason by the same king. Awaiting the council, Clement took up residence in a nearby papal possession that had figured little in the travels and residences of the popes since its cession by Raymond of Toulouse to the papacy in 1229 in the treaty that ended the Albigensian Crusade. On March 9, 1305, Pope Clement entered the papal territory of the Comtat Venaissin and Avignon, the city of his vassal, the king of Naples and the Angevin count of Provence.

The Roman pontiff's taking up residence in any city other than Rome—even for an extended period—meant nothing extraordinary to his contemporaries. Between 1100 and 1303 the popes had spent 122 years outside of Rome, against 82 years actually in residence there. This had mostly been in cities of the Papal States—Viterbo, Perugia, Orvieto, and Anagni—but it also included long travel through Tuscany, Lombardy, and the kingdom of Naples, in France, and in Provence itself. Avignon was, after all, just outside the bounds of the kingdom of France, and thus away from King Philip's control, and just as remote from its ultimate overlord, the German emperor. What is more, because of its position on the central Rhone valley, it was not only perfectly situated to keep an eye on developments in the main hot spot of the time—the English-French border in neighboring Gascony—but also close enough to the lands of Italy: to Lombardy and Tuscany by land, and to Rome and the south by ship via Marseilles. In five days a messenger could get from Avignon to Paris or Metz, in eight days to Bruges, in ten to London, and in thirteen to Venice, Rome, or even Naples. Avignon was at the center, rather than the periphery, of a European—as opposed to a Mediterranean—Christendom. No papal possession, even Bologna or Rome itself, was better suited to the pope's present needs for quick diplomacy.

In addition, Avignon's climate was far more healthy than Rome's, and its population had lost its last trace of independence more than fifty years earlier. Unlike the Roman commune, it did not offer a persistent threat to the pope's political status and personal safety, nor put forth a long list of claims to republican traditions and imperial glories. Avignon's population grew as the papal administration did and generally came from the same regions. The city's wealth and fame increased with the growth of the papal court. Avignon's patriciate had all but disappeared as a political force during the Albigensian wars and never had the kind of extended familial or territorial power bases within and without the city that Rome's nobility claimed. And so what began as a brief stay in a papal possession became instead a papal exile that was to last with few interruptions for over seventy years. From 1305 to 1377 seven popes—Clement V, John XXII, Benedict XII, Clement VI, Innocent VI, Urban V, and Gregory XI—made Avignon their capital through the period dubbed by Petrarch the "Babylonian Captivity."[3]

On April 25, 1342, Benedict XII died. This frugal, austere, personally cold, and ultraorthodox reformer was quickly replaced by Pope Clement VI,[4] a man entirely his opposite. Born in 1290/91 at Maumont (Corrèze), Pierre Roger had been raised among the lesser nobility of the Limousin region in France. In 1301 he was placed at the Benedictine abbey of La Chaise-Dieu, where he made his religious profession, and in 1307 his superiors sent him to Paris, where he studied theology and canon law. Roger quickly emerged as one of the leading conservative intellectuals of the early fourteenth century and engaged in heated debate—both against the Scotism of François de Meyronnes, a leading intellectual at the court of Naples, and against the Spiritual Franciscans—defending Pope John XXII's position that condemned the absolute poverty of Christ and the apostles. By 1323 he had been named a master of theology at Paris, and by 1326 abbot of Fécamp in Normandy. In that post he quickly also won the favor of the French court; and thereafter his rise was certain. He was named bishop of Arras in 1328, archbishop of Sens in 1329, and archbishop of Rouen and chancellor of France in 1330. On December 13, 1338, he was the sole cardinal created by Benedict XII, who raised him again to the title of cardinal priest of SS. Nereo e Achilleo on May 5, 1339.

But the new pope was something of an enigma to his contemporaries. Judging from his several portraits that have survived, including the tomb sculpture at La Chaise-Dieu and several manuscript illuminations, he was not a handsome man. Bearded as on the dedication page of Bartolomeo da Urbino's *Milleloquium Sancti Augustini* (fig. 12) or clean-shaven as on his tomb, he was broad-faced with a prominent nose, and large, almond-shaped eyes set fairly close together. Yet he was known for his great charm and suave manners. Clement considered himself a French prince and used the vast wealth accumulated and not spent by Benedict XII to make his court at Avignon the political, intellectual, and artistic capital of Europe.[5] Often called an early humanist pope, he was more a medieval polymath. His interests ranged from crusading history to astronomy; and in the papal library he supplemented the liturgical, legal, and theological collections of John XXII and Benedict XII with the classics, especially Cicero, but also Pliny, Valerius Maximus, and Macrobius, and with books in Hebrew and Arabic. Yet while his many sermons also quote Seneca, Cicero, and Boethius, they reveal not a secular man but one deeply familiar with Scripture, the early church fathers, and Bernard of Clairvaux. Clement was also a great patron of learning and the arts, and his generosity to both office seekers, such as Petrarch, and diplomatic guests was unmatched, his reputation for opulence unrivaled, his ceremony, feasts, and festivals the envy of all other European princes. The "New" Palace that Clement ordered to be built to house all this was, in the words of Jean Froissart, the chronicler of the Hundred Years' War who visited it in the 1360s, "the strongest fortress and most beautiful building in the world."

The presence of the Roman bishops had by the year 1342 made Avignon not only the center of European Christendom and the site of its most elegant court and sophisticated administration but also a city of great economic wealth and social diversity. It has been estimated that between 1342 and 1346, the years of Cola's embassy, the area within the city's walls held between 40,000 and 50,000 residents: an immense number of cardinals and princes, clerics, merchants, office seekers, ambassadors, artists and craftspeople, musicians and composers, prostitutes, notaries, lawyers and thieves, grocers, jewelers, furriers, butchers, fishmongers, horse traders, students, and friars all squeezed within a wall circumference of about five kilometers, on unpaved, mud-filled, and refuse-choked streets. It was a city from which the papal court never departed; for which there never was an off-season, and whose rhythms kept pace with the flow of treasure into the papal palace and the dispensation of spiritual and material largess from it.

The following is an accounting of the food served on November 22, 1324, at the dinner given by Pope John XXII to celebrate the marriage of his great-niece, Jeanne de Trian, with the young Guichard de Poitiers:

On that occasion they ate 4,012 loaves of bread, 8 3/4 oxen, 55 1/4 sheep, 8 pigs, 4 boars, a large quantity of different kinds of fish, 200 capons, 690 chickens, 580 partridges, 270 rabbits, 40 plovers, 37 ducks, 50 pigeons, 4 cranes, 2 pheasants, 2 peacocks, 292 small birds, 3 cwt, 2 lbs. of cheese, 3,000 eggs, a mere 2,000 apples, pears and other fruits; they drank 11 barrels of wine. In 1323, at the wedding feast of Bernarde de Via, the great-niece of John XXII, and in 1324 at that of the pope's brother Pierre, more than 931 and 720 florins respectively were spent, that is about 70,000 and 54,000 francs in gold coin. (*Introitus et exitus* accounts, cited in Mollat, *Popes,* 311)

Nor should we imagine that the pope and cardinals lavished expense and luxury only on relatives: there was their own status and power to consider. An Italian eyewitness reports a reception given for Pope Clement VI by Cardinal Annibaldo de Ceccano of Naples in 1343, the year of Cola's embassy:

The pope was led into a room hung from floor to ceiling with tapestries of great richness. The ground was covered with a velvet carpet. The state bed was hung with the finest crimson velvet, lined with white ermine, and covered with cloths of gold and of silk. Four knights and twelve squires of the pope's household waited at table; the knights received from the host a rich belt of silver and a purse worth 25 gold florins; and the squires, a belt and a purse to the value of 12 florins. Fifty squires from Cardinal Annibaldo's suite assisted the papal knights and squires. The meal consisted of nine courses each having three dishes, that is a total of twenty-seven dishes. We saw brought in, among other things, a sort of castle containing a huge stag, a boar, kids, hares and rabbits. At the end of the fourth course, the cardinal presented the pope with a white charger, worth 400 florins, and two rings, valued at 150 florins, one set with an enormous sapphire and the other with an equally enormous topaz; and last of all, a *nappo* worth 100 florins. Each of the sixteen cardinals received a ring set with fine stones, and so did the twenty prelates and the noble laymen. The twelve young clerks of the papal household were each given a belt and a purse worth 25 gold florins; and the twenty-four sergeants-at-arms, a belt worth 3 florins. After the fifth course, they brought in a fountain surmounted by a tree and a pillar, flowing with five kinds of wine. The margins of the fountain were decked with peacocks, pheasants, partridges, cranes and other birds. In the interval between the seventh and eighth courses there was a tournament, which took place in the banqueting hall itself. A concert brought the main part of the feast to a close. At dessert, two trees were brought in; one seemed made of silver, and bore apples, pears, figs, peaches and grapes of gold; the other was green as laurel, and was decorated with crystallized fruits of many colors.
The wines came from Provence, La Rochelle, Beaune, St. Pourçain and the Rhine. After dessert the master cook danced, together with his thirty assistants. When the pope had retired to his apartments, wines and spices were set before us. (Cited in Mollat, *Popes,* pp. 313–14)

Here, indeed, was wealth of a different kind; for the court and the papacy of Clement VI that Cola and his Roman companions saw were the most sophisticated, lavish, and complex that had yet existed in Europe.

While display—of status, wealth, and educational level—has always been of importance to any society; in the late Middle Ages visible displays of wealth manifested a prince's power and his ability to provide for his court. In an age bound to the soil and to its hard metals and brilliant hues, how else to express a realm's wealth if not in the extravagance of its materials, its ability to dispense and to flaunt wealth; how better to inspire loyalty among friends and dread among enemies than to parade this wealth: of food, clothing, weaponry, the ability to reap and to fashion, and to waste?

Avignon was a city of spectacle and waste, its year filled with the major feast days of the Christian liturgical calendar, of the saints dear to the families of cardinals, prelates, and nobles, of papal processions; of the pope's Holy Week blessing from the Indulgence Window in the courtyard of the New Palace; of Christmas Day gifts and awards to favored lay lords. Funerals with their elaborate corteges and solemn processions, passion plays, popular devotions, the arrivals of pilgrims, the preaching of the popes themselves in the cathedral of Notre Dame—all added to the sense of a deep and vibrant religious life. But nothing compared to its court spectacles, its lavish feasts, or the annual awarding of the Golden Rose. This prize—worth over 100 florins and created by Tuscan craftsmen from sapphire, pearl, garnet, and gold—was bestowed by the pope on the fourth Sunday of Lent to the prince of the pope's choosing and would often climax the arrival of a great, and politically important, visitor. It was, in 1368, even granted to a woman, Queen Giovanna I of Naples.

Yet cultural life in this papal city naturally went deeper than spectacle and ceremony. The home of some of the brightest and most influential men in Europe, the Curia was a center of intellectual creativity and exchange: in law and theology for the most part, but from an early date the new international humanism pioneered by Petrarch. Poetry, letter writing, history, and classical literature found avid supporters. While there is no record of grammar schools in Avignon, the substantial number of educated heads of households—lawyers, notaries, advocates, diplomats, and others of every type—made the presence of several schools indispensable. A university had existed since 1303, and this soon specialized in what best served the needs of the Avignon papacy: law. The palace also had its own school, with the status of a *studium generale,* and supported a master of theology, generally drawn from the Dominicans, who lectured on the works of Thomas Aquinas.

If Avignon was so well positioned for trade and communication, during an era in which artistic influence traveled with an artist's eyes, paint box, and tool kit, it was also a key focus in the development of the *ars*

nova in music and of what would come to be called the International
Gothic style best exemplified by the arrival of Simone Martini, the leading exponent of the new school of Giotto, to Avignon in 1339. The construction of the papal palace drew on the talents of artists from all over
Europe: thirty-five painters were hired by John XXII in 1321–22 for his
temporary palace alone; fifty-four by Benedict XII when he began the Old
Palace; and Italian painters formed the avant-garde. They included Martini, his brother Donato Martini, Simone's brother-in-law Lippo Memmi,
and, in 1343, Matteo Giovanetti, prior of San Marco in the papal city of
Viterbo. Matteo was to become the official court painter for the next
twenty-five years and would direct the overall decoration of the papal
palace throughout that time. Within his atelier were Riccone and Giovanni d'Arezzo, Giovanni da Lucca, Niccolò and Francesco da Firenze,
and Pietro da Viterbo.

The oldest part of the papal palace was built between 1335 and 1337 in
the austere Cistercian style that suited Benedict XII. But the New Palace
owes its elegant gothic internationalism to Clement VI. Immediately after his elevation, in fact in 1342–43 during Cola's embassy, Clement VI began to embellish the old papal apartments of Benedict's fortress-convent.
He had Jean de Louvres build what came to be known as the Tower of
the Wardrobe, just to the south of the Angel Tower and connected to it
via the pope's bed chamber. Clement had a sophisticated bathhouse in-
stalled in the basement, private wardrobes on the next two floors, and,
above that and connecting to the papal chamber in the Angel Tower, the
Room of the Stag.

That room and its gorgeous decorations survive today, almost intact:
a simple space paved in terra-cotta tile, with a large fireplace (an avant-
garde housing feature for the Mediterranean in the mid–fourteenth century) set catty-corner at one angle. Its large expanses of wall were painted
in 1343, perhaps by Robin de Romans but more likely supervised by Matteo Giovanetti, who arrived in Avignon that year. They consist of a series
of scenes of the hunt and falconry: courtly, elegant figures of nobles with
their servants and dogs, set amid a lush background of flowers, brambles,
and trees. The palette is rich in earth hues and the brilliance of flowers,
fine cloth, and silks; the overall effect, though naturalistic, is closer to that
of a northern French or Flemish tapestry: Arras has been suggested as a
visual source. But the frescoes are not simply tapestry in paint: the naturalistic understanding of the world suggests a deeper secular spirit. Religious themes are absent here in Pope Clement's private study: instead,
one finds a sophisticated, pleasant openness, not at all unlike the sophis-

ticated, cultured man they were created for. But, like him, they breathed the air of the chivalrous north and the French court of Paris: game and the hunt, not the classical landscapes that Petrarch was then commissioning from his friend Simone Martini for the frontispiece of his copy of Virgil.

While all the administrative and religious functions of the Roman pontiff could easily be performed by the popes in their new home, some deeply spiritual ones were essential to their role as bishops of Rome.[6] These could not so easily be duplicated away from the sacred soil of Rome itself. But this does not mean that the Avignon popes did not try. The chapel of St. Michael, atop the Tower of the Wardrobe, was called "Roma" almost from its dedication in 1344. But perhaps the most striking example of their attempt was the creation of three chapels intended to replace Rome's great basilicas as the focus of papal—and thus Roman Catholic—cult practice: St. Peter's in the Vatican, San Paolo fuori le Mura, and St. John Lateran. In their place papal architects would eventually design two chapels: of St. John and of St. Peter and St. Paul. Papal coronations took place just outside the chapel of St. Peter, and papal processions often recalled the route from one Roman basilica to another while remaining completely within the palace. There was even a loggia of benediction to take the place of that at the Lateran, the Indulgence Window tucked into the southwestern corner of Clement VI's Great Court, just off his Great Chapel. Thus, one of the most important functions of this new palace was its symbolic recapitulation of the Old Rome that the popes had left behind and to which some, like Clement VI, seem to have had no intention of ever returning.

But the new Roman delegation had arrived in Avignon to persuade its lord, the mightiest, wealthiest, and most brilliant monarch of his age, to do just that: abandon his court; abandon his new palace, with its charming study, its fireplaces, and its dazzling frescoed halls; abandon the safety and financial security of the Rhone valley and the protection of the king of Naples and the count of Provence; abandon them all to return to a malaria-infected, crumbling, mob-infested, and baron-torn wreck. But there was more at stake than simply the material comfort and convenience of the pope. Clement VI shared in the long tradition of absolutist papal monarchy begun under Gregory VII (1073–85), fulfilled by Innocent III (1198–1216), and defined most dramatically by Boniface VIII. As vicar of Christ on earth, he was truly the lord of the world and claimed ultimate sovereignty over all matters both spiritual and temporal. As bishop of Rome the pope at Avignon assumed the position of universal pontiff, and no mere physical absence could cause him to abandon that claim. Though a conservative on these matters, Clement VI was a subtle thinker who could put fresh interpretations upon the venerable tradition. He had consciously taken the unprecedented step of choosing Pentecost day, May 19, 1342, for his coronation to demonstrate that just as the Holy Spirit had brought revelation to Christ's apostles, so, too, was the Holy Spirit the source of his unchallenged authority on matters of church teaching and authority. When it came to the delicate matter of being an absentee bishop of Rome, Clement employed one of his favorite motifs: the image of the bridegroom coming to meet his bride, the city of Rome. Yet he presented this topos in a double light: as the twin marriage of the pope to the church both as universal pastor and as the particular bishop of the city of Rome itself. Thus while his authority depended not so much on his presence in Rome as on his first function as universal pastor, he retained his essential tie to the *caput mundi* as its bishop and human lord. It was a tendentious argument; and the Avignon Curia knew it; thus its more-than-unusual defensiveness against any claim that might impugn its distant power and shaky authority. But where ecclesiology might appear less than solid, temporal power and court ceremonial could dazzle and intimidate any challenges.

On that Sunday, January 27, 1343, as Cola di Rienzo entered the grand Consistory Hall to present the congratulations and petition of the Thirteen Good Men, he faced the papal court in its full brilliance, the pope beneath his regal canopy; the cardinals, prelates, abbots, and bishops; the princes, high-ranking knights, courtiers, and servants; the priests and choir arrayed all around him and against the long walls of the hall. Who in that vast and exalted assembly would heed his words, even take them seriously? Who there were his enemies? Surely the two sons of Stefano il Vecchio, the leader of the Colonna clan.

Giovanni Colonna, powerful and, like all the Roman barons, vengeful if need be, headed the Roman faction in Avignon.[7] Cardinal from 1327 to his death in 1348, he was the leading cleric of the family and nephew of Cardinal Pietro Colonna, one of the leaders of the Colonna revolt against Boniface VIII in 1297. Giovanni, described by Petrarch as cultured, forward-looking, and sweetly tempered yet of a strongly authoritarian disposition, especially in defense of his family's interests, was probably the second son of Stefano il Vecchio (table 1). He had already come to the attention of Italy as a young boy when, on November 10, 1290, the Polentani kidnapped him from the train of his father, then acting as the papal rector of the Romagna. Giovanni probably studied law at Bologna, the family's university of choice, and seems to have gone on from there to

TABLE I. The Colonna of Palestrina

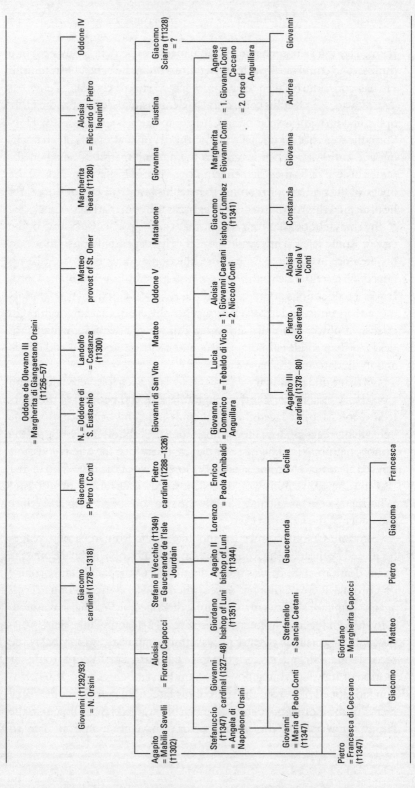

serve as Rome's chief judge of civil cases. On September 8, 1327, he was named a papal notary; then suddenly, on December 18, 1327, he was raised to the cardinalate by John XXII, probably to fill the family slot vacated by the death of his uncle Pietro Colonna on January 7, 1326. Giovanni was named cardinal-deacon of Sant'Angelo in Pescheria, the heart of Cola's Rome. In the manner of most highly placed barons in the church hierarchy, Giovanni soon amassed a wealth of benefices. These ranged from the traditional Colonna canonry at Marseilles, to a chantry at Bayeaux in Normandy, to canonries at Noyon and Tours, to ones closer to home: at Sant'Eustachio and Sta. Maria Rotonda (the Pantheon), an archpresbytery at Sta. Maria Maggiore and perhaps at the Lateran even before his elevation.

The Colonna *livrée,* their palace complex in Avignon, was also at times the residence of Giovanni's younger brother, Giacomo, the bishop of Lombez. Born between 1300 and 1301 in France, where Stefano il Vecchio had fled to escape Boniface VIII's "crusade" against the Colonna, Giacomo was set on an ecclesiastical career from an early age. By 1316 he already held canonries at Noyon and at Chalons-sur-Marne in France. Canonries at Cambrai and at Lubiana followed, this last previously in the hands of his uncle Cardinal Pietro. At some point during this period he also became a canon at the Lateran in Rome. From 1322 to 1326/27 he studied law at Bologna along with his brother Agapito, the future bishop of Luni, and there met his fellow student Francesco Petrarch, who was to become his lifelong friend. Giacomo then returned to Rome and, on April 22, 1328, it was he who nailed the papal excommunication of Emperor Lewis of Bavaria to the door of the Colonna church of S. Marcello. This was a brave act, indeed, considering that the emperor and his German troops then controlled the city and his uncle Sciarra was an active imperial commander. In recognition of his act, on May 28, 1328, Giacomo was named bishop of Lombez by John XXII, who set aside the major impediment to this appointment: Giacomo was not yet a priest. The pope's choice of Lombez was not by chance: its diocese was created by John himself only in 1317; and its region was the power base of the family of Giacomo and Giovanni's mother, Guacerande de l'Isle Jourdain. On the verge of his appointment as patriarch of Aquileia, Giacomo died in 1341, much to the shock and grief of friends and family.

But still here in Avignon were Giovanni's elder brother Stefanuccio Colonna, one of the leaders of the delegation sent in May 1342 by the Roman government that the Thirteen had displaced, and then Cardinal Giovanni Orsini, the archbishop of Naples and the papal legate for Italy; and how many others among that first delegation now about to be publicly repudiated? Cola already knew of the College of Cardinals' opposition to any return to a now-foreign Italy. And what of this papal court and its hundreds of *courtisans* from every part of France: Would they "return" to Rome?[8]

And who among the throng were his friends? Members of the Roman delegation had already made their solemn entry into Avignon and the papal court with a grand procession and great public ceremonial. They had no doubt already been treated to a sumptuous papal banquet and there and at the numerous receptions surrounding their embassy canvassed the papal court days before the formal address was scheduled; and a copy of Cola's address may have already circulated through the Curia. Cola knew well the art and technique of public speaking. He was regarded even then as the best orator in Rome and would soon be known as the best of his age. But friendly faces helped. Perhaps Lello di Pietro di Stefano dei Cosecchi, Petrarch's friend "Laelius"; and then perhaps Petrarch himself was somewhere in the hall. The poet and scholar was, after all, a member of the papal court, a member of Cardinal Colonna's *familia,* and an ally of the Romans then visiting Avignon. He had already intervened for the first delegation, sending Pope Clement a letter in verse, seen by many, encouraging the pope's return to Rome. And then, of course, Petrarch himself had every reason to join this Roman delegation as well. He was now a citizen of Rome, crowned only two years ago, at Giovanni Colonna's suggestion, on the Capitoline itself.

Cola and his legation now were ready to present their credentials and their "powers" and to deliver their first formal address. Rienzo rose when bidden, approached the papal throne, and then began. We do not have a copy of his address or of his instructions from Rome; but Brother Bernardo of Orvieto, an Augustinian Hermit who was present in the hall that day, set down a transcript that recorded faithfully the main points of Cola's speech and the pope's reply. Cola appears to have known the new pope's positions and their symbolic presentations well. He may have been informed of them by friends of Rome at the Curia. Cola began in the best tradition of the *ars arengandi,* with his formal salutations befitting the most exalted position of the pope and his court. Then, as part of his exordium or *captatio benevolentiae,* he expressed the delegation's and the city's filial devotion to their lord the pope and asked paternal pardon, presumably for the revolution that had put the Thirteen Good Men in power and brought Cola to Avignon. He added an expression of universal joy at the pope's election. Cola then continued with his *narratio,* or exposition of the condition of Rome and the creation of its new government under the Thirteen Good Men, before coming to his *petitio,* the statement of the delegation's main purpose. In this petition Cola made the case for the pope's return to his true home and for the granting of the Jubilee in 1350; finally, coming a bit discreetly at the end of the address as it did, he offered the pope the "general lordship of the Roman government," before coming to the fifth and final part of his address, the *conclusio.* When he had completed his address, Rienzo made the proper bows and obsequies and returned to his seat along the wall.

The pope's answer was more fully recorded by Fra Bernardo.[9] Clement was a skilled orator: 120 of his sermons, as well as 30 of his *collationes* preached in consistory, survive. But like most papal documents, this address was composed by one of the pope's staff. We know who that probably was, the notary and clerk of the Apostolic Chamber, Michele Ricomanni. Paleographical evidence attaches him to several other documents composed that day at the papal palace, including the bull *Unigenitus Dei Filius.* That bull marked a milestone in the history of Western Christianity, for here Clement defines the "treasury of merits" *(cumulus meritorum),* the reserve of spiritual grace accumulated by Christ and the saints, which the prayers and works of the faithful can draw from to apply to their own and to the souls of the deceased to shorten the punishment due to their worldly sins. The granting of these "indulgences" had formerly been applied generally only to crusaders, but now Clement extended them to the Jubilee pilgrims for certain set stays and visits to certain shrines in Rome during the Holy Year. Even though some form of both the Romans' petition delivered by Cola and Pope Clement's reply could have circulated in written form before their presentations, the medieval sense of formality would not have considered either valid unless presented in public ceremony and according to the proper procedures. Ricomanni, therefore, would have composed the reply following the specifics laid out by Pope Clement, but, being a notary, he would have known exactly how to compose and order them according to the proper forms of the *ars arengandi,* so that the pope's address would have the proper diplomatic form and ceremonial impact.

The pope's reply addresses the Romans' petitions one by one, recognizing their filial reverence, their request for paternal pardon, their joy at his election. This takes up the first 50 lines of the printed edition. Clement then went on in the next 193 lines to respond to the delegates' arguments for his return to the Eternal City: a spouse's love for his bride (Eph. 5:25–27); the need to fully realize his authority, to manifest the power of his episcopal seat; veneration for the apostles Peter and Paul and all the saints; the need of his presence in order to call a new crusade, to better govern the lands of the church, and to silence the voices of vituperation and reproach at his absence. Using the dialectic methodology so dear to late medieval scholastic philosophy, Clement took up the pros and cons of each of these points, often citing scriptural examples of marital love—the Song of Songs and the Genesis story of Jacob and Rachel— but then went on to cite a scriptural rebuttal. During the storm at sea, Peter alone left the safety of the bark, or *navicella,* while the other apostles kept their seats. So must the successor of Peter leave Rome to seek out peace in the growing conflicts between England and France, Aragon and Majorca. As much as the pope desires it—*desidero videre vos,* "For I long to see you," he repeats from Romans 1:11–12 throughout his address— it is not yet possible.

On the next point, however, taking up 280 lines, Pope Clement is far more encouraging: practical, moral, even scriptural reasons concur that the Jubilee ought to be held every fifty, rather than every one hundred, years. Finally, and somewhat abruptly considering the diplomatic occasion and form of his speech, Clement turned to address the last point of Cola's and the delegation's speech: the grant to the pope by the new government of "the general lordship of the Roman government." Clement's reply is direct and bluntly lacking in any diplomatic form. Even the pope's polite and charming *desidero videre vos* is missing. Clement intended to counter Cola's exaltation of Rome and its past glory, and he takes up a mere 10 lines in the printed Latin:

You come to offer us the general lordship of the Roman government. You Romans who have subjugated the world to you through your wisdom, you who have governed the world through your prudence, is it true that you offer to us an office that is already ours, since that City is ours? And you offer to us the Senate, captaincy, consulship and title of Defender of that City; and we accept them on this condition, that this acceptance in no way prejudices the rights of the Roman church. (ll. 525–35, Schmidinger "Die Antwort")

Then, presumably turning to the papal secretaries in attendance, he adds: "And you, notaries of the Apostolic Chamber, put all this into proper form." "And then," Fra Bernardo records, "those in attendance began the *Te Deum laudamus* in alta voce."

The effect must have stunned the Romans and left them speechless. Their reaction, and the reaction throughout the great Consistory Hall, can only be imagined. The Romans, Cola at their head, must have risen from their seats to protest: they had not meant to offend their lord. Of course these Roman offices and titles that they were offering were already his; they were only following ancient custom. But any pleas were immediately muted: all those in attendance, on a cue from some master of protocol, had already broken into the *Te Deum,* drowning out any possible protest. The pope had concluded his remarks and shut off any further discussion with the grand solemnity and frightening majesty of papal ceremony. Amid the throng of papal adherents the Romans would have had no choice but to leave the palace, still wondering whether their best efforts to win the pope's return to Rome had proven a dismal failure.

If Cola di Rienzo or any of his delegation thought so, their misgivings were not revealed in the official correspondence they sent to Rome the very next day.[10] For Cola's letter of January 28, 1343, resonates with imagery of rebirth, of emerging from a dark age, of the return of a golden age that quotes both Scripture and the classics, in this case Virgil's famous fourth *Eclogue,* seen by medieval people as the prophecy of the new Christian era, and the pagan prophecy of the Tiburtine Sibyl invoked in the legend of the Aracoeli in Rome: "With extraordinary and special veneration, let Rome, the nurturing, the holy, erupt into praise; and, devoutly on her knees, let her proclaim with the life-giving adoption of such sons that 'the virgin and the reign of Saturn [the Golden Age] has returned' and that the lamb of God, who has taken away the sins of the world, sits on the Apostolic Throne!" (1, BBCR 2.3:1–4, ll. 6–9).

That day, or very soon afterward, Cola dispatched a second letter to the Senate and People of Rome, repeating the good news of the delegation's success in obtaining the Jubilee for the year 1350 but adding some impressions of the pope's reaction to his speech. The letter is infused with a spiritual vocabulary of renewal and resurrection that would become a hallmark of Cola's thought:

Let the City of Rome rise again from its fall and long decline, ascending to the throne of its accustomed majesty. Let her take off her mourning widow's weeds and put on the royal purple wedding dress! Let her adorn her liberated head with a diadem. Let her grace her neck with jewels, let her take up the scepter of justice once again. Supported on every side and renewed with every virtue, let her be prepared like a jeweled bride, dressed for her husband's pleasure. . . .

For, behold, the heavens have opened [Apoc. 21:1], and from the glory of God the Father, the rising day of Christ, pouring out the light of the Holy Spirit, has prepared for you, who have been living among the gloomy shadows of death, a grace of unexpected and wondrous clarity. (2, BBCR 2.3:4–8, ll. 4–18)

With his reference to the bride dressed for her husband, Cola also invokes the powerful language of Apocalypse 21:2, which describes the descent of the New Jerusalem. He thus sets Rome's rebirth in deeply apocalyptic terms. But Cola had other reasons for citing this passage: the image of the bride was, as we have seen, a favorite of Pope Clement himself, and around that image focused much of the discussion—and debate—about the Avignon popes' proper relationship to the city of Rome. But there may be another reason for Cola's use of this topos. The image of Rome as a widow derives from a long tradition of lamentations in Judeo-Christian history and also goes back to antiquity, at least to Lucan's *Pharsalia* (1.183ff.) and was then used by the early church fathers and so entered the mainstream of medieval letters. But Cola did not have to look far to find examples. In Dante Alighieri's Letter 5 to the princes and peoples of Italy, "Behold now is the accepted time" [2 Cor. 6:2], and his Letter 8 to the Italian cardinals, "How doth the city sit solitary that was full of people" [Lam. 1:1], the poet employs images of Rome as both bride and widow, awaiting deliverance by the return to Italy of either emperor or pope. In both letters Dante also makes explicit his comparison of Rome to Jerusalem and implicit that of Avignon to Babylon, thus underscoring the apocalyptic imagery of his appeals and the notion of Rome as the New Jerusalem. In Letter 8 Dante presses the image of Rome as bride, calling on the Italians in the Curia "to fight together manfully for the Spouse of Christ, for the Seat of his Spouse, which is Rome." As we shall see again and again, Cola was long familiar with Dante's works and may have used an allusion to the great poet's authority to bolster his own arguments just as he mirrored Pope Clement's imagery.

After repeating his news that the Jubilee had been decreed for 1350, Cola urges the Romans "to set up [Clement's] sculpted image in purple and gold in the Colosseum or on the Capitoline, so that the eternal, joyful, and glorious memory of that most clement father of fathers, the author and liberator of the City, may live on in posterity and may not perish throughout the long duration of the ages" (2, BBCR 2.3:4–8, ll. 53–57). Rienzo then proposes a triumph for Clement as a Roman conqueror, not by the sword but "through words alone . . . armed with spiritual weapons." He signs the letter, "Nicholas di Rienzo, Roman consul of the orphans, widows and the poor, the sole legate of the people to our lord the Roman pope. Signed with his own heart and hand" (ll. 84–86). It was a lofty claim, but one with plenty of precedent in recent Roman history. From at least the thirteenth century Rome had appointed a *iudex orphanorum et viduarum et pauperum*, a "judge of orphans, widows, and the poor," to act as a public advocate on their behalf; and in the Roman Statutes of 1363 provisions were made that clarified this position. Cola may well, therefore, have been entrusted with these duties by the pope himself acting as the city's lord.

If Cola had any doubts about the success of his mission, he hid them from his readers. But he had little apparent reason to do so. While Clement's response to the offer of Roman sovereignty had been blunt and dismissive, the new government already knew the risks it had run in sending a second delegation and making such an offer. It was, no doubt, one of the main reasons they had sent their most eloquent spokesman. In his second letter from Avignon, Cola confided to the Romans that Pope Clement "also, with unspoken emotion, with word, facial expression, hands, with his entire body language, and with every exterior sign, promised—more than he was able to say—a visit to the Apostolic See after the scandals of the French [and English war] have been set to rest." Indeed, whether Cola was accurate in reading the pope or simply projecting his own sense of success for the consumption of the Roman government, Clement was never really inclined to leave Avignon. He did, however, seem to be moved both by Cola's arguments and by his personal charm. The Anonimo romano recalls what impression the event left with contemporaries: "The speech he made there was so highly developed and beautiful that it caused Pope Clement to fall in love with him at once. The pope greatly marveled at the beautiful style of Cola's language. He wanted to see him daily" (AR, XVIII, ll. 29–32, Porta, p. 144).

And so Rienzo became a favorite of the new pope.[11] The first reference to his new status dates from a letter written by Pope Clement to the Roman senators on August 9, 1343, in which Clement calls Cola *familiaris noster,* a member of the papal *familia* or personal household staff. Rienzo must have been granted this status soon after their first meeting. Around that time as well Cola, now a resident of the papal palace, may have first struck up a friendship with Francesco Petrarch.

Petrarch had been a resident of Avignon since his parents moved there in 1312, and, after studies in Montpellier and Bologna, he returned to the city in 1327, where he became part of the Colonna *familia* as a chaplain in 1330. Although he remained a full-time member of the cardinal's staff only until 1337, when he bought a house in nearby Vaucluse, he remained in Colonna's *familia* and continued to perform a variety of functions through the 1340s. When he was in Avignon he may, therefore, have lived close by the papal palace in Giovanni Colonna's *livrée* on the site of the ancient forum. The Colonna *livrée,* or palace complex, was a center of Roman and

Italian life at Avignon; and attached to the cardinal's *familia* were a number of Rome's favorite clerical sons, as well as several sons of notable families from the Colonna lands around Palestrina. Here also lived some of the leading musical and literary personalities of the time.

Here, certainly, the Roman embassies must have been entertained, and here it is quite possible that Cola first met Petrarch. The proximity of their lodgings in this city of high political contacts and mutual Italian interests easily allowed Petrarch and Cola to meet and to talk about things dear to them: the papacy's return to Rome and the revival of the city's ancient glory. In one of the many private letters that Petrarch wrote but never circulated, letter 7 of the *Epistolae sine nomine,* or "Letters without Names," the poet describes a meeting with an unnamed companion in the nearby church of St.-Agricol. The recipient of the letter is debated, but the mood and imagery make it plausible that Petrarch is addressing Cola:[12]

I glow with such zeal that I consider your words those of an oracle issuing from the innermost recesses of that temple. I seem to have been listening to a god, not to a man. You bemoaned the present conditions—no, the very fall and ruin of the republic—in words of such divine inspiration, and you probed our wounds with the shafts of your eloquence to such depths that whenever I recall the sound and the meaning of your words, tears leap to my eyes, and grief again grips my soul. . . . Despair seizes me one moment, hope the next; and with my soul wavering between the two, I often murmur to myself: "Oh! if ever. . . . oh! if it would only happen in my day. . . . oh! if I could only share in so noble, so glorious an enterprise!" (BBCR 2.3:9–11; CRCR, 4–6; Zacour, 64–66)

Their friendship had become common knowledge, and with Petrarch's help no doubt Cola had quickly become a trusted, and daily, adviser to the pope on Roman affairs. But his position, like Petrarch's, was tenuous:

And so Cola stayed on and said that the barons of Rome were highway robbers; they consented to homicides, robberies, adulteries, and every evil. They wanted their city laid low and desolate. The pope conceived many plans against the barons. Then, at the petition of Lord Cardinal Janni [Giovanni] della Colonna, Cola fell into such disgrace, such poverty, such infirmity, that he came close to having to enter a church hospice. With his little tunic on his back he stood there like a snake in the sun. (AR XVIII, ll. 32–41, Porta, p. 144)

The Anonimo romano could not have put it more succinctly or cruelly. On May 15, 1343, Clement VI named Matteo Orsini and Paolo Conti of the Torre delle Milizie, two Roman barons, as his new senators for the next six months. The pope's appointment was more than a mere formality, for in restoring the rule of the senators Clement was also now realigning with the Colonna faction in Avignon and annulling the government of the Thirteen Good Men, thus overturning the coup that had brought Cola's delegation to Avignon. In July the rest of this Roman delegation returned to the city, leaving Cola alone and at the mercy of Rome's barons, whose chief representative, Cardinal Giovanni Colonna, held enormous influence both in Avignon and in Rome. The barons had apparently begun both a smear campaign against Cola through Cardinal Colonna in Avignon and legal actions against him, his family, and his property back in Rome. But Petrarch seems to have intervened with Giovanni Colonna sometime soon after that. The Anonimo romano reports it succinctly: "'He whom He has brought low, He also exalts' [cf. Ezek. 21:26]. Lord Janni della Colonna sent Cola back to the pope. He returned to grace and was made notary of the Chamber of Rome." On August 9, 1343, Clement wrote from his summer home at Villeneuve to his two new senators:[13]

A little while ago, Nicholas di Rienzo, a member of our household, sent, as he asserted, to our Apostolic See by our beloved sons the Consuls of the Guilds and other popular elements of the same City, prudently and elegantly laid out before us and our brothers in Consistory matters regarding the reform of the condition of the same City and the liberation of its people from the oppressions of its barons. He also set forth the complaints and oppressions reported to have been imposed on the same people. In declaring them he could not have been more straight-forward. . . . (Theiner 130, 2:119)

Clement's position was unequivocal. He and the College of Cardinals believed Cola's allegations; and he ordered the barons to cease all legal proceedings and revoke all penalties against him. Clement also stood firmly behind Cola's plans for Rome's reform: re-creating the *buono stato*. This concept of political reform and renewal was a venerable one in medieval political thought, and the notion had antecedents in medieval political discourse; but the fact that here Clement is throwing back at the senators a term prominent in Cola's political lexicon indicates that Rienzo's and the pope's political agendas for Rome had found common ground. Cola was now Clement's declared protégé.[14]

But Giovanni Colonna finally had had enough of both Cola's plans for a revived republic and of his alliance with Petrarch. By a sad coincidence of events, news of the death of King Robert of Naples, on January 19, 1343, created an opportunity for Pope Clement to send an embassy to the court of Robert's granddaughter and successor, the young Queen Giovanna I (table 2). Ever since Pope Clement IV had sanctioned Charles of

TABLE 2. The Angevins of Naples and Hungary

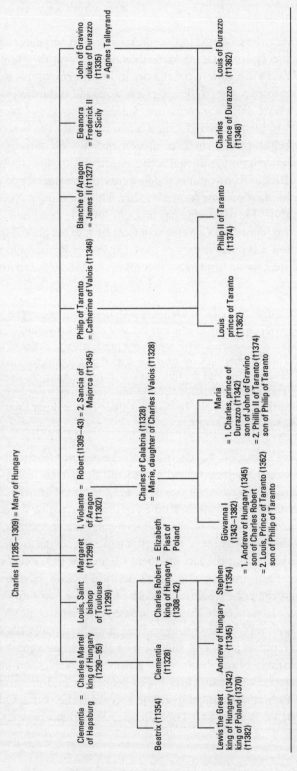

SOURCE: © Italica Press.

Anjou's invasion of Naples and his overthrow of the German Hohenstaufen there in 1266, the ruler of Naples had been the pope's feudal vassal, and Clement VI had the right to advise that ruler, especially since she
was a young woman beset by threats at home and challenges to her throne
from abroad. Robert's heir, Charles of Calabria, his son by Violante of
Aragon, had predeceased him in 1328, and while still alive Robert had
arranged to have his granddaughters, Giovanna and Maria, married to
the Angevin heirs to the throne of Hungary. Robert's widow, the child-
less Queen Sancia, had immediately stepped in to assume the regency, accompanied by several of her closest Franciscan advisers, but she yearned
to retire to the Clariss convent of Sta. Croce, where she died on July 28,
1345. Giovanna had married Andrew of Hungary on January 22/23, 1343;
but the widows of Robert's two younger brothers, the princes of Taranto
and Durazzo, also put forward claims to the throne on behalf of *their*
Angevin sons. The situation for the young queen, and for the wealthy papal fief of Naples, was critical.

At Colonna's influential suggestion, Petrarch was named papal ambassador and ordered to leave Avignon, which he did in mid-September
1343. The pope had good reason to choose him. Petrarch had been
crowned poet laureate through King Robert's intervention, and he had
visited and made a strong impression on the king and his court. In addition, Petrarch's close friend since his first days at Vaucluse, Philippe de
Cabassoles, bishop of neighboring Cavaillon, was the head of the board
of regents appointed by the pope for the young Queen Giovanna. Could
the pope have sent a more important legate? Certainly. In fact, one of Avignon's leading figures, Cardinal Annibaldo de Ceccano, whose hospitality Clement had so abundantly enjoyed, had been the archbishop of
Naples from 1326 to 1328, and he was well connected to the court. Several other high-level candidates might have been chosen as well, including the present archbishop, Giovanni Orsini, who had also served as a papal legate to Italy. But the choice of a low-level, *cultural,* figure — who also
had considerable Italian experience — may have suited Clement's purposes
better: to size up the situation in the kingdom and to report discreetly to
the pope. Giovanni Colonna probably made such arguments to the pope
and would have added that Petrarch could travel there to secure the release from prison of some political allies of the Colonna. But King Robert
had died on January 19; and a courier bearing the news would have taken
only about two weeks to reach Avignon. The pope and his court should,
therefore, have been making plans for this most important fiefdom early
in February at the latest; and Petrarch's appointment only a few weeks

after his intervention on Cola's behalf and Clement's letter of support for Rienzo reinforces the role of Giovanni Colonna in sending him from Avignon after these events.

The upshot of Petrarch's departure was that Cola was left isolated and alone in Avignon; and as the last and most outspoken vestige of the communal government, he had made an enemy of the powerful Colonna cardinal, while back at home the barons were already plotting his destruction. But Rienzo took the first of many tacks in these newly stormy waters. He remained behind in Avignon until June of 1344. There was little need for him to return to Rome quickly. The chief goal of his mission had been achieved: the Jubilee was set for 1350; but the republic had foundered, replaced at the stroke of a pen by Pope Clement. Despite the pope's warning to the barons, Rome was still dangerous for the young notary, whatever status he might hold at the papal court. He therefore waited, biding his time; and, judging from Clement's later description of Cola as *dilectus filius,* "beloved son," no doubt he remained visible at the papal court, serving Clement on Roman matters in whatever capacity he could. He realized that the term of the pope's senators in Rome would expire at the end of April. The situation would be fluid, or at least open to some form of political maneuvering while the pope made his decision to appoint or approve two new senators from the rival baronial clans. Cola could not hope to supplant the pope's vicars, but he just might be able to exercise enough influence on Clement to salvage his own position and, if need be, his life.[15] In early April 1344, Cola therefore presented the pope with the following petition:

that he can live in the said City more secure from loss of his person and of his properties, together with your officials: that is, as one of the chamberlains appointed to the Chamber of the same City by your aforesaid Holiness.

May you deign to provide to the same Nicholas, a public notary with the approval of the aforesaid common people, the office of Notary of the said Chamber, at the pleasure of your aforesaid Holiness, and until he shall command him to be recalled, just like the said chamberlains, with the usual salary of five gold florins a month, at your pleasure, and with the usual advantages and honors and wages, along with the appropriate terms. (4, BBCR 2.3:12, ll. 7–16)

The request was a dangerous one: Cola had come to Avignon as the representative of the people of Rome to their bishop and lord. He had lost his status overnight when the pope dissolved that government and appointed two barons as senators. But Cola was now asking the pope to appoint him a salaried *papal* representative to return from Avignon to

Rome. Could he rely on Clement's continued goodwill for this complete about-face? Would the pope see any purpose in granting it? On April 13, 1344, Clement named Giordano Orsini and Giovanni Colonna the Younger his new vicars as senators and captains for a six-month term beginning July 1, granting them a salary of 3,000 florins, plus a staff of "judges, notaries, and officials." The barons' hold on the city was now solid, with a Colonna sharing the reins of government.

Yet in a gesture quite fitting Clement VI's political adroitness and sophisticated sense of irony, on the same day the pope wrote to Cola di Rienzo. The letter reads as a personal vindication of Cola's entire stay in Avignon. In a passage that must have revealed the pope's silent smile at his *familiaris* "more than he was able to say," Clement finally answered Cola's very first speech in Avignon with the courtesy befitting a trusted member of his personal household. The pope "gratefully accepts" the Roman people's offer to him of the titles of senator, captain, syndic, and defender, with all their offices, authority, and so forth. Clement notes that he has appointed two senators for six-month terms with set salaries and staffs, but he has now also agreed to Cola's request. He recognizes Rienzo's "praiseworthy actions and the merits of your competence," and so that "you may return to the City suitably more secure and honorable in the protection of a status infused with our favor for you," Clement appoints him: "Notary of the City Chamber, with a monthly salary of 5 gold florins, as a notary public with all the usual benefits, honors, and wages, appointed at the pope's pleasure, and by his special grace" (5, BBCR 2.3:13–14, ll. 24–30; Theiner 139, 2:141).

Cola, a taverner's son, was now a papal notary, the first office that Cardinal Giovanni Colonna himself had held in Rome. The irony of the pope's appointment must have grated on the powerful Roman churchman and alarmed the new senators, for by tradition only they could name the notary of the Chamber. Two months later, on June 17, just before Cola departed for Rome, Clement sent him a second letter, confirming his appointment but noting that even had Cola's appointment actually been coterminous with that of Matteo Orsini and Paolo Conti, as the letter of April 13 seemed to imply, the pope is now extending Cola's appointment not only through the term of the newly appointed Giordano Orsini and Giovanni Colonna, "but that you may be able to administer it freely and legally, until the concession so granted to you specially by us is revoked" (6, BBCR 2.3:15–16, ll. 36–39; Theiner 140, 2:141–42).

Clement was too clever a ruler and politician not to have been aware of Cola's, and his own, coup. The barons might hold the reins of power under the restored oligarchy; but they did so as the pope's vicars, and their official positions were terminated every six months. On November 26, 1344, Clement had already named two new senators—Bertoldo Orsini and Orso degli Anguillara—and shifted power once again. While that power remained within the baronial families, divisions among them were strong and bloody: only such a rotating arrangement could check the rival factions and preserve some form of equilibrium in the city. Yet now a papal agent had been inserted into the equation, and a brilliant and potentially dangerous one at that. Cola di Rienzo had now become the Notary of the City Chamber: no great post, as his annual salary of sixty florins indicates, but in that capacity a sitting member of Rome's governing council. It was a limited position, but it had one great strength and advantage over the barons: its continuity. For although the barons came and went on the city's council, Cola sat in the government at the pope's pleasure, and without a set term. He therefore was able to start doing what clever and long-tenured politicians have always done: working carefully and modestly behind the scenes, looking into the city's finances, expanding his contacts and his network of favors, building his own power base while the barons continued to chip away at one another's. Best of all for Clement: Cola was a known quantity, charming, intelligent, courageous, trusted, and capable of serving the interests of the pope while pursuing his own and the papacy's agenda: Rome's revival and the pacification of its warring factions.

For Clement the risks to his own position and prestige were relatively small and the opportunity great. For Cola the opportunity was also remarkable: he had come to Avignon the legate of the new republic, had seen it run aground on the political shoals of the papal court, founder, and sink. But he had survived the shipwreck. Now fitted out anew, with a mandate from the city's former and present lord, he was ready to return to Rome to work his plan for its revival and the return of the Golden Age. Only one thing could stop him: the barons.

CHAPTER 5

Cola and the Barons

Cola returned to Rome very joyfully; but between his teeth
he made threats. As soon as he returned from the pope's
court, he began to perform his office like a member of the
court. He recognized clearly the robberies of the dogs of the
Campidoglio, the cruelty and injustice of the barons. He saw
how great the danger to the commune was, but he could not
find a good citizen who was willing to aid him.

Anonimo romano, XVIII, ll. 45–52, Porta, 144

And so Cola di Rienzo returned to Rome, and as Pope Clement had perhaps expected, Rienzo alone seems to have survived the shipwreck of the
Thirteen Good Men. His task would be a long and hard one: reestablishing the coalition that had brought about the revolution and had sent
him to Avignon. But now he had the backing of the pope and an official
position within Rome's government, a minor one, but one from which
he could reestablish his contacts and build support, and one that would
protect him from the power of the barons.

Reviewing all the forms of government then known to political
thinkers, Cola's contemporary, Bartolo of Sassoferrato, wrote in his *Treatise on City Government*:

There is a seventh method of government, one current in the City of Rome: the
worst. For in that City there are many tyrants just strong enough in the different
rioni of the City that one cannot prevail against another. For the communal government of the City as a whole is so weak that no one can do anything against any

83

of these tyrants nor against any of their adherents, without himself suffering the consequences. Aristotle did not propose this form of government, and for good reason: for it is something monstrous. (I, ll. 65–71)

Bartolo's focus on baronial faction as the root cause of civil strife built on a long legacy of Italian analyses of moral depravity, the influence of the spheres, class conflict, and the papal-imperial struggle, but it understood the Roman situation well.[1] The Anonimo romano provides the hard details of Bartolo's monster:

The City of Rome was living through great troubles. It had no appointed rectors. Combat raged every day. People were robbed everywhere. Virgins were defiled. There was no protection. Little old maids were assaulted and led off to dishonor. Wives were seized from their husbands in their own beds. Farm workers going out to labor were robbed. Where? Within the gates of Rome. Pilgrims, who had come to the holy churches for the good of their souls, were not defended but were robbed, their throats slit. Priests began committing crimes. Every lust, every evil, no justice, no restraint. No longer was there a remedy. The individual was perishing. The man who could wield the sword best was the one who had most claim to the right. There was no safety unless each man defended himself with the help of his relatives and friends. Every day saw musters of armed men. (AR, XVIII, ll. 290–308, Porta, p. 153)

Far from imposing a "cohesive force" or the peace of "self-help," as some anthropologists have characterized the feud, Rome's barons fought an endless cycle of violence and vendetta. On May 6, 1333, Stefanuccio di Sciarra Colonna personally murdered Bertoldo Orsini during a roadside encounter in the Campagna. Feuding became uncontrollable and disrupted every aspect of life in a civil war that would involve almost all of Rome's powerful barons, continue through the next decade, and make Rome the very image of anarchy for contemporary Italians.

Yet one cannot discuss Cola's Rome without focusing on the barons and the nexus of power, patronage, and family that kept Roman society together. Although Rome had its emerging mercantile class of large traders and its many smaller shopkeepers, its long tradition of bankers and moneychangers, and of course the papal court and its followers, and though it had a long history of civic government under the various reincarnations of its commune from the 1140s on, it was the barons who formed the core of Rome's political and social structure.

The Latin word *baro* had, by the twelfth century, come to mean a magnate, a tenant-in-chief, a "baron" throughout feudal Europe, and almost universally implied the possession of fiefs and vassals. In Rome, however, it more accurately came to mean one who possessed great landholdings and only secondarily the vassals, tenants, wealth, and power that such holdings implied. And while Rome had long had its *milites, nobiles viri,* or *cavallerotti* who had sprung from ancient lineage or had acquired sufficient wealth in the course of the eleventh and twelfth centuries to form the nucleus of the city's patriciate, by the fourteenth century the barons had become a class apart. These *magnifici viri, magnates,* and *barones* soon formed a small circle of about a dozen families whose great fortresses, *fortilizie* and *case-torri,* sprung up from Rome's great ruined monuments or around the skyline of towers encircling the *abitato.* These men dominated the city's government, finances, and society.

Unlike the rise of the barony in Tuscany, Lombardy, or the Veneto, the great paradox of the feudal order within the Papal States is that it arose not at the expense of—but precisely in support of—the public authority, here wielded by the pope and Curia. With the thirteenth century and the consolidation of unquestioned papal government over Christendom, along with its newly unparalleled sources of wealth and influence, a series of Roman and Latin families ascended to the papal throne. Between 1241 and 1303 there followed a steady stream of cardinalates showered upon their relatives and friends. These cardinals, in turn, brought power and prestige to their families and support to the popes.[2]

With papal ascendancy over Rome's government, recognized in the treaty of 1188, the pontiff was eventually authorized to name a single senator as his vicar. From then on the shape and fortunes of the baronial class were set. While this arrangement varied broadly throughout the thirteenth century, between 1230 and 1347, the year of Cola's revolution, the pope recognized 168 senators with origins in Rome and Lazio. Of these, 50 came from the Orsini clan, 28 from the Annibaldi, 24 from the Colonna, 17 from the Conti, 15 from the Savelli, 8 from the Stefaneschi, and 5 from the Anguillara. These had joined the ranks of only a handful of other families of similar power and wealth: the more ancient lineages of the Crescentii, Frangipane, Pierleoni, Capocci, and Normanni; and were soon joined by the Cenci and Caetani. Unlike the rest of Italy, especially the center and north, where the thirteenth century saw the gradual restriction of the urban nobility to certain set families, Rome remained fairly fluid, with its *nobiles viri* always ready to rise up to join the highest level of *barones Urbis,* while old baronial families could just as easily slide into oblivion or extinction.

While our sources for the history of these baronial families are fairly rich for the thirteenth century, by the early fourteenth century they become scarce and fragmentary; and only in the decades after Cola's revolution do rich *fondi* of notarial documents for both the city and the countryside become available. We can best look at the great baronial families by charting their islands of power and influence across thirteenth- and fourteenth-century Rome (see map 1). The resulting map is medieval in every sense: its coordinates not easily laid down, the names and formations of its major centers shifting over time, much of our information derived from ancient tales recorded only partially and imprecisely; much of the record lost.[3]

The Orsini were the oldest Roman family whose rapid rise to baronial status can be tied directly to a papal connection. Two neighborhoods in the city's *abitato* became the foci of their slow and careful process of acquisition: the area between the Theater of Pompey, the Piazza dei Satiri, and the Campo dei Fiori to the east; and the stretch of Rome at the western point of the *abitato:* from Monte Giordano (fig. 13) west along the axis of via dei Coronari, through the *rione* Ponte, across the Ponte S. Angelo, and into the Borgo around the Vatican. They soon controlled a strip through the center of Rome from the Castel Sant'Angelo (see fig. 1) eastward to the edges of the Cenci territory in the *rione* of Sant'Angelo in Pescheria from today's Piazza Mattei to the church of Sant'Angelo itself (see fig. 3).

Their great rivals, the Colonna, controlled a broad swath of the eastern *abitato* between the Tiber and the Mausoleum of Augustus, through the modern Piazza Colonna, Montecitorio, and south through the area of SS. Apostoli, and culminating in their palace on the western outcropping of the Quirinal. Here, just as via del Plebiscito turns sharply to mount the Quirinal, a Colonna palace has stood since at least the ninth century. It had originated in a hodgepodge of fortified loggie, houses, and outbuildings carved into the ruins of the Temple of Serapis on the Collis Latiaris (see fig. 7). By the early twelfth century the Colonna had succeeded the counts of Tusculum, and the family of Alberic before them, to control the Quirinal and a large part of the *rione* Monti. By 1167 they were in possession of some form of fortification built atop the Mausoleum of Augustus. Petrus de Columna, a descendant of the counts of Tusculum, seems to have begun the baronial dynasty. He took his family name either from the Column of Antoninus or from the town of Colonna in Lazio. While the Colonna were always firmly grounded in Roman properties, their chief power came not from Rome's cattle, commerce, and banking, as did that of so many other magnate families, but from their country fiefs concentrated along the via Prenestina and via Casalina, especially around their chief seat of Palestrina. Here, in the ancient Praeneste, site of the immense sanctuary and oracle of Fortuna Primigenia, the counts of Tusculum had become the chief feudatory by the tenth century. By the twelfth century their only surviving heirs, the Colonna, had inherited the high-perched *castrum* set amid the remains of the sanctuary.

By 1252 the family had grown rich and large enough for a formal division between the branches of Oddone di Giordano and Pietro di Oddone. By the beginning of the fourteenth century there were also Colonna branches of Gallicano, Genazzano, and Riofreddo. Yet the meteoric rise of the Colonna on the eve of the fourteenth century was due in large part to their alliance with Pope Nicholas IV (1288–92), who rewarded them not only with, and for, their papal offices in the government of the Papal States but also for the role that Cardinal Giacomo Colonna had played in his election. During Nicholas's reign the Colonna of Genazzano and Palestrina gained control of two cities, thirty castles in Lazio, ten in the Regno of Naples, and six in Romagna, grants of feudal rights and jurisdictions that generated enormous wealth and power for them. By 1328 the family's control of the eastern *abitato* was so firm that Giacomo de Sciarra Colonna could enter a Rome then held by the pope's enemy, Lewis of Bavaria, read the papal excommunication of the emperor from the security of the Colonna quarter, and then beat a hasty retreat to the safety of Palestrina.

And yet it was not their wealth and power alone that made the Colonna a special force in Roman politics and society in the early fourteenth century. The family could and did make claims both upon its ancient roots in Rome and upon its spiritual affinities to the city and its history: Cardinal Giovanni Colonna (1206–45), his grand-niece, the Blessed Margherita Colonna (1255–80), her eldest brother, Senator Giovanni Colonna, the author of her *Vita,* and Giovanni's granddaughter, another Margherita, the daughter of Stefano Colonna il Vecchio (d. 1349), the widow of Giovanni Conti and benefactor of the hospital of Santo Spirito, matched their physical with a spiritual power.

While no Colonna was to sit on the papal throne until Oddone Colonna of Genazzano became Martin V in 1417, Colonna cardinals long played a pivotal role in the Curia. From the papacy of Celestine V, Cardinals Giacomo and Pietro, along with Napoleone Orsini, had been aligning themselves with the Spiritual wing of the Franciscan order. This not only fit their reform ideals—insistence upon the absolute poverty of Christ and the apostles—but also admirably dovetailed with their own politics; for Boniface was perceived as the sworn enemy of the Spirituals; and the millennial histories and reform critiques that poured out from the Spirituals against their persecutors could only help the Colonna campaign to smear the orthodoxy of their Caetani enemy. Thus at Avignon under Clement V and John XXII, Giacomo Colonna, the mystical as well as physical brother of the Blessed Margherita, became a key figure in the history of the Spiritual Franciscans, taking the leader of the Italian Spirituals, Angelo Clareno, under his protection. During the first four decades of the century, the *livrée* of the Cardinals Giacomo, Pietro, and then Giovanni (cardinal 1327–48) was a focus of the religious and cultural life at Avignon that included Petrarch. In Rome, meanwhile, Giacomo's older brother, Stefano the Younger, or "Stefanuccio," played host to Petrarch on his first trip to the city in 1337; and in 1341, after Petrarch had been crowned poet laureate and lauded by Stefano Colonna il Vecchio, the Dominican Giovanni Colonna was his touring companion through Rome's ancient remains.

To see the barons of Cola's Rome as simply a collection of medieval gangster families set upon dividing up the city into their own territories would be only part of the truth, a caricature that ignores aspiration, personality, and emotion. It would also be a mistake to see the baronial families, or even the lesser nobility, restricted or restricting themselves to small sections of the city, or even to a single *rione*. Their properties, and their influence, overlapped those of other families. While the definite lines of such clientage with a baronial family's *vicinantia* are difficult to document, they remain very real; and widely spread property holdings and clients throughout the city guaranteed not only economic diversification but also family prestige. The Savelli, for example, held properties and clients within the area of the Arenula controlled by the Cenci. As the Anonimo romano tells us, one of their clients, who had become a feudal vassal of Francesco Savelli, was Cola di Rienzo. The barons' tombs, the canonries held by members of their families, the chapels they endowed, especially at such great basilicas as the Aracoeli, the city offices they held, and the clients who bound themselves to them all point to a broader consciousness of being "Roman" in a wider political and social sense.

The barons could even see their unceasing penchant for bloody civil war as a social virtue: war waged for peace, not vendetta, and on behalf of the common good. Writing on September 8, 1348/49 (*Fam.* VIII.1), Petrarch reminded Stefano il Vecchio, the powerful head of the Colonna clan, of a pleasant afternoon walk they had once taken through Rome in 1337. Late in the day they found themselves on the via Lata (today's Corso), in the center of the Colonna district:

It so happened that mention was made of one of your sons with whom at that time you were angry, I believe, because of the evil tongues of troublemakers rather than because of a father's normal anger. But you favored me with your kindness, and you allowed me to do what you had never previously permitted others to do, to prevail upon you to have your son return into your graces. In any event, after you had complained about him to me in a friendly fashion, with a changed expression you finally added words more or less like these. . . . "Among the first accusations leveled against me [by my son] was that I had become involved in more battles than I ought to, considering the dignity of my advanced age, and thereby would I leave my children a legacy of hatred and of discord. I call on God to witness that I have undertaken wars for no other reason than my love of peace. Both my advanced age and my spirit now growing cold in this bosom, which is of the earth, and my long experience with human affairs make me eager for peace and quiet. On the other hand, I remain firm and determined not to turn my back to hardship. I would prefer a more peaceful existence, but if destiny ordains it I would prefer to go to my grave fighting than learning how to be a subservient old man. As for what they say concerning my legacy, I wish to answer only this (and I beg you to pay the closest attention to my words): Would that I could leave my children some kind of legacy, but contrary to my personal wish, fate decreed otherwise; and—I say this with great sadness—the fact of the matter is that, contrary to the natural order, I shall be the heir of all my children." While you said these things you turned your tearful eyes away. (PLFM 1:391–92)

Like the elder Stefano, the other great barons of Rome—Orsini, Anguillara, Savelli, Caetani—also saw their actions as in the best interests of the whole. They saw themselves as *barones Urbis* or *de Urbe,* or as *milites romani,* descendants of a noble order of citizens ever ready to defend the interests of Rome—which almost universally they identified with those of their own family and faction. Only a rare and insightful source, such as the Anonimo romano, could label them *baroni de castella,* the big men in the castles who were thus identified not with civil life but with violence and civil strife.

Any visitor to Cola's Rome could gaze upon the superstructures of the barons' fortresses rising atop the wreckage of the Colosseum, the Capitoline, the Temple of Serapis, the Arch of Titus, and the Mausolea of Augustus and Hadrian: sprawling amalgams of precious stones and marbles, columns, entablatures, and inscriptions: the *spolia* of past power among the mansions, towers, porticos, loggie, and *cortili* of what came to be known as Rome's *fortilizie,* the fortresses.[4] Since the 1050s they had proclaimed the wealth of the barons and their mastery of—and even greater dependence upon—the glory and traditions of classical and Christian Rome. Like the Torre Anguillara in Trastevere or the sprawling Orsini complex atop Monte Giordano (see fig. 13), these could include *torre* but also *palatie* (residential palaces), *munitiones* (strongholds), and *claustrae* (compounds of interior courtyards).

In whatever part of the *abitato* or *disabitato,* the pattern was familiar: the central *casa-torri* was protected by slowly acquiring the properties of clients and friends all around. Unlike even the palaces of the lesser nobility, which greeted the street and the city with open porticos, loggie, and "civil" facades, the *fortilizie* showed the rest of the city little more than their barred gates and frowning walls. Such fortified complexes put off strangers, yet they served as havens for friends and relations; and they acted as imposing defensive works in ongoing civil wars. From fortress to fortress within a *vicinantia,* a baronial faction could quickly erect barricades and roadblocks, the *sbarre* that play so prominent a part in Cola's description of the street fighting around Henry VII's battle for the city. The sources agree on the destructive effectiveness of these fortresses: the street-to-street bloodshed that ebbed and flowed through Rome like the waters of the Tiber in flood; and the mighty destruction done to the urban fabric by opposing factions holed up in their castles and towers.

If the barons held their *fortilizie* within Aurelian's walls, outside in the Campagna they had also accumulated a wide array of rural settlements, the *castra* and *casali.*[5] By the fourteenth century the barons had acquired about four hundred grand estates across Lazio. Over the course of the thirteenth century the barons alienated hundreds of *castra* and their feudal fiefs from the estates of Lazio's monastic houses—especially Farfa and Subiaco—and from Lazio's lesser nobility. Many more were acquired outright as "allods," or freeholdings, a phenomenon common in Italy and widespread in Lazio.

The vast majority of the *castra* in Lazio were built by the barons themselves in the late thirteenth and early fourteenth centuries. Many of their motives are obvious: to hold down their newly acquired estates, guarantee both rural income and human loyalties, and ensure military security in an era of papal-imperial conflict and communal wars. Others were less apparent. For most baronial holdings there existed, in the phrase of Sandro Carocci, a "topographical rapport" between their urban *fortilizie* and their rural *castra.* That is, the barons tended to build their countryside castles along the routes that tied their major urban holdings, their *vicinantia,* to their rural estates, even if these castles were not always directly on the shortest modern axis between the two points. Thus the Colonna's major holdings in the east and north of Rome were tied to their country estates to the east and north: at Palestrina, Colonna, Gallicano, Genazzano, and elsewhere by *castra* along the via Tiburtina, Prenestina, and Appia; the Normanni, Bonaventura, and Stefaneschi of Trastevere held *castra* strung out along the via Portuense and Aurelia; and the Capocci holdings on the Quirinal were linked by towers along the via Salaria, Nomentana, and Tiburtina. One might have to pass the towers of many another baronial family on such a journey; but this is why, in this mortar and stone game of "Go," so many baronial families kept such good ties with their friends and kept potential rivals close at hand.

This also explains why Rome's bridges were so essential to the political, as well as the economic, life of the city. For not only did the Ponte Nomentana and Milvio bring goods and pilgrims to Rome from the north and east; they also held the balance of power for many the city's baronial families and their ability to communicate with their estates and vassals. They were constantly the object of baronial seizure and thus of papal and communal anxiety. Between May 1333 and March 1336, with only brief truces, the city had erupted into a brutal civil war, the factions clustering around the Colonna and the Orsini. One of the chief objects of the warfare was control of Rome's bridges. After careful negotiations, in a letter of March 18, 1336, Benedict XII was able to arrange a peace settlement in which the bridges figured prominently, "of which bridges four are held by the said Stefano Colonna, a fifth by the said Jacopo Savelli, and several others by the said Orsini." The pope called for repairs to Ponte Molle and Rome's other bridges and their restoration to public control. The papal letter was dead on arrival, and Benedict had to follow up his arrangement with further entreaties on April 13.

Still other factors multiplied castles and towers in the countryside. They served as rest stops on the road between town and country; safe havens for the family's ladies, its wagons of grain, and its rents; and then, especially in the fourteenth century, as seats for the newly exploding branches of many of the baronial houses. For the youngest grandson of a collateral Colonna or Orsini branch, owning a castle in the countryside would assure him and his own family the status and prestige that only property could convey, no matter how modest the "castle" might be. And modest many of them were: the size and importance of such estates could vary widely from wooden structures with a dozen dependent villagers, to important centers like Palestrina, Vicovaro, and Cave, to cities like Ninfa and Nepi.

It was here in such rural communes as Ninfa and Nepi, and not in the crammed and highly visible life of Rome, that the full impact of the barons' acquisitions becomes clear. By the 1290s a similar pattern had emerged in the frenzy to acquire holdings, which brought to bear the barons' economic, political, and military power on their weaker neighbors and set a precedent for their strategies of domination in Rome itself over the next fifty years. In order to counter the growing influence of the Caetani in southern Lazio and the Marittima, for example, the Colonna decided on the wholesale takeover of the free commune of Ninfa. In 1293 Agapito Colonna, the brother of Cardinal Pietro Colonna, arranged to have himself appointed podesta of the city. But rather than relinquish power at the end of his official term, he used the threat of military force and political influence to arrange to have his term extended. The *popolo* who "elected" him were thenceforth reduced to assenting to his decrees, *pro bono statu, pace et quiete dicte terre,* "for the good condition, peace, and quiet of the said holding." While the commune's statutes remained on the books, all effective control passed to the Colonna; and when in 1300 the supremacy of the Caetani appeared unstoppable, the citizens of Ninfa were easily persuaded, for a sum of 200,000 florins, to sell all their properties and urban rights to the family of Boniface VIII. The Caetani then became the manorial lords of these formerly free citizens.

At Nepi, another free commune, the process was not even as subtle. As part of a settlement with the Anguillara and lords of Vico, the Colonna purchased the entire city, its properties and rights, without the consent of any of its 330 citizens, for 48,000 florins. The reason is not difficult to find: as one communal resident put it, it was impossible to oppose "the horsemen and the raiding parties constantly launched against people, *castra,* and communes." In Lazio, especially with the lord pope absent or determined to enrich his own family at their expense, country folk were isolated and small communes impotent to defend themselves, and unlikely to find help from any of the constituted authorities. They might raise their voices to protest, or even organize civil committees; but like the citizens of Selci who spoke out against Riccardo Iaquinti's refusal to relinquish the office of podesta in 1304–5, they found themselves beaten by his armed retainers or jailed as menaces to the public safety. Only rarely would resistance succeed, as in the case of Caprignano, where in 1298 the entire commune voted to destroy its walls, sell their properties, and move to an allied town rather than allow a baron to make a hostile takeover.

On the whole, however, most rural residents had little choice but to submit to the domination of the strong. There were even incentives for becoming part of a baron's holdings: membership in a larger economic unit, easier access to a lord's mills and markets, and cash buyouts. There was also the prospect that once the takeover by a Colonna or an Orsini was complete, the baron would want to see his properties well managed and profitable and thus would invest in infrastructure improvements: cleared marshes or streams, larger castles, busier roads and inns. There were mighty incentives for the rural middle class and poor to remain silent in an age slipping rapidly into economic and political crisis.

By the same token, at the close of the thirteenth century many of Rome's barons, long used to political independence and the outright ownership of their "allodial" lands, found themselves becoming the vassals of their near neighbor to the south and east: the king of Naples. It was a legal arrangement that they soon came to regret, since the Angevin monarchy, like the Norman and Hohenstaufen before it, took seriously the feudal obligations of its 3,455 vassals-in-chief; and that meant participation in the kingdom's feudal levy in war and the duties of attendance at court. It also meant that the fiefs it held under the "Frankish custom" could not as easily be sold. With the appointment of King Robert the Wise as senator of Rome from 1313, as captain general of the army of the Patrimony of St. Peter from 1316, and then as head of the Guelph Party in Italy, both barons and free communes faced an even stronger threat to their traditional liberties. King Robert could count on normal revenues of 700,000 florins a year; and he often used his vast resources to intervene actively in the affairs of Rome and the Papal States.

Nevertheless, there were aspects of the traditional feudal and manorial systems that the barons found quite attractive as they spread out over the Roman Campagna. The archives of Rome are full of notarial acts documenting the sale and purchase of rural properties and clearly reflect their great increase in value in the century prior to Cola di Rienzo. Around 1200 a modest-sized *castrum* might cost 1,000 lire. By 1250 the same- sized estate could fetch 5,000 to 6,000 lire; while by 1270 it would bring its seller 10,000 lire. By 1291 Cardinal Boccamazza was paying 22,500 florins for three-quarters of Ponticelli; and by 1300 the Caetani were paying an immense fortune for their holdings in Lazio: 150,000 florins for Sermoneta, Bassiano, and the lands of S. Donato; 26,500 florins for three-quarters of Norma; 27,000 florins for Spurgola, and the same for Trevi, Filettino, and Vallepietra; 30,000 for half of Astura; 40,000 for Gavignano; and over 200,000 for Ninfa.

If the prices were high, so, too, were the income and rights. These included the manorial lord's jurisdiction over his tenants and vassals and court fees, the incomes of mills, labor and rent services: the *corvées* of northern Europe. Lords could avail themselves of a vast array of tributes, censuses, donations, services and monopolies, rights to hospitality, to game, to banalities from mills and ovens, exactions, indirect taxes on commerce, ordinary and extraordinary levies, such as the aids granted on the marriage of the lord's children, *gabelle,* and tolls on merchants' goods and on passage through his lands. All these, in addition to the regular incomes from the barons' agricultural estates, made the acquisition of rural properties irresistible.

The barons also possessed a resource that few could match: an enormous pool of vassals to provide military service. The *milites* or *nobiles castri* of Rome's barons were bound by their feudal oaths to provide specific service in defense of their lord, his family, and his friends, in the city as well as in the countryside. In addition to these vassals, who were normally mounted knights, they could also call out rural levies of hundreds of *pedites,* or foot soldiers. Thus, according to the reckoning of the Anonimo romano, on the eve of the battle of Porta San Lorenzo in November 1347, the Colonna alone could call up seven hundred mounted knights and four thousand foot. Though these numbers may be exaggerated, they take on real meaning when opposed to a city with a total population of men, women, and children of less than thirty thousand. Thus the barons not only held sway over Rome's ancient monuments, waging their factional wars and arranging their dynastic alliances, all the time collecting their rents and selling the produce of their farms, flocks, and vast herds; but they also brought to bear on the citizens of Rome those other resources of their urban positions and their country estates: enormous revenues and the loyalty of hundreds, even thousands, attached to them by ties of feudal service.

Nonetheless, it was not arms but property and money that made a Roman magnate; and it was this very property and wealth that captured them in a net of mutual dependence and physical proximity.[6] Several families of one clan, for example, might share the same rambling urban *fortilizia* or rural *castrum,* a common life as often as not infused with real affection and loyalty. Ultimately, as Robert Brentano remarks, these barons were also "caught together on their common property like flies on a piece of fly paper." It was the family, not the individual, that mattered most for medieval people, and the barons, though grander and mightier, were no exception: their "clustering corporate behavior" determined the lives and acts of even a Boniface VIII, a Margherita Colonna, or a Napoleone Orsini. Such tightly packed cores of nuclear families reached out to their extended kin with accumulated self-interest and in broad links of interconnectedness, sharing common blood, common name and history, and common households and properties that identified them to themselves and to the world at large. As the *Vita* of the Blessed Margherita Colonna shows, the baronial families could tenderly nurture their individual members and their most unworldly ambitions; and they did so both out of familial affection and out of a sense of preserving all members of the family and its common inheritance. As in the case of Margherita and many other baronial daughters and sisters, women were not forced to marry— as beneficial as such alliances could often be—thus combining a personally enlightened respect for each family member's wishes with a broad corporate interest in passing on undivided patrimonies.

Yet this family devotion was also the chief weakness of the Roman barons: for if family were the route to power and wealth, it marked a dependency that the fortunes of a pope or cardinal could make or break. In addition, in Lazio and in Rome the ancient authority granted the paterfamilias over even adult and senior male children was unquestioned. As long as a father or grandfather lived, he ruled supreme within a household and a clan; even mighty heads of nuclear families, living within the same urban fortress or rural castle, would be bound by his authority and would bind their own children to it. Independent policy was thus as rare as independent family life. Members of the great extended families adopted strategies of accommodation, negotiating their family relationships as diplomatically as their public lives.

Despite the lack of primogeniture rules and inheritance among all male heirs, many baronial families resolved potential problems in much the same way as the rest of feudal Europe did: by younger sons entering the clergy; and in Roman society this was very often a road to immense wealth and power. Thus in the late thirteenth century five of the seven sons of Stefano Colonna il Vecchio were clerics, as were three of the four sons of Buccio Savelli. The equal rights of all male members could often create complex patterns of inheritance and rather twisted branches on the family tree. By the mid–thirteenth century the Colonna had sprouted three main branches (see table I); the Conti eventually devolved into four; the Savelli into two; and the Annibaldi into seven or eight. The Orsini had an even more complex family tree. And while *castra* in the countryside might be firmly divisible among male heirs, in the city their holdings tended to be divided only for set periods.

The barons also took proper steps to protect themselves from external enemies by constantly and carefully renewing their complex web of family alliances.[7] Given the fluid and constantly changing power relationships among the baronial families, and the added pressures of Italian and European, especially papal, policies upon Rome, the Colonna, Orsini,

or Savelli looked to strengthen family ties and strategic alliances where
they could find them, and where they would best serve their dynastic interests. Thus by the late thirteenth century the main Colonna line not only
could claim a clear descent from the counts of Tusculum but also could
boast of their Orsini grandfather. They were thus as much Orsini as
Colonna, and clear-cut loyalties and strategies were often difficult to chart
out. Such alliances bound together all the great Roman families and linked
them not only to one another but also to families of the lesser nobility,
and sometimes to the wealthier merchant class. These alliances were often
sealed with quite substantial dowries, such as the 4,000 florins exchanged
in the triple alliance among the Colonna, the lords of Vico, and the Anguillara in 1293.

By the same token, these very practical men did not allow themselves—
or their city—to be permanently divided by the Guelph-Ghibelline wars
that continued to eviscerate many of the great Italian communes throughout the late thirteenth and early fourteenth centuries. Though some families certainly identified with one side or another, these tended to be party,
and not ideological, rifts, and these were often crossed when momentary
advantage or shifting situation called for it. Some, like the Annibaldi, had
even—disastrously—divided into rival Guelph and Ghibelline branches.
On February 7, 1324, the Aragonese ambassador to the papal court of Avignon dispatched a report to his lord, King Jayme II, on recent events in
the Curia: in Consistory one day Pope John XXII, reviewing the Italian
situation, turned to Cardinal Napoleone Orsini and chidingly accused him
and his family of being antipapal Ghibellines. Orsini replied to John XXII:
"Truly, Holy Father, I am neither Ghibelline nor Guelph, nor do I understand what the words mean. . . . Truly Romans have many enemies
and friends, and they help their friends, whether they are Guelph or Ghibelline. They help and love their friends, but you will not find that any
true Roman is either Guelph or Ghibelline." One can picture the great
cardinal's typically Roman reply, accompanying the words by the most
subtly raised shoulders and softly shaking head as he gracefully shrugged
off a potentially dangerous diplomatic situation: the pope was still
seething from the defeat of his Guelph army by the Italian cities of northern and central Italy and the loss of nearly 3 million gold florins in an attempt to reconquer the Papal States.

But Orsini's remarks also masked a terrible reality: the fourteenth century was one of grave crisis for the barons of Rome. Despite a general stability of family and position that would last for about another fifty years,
these positions were themselves at the mercy of gravely deteriorating so-

cial, economic, and political trends that Orsini's picture of loyalty to friends and family only underscores by its very parochialism. While the precise details of the dilemma have yet to be filled in, its broad outlines have long been clear: the crisis of the early fourteenth century that affected all of Europe also troubled central Italy. Overpopulation, repeated droughts and climatic shifts, a decline in agricultural output, the frenzied race to acquire and exploit broader and more marginal agricultural lands, repeated famines and epidemics that reached their climax in the Black Death; these trends were already well under way. So, too, were the economic and political crises that marked the end of communal Italy and saw the rise of the *signori* and tyrants: what historians have seen as the economic and political crisis of the early Italian Renaissance. The flight of the papacy to Avignon, the ineffective rule of the papal vicar King Robert of Naples through his appointed agents from 1313 to 1335, and the consequent loss of any effective control over the barons' ambitions only exacerbated the situation. By the 1350s these trends would be clear to everyone: depopulation, the wholesale abandonment of country estates, their sale to members of the haute-bourgeois *bovattieri,* the antimagnate legislation passed in the cities, and the military reconquest of the Papal States by Cardinal Albornoz lay just beyond Rome's crumbling skyline.

But for the time being the barons clutched onto their status and their families and friends, and they competed with their rivals for territory, position, and wealth. If they fretted in private, they showed little of it to their urban neighbors: the very notion of the Roman baron was intimately connected with a public display of haughty indifference to either person or law and was embellished by an elaborate code of behavior that combined chivalric ritual with an almost liturgical insistence of their role as the pope's vassals.[8] If the barons were hardly distinguishable from their neighbors in their *rione,* living as they did cheek by jowl among innkeepers, coppersmiths, butchers, notaries, canons of local churches, or bankers, they could claim uniquely to be those entitled to go about the city on horseback and to participate prominently in its many rituals and spectacles: in the mounted games on Monte Testaccio and in the ancient Agone, the Piazza Navona, by their participation in high church rituals, such as the consecration of Boniface VIII described with great attention to family rank and order by Jacopo Stefaneschi in his *De coronatione;* by their prominent role in the ceremonies of Holy Week; and by their lavish expenditures on somber robes, candles, incense, and masses at their funerals, and on food, clothing, "inventions," public entertainments, and gifts at their banquets and weddings.

All these were powerful propaganda tools that emphasized the barons' nobility, ancient lineage, wealth, and military prowess for both the barons themselves and Rome's ordinary citizens. Ritual and public display thus underscored what for the hierarchical mind-set of medieval people, even those critical of the barons, was their "natural" superiority, their legitimate claim to command, and their *onore* and *virtù:* traits that put them at the forefront of the entire commune as symbols of their city and its ancient traditions. Yet a self-consciousness that so projected itself into the public domain could easily collide with that same public interest and sensibility. J.-C. Maire Vigueur has speculated that as popular governments and their haute-bourgeois exponents gained more and more control over urban life, the reaction of the barons was to demonstrate their status by increasing levels of violent, antisocial, and provocative forms of public behavior. Such behavior is well documented, and in Rome it coincides most appropriately with those most public of forums: the Senate, City Council, and other agencies of Rome's civic constitution.

Although the pope remained the nominal lord of Rome, even for most of its communal periods, determining who exactly did govern the city could be a difficult task.[9] The barons certainly wielded power, if not authority, to govern, and the ancient merchant guilds, the *scholae,* did exist, as in other cities, but they were weak; and the voices of the *cives,* the *bovattieri,* and the *Romani plebei populus* were often hard to hear. A civic militia had existed within the city, divided among its fourteen Augustan *regiones,* and then its twelve medieval *rioni* since at least 648 (see map 1). While counts of the Campagna and prefects of the city survived the Byzantine period, the military *dux* and the administrative *consul* soon disappeared; and with the communal revolt of 1143, the new communal council revived the Senate. It appears that most of the senators came from the trade and craft classes, though as was the case throughout Italy, some noble families participated in the new government.

From the mid–twelfth through the mid–fourteenth century, the Senate in its palace atop the Capitoline remained the focus of Rome's government (see fig. 6). It summoned the army and made treaties, established weights and measures, struck coins, and pronounced legal and legislative decisions. It and its agents administered justice, both criminal and civil, and acted on the legal advice of jurists experienced in Roman law. The entire body of senators, the *consistorium,* elected the *consiliatores* or *procuratores* of the republic, who wielded the commune's executive powers. Over the course of the thirteenth century the papacy was able, with the help of the new baronial class, to regain control over the city largely through co-opting the Senate. By the end of the thirteenth century the popes were themselves being named senator for life and appointing their personal vicars. Boniface VIII decided on a new formula that was to remain in force into the 1350s. On October 23, 1298, he appointed Fortebraccio Orsini and Ricardo Annibaldi as senators and his vicars for a term of six months. Papal letters preserved in papal and communal archives faithfully record this continuing semiannual round. Thus on November 26, 1344, the pope named Bertoldo Orsini and Orso Anguillara as "counts, senators, and captains of the City." On May 20, 1345, his choice fell on Rainaldo Orsini and Niccolo Annibaldi, rotating rule among the baronial clans, preventing violence and too great an accumulation of power and influence by any one faction.

In the beginning the *senatores* were elected by the people—the *Romani plebei populus*—but what exactly this meant is hard to say. In Arnold of Brescia's time sources mention some two thousand electors, presumably male heads of households, but details are lacking. The *populus* does seem to have had a role in electing the senators, and in approving their acts. By as early as the mid–thirteenth century they were being summoned to the Capitoline by bells and trumpets, and by the voices of heralds. Here, in the piazza of the Capitoline, on the site of the medieval marketplace, they constituted the *parlamentum,* but what they did aside from approving the acts of the Senate remains a mystery, especially in the age of the one- or two-man Senate acting as the pope's vicars. Day-to-day affairs were left to the city's nascent bureaucracy, the *consilium,* which would be constituted as *generale* or *speciale* according to the business at hand and the administrative and consultative needs of the senators. Large councils would meet in the Aracoeli atop the Capitoline, imitating, as the *Marvels of Rome* indicates, what was believed to be the Senate hall of ancient Rome. Smaller *consilia* would meet in the Senators' Palace across the piazza.

We know that the Senate, the Consistory, and the Council had at their disposal a permanent judiciary and a magistracy, much of whose activities are revealed only in the texts of the fourteenth century. Courts met regularly to pass judgment in civil and criminal cases, arrange settlements, arbitrate agreements out of court, and impose sentences and fines. In the fourteenth-century statutes, which reveal a deep antiaristocratic bias, murder appears to be the central problem of civil society, ranked at the top of the capital crimes that included arson, incest, sodomy, rape, and the kidnapping of children (but not of adults who could provide useful ransoms and who had the legal and moral authority to offer their own pledges of good faith). Yet in a society where the feud was sanctioned by custom and personal oath to take up arms against a lord's enemies, capital punishment was often avoided in the hope of preventing further acts of vengeance. Instead, Romans imposed a carefully graduated system of fines and confiscations: the higher one's status in society, the heavier the fine imposed. This made sense in a system where the fines were often divided, so many parts for the victims or accusers, so many parts for the public treasury: those who could were made to pay substantially; and property, not persons, was the major target of justice. But when corporal punishment was imposed, in keeping with many urban codes through the medieval West, repeat offenses were punished in increments: from fines to mutilations, to greater mutilations, to capital punishment. Despite the great violence of the age and the tendency of families to inherit feuds and vendettas, minors were treated more leniently, both out of Christian piety and from a hope that early mercy would reap its harvest in later acts of mercy among those forgiven.

Senators, councils, and courts were only as effective as the daily implementation of their laws and decisions; and here fourteenth-century Roman society seems to have already become what modern Italy has long appeared to its observers, a self-governing, self-regulated complex that worked not on the grand level of government but on the small accumulated detail of city management: cleaning streets, removing obstructions, arbitrating property and personal disputes among neighbors and friends. Not that the Romans of Cola's time avoided formalization and final agreement: far from it. The huge *fondi* of notarial acts that begin to accumulate from the 1350s on contain almost nothing but the record of these formalizations and agreements. But here is precisely the point: the Romans governed themselves and appealed to government only as a resource for third-party arbitration or judgment when the far more normal processes of agreement somehow broke down. What worked for the fish sellers of the portico at Sant'Angelo also worked for the mightiest barons; magistrates and vicars were called in only when all other remedies seem to have failed.

The notaries whose acts were so important to every aspect of Roman life were also essential to every department of government. There were notaries who accompanied the Masters of the Buildings and Streets of the City on their day-to-day inspections of streets, building lines, vacant lots, rubbish fires, fetid sewers, and illegal dumps, who recorded their inquests, their decisions, and the implementation of their ordinances. There were notaries of the Chancellery, the Senate, the various civil and criminal courts; there were notaries who sat on the Council and some who apparently, because of their high level of education and connections, performed more than scribal duties, often sharing in deliberations and decision making.

It was here, in the chambers of Rome's government, that the barons still had to contend with the remnants of the revived communal movement that had elected the Thirteen Good Men and sent Rienzo to Avignon. Cola had returned to Rome shortly after his appointment as Notary of the City Chamber on June 17, 1344.[10] He probably arrived about four weeks after that and was ready to assume his new responsibility by the fall of 1344, protected by the pope's friendship and appointment, reasonably well salaried with sixty florins a year and "all the customary emoluments" that city offices brought. For all that, however, Cola returned to Rome isolated and only partially successful. He had managed to obtain the Jubilee, and to save his own life, career, and properties from the attacks of the barons; but the popular government that had sent him north had fallen: he alone remained to face the full opposition of the barons in the chambers of government and to feel the humiliation of their social disdain in the city's banquet halls.

It had been oratory and public display that had first won Cola attention and respect among the Romans; and it was the uses of public image and propaganda that he understood so well. He therefore set out once again to make himself his own best argument against the rule of the barons. He would "perform his office like a member of the court," fulfilling his duties as notary and papal representative and participating in the governance of the city to the full extent that his office and his papal mandate allowed. On an official level this did not leave much room for maneuver: as Notary of the City Chamber, Cola may not have performed the duties of a clerk, transcribing sessions, resolutions, and votes and putting legislation into proper form—this might be the work of one of his staff—and his duties were not merely consultative: he would provide the proper form for such a law, its precedents in Roman law and tradition, the appropriate language and order in which to frame and present it. But his role was limited.

Cola continued to act as a notary and scribe for the Chamber and developed a solid reputation in this office. In a letter of July 29/30, 1347, Bishop Ildebrandino Conti of Padua reported that Cola was "a notary, competently literate in grammar, eloquent enough in speech, prudent and diligently exercising his office." We still have extant a document dated

March 28, 1346, in the name of Senator Orso de Jacobi Napoleone Orsini confirming Rome's Statutes of the Merchants. The document was drawn up for Orso Orsini by Cola himself; and it is in Cola's hand and signed by him in his capacity as notary of the City Chamber (fig. 14). Cola may have continued to serve in a diplomatic role as well, as he had for the government of the Thirteen Good Men, setting out formal letters to the city's lord, the pope, to Rome's neighbors, and to its subject communes and territories, addressing their councils and great barons, all in the forms proper to their dignity and rank. But official position was only a foot in the door of power. As a member of the government, as the man who had so impressed the pope and cardinals at Avignon, who had sung of Rome's ancient glory and dignity, who had won the Jubilee and its promised wealth for the city, Rienzo could enjoy a wider reputation and influence.

At first Rienzo seems to have held an uneasy peace with the barons; Cola's "muttering threats between his teeth" is, in the world of the Anonimo romano, not the empty recrimination of a dismissed servant but the first sign of plans yet to be revealed. Neither side could afford to demonstrate its opposition to the other's policies, nor the hatred they bore each other. As the pope's protégé and the city's new favorite, Cola moved within the highest circles of Roman society, for the time being at least.

In those days he used to dine with Janni [Giovanni] Colonna and the lords of Rome. The barons used to make fun of his speech-making. They made him rise to his feet and deliver his sermons. And he would say, "I shall be a great lord, or emperor. I'll persecute all these barons. This one I'll torture; that one I'll behead." He judged all of them. At this the barons burst out laughing. (AR, XVIII, ll. 203–11, Porta, 150)

The very reason that he was probably chosen by the Thirteen Good Men to represent Rome played again to Cola's benefit: as good a speech-maker as he was, the notary and son of the taverner was not considered serious enough to pose any great threat. Speeches, no matter how eloquent and laced with references to the glories of ancient Rome, were no match for money, friends, and armed retainers. The stage was set for Cola to act, and he did so without long delay. As one of the city's papal officials, he held a seat on the *consilium*. Although the Anonimo romano does not provide the details of the time and place, he does tell us that shortly after Cola's return he decided to push the issue of the barons' misrule at the assembly of councilors. It was a theme he had raised repeatedly to the pope, and his position was already well known; he therefore could not have gained by delaying his first attack; indeed, the losers in any confrontation would surely be the barons. There on the Capitoline, in the Franciscan church of the Aracoeli, Cola chose to make his case public:

Therefore he rose to his feet one time in the Assembly of Rome, where all the councilors were, and said, "You are not good citizens; you suck the blood of the poor people and refuse to help them." Then he warned the officials and rectors that they should provide for the good new state *[buono stato]* of their City of Rome. When this sparkling statement was done, one of the Colonna, named Andreuzzo de Normanno, who was then Chamberlain, rose up and gave him a loud slap on the cheek. Then there rose a scribe of the Senate—his name was Tomao de Fortifiocca—and made the obscene tail at him. This was the result of his speech. (AR, XVIII, ll. 52–64, Porta, 144–45)

Though the Anonimo romano records the story of Cola's dinners with the barons two chapters after this, no one conscious of his dignity in fourteenth-century Italy could have accepted the affront of a physical assault and then an invitation to dine. The dinners and laughter must have come first, then the public confrontations over public policy, and then the open—and physical—hostility. The Colonna had reacted as their class was reacting increasingly, meeting challenges to their public status with violence and contempt. In so acting, they were playing directly into the hands of one who had secretly sworn to destroy them. Cola had now condemned them all openly, and in his threats he seemed to have pictured a cataclysm of universal dimensions. But the barons were not yet aware of how carefully Rienzo was planning their apocalypse.

CHAPTER 6

Preparing for the Apocalypse

As a result Cola admonished the rectors and the people to good actions using an image that he ordered painted on the palace of the Campidoglio in front of the market.

Anonimo romano, XVIII, ll. 65–68, Porta, 145

Cola was quick to take his dispute with the barons out from the privacy of the banqueting hall and the closed debates of the Council. We do not know how long his behind-the-scenes maneuvering lasted after his return from Avignon and before the breach with the barons had become too well known and too humiliating for him not to answer it publicly and promptly. If Cola had returned to Rome in July 1344 and taken up his new position by the fall, his status as a member of the Civic Chamber and Council did not give him much time to organize the remnants of the now defeated communal revival into anything like a working political movement. He alone, it seems, still carried the banner of the Thirteen Good Men. Rienzo therefore decided to focus public attention, sympathy, and condemnation upon a chosen set of issues. He had already used oratory to bring himself and his reform program to the attention of policy makers; but political oratory could have only limited scope and short-term impact on a still-inchoate civic society generally indifferent to the non-religious word. Cola therefore decided to use another tool of persuasion readily available to him: the visual arts. He carefully selected a series of images to symbolize for his contemporaries the issues he wanted to bring into public focus and discussion:

On the outer wall above the Chamber he hung an image in this form:

There was painted an immense sea, the waves horrible, very turbulent. In the midst of this sea there was a ship just about to sink, without rudder, without sail. In this ship, which was in this danger, there was a woman, a widow dressed in black, bound in a belt of mourning, her gown ripped from her breast, her hair torn, as if she were about to weep. She was on her knees, her hands piously crossed over her breast, praying that her danger would pass. The inscription said, "This is Rome." Around this ship, in the level below, there were four ships foundering in the water, their sails fallen, their masts broken, their rudders lost. In each one was a woman, sunken and dead. The first was named Babylon, the second Carthage, the third Troy, the fourth Jerusalem. The inscription said, "Because of injustice these cities fell into perils and diminished." Among the dead women there spread a caption that said: "Once you held high dominion over all. Now here we await your collapse."

On the left side there were two islands. On one was a woman, who sat in shame; the caption said, "This is Italy." This woman was making a speech and saying the following: "You took away the power of every land, and you kept only me as your sister." On the other island were four women with their hands on their cheeks and on their knees in an attitude of great sorrow, and they were saying: "Once you were accompanied by every virtue. Now you wander abandoned through the sea." These were the four Cardinal Virtues: Temperance, Justice, Prudence, and Courage. On the right side there was a small island. On this islet there was a woman kneeling. She was stretching her hand up to heaven, as if praying. She was dressed in white. Her name was Christian Faith. Her verse went: "O greatest father, leader, and my lord, if Rome should perish, where then shall I remain?"

On the right side of the upper level there were four orders of different animals with wings who were holding horns to their mouths and blowing as if they were the winds who made the tempest in the sea and who ought to have aided the endangered ship. In the first order were lions, wolves, and bears. The caption said, "These are the powerful barons and evil rectors." The second order were dogs, pigs, and roebucks. The caption said, "These are the bad councilors, followers of the nobles." The third order were rams, dragons, and foxes. The caption said, "These are the false officials, judges, and notaries." The fourth order were hares, cats, goats, and monkeys. The caption read, "These are the *popoli:* thieves, murderers, adulterers, and plunderers."

In the section above was Heaven. In the middle was the Divine Majesty, as if come in judgment. Two swords issued from of His mouth, in one direction and the other. On one side stood St. Peter, on the other St. Paul praying. When the people saw this image, each individual marveled. (AR, XVIII, ll. 68–132, Porta, 145–47)

Logically enough, Cola chose the Campidoglio to begin his campaign, with an image of the Navicella on the very facade of the Senators' Palace (see fig. 6).[1] He probably chose the wall above the loggia of the upper chamber, facing the marketplace. Not only was the palace the seat of official government and thus the logical point at which to begin his confrontation, but it dominated the city physically as well. For centuries before the Vittorio Emmanuele monument to the Italian Unknowns rose above the ancient arx to block them, the Senators' Palace and the Aracoeli were the most prominent landmarks visible from the *abitato*. Thus, even if the painting itself (and we do not know how large it was) were not readable from the city below the hill, the fact that everyone in Rome knew of its presence as they gazed up at the Capitoline must have made a powerful impression. The Anonimo romano takes on the subject of Rienzo's propaganda campaign in minute detail in the next few sections of the *Vita* and makes it clear that his actions and works were carefully thought out in images "that he ordered painted." Acting as a public official, and contracting the best talent then in Rome that he could find, Rienzo commissioned what appears to have been a large panel painting, its themes and images carefully worked out and designed to reach the largest possible audience with the most powerful message.

By the mid–fourteenth century Italian religious art had long been using a clear symbolic language;[2] and the forms of public, secular art had become more regularized, and the lay viewing public became more skilled in, and accustomed to, viewing and "reading" visual programs with an accessible visual grammar and language of what Hans Belting has called a "public rhetoric of wall painting." It thus became possible for even public officials like the notary Francesco di Bardolino to compose his *Documenti d'amore* to spell out artistic programs relating to secular time and space and in it "invent" a series of visual programs for painters of public art and instruct them in what was becoming by then a standardized language of political symbols. Painting, even monumental painting cycles on church walls, was no longer viewed exclusively as illustrative of sacred texts but also as a reflection of external and everyday reality. As imagery began to take on a reality independent of a viewer's memory of the sacred text— their *recordatio*—viewers began to understand painting and its imagery on a new level, as an independent medium that could convey not only secular *historia* (persons and events) but also *allegoria* (the deeper meaning of what the artists had portrayed). By the mid–fourteenth century Italian public art had attained a message and a medium of the highest symbolic complexity meant for a public well educated in both the visual and the verbal signifiers that it contained.

Thus, throughout Italy, from the middle of the thirteenth to the middle of the fourteenth century, the free communes had become the scene of a long tradition of public, political painting. Many, such as the one by Giotto commissioned for the Palazzo del Podestà (the Bargello) in Florence, no longer exist. We can, however, still see what remains of one of the Trecento's most dazzling pieces of public art, secular or religious: Ambrogio Lorenzetti's *Good and Bad Government* in the Palazzo Pubblico in Siena, painted sometime between 1337 and 1339.[3] Its rich shades of ocher and rose, the stonework, shutters, crenellations, and windows of Siena's houses, their loggie and porches, carefully reproduced vegetation, birds, wild animals, the tilled or devastated earth, citizens carrying out peaceful acts of commerce, conversation, travel, song or dance, the details of their clothing, their goods and pack animals, were not mere decoration meant only for the eyes of the city councilors but were placed where any citizen having business in the town hall could see them. Both the *allegoria* of Good Government (fig. 15) and its attendant virtues and its effects in the *historia* of the real city and *contado* (fig. 16) governed well under peace and justice; and their opposites—the *allegoria* of Tyranny (fig. 17) and the city and country in anarchy and desolation, reality beset by Cruelty, War, Treason, and Division—needed no clergyman or monk to explain their meaning, even to the illiterate. For most Sienese viewers even those inscriptions placed beside the allegorical figures, the word *concordia* next to Concord (see fig. 15) holding the "chord" of unity, for example, would have been less a necessary sign than an added visual and textual pun to both delight and reward the attentive citizen.

Rome itself was a center of the new arts from the third quarter of the thirteenth century on, and so it is more than likely that Cola saw and appreciated much of the new style, just as it is likely that he knew well the Apocalypse cycle in the crypt of Anagni's cathedral (see fig. 4). Although no artist or workshop of any note remained in Rome after the first decade of the fourteenth century and the departure of the papal court to Avignon, Cola certainly would have had access to the sketchbooks and sample books of Italy's itinerant masters because Rome remained a stop on the artistic itinerary between Avignon and the court of Naples. Naples offered an especially rich source of both famous painters and political and apocalyptic themes to draw from, supported and given programmatic direction by King Robert and Queen Sancia themselves. Everyone from Giotto to Simone Martini to Pietro Cavallini, Lello da Orvieto, to Roberto Oderisio painted in the Angevin capital, while the monastic center at Cava de'Tirreni attracted a steady stream of manuscript illuminators and scribes from as far afield as Bologna. Marino Sanudo and Paolino da Venezia, well known for their histories, maps, and manuscript work, also traveled widely between Naples, Venice, Rome, and Avignon. Contacts with the major artistic capitals of Italy thus were uninterrupted as long as patrons remained in Rome. As a notary well known for his written and oratorical skills, who was to become the chief ambassador of Rome by 1342, Cola is also likely to have been employed on a variety of smaller missions and embassies in Lazio, Tuscany, and even beyond, during which he may well have seen masterworks of Giotto, Lorenzetti, Martini, and others. Certainly at Avignon Cola had the opportunity to see Martini's work at the papal palace, and there to discuss the meaning and proper form of the visual arts with his friend Petrarch, who was to begin the Renaissance tradition of art criticism.

Even more public and immediate in its impact on the Italian urban population, and less dependent on any critical apparatus for viewing or assimilating art, was the *pittura infamante,* or "infamy painting."[4] As its name implies, this was a genre of public art, often in fresco, that a town or city would commission to be painted to commemorate some horrendous crime against the commune and the criminal's subsequent infamy. Taking their cue from the new type of religious painting that placed the recent lives and deeds of local saints into easily recognizable cityscapes— St. Francis's renunciation of his father's wealth in front of the church of Sta. Maria, the former temple of Minerva, in Assisi, for example—*pitture infamanti* would name names, show faces, and locate crimes and criminals in a set time and place. The genre also had its remote origins in the ubiquitous paintings of the Last Judgment, which, especially under the influence of Dante's *Divine Comedy,* began to become more and more detailed and particular in rendering individual crimes and their very appropriate—and contemporary Italian—punishments.

Pitture infamanti first appear in Parma about 1261 and Bologna in 1274 with the painting of wrongdoers' names on exterior walls, most often on the palace of the podesta. In fact, their earliest name was "pictures painted on the palace of the podesta"; and the practice appears to have spread with the employment of the podesta by the Italian communes. By the end of the century Italian communes had taken up the practice of painting the actual effigies of public criminals. They appear in San Gemignano in 1274, in Florence by 1283, in Siena several times between 1302 and 1310, and in Prato in 1312 and reached about two dozen cities in late medieval Italy. Generally the flight of the lawbreaker occasioned his punishment in effigy, a kind of magical retribution substituting the lawbreaker's image for the person, just as the cloth used by Veronica to wipe the face of Jesus during his passion, the *sudarium* of Christ's sweat and blood, was also the *vera icona* preserved at St. Peter's. Such sacred meanings of art combined with the destruction of that most important asset of the urban Italian: one's reputation and one's dignity. Throughout the fourteenth century, criminals, especially traitors, suffered the uniquely humiliating fate of having their images, their *similitudini,* publicly hung upside down. One need only recall the fate of the usurious Pope Nicholas III in canto 19 of Dante's *Inferno* to understand the intensity of this punishment by inversion, as befitting someone who so turned the proper order of things topsy-turvy.

On a deeper level, however, the "infamy painting" presented the viewer with a different type of *recordatio,* not the sacred *vita* of the local saint as an object of meditation and imitation but *historia* now turned to the service of the "social memory" of the commune. At Reggio Emilia in 1315, for example, after the banishment of the entire Della Paluda family for terrorizing the city's *contado,* not only were their images and names prominently displayed for all to see *de litteris grossis,* but their *pittura infamante* also included the *historia* of the destruction of their family castle by the Reggian army. If the birth and Passion of Jesus could be commemorated over and over again in the viewer's active meditation upon the sacred cycle of salvation history at the Arena chapel at Padua, so, too, could the crime and punishment of prominent wrongdoers become the objects of secular, political discussion and reflection. Thus it was entirely appropriate that when a public building was not available, *pitture infamanti* would often be displayed either on the blank facade of a church or even, for a time, within the church itself, most likely on *tavole* or movable and removable painted surfaces. In fact, most *pitture infamanti* were designed and executed to remain up only temporarily. In Siena every year from 1305 on, the podesta would ask his council whether such a painting should remain in situ, and depending on the seriousness of the crime commemorated, the strength of the infamy, and even the fame and skill of the artists, the council might vote to take down or paint over the image. One painting recently rediscovered in Siena and attributed to the master Duccio di Buoninsegna remained on display for fifteen years before being painted over. Some *pitture infamanti* had far longer lives, due to the horrendous nature of the crime depicted. Thus the painting commemorating the treason of the duke of Athens, who had set up a tyranny in Florence, and his overthrow on July 26, 1343, was kept prominently displayed on the walls of the Bargello, Florence's own palace of the podesta, for nearly two hundred years and was still visible in Vasari's day.

Yet such publicly commissioned and displayed paintings were not the only kind of public art created in the fourteenth century that conveyed political and historical themes. Since the eleventh century and the large-scale propaganda war that accompanied the struggle of the popes and the German emperors in the Investiture Conflict, art had become one of the primary agencies for putting forth the historical claims of both pope and emperor. Frederick II's gate at Capua spoke as elegantly of imperial aspirations and theoretical claims to ancient glories as the Silvester and Constantine cycle at SS. Quattro Coronati spoke of papal claims to spiritual dominion. Not sacred biblical history but historical events of a more secular nature intended for public consumption, these cycles of fresco, sculpture, or mosaic had a long tradition before Cardinal Jacopo Stefaneschi commissioned Giotto to create a new, public statement of Pope Boniface VIII's most exalted claims to worldwide domination as the vicar and sole mediator of Christ.

The location and the program of Giotto's *Navicella* mosaic spoke admirably to these propaganda themes. Giotto di Bodone (c.1267–1337) came to Rome to receive the commission for another of Stefaneschi's projects, the altarpiece for St. Peter's, for which he was paid 800 florins. But this new work, if not completed for the Jubilee of 1300 then certainly finished close to that date, and for which Stefaneschi was eventually to pay Giotto the staggering amount of 2,200 florins, was something newer and bolder in concept, design, and content. It was recognized as Giotto's most important work by contemporaries. The mosaic, which was removed in 1562 to make room for Carlo Maderna's present facade of the new St. Peter's, rose above the eastern wall of the atrium of the old St. Peter's, above the gatehouse, and thus behind the pope's loggia and facing the apocalyptic facade of St. Peter's itself. Several reproductions of the mosaic survive (fig. 18). Stefaneschi and Giotto chose as their theme the text from Matthew's Gospel (14:22–33) of Jesus walking on the waters of the Sea of Galilee, one of the miracles whereby Jesus manifests his divinity to his doubting disciples and reveals his powers over nature. In this context, however, it was also a revelation of the universal power and authority over the world delegated to St. Peter's successor.

Cola's painting thus evoked the *Navicella* and combined *historia, allegoria,* and *infamia* in a style and a rhetorical language that would be immediately readable by his viewers.[5] Giotto had already provided the "tremendous sea with horrible waves, storming violently," as he had the storm-tossed ship. But Rome here is not the eternal Church but the earthly city, sail-less and rudderless, about to founder. Instead of the apostles of sacred history, Rome herself sails the choppy waves of secular history, amid the shipwreck of earlier empires: the successive *tempora* of secular history.

While the image of the shipwrecked Rome goes back at least to Gregory I, Cola's inspiration was more direct: in 1335 Petrarch had written a lengthy letter in verse, his *Epistola metrica* (I.2) to Pope Benedict XII, urging him to return the papacy to Rome, personified as a distressed and disheveled matron. In 1342, with the arrival of Stefano Colonna's deputation at Avignon, Petrarch wrote another *Epistola metrica* (II.5) to the newly elected Clement VI warning of the impending shipwreck of the Roman church, which he portrayed again as a distressed matron.

The twin towers to the left of Giotto's *Navicella* are here replaced by two islands: Italy, as the caption reads, and the four virtues. On the right, on another "island," a kneeling woman replaces the image of the pope in Giotto's *Navicella,* but here the symbol of the power of the bishop of Rome is replaced by that of the suffering Christian faith as a whole, whose safety and well-being, her verse reveals, depends not on the pope's divine connections but on the health and safety of Rome itself. Devils might beset the universal Church on the cosmic level in Giotto's painting, but here in the real Rome, more earthly beasts replace the tempests and threaten to wreck the city and its church, beasts that not only carry the marks of medieval symbolism common both to humble bestiaries and to Dante's mighty opening canto but also are uncomfortably close to the heraldic devices of Rome's baronial families: lions, bears, wolves. But the barons are not alone in sharing a place in this *infamia*. Less powerful, if still dangerous, creatures also have their inscriptions, and every social status, every profession responsible for Rome's present corruption, is put up for public condemnation.

The art historian Amy Schwarz has suggested other sources that might have inspired Cola's program. The image of the widowed woman was a well-known Christianization of the Roman city goddess, used by Dante in the *Purgatorio* (VI.112–14) and his letter to the Italian cardinals, as well as by Petrarch. This female figure also plays a prominent role in a splendid illuminated text known as the *Panegyric to Robert of Anjou from the Citizens of Prato* (fig. 19). The manuscript, now in the British Library (Royal 6E.IX), was probably completed by Neapolitan artists in Prato about 1335. In it the citizens of Prato use the image of Rome as the widow dressed in black to urge Robert to rescue justice, bring the papacy back to Italy, and restore Rome to its proper place. Here the Widow Rome herself tells the story of the sinking, storm-tossed ship and the spiritually desperate condition of the city. Long attributed to Convenevolo da Prato (c.1270–1338), Petrarch's Latin teacher, the text is now believed by some to be Petrarch's.

Thus far well-known precedents provided easy visual understanding. But one final image, if we read the Anonimo romano correctly, brought true amazement to the entire painting: there at the top of the scene, replacing the prophets and the historical Jesus of Giotto's Gospel scene, was the Cosmic Christ of the Last Judgment. The first act in Cola's public drama to reform and renew Rome focuses appropriately on the figure of Christ, sword issuing from his mouth, surrounded by the seven candelabra from Apocalypse 1:12–18. The scene had been represented countless times all over Europe throughout the Middle Ages. It had one of its most forceful representations in Italy in the crypt of the cathedral at Anagni (see fig. 4), where Cola had grown up. Here in Rome, however, Cola added two figures: Peter, symbolized by the keys, and Paul, by the sword. For Romans of the fourteenth century the two apostles held enormous power and prestige, not only because their bones rested in Rome but also because Peter and Paul represented the two *limites* of the pilgrim city. They occupied the opposite ends of the sacred axis formed by the route between St. Peter's at the Vatican and San Paolo fuori le Mura, the axis around which medieval Rome's *abitato* had formed after the collapse of the pagan city. It was this symbolic association, and this physical route, that had brought prosperity to Cola's parents and to all of Rome's innkeepers, merchants—and churches—throughout the city's history, culminating in the first Jubilee of 1300.

In another sense, as Antonio Thiery has speculated, the pilgrim coming to Rome, especially for Boniface's Jubilee in 1300 and for the one arranged by Cola for 1350, would physically retrace in his journey to Rome's three major churches—St. John Lateran, St. Peter's, and St. Paul's—the entire history of the earthly Church: St. John the Baptist, the precursor and prophet of the past age of the Church; St. Peter, the earthly vicar of the present, institutional church; and St. Paul, who truly stands "beyond the walls" of Rome, who could be taken to represent the Church of the future and its mystical expansion, just as he had represented its historic expansion beyond the boundaries of Palestinian Judaism. Cola's viewers could well be amazed; for whatever the complex of interpretation they derived from these powerful and multivalent symbols, no one could have come away from the painting without the sense that the Apocalypse loomed over, behind, and beyond the events, institutions, and personalities of Rome's history.

• • •

Not much time had passed when Cola admonished the people with a beautiful speech in Italian, which he made in

St. John Lateran. Behind the choir, on the wall he had fixed a
magnificent metal tablet written with ancient letters, which no
one else but he alone knew how to read and interpret. Around
this tablet he had figures painted, [showing how] the Roman
Senate conceded authority to Emperor Vespasian. There, in
the middle of the church, he had a speaker's platform built of
planks, and he had wooden steps made high enough to sit on.
He also had it decorated with carpets and bunting. He brought
together many of the nobles of Rome, among whom were
Stefano della Colonna and Janni Colonna, his son, who was
one of the most shrewd and magnificent men of Rome. There
were also many learned men, judges and decretalists, and many
other people of authority. Cola di Rienzo mounted his pulpit
among so many of these good people.

Anonimo romano, XVIII, ll. 136–54, Porta, 147–48

Perhaps more so than any other in medieval Christendom, Italian society in Cola's time sensed and lived a unity of the sacred and the secular
planes. The lives of its countless holy hermits, of St. Francis of Assisi and
his followers in the new mendicant orders, of the numerous lay religious
confraternities and their public rituals of penance, peace, and reconciliation were all aimed at the reform of *civic* life, as well as of the salvation of
personal, individual life. If this unity of secular and sacred worked in the
present age, so must a return to the purity and grandeur of ancient Rome
also fuse the religious with the political, the imperial with the holy. The
reform of Rome's civic life must surely go hand in hand with a reform of
its moral and spiritual life; this is the approach that Cola took as he unfolded his propaganda campaign to win over Rome's people and their
rulers to the city's renewal. He chose as his next site and text two of the
most potent symbols in the history of Rome.[6] The church St. John Lateran meant for Romans not only the seat of their bishop but also the very
act whereby Constantine had transferred, "donated," to the pope both
spiritual authority and political power over the western empire. Here on
the foundation of an ancient imperial palace, where—as the *Mirabilia* also
records—were stored the treasures of the Temple of Jerusalem, the popes
both ruled Rome and brought together a collection of ancient Roman
art that underlined their inheritance of imperial power: the monumental
equestrian bronze of Marcus Aurelius, long believed to be Constantine
himself; the colossal head and hand of Constantine now in the Capitoline Museums; the Capitoline wolf, the symbol of the city of Rome and
its people; and the bronze tablet of Vespasian, commemorating the act

in December 69 C.E. whereby the Senate and People of Rome transferred to the emperor their power and authority.

Significantly, Cola chose not the nave of the Lateran from which to deliver his speech on the tablet but the very choir of the cathedral: the most ancient portion of the Constantinian church and that part generally reserved for the clergy. In choosing the spot, Cola intended to reveal that this performance was unlike his painting on the wall of the Senators' Palace. That had been open to all and visible all over Rome. Its message had been intended as a public discourse on the condition of the city and its church, in a visual language clearly understood by the average citizen. Instead, here in the venerable and highly exalted space of former imperial palace and papal church, Cola would deliver a sermon to an invited elite, presumably with the approval of the distant pope and his vicar in the city. His theme would touch matters dear to the few who governed Rome: the very foundational authority of their power.

Cola's installation was a marvel in itself, a work of interactive art whose brilliance can be understood only on reflection. In the midst of the piece was the surviving bronze tablet of the *lex de imperio Vespasiani*,[7] inscribed in a Roman majuscule easily read by any literate Roman of the first century, as by any student in the Renaissance, but indecipherable to the eyes of the twelfth-century *Mirabilian* authors, used as they were to the "Gothic" public lettering used into the fourteenth century. Cola had the tablet set up on one of the walls of the choir, whose horizontal planes below the springing of the apse were appropriate to just such tableaux. Around this magical object of political veneration he then imposed a painted *recordatio,* a visual meditation on the meaning of the inscription that not only explained its hidden meaning to an audience variously learned in classical history but also, by reflection, placed it within the *historia* that was being portrayed and thus made the entire work a kind of memory palace. For, if true to late medieval practice, Cola depicted the Roman senators transferring authority to the emperor via some visual sign, he most likely had them painted in the contemporary dress of Rome's fourteenth-century *senatores,* one of whom is still visible for us in the mosaics of the Santa Rosa chapel in the Aracoeli. The emperor was also painted there, probably in the garb of the German emperors of Cola's day in their odd mélange of Roman, Byzantine, Sicilian, and German regalia. The effect would have been startling and immediate, and the message could not have been lost: here the present meets the past—now made all too contemporary by the skill of the artist—and in a sense it had a chance to repeat, or undo, the actions of the past in an act of perfect symmetry.

For what the Senate could give in the name of the Roman people, it could now take back. So Cola read his transcription of the tablet—the Anonimo romano is clear that he used a *carta*. He spun his secular sermon from atop his pulpit as he bade the assembled senators, officials, and professionals contemplate the historical scene, the center of which was the very reality that the painted *historia* portrayed, the very tablet by which such authority had been granted: the sacrament of political authority—externally signifying its very essence—whose power heretofore only the popes in their Lateran Palace had seemed to understand.

Cola's lecture has been seen by scholars as the first example of the Renaissance's understanding of ancient inscriptions and historical sources in their proper civic context; and Cola may have had sections of the inscription no longer available to modern scholars; but his own legal knowledge and that of several of his closest advisers made even this unnecessary. The theory of a *lex regia,* which had granted authority to the emperors, was actively debated among Cola's contemporaries. But Rienzo's own take on the event and his reliance on an actual inscription to document his interpretation underscore his attempt to reverse the church's co-optation of this legislative concession and to return it to its historical, civil context and use. As he later wrote to the archbishop of Prague, the minister of the German emperor Charles IV, in August 1350:

Among these ancient inscriptions and personal documents there appeared a great tablet of bronze, inscribed with ancient lettering, which Pope Boniface VIII had hidden out of hatred for the empire. He had a certain altar made from it, with the lettering hidden toward the inside. But before I assumed the tribuneship, I placed it in an ornate setting in the middle of the Lateran cathedral, in an eminent position, where it could be inspected and read by everyone. Thus fitted out, it has survived intact to this day. (57, BBCR 2.3:258, ll. 726–33)

Cola's account was probably meant to flatter the German emperor, since the tablet had been on public display at the Lateran for decades. On the other hand, Boniface had recently removed it from its prominent position, perhaps as a sign of contempt for secular claims to authority. At any event, the oration's nature as both liturgy and theater was underscored by Cola's arrangement of the space. He set up a series of wooden bleachers decked out in rich tapestry, recalling the interior spaces of the Theater of Marcellus and the settings of contemporary mystery plays: public spaces in which the great *agonia* of Rome's past and of Christianity's triumphs were played. Just as Cola's secular *Navicella* had spelled out a religious and moral message upon the walls of Rome's secular capital, so now his secular political message was delivered within the sacred space of the former imperial—but now papal—palace. Just as the communes and lay confraternities took over much of the role and authority of the clergy and church in late medieval Italy in what historians have termed "civic religion,"[8] so, too, now Cola called on Rome's lay leadership to record and take back its long-abandoned rights and duties to govern the city.

Lengthy lectures and a warm, darkened room will persuade members of an audience to let their eyes and minds wander across the spaces and discreetly fix upon images painted or projected onto walls. Skilled speaker that he was, Cola knew and had planned this. As the Virgin and the saints stared down upon the senators and officials of Rome, and as they in turn stared at those images of Vespasian and the senators, dressed in their own clothes, in settings probably drawn from familiar Roman scenes, they recognized themselves handing over their power and authority to some far-off emperor—who in turn had given it to the pope—and they absorbed Cola's words. Nor were these empty evocations of the distant past, or some high-minded claim of imperial authority like Dante's recently published *De monarchia*. Rule over Rome, Cola stressed, meant real rule and effective power: over legislation and treaties, over country fiefs and estates, over taxation and finance, war and peace, public works, and the supply of food and provisions, just as the tablet of Vespasian spelled out. Most important, Cola reminded his listeners, it meant jurisdiction over the coming Jubilee that he had recently won for them: the Jubilee and its promise of vast blessings for the city, and even vaster throngs of pilgrims remaining in Rome long enough to visit its chief sites and gain their indulgences, pilgrims buying at its souvenir and icon shops, its vegetable and meat counters, its fish and poultry stands, from its vendors of cheese and bread and wine.

When this document had been read, and these chapters, he said, "My lords, so great was the majesty of the people of Rome that it gave authority to the Emperor. Now we have lost it." Then he leaned forward toward them and said, "Romans, you do not have peace. Your lands are not ploughed. The Jubilee is approaching on good faith alone. You are not provided with grain or provisions, and if the people who are coming to the Jubilee find you unprovided, they will carry off the very stones of Rome out of hunger. Even the stones are not enough for such a multitude." (AR, XVIII, ll. 185–95, Porta, 149)

Then, just as suddenly, Cola brought his listeners out of the world of antiquity, out even from the world of future profits, with a startling conflation from the Gospels: "Even the stones are not enough for such a multitude." Had not the "multitude" been fed only by a miracle of Christ, that of the loaves and fishes? Any Christian with eyes to see and ears to hear would have recognized this allusion to loaves and multitudes, but the elite and professional class in the bleachers would also have connected it immediately to the great mosaic of the *Navicella*, for Christ's walking on the waters had taken place just after this miracle of the loaves and fishes. But Cola's words carried even more meaning, for had not turning stones to bread been the very temptation that Satan himself had offered Christ in the desert, and had not Christ replied, "Human beings live not on bread alone but on every word that comes from the mouth of God"? And so the cycle was complete. Cola had brought his audience to the origin of Rome's imperial conundrum and had painted a vivid picture of its future profit or chaos. He now laid out what could be the only political solution for the present: the words of the Gospel, the rejection of Satan and his sins that must be the prelude to any conversion and to the moral and spiritual reform of the city that alone will bring it peace and stability and guarantee the Jubilee.

The Jubilee.[9] No one could forget for a moment that all of Rome's hopes, for income, for spiritual grace, for the renewal of its institutions, even perhaps for the return of the pope, depended upon the successful events of the year 1350. Cola and his delegation had made it among the chief goals of their mission to Avignon in January 1343; and the pope's granting of the fiftieth-year indulgence had been greeted with great joy by the envoys and their fellow Romans. But could they live up to the great expectations of the last Jubilee declared by Boniface VIII in 1300, when contemporary chroniclers put as many as two hundred thousand people in the city on any given day, and when as many as two million men, women, and children may have made their way to Rome from all over Christendom?

Joshua had commanded the priests to take up the ark and ram's-horn trumpets, *iubileorum buccinas,* and to march around Jericho until its walls collapsed (Josh. 6:6). *Yobel,* the horn, also called all the Hebrew people together to the festival of reconciliation and forgiveness held every seven-times-seven years, a mystical number denoting a new era. In the same sense Jesus announced the "acceptable year" at the beginning of his ministry. By the year 1200 the term *jubileus* was being used synonymously with the peace and renewal associated with penitence, reconciliation, and the forgiveness of sins on a personal level. The jubilee of 1300 had been as overwhelming as it was unplanned, arising, it seems, from a unknown preacher's impromptu sermon to a group of pilgrims viewing Veronica's veil at St. Peter's. The effect was electrical: the idea of a pilgrimage for the coming year 1300 spread across Italy and beyond. Within months hundreds and thousands were making their way spontaneously toward Rome, just as they had in the movement of the Flagellants in 1260. Caught by surprise—and not by the greed for pious donations as nineteenth-century historians assert—Boniface VIII consulted with his cardinals and on February 22, 1300, issued the bull *Antiquorum habet fida relatio,* granting the plenary indulgence to all those pilgrims who came to Rome's great churches and the shrines of its saints from the city itself, from Italy, and from beyond Italy. Such an indulgence remitted not the sin, the guilt of which had to be confessed and forgiven, but all the temporal punishment due in purgatory. It was therefore a treasure far greater than anything earthly.

Yet another factor that Boniface could not have planned lay behind every aspect of the Jubilee year and the pilgrims who made their way to Rome even before the Jubilee bull. The Jubilee horn and the turning of the ages were inseparable; and the newness of the century meant the renewal of all things and the forgiveness and reconciliation of old debts and sins, old hatreds and violence. Nor could anyone in the Middle Ages escape the association of the Jubilee horn announcing the seven times seven with the seven trumpets blown by the seven angels of the Apocalypse (8:6, 12).

The word "apocalypse" today carries so much terror, speaks of such violent cataclysm, the destruction of the old order, the punishment of the vast majority of sinners, and the rewarding of those very few elect who adhere to one form or another of the Christian message.[10] Yet in antiquity and for most thinking people of the Middle Ages, the word had meanings far more nuanced, and far more open to the rational investigations of speculative thinkers, than we might imagine. *Apocalypse* literally means "revelation" in Greek, and the book composed by John of Patmos, called the Divine (c. 95 C.E.), is essentially a group of visions of things hidden and now revealed in a series of rich and multivalent symbols. The book's historical context of Roman persecution of the weakened Christian church is only secondary to the great cosmic struggle between the new people of God and the forces of Satan. Rome might be symbolized by Babylon, but Babylon itself is the great symbol of the oppressive forces of a world that turns against the true religion and is ultimately destroyed by God. The series of invasions, plagues, and natural disasters that John prophesies against Rome can all be related to ancient events and peoples in one way or another, but such literalness would miss the essence of the book. It is God who cares for and protects his people. Those who remain faithful may suffer tribulations, but God will triumph over Satan and his minions.

Since apocalyptic writing offers both consolation to the oppressed and exhortation to resist these very same forces, it can be seen, among other things, as a form of political rhetoric. At its core of meaning in the "opening up"—through opened books, seals, visions—apocalyptic also reveals a "second reality" that transcends the secular. Apocalyptic opens those who understand its symbols and rhetoric—those who can "read the signs of the times"—to new planes both vertical and horizontal: the vertical in the divine world above and around us, and the horizontal in the sacred end of time beyond our own.

Apocalypse has also, especially in modern discussion, been confused with the notions of eschatology, the millennium, and chiliasm. But *eschaton* is merely the Greek word for "the end," the fulfillment of linear time, the conclusion of the ineluctable progress through earthbound time and space for both societies and individuals. Much more problematic for the history of Christian thought has been the notion of the millennium. Chapter 20 (1–3) of John's Apocalypse describes the chaining and sealing up of the dragon, "which is the devil and Satan," for one thousand years: *annos mille* in Latin, the root of "millennium"; and *chilia eite* in Greek, the root of "chiliasm." The "thousand years" between the defeat of the dragon would be an age of peace and the triumph of the elect. This, in turn, would end with the release of the dragon, the unleashing of the forces of Gog and Magog, and their final assault on the earthly city of the elect, until Christ enthroned returns for the Last Judgment, the devil is cast down, the dead appear before the throne, the book of life is opened, the seas, death, and hell give up their dead who are "judged each one according to their works." Suddenly John sees "a new heaven and a new earth," as the old passes away and the New Jerusalem descends from heaven, "prepared as a bride dressed for her husband." The New Jerusalem is the perfect city, the fulfillment of all human society and history, whose walls are jade, studded with precious stones, whose gates are pearls and whose main street is paved with gold (Apoc. 21).

Thus the millennium is not the end of the world but the period *in between* the defeat of the dragon Antichrist and the great tribulations and Christ's Second Coming, the Last Judgment, and the end of time. While the body of John's series of visions fit firmly within a long tradition of apocalyptic vision, the final chapters of his *Revelation* immediately became problematic for the early Church. What had the Apocalypse meant by that "thousand years"? Had it already passed, or was it to stretch out ahead into the future? Was it to be taken literally, and for how long? By the fourth century and the triumph of Christianity, the chiliastic view of church history that posited the millennium as a literal one thousand years had become an embarrassment both for the sophisticated Greek-educated apologists of the Eastern Church and for Western thinkers like Jerome. Augustine labeled belief in the literal millennium "ridiculous" and advised his readers to "relax your fingers" and stop trying to calculate the date of its arrival and duration. His view came to dominate the early Middle Ages.

It was not until the twelfth century that religious thinkers began to approach the Apocalypse in a new way, more in keeping with the age's historical consciousness, more in key with its attempt to return to evangelical models in order to bring about institutional change and personal reform. The most important figure in this new interpretation was Joachim of Fiore (c.1135–1202), whose biblical exegesis used a series of concordances in the time-honored medieval method of *symphonia* between the Old and New Testaments.[11] Thus Adam is to Jesus as Eve is to Mary, the twelve patriarchs to the Twelve Apostles, and so on. Yet Joachim took these concordances and reapplied them in a dynamic system of typologies that fit them into a *historical* interpretation. He took the existing notions of seven ages *(aetates)* going back to Augustine and that of two *tempora* of salvation history—the Old and New Testaments, each with forty-two generations of thirty years each—and applied to them a series of his *concordia*. Each of his first two *tempora* were thus also subdivided into seven *aetates* each.

In addition to this twofold concordance, Joachim also used a Trinitarian model that spelled out three great *status,* or "ages": the first *status* of the Father, of the Hebrews, of laws, and of married men and women; the second *status* of the Son, of grace, and of unmarried Christian clergy working in the world; and a third *status* of the Holy Spirit, marked by full grace, understanding, and the spiritual contemplatives, the monks and hermits of his own time who would bring the Christian life to full perfection. The church of the second *status* would be not so much replaced (by any revolutionary change) as spiritualized and fulfilled. Joachim wanted to make it clear that his third *status* was not to be confused with the millennium: it was an era of reform within the continuum of history.

It was difficult, however, for many of those living in the wake of Joachim to refrain from reading his biblical exegesis as a literal outline of events and a prophecy of groups and individuals. With the 1310s and 1320s conflicts arose over the adherence to Francis's strict rule of poverty that began to tear apart the Franciscan order. Many of the stricter faction, soon called "Spirituals," began to face persecution from their fellow Franciscans and arrest and inquisition as a result of a series of papal bulls attempting to settle the dispute.[12] But rather than adopt what ultimately became the orthodox position of their "Conventual" opponents within the order, the Spirituals quite early embraced and reinterpreted Joachim's "prophecies" of the apocalyptic tribulations that the elect must suffer. This combination of "prophecy and poverty" became a self-justifying intellectual and ethical stance that had an enormous impact on Franciscan life and the Church in general into the fifteenth century.

In the fifth and sixth *aetates* of the second *tempus* and the second *status*, the Spirituals believed, the Church and all its institutions would find themselves in a state of deep corruption and decline. Only those very few "spiritual" men would embody the true message and life of the early Church, of Jesus and his apostles. In the present age, however, Francis of Assisi had revived the pure life of the early Church and pointed the way to reform and renewal through his *Rule* and his life of humility, patience, and apostolic poverty. But just like Elias and Elijah, just like Jesus and his disciples, Francis went unheeded, and his followers began to suffer a series of increasing tribulations at the hands of the forces of Antichrist within the Church.

The Spirituals and their message attracted many followers not only from among their fellow Franciscans but also in high places. We can focus on only a few examples. I have already noted Cardinals Pietro and Giacomo Colonna's embrace of the Spiritual cause in the 1310s and 1320s. One of their protégés, Angelo Clareno OFM, was a major influence on the Neapolitan court of King Robert the Wise and Queen Sancia. Clareno's followers had also long been a distinct presence in Rome.[13] From as early as 1295, the church of Sant'Eusebio is singled out for a pious bequest by Pietro Sassone, whose will mentions it as housing the "friars of Fra Pietro da Morrone," the Poor Hermits of Celestine formed by Clareno and his companions in 1293. By the year 1300 the house of S. Pietro in Montorio, on the Gianicolo Hill above Trastevere, hosted a community of eight of the Poor Hermits. Despite the pressures of the Inquisition, directed from the Franciscan church of the Aracoeli, Clareno's followers continued to survive in Rome. Clareno's *Letters* also reveal Spiritual communities in the houses of San Giovanni a Porta Latina as early as 1312, at San Lorenzo in Panisperne on the Viminal Hill, in Rieti, and elsewhere in undisclosed locations in and around Rome.

The Spirituals in Rome came into prominence with the crisis spurred by the descent on Italy by the emperor Lewis of Bavaria in 1327–28. Pope

John XXII was the emperor's mortal enemy, and Lewis's entry into Italian politics threatened not only to upset the papal ascendancy but also to revive imperial hopes throughout the peninsula. Lewis's journey to Rome to obtain his crown at St. Peter's was relatively easy and his entry into the city virtually unopposed. To maintain Rome's loyalty and to exploit the papacy's exile in far-off Avignon, Lewis decided that he should call on the pope to return to his see; failing that, he claimed that the Romans had the right to elect their own pontiff. On May 12, 1328, a new college of cardinals, puppets of the emperor, elected Pietro Rainallucci da Corbara antipope as Nicholas V. Pietro, a Franciscan from the Aracoeli convent, had been one of the few friars to ignore the interdict that John XXII had placed upon Rome for accepting Lewis, and for the next five years Pietro served as the emperor's willing agent in his Italian schism against John XXII. Abandoning any pretense to the Spiritual embrace of voluntary poverty, he quickly amassed a fortune, assembled an elaborate papal court, and lived a private life of sexual excess, according to hostile sources.

Lewis soon thereafter abandoned Rome. While Pietro abdicated his throne in 1330 and ended his days a prisoner in the papal palace at Avignon in 1333, his "schism" points to the wide penetration of Spiritual Franciscan individuals and ideas in Rome. While the Romans did eventually drive the emperor and his adherents from the city, they seem to have had no quarrel with the ideals of a purified and chastened papacy. On the contrary, it was Pietro da Corbara's very corruption that hastened his demise. The ideals of apostolic poverty and apocalyptic expectation that the Spirituals espoused lived on as potent reform motifs; and even after Angelo Clareno's own death in 1337, his followers remained active throughout the region.

Lewis's descent on Italy and the episode of Pietro da Corbara impressed not only Clareno and the Roman Spirituals with the grave tribulations of the times. Back in Avignon the new pope, Benedict XII, decided on his coronation in January 1335 that Italy and Rome were far too dangerous places to even consider returning the papacy there. It was Benedict who therefore decided to build the permanent papal palace at Avignon. But, as Roberto Rusconi has pointed out, Benedict's decision sparked a reaction of another kind back in an expectant Italy, that of the "peace pilgrimage" of Fra Venturino da Bergamo, OP.[14] By the beginning of 1335, Venturino's sermons on personal repentance and reconciliation of enemies had begun to attract such a large following that Bergamo's churches and streets could no longer hold the throng of listeners, and so he moved his sermons to the open countryside and announced that the true goal of his preaching was to be a pilgrimage of penance, peace, and reconciliation to Rome. According to contemporary sources, miracles and visions began to attend Venturino's sermons.

Peacemaking was central to Venturino's movement; he himself referred to one of the goals of the pilgrimage as *totius Ytaliae pax reformatio,* "the peace reformation of all Italy." Other sources, including the Anonimo romano, specifically mention the apocalyptic aspects of Venturino's *peregrinatio romana,* most especially the pilgrim's white robes, a visual quotation from Apocalypse 19:14, and the mark of the "Tau" in reference to Ezekiel. Their progress to Rome was rapid: departing Bergamo on February 2, 1335, the peace pilgrims streamed through Milan, Lodi, Cremona, Mantua, Ferrara, Bologna, Florence, Siena, Montepulciano, Orvieto, and Viterbo, everywhere giving rise to the same acts of penance and reconciliation, the (temporary) end of wars and feuds, the release of prisoners from jails, and the same apocalyptic expectations. For the year 1335 was another of those magical dates prophesied by Daniel (12:9–13) currently being associated with the millennium.

The peace pilgrims reached Rome on March 21, 1335, to be met with a flood of pilgrims from all over Italy who had come to see and hear Venturino's miraculous preaching. But Venturino's stay was problematic from the start, as he mixed criticism of absentee popes with contacts with high-ranking papal opponents both clerical and lay. Venturino's surviving letters also reveal an interest in the writings of the Franciscan Joachites. One can imagine the pope's growing fears. On April 8, 1335, therefore, Benedict XII dispatched a letter warning his vicar and Rome's government against Venturino's *illusio diabolica* and the schisms and errors that his movement threatened. But before the papal letter could reach the city, Venturino and his movement had evaporated into thin air. By April 30 Venturino was in Mantua, where his preaching became the center of immense devotions. The friar's enemies soon turned him over to the Inquisition, however, and he was sent off to Avignon to await trial for heresy, silenced, and sent into internal exile in Provence. With the election of Clement VI in May 1342, Venturino's case was reviewed; in February 1343 he was rehabilitated and given a license to preach *ultra montes.* Just as with Cola di Rienzo, Clement VI had a hunch that he could make use of this talented and charismatic leader, and so in January 1344 the Dominican was sent to Lombardy to preach a new, armed, crusade against the Turks. Venturino died at Smyrna, in Turkey, on March 28, 1346.

Had he and Cola met at the papal palace or in the streets of Avignon? Did Cola have access to the *Legenda* published shortly after Venturino's death? He surely did know of events during Venturino's later crusade to Smyrna and speaks of them in a letter to Clement VI dated July 8, 1347. It would therefore be highly improbable that while in Avignon from January 1343 to June 1344, the young and famous Roman, the champion of reform and rebirth, would not have sought out the man who had turned Cola's city into the center of the highest religious drama of the first half of the fourteenth century, had made it the center of his great pilgrimage to bring a "peace reformation" to all of Italy, and had awakened the apocalyptic expectations of tens of thousands. But neither Cola nor Petrarch speaks of the man or his stay at Avignon.

Apocalyptic influence was not confined to religious thinkers and popular movements. Recent studies on Dante and his *Divine Comedy* have begun to show how deeply indebted fourteenth-century literature was to the same apocalyptic traditions that influenced Venturino and his contemporaries.[15] Dante's meeting the simoniac Pope Nicholas III in *Inferno* 19, for example, raises the image of Simon Magus, for many the preeminent symbol of Antichrist. *Purgatorio* 29, 32, and 33 and *Paradiso* 11 reverberate with Apocalypse 12 and 13. Dante's condemnation of the Avignon papacy in *Paradiso* 27 used the same apocalyptic Babylon-Jerusalem dichotomy that appears in his letters concerning the Avignon papacy and the need for the popes to return from exile to Rome. Scholars point to such passages and find the influence of Joachim of Fiore through intermediaries, such as the Tuscan Spiritual leader Ubertino da Casale and the series of pope prophecies, the *Vaticinia de summis pontificibus,* probably composed in the circle of Angelo Clareno.

In the next generation Petrarch also reveals the deeply apocalyptic influence of the time. In his contemporary commentary on Dante, Benvenuto da Imola remarked how Petrarch had based his criticism of Avignon on that of "the great Babylon" of the Apocalypse. In three sonnets inserted into his *Rerum vulgarium fragmenta* of 1346–47 and in the *Sine nomine* letters, Petrarch explicitly compares the Avignon papacy to the Whore of Babylon. *Rime* 114 presents the image of Avignon as the "mother of fornication and lust and drunkenness, full of abomination and of all filthiness, and seated upon the rushing waters of the Rhône, the Durance, and the Sorgue. And her prelates are indeed like the Scarlet Woman, clothed in purple and gold and silver and precious stones, and drunken with the blood of the Martyrs and of Christ." Petrarch's condemnation in *Sine nomine* 18 repeatedly addresses Avignon as the Whore of Babylon from Apocalypse 17 and 18.

"Babylon the Great is fallen" (Apoc. 18:2). And so in words Petrarch had painted an image as startling as Cola's secular *Navicella,* of Babylon and Carthage and Jerusalem all fallen and lost. But if Petrarch had meant to heap coals and ashes upon the ruins of Avignon, his words could only bring to mind the fact that for John's Apocalypse Babylon had stood as symbol of the true city of Satan: Rome itself.[16] Babylon the Great, the cosmic antithesis of the heavenly Jerusalem, was the seven-headed beast described in Apocalypse 17:9: "The seven heads are the seven hills" on which the Whore of Babylon rests. Rome as the destroyed and fallen Babylon, a city of toppled columns and turrets, "the haunt of devils and a lodging for every foul spirit and dirty loathsome bird" (Apoc. 18:2–3) always lay behind the medieval dread of its magical, haunted ruins.

In his *Reading on the Apocalypse* the Provençal Spiritual Franciscan Peter John Olivi (d. 1298) identified Rome with the apocalyptic Babylon and predicted its destruction as a punishment for Antichrist's persecution of the faithful. Just as Emperor Augustus's vision of the *ara coeli* recounted in the *Mirabilia Urbis Romae* foretold the toppling of the pagan gods and the victory of Christ, so, too, did a long series of medieval illustrations show the victory of Christ and his martyrs by the striking visual image of the collapse of Rome's triumphal columns, their shafts splitting in two, their pagan gods, now deformed demons, toppling from their heights. This visual tradition later found great currency in the propaganda of the Protestant Reformation, where the image of Rome clearly stands in for the apocalyptic Babylon.

Similar in naturalistic intent and close in style to Giotto, but far different in its spirit of ghostly evocation, is the fresco by Maso di Banco in the Bardi di Vernio Chapel of Sta. Croce at Florence (fig. 20). Working between the 1330s and 1350—contemporary to Cola's career in Rome—Maso paints scenes from the legend of Pope Silvester, the recipient of Constantine's "donation." Two parallel incidents in what are really three scenes, more like a dream sequence than real time, play out against a background clearly meant to be the haunted ruins of Rome's Forum. In a desolate landscape of shattered walls and broken vaults and arches, empty palaces engulf the viewer in distorted perspectives, and a lonely column stands amid a pile of rubble against the viewer's plane, erasing the distance between the present and legendary time. In a sequence derived from the *Golden Legend,* the priests of Rome's pagan gods entreat the emperor to save the city from a dragon buried deep in a pit, forty steps underground, whose breath of fire has already slain three hundred citizens. At Constantine's request, and on instructions from the Holy Spirit, Silvester enters the deep pit to find the dragon, Satan himself, and there binds the beast and seals the pit. The scene is a clear evocation of the binding of the beast and his false prophet in Apocalypse 19. In the central scene to the right he revives two Roman wizards, underscoring the connection to Simon Magus and the apocalyptic text. Finally, on the extreme right, Rome's emperor and his people witness Silvester's healing powers, based not on Rome's magical arts but on the new strength of the Christian faith. Further pagans are converted and "delivered from a twofold death, namely from the worship of the devil and the dragon's venom."

Rome's hellish landscape continued to evoke the apocalyptic "haunt of devils and a lodging for every foul spirit"; but like the Romans beset by evil and violence in the time of Silvester, Cola could now convince the Romans of his own day, seated in Silvester's and Constantine's church, that the time for the conversion of individuals and society had arrived. Soon after his Lateran lecture Cola displayed the last of his grand prophetic paintings:

He had painted the following image on the wall of Sant'Angelo in Pescheria, a place famous throughout the world. In the left-hand corner of the picture was a very intense fire, its smoke and flames rose up to heaven. In this fire were many people and kings, some of whom appeared half alive, others dead. And in this same fire was a very old woman; and because of the great heat two parts of this old woman's body were blackened; the third part remained unharmed. On the right side, in the other corner, was a church with a very high campanile. Out of this church came an armed angel, dressed in white. His cloak was of scarlet vermilion. In his hand he was carrying a naked sword. With his left hand he was taking this aged woman by the hand, because he wanted to free her from danger. At the top of the bell tower were standing St. Peter and St. Paul, as if they had come from heaven, and they were saying this: "Angel, angel, help our inn keeper."

Then the painting showed how many falcons were falling from the sky; and they were falling dead in the midst of the raging flames. High up in heaven was a beautiful white dove, which held a crown of myrtle in its beak, and it was giving it to a tiny sparrow-like bird; and then the dove drove the falcons from heaven. The little bird was carrying the crown and placing it on the head of the old woman. Below these pictures was written, "The time of great justice is coming, and you await the time." The people who poured into Sant'Angelo looked at these figures. Many said that they were a vanity exhibit and laughed at them. Some said, "It will take more than pictures to rectify the condition of Rome." Someone said, "This is something important. It has great meaning." (AR, XVIII, ll. 213–49, Porta, 150–51)

If Cola's two previous paintings on the Capitoline and in the Lateran had used visual language appropriate to the centers of Roman secular and spiritual power, his fresco on the wall of Sant'Angelo in Pescheria (see fig. 3), in the heart of his old neighborhood amid the fish mongers and the taverns, spoke to the Roman people directly and in a language they could understand.[17] Cola's image here contained neither lofty *historia* drawn from the annals of ancient Rome nor the *allegoria* used in his secular *Navicella*. Here instead the images were direct, the church portrayed was Sant'Angelo itself with its well-known and lofty campanile, built in 1290/91 and dedicated to the Archangel Michael. Cola's symbolism was simple: the image of final conflagration, the destruction of Babylon in a blaze of heavenly fire common to countless Last Judgment scenes all over Europe and Italy. At least two fresco cycles illustrating Apocalypse 18 and 19 survive within a day's journey of Rome: at Anagni to the south, and at Castel Sant'Elia to the north.

If the Anonimo romano does not seem to have gotten the reference to John's pun, "for ever and ever" upon the imperial title *Roma aeterna,* he also has missed the central images of Cola's painting: for the "armed angel" who emerges from the church on the right-hand side is no ordinary supernatural but a conflation of the Archangel Michael, for whom an association with Sant'Angelo would be appropriate, and the central figure of the next chapter of the Apocalypse, the Christ of the Second Coming (Apoc. 19:11–18).

Many medieval illustrations of the scene, from the Angers Tapestry of 1377–82, to the Estense Apocalypse (a block book of c.1450), to Hans Holbein's woodcut of 1523 show Christ with sword in hand, just as in Cola's fresco. And so the forces of the beast, of the false prophet Antichrist, and the kings of the earth and their followers are defeated. The beast and prophet are "cast alive into a lake of fire burning with brimstone" (Apoc. 19:21). But again the Anonimo romano mistakes his apocalyptic imagery, for the fowls are not being cast into the flames, but as the Estense Apocalypse and the Angers Tapestry show, they are descending upon the defeated amid the flames to devour them. Finally, in verses immediately following (Apoc. 20:1–2), John reveals, "I saw an angel come down from heaven, having the key to the bottomless pit and a great chain in his hand. And he laid hold of the dragon, that old serpent, which is the devil, and Satan, and bound him a thousand years." This was the millennium: "The time of great justice is coming, and you await the time," Cola's caption read.

But here and throughout the fresco Cola has introduced an imagery that brings the events of apocalyptic prophecy back into contemporary time: for the Church is ever-present, symbolized by the church building, by Christ emerging from it, and by Sts. Peter and Paul, themselves symbols of justice and peace, invoking divine aid. Foreign to apocalyptic imagery are the old woman, two-thirds burned and one-third still free of harm, led from danger by Christ, as well as the image of the dove with the myrtle crown and the tiny sparrow, which in turn places the crown on the head of the old woman. The old woman could symbolize many things, including the same Rome who appeared in Cola's *Navicella* painting. Most uses, however, were different facets of the same symbol: the Church, the bride of Christ. In another guise, especially in this apocalyptic context, she is the *mulier amicte sole,* the "woman clothed with the sun" of Apocalypse 12, with the moon under her feet and the crown of twelve stars upon her head, the Holy Spirit about to give birth to the child, the symbol of the Messiah. Mother and child are pursued by the dragon, Satan, and forced to flee into the wilderness, "where she hath a place prepared of God, that they should feed her there a thousand two hundred and three score days" (Apoc. 12:6), the 1,260 of the Apocalypse that was to cause endless speculation for medieval date watchers.

According to certain Joachite interpreters of the Apocalypse, such as Peter John Olivi, however, the mother with child is the Church of the present age forced into the wilderness of tribulation just as she is about to give birth to the church of the third *status.* In this light the woman burned over two-thirds of her body, "while the third part remained unharmed," makes some sense, since it is in the third age that Christ will come again to save the remnants of the Church so badly persecuted by the forces of Antichrist. In certain representations, the Estense Apocalypse, for example, the *mulier amicte sole* is shown in the midst of a huge mandorla of flames, and once more the Anonimo romano may have missed his visual cues.

Peter and Paul are, of course, the symbols of the church of Rome and may symbolize Roman replacements for the two witnesses who stand atop the church and in Apocalypse 11:1–3 witness the measuring of the Temple: "And I will give power unto my two witnesses, and they shall prophesy a thousand two hundred and three score years; clothed in sackcloth. These are the two olive trees, and the two candlesticks standing before the God of the earth. And if any man will hurt them, fire proceedeth out of their mouth, and devoureth their enemies." In the Joachite tradition the two witnesses were also the founders of the two great mendicant orders, Francis and Dominic, "clothed in sackcloth," who have renewed and reformed the church at the end of the second *status* and who look forward to the contemplatives of the third *status*. Witnesses to Venturino da Bergamo's preaching recall that "as he preached flames of fire were seen to burst from his mouth," and beside him appeared two men: the apocalyptic witnesses.

Since the Gospel of Matthew's description of the baptism of Jesus (3:16), the dove had been used to symbolize the public manifestation of the Holy Spirit descending upon the earth. In Venturino's *Legenda* the friar is also seen with the dove "descending several times to the head of the preacher," as the crowd looked on and wondered. Thus Cola's Joachite symbolism remains consistent. In the third age, that of the Holy Spirit, the conflict and tribulation of the second is replaced by that of peace, the Spirit places the crown of myrtle, which in Isaiah's prophecy (55:13) replaces the nettles of tribulation, upon the head of the Church in the time to come. The dove does not do this directly but via the humble sparrow, presumably dressed in brown, the symbol of the simple Franciscans of the third age who would renew the Church.

Some Romans were convinced by Cola's visual arguments, some thought them meaningless and mockable; and some thought that art and symbols alone could not change society. But Cola had finally achieved what he wanted: everyone in Rome who "poured into" the exhibit at Sant'Angelo came out talking not art but politics and religion. In bringing the Romans to openly discuss and to debate what most had given up for dead—the basis of a just society, the *buono stato*—he had achieved what he had come back to the shattered city to do: to make possible once again what three decades of depression and civil war had destroyed, the common ground of civil society, from which he knew all else must follow.

CHAPTER 7

Pentecost

Cola's campaign to rebuild a civic culture in Rome took nearly three years: from his return to the city in June 1344 to the spring of 1347. But as his speeches gained circulation and his apocalyptic images grew on the consciousness of the Romans, he became more and more confident in his ability to restore power to the communal government.

He also predicted his ascendancy in this way. He wrote a placard and affixed it to the door of San Giorgio della Chiavica [in Velabro]. The placard said: 'In a short time the Romans will return to their ancient *buono stato*.' This notice was posted on the first day of Lent (AR, XVIII, ll. 249–55, Porta, 151).[1]

The Romans did not have to wonder what Cola's placard meant. Lorenzetti's *Buon Governo* (see figs. 15 and 16) is only the best known of the images of this tangible political force to have come down to us from fourteenth-century Italy. A more detailed description will give us some idea of what resonances Cola's *buono stato* had with his urban audience.[2] On the end wall, opposite the windows of Siena's Sala de' Nove, Lorenzetti's painting is dominated by two figures. On the right, the monumental Common Good, the *buon comune,* personified that most cherished of medieval political notions inherited from Aristotle in his *Politics,* passed on to medieval political thought, and systematized by Thomas Aquinas (1224–74) in his *Summa Theologica* [Q.96, art. 4] and other works. In the political lexicon of the fourteenth-century Italian communes, the terms used by Aquinas—*communitas, comune,* and *governo*—all translated into the same reality; and the good government, the *buon governo,* was synonymous with the "common good" and its mirror image, the "good commune." Lorenzetti painted in tangible form and color what this tradition had sketched out in theory. Justice forms the center of the composition in both her "distributive" aspect, which punishes wrongdoing and rewards virtue, and her "commutative" form, which grants power and wealth. Concord herself sits at Justice's feet (see fig. 15a) to indicate that only through the strict application of Justice can "political union" be achieved, order restored, and liberty ensured. Concord holds in her lap a carpenter's plane, but not just any kind. This is a large, two-handled tool, meant either to smooth down newly joined planks or to "re-form" a roughened surface made ragged by age or injury. The rhythm of the plane is another reminder of the necessity of harmony and cooperation: the plane is guided properly only by two people standing on opposite sides of the surface, working in a reciprocal, back-and-forth motion. Concord holds the tool in potentiality, awaiting worthy hands.

Below Concord begins a procession of twenty-four of Siena's citizens, a visual *memoria* of the form of the city's communal government from 1236 to 1270. On another level, these men are linked, "twelve by twelve," like the pilgrims in Fra Venturino's peace pilgrimage, with a *chorda* held by Justice and passed along by Concord as it moves toward the right side of the painting and to the figure of the Common Good, concretizing Thomas Aquinas's notion of the perfect community. Enthroned on a long couch on both sides of the Common Good are Christian virtues—Peace (at the center of the entire composition); Prudence and Fortitude to the Common Good's left; and Magnanimity, Temperance, and Justice on his right. At the Common Good's feet the twins Senus and Aschimus—Siena's Romulus and Remus—nurse at the she-wolf. Above the Common Good hover Faith, Hope, and Charity. The Common Good is linked to the figure of Charity, since this is the ideal of medieval rule: the harmony and peace of all members of society, fraternity bound by the charity preached by St. Paul. Wisdom hovers above the figures of Commutative and Distributive Justice that dominate the fresco's left. Lorenzetti thus reminds his audience that only through common effort to create the *buon comune* can the Christian virtues survive and flourish.

On the right wall of the Sale de' Nove, Lorenzetti set out the *Effects of Good Government in the City* (see fig. 16). Here, in the most arresting urban landscape of the fourteenth century, the city of Siena rises in peace and harmony: cathedral, school, shops, an inn, houses of every type; its people: men, women, and children enjoying the benefits of peace and concord. At the center of the scene a group of young women dance hand in

hand to the rhythm of the tambourine and the song of their leader, perhaps in celebration of a wedding procession to the left (see fig. 16a). Their
dance is a visual portrayal of the Justice described by Dante in *Paradiso*
VI, 118–26 and reminiscent of Dante's vision of the souls in *Paradiso* XIII,
20–31. Their dance and song give visual form to the *harmonia* and *concordia* that thrive in the *buon comune.*

Beyond the city's walls, in the *contado,* the fields are well tended and
busily cultivated, and peasants enter the city with their harvests. The nobility, suavely dressed, occupy themselves in the peaceful pursuits of the
hunt, not in war—but likewise not in the government of the city. Merchants arrive with their wares along fine roads and across a well-built and
well-maintained bridge; villages and hamlets rest in peace and prosperity. Above the panorama the winged figure of *Securitas* watches over all
(see fig. 16b), in her right hand displaying a scroll that tells the viewer:

> Without fear, let each man freely walk,
> And working let everyone sow,
> While such a commune
> This lady will keep under her rule
> Because she has removed all power from the guilty.

In her left she holds up the figure of a hanged man, a warning that the
law has long arms and will punish the evildoer.

Across the hall, on the left wall, the Sienese faced their other choice:
the *Allegory of Bad Government* or *Tyranny* (see fig. 17). Here at the center of the composition the horned and devilish figure of Tyranny replaces
the Common Good; at his feet the goat, symbol of lechery and unbridled lust for power; above him Vainglory, Avarice, and a winged figure
in red holding an exposed sword and empty yoke: *Superbia,* the figure of
pride mixed with force that replaces Charity, just as private interest over-
powers the public good. The lopsidedly swaying yoke recalls and repu-
diates the balanced scales of Justice, while the yoke itself—symbol of humility and the devotion to public duty—is empty and points to the
barrenness of Pride. Below Tyranny's throne Justice lies bound and prostrate (see fig. 17d)—in what might be a burial shroud—while scenes of
violence, rape, and robbery fill the viewer's gaze. Swords are everywhere.
Flanking Tyranny are the vices associated with him: Cruelty, Betrayal, and
Fraud attend on the left; Fury, Division, and finally War to the right. *Di-
visio*'s large carpenter's saw acts as another powerful signifier. Used for
cutting planks from rough timber, it can be worked only by two carpenters, again in a reciprocal, back-and-forth, rhythm: harmony alone can accomplish its task. Here the tool is misused, usurped by a single will, to

ridiculous and pointless effect. The Sienese who viewed the painting would have realized that in the *buon governo* both the saw and the plane must be used together to create the order of a useful and beautiful good from the unshaped and natural state.

On the same wall Lorenzetti painted the *Effects of Bad Government*. Here *Timor,* Fear (see fig. 17a) rules the day, a black and deathlike demon dressed in tattered robe, wielding in one hand a sword and in the other a scroll that reads:

> From the desire for the private good,
> in this land Justice submits to Tyranny,
> so that on this road
> no one passes without the fear of death,
> for he is robbed both inside and outside the gates.

Behind her a countryside lies desolate: brown and uncultivated, sterile except for a few deserted groves and isolated huts. Everywhere collapsing walls, broken arches, empty windows, and cracked doorways summon up the ghostly images of haunted desolation of Maso di Banco's Silvester fresco (see fig. 20). Villages erupt into flames as musters of armed men stream across the countryside looting and burning. *Timor* rushes from a city deserted except for a few soldiers aimlessly dismantling wood and brickwork with their swords and axes. Amid empty shops and streets littered with rubble, only one artisan works: a weapons manufacturer (see fig. 17b). Just outside the gates those unlucky last ones to flee are captured by marauding soldiers (see fig. 17c). As the painting moves to the right, from *historia* to *allegoria,* these scenes are repeated beneath the very throne of Tyranny and the figure of *Guerra* or war.

The Anonimo romano has already given us a vivid description of tyranny. Cola himself was soon to describe the same effects of bad government under the barons, "the depraved and cruel rectors," in a letter of May 24, 1347, to the city of Viterbo:

Justice mortified, peace expelled, liberty prostrate, security stolen away, charity damned, mercy and devotion profaned, to the extent that foreigners and pilgrims, indeed Roman citizens themselves, and our dearest countryfolk and members of our commune could never come nor remain secure in one place without there occurring everywhere, by land and sea, in the most unrestrained manner oppressions, sedition, hostilities and wars, the destruction of livestock, arson inside and outside the walls, with great danger for the holy City itself and the entire province of Rome, with the loss and harm of souls, of goods and bodies, and with no small detriment to the entire Christian faith. (7, BBCR 2.3:17–27, ll. 35–56)

Such condemnations, neither radical nor unheard of for the time, fit the mainstream of Italian political thought and further threw the anarchic behavior of the barons into sharp relief. Three years of highlighting the city's problems, of isolating out the barons as their chief perpetrators, and of offering the Romans a stark comparison between the hopes of good government and the disastrous consequences if the ship of state remained on its present course, now began to yield results.

The placard at San Giorgio in Velabro appeared on the first day of Lent, or February 14, 1347. By the spring Cola had built a viable political movement around him. The Anonimo romano tells us that his support came not from the poor and disenfranchised but from the middle classes: "discreet Roman plebeians and goodmen," as well as from "plebeian knights," that is, from the lower, nonbaronial nobility, and from "many discreet and rich merchants." Cola thus managed to bring together Rome's emerging class of *mercanti, bovattieri,* and *cavallerotti,* the merchants, families who gained their wealth in Rome's cattle market and other trading, and knights of the lower nobility, all of whom made up Rome's *popolo minuto.*[3]

While always a presence in late medieval Rome, by the early fourteenth century these classes, especially the merchants and *bovattieri,* were beginning the supplant the barons in economic and political importance, and they would do so completely by the end of the century. But with the papacy in Avignon these first two groups had suffered serious economic setbacks. With the absence of any strong papal government over the Roman *contado,* the lower nobility, always assured of steady title and position in the papal administration, also felt growing insecurity.

The Anonimo romano and Villani seem to agree that Cola first brought these political groups together at a *parlamento* to discuss the city's condition. Bishop Ildebrandino Conti of Padua stresses that Rienzo was the "author, promoter and mediator" of the movement. He notes that "neither was it a secret affair. Indeed it was known to many barons and in the beginning held in disdain by certain of them." But Cola still waited until he was certain of his power base. He soon called another meeting with "these good and mature people" in the security of "a secret place" on the Aventine. Cola probably chose a smaller group from among the assembly of *mercanti, bovattieri,* and *cavallerotti,* a group that would form the basis of his executive council. Ildebrandino again fills in missing details: Sta. Sabina was the meeting place, near the cell long claimed to be that of St. Dominic himself. The Friday before Pentecost was the day, and the gathering consisted of about one hundred people.

Cola was far from secretive with his co-conspirators. After delivering an emotional speech on Rome's present "misery, servitude, and danger" and of its ancient "peaceful and illustrious government," stressing the need to restore "peace and justice," he revealed what had lain at the heart of his and Pope Clement's campaign for the past three years. Clement had named Cola Notary of the City Chamber and had placed his young ally and agent at the heart of the city's government and finances. Cola had used his position admirably and not only had solidified his own position and made many and powerful allies but also had taken the time to examine the city's records and to prepare a thorough review of Rome's wealth, its sources of revenue, and its methods of taxation. He told the gathering, "Do not worry about money. The Chamber of Rome has many inestimable revenues." What he reported would have been enough to encourage any group of responsible and ambitious citizens. Rome's potential wealth—if we believe Cola's biographer—was immense: nearly 400,000 florins from the city and its *contado*.

Cola's speech was designed to gain the support of his diverse coalition: to the merchants and traders he promised the reform of the city's finances and taxation; to the knights the reestablishment of Roman control over the countryside, a campaign in which they would lead Rome's militia and from which they would regain landed title, office, and wealth. But what Cola then told his companions explained to many where he had gotten the wherewithal to support himself and his campaign for Rome's reform on a salary of only 60 florins a year: "For the present we shall begin with 4,000 florins, which my lord the Pope has sent, with the full knowledge of his vicar." Cola must have sensed the shock, disbelief, and excitement among the conspirators, for then he added, "Gentlemen, do not believe that it is with the permission of the Pope that many citizens do violence to the goods of the Church." The intentions of the pope and his protégé were plain. Emboldened by his words, and by his revelation of papal funding and support, the conspirators heard Rienzo's plans for the restoration of the *buono stato* and then allowed Cola to administer a written oath of allegiance to each of them, binding them to the commune, the *buono stato*.

There was no turning back for the sworn conspirators. Time was passing quickly. It was now mid-May of 1347. The barons were not in Rome. The first harvest of the year was under way. Unlike the labors of the months portrayed on the tympana of French cathedrals and in late medieval books of hours, not June and July but April and May in central Italy are the months of first harvests and threshing. Stefano il Vecchio Colonna had taken the militia to Corneto, the Etruscan Tarquinia, "to gather this grain." The medieval town sits on a ridge overlooking gently sloping fields that meet the Tyrrhenian Sea glimmering to the west. To its north and east stretch the rich agricultural lands that had given the region the name *horreum Urbis,* "Rome's Granary." The town rises above the via Aurelia, about 100 kilometers north and west of the Capitoline, the distance a very fast courier or a ship laden with grain might travel in two days, but which a wagon train laden with grain might take a week to cover. Completing the task of overseeing the harvest and arranging for its transport to Rome was no easy undertaking. Corneto was in revolt against Rome, and the barons were besieging the city. The senatorship for that six-month term was being shared, as usual, by two men from rival baronial families: Bertoldo Orsini and Pietro di Agapito Colonna. But the organization of the expedition fell naturally upon the de facto ruler of Rome, Stefano il Vecchio, Pietro's uncle and the leader of the Colonna clan.[4]

Stefano was one of eleven brothers and sisters, the children of Giovanni Colonna and of an Orsini bride whose first name has not been recorded (see table 1). Born c. 1265, in November 1285 he had married Guacerande di l'Isle-Jourdain, a daughter of the French nobility of the Toulousan and of the Angevin kingdom of Naples, thus becoming lord of fiefs as far south as Calabria and Apulia and also a vassal of the king of Naples. Through this alliance the Colonna received many more fiefs in the Regno in the years to come, worth thousands of florins in annual income. Guacerande and Stefano produced twelve surviving children, including the eldest, Stefanuccio; Cardinal Giovanni, Petrarch's patron and Cola's enemy in Avignon; and Giacomo, the bishop of Lombez, who had died in 1341.

Stefano rose to prominence as the embattled rector of the papal Romagna. In May 1292 he was named one of the two senators of Rome, along with Matteo Orsini. It was Stefano who carried out the infamous attack on Boniface VIII's treasure train on May 3, 1297, that resulted in the condemnation of the Colonna cardinals and a papal crusade against his family, the destruction of Palestrina, and the submission of the leading Colonna to the pope at Rieti. As part of his penance Stefano was sent off on pilgrimage to Santiago de Compostela in Spain and remained in exile for five years, largely in southern France, at Narbonne and Arles. Here Stefano may have met his younger brother Sciarra in the early months of 1303 to hatch with French minister Guillaume de Nogaret Boniface VIII's kidnapping.

Stefano was not at Anagni for that affair, however, and returned to

Rome only after the pope's death. By September 1304 he was serving as papal captain and podesta at Viterbo, and by 1306 he was again senator in Rome. By 1306 Clement V had also lifted Boniface's excommunication of the Colonna and allowed them to rebuild Palestrina; but the war with the Caetani continued, by their own account costing the Caetani 940,000 florins. Having staked out their claim to be the most antipapal family in Italy, the Colonna had every right to claim pro-imperial credentials. Stefano probably commanded a contingent of imperial troops during Henry VII's coronation expedition to Rome in 1312 but seems to have realized that the Colonna's imperial and Ghibelline sympathies were only prolonging the civil strife in the city, and he refused an imperial investiture.

Throughout the 1310s Stefano led his family's war against the Orsini for control of the Campagna; by the 1320s he had shifted his loyalty from the Ghibellines to the Guelphs and the royal house of Naples, allying with Robert the Wise as vicar in Rome. This affiliation put him at risk during Lewis of Bavaria's expedition to Rome in 1327 and at open war against his own brother Sciarra, Lewis's ally in the city. With the naming of his son Giovanni as cardinal, Stefano's alliance with the papacy was solidified, and in March 1328 he attacked the imperialists in Rome with an army of four thousand Angevin troops. Upon the emperor's withdrawal he was welcomed into the city and with Bertoldo Orsini was again named senator. A man of enormous prestige, imposing physical presence, and immense personal authority, Stefano continued to play a central role in Roman politics into his eighties. He served as Angevin royal vicar for Rome in the 1330s, envoy to Avignon, senator again in 1339 and 1342, and official witness to Petrarch's coronation on the Capitoline in 1341. Petrarch places Stefano in his *Triumph of Fame* (II) next to Saladin and Robert of Anjou as "my great Colonna, constant and generous, and of noble heart."

But Stefano and his clan, and most of the barons, were away from Rome that late spring; and so on May 19 Cola acted.[5] Bishop Ildebrandino Conti wrote that throughout Saturday, the day after the meeting on the Aventine, the entire city remained "in suspense." Rienzo had sent a trumpeter throughout Rome summoning the citizens to rally to the *buono stato* at the ringing of the tocsin. At the sound of that bell the citizens were to assemble at the heart of Cola's Rome: the church of Sant'Angelo in Pescheria (see fig. 3). But this was to be a revolution unlike any that Rome had known: for the herald urged the Romans to assemble unarmed.

Cola had chosen no ordinary day in May but the eve of the Pentecost, when the Christian Church celebrates the descent of the Holy Spirit upon Jesus' followers and the new age of grace, the new dispensation that had then transformed the secular world of people and politics. Just so now, Cola would act as a herald to the new age. Not coincidentally, May 19 also marked two important anniversaries in Cola's spiritual world. The first was one widely celebrated, especially among the Spiritual Franciscans, the Fraticelli, and their brethren among Rome's Poor Hermits: the feast day of that most spiritual of popes, Celestine V, canonized by Clement V in 1313. The second marked the anniversary of the coronation of that most worldly of popes and Cola's own patron: Clement VI, crowned by Napoleone Orsini on Pentecost Sunday, 1342. And so in the church of the Holy Angel, in the night and early morning of Pentecost Sunday, May 20, 1347, beginning at midnight, Cola heard thirty masses of the Holy Spirit in preparation for his new role. By "mid-tierce," that is, late enough in the morning of Pentecost Sunday for all of Rome to have heard of his all-night vigil and to have responded to the trumpet and the bell, he and his co-conspirators were ready.

It was the morning of May 20. Cola di Rienzo emerged from the church like the angel in his fresco there: a knight in full armor. Then behind him, from the darkness of the church, there emerged twenty-five companions, also armed. Cola knew how to rouse the public and to begin a mass demonstration: by the time Cola's group emerged from Sant'Angelo, it was already shouting his slogans and rallying calls. Ildebrandino reports that a hasty attempt was made to squash the demonstration, but it proved unsuccessful. A procession quickly formed amid the throng of sympathizers and onlookers. The model was that of Italy's lay religious confraternities and of the Flagellants. At the head of the procession marched three "men of his conspiracy" carrying banners, *gonfaloni*. Cola Guallato, known as a good public speaker, carried the first: large, red with gold lettering, bearing an image of Rome as the ancient city goddess seated on her throne. On either side of her a lion; in her left hand the orb of the world; and in her right, the palm of victory. "This was the banner of Liberty," the *Anonimo* records. Guallato is Romanesco for Vallati, a family of the lower nobility with a long presence in the *rione* Sant'Angelo. They possessed a small palazzo that was built in the fourteenth century and still stands, and a very small chapel in Sant'Angelo in Pescheria, where a Francesco Vallati was a canon in 1327. A Lello Vallati was still active in the reform of the commune in 1358. Next came Stefaniello, called Magnacuccia, like Cola a professional notary. He carried a white *gonfalone*, and on it was the image of St. Paul, holding both his sword and a crown of justice. The third conspirator, unnamed by the *Anonimo*, carried the banner of St. Peter, holding his usual attribute, the keys. Here these also represented concord and peace.

And then, probably also because Cola had long ago also enlisted the members of a confraternity dedicated to him, most likely from the nearby church of San Giorgio in Velabro, there came a fourth conspirator bearing the banner of St. George. As was normal, St. George (like St. Michael) was dressed as a *cavaliere,* slaying the dragon, the symbol of the apocalyptic beast, and rescuing a woman representing the Ecclesia Romana. The banner was the one made for Cardinal Jacopo Stefaneschi in 1295 and carried in the processionals of Boniface VIII. Because of its great age it had been housed and carried in a glass case. The banner has survived and is now housed in the Sala delle Bandiere in the Palazzo Senatorio on the Capitoline.

What happened next must have further amazed the crowd pressing in on either side of the procession: for Cola was joined openly by Raymond de Chameyrac, bishop of Orvieto since 1346 and the papal vicar in the city. The Anonimo romano, who could have discussed these events with Cola or those close to him before he wrote, records that though "still somewhat fearful, Cola gathered his courage and set out." The goal of the procession was quite close—the Capitoline and the Senators' Palace. The sources agree on the sense among the people: the shouting of Cola's own soldiers became general as the procession reached the palace, for even Villani records the *"grida di popolo,"* the popular clamor that pushed Cola and his companions forward. The Senators' Palace atop the Capitoline stood directly above the route. The chanting and the cheering of the crowd along the sidelines must have confirmed what the senators' spies had told them: all of Rome was on the march and aiming for the palace. Cola himself, writing years later to Emperor Charles IV in Prague, records that "the senators of the houses of Orsini and Colonna, who then shared rule, fled the palace. As a result, on the same day, all the Roman barons without exception were expelled far from the City solely by the lion's roar of the people. As all the people cried out in praise, I ascended the Capitoline and restored the glory of the ancient tribunate" (50, BBCR 2.3:204, ll. 203–7).

By the time the procession reached the summit, Cola had a force of about one hundred armed supporters. But arms were of no importance that day: all Rome had turned out, and the Capitoline was overflowing with people. Cola mounted a speaker's platform that stood in front of the Senators' Palace (see fig. 6). There he delivered a speech on "the misery and servitude of the people of Rome. He said that he was exposing his person to danger for the love of the pope and the salvation of the people of Rome" (AR, XVIII, ll. 343–45, Porta, 154).

The Romans who filled the piazza and listened were no longer a passive mob, the victims or subjects of the barons, but now the agents and writers of their own history, the people of Rome restored to their proper place, mingling among friends, neighbors, and strangers, all sharing the same sense of rebirth and renewal.[6] Cola himself, in his first official letters, to Viterbo and to the cities of Italy, on May 24 and June 7, was to call the people's assembly, "its public and most solemn parliament." The Romans had accomplished what no German emperor could: they had retaken the city torn apart by the strife of arms and the endless cycle of bloodletting and had put an end to violence, without violence. So Cola himself understood the event. Four days later he wrote to the commune of Viterbo that his and the Romans' actions were taken "through the inspiration of the Holy Spirit. . . . Although we recognize that our own shoulders are too incapable and weak to bear the weight of such a burden, we also most openly realize that by the Lord this has been done, and it is wonderful in our eyes" (7, BBCR 2.3:16–27, ll. 94–96, 114–20).

The quotation from Matthew 21:42–44 was unmistakable. In the messianic parable of the vinedressers, the owner of a vineyard sends his servants to receive the grapes from his tenants, but the tenant vinedressers beat these and more of his servants and send them off. Finally the lord sends his son, trusting that they will respect him. But the vinedressers decide to kill the son and take his inheritance.

When Jesus asks his disciples what the owner will do upon his return to the vineyard, the apostles reply:

"He will utterly destroy those evil men, and will let out the vineyard to other vinedressers, who will render to him the fruits in their seasons." Jesus said to them, "Did you never read in the Scriptures [Ps. 117:2, Is. 28:16]:

'The stone which the builders rejected,
has become the corner stone;
By the Lord this has been done,
and it is wonderful in our eyes'?

Therefore I say to you, that the kingdom of God will be taken away from you and will be given to a people yielding its fruits. And he who falls on this stone will be broken to pieces; but upon whomever it falls, it will grind him to powder."

Cola's identification with the rejected stone, the young son of the taverner mocked and threatened by the barons, is clear. So is the apocalyptic sense of the return of the Lord to his vineyard and of final justice. Now

Cola has become the cornerstone of the new republic, the kingdom of God wrested from the barons and given to a new people. Cola's profound knowledge of Christian Scripture and his familiarity with classical history deepen his imagery: for it was here, upon the Tarpeian Rock of the Capitoline, below which his procession had just passed, that traitors to the ancient Republic were cast down and "broken to pieces."

Sometime after Cola's founding the *buono stato* and the flight of the barons from the city, he and the papal vicar appeared before an assembly to ask for confirmation of their acts and for the approval of new titles for himself and Bishop Raymond: "Tribunes of the People and Liberators." The contemporary *Chronicon Estense* remarks that Cola was elected tribune by "divine providence" and that "the Roman people confirmed his government of the said city." Whether or not he later asked for the people's approval, Cola seems to have had adopted his titles from the very beginning of the revolution. In his first letter to the city of Viterbo on May 24, 1347, four days after Pentecost, and in his circular letter to the major powers of Italy dated June 7, 1347, Cola employs the honorary titles that he would use throughout his tribunate: "Nicholas the severe and the clement, tribune of liberty, peace and justice and liberator of the sacred Roman republic."

Amy Schwarz has noted that, in addition to his readings in Livy (II.33–34) and other classics, Cola's sources for the ancient tribunate might have included the medieval French historical cycle on Roman themes known as *Li Fets des Romains,* which used such sources as Sallust, Caesar, Suetonius, and Lucan and which explained how the Senate had appointed Caesar military tribune. An Italian translation of the work was written in Romanesco during the reign of Martin IV (1282) and called *Liber Ystoriarum Romanorum* or *Storie de Troja et de Roma.* A manuscript survives that also provided a series of vivid illustrations (fig. 21). This manuscript once belonged to Senator Pandolfo Savelli. Francesco Savelli may well have made it available to his retainer and neighbor, Cola di Rienzo.

Cola's intent in restoring the tribunate was clear: the people would now have their own head, elected by those who, like the ancient Roman plebeians, had sworn their oath of allegiance atop the Aventine. And he would be a man of the people: the senatorial class was to be excluded from power. In addition to the military meaning, there was yet another meaning of the term that Cola could well have known. Gregory the Great had written in his *Exposition on 1 Kings* that "tribunes can also be understood as spiritual men *(spirituales viri),* simple in earthly knowledge, but inflamed by the love of God and their neighbors." Thus Cola would again conflate ancient Roman republicanism, the traditions of Christian Rome, and the apocalyptic connotations of the "spiritual men."

Writing from Avignon in June 1347, immediately after he had received news of the revolution in Rome, Francesco Petrarch congratulated and encouraged his friend and the rest of the Roman people by comparing Cola's action to that of the first Brutus who overthrew the rule of Rome's ancient tyrants:[7]

He was Consul, you are Tribune. If we compared the two offices we would find that the consuls performed many acts hostile to the welfare of the Roman plebs; indeed—and I will speak out bravely—they often treated it harshly and cruelly. But the tribunes were always and constantly the defenders of the people. If then that consul slew his own sons because of his love of liberty, realize what is expected in all circumstances from you as a tribune. (*Variae* 48 [Hortatoria], BBCR 2.3:63–81; CRCR, 9–24, at p. 17)

And now the Roman people stood atop the Capitoline as they listened to Cola's words, watched him, the pope's vicar, and the other leaders at the rostrum. Receiving the powers granted to medieval emperors during their journeys to Rome, Cola used them to reestablish the Roman republic. He had reconfirmed powers that the original commune of 1143 had seized from its overlord, the bishop of Rome, and he had ended the long century of rule by the barons acting as the "senators" of the pope. The *buono stato* had been born and with it, it seemed that day, the good new age of the Holy Spirit.

FIGURE 1. Castel Sant'Angelo and Tiber bend, c. 1495. The view shows the heavy fortifications around the Vatican Borgo and the stream of pilgrims across the Ponte Sant'Angelo. The Castel was a major fortress of the Orsini del Monte in the fourteenth century. Note the sculpture of St. Michael atop its tower. Codex Escurialensis. 28.II.12, fol. 26v. Escorial. Biblioteca del Monasterio. Copyright © Patrimonio Nacional.

FIGURE 2. Floating mills on the Tiber, looking downstream to Ponte Fabricio between the sandy hillock of the Arenula (*left*) and the Tiber Island (*right*), c. 1495. Towers, largely truncated, still dominate the skyline. Codex Escurialensis. 28.II.12, fol. 27v. Escorial. Biblioteca del Monasterio. Copyright © Patrimonio Nacional.

FIGURE 3. Sant'Angelo in Pescheria, drawing by Jan Miel, c. 1650. The market uses the ancient arcade of the Portico of Octavia. The medieval campanile rises behind it. Musée du Louvre, Départment des Arts Graphiques, inv. 22700. Copyright © Réunion des Musées Nationaux/Art Resource, NY.

FIGURE 4. Apocalyptic Christ, *majestas*, Anagni Cathedral crypt, Chapel of St. Magnus, c. 1250. Many of the standard symbols are present: the sword issuing from Christ's mouth, the seven stars in his hand, the seven angels, and the seven candlesticks around the mandorla. Istituto Centrale per il Catalogo e la Documentazione. Ministero per i Beni e le Attività Culturali. Rome.

FIGURE 5. Santa Maria in Aracoeli from the Campidoglio market, drawing by Marten van Heemskerck, c. 1535. The 1348 stairway is on the left but is hidden by the retaining wall. Staatliche Museen zu Berlin–Preussischer Kulturbesitz, Kupferstichkabinett. Photo: Joerg P. Anders.

FIGURE 6. Senators' Palace, c. 1300, isometric drawings by Mario Melis, 1959. The bell tower is on the left. The place of the Lion is just to the left of the entrance ramps. The walls show the coats of arms of Rome's barons. From Carlo Pietrangeli, "Il palazzo Senatorio nel Medioevo," *Capitolium* 35 (1960): 3–19.

FIGURE 7. Colonna Palace on the Quirinal, the ancient Temple of Serapis, drawing by
Marten van Heemskerck, c. 1535. *Spolia*—fragments of statuary, columns, a trabeated loggia of ancient columns, and architrave embedded into the ancient ruins—lend the palace
dignity and pedigree. Museum Kunst Palast, Sammlung der Kunstakademie (NRW),
Düsseldorf.

FIGURE 8. Arch of Constantine, c. 315. The arch remained a rich archive of graphic information on ancient Rome, from inscriptions to costume and insignia to scenes of imperial ceremony. C 5124. Istituto Centrale per il Catalogo e la Documentazione. Ministero per i Beni e le Attività Culturali. Rome.

FIGURE 9. St. John Lateran, north portal with Palace wing, equestrian statue of Marcus Aurelius, Loggia di Benedizione, and piazza, drawing by Marten van Heemskerck, c. 1535. Staatliche Museen zu Berlin–Preussischer Kulturbesitz, Kupferstichkabinett. Photo: Joerg P. Anders.

FIGURE 10. *Left.* Portrait of Petrarch, from his *De viris illustribus,* c. 1375. Paris, Bibliothèque Nationale. MS Latin 6069 F. Cliché Bibliothèque Nationale de France, Paris.

FIGURE 11. *Bottom left.* Portrait of Cola di Rienzo, late fourteenth century. From Edward P. Cheyney, *The Dawn of a New Era, 1250–1453.* New York: Harper and Row, 1936, fig. 22.

FIGURE 12. *Bottom right.* Portrait of Clement VI, from Bartolomeo da Urbino's *Milleloquium Sancti Augustini.* Paris, Bibliothèque Nationale, Ms, Lat. 2120, fol. 1r. Cliché Bibliothèque Nationale de France, Paris.

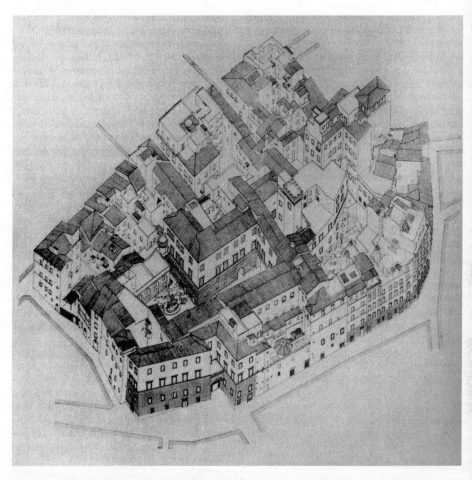

FIGURE 13. Monte Giordano, c. 1950, isometric drawing by M. P. F. Asso. A complete urban complex or *fortilizia*—including palace, fortifications, towers, chapels, *cortili*, shops, stables, and living quarters—this was the chief residence of the Orsini del Monte in the fourteenth century. From M. F. P. Asso, "Monte Giordano," *Quaderni dell' Istituto di Storia dell'Architettura* I (1953): 12–15, and figs. 19–20.

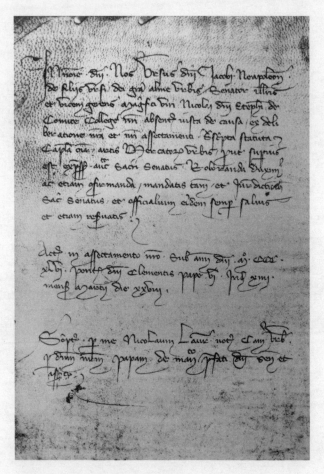

FIGURE 14. Document dated March 28, 1346, in the name
of Senator Orso de Jacobi Napoleone Orsini confirming
Rome's Statutes of the Merchants, drawn up and signed by
Cola di Rienzo as Notary of the City Chamber. Giuseppe
Gatti, ed. *Statuti dei Mercanti di Roma,* tab. II.

FIGURE 15. Ambrogio Lorenzetti, *Allegory of Good Government*, Palazzo Pubblico, Siena, c. 1339. A. Concord; B. Peace; C. Common Good; D. Justice. Copyright Scala/Art Resource, NY.

FIGURE 16. Ambrogio Lorenzetti, *Good Government in the City and Countryside*, Palazzo Pubblico, Siena, c. 1339. Detail. A. Dance of Harmony; B. Securitas. Copyright Scala/Art Resource, NY.

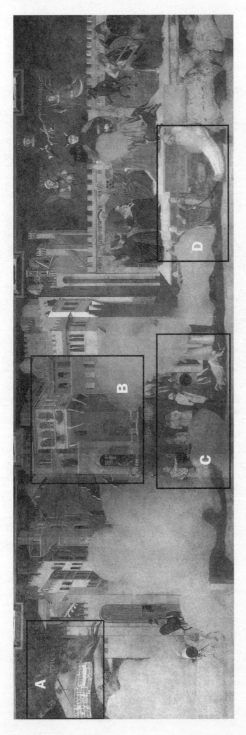

FIGURE 17. Ambrogio Lorenzetti, *Bad Government in the City and Countryside*, Palazzo Pubblico, Siena, c. 1339. Detail. A. Timor; B. Soldiers and arms maker; C. Refugees at the gate; D. Justice bound. Copyright Scala/Art Resource, NY.

FIGURE 18. Giotto, *Navicella* mosaic, c. 1300; engraving by Nicholas Beatrizet, c. 1559.

FIGURE 19. Rome as an aged widow. From the *Panegyric to Robert of Anjou from the Citizens of Prato*, c. 1335. British Library. Ms Royal 6.E.IX, fol. 11v. By permission of the British Library.

FIGURE 20. Maso di Banco, *The Legend of St. Silvester,* fresco, Bardi di Vernio Chapel, Santa Croce, Florence, c. 1340. Copyright Scala/Art Resource, NY.

FIGURE 21. Triumph of Caesar. From *Storie de Troja et de Roma*. Hamburg, Staatsbibliothek, Cod. 151, fol. 90v. c. 1282. Used by permission.

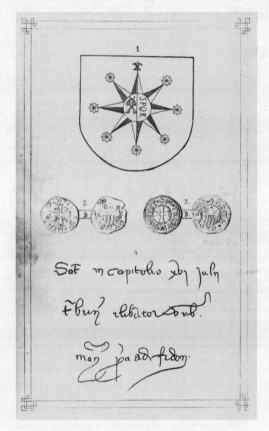

FIGURE 22. Coat of arms, coinage, and signature of Cola di Rienzo. From Felix Papencordt, *Cola di Rienzo und sein Zeit* (Hamburg: A. Perthes, 1841), appendices.

FIGURE 23. Porta San Lorenzo, engraving from Giuseppe Vasi, *Delle Magnificenze di Roma Antica e Moderna*, book 1 (Rome: Chracas, 1747).

FIGURE 24. Emperor Charles IV giving and receiving relics. Karlstejn, Chapel of the
Virgin Mary, c. 1357. *From left:* Charles IV and Charles V of France; Charles IV with Peter,
king of Cyprus and Jerusalem; Charles IV as Emperor of the Last Days, preparing to lay
down his crown in Jerusalem. By permission of National Institute for Monument Care,
Prague, Czech Republic. Photo © Iva Tuhácklová.

CHAPTER 8

The *Buono Stato*

> Then Cola had a document read containing the Ordinances
> of the *buono stato*. Conte, the son of Cecco Mancino, read
> them briefly. . . . The people were extremely pleased with it;
> they all raised their voices high and with great joy they voted
> that he remain lord there in union with the pope's vicar. They
> also gave him license to punish, execute, pardon, to remove
> from position, to make laws and pacts with peoples, and to set
> boundaries of communities. They also gave him unhindered
> and free imperial power as far as the [jurisdiction] of the people
> of Rome extended.
>
> Anonimo romano, XVIII, ll. 345–404, Porta, 154–56

Cola and his supporters knew that for the revolution to succeed and the
renewed commune to survive, they not only must promulgate a new constitution but also must form new institutions to embody their ideals. They
also must spread the news of Rome's rebirth far afield both to gain practical support and to fulfill the promise embodied in their attempt to renew the world. Cola and his supporters had been working and preparing for months. Now "in their season," they produced the first fruit of
their labors: the proclamation of the Ordinances of the *buono stato*.[1] It
was a natural first step and one eminently suited to a city and a people
that had lost all sense of civic life and mutual trust, the basis of a new urban culture.

Like most of Cola's political changes, the new Ordinances brought
Rome back into the mainstream of contemporary Italian communes. Al-

though the Anonimo romano chose to record only "a few of their titles" and seems to have listed them in no particular order, fifteen of the articles survive. We can get some idea of the 1347 constitution by examining an earlier set of ordinances from 1305 and the later set from about 1363 that incorporates the first. But the Ordinances of 1347 are less important for the minute details of regulation than for the broad principles of government that they embody, for they also contain most of the powers set forth by the tablet of the *lex de imperio Vespasiani* that Cola had interpreted for Rome's rulers at the Lateran.[2] This is not to say, however, that Cola sought to assume imperial rule. More to the point of the Ordinances and of his repeated statements to the pope: he and the Romans had reasserted claim to the powers of Rome, and not of any one individual, whether emperor, pope, or tribune.

We can group the Ordinances themselves into several distinct categories. Each of these reflects one of the chief aspects of Italian *buon governo*. The first group—articles 1, 2, 3, and 15—deals specifically with issues of legal justice: capital punishment and rules of evidence and accusation, civil litigation, and a prohibition that "no house in Rome should be torn down for any reason, but should become the Commune's."

The second group—articles 4, 6, 8, 9, 10, 13, and 14—brings together ordinances that sought to reform the city's armed forces and general security: rional levies and pay levels of the urban militia, both horse and foot; compensation for death in combat; protection of waterways and shores, along with travel and commerce; the city's direct control over "castles, bridges, ports, gates, and fortresses" and the stripping from the barons of control over these, and the District of Rome's cities and lands; the confiscation of their *fortilizie;* the barons' draft into public service as guardians of roads and a specific prohibition against their harboring enemies of the commune.

The fourth article reestablished the standard communal practice of maintaining a public army, drawn from the citizenry within each *rione,* and not made up of the barons' feudal retainers.[3] Both infantry and cavalry were to be funded by the public treasury, again a deep blow to the feudal system of largess and plunder practiced by the barons, ultimately at the public's expense. The force is also substantial: 1,400 infantry and 350 cavalry as a standing militia, excluding the emergency musters that were a frequent aspect of Italian communal life.

The ordinances also indicate that the *buono stato* anticipated armed resistance from the barons. Citizens killed in battle were to receive full compensation from the commune's treasury (the *paga morta* of cities like

Venice, for example), thus rewarding public service and undermining the private loyalties of the *cavallerotti*. The Ordinances also took the bold stroke of stripping the barons of their strategic hold on the city. They were to give up their fortified strongholds within Rome, but outside its walls and in the *contado* they were to act not as feudal lords over fiefs and demesnes but as civil servants keeping roads secure and guaranteeing the safe provisioning of the city and the peace and security of the country-side. (see fig. 16). The *buono stato* intended to make good its promises to the *cavallerotti* to retake effective control of cities and lands within the Roman district.

Finally, a series of ordinances—articles 5, 7, 11, and 12—dealt with the role of the civil government in ensuring the life of Christian virtue and works of mercy, what modern historians have termed "civic religion." Articles 5 and 11 (aid to orphans and widows; public support of religious houses) were probably only two of several that spelled out the role of the commune in guaranteeing the support of the Christian life, maintaining a long-standing tradition of public assistance to the needy, such as those in Florence administered through its confraternities and in its patronage of the city's religious institutions. Article 12 (the establishment of granaries in each *rione*) had a venerable tradition within Rome: the provision of grain had been a primary function of government since the ancient republic; and the *stationes annonae,* or grain stations, were among the first imperial responsibilities assumed by Rome's bishops from Gregory the Great on. Cola thus reasserted the civil role of government and devolved many of its powers back to the *rioni*.

Article 7 legislated what Cola had promised his supporters on the Aventine: that the vast resources of Rome's taxes, both its direct hearth taxes and its indirect taxes, or *gabelle,* would be devoted not to the private coffers and interests of the barons but to the public good. "The hearth tax pays four [soldi] per fire," or 4s per household, "from the Ponte di Ceperano all the way to the Ponte della Paglia," that is, from the southern to the northern boundaries of the District of Rome.[4] "This totals 100,000 florins," as Cola had revealed to the members of the *buono stato*.

How realistic were Cola's claims? The city of Rome certainly had the traditional authority to levy such taxes, They were first mentioned in 877 under Emperor Charles the Bald, but there is little evidence for their existence until the twelfth century. It was not until the reign of Brancaleone in the mid–thirteenth century that these revenues became a steady base of Roman government. Throughout the thirteenth century popes and communes struggled over their authority to raise and spend these funds; and by 1284 Pope Martin IV had appointed a special *camerarius* in charge of receipts and expenditures for the district. Cola's promises of revenue are hard to substantiate. Even if economic historians could agree on the true equivalents of the currency values he discusses, they would still have to accept a standard multiplier for the average household size in fourteenth-century Lazio. Even then, estimates of the total number of households (hearths, fires, *focolari*) in Lazio during Cola's age have varied from about 32,500 to about 72,500. Tallies of the district's population using salt-tax records of the City Chamber—from 1416, for example—range from 200,000 to 500,000.

But Cola's speech also reflected a new trend in the Italian city-states: the replacement of declining hearth-tax revenues with a whole new series of forced loans, *prestanze,* and indirect taxes called *gabelle.* These were developed quite early in the history of the communes, but they grew dramatically as military threat, rising poverty, famine, and debt repayment began to overtake the free communes at the end of the thirteenth century. Passed by communal councils more and more frequently through the fourteenth century, they included a wide variety of sales and exchange taxes on a host of items and transactions ranging from salt to contracts, from livestock to wine in the cask and in bottles, to passage through a city's gates. In Florence Villani lists thirty *gabelle* for 1338; and between 1340 and 1360 these taxes reached an unprecedented level as a result of stresses on the commune. The *dazi* levied by the Venetian senate fill its records during this period. The urban population reacted to these impositions with a variety of tactics ranging from fraud and noncompliance, to removal of businesses outside the city walls, to pleas of poverty, to organized demonstrations, protests, and riots. Such consumption taxes were regressive in nature: falling hardest on those least able to pay: small businesspeople, wage earners, and the unemployed, for whom these expenses represented a far greater proportion of their total incomes.

But revenues there were, waiting to be collected. "Again, from the salt tax," Cola noted, "100,000 florins; also from the gates of Rome and the castles of Rome 100,000 florins; and from the tariff on livestock and from penalty fines 100,000 florins." Considering that John XXII had spent 2,390,433 florins on Italian wars in the decade between 1321 and 1331, total potential revenues of 400,000 florins a year were large indeed, larger than those of Florence, with an urban population of almost one hundred thousand. But even if Cola exaggerated their potential—Rome's population could only have been about thirty thousand—they were certainly large enough not only to guarantee the city's security and the safe passage of people and goods through its territory but also to actively go about aiding its needy, supporting its religious institutions and their buildings, preparing for the Jubilee, and funding Cola's *buono stato*. In his letter to Pope Clement VI of July 8, 1347, Cola claimed that he had already, barely a month after taking power, raised the revenues of the salt tax to 30,000 florins a year; and the hearth tax, which "thanks to the good rectors had been uncollected and abandoned," had gone from 26 denarii "of the old money" to 1 carlin 4 denarii, or 52 denarii of Provins, double the old amount. By reorganizing regular taxation, Cola told the pope, he was also able to reduce or eliminate most toll, gate, and passage taxes. All this, he said, had been done with the approval of the taxpayers, since they recognized that the revenues were going to the public treasury and not to the profit of the barons. The tribune's fiscal reforms were so popular with the Romans that they would be enshrined in the Statutes of 1363.

To many over the years between Cola's return from Avignon and his reestablishment of the commune, the *buono stato* must have seemed little more than an empty political slogan.[5] It had been used in Lazio as recently as 1293 in Ninfa, for example, to describe the hostile takeover of that commune by the Colonna. It was a common expression of governance in Venice from the 1330s on. In his letter to Cola of August 9, 1343, Pope Clement expressed the purpose of Cola's embassy and return to Rome as the formulaic *pro bono et pacifico statu Urbis predicte in melius reformando,* "on behalf of the reform for the better of the good and peaceful condition of the said City." But neither papal political writing, dependent on a long tradition of imperial and church theory and ancient Roman law, nor the relatively new discourse of the Italian communes had ever used the phrase *"buono stato"* in Cola's sense. Instead, the communes had used the language that we have seen in Lorenzetti's painting of the *buon governo* in Siena or in the political theory of Remigio de' Girolami: the good commune *(buon comune)* as the manifestation of the common good, peace and concord, justice and tranquillity.[6]

Political theory in the early Middle Ages had spoken of government in the Augustinian terms of *civitas* or the Carolingian *respublica christiana, societas* or, during the Investiture Conflict as a *regnum* as opposed to *sacerdotium.* With the twelfth century and the revival of ancient political theory through the rediscovery of Aristotle and his Christianizing by Thomas Aquinas, a whole new vocabulary became available to describe an autonomous secular government. Though translated as "state" by modern students, Aquinas's terms *civitas, civilitas, communitas,* and *bonum com-*

munem derived more from his Italian communal culture than from his sources in Aristotle's *Politics*. Only when comparing forms of this *civitas* would Aquinas employ a phrase such as *status popularis,* not to mean a "people's state" but a government in a popular *mode* of governance, with the emphasis of *status* placed upon the condition of the government, and not the government itself. This is also the sense in which it appears in contemporary Venetian senate records describing the condition of Venice's maritime empire. That commune preferred such terms as *regimen* or *dominium* when describing its actual government and its operation. Even when distinguishing monarchic from democratic governments, Aquinas contrasted the *regimen regale* to the *regimen politicum,* a term he invented to match the new reality of the communes.

Such usage remained constant and consistent throughout the fourteenth century in the writings of Bartolo da Sassoferrato, Remigio de' Girolami, Dante, Marsiglio of Padua, and William of Ockham. Giovanni Villani would describe events in Florence in the language of the communes: words like *signoria, giustizia, sicurtà, comune, popolo minuto,* and even *imperio* still speak the language of Lorenzetti's *Buon Governo.*[7] Political theory had to await Nicolò Machiavelli's coining of the Italian term *stato* in his *Prince* (1516) and *Discourses* (1519, published 1531); not until 1538 does the word first appear in English with anything like the meaning of the modern "state."

Why, then, did Cola, or the Anonimo romano after him, choose to describe his government in terms of *stato* and not *governo* or *regimen*? One can find several precedents for Cola's slogan in his classical reading: of Cicero's *De republica* and Valerius Maximus (4.1.4), for example, and more immediate sources in Dante (*Paradiso* 16.46–51). In this classical tradition the term *status* is most often used not as a substantive thing in itself but as a descriptive of something else, as in *status rei publicae,* "the condition of the republic."

Status was also the widely accepted term used by Joachim of Fiore and subsequent Joachite writers to describe not a political state but a moral condition tied to the passage of historical time, the gradual progression of sacred history. Thus in the religious sense *status* is not exactly our sense of a time period. That idea remained best transmitted by the Latin term *aetas* so widely used in the medieval Augustine tradition. *Status,* on the other hand, was understood more appropriately as "age" in the sense of a progressive step, a stage in a ongoing process of salvation, a position in time that also connotes the moral and religious "status" of the people who would come to the fore within it. The Franciscan Spirituals, poets such as Dante, even the king of Naples, Robert of Anjou, were familiar with this usage.

While we have no evidence of any contacts between Cola and Petrarch after the latter's departure from Avignon in September 1343 and Cola's revolution in May 1347, when the news reached him at Avignon, Petrarch sent Cola and the Romans a congratulatory oration, the *Hortatoria* (*Variae* 48, dated June 24–27, 1347). Cola's act has brought new life to the Romans: "You seem to have awakened at last from your heavy sleep," the poet laureate tells them. He then introduces elements that relate Cola's *buono stato* to historical progressions that secularize both the concordances of Joachim's three ages and his notion of a "double progression":[8]

There are now three named Brutus celebrated in history. The first exiled the proud Tarquin [to establish the first age of the Roman republic]; the second slew Julius Caesar [to revive the decayed republic]; the third [Rienzo] has brought exile and death to the tyrants of our own age. Our third Brutus, then, equals both the others because in his own person he had united the causes of the double glory that the other two divided between them. (*Variae* 48, *Hortatoria,* CRCR, 13)

Roman reform proceeds not along the lines of the *buon comune* but along grand historical axes, through great acts worthy of the progress of Roman history from grandeur, to decline and sleep, to reawakening.

Thus Cola's *buono stato* seems to have taken up contemporary meanings of the condition of good government but to have joined them with the rich connotations of religious renewal and reform. Rienzo leaves no doubt that he is thinking in terms of a new age. On July 1, in his letter to Giovanni de Randazzo, the son and viceroy of Frederick II of Sicily, Cola uses a new dating element— *liberate rei publice anno primo,* "In Year One of the liberated Republic"—that breaks with both dating systems used in papal correspondence: the regnal year and the Roman kalends.

Along with Cola's first diplomatic letters to the communes and princes of Italy, his diplomatic couriers also bore one of his powerful visual symbols. This was the new coat of arms he had devised for the *buono stato,* and which he had placed prominently on the wall of the Senators' Palace facing the market square and the Aracoeli. It was still in place when Teodor Amayden (1586–1656) described it in his *Storia delle Famiglie Romane* (1:316–18). A distorted image of the arms has survived in a manuscript drawing (fig. 22). At the center of this new emblem an orb is equally divided into two fields. The right half bears the SPQR, ancient emblem of the Senate and People of Rome, readopted by the first commune in 1143, and the left bears the crossed keys of the papacy. The orb forms the

center of an eight-pointed star, much like a modern compass rose, with
the fleur-de-lis at the top, and on each of the other seven points a star.
While there is some evidence that this was a device used by Boethius
Severus, the philosopher and consul of Rome (d. 524) who was a hero to
Cola, the seven stars are also a rich Christian symbol, carrying strong apocalyptic resonance. In the Anonimo romano's description, moreover, the
figure at the top is not a fleur-de-lis but a dove holding an olive branch
in its beak. The figure is the redolent symbol of the Holy Spirit and as
such was also associated repeatedly with such apocalyptic movements as
that of Venturino da Bergamo.

Thus, when the Romans listened to Cola's speeches and helped him
form his *buono stato,* they probably had in mind something far closer to
"the good New Age" than anything a straightforward translation like
"good state" or "good estate" could ever provide. The *buono stato* not only
described the reform of the city of Rome and its government but also set
Rome apart as something special in the world of the Italian commune:
not a simple *regimen,* or even a *buon governo* or a *buon comune,* but a sacred city that recalled both the ancient *status* of the Roman republic and
looked forward to the new *status* that Joachim and his followers had
predicted. The *buono stato* thus found its origins in both Roman history
and medieval apocalyptic thought; while its mission of reform and renewal brought the ideals of the medieval *buon governo* to a new level of
self-awareness and high purpose. More than a simple political slogan and
the rallying cry of Cola's four-year campaign to topple the barons, the
buono stato also described and enshrined the politics of the new age.

But Cola and his new government must first attend to the chief priority
of the *buono stato:* peace and justice. The initial threat to the renewed commune came from where anyone might expect it.[9] Stefano Colonna heard
the news of Cola's uprising while at Corneto and thundered off toward
Rome with a small band of retainers. The via Aurelia, along the coast, was
the shortest route, about one hundred kilometers. It must have taken him
nearly two days, up and down the rolling hillsides along the coast, then
south and east. He probably arrived at the gates of Rome on or around
May 22. The imposing patriarch of the Colonna clan, by now about eighty-
two years old, was accustomed to command, and he had both the personal authority and the might of the Colonna and their allies to back him
up. He rode confidently to the heart of the Colonna section of Rome, Piazza San Marcello, on the via del Corso just north of the Palazzo Colonna,
and announced "that he did not like what had happened." Stefano prob-

ably then retired to one of the Colonna *fortilizie* in the neighborhood to await Cola's arrival. But neither Rienzo nor an answer came.

Instead, Cola let the sun set on the baron's anger and early the next morning sent the old man an edict banishing him from Rome. Stefano flew into a rage and "took the note and tore it into a thousand pieces, saying, 'If this madman provokes me any further I'll have him thrown out of the windows of the Campidoglio.'" Cola had anticipated Stefano's reaction. As soon as the news reached him on the Capitoline, he had the tocsin rung and the members of the *buono stato* turned out. As the militia gathered, Stefano realized that Cola had the force to back up his words. Alone, and apparently deserted by one and all in the city, Stefano suddenly felt what he had not felt in years: fear for his life. "Signore Stefano mounted his horse. Alone, with only a footman, he sped out of Rome." Stefano had one thing in mind: the protection that only his family could give. He headed directly for the Porta Tiburtina. "In great grief, he stopped for a bit at San Lorenzo fuori le Mura to eat some bread" and then continued quickly out along the via Tiburtina, an easy day's ride to the safety of the Colonna lands and the family's newly rebuilt fortress at Palestrina.

At Palestrina the elder Stefano found both his son Stefanuccio and his grandson Giovanni. The old man recounted the events of the past few days, but it is impossible to tell how much the other Colonna already knew. Had they been in the city on May 20, along with their cousin Pietro, Agapito's son, one of the two senators who fled the Campidoglio on news of the revolution? The Anonimo romano recounts only that the "old trooper poured out his grievances to his son and his grandson." At Cola, too, perhaps; but if he caught himself in self-pity, the venerable and heroic figure must have soon recovered, turning his "laments" into upbraiding his son and the rest of his family for their inactivity and lack of nerve.

Meanwhile, Cola pressed his advantage on the news of Stefano Colonna's flight. "And so, Cola di Rienzo sent commands to all the barons of Rome that they leave the City and go to their castles; and that they did immediately." The following day all the bridges within the city's circuit were surrendered to the commune; effective control now lay with the *buono stato*. Dispersed and downhearted, the barons roamed outside the walls. Petrarch wrote quickly to warn Cola and the Romans against allowing the wolves back in: "They now thirst equally for the blood of both the flock and the shepherd."

The barons attempted to hatch a plot against the new government, but they lacked that essential virtue of any good commune: *"non fuoro in con-*

cordia," they were not in concord and, in fact, were mired in *discordia*. Cola got wind of the conspiracy and took the bold stroke of summoning them to the Capitoline. The move must have been as stunning to the disunited barons as it had been to Stefano il Vecchio the day he had ridden alone into Rome, but they obeyed. The first to arrive was Stefanuccio Colonna, the eldest son of Stefano il Vecchio, born at Palestrina around 1300 and therefore Cola's senior by many years.[10] This younger Stefano had served as royal vicar of Rome for Robert of Naples in 1332 and seems to have been the leader of the Colonna war against the Orsini in the 1330s, which ended only with the truce arranged by the papal legate Bertrand de Déaulx in the fall of 1337. As a result of this agreement, Stefano the Younger was invited to Avignon in March 1338 and awarded the coveted Golden Rose. Stefanuccio returned to Avignon in 1342, the head of the delegation that included Bertoldo Orsini, his partner as senator and captain of the people, sent by the Romans to implore the pope's return. Stefanuccio had good reason to know and respect Cola's abilities. He was in Avignon when Cola arrived at the head of the delegation for the Thirteen Good Men who had overthrown his government. He, along with his son Giovanni, were among those invited by Cola to attend his lecture on the *lex de imperio* of Vespasian at the Lateran.

But now, as the Colonna baron approached the Capitoline, he noticed that its habitual bureaucratic chaos was gone. "Stefano entered the palace with a few men. He saw that everyone was receiving his due. There were many people up at the Campidoglio; and he grew afraid and he marveled greatly at the strength of this multitude." Soon the tribune came down and appeared to Stefanuccio fully armed. His dress was "scarlet, flaming like fire; his face and his appearance were terrible to behold." At Cola's command Colonna swore upon both the Bible and the Eucharist placed on the altar of the palace chapel and promised to uphold the Ordinances and be ready to answer the commune's summonses for military duty. One after another the fearful barons arrived to swear fealty to the *buono stato:* Rainaldo and Giordano Orsini, the brothers of the Marino branch of the family; then Stefano il Vecchio himself; and then, in what must have been the final sign that a new day had arrived, Francesco Savelli, Cola's own liege lord. Such oaths were not unusual in fourteenth-century Italy: their inclusion in Florence's Ordinances of Justice of 1295 was a sign that rule of the city had passed to the guilds. Even a great commercial city like Venice regularly required them from its feudatories. The Roman barons all swore fealty to the *buono stato,* and they offered their persons, their fortresses, and their own vassals in support of the city. In his letter of July

1, 1347, to Viceroy Giovanni Randazzo of Sicily, Cola stressed these details for the public record.

. . .

> Cola served unrelentingly, without mercy. He appointed his
> officials. He seized one man and then another; this one he
> tortured, that one he beheaded without mercy. He judged all
> the defendants cruelly.
>
> (AR, XVIII, ll. 431–34, Porta, 157)

If the *buon governo* rested on the bedrock of Justice, Justice itself depended on her willingness to use force to punish wrongdoers.[11] Lorenzetti did not create his forceful images in Siena without precedent. At the beginning of the century, at Padua in the Scrovegni Chapel, Giotto himself had painted a series of monochrome panels representing the virtues and vices, each matched with its opposite across the hall. Here Justice sits enthroned. In the best tradition of Aquinas, she holds in each hand a scale, each with one type of justice: distributive, which rewards and crowns, and commutative, which punishes. The figure in her left hand swings a sword over his shoulder, ready to behead a criminal bound and on his knees. Justice swift and harsh. Yet the results of just reward and punishment are plain; and the alternatives depicted—robbery, murder, rape—too horrible to consider.

One example of Cola's harsh justice assumed the personal tone of much medieval governance: his beheading of one of the clergy of the monastery of Sant'Anastasia in Arenula, right in the middle of Cola's own neighborhood. What crimes the cleric had committed are unlisted, but they must have been well known in the *rione,* for the Anonimo romano declares that the monk was *persona infamata,* an obvious public criminal. Even more important, however, is that Cola dared lay hands on a cleric at all: this had been one of the key elements of the conflict between the *regnum* and the *sacerdotium* during the Investiture Conflict, and popes had defied and toppled kings and emperors over just such clerical immunity. Yet in a world where the Italian commune controlled many aspects of the religious lives of its citizens, and clerics mingled easily within the complex social world of the city, their special status was mitigated by custom and law. Indeed, in the political treatises of contemporaries like Remigio de' Girolami, uncontrolled strife between clergy and laity is spelled out as one of the causes of a commune's destruction. By the standards of fourteenth-century Italy, Cola's zeal to rein in private interest and to conform to new standards of law was the very model of a just government. In Siena's *Buon Governo* Lorenzetti painted a vivid image of contemporary notions of Justice (see fig. 15d). The figure herself sits, sword upright in her right hand, resting on the head of an executed criminal. Below her, mounted cavalry and foot soldiers, all carrying lances, hem in a group of prisoners, bound and awaiting sentence. The defendants come from every social class, gentlemen at the fore on their knees, knights, merchants, peasants, and the poor in a huddled mass, a stark contrast to the twenty-four citizens immediately opposite them, on the other side of the Buon Comune. The laws of the commune of Siena, embodied in its *Constitutio* of 1232–1338, reinforce this image: "The most excellent part of justice, which exceeds all other virtues, and which ought to be the main duty of all lords, governors, and citizen bodies, is to strike at, and punish, those who breach the law, above all through betrayal and rebellion, which bring danger, death, and injury for the public as well as for private individuals" (Siena, AS, 23, f. 477).[12] In his letter to the Romans of June 24, 1347, Petrarch also urged very harsh measures against the barons: "The republic must be relieved of these as a body would be freed of its poisonous excretions. Thus the republic, though diminished in numbers, will be stronger and healthier" (*Variae* 48 *[Hortatoria]*, CRCR, 17–18).

The metaphor of the body, "relieved of its poisonous excretions," was a common one to medieval society. It justified the persecution of heretics, witches, and homosexuals, and it served — as Foucault, Ester Cohen, and other students of ceremonies of punishment emphasize — to provide one of the deeply symbolic underpinnings of the communes' extreme treatment of criminals and political traitors into the Renaissance. Public punishment, harsh and violent, played out a ritual of both purification to the body politic and warning to future malefactors. Thus punishments included the removal of tongues for blasphemers, amputation of hands for notaries or accountants who kept false records, or castration for sexual crimes. All displayed a symbolic retributive justice as symmetrical as the opposing processions of just and criminal citizens in Lorenzetti's painting. Even graver crimes merited more public and extreme measures: the destruction of the homes, towers, and properties of traitors; the commissioning of the *pitture infamanti;* and a wide range of capital punishment depending on the crime and the social status of the criminal: decapitation for nobles and for crimes against the state (the "capital" crime par excellence), hanging for those of lower social status or crimes considered less severe — for theft or rape, for example — and finally burning at the stake for crimes considered the most "poisonous" to the body politic and civic. Heretics, witches, and homosexuals all met the same fate in the flames that were seen both to cleanse society and to preview the fires of hell to which medieval society believed these marginalized groups were surely headed and of which countless paintings of the Last Judgment in their churches provided vivid examples. In the next century the sermons of Bernardino da Siena continued to excoriate these—and members of factions—as poisons to the body politic.

The fate of the executed criminal's remains was also a matter of consistent and ritualized ceremony. The ashes of those burned at the stake were without exception dispersed to the four winds, both as a guarantee that they would never see burial in consecrated ground and, as in the case of Arnold of Brescia, so that heretics' ashes would not become venerated relics and centers of cults. Those other criminals hung, drawn and quartered, or decapitated were stretched out on the *furca*, or cross-rack, and very often left hanging for days. Sometimes (as in the Florentine case of the Pazzi conspirators against Giuliano and Lorenzo de' Medici in 1479) they were left for weeks, until their flesh rotted off their bones or was eaten by carrion birds and vermin. Even before being hoisted up as both public mockery and warning, their bodies might be mutilated beyond all recognition by countless knife wounds, dragged through the city streets, or become the object of boys games: the target of rocks and mud. Finally, whatever of the condemned remained was cast to the dogs and pigs, their *infamia* throughout the city and *contado* complete. Or nearly complete. Contemporary chronicles speak—perhaps suspiciously by formula—of the very bones of the condemned being turned into dice or the handles of cutlery for their judges and living enemies: a final ritual remembrance of their humiliation and the triumph of society. Unsubstantiated tales of ritual cannibalism against their remains were not uncommon.

Over the course of the fourteenth century the more extreme of these measures fell by the wayside. The implementation of consistent criminal codes influenced by Roman law and the substitution of money fines by cash-strapped communes combined with a civil reaction against punishments that made a city appear barbarous to both religious sensibility and new standards of civil life in Italy. By midcentury a new type of confraternity had grown up, the Confraternities of Justice, whose members devoted their public works of mercy to assisting and comforting the condemned and their families, to ensuring proper Christian burial for their remains, and through their work to symbolize and effect public reconciliation and peace, both between the commune and those who committed crimes against it as well as among victims, their families, and those of the perpetrators. The net effect was to diminish archaic codes of eye for eye.

So Cola's new justice had its effects. "A few days later the judges of the city came and swore fealty to him and offered their services to the *buono stato*. Then came the notaries and did the same, then the merchants. In short, in line, their souls at rest, without arms, each swore allegiance to the common good new state" (AR, XVIII, ll. 473–78, Porta, 159). They came, in line, *per ordine,* like the twenty-four in Lorenzetti's fresco. "And so these measures began to please everyone; and armed conflicts began to cease." Sometime in June, before the feast of St. John on the twenty-fourth, Cola even moved against Martino del Porto, the nephew of both Cardinal Annibaldo de Ceccano and Cardinal Giacomo Caetani. A former senator, Martino was husband of the beautiful widow Macia degli Alberteschi. Well known for his depredations in the countryside, he gained widespread *infamia* for having robbed a galley from Marseilles that had been stranded on the Roman shore.[13] The incident had become a major scandal in Rome as well as in Provence. On February 1, 1347, Pope Clement VI himself had written to the senate and people of Rome, commanding them to restore the stolen goods and monies, some of which belonged to Provençal merchants, but much also to Cardinal Bertrand de Déaulx to fund his legation to the kingdom of Sicily. Clement was so adamant about the case that he wrote again, on April 27, to his vicar Raymond de Chameyrac and to the then senators of Rome — Stefano Colonna and Nicola Orsini — ordering them to force Martino del Porto to make full restitution.

Cola saw the robber baron as a threat to *securitas* and had the young noble, then immobilized by a severe case of dropsy, seized from his palace, the home of the Alberteschi on the Ripa Romea in Trastevere, and dragged to the Campidoglio. There, below the statue of the Lion (then on the lower stairway to the palace and now in the garden of the Palazzo dei Conservatori), he was stripped and bound on his knees. Cola called an assembly and read off the death sentence. Instead of decapitation, the usual sentence for noblemen, Martino was condemned to the gallows: a humiliation for common thieves. There on the *piano* of the Campidoglio, probably on the Tiber side of the marketplace, Martino hung for one night and two days. "His wife, far off, could see him from her balconies. . . . Neither his nobility nor his being related to the Orsini could help him" (AR, XVIII, ll. 604–6, Porta, 163–64).

Soon "a horrible fear entered the souls of the thieves, murderers, malefactors, adulterers, and every person worthy of *infamia.*" They left the city under cover and fled secretly, clearing Rome and its district. Martino de Porto's execution terrified the barons, who fell into mutual distrust as their own arrogance crumbled. The countryside began to flourish again, pilgrims returned and merchants traveled unharmed, the streets were cleared of barricades, people moved freely about day and night; and "no one dared to carry arms." The streets became so safe, in fact, that deliverymen could leave their carts unattended and find them untouched when they returned. Rome's Statutes of the Merchants seem to have been fairly and effectively enforced, the guilds of butchers and fishmongers for once began complying with regulations governing the labeling and grading of their meat and fish. Cola paid special attention to the city's business climate. On June 27 he approved the statutes of Rome's cloth guild, the Arte della Lana, in a document drawn up by Ceccho Petri Rosarii, the protonotary of the Capitoline; and on September 2 he ratified a new issuance of the Statutes of the Merchants in a document drawn up by Egidio Angelerii, notary and *dictator* of the City Chamber.[14]

Justice was visibly and forcefully the most tangible effect of the *buono stato*. The Anonimo romano devotes nearly one-quarter of his description of all the events and personalities between the revolution on May 20 and Cola's knighting on August 1, 1347, to examples of Cola's works of justice. He employs the classic language of the Italian city-states to describe the *buon comune*, and he applies it unsparingly to Cola's actions, even when, it seems, the hindsight of events has caused him to nuance his narration with forewarnings of troubles to come and the effects of later judgments. The dramatic contrasts between his picture of the city during the rule of the barons and after Cola comes to power are verbal equivalents to the images of the *Mal Governo* and *Buon Governo* painted by Lorenzetti.

Yet, if Justice had a place of honor on the extreme right of the dais with the *Buon Comune* in Lorenzetti's fresco, so, too, did Peace upon the extreme left.[15] Peace was the constant companion of Justice in both communal thought and Christian doctrine. "Peace" meant many things in the Middle Ages; but in Cola's *buono stato* peace took on a position both remarkable and perplexing, and it would become central to Rienzo's political fortunes and to the image that the tribune would forever bear in history.

Peace in Lorenzetti's *Buon Governo* (see fig. 15b) takes her place among the images of the other Christian virtues; yet her posture, gracefully relaxed and reclining on her throne, and the olive branch that she holds in her left hand reveal much of her lineage. For this *Pax* is modeled after ancient statuary and is meant to convey to Lorenzetti's viewers the classical Roman peace that is inextricably linked with earthly Justice and with Security who hovers over the gates. For much of the Western tradition after Augustine the notion of peace was one borrowed largely from Roman concepts of *pax* as the absence of war; as the order of tranquillity imposed by the victor upon the defeated, by the treaty ensuring such tranquillity, and by the resultant security that armed vigilance would guarantee: all meanings contained in the notion of the imperial *pax romana*.

But while Cola's sense of justice owed very much to Roman history and the traditions of the Italian commune, his notions of peace were as strongly influenced by the religious movements of his time: such phenomena as the Great Alleluia of 1233, the Flagellant confraternities born in 1260, and the "peace pilgrimage" of Venturino da Bergamo in 1334. Rienzo attempted to bring harmony among these traditions in an institution new to Rome: the House of Peace and Justice. Already well developed in Genoa from as early as 1169, and in Florence, Siena, and elsewhere in Tuscany by the fourteenth century, it had appeared diversely as the new confraternities of justice or as Venice's "Office of Justice." Contemporary chronicles rarely described the process elsewhere, perhaps because it was so well known, but the Anonimo romano records it at length:

[Cola] established the House of Peace and Justice and in it he set up the *gonfalone* of St. Paul, on which was portrayed the naked sword and the palm of victory. In charge of this office he placed the most just men from among the *popolo,* the Good Peacemakers, who were to supervise the peace. These are examples of how the office worked:

Two enemies came and gave pledges to make peace. Then, according to the nature of the injury dividing them, the aggressor was made to suffer the same injury he had inflicted on the victim. Then they gave each other the kiss of peace, on the mouth, and the man who had been offended made complete peace.

One man had blinded another. He came forward and was brought up to the stairs of the Campidoglio. He remained there on his knees. Then the man who had lost his eye arrived. The malefactor wept and prayed to God to pardon him. Then he turned his face up so that if the blinded man wanted to, he could pluck out his eye. Well then. He did not blind him, but he was moved by pity, and he forgave him the injury. Civil cases were resolved expeditiously as well. (AR, XVIII, ll. 479–99, Porta, 159–60)

The practice made a deep impression on the Romans, who maintained Cola's ceremony of peace and reconciliation into the next decade. Clear evidence comes from the notarial archive of Sant'Angelo in Pescheria among the cartularies of notary Antonio di Lorenzo Stefanelli de Scambiis, who worked around the fish market and church. In September 1364 de Scambiis was asked to document just such a ceremony of reconciliation between Fra Paluccio Cole Guetarii of Trastevere and his enemy Amatore Porcari. The elements of the reconciliation—a neutral public place, official witnesses, the perpetrator's ritual humiliation, the embrace, the kiss of peace, and the exchange of pledges and the notarized record—were all common in contemporary Italy. But the ceremony makes clear reference to two survivals of Cola's *buono stato*. The first is to the *Statuta Urbis* of 1363 (II.20–21) and the various means of facilitating a peace settlement, which might include the sharing of a strong glass of wine, the kiss of peace *(hosculum pacis),* a public ceremony, and a written *instrumentum pactorum*. The second—a necessity for an urban society so beset by feud—is to the public reading of the legal instrument, in this case before the house of Matteo de Baccariis, who was one of Cola's ambassadors to Florence in June 1347 and was to go on to a distinguished public career in Rome.

While Cola's *buono stato* shared many of the characteristic behaviors of the *buon comune,* and if its ideals of justice, security, and peace had much in common with contemporary communal practice, in Cola's mind the new age was also one of Christian peace, of reconciliation, mercy, and justice played out on a higher level: the justice spoken of in the Bible. If his actions against criminals and traitors were as harsh and swift as those of other Italian communes, his institution of the House of Justice and Peace reveals influences that went far deeper into the religious substrata of fourteenth-century Italian life and that indicate the influence of both urban peacemaking and the popular religious movements that had developed independently of papal Rome. And if Cola's *buono stato* was marked by a high degree of political prudence, realizing full well that a new day could bring any number of new plots and violent threats from the deposed barons, it was also born out of the expectation that the new day would bring the reform and renewal of both political and religious life to Rome and to Italy. Thus, like Cola's new coat of arms, his *buono stato* combined both the *buon comune* and the heavenly city: the ideal *civitas* whose liberation and renewal Cola had described in terms borrowed directly from the Apocalypse.

CHAPTER 9

Cola and the World

> Then the Tribune called a general council and wrote most
> eloquent letters to the cities and communes of Tuscany,
> Lombardy, Campagna, the Romagna, and Marittima; to the
> doge of Venice; to Messer Luchino, tyrant of Milan; to the
> marchese of Ferrara, to the Holy Father Pope Clement; to
> Lewis, duke of Bavaria, who had been elected emperor . . . and
> to the princes of Naples. In these letters he prefixed his name,
> with a magnificent title, in this form: "Nicholas, Severe and
> Clement, Tribune of Liberty, Peace and Justice, and Illustrious
> Liberator of the Holy Roman Republic." In these letters he
> announced the peaceful, just *buono stato* that he had begun.
>
> Anonimo romano, XVIII, ll. 523–37, Porta, 160–61

Cola's *buono stato* had restored the peace, security, and prosperity of
Rome's *buon governo,* it had awoken the slumbering grandeur of the ancient republic, and it had ushered in a new era in which Rome would be
restored to its rightful place as the New Jerusalem, the light and beacon
for the faithful. But, as Jesus had told his disciples, no light can remain
hidden under a bushel, and his new people must stand forth like a "city
on a hill," a new Zion. It followed that Cola's *buono stato* would manifest
the deep and dramatic changes taking place in Rome and propagate these
to the rest of Italy and the world. To do this Cola envisioned a clear and
consistent foreign policy and diplomacy.[1] This was threefold: to manifest
the deeply apocalyptic underpinnings and goals of his *stato,* to spell out
the practical results of the *buono stato* in a language understood by the

Italian communes, and to proclaim the renewal of the Roman Republic and of the ancient liberties and greatness of all Italy.

Cola relied on standard medieval institutions and methods of propaganda to implement this diplomacy: Rome's chancellery produced a steady and consistent stream of letters that set forth his program to the rest of Christendom; a reliable and quickly expanding core of diplomats, ambassadors, and couriers spread this message; a new series of political symbols and slogans made it readily recognized and understood. Finally Rienzo marshaled the material resources to back up his diplomacy: the new wealth of Rome and a series of political and military alliances with Rome's Italian neighbors and with foreign powers.

Yet Cola was also setting Rome's ship of state on the tumultuous waters of Italian, papal, and imperial politics in an age of increasing international insecurity: the outbreak of the Hundred Years' War between England and France, the attempts of the Avignon popes to regain the Papal States by either diplomacy or outright war, the creation of the territorial Italian states of central and northern Italy, including the rise of the new *signorie,* and the sudden crisis that overcame the Angevin kingdom of Naples on Rome's borders upon the death of King Robert the Wise in 1343. Cola had many friends inside and outside Rome, and yet he would soon also have many enemies, including those like the Angevins and the papacy, whose interests and claims could not long abide an independent and active new power in Rome.

Cola began Rome's diplomatic mission as early as his first letters and dispatches just days after Pentecost. His surviving letters, culled from his own copies, the city and chancellery fondi of Italian communes, papal archives, and Rome's own records, indicate that as early as May 24 he was already announcing the *buono stato* to Viterbo, Rome's sister city in the Papal States. On June 7 he followed this with a general letter. Its numerous copies and the Anonimo romano tell us the extent of Cola's reach: within the Papal States to Tivoli, Velletri, Corneto, and Gaeta; to Amelia, Todi, Terni, Spoleto, and the cities of the duchy of Spoleto; to Rieti, Foligno, Assisi, and Perugia; and in Tuscany to Florence, Siena, Pisa, Lucca, Arezzo, and Pistoia, as well as to Tuscia, the communes of southern Tuscany that lay within the Papal Patrimony, including Tuscanella. These were Rome's natural allies, They had much in common: an association with the Papal States, a frequent Guelph allegiance, and geographic and economic connections along the Tiber and its tributaries. But Cola also went further: to the lords of the Romagna, the heads of the new *signorie* that had replaced the communes of the former papal possessions: to the Pepoli of Bologna, the Obizzo of Ferrara, the Carrara of Padua, the Ordelaffi of Forlì, and the Malatesta of Rimini. Rome's couriers delivered the new message of revival even to the della Scala of Verona, the Gonzaga of Mantua, and Lord Luchino Visconti, the tyrant of Milan.

As Cola might have expected, these new *signori* either ignored or derided the pretensions of the new republic. But not all opposition to the *buono stato* came from hostile governments. In southern Lazio, in the port city of Terracina, a notarial document dated September 27, 1347, records a popular vote to send ambassadors to Rome to protest "before the most clement and illustrious Lord Nicolo, the severe and clement, and the illustrious liberator of the sacred Roman republic, that the city of the commune of Terracina and the men of the said city are exempt from any Roman jurisdiction." Farther to the south Cola embarked on a much grander, and far more dangerous, diplomatic initiative. Letters offering friendship and alliance went not only to the Aragonese rulers of Sicily but also to both the adherents of Queen Giovanna of Naples, the Angevin heir of Robert the Wise, and to her sworn enemy, her brother-in-law, Lewis of Hungary. In the midst of all this, Cola also managed to supply Pope Clement VI in Avignon with an uninterrupted series of reports on his activities on the pope's behalf and to correspond actively with his friend Francesco Petrarch. The letters provide an unmatched record of the *buono stato*'s ideals and goals. Cola's words and policies are confirmed by independent sources: the Anonimo romano in Rome and Giovanni Villani in Florence; the letters of the pope and his vicar; the replies of other Italian communes; the testimony of such early humanists as Petrarch and Barbato da Sulmona; such well-placed Romans as Cochetus de Chotiis; and the records of notaries and other witnesses.

Rome's chancery consistently spelled out Cola's threefold vision. Rienzo is the tribune of peace, justice, and liberty, the "illustrious liberator of the sacred Roman Republic," a letter of June 11 informs Guido Gonzaga. He is the "Zealot of Italy, the Lover of the World," adds a general letter of August 1, 1347. Cola and his revolution, a letter of June tells Florence, have achieved the "reformation and renewal of justice, liberty, security and the peaceful condition of the province and City of Rome." Cola and his *buono stato* have brought about the restoration not only of civil government and its functions but also of the deeply religious purpose of medieval Roman rule, the "consolation of pilgrims and of all faithful Christians." "By the inspiration of the Holy Spirit," the Lord Jesus Christ himself has "recalled the Roman people to unity and concord and inflamed them to the desire for liberty, peace, and justice." Justice, based on divine foundations, now reigns in Rome, and even the barons have taken sacred oaths upon the Eucharist to preserve the *buono stato,* Cola tells the government of Lucca on June 23. With his authority and just power, Cola has set upon the "renewal" of the "sacred Roman people."

This is only right, for Rome itself is the *caput mundi,* "head of the cities of the entire world and of all of sacred Italy," he tells Guido Gonzaga. The *buono stato,* therefore, has brought reconciliation, peace, and justice both to Rome and to all of sacred Italy. Simultaneously Rome's revival has achieved the *renovatio* of ancient friendship between Rome, Florence, and the other republics and the "enervation and extirpation" of tyrants. Cola delivers this message to the tyrants themselves: to Guido Gonzaga, for example. On July 1, Cola also tells the viceroy of Sicily that the "nourishing City will miraculously eject tyranny."

But if, as Cola claimed, Rome's *buono stato* was founded on the direct inspiration of the Holy Spirit, then it was unlike any state that had yet existed. For in the long tradition of medieval political thought, all authority found legitimization only through the intermediaries of church and pope. But Cola seems deliberately to have put Rome and its people on equal footing with both papacy and empire: for now Rome and "sacred Italy" have taken on an authority of their own. By stripping politics of mediation, Cola ultimately legitimizes the authority of the people before God. He thus shares much with a tradition of Italian communal thought that had recently found its clear exposition in Dante's *De monarchia* and Marsiglio of Padua's *Defensor pacis.*

Soon, as the Anonimo romano makes clear, the "fame and terror of Cola's excellent government spread into every land." The *buono stato* had attracted many in the professional and business classes of Rome, her best and brightest.[2] "The Tribune had many writers and scribes who kept writing letters day and night. . . . Many were the most famous of the district of Rome." Did these talented people merely copy Cola's texts, or did they "flesh out" his key ideas and political slogans with their own professional knowledge of the *ars dictaminis* and inform them with their own political— and religious—concerns? Enough material survives to clearly distinguish Cola's personal themes from his more formal state letters, yet the consistency of ideas among them seems to point to Cola's close supervision of his chancery's output. While their elegance of imagery points to a new synthesis of political and religious vocabulary, his medieval Latin retains the notarial metric *cursus,* and most of Cola's surviving letters continue to employ the *stilus rhetoricus* of the late medieval *ars dictaminis.* Some are even in the *volgare,* an Italian meant to be read by, or to, the urban classes of Italy's communes.

Roman couriers and ambassadors, drawn from the same professional and wealthy merchant class, began to crisscross Italy. Like most medieval ambassadors, they went unarmed, protected by diplomatic immunity. Rome's couriers were accorded "great honor, and they were given gifts." As the city's prestige and power grew, their position became more and more attractive. Some ambassadors were important enough for their names to be recalled: Pandolfuccio di Guido di Pandolfo de' Franchi, Matteo de Beccariis, Francesco Baroncelli, Stefanello de Boetiis, and the Messer Giovanni of Petrarch's *Variae* 40. They and Rome's diplomatic couriers bore both the "silver-plated wooden wand" of the ambassador and the *buono stato's* new coat of arms: "a certain *gonfalone,* azure or celestial blue in color, on which was depicted a golden sun with golden rays and stars," as the notary Pietro Ciccoli Pizzaluti of Todi witnessed and recorded in August 1347. According to one unnamed courier who returned to Rome after a far-flung mission: "I have carried this staff publicly through the woods and through the streets; thousands of people have knelt before it and kissed it with tears of joy for the safe highways, free of robbers" (AR, XVIII, ll. 556–60, Porta, 162).

We have an example of this diplomacy in the record of the delegation to Florence that on July 2 persuaded that republic to send to Rome one hundred knights for three months. Florence again responded positively to Cola's request of July 19 for military alliance against Janni di Vico, the rebellious prefect of the city. Giovanni Villani provides some details that bear out both Cola's letter and the record of the ambassadors themselves:

Cola sent letters also to all the chief cities of Italy and one to our commune with many excellent rhetorical turns *[dittato].* And then he sent to us five solemn ambassadors who did glory to themselves and then to our commune: how our city was a daughter of Rome, founded and built by the people of Rome; and he asked for aid for their army. To these ambassadors great honor was accorded; 100 knights were sent to Rome to the tribune, and more aid was offered, whenever there might be a need. (Villani, *Cronica* 90, p. 277)

Cola's impact on the thought and action of the governments of Italy was no less profound.[3] The author of the *Cronaca Senese,* Agnolo di Tura del Graso, recorded that on July 22 his own city of Siena agreed to the request of Rome's ambassadors and sent fifty knights. Perugia sent sixty. Gaeta, closer to home, sealed its alliance with Rome with a subsidy of 10,000 florins. Tuscanella renewed its tribute, commuting a lapsed payment of £1,000 with a guaranteed annual shipment of one hundred pounds of grain for Sta. Maria in Aracoeli, while the other towns of the Patrimony in southern Tuscany "offered themselves to the *buono stato.*"

But such aid had its limits. In the postscript to a letter to Florence dated August 5, Cola notes the Florentine ambassadors' refusal to allow their troops to be used outside the boundaries of the Roman Campagna, against the count of Fondi, then at Gaeta; and in a letter of August 6 Cola acknowledges similar conditions imposed by the ambassadors of Todi. Florence's policy seems to have been matched by many cities of Tuscany and Umbria. According to Agnolo di Tura, Siena's contingent returned home on September 12; and on October 18 Cola sent another embassy to explore the formation of a military league. The Sienese refused the offer. These policies made sense: the cities of Tuscany and Tuscia on Lazio's border were threatened by Janni di Vico's expansionism. Politics in southern Lazio concerned them far less.

If Cola's new diplomacy had to confront the rough realities of Italian politics, the impact of his message on Italy's intellectuals was another matter.[4] This is illustrated by the response of two humanists: Petrarch himself and his friend Marco Barbato da Sulmona, one of the widening circle of artists, intellectuals, and religious reformers who had been supported and nurtured by King Robert and Queen Sancia of Naples. Sometime in the summer of 1347, Barbato published his own *Romana respublica urbi Romae* (The Address of the Republic of Rome to the City of Rome). In this epistolary allegory, tinged with traces of the medieval rhythmed *cursus,* ancient Rome calls on her present-day descendent, lamenting that after the great age of Rome's ancient heroes, the city—without laws, beset by wars, fallen and abject—has not had faithful friends for centuries. Yet all is not lost, ancient Rome declares, for today two men have arisen to revive the city's fortunes: Petrarch and Rienzo. Rome exhorts her children to "commit yourselves and your possessions to the Tribune and to these two completely and without reservation, so that whatever the Poet Laureate advises, the Tribune may carry out." The reform language of the early Renaissance is already in place: two lights amid the darkness of the age, Petrarch and Cola bring new life to the ancient city.

Petrarch gives us the clearest image of the impact of Cola's revolution on the court at Avignon. On July 24–26, 1347 (*Variae* 38) he wrote Cola:

Do not suppose for a moment that the letters that you write from Rome remain long in the possession of those to whom they are addressed. On the contrary, everyone rushes to make a copy of them with as much earnestness, and circulates them around the pontiff's court with as much zeal, as if they were sent not by a man of our own race but by an inhabitant of another world, or of the Antipodes. (CRCR, 40)

But he cautions Cola that his news is already beginning to meet a mixed reception and that he should "display greater and greater care in the future." Petrarch refers to Cola's work on behalf of "truth, justice, peace, and liberty"; he praises his adoption of the "Year One" as his dating element; and he asserts that Cola's message is reaching "every land."

The farther Cola's letters went beyond the old boundaries of the Papal States and Roman Campagna, however, the less impact they had. If Luchino Visconti wrote a polite response to Cola's news of a new age in Rome, advising him to rule wisely, most of the lords of the Romagna greeted his diplomacy with outright derision, revealing their contempt for the old communes and their fears that a revived Roman power would reestablish its claims to domination over their part of the old Papal States. Others, such as the lords of Verona, Mantua, and Padua, ignored Cola as best they could. On August 1 Cola wrote the heir and viceroy of Aragonese Sicily, Infante Giovanni. Trading history for the present realities of geopolitics, Cola reminded Giovanni that in ancient times Rome had saved Sicily from Hannibal and his Carthaginians: the island then became a province of Rome. The tribune therefore asks the viceroy to provide a contingent of galleys to aid in Rome's upcoming military operations.

From the start Cola also felt the necessity of involving Rome in the politics of Angevin Naples.[5] His decision may have been a logical and necessary one at the time, for ever since the founding of the dynasty in 1266, the kings of Naples had exercised inordinate influence on Roman politics as papal vicars for the city and then for Italy, as the feudal lord of many of Rome's great baronial families, and then as a rich and ambitious territorial dynasty eager to expand the influence of the Regno into whatever power vacuum either pope or communes had left in the Papal States. Moreover, instability in the enormous and very rich kingdom to the south and east of Rome could only harm the growth of the republic; but clever interference in the politics of Naples might actually work to Rome's advantage.

On the death of King Robert in 1343, the kingdom was inherited by his eldest granddaughter, Giovanna, the daughter of his only son, Charles of Calabria (d. 1328) (see table 2). The young queen was beset by rivals from within her own family: Louis, prince of Taranto, and Charles, duke of Durazzo, were both legitimate male heirs, grandsons of Charles II of Naples; and the succession of women in the French royal houses had always been problematic. Heirs, too, were the great-grandsons of Charles II, through the direct line of King Robert's elder brother, Charles Martel, king of Hungary (d. 1295). Lewis, king of Hungary, and Andrew, his younger brother, had to be dissuaded from any potential claim to the kingdom of Naples, and the best way to do that was to arrange a marriage alliance. In 1332 King Robert and Pope John XXII had agreed that Giovanna would marry either available brother. On September 26, 1333, Giovanna was therefore engaged to Andrew; the couple was married on January 22, 1343. Clement VI immediately attempted to prevent Andrew from assuming the title of king, except as consort, and the great power of Hungary from absorbing Naples. Clement dissolved the regency council of Robert's widow, Sancia, on threat of excommunication, received the oath of homage from Queen Giovanna, and assumed the regency of the kingdom himself through his legates.

Giovanna was not fond of her distant cousin, now her husband; rumors circulated that she preferred the company and bed of a lady-in-waiting. She certainly had a succession of male lovers throughout her reign; and when Prince Andrew was summoned from his chambers in the castle of Aversa on the night of September 18, 1345, and strangled by unknown assassins, sexual rumor and Hungarian political purpose conspired to place the blame squarely on Giovanna's supposedly depraved head. The crime became the scandal of Europe: Clement VI acted quickly to quell the rumors and the wrath of Lewis of Hungary, who was already demanding Giovanna's trial and deposition, as well as the crown of Naples. Clement stalled for time, and on November 4, 1346, he excommunicated the unknown assassins and appointed Cardinal Bertrand de Déaulx to head an official investigation into the actions of the queen and the princes. Bertrand had had a long career in diplomacy when, on March 30, 1346, he was named vicar general for the Papal States and, on August 26, 1346, legate to Sicily.

Meanwhile, Louis of Taranto and Charles of Durazzo saw their opportunity to foment a popular uprising against the "shameless" queen. Giovanna was forced to surrender many of her closest advisers and political allies to the chopping block. In the meantime, however, the queen had given birth to an heir, Charles Martel, who received the homage of her subjects in February 1347. Giovanna soon decided to defy Cardinal Bertrand's investigation. She quickly exchanged her young lover, Robert of Taranto, for Louis of Taranto himself and defied her accusers. Bertrand, never a brave man, lost his nerve and soon fled Naples. Lewis of Hungary announced his intention of avenging his brother Andrew's death and prepared an invasion of the kingdom. His route would be an easy one: Hungary then included not only the territory of the modern nation but also most of modern Croatia and Bosnia. To the great anxiety of the Venetian senate, Lewis controlled much of the eastern Adriatic from the borders of Venice to Durazzo, long a possession of the Angevins of Naples.

The natural course of invasion would therefore bring the Hungarian army across Venice's colonial empire and the Adriatic and to the March of Ancona, link up to the main road through the Abruzzo via L'Aquila and Sulmona, and thence south and east to Naples itself. By the early summer of 1347, representatives of the Hungarian king were already posted at L'Aquila, just outside the Papal States. Clement VI, in far-off Avignon, could do little but berate Cardinal Bertrand for inaction and vainly urge the diplomacy of King Philip of France and Charles IV of Bohemia to prevent Lewis's invasion.

At this point Cola di Rienzo decided to intervene. On July 8, 1347, he informed Pope Clement that he has sent ambassadors to both Anjevin factions in an attempt to prevent war from breaking out. His decision might have struck the pope as foolhardy, impertinent of his own prerogatives, and disruptive of years of papal diplomacy; but Cola may well have reckoned that he had nothing to lose, given the threat to Rome, and much to gain in influence and tangible political benefits. One such benefit, Cola informed the pope, was to reopen Naples to Roman diplomatic missions. Another was less ambiguous: on July 27 Cola informed Clement that Lewis of Hungary had offered Rome a paid force of five hundred knights and then had upped the offer to one thousand knights in exchange for Cola's support against Giovanna. Cola reports that he had refused the offer out of loyalty to Clement. But such a threat to Clement's position and to his support for his vassal Giovanna could not go unanswered. Clement therefore dispatched Bertrand de Déaulx to prevent what he believed were the tribune's active plans to supplant the queen in exchange for a substantial Roman role in the affairs of the Regno.

So important was this role already that all parties in the conflict actively courted the Roman tribune. Charles of Durazzo sent letters addressing Cola as "our dearest friend." Giovanna herself, the Anonimo romano reports, sent Cola's wife, Livia, a present of 500 florins and an assortment of jewelry. Early in August both King Lewis of Hungary and Queen Giovanna sent ambassadors to Rome to argue the case of Giovanna's complicity in King Andrew's death before Cola and a Roman tribunal. Briefs were filed and a decision promised after due consideration. One incident during this embassy sheds much light on Cola's intellectual and diplomatic abilities. On Giovanna's behalf, Louis of Taranto sent a magnificent embassy to Rome, consisting of a Franciscan theologian and archbishop, probably Giovanni Orsini of Naples, a knight "with golden spurs," and a judge. The archbishop began his diplomatic oration in a manner common to many such addresses, with a quotation from Scripture, "He sent men to renew the amity," a direct quotation from 1 Maccabees 12:1, con-

cerning the mission from the hard-pressed Jews to request the alliance
and aid of the Roman people. "Without any preparation"—and without
missing a beat—Cola responded with these words: "Far be the sword and
arms from us, let there be peace by sea and by land." The tribune's response won the dumbfounded archbishop's admiration, for Cola not only
had recognized the quotation from Maccabees but also was able to pick
up the text from memory and to respond in kind to the biblical passage:
the Romans would stand by their alliance.

Cola had established himself and Rome as a font of learning and political wisdom.[6] Kings and potentates sought him out; other communes
rushed to his aid. Rome became a court of appeals from many parts of
Italy. Even beyond the Alps and the Mediterranean, Cola and Rome's reputation began to assume mythic proportions. Rome was, after all, the legitimate seat of Christian unity; and whether or not the popes in Avignon liked it, Rome still held a magic fascination for medieval people.
Philip VI of Valois, the king of France (1328–50), "sent a letter by an archer.
It was written in the vernacular. It was not pompous, but it was like a
merchant's letter." Sent by express courier, intended for Cola and his Roman people, it had been preserved, according to the Anonimo romano,
in the Roman chancellery. Even Lewis of Bavaria, the emperor crowned
by Pietro da Corbara in Rome in 1328 and deposed by John XXII, sent a
secret letter to Cola asking him to intervene with the pope to arrange a
reconciliation and the lifting of his excommunication.

Rome held magical sway even among Christendom's enemies:

There was a Bolognese who had been a slave of the sultan of Babylon [the caliph
of Egypt]. As soon as he could gain his freedom, he hastened to Rome as quickly
as possible. He said that the great Peraham had been told that in the City of Rome
there had arisen a man of great justice, a man of the people; he answered, fearing
for himself, and said, "Mahomet and holy Elinason help Jerusalem," by which he
meant the land of the Saracens. (AR, XVIII, ll. 633–40, Porta, 165)

Cola confirmed the Anonimo romano's story in a letter from Prague in
1350. Was it just possible that the rumor of the revived Roman Empire
and its "arisen" lord had touched a memory among Muslims, as among
Christians, of widespread Joachite prophecies of a "Last World Emperor"?
In the end of time that man would arise again in Rome to unite the Christian world in peace, justice, and liberty and then set off for the Holy Land
to finally retake Jerusalem before the coming of Antichrist.

Before the final days, however, Cola must still serve his own lord, Pope
Clement.[7] Most of Cola's diplomacy therefore focused on Avignon. Pe-

trarch had testified to the Curia's intense interest in Cola's *buono stato;* and Cola seems quite conscious of the public nature of his private correspondence. On July 15, 1347, he confides to an anonymous friend at court the purpose and achievements of his government: "Who could have believed that the Roman people, until now full of dissensions, of every type of sordid vices, could be brought back to a feeling of such great unity, to such a great love of justice and honesty, of virtue and of peace in such a brief time, and that its tyrants would have been subdued; its hatreds, attacks, murders and rapes ended?" (18, BBCR, 2.3:53, ll. 8–13).

The tribune emphasizes that he has done these things not out of "ambition for dignity, office, fame, honor or earthy gold, which I have always abhorred like filth; but the desire for the common good of the entire Republic of this most holy *status* has induced us to bend our neck to the yoke." Neither he nor any of his relatives have profited from this: "God be my witness for these things that we have done for the poor, the widows, the orphans and the wards of the City. Cola di Rienzo used to live more quietly than the Tribune does now; but we consider every labor for the love of this holy *status* a form of quiet" (18, BBCR, 2.3:54, ll. 37–41).

Despite reports to the contrary, he is so lacking in ambition "that the other day in Council, we requested that this office rotate among different persons every three months. Those who were at the Council meeting ripped their clothes in distress, and all tearfully replied: 'Each and every one of us will die first before this most sacred *stato* and this government is passed on to another man!'" (18, BBCR, 2.3:55, ll. 52–59).

But attempts to defame him continue. Cola, however, maintains his faith in God, despite the opposition of men: "We live certain that the more this most sacred *stato* is attacked by men on earth, all the more is it strengthened by God in heaven. . . . The seas surge in vain, the winds rage in vain; fire crackles in vain and turns into lifeless ashes against the man who trusts in the Lord. Like Mount Zion, he shall not be moved" (18, BBCR, 2.3:57, ll. 95–117). The psalm (124:2) continues: "Mountains are all around it: so the Lord is round about his people." Thus Cola repeats the central imagery of his first letter to the Romans from Avignon in 1343, an image that consciously repeats one of Pope Clement's favorite ideological themes: Rome is Jerusalem, the apocalyptic city of the Last Days.

Rienzo had now launched his campaign of image, slogan, and propaganda against even Avignon. Pope Clement, who for years had been secretly funding and encouraging his *familiaris,* must now have begun to feel uneasy with Cola's new claims and diplomacy.[8] Yet he still had no reason to doubt the tribune's loyalty, nor to deny the solid achievements of the *buono stato*. The pope, in fact, was in an ideological bind: he could not deny—much less condemn—Cola's claims for the *buono stato,* because the exiled papacy's own claims to spiritual supremacy and temporal universality depended precisely on Rome's universal stature and imperial inheritance. The perceived illegitimacy of the Avignon papacy made this continued reliance on Rome even more imperative; and Clement's own stress on Rome's apocalyptic associations with the New Jerusalem validated Cola's claims. The pope could not therefore undermine the concept of the *buono stato* directly. He could, however, begin to apply subtle and indirect pressure to remind Cola that the pope, not the tribune or the people, actually ruled Rome. Clement therefore set out a strategy of his own with clear and consistent positions that focused on issues of day-to-day governance: the pope has held, and still holds, all the major offices of the city; Cola and the papal vicar are acting solely as his "rectors." He also decided to hedge Cola in with other papal appointees and to raise the issue of the Jubilee and its dependence on the pope's good graces and the loyal cooperation of the Romans.

Clement began his campaign with a letter dated Avignon, June 27, 1347. After congratulating Cola and the vicar on the events of Pentecost, he quickly moved to counter Cola's most important slogan, that of the *buono stato*. Clement tells his rectors that they can be proud of establishing not the *bonum statum* but the *statum pacificum,* merely the "peaceful condition" in the city. Clement reminds Cola that the pope alone holds the titles of Senator of the People, captain, syndic, and other "frequently used offices of the City," which the people had granted him for life. Clement therefore grants Cola and the vicar the title of "Rectors of the City and its district" and commissions them to perform their offices diligently for the "cult of justice, fidelity, and peace."

Clement reiterates this point in a second letter of June 27; but here the pontiff begins to refer to Cola's government as a *regimen,* the standard term for a secular government. Clement avoids the use of the terms *status* or *bonus status* in any form. Nor is this an accidental or isolated instance. In this and other letters Clement uses this terminology repeatedly: he speaks of Cola's duty as exercising the *regimen* of the said city and its district, encourages the care of the *regimen,* promotes policies for Rome's good and useful *regimen,* while condemning the bad *regimine* of the barons.

Far from putting forth high theoretical claims for the papacy and its dealings with Rome, Clement VI appears to have countered the high claims of the *buono stato* with the mundane concerns of papal jurisdictions and privileges. A battle of slogans and public image therefore began: the *buono stato* versus the reestablishment of the papal *regimen*. As Clement continued to reserve all important titles to himself, Cola continued to claim ever new ones. To Cola's "Tribune," the pope countered with "Rector," to which Cola retorted that it was the "depraved and cruel rectors" who were responsible for the destruction and ruin of Rome and its provinces under the barons. Ambassador Francesco Baroncelli had already used a similar play of words on the *rectores* in his speech to the government of Florence on July 2. Cola also reminds the Romans that the barons had bandied about these same hated papal titles—"senators, captains, militia"—as the hypocritical slogans for their oppression.

But the pope had more than slogans at his disposal. In his second letter of June 27, Clement mentions, almost in passing, his appointment of Bertrand de Déaulx as legate to carry out papal decisions "for the good and useful government *[regimine]* of the said City." Furthermore, the pope will soon name a "certain person" to handle all matters relating to the upcoming Jubilee. Bertrand's presence in Rome could only serve to diminish the papal vicar's own authority and to curtail Cola's. With the naming of a third official, to manage the Jubilee, Clement also diminished whatever prestige Cola had won from his mission to Avignon in 1343 that finally secured the event.

On July 8 Cola wrote Clement to report that he has also forbidden the heralding of any lord but the pope within Rome and the exhibition of any heraldic devices—especially the arms of the Orsini, the Colonna, and the Savelli—upon Roman dwellings, or upon shields, "except for the arms of the Holy Roman Church, of Your Holiness, and of the Roman people." The tribune then describes how these *depicciones* were abolished and deleted, and how no other lordship of Rome was named "except for that of the Holy Church and of Your Holiness." Cola goes on to describe his reform of the city's finances—of the hearth tax and of the salt *gabelle*—and to defend himself against charges that he had abused these longstanding and jealously guarded papal prerogatives. In another of Cola's brilliant associative leaps, the tribune then describes how his regime has protected the poor, the powerless and oppressed, those who mourned, the just, the humble, the good, the peaceful, the gentle—all the categories of those who had been blessed by Christ in the Sermon on the Mount (Matt. 5:3–12). Cola thus silently invited Clement to make the connection to the conclusion of the sermon in Matthew: "You are the salt of the earth" (5:13), thus bringing the pope up short, in his obsession with salt taxes, with the true meaning of people who live in justice and peace.

Cola's reference also reinforces his sense of Rome's "good new age," for Matthew continues: "You are the light of the world. A city set on a hill cannot be hidden. Neither do men light a lamp and put it under a bushel, but upon the lamp-stand, so as to give light to all in the house" (5:14–16).

The passage is also a prelude to Jesus' most explicit statement of his mission and the coming into a new age: "Do not think that I have come to destroy the Law or the prophets. I have not come to destroy but to fulfill" (Matt. 5:17).

It would have been difficult for a well-read and intellectual churchman to miss the point. On July 14 Clement wrote Cola a strange letter, supposedly in response to the tribune's request, forgiving his sins and agreeing to act as Cola's personal confessor. Although we do not have Cola's original request and can only guess at its content, its context may be clarified by Cola's letter of July 15 to a friend in Avignon in which he alludes to a plot to assassinate him. It would then have made sense that the tribune had secretly informed the pope of these plans and of the danger of his impending death, asking for the forgiveness of his sins as a spiritual preparation for the martyrdom he felt close at hand. Whatever their content, these letters earned Cola's reentry into the pope's favor and good graces, for on July 26 Clement writes, addressing Cola with his old titles; and while reminding him and Vicar Raymond that they are only rectors, he calls Cola "our beloved son, Roman citizen, member of our family."

By the end of July, Cola's diplomacy had succeeded: he had won the alliance of Italy's major free communes, the respect or caution of its tyrants, the attention of Europe's kings, and the entreaties of the rivals to the throne of Naples. He had managed to maintain the pope's approval for these actions. In Petrarch and Barbato da Sulmona he had found brilliant supporters who could spread his fame and that of the Roman republic. Now he only had to consolidate these gains, and he chose a method of doing so that fit perfectly with both the practice of medieval diplomacy and the fundamental nature of his thought and government: the Roman Synod of August 1347.[9]

From the start of his *buono stato,* Cola planned a Festival of Italian Unity in Rome that would take place over the two weeks between the feast of San Pietro in Vincoli on August 1 and the feast of the Assumption of Mary on August 15. To it he would invite the ambassadors of all the cities and the princes to whom he had begun to spread the news of Rome's revival; in fact, the invitation to this festival accompanied the news. Cola realized that the pomp and circumstance involved in public display and ceremonial were the very lifeblood of Rome on both the spiritual and the material level. Even his choice of the word "synod" co-opted the term for a sacred church council. Cola also knew that his Roman Synod would manifest his *buono stato* to the rest of the world. It therefore had to contain many of the usual elements of medieval diplomacy and government display: elaborate ceremonial, feasts, processions of dignitaries and leading citizens in their finest, entertainments and public games, the granting of largess to the people and special gifts to ambassadors. If Avignon were to function so splendidly, how could Rome itself do anything less?

The tribune's keen sense of ceremony and display was revealed as early as the feast of St. John the Baptist, on June 24.[10] All Rome usually turned out for that yearly celebration at John's church of the Lateran. Cola also made his way across the city with great pomp: "He rode with a great company of knights. He sat upon on a white war horse. He was dressed in white silk vestments imbedded with ivory and decorated with gold lace. His look was handsome and terribly strong. Before his horse went the hundred sworn infantrymen of the *rione* of Regola. A *gonfalone* was carried above his head" (AR, XVIII, ll. 644–51, Porta, 165). While the Anonimo romano would later criticize Cola's expensive wardrobe as a descent into oriental despotism, the vast outlays spent on medieval costume were a necessary outward sign of status; and Cola's new display befit his new station and his role as symbolic leader of the *caput mundi*.

On another occasion Cola reversed the usual papal procession route along the via Papalis from the Vatican to the Capitoline and thence to the Lateran and led a splendid procession to St. Peter's *from* the Capitoline, just as early Christian and Byzantine imperial processions had done. The procession included a militia of knights, officials, judges, notaries, chamberlains, chancellors, Senate scribes, public officials, Cola's peacemakers, and syndics. An official, Janni de Allo, then marched with a silver goblet carrying Cola's eucharistic offering "in the fashion of a senator." More horsemen followed. Then came the symbols of the *buono stato:* the naked sword of justice carried by Buccio, the son of Giubileo, a knight who would remain loyal to Cola throughout his life. Another official, Liello Migliaro, dispersed money to the crowd, "as is done in the emperor's processions." Then the tribune, alone and dressed in fur-lined silk in yellow and green, rode on a great warhorse. In his right hand he carried a highly polished steel rod, a standard topped with the orb of the world, surmounted by a cross containing a piece of True Cross and inscribed with the words *Deus* and *Spiritus Sanctus*. Directly behind, Cecco d'Alesso carried above Cola's head his special standard with the sun, seven stars, and dove holding an olive branch in its beak. On his left and right marched fifty pikemen from Vitorchiano, the "Faithful," in bearskins. Finally, there followed all the citizens of Rome: the rich, the powerful, counselors, allies, and many "honest people." The procession crossed Ponte Sant' Angelo, "while everyone waved." Cola's triumph proceeded to the Vatican Borgo, where it was greeted solemnly and with great rejoicing by clergy of St. Peter's, who entrusted him "with possessions of St. Peter's."

Nor was the procession empty display: like much of medieval symbol and liturgy, it was meant to effect on the plane of reality what it revealed on the level of sign. Thus the Anonimo romano notes that "the gates and the barricades had been torn to the ground, the streets were open and free." On the most basic level this procession announced the reclaiming of the streets and public spaces for civil society: the demolition of the barricades was a sign that civil authority now ruled. The study of Italy's confraternities done in recent years also reminds us that such processions and elaborate feasts were the stuff not only of princes and popes but also of popular piety, and not merely the display of earthly pomp and largess— the richness of a prince or commune—but also an outward sign, a sacrament, of the love and concord that reigns in heaven and that humans can strive for here on earth. In this sense medieval processions also served as the ideal image of the heavenly city.

The procession performed other important functions: to bring together all the classes in Rome as a sign of unity and harmony, like the procession in Lorenzetti's *Buon Governo,* and to recall ancient Roman triumphs. We know that a copy of the Italian version of the *Storie de Troja et de Roma* or the *Lyber ystoriarum Romanorum* (Hamburg, Staatsbibliothek, Cod. 151) was produced in Rome in the reign of Martin IV (1282), perhaps at the papal chancellery, and that it contained images of classical triumphs, including one (fol. 90v) of Julius Caesar in a chariot being drawn by white horses, while an angel of Victory hovered behind him holding triumphal wreaths (see fig. 21). Its ownership had passed to the Savelli, Cola's Roman lords, and was probably available to Cola. Thus Cola's literary sources, the depictions of triumphs on the arches of Titus and Constantine, and the illuminations of contemporary manuscripts all provided classical models that were reinforced by medieval imperial ceremony. On the deepest symbolic level, on which Cola moved so easily, he had again combined diverse elements harmoniously: the revival of ancient Roman imperial glory, the restoration of communal *buon governo,* and the apocalyptic symbolism of the new age: a threefold synthesis of past, present, and future.

And so it was to be with the Roman Synod. Cola's knighting on August 1 would give him legitimacy in the eyes of Italian communal culture; his crowning as tribune on August 15 would revive the practice and glory of ancient Rome; and his imperial summons would usher in the Last Days as the new emperor would be elected in Rome to bring about a final age of peace, justice, and liberty. That the Roman Synod would stretch out over two weeks—from the knighting to the coronation and summons—was neither unusual nor extravagant, considering Rome's legacy of grand festivals and the need for those traveling from Italian communes and principalities (and even farther from across the Alps) for the pageantry to be worth the trip. The planning stages were announced as early as Cola's letters of May 24, as he invited the Italian governments to send ambassadors for this "Roman Synod" on August 1 "for the salvation and peace of our entire [Italian] province." From July 9 Cola's letters include notice of plans for his knighting and subsequent crowning with the tribune's laurel. By August 1, as the synod had begun, its program was fully spelled out.

August 1 carried immense significance in the Roman religious and mythic calendar, for it represented one of those great turnings of the ages on which Roman history hinged: the ancient festival marking the transformation of the pagan Octavius into the emperor Augustus. As Augustus watched, entranced, in the Senate house atop the Capitoline, the Virgin had appeared with the Christ child on the "altar of heaven," now the site of Sta. Maria *"in ara coeli."* During the early Middle Ages, August 1 took on another feast that celebrated Empress Eudoxia's donation to the city of the very chains, the *vincula,* with which St. Peter had been bound. The twelfth-century *Mirabilia* (II.6) gives an account of how this feast day thus symbolized the Romans' liberation from the old age of pagan sin and their rebirth into the age of Christian grace. Cola knew the *Mirabilia* well, and years later in his letter to the archbishop of Prague of August 1350 he quoted this very chapter. August 1 was therefore a natural date for Cola to celebrate Rome's liberation from the tyranny of sin and its entry into a new, third, *status,* his "good new age."

The ambassadors began arriving in the last week in July. According to the Anonimo romano: "Now foreigners grew thick; the inns were filled with the throngs of so many foreigners; abandoned houses were repaired; people flocked to the market. . . . All Rome was happy, it laughed again, and it looked like it had returned to better years past" (AR, XVIII, ll. 1039–57, Porta, 178). The *Chronicon Mutinense,* writing in far-off Modena, reported that over two thousand ambassadors and other guests attended shows of horsemanship, dances, and games.

It was the beginning of a highly charged diplomatic, civic, and religious time that filled the city and its inns with an atmosphere that must have recalled the Jubilee of 1300 and given the Romans a foretaste of 1350. Cola was determined to fill what might otherwise have been a standard round of medieval celebration with potent religious-civic symbols and diplomatic acts of substance: hosting an arbitration to the dispute over the crown of Naples and laying plans for settling the contested imperial election were only the most important. He received appeals from all over Italy, promised justice, and demonstrated that Rome was now living in the state of peace, justice, and liberty. This is why the Anonimo romano interrupts his description of the synod with a section devoted to "notable examples of the good justice of the tribune," because such justice, coupled with great pomp and display of wealth, was the proof of the *buono stato* that the rest of Italy had come to see, and remarkable proof it must have been.

There is evidence that Cola had also begun striking his own coinage, as various Roman communes had done since 1143.[11] For much of its history the commune minted a silver currency, based on the solidus from Provins in Champagne. Coins minted for Brancaleone degli Andalò in the 1250s and by Senator Pandolfo Savelli in the 1290s had depicted *Roma caput mundi,* a female figure sitting enthroned between two lions, holding a palm leaf signifying peace in one hand and in the other a T-O map dividing the world into three sectors formed by a "T" imposed within an "O." Cola's first coinage used this model (see fig. 22). But with his knighting on August 1, Rienzo struck a new issue, retaining the obverse but suppressing the *V.R.B.S.* on the reverse and replacing *ALMVS.TRIBUNAT[us]* with the more personalized *N[icolaus]•TRIBUN[us]• AUGUST[us]•.* Rienzo's new coinage would soon become a major issue in Avignon.

Cola chose the Lateran for the site of his knighting on the evening of July 31.[12] In preparation he ordered the expropriation of the planks and timbers that the barons had used to construct barricades and the stockades of their *fortilizie* and had them brought to the Capitoline. There he put them to two uses: to fortify the Senators' Palace, filling in the openwork colonnades on the facade (see fig. 6), thus symbolically expropriating the disruptive power of the barons and their private interest to the common security and good of the *buono stato,* and at the same time to weaken the barons' ability to protect their retainers. In fact, the Anonimo romano reports that Cola even entered Stefano il Vecchio's *fortilizia* to arrest robbers, "whom he hanged."

Cola also had many of the timbers brought to the Lateran. Here he had them joined together at the Lateran Palace to form the dining tables for his feast of Italian unity. On one level the act was a practical sign of unity built on the very elements of disunity; but Cola's action also worked on the deeper symbolic level of Lorenzetti's *Buon Governo* (see fig. 15a), where *Concordia* holds both the *chorda* and the large carpenter's plane, the "joiner's" plane used for just such tasks. Cola worked most effectively on this symbolic level: his language, his gestures, his paintings, his costumes, his conceptions were far closer to the mind of an artist than to the calculations of a politician. This has been often overlooked by historians; but it is precisely what explains Cola's remarkable rise and appeal to his contemporaries—to the Romans, to the pope, and to thinkers like Petrarch—and the disdain and loathing that he inspired among the barons and other men of power.

The ceremonial of the knighting was quite elaborate and well attended by all Romans and visitors: it began with a procession outside the Lateran led by foreign dignitaries, its main groups interspersed with musicians and trumpeters. Next came Livia with her mother, preceded by a young man holding a golden bridle, the symbol of humility and moderation, and then the ladies of Rome: "Many well-born ladies accompanied them because they wanted to please them," according to the Anonimo romano. Next came more musicians, then equestrian players. Cola's own entourage followed: he was preceded by a man carrying a naked sword (of justice) and by another carrying a banner with Cola's apocalyptic arms. Cola strode with his scepter; then marched the pope's vicar; and finally strutted the Roman nobility. That evening Cola gave a brief address announcing upcoming events and extending his invitation to all to return the next day.

After the crowds had gone home for the evening, the knighting followed a rather standard procedure: mass, solitary prayers by the candidate, a ritual bath, and solitary sleeping. In a letter to his patron, Rainaldo Orsini, of August 2, 1347, Cochetus de Chotiis adds that "at this baptism all the aforesaid ambassadors attended in person." The next day's schedule called for Cola's ceremonial dressing with the sword, spurs, and belt, to be followed by public events open to all, again at the Lateran. A remarkable aspect of this evening's ceremony, however, was Cola's appropriation of one of the chief symbols of Constantine, the first Christian ruler and the archetypal Christian "knight": "When all the people had departed, the clergy celebrated a solemn office. Then the group entered the Baptistry and he bathed in the basin of the Emperor Constantine, which is of the most precious basanite. This is an astonishing thing to speak of, and it caused people a lot of talk" (AR, XVIII, ll. 1286–91, Porta, 186).

The reason for this astonishment and talk, which was later to become a centerpiece of the pope's campaign against Cola, was the special place of that basin in Christian symbolism. While Constantine was actually baptized near Nicodemia in Asia Minor shortly before his death in 337, according to the tradition preserved in *The Golden Legend* 12, in this basin Constantine received both the cure for the leprosy caused by his persecution of the Christians and his Christian baptism at the hands of Pope Silvester. Constantine's baptism was a well-known theme in Italian art. It is central to the Constantine-Silvester cycle at SS. Quattro Coronati in Rome; Maso di Banco included it in his Silvester cycle at Sta. Croce in Florence; and it was illustrated in the *Liber Ystoriarum Romanorum* that Cola probably used in the Savelli library in Rome.

Again, the bath itself was nothing unusual. Medieval Italian communes had seen many of their younger patricians dubbed "knight of the bath," or "of the garter," or "of the fleece" in ceremonies derived from both the chivalric romances of France and the symbols of their own civic past, real or imagined. There is some evidence that in 1326 the Roman people honored Senators Stefano Colonna and Poncello Orsini with just such a ceremonial bath. But Cola's motivation in using this basin was clear: in reviving the Christian Roman Empire that Constantine had founded and in bringing back the glory of Roman antiquity, what better symbol of rebirth than this ancient font of Christian virtue?

But Cola's very pointed comparison of himself to Constantine was what would so unnerve the papal vicar and Pope Clement in Avignon, for the rebirth of *imperial* authority within and from Rome was precisely the greatest threat to the papacy's temporal claims on the city. It was very well and good for a German emperor to travel to Rome once in a generation to receive imperial coronation and popular acclamation, and then to retreat quickly north. It was something else again for a Roman and the Romans to revive the images, ceremonies, and legal claims of empire that Constantine had supposedly relinquished to the popes forever at this very Lateran Palace. And so, even at his moment of triumph, Cola was visited by portents of disaster, at least in the Anonimo romano's later reflections. In the center of the fifth-century baptistry, within the circle of eight ancient porphyry columns, the bed set up for his vigil night partially collapsed, leaving the Knight of the Holy Spirit angled somewhere between heaven and earth, "and so he remained in the silent night."

Early the next morning, August 1, papal vicar Raymond de Chameyrac celebrated mass in the *parlatorio* of the Lateran. Then, in what the Anonimo romano calls the Chapel of Boniface VIII at the Lateran, Cola received the belt of knighthood from Goffredo Scoto, a "syndic of the Roman people especially appointed for this." This chapel probably would have been the remodeled east wing of the papal palace, where the ninth-century banqueting hall looked out over the Piazza di San Giovanni. Around 1299 Boniface remodeled the east wing's balcony into a three-story *loggia di benedizione* (see fig. 9).

Here the theater of Rienzo's synod unfolded. After the public knighting Cola made an appearance on the papal loggia. There, dressed in scarlet trimmed with fur, he made his most startling declaration to date: his Decree on the Sovereignty of the Roman People.[13] Cola began his address by adding a new title to his panoply, one that had resulted from his dubbing: *candidatus Spiritus Sancti miles,* "the white-clad soldier of the Holy Spirit." The title is another wonderful example of Cola's rhetorical synthesis of the revival of the ancient Roman Republic, the Italian communal world, and the Joachite new age. For *candidatus* derived first from the ancient Roman candidate for office. For both the Roman and medieval communal political worlds, *miles* indicated the equestrian class that generally was the minimal social status required for public office. Finally, *candidatus* also meant "whitened" or "dressed in white" and thus referred back to the apocalyptic soldiers of Apocalypse 19:14: "And the armies which were in heaven followed him upon white horses, clothed in fine linen, white and clean." Few Romans could have forgotten the angelic figure of Cola's own apocalyptic painting at Sant'Angelo in Pescheria: "An armed angel, dressed in white, was coming; his cloak was of scarlet vermilion; in his hand he was carrying a naked sword."

The newly dubbed knight then confirmed this threefold symbolism with a speech unlike any that he had given since his return from Avignon in June 1344:

We, Candidate of the Holy Spirit, Knight, Nicholas, Severe and Clement, Liberator of the City, Zealot of Italy, Lover of the World and Tribune Augustus, wishing and desiring that the gift of the Holy Spirit be received and increased in the City as well as throughout all Italy, and imitating—as much as God permits—the good will, kindness, and liberality of the ancient Roman princes, make known to all that recently, after we had assumed the office of tribune, the Roman people learned again on the advice of each and all the judges, wise men and advocates of the City, that it still has that authority, power, and jurisdiction over the whole world that it had in the beginning and that it had when the aforesaid City was at its height; and it has expressly revoked all privileges made to the prejudice of such right, authority, power, and jurisdiction.

We, therefore, on account of the ancient authority, power, and jurisdiction and the present power granted to us by the Roman people in public parliament and by our Lord, the highest pontiff recently, . . . do with the authority and grace of God and the Holy Spirit and in every way, right, and form, decree, declare, and pronounce the holy Roman City, the capital of the world and the foundation of the Christian faith, and the governments of Italy, one and all, to be free. We have and do give the same cities the security of full liberty, and the individual peoples of the whole sacred Italy we decree to be free. And from now on we make, declare, and pronounce all the aforesaid peoples and citizens of the cities of Italy Roman citizens, and we wish them to enjoy the privilege of Roman liberty as well.

Likewise, with the same authority of God and the Holy Spirit, and of the aforesaid Roman people, we say, confess, and also declare that the election of the Roman Emperor—and the jurisdiction and monarchy of the entire holy empire—belongs to that beloved City and its people and also to the whole sacred Italy. To them this has devolved legitimately for many causes and reasons that we will cause to be declared in their place and time. To one and all the prelates, emperors elect and electors, kings, dukes, princes, counts, margraves, people, associations, and any others who are in particular or in common of any prominence whatsoever, who wish to gainsay this or pretend authority and power in the aforesaid election and in the empire itself, we assign and fix in these writings that from now until the coming feast of Pentecost [June 8, 1348] they should appear with their claims before us and other officials of the Lord Pope and the Roman people in the beloved City and the sacrosanct church of the Lateran. Otherwise, we shall proceed from the aforesaid deadline according to right and as the Holy Spirit shall minister.

Moreover, in addition to all the aforesaid, we cause to be cited in particular the illustrious princes mentioned below: the lord Lewis of Bavaria and the lord Charles, king of Bohemia, who assert that they are emperors of the Romans; the lord duke of Bavaria; the lord duke of Austria; the lord margrave of Brandenburg; the lord archbishop of Mainz; the lord archbishop of Trier; the lord archbishop of Cologne; the lord duke of Saxony. They should appear personally before us and the other officials of the Lord Our Pope and of the Roman people in the said city and place within the aforesaid time limit. Otherwise, we will proceed as is stated above, their absence and refusal to appear notwithstanding.

In all the aforesaid and in every one of our acts, processes, and executions, we in no way wish to abjure the authority and the jurisdiction of Holy Mother Church and of Our Lord Pope and of the Sacred College of Cardinals; in fact we wish always to direct our acts to their augmentation and honor; and as we are so bound, we wish to be imitated in everything. (27, BBCR 2.3:100–106, ll. 11–77; DKPSP, 205–6)

The Anonimo romano confirms the general thrust and particular elements of Cola's speech but then adds some details of his own: "After he made this citation, letters were immediately prepared and couriers were sent on their way. Then Cola drew his sword from its sheath and divided the air into the three parts of the world and said: "'This is mine, this is mine, this is mine'" (AR, XVIII, ll. 1321–26, Porta, 187).

For medieval people the world was divided not into four quarters but into the three major divisions of its lands: Europe, Africa, and Asia, just like the T-O map in Rome's hand and as Cola himself would write years later in his commentary on Dante's *De monarchia*. The Mediterranean was literally that: the sea in the center of these earthly realms that opened out like the crossing point of the "T" from the earth's focal point, Jerusalem. With his gesture Cola was not launching off into megalomania but simply repeating a standard part of the imperial coronation ceremony that his contemporary Romans had seen several times during their lifetimes.

The reaction of papal vicar Raymond was predictable: "Stunned and dumbfounded . . . nevertheless he protested." As Raymond wrote the pope on August 1, Rienzo had made his decree "without my advice or knowledge." He declared that "hearing and understanding them I was astonished, and as the Judge of hearts knows, I was so upset and confused that I lost heart and chose not to go up to the Lord's altar for the divine sacrifice that morning." But Raymond regained his senses, he tells the pope, and "I chided Cola bitingly for his temerity, his audacity, and his presumption. And since it appeared to me that his ordinances proceeded from the greatest fatuity and that they were issued against the liberty of the Church, I protested in the name of Your Holiness." The vicar, a well-known canon lawyer, insisted that Cola neither make, publish, nor sign these decrees, and "in the presence of the people and before the people had left the spot I demanded that he rescind, retract, remove, empty, annul and void them with all his might" (Papencordt, xvi–xvii).

Raymond further tells the pope that he warned Cola that these decrees had no validity "unless they proceed from the will of Your Holiness." The vicar ordered Pietro Viscardi de Gonessa, an imperial notary and his scribe, to make a public instrument of his statement, which Raymond then proceeded to record: "Done in Rome on the Loggia of the Lateran Basilica, after the solemn Mass, in the year of the Lord 1347, 15th Indiction, in the Sixth Year of Your Pontificate, the first day of August." He then named thirteen witnesses, most of whom had just participated in Cola's knighting. He had Pietro the notary sign and seal it.

Raymond followed his legal instincts, had a notary draw up an official letter of protest, and read it before the assembly; but the Anonimo romano adds some characteristic detail. As Pietro Viscardi "shouted out these protestations to the people in *alta voce*," Cola commanded a cacophony of "trumpets, kettledrums, and cymbals" to drown out the protest. "The larger sound covered over the smaller. Vicious buffoonery!" Yet here Cola's action may not have been buffoonery but the completion of another of those long-festering, well-planned, and highly symmetrical acts of vendetta at which medieval Italians were so skilled, the repayment of debt with principal and interest. Had not Raymond's lord, Pope Clement, just days after his own elevation in Avignon, just as Cola and the Roman delegates had concluded their heartfelt appeal for the pope to return to Rome and to grant the Jubilee, drowned out the Romans' final appeals in the midst of the audience hall with a curt and summary command to the choir to burst, *"alta voce,"* into the *Te Deum laudamus?*

The vicar's protest—legalistic, public, and on the record—decided Cola's next political move. The Anonimo romano puts it bluntly and places it *before* the Roman Synod, as if to deliberately emphasize Cola's personal motivations: "Wishing to be the sole lord in such a prosperous time, the tribune dismissed his colleague, the pope's vicar." It would have been impossible after Raymond de Chameyrac's protest either for him to stay on and retain any credibility with the pope, or for Cola to maintain their political partnership. Raymond also knew that Clement was to appoint both a new legate and a vicar to take charge of the Jubilee. But for the time being he remained at his post.

There were a good number of witnesses to these events. The next morning, August 2, Cochetus de Chotiis sent a detailed account to Rainaldo Orsini, the papal notary:

At the sound of the bell and the voice of the public crier, the Lord Tribune had assembled on the Capitoline all the ambassadors of over twenty-four lands, cities and provinces to celebrate his Mass of the Holy Spirit. On the altar he had placed and consecrated four *gonfaloni,* namely the standard that had the arms of Constantine: a white eagle with a crown in its mouth and a palm in his right claw. He had this taken up and with his own hand he gave it to the ambassador of Perugia as a sign of love and fraternity.

He gave a standard with the figure of Rome to the Florentine ambassador. On one side was depicted Christian Faith and on the other Italy with the letters S. [P.Q.R.].

To the ambassador of Todi he gave a standard with the arms of the Tribune and the Roman People, the she-wolf and Romulus and Remus.

To the ambassador of Siena he gave the standard of Liberty, and for all the aforesaid ambassadors and to all the others he put golden rings on their fingers, as a sign of Fraternity, Peace, and Love; and there were more than 200 of these rings. (Papencordt, *Cola di Rienzo,* xvii–xix; BBCR 2.4:21–26)

Giovanni Villani, who must have seen the Florentines' *gonfalone,* describes it as "an old women enthroned representing Rome, and in front

of her stood a young woman holding a globe in her hand, representing
the city of Florence, which she was offering to Rome." He adds that the
syndic of Florence did not step forward to accept it. Cola had it placed
upon the altar, declaring that "he'll come soon enough to take it in his
due time and place." The syndic of Perugia received a *gonfalone* "with the
arms of Julius Caesar: a golden eagle on a field of vermilion." The *Chronicon Estense* also offers a detailed description of the ceremony.

Cola's letters to the pope and to the cities of Italy confirm these accounts
and his difficulties in persuading the communes to accept what could be
taken as symbols of their fealty to Rome. The envoys of Todi recorded their
reservations in accepting "the *gonfalone* with the golden sun now in the
archive of San Fortunato" in a notarized form drawn up by their fellow
citizen, the notary and judge Pietro Ciccoli Pizzaluti. Todi's envoys might
well have had misgivings, because Cola wished to give them what were
described as "the arms of the Tribune": the apocalyptic symbol of the sun,
rays, seven stars, and dove. They were not alone in their suspicions that
they were becoming vassals of Rome. On August 5 Cola wrote to the government of Florence, explaining that his gesture was intended only as a
gift, a seal of friendship, and implied no further relationship.

Meanwhile, the agenda of the Roman Synod continued to unfold.
Chocetus reports that Cola also sponsored a "show of arms" in the Piazza Navona, the traditional site in medieval Rome for such games. All
the Roman and foreign knights attended, along with fifty foot soldiers
from each *rione*. Chocetus concludes: "There's no further news from the
City, except that the Romans together and individually are happy with
their Lord. Recommend me and my family to Your Lordship. And if it
pleases you to recommend me through your letters to the said Lord Tribune, include me in your recommendation, so that I can have an audience with him some time." If Cochetus had any underlying criticisms of
Rienzo's government, he kept them hidden from the papal notary and
did not let them interfere with his own hopes of working for the tribune.
He was probably representative of a large class of Rome's young nobles
or prosperous merchants, some genuinely attracted to Cola's vision of reform and rebirth, others by the opportunities a new and expanding government and economy could provide.

The round of feasting, games, processions, liturgies, and ceremonies,
set before a backdrop of real diplomacy, culminated on August 15 with
Cola's coronation as Tribune of the Roman People.[14] The Anonimo romano, either through a confusion with the knighting ceremony on July 31
or through some textual corruption, seems to conflate the two events and

to omit most of the details of the coronation. But we do have two accounts of the coronation liturgy itself from manuscript sources, one from the *Chronicon Estense,* as well as another letter by an anonymous source, perhaps Cochetus de Chotiis, sent from Rome and dated August 18. This reports that the ceremony took place on "Friday, the fifteenth of this month, on the feast of the Blessed Virgin in the church of Sta. Maria Maggiore." An anonymous manuscript source, the Cod. Torinese c. 182 A, offers details:

The coronation of the tribune proceeded as follows: The first crown was of oak, and was presented by the prior of the Lateran church, with the words: "Accept this crown of oak, since you preserve the citizens from death."

The second crown was of ivy, and was presented by the prior of the church of St. Peter, with the words, "Accept this crown of ivy, since you love religion."

The third crown was of myrtle, and was presented by the deacon of the church of San Paolo [fuori le Mura], with the words, "Accept this crown of myrtle, since you cherish your office and learning, and hate avarice."

The fourth crown was of laurel, and was presented by the abbot of San Lorenzo fuori le Mura, with the words, "Accept this laurel, since you cherish your office and learning and hate avarice."

The fifth crown was of olive, and was presented by the prior of the church of Sta. Maria Maggiore, with the words, "Humble man, accept this crown of olive, since you overcome pride with humility."

The sixth crown was of silver. It, together with a scepter, was presented by the prior [Giacomo] of the church of Santo Spirito in Sassia, with the words, "Tribunus Augustus, accept the gifts of the Holy Spirit, with the crown and scepter. Accept also this spiritual crown."

The apple, however, was presented by Lord Godfredo [Scoto], a knight, with the words, "Tribunus Augustus, accept this apple and cultivate justice; grant liberty and peace." And he kissed him.

The vicar of the cardinal of Ostia disposed of the crowns. The lord archbishop of Naples did not allow him to take away the silver crown.

While the aforesaid tribune was being crowned, he kept with him a pauper dressed wretchedly as a sign of humility. The Lord Tribune asserted that it was an ancient custom that when the Roman emperors returned in triumph they would tolerate and endure all the insults spoken to them by anyone on that day. (Gabrielli, *Epistolario,* 245–47; BBCR 2.4:36–38; DKPSP 214–16)

The anonymous letter of August 18 confirms that among the officials performing the crowning were the prior of Sto. Spirito in Sassia, the vicars of the lords cardinal, and the archbishop of Naples. The letter says, however, that the *fourth* crown was of olive and the *fifth* of laurel, and that the sixth was the "last crown." "After all of these Cola received the golden apple of justice." This source then goes on to say: "After all this was completed, the Lord Tribune spoke to the people in public and in his chambers and once again cited the lord duke of Bavaria and Lord Charles the king of Bohemia who either call themselves Roman emperors or were just elected to the imperial office, and after that he summoned all the imperial electors by name" (Papencordt, *Cola di Rienzo,* xx; BBCR 2.4:32–35). Thus Cola made *two* citations to the imperial candidates, one of August 1 and the second on August 15, and this could explain the confusion in the Anonimo romano's account and in his chronology of events.

With the participation of St. Peter's, St. Paul's, the Lateran, San Lorenzo fuori le Mura, and Sta. Maria Maggiore, Cola had representatives of the city's main churches and greatest pilgrimage sites. With Prior Giacomo of Sto. Spirito in Sassia he also included among his supporters the major confraternity of the city and its most important charitable organization. This would have been a natural alliance, both because of Cola's reestablishment of peace, justice, and the free access of pilgrims and because of these churches' hopes for the return of the papacy that Cola's rule promoted.

There exists another version of this coronation ceremony, which contains commentaries on some of the symbolic meanings of the objects. The text, for example, makes clear the symbolism of the silver apple: "He held the silver apple in his hand in the style of emperors seated in majesty, holding the orb in their hands, since the round shape is always suitable for motion, and in the manner of the Roman prince since Caesar; since Rome was the capital of the world" (Gabrielli, *Epistolario,* 247). More important, this manuscript (Vatican, Cod. arch. Vat. c. 3 A) contains a series of readings that accompanied the acts of crowning described earlier: Lucan's *Pharsalia* (1.357–58); Persius's *Saturae* (Prologue); Virgil's *Georgics* (1.24–28); Dante's *Paradiso* 1.22–30; and finally Prudentius, *Dittochaeon* 3 (*Archa Noe* 5.10), describing the dove holding the olive branch in its beak. The text from Dante demonstrates Cola's familiarity with the poet and his imagery, including the apocalyptic passages at the end of *Purgatorio* just before these verses. We do not know the exact date of composition of this manuscript, and it might have been composed after the fact and not by any of the principals involved; but Cola was quite capable of assembling these texts himself.

Rienzo's coronation thus made clear his threefold political and religious program. The tribuneship imitates the model of the ancient Romans, thus re-creating their world as much as possible. In the second sense, Cola reclaims the medieval prerogatives of Rome as the *caput mundi,* specifically the right of the Romans to elect the emperor. Finally, Cola's mixture of symbolic liturgy and imperial summons reintroduces the Joachite overtones of Rome as the seat of the emperor for the "whole world" in the Last Days. Yet if one assumes Joachite elements to Cola's political program and symbolism, one would naturally be led to ask why the tribune was granted only *six* crowns, not seven, the number of the Holy Spirit and one of Joachim's numeric keys. Was the scepter the seventh gift of the Holy Spirit, or was it the apple? There might, in fact, be another explanation. The Anonimo romano concludes his account of the Roman Synod with two curious details: "I won't forget the thing that he arranged for while he prospered. He made a chest with a hole in its top. Then it was expensive, but it was later reviled. He also had made a hat all of pearls, very beautiful, on top of which was a little dove of pearls. These various vices caused him to be overthrown and in this way bound him to destruction" (AR, XVIII, ll. 1373–80, Porta, 189).

The hat with the symbol of the dove, as luxurious as it was, was perhaps yet another, *seventh* tribunal crown that the *Anonimo* had earlier said he would describe. Worthy of the splendor of Rome and of medieval imperial regalia, it also bore the chief symbol of Cola's coat of arms and his government: the dove of the Holy Spirit. The parallel coronation text derived from Prudentius's description of the dove reinforces this assumption, as does a textual variation to Cola's letter to the Florentines of November 20, 1347, which reads that his *seven* crowns and the apple symbolized the seven gifts of the Holy Spirit.

The other item that Cola had made for himself, the "chest with a hole in its top," seems to have gone unexplained not only by the Anonimo romano but also by all subsequent students. It, too, had associations with the Holy Spirit, but these were indirect and subtle ones in the context of the Roman Synod, into which the Anonimo romano places it. We know from Cola's letters that he had planned to summon the German electors to Rome for a final ballot on the imperial throne on Pentecost day, June 8, 1348. Not that the German emperors had ever been elected by "ballot" per se. But Cola did have an ancient precedent among his favorite authors, including Cicero. Ballot boxes were a standard feature of all Roman municipal elections; into them the ballots, or *taballae,* of every form and level of election were placed. Once again Italian communal practice also informed Cola's innovation: a Venetian senate decision of April 26, 1350, for example, clearly spelled out the balloting procedures used for nominations to high office in that republic. Notaries like Cola played a major role in such proceedings. Thus Cola's precious and reviled invention may have been the ballot box into which the German electors were to cast their votes to settle the imperial succession and bring both emperor and pope back to Rome in the Last Days.[15]

Heated discussions followed among the assembled foreign visitors and Romans over Cola's knighting, his bath in Constantine's font, and his imperial summons: "Some rebuked him for his audacity, some said that he was a dreamer, a madman," the Anonimo romano reports.[16] But political discussion soon gave way to a splendid feast at the Lateran Palace to which all of Rome and its visitors were invited. "There was no order there: plenty of abbots, clerics, knights, merchants, and other people." "Water was more scarce than wine," and the wine flowed continually from a remarkable fountain devised inside the bronze horse of Constantine out in the piazza, from its belly through its nostrils, out into a fountain below, from which all could drink their fill. Sturgeon, that most royal of fish, was served in abundance to all comers, as were other foods generally restricted to the nobility either by price or by sumptuary law: "delicate" fish, pheasant, and kid. And why not? Such social mixing was a common feature of medieval festival; and Cola certainly did not intend any social revolution through his acts; but with such mixing of the classes and of Roman and foreigner he meant to make manifest the Romans' special place in the scheme of things, to recall the days of the city as imperial and papal capital, as the bustling and rich goal of pilgrims and merchants, clerics, and ambassadors from every land; a living tableau of the *buon governo;* the realized dream of the taverner's son as well. *Refudio,* "leftovers," were plentiful and freely given away; they must have found their way into every Roman household that night.

While Cola and vicar Raymond sat at the pope's marble table and presided over the feast for the ambassadors and Rome's mixed classes in the Old Dining Hall, Livia and the ladies dinned in Pope Boniface's new banquet wing. The separate feasts were a standard division by gender and one taking its cue from many a royal feast during that century. Cochetus de Chotiis, in fact, remarks in his letter of August 2 that "no emperor could have done as much." Musicians and dancers circulated among the guests. The Anonimo took special note of one that impressed him strangely that night: a man dressed in an ox's hide, horns and all. "He played and leapt." When the celebrations were over, Cola, still in scarlet, rode off with a large mounted escort to the palace on the Capitoline.

But there were some guests who had been invited to these two weeks of festivities who decided not to come: the Colonna, the Orsini, and their allies. Vicar Raymond de Chameyrac lodged his official protest in the midst of the festivities and disappeared from the Roman scene shortly thereafter; and some others learned the details only after the fact, including Cola's lord and master, Pope Clement VI.

In a letter written between July 27 and August 5, 1347, in the midst of his synod, Cola informed the pope of administrative and fiscal matters and of much of the recent political events in the city: his conflicts with the prefect Janni di Vico and other barons. Cola reiterates that despite what the pope may have heard, his tribune remains constant in his goals of justice, peace, liberty, and security under the *buono stato*. Cola further defines this *buono stato* as "a most sacred" state as well. This was a propaganda and political gambit, for Cola must have realized that only the church could claim such a formula. Even the imperial use of *holy* had caused much conflict with the popes; and Pope Clement in Avignon was particularly jealous of all papal rights and claims. Realizing the pope's probable reaction, Cola then repeats his offer to resign, his proposal that the tribuneship be rotated, and the dramatic refusal of the Council to accept his offer:

Everyone on the Council, this one ripping his clothes, that one dripping with tears, another tearing his face with his nails, all cried out with grief: "Each and every one of us would rather die than have any other government but yours; for we have experienced well enough with our destruction and servitude the quality of another government; and we can see with our own eyes that the Holy Spirit has worked so many miracles in this City through you that in these days we live and we shall live in justice and peace and sweetest liberty." (28, BBCR 2.3:106–16, ll. 128–36)

He then reminds Clement of his popular appeal and his achievements, goes on to ask the pope to agree to his reining in the officials of the Patrimony and the Campagna, and then informs his lord that the day before the captain of the Patrimony had suddenly died: "And so I believe without a doubt and I hope most firmly in God, whose judgments are hidden, that the same should happen to each and every one who presumes to oppose this holy *buono stato*" (ll. 147–49).

Reports would, no doubt, soon be reaching the pope of the events of the Roman Synod. Cola must have known that on August 1 Raymond de Chameyrac would have sent a messenger to Avignon with news of his public protest against the tribune's imperial decree. He might not have known of Chocetus de Chotiis's letters, but he could have assumed that there would have been such independent reports. And so, in a first postscript of his July 25 letter, dated August 5, Cola informs the pope of the events of the past week and conveys his hopes that all this is merely a prelude to the return of the papacy to Rome in the Jubilee year, and that the emperor will join the pope there. This is the work of the Holy Spirit, he states, and the result of his actions will be that "there will be one flock and one shepherd, through the unity of the same grace of the Holy Spirit." He thus reveals a Joachite expectation of the Angel Pope and Last World Emperor coming together for that apocalyptic event: the Jubilee.

On August 5, 1347, Cola sent a second postscript. Here he claims that "the Spirit of the Lord works for the growth of this *buono stato*." He goes on to describe his Roman Synod or Festival of Italian Unity and his public diplomacy with the Italian states. He defends himself against charges that he has burdened the clergy with taxes, and he concludes with some political news that must have threatened the pope as much as Cola's religious gestures: his report on relations with the king of Hungary and the Neapolitans.

Thus, by the time the first news of Cola's knighting and summons of the Germans to Rome had reached him in Avignon, probably just before August 15, Clement may well have begun taking Cola's actions not only as a policy reversal but also as a bitter personal betrayal. The pope appreciated his lieutenant's deep learning and his quick wit; he had protected him against even such powerful cardinals as Giovanni Colonna and had staked much of his personal Roman capital upon Cola's loyalty. And now Colonna was probably telling him that he had made a disastrous error of personal judgment where straightforward power politics alone should have counted. Now the person he had described as his *familiaris* was plotting against him to take control of Rome for himself and his *buono stato*. The reaction of this urbane and worldly man therefore fit his personality: the pope began carefully, delicately plotting Cola's downfall and seeking his personal humiliation, as well as his public *infamia* as a traitor and a heretic.

The atmosphere at Avignon and the papal palace soon began to reflect the pope's growing suspicion and anger. By the end of August, Petrarch was still writing Cola daily. In a letter of August 21–25 (*Variae* 40), the poet tells the tribune that he had taken to forthright defenses of him against mounting criticisms in the Curia, losing many an influential and longtime friend in the process. "Homage begets friends; truth, enemies." Petrarch then speaks to Cola in a symbolic language that he knew the tribune would comprehend. The poet had dreamt a vision of Cola on a great height, above everyone else, already earning the jealousy and enmity of Phoebus and of traitors within his own midst plotting his over-throw for their own advantage. Petrarch tells Cola that this is because he had disturbed the natural order of the universe. "I listened, and be-hold! the deep thunder of a distant cloud—like the warning of an ap-proaching storm." By the end of August, with news from Rome of Cola's coronation and his synod causing great consternation at Avignon, Pe-trarch was still openly supporting Cola and singing his praises in his *Eclogue* 5, "The Shepherds' Affection." He accompanies this with a let-ter, *Variae* 42, explaining the allegory of the poem: Cola's displacement of the outmoded government and empty political slogans of the Colonna and Orsini factions.

But the hopes of a poet and a visionary had to be tied to real political clout. By August 17, perhaps not yet informed of Raymond de Chameyrac's dismissal, Clement sent a letter to his Roman "rectors." He calls Cola "our beloved son and member of our household family." The pope acknowl-edges Cola's accomplishments, "tending to the praise of God, the honor and reverence of the Apostolic See and of Holy Mother Church and the peaceful condition *(statum)* of the City and the advantage of the Repub-lic." Then, without muttering an open word of hostility, Clement launches his campaign to depose the tribune. He informs Cola and Raymond that he has appointed his representative "for the planning of the fifty-year Ju-bilee." This is Matteo, bishop of Verona, "a man both endowed with pro-found learning and conspicuous in his uprightness, maturity and discre-tion." Matteo carries with him the letters for the aforesaid Jubilee year and is fully informed of the pope's intentions for this. The pope asks the discretion and cooperation of Cola and the vicar and their attention to Matteo's advice and helpful suggestions. Had Clement already heard of Cola's knighting and Raymond's protest and chosen not to raise the is-sue until he had received confirmation from the tribune? This may well be, but in any case the pope seems already to have decided he needed to replace Raymond and to hem in Rienzo.

Cola soon realized, either from Petrarch or from his other sources in Avignon, that opposition to his rule was gaining ground. He therefore dispatched a letter to Clement VI, dated August 20, to counter these "ru-mors, fallacious words," and to "declare the truth." Cola gives a brief re-port of his tribunal coronation. He then asks the pope to send an inquisitor to investigate whether he has done anything contrary to the church's in-terests. But it was already too late, and no inquisitor was needed. On Au-gust 21 Clement wrote to Bertrand de Déaulx, his legate for the affairs of Naples and already named special legate to Rome. By now definite news had come from Rome, and it had been confirmed by Rienzo's own pen. The pope therefore began actively to plot the tribune's destruction:

From these facts [reports of the Roman Synod] it is palpably evident that Cola is aiming at the occupation and the usurpation of the territory of that same Church, to withdraw it from the dominion of the said Church, and to subject it to the sway of the Romans.

It is likely, we suppose, that these and other innovations instituted in that City have come to your notice; and unless an opportune remedy be quickly applied, perilous scandals and serious dangers may arise from these—as your discretion can readily understand. Therefore, desiring to prevent such scandals and such dangers and hoping that a timely and effectual remedy may be employed by the exercise of your foresight and by the grace of God, we, by this apostolic letter, bid your discretion that without delay you get ready to go at a moment's notice as far as the City or its vicinity, provided this can be done without serious prejudice to the conduct of those affairs in the kingdom of Sicily that have already been entrusted to you. We bid you go there that you may provide against such innovations and for the safety of the City in accordance with the power conferred on you by your liege lord and that you may diligently strive to provide a remedy in due season. For every possible avenue must be closed to the dangers and the evils that can arise.

We shall unhesitatingly dispatch to you whatever letters seem necessary to you for this purpose, whatever letters, indeed, you yourself will ask for and dictate. . . .

In order, however, that you may be more fully informed regarding what has already been done in these matters, we enclose copies of letters that we have recently forwarded to the bishop, to Cola, and to the Roman people, and we also enclose copies of other letters. Finally, we have sent a full statement of our information concerning the above-mentioned matters to our venerable brother Matteo, bishop of Verona, and we have provided that he be assigned to the City and ultimately to you. (Theiner 175, 2:179–80; CRCR, 69–71; DKPSP, 216–17)

Cola had declared himself the "lover of the world," and now the world had begun to engage him. It was the barons who were to make the first pass.

CHAPTER 10

War with the Barons

And so Cola organized the militia of the knights of Rome in
this order. For each *rione* of Rome he mustered infantry and
30 cavalrymen, and he issued them pay. Each cavalryman had
a destrier and a pack horse, protection for his horses, and newly
decorated armor. They were a good match for the barons.
He also organized and equipped the infantry and gave them
gonfaloni. He devised the *gonfaloni* according to the symbols
of their *rioni,* and he issued them pay. He commanded them
to be ready at the ringing of the bell; and he made them swear
fealty. There were 1,300 infantrymen and 360 cavalry, select
young men, masters of war, well armed. When the tribune
saw that he was armed with the militia he had thus created,
he prepared to make war against more powerful people.

Anonimo romano, XVIII, ll. 738–51, Porta, 168

The *buono stato* had been established, but it needed both a regular system
of taxation and a defense force to maintain peace and justice. The papacy's
flight to Avignon had shifted power and control over the city's finances
to the barons. What public funds the commune did command—*gabelle* on
trade and business and the *focatico,* the hearth tax on households—either
had been left to lapse or had been diverted from the public sector into
the hands of powerful private interests. Thus military supremacy and the
reestablishment of taxing authority went hand in hand with any reform
of the city's public life and government. "So they gathered the ancient
census of the people of Rome; and every day so much money came to

Rome that it was hard work just to count it," the Anonimo romano reports. The actual figures may have approached Cola's estimates: annual income from the salt tax at 100,000 florins, and by his letter of July 18 to Pope Clement, he boasted of having levied 30,000 florins.[1]

Compliance was high: both Romans and subjects of the district now felt that their taxes would go to pay for security, the administration of justice, road maintenance, and other public works that marked any *buon governo*. The cities, towns, and communes of lower Tuscany, of the Campagna, and of Marittima prepared to levy and transfer payments to Rome, while the barons "obeyed graciously." But the barons' submission to a change in government atop the Capitoline, to someone who had the pope's blessing and who might keep the streets clean and prevent their enemies from gaining supremacy within the city, was one thing. The reimposition of taxes and submission to an aggressive government over the district of Rome where the barons had enjoyed a free hand for half a century now, was something else again. If Cola had reformed the city militia and turned it into a powerful and well-disciplined fighting force to confront the barons, his new taxes provided these barons with the perfect excuse to resist.[2]

"Two alone assumed the spirit of rebellion," wrote Cola to Clement VI on July 8. "These were Janni di Vico,[3] formerly prefect of the city, and [Nicola Caetani] the count of Fondi." The Janni in question was Giovanni, lord of Vico on Lago di Vico, about forty kilometers east-northeast of Rome, just off the via Cassia. The lords of Vico had long been the hereditary prefects of the city, an office that dated back to the reign of Emperor Augustus. But like most of the barons, they derived their main strength from their wide holdings in the district of Rome. Their origins are uncertain. By the beginning of the tenth century they were already a powerful and important family in Rome, exercising the prefecture through hereditary right and holding properties in Trastevere and on the Isola Tiberina. By that date they already held some castles in the province of Tuscia, including one at Vico. A policy of aggressive aggrandizement combined with a long-term "politics of waiting" marked the family from the start.

In 1337 Giovanni III (Janni) became count of Vico and prefect. In the course of his rise he either ordered the murder of or himself murdered his own brother Faziolo to seize from him the lordship of Viterbo, an office conferred by their father, Manfredo. By the mid–fourteenth century Janni was carving out a principality along the northern and western borders of the Patrimony of St. Peter that spread outward from Vico and would eventually center on Viterbo and include territories belonging to

Bolsena, Orvieto, Todi, Narni, and Amelia inland and even absorb Civitavecchia and Corneto on the coast. He thus created an enclave within the Papal States that threatened to cut off not only Rome's access to its grain supply around Corneto but also its lines of communication with Tuscany and Umbria along the via Cassia and via Flaminia.

The prefect's plans did not go unchallenged. Here, around Lago di Vico and Lago di Bolsena, the lords of Vico ran into the competing claims and ambitions of two of Rome's great baronial families: the Anguillara and the Orsini. The first had their base of estates, *terre* and *castre,* at Anguillara on Lago di Bracciano to the south of Lago di Vico and reached out from there north as far as Ronciglione, only a few kilometers from Lago di Vico, west to the valley of the Biedano at Barbarano Romano, and east and north toward the Tiber Valley, including holdings at Magliano Romano and around the slopes of Monte Soracte. Their holdings, like those of most of the baronial families, were not compact territorial units but sometimes contiguous, sometimes isolated fiefs; thus they were interspersed with and interrupted by those of the other main family of the region, the Orsini. Their branch centered at Soriano, just north of Lago di Vico, and held a wide swath of territory between the via Cassia on the west and the via Flaminia on the east. It stretched from Mugnano in the Tiber Valley at the northern border of Lazio, skirted past Lago di Bolsena and Viterbo, and made its way parallel to the river past Magliano Romano, Formello, and Isola, now Isola Farnese, the site of the ancient Veii.

As was the habit of the competing baronial families of Rome, the counts of Vico long had strong marriage ties with their rivals. Bertoldo Orsini, of the Castel Sant'Angelo branch, had married Mabilia di Vico, while in 1320 Giovanni (Janni) fathered an illegitimate son with an Orsini daughter and a sister of Giordano. This son was to become the famous Briobris, or Brisse, the military leader who died in 1353 and whose tomb still rests in San Francesco at Vetralla. In 1345 Lodovico, Giovanni's brother, wedded Venozza Orsini, daughter of Andrea and the cousin of Giordano, and further solidified the alliance between the two families.

Exchanges, sales, alienations, and "hostile takeovers" among baronial families were also as common here as they were south of the Tiber between the Colonna and Caetani. In 1314, for example, the Orsini purchased from the Anguillara for the sum of 3,300 florins a large share of the castle of Magliano Romano. By the mid-1340s competition among the barons of northern Lazio had come to a head. On August 1, 1346, Clement VI ordered Andrea Orsini, son of Orso of the Orsini di Campo dei Fiori, to desist from building a *fortilizia* in the papal *castrum* of Vetralla. At the same time he warned Janni di Vico not to purchase the same *castrum*. The pope's words had little effect. A new government in Rome led by a taverner tribune and a ragtag army must therefore have made little difference to the barons and their family strategies.

And so when Cola summoned Janni di Vico to appear in Rome, as the other barons had done, and swear his fealty to the *buono stato,* the prefect of the city refused the summons "a thousand times." At the same time Janni fortified the recently "acquired" Vetralla and seized another position of great strategic importance, the *rocca,* or fortress, of Respampani. The intentions of the lord of Vico were clear: to exploit what he saw as the weakness of Rome's new government in order to consolidate his territorial gains on Lazio's northern and western borders. The war against the barons had begun. Its first theater of activity was to be the point where the via Cassia toward Siena and Tuscany intersected the road that led from Corneto inland to Viterbo and the Tiber Valley, a wide stretch of territory between Blera on the south of the Cassia, Vetralla, Lago di Vico and Viterbo, the center of Janni di Vico's *signoria,* to the north.

Viterbo itself lies at a crossing of the routes between the coast and the Tiber Valley and between Rome and southern Tuscany, about one hundred kilometers north-northwest of Rome on the via Cassia. Because of its centrality within the papal territories, its safety from both the Romans and German emperors visiting Rome, and its long-standing hostility to the Roman commune, the city served as a major papal center. Throughout the thirteenth century, however, it was gripped by party struggle between its two main baronial families, the Gatti and the Vico, a struggle that boiled over after the papacy's flight to Avignon. By 1341 Janni di Vico had emerged as Viterbo's sole tyrant.

At the other end of the theater of war stood Vetralla, a key strategic site in northern Lazio. The city caps a long, steep spur above the via Cassia, which makes an almost ninety-degree turn sharply around the town and heads east and south toward Sutri and the Monti Sabatini. To the west the city offers a sheer cliffside crowned with walls; its long, steep southern flanks were guarded by walls and towers; while its more gradual eastern slope was defended by a *rocca* built only recently by the Orsini at the town's southeast. This broad, seven-story structure culminates in a massive, crenellated, round tower on its northeastern corner. Commanding the border to Tuscany and the Patrimony from its rise above Tuscia's rolling chalk flats and farmlands, Vetralla lies only ten kilometers west of Lago di Vico, on the via Cassia, eighty kilometers from Rome,

and it controlled east-west communication between Viterbo and the sea
at Corneto, and north-south communication between Rome and Tuscania. Holding it was therefore a strategic goal of Janni di Vico, and here
he threatened to cut off the logistic and diplomatic axis from Rome to
the north.

Cola therefore decided to act swiftly on several fronts: the military, the
judicial, and the diplomatic. In a letter to Clement VI of July 8, 1347, the
tribune had already explained his actions to the pope:

This Janni di Vico I have condemned by just sentence as an enemy of God and
the apostles Peter and Paul, whose cause my work pursues. I deprived him of every
dignity and office in full and public parliament. Nor did I set aside equity and
gentleness in case he might want to humbly admit to the impudence of his error
and freely and devoutly restore, as an offering to the City Chamber, the Rocca
Respampani, long and unhappily occupied by him—and concerning which I often
acted by appropriate means to demand from him. I shall be ready to treat him
with mercy. (15, BBCR 2.3:44–45, ll. 77–86)

Medieval military logic was often quite different from modern strategy. The Rocca di Respampani is a case in point. Throughout his campaign against Janni di Vico, Cola's letters are preoccupied with the
fortress. Called "La Roccaccia" by the medieval Romans, the fortress had
formed an essential part of the defensive system of the Byzantine duchy
of Rome and had long counted among the special possessions of the city.
Rome seized it from Viterbo in 1228 and rebuilt the fortifications early
in the fourteenth century. On the site of this *rocca* there now stands the
newly restored "hunting lodge" of Pope Paul V (1605–21), but behind the
noble facade and grand wings of the lodge there still rise the remains of
the fourteenth-century *rocca*. The fortifications of Cola's time are not imposing: low walls of about five meters, protected by a moat no wider than
seven meters and accessed by a stone, two-spanned bridge that leads into
a modest gatehouse. But the *rocca* depended far more on its location at
the head of a steep prominence over the confluence of two tributaries of
the Marta: the Respampani and the Blera. It dominates the bridgehead
of the medieval road from Norchia west that still spans the Respampani
at the southeastern foot of the cliff.

Even today, where thick forest covers the slopes of the hills to the south
and west, the view from the lodge's tower extends as far north as Tuscania and Marta on Lago di Bolsena. But if the current tree cover were absent, the garrison lookouts could have seen as far south as Corneto itself.
This was probably the case in the fourteenth century, when drastic over-

population forced the farming of every bit of arable land, including steeper hillsides that have since reverted to waste and forest. The site shows up quite distinctly as "Rocca Respampani di S. Spirito" on a 1547 map of the Campagna Romana, in which it is the only habitation between Tuscanella and Corneto, and around which the countryside is devoid of forest for miles. Its location thus tells us much of medieval notions of strategic importance. A strong fortress here, garrisoned by a large company of mounted knights, could disrupt traffic and communication throughout the region.

Tuscanella itself was long part of the Patrimony and was thus hotly contested between the Orsini and the Anguillara throughout the thirteenth century, and between the papacy and the lords of Vico in the fourteenth. As a result of an unsuccessful rebellion against Boniface VIII, the defeated city's name was changed from Tuscania to the diminutive Tuscanella. Cola mercifully commuted Boniface's onerous annual tribute of £1,000 to a gift of one hundred pounds of grain for the church of Sta. Maria in Aracoeli. His clemency had its practical effect: it gained Tuscania's alliance against Janni di Vico and helped encircle his lands. Thus the position of the Rocca di Respampani was vital if communication with Tuscania and the papal Patrimony of southern Tuscany were to be maintained. Its possession also guaranteed command over the rich agricultural lands of the Cornetan uplands, and thus the "granary of Rome." The war with di Vico was thus not only a first test of strength but also in the vital and long-term interests of republican Rome.

Cola also used the campaign as an opportunity to solidify his alliance with the barons who had already sworn allegiance to the *buono stato.* He appointed as captain general of the army Cola Orsini, lord of Castel Sant' Angelo near Rieti. This Orsini was probably a Nicola from the Tagliacozzo branch of family, the son of Napoleone, the younger brother of Giacomo. Cola also named Giordano Orsini his assistant. This was Giordano of the Monte branch, the son of Poncello, younger brother of Bertoldo. The choice of the Orsini was a good one. Within Rome the family had long dominated the *rioni* where Cola had grown up and then lived and worked; to a certain degree they and the Savelli were Cola's protectors, and he, in turn, felt a certain loyalty to them. His choice was also natural given the Orsini estates and interests in the area of Vetralla and Viterbo and their rivalry with the lords of Vico. In the world of the local feudal levy and the privately held castle, they were strategically well placed to wage the war and to defend whatever territory the Romans won from the prefect. Because they would also bear the brunt of any countermeasures launched by Janni di Vico from Viterbo, it made great sense that they be entrusted with the military operations in that theater.

Cola described the opening operations of the campaign in his letter to Clement VI dated July 27–August 5:

By the grace and favor of the Holy Spirit this army occupied Vetralla after the first horrible assault. To take the *rocca* by storm, which he had constructed recently to more freely hold the city in servitude and tyranny, the army built trebuchets, asinells, and other kinds of different war machines and also built underground mines. Rocks rained down thick from the trebuchets, they hurled day and night without cease; they smashed the walls of the *rocca* and they demolished the rampart fortifications of its tower, so that inside it there could be neither hope of protection nor an hour of rest. Nor should I omit the continuing campaign of scorched earth against Viterbo, because the Viterbesi, who had committed rebellion, had been fined more than 40,000 florins. (28, BBCR 2.3:106–7, ll. 16–27)

Cola also reported the participation of troops from Corneto under "Manfredo, their lord," and from Perugia, Todi, and Narni, as well as those of the Roman barons. The initial attack must have taken place sometime before June 17. The Anonimo romano confirms these details, including the use of the asinell, but adds: "Night fell. Those in the *rocca* mixed up sulfur, pitch, oil, wood, turpentine, and other things, and threw this mixture on top of the edifice. The asinell caught fire that night. In the morning it was found in ashes" (AR, XVIII, ll. 788–92, Porta, 170).

Cochetus de Chotiis wrote to his patron Rainaldo Orsini:

The *rocca* was held by the prefect, however, so that the army remained around the said *rocca* building trebuchets and manganels for twenty-seven days [June 18?–July 15?]. Meanwhile the same captain [Nicola Orsini your nephew] often rode with the militia to the city of Viterbo, bearing off wheat, barley and other grains belonging both to Viterbo and to the people of the Biedano valley, so that the prefect answered the summons and was detained on the Capitoline [July 16] until the Rocca Respampani . . . was returned to the hands of the Chamber. And yesterday [August 1] the Tribune sent as castellan of Rocca Respampani Lello de Camiglianis, a good commoner.

Upon the return of the captain with the militia to the City on the feast of Saint Mary Magdelene [July 22], as he entered Rome, Nicola [Orsini] received great honor as the people waved olive branches. Triumphal arches of stage scenery were made in his honor through the City all the way to the Capitoline. The Lord Tribune made a speech in the parliament on the Capitoline commending him and the militia, the horse as well as the foot. (Papencordt, *Cola di Rienzo,* item 9, xvii–xix)

Rienzo had ensured that Janni di Vico would be cut off from reinforcement and encircled. On July 15 Cola had written to an unnamed friend in Avignon that Rome had received reinforcements from "all the cities of Tuscany." In a letter to Florence of July 19, he had informed the government that Roman agents had discovered that di Vico had recruited mercenaries in Lombardy to aid his rebellion against Rome. Cola therefore emphasized the danger this posed not just for Rome but for all of free Italy and requested that the Florentines intercept these reinforcements as they passed through Florentine territory. The Vetralla campaign coincided with Cola's diplomatic outreach for the Roman Synod of August, and the attendance of so many ambassadors from the free communes of Tuscany, Umbria, and Lazio makes even more sense in the context of the common danger posed to them by Janni di Vico's expansionist policies.

The swiftness and directness of the campaign, the numbers of troops that Rome and its allies were able to field—one thousand cavalry and six thousand foot, according to the Anonimo romano; eight hundred knights and unmentioned infantry, according to Bishop Ildebrandino Conti of Padua—and the devastation done to his holdings probably would have forced Janni di Vico to come to terms in any case, but the threat of Cola's personal participation in the siege and the surge in morale that this would bring the Romans finally forced di Vico to concede. Negotiations were begun by the middle of July, at first through Ser Gianni, an ambassador of Janni di Vico, and through Fra Acuto of the Hospitallers of Assisi, a respected religious who had founded the Hospital of the Cross of Sta. Maria Rotonda in Rome. We are fortunate to have a transcript of the hard personal bargaining between Janni and Rienzo, signed by Cola di Rienzo himself and dated July 16, 1347, now preserved in the Spanish College in Bologna.

At Cola's insistence, the deposed prefect came to Rome, probably no sooner than July 18. According to the Anonimo romano,

It was the ninth hour, at midday. He entered the Campidoglio and placed himself in the tribune's custody. In his company he had a force of sixty men. Then the gates of the Campidoglio were sealed, the bell was sounded, and the men and women of Rome gathered outside. The tribune held a parliament in which he announced that Janni di Vico wished to obey the people of Rome. (AR, XVIII, ll. 809–17, Porta, 170–71)

Cola provided the details of the ceremony to Clement VI on July 27:

Giovanni di Vico, . . . in most solemn parliament, prostrate at my feet, humbly and reverently begged forgiveness, and he swore to the commands of Holy Mother Church, of Your Holiness, to me and to the Roman people upon the most sacred body of Our Lord Jesus Christ and upon the head and the standard of Saint

George, knight and protector. And once he had accepted the commands, clemently I restored him to the office of the prefecture and to each of his honors. (28, BBCR 2.3:107–8, ll. 31–37)

Only upon the surrender of Respampani to the Roman castellan, Lello de Camiglianis, on August 1, was the last of the Roman army ordered back from Viterbo and Janni and his son Francesco released from custody in Rome, a fact related by the letter of Cochetus de Chotiis of August 2. The *Chronicon Estense* offers some further motivation for di Vico's submission: Cola had offered a bounty of £1,000 to anyone who had killed the prefect in the meantime.

As part of the peace settlement, the tribune also arranged the reconciliation of Janni's son Francesco with his estranged wife, Perna, the daughter of Giordano Orsini. Cola and the Romans also regained a series of castles throughout Lazio, several of which had long been possessions of the city. These included the castle of Ceri in Marittima (about 5 kilometers due east of Cerveteri) in Anguillara and di Vico territory; of Monticelli, about 10 kilometers north of Tivoli, on the slopes on the Monti Cornicolani; and Sant'Angelo Romano, about 6.5 kilometers south of Palombara, in the center of an Orsini district. Vitorchiano, 10 kilometers northeast of Viterbo, lay at the heart of di Vico and Orsini lands. The castle of Civitavecchia was not only Janni di Vico's window on the coast but also a major port for travelers to Rome from northern Italy and Provence. Piglio, in the Ciociaria region of the Campagna, lies in Colonna lands about 20 kilometers east of Palestrina at the foot of the Monti Ernici. It and its *rocca* stand astride a narrow, winding mountain road that crosses from Lazio to the Abruzzi and into the kingdom of Naples through the Monti Simbruini. Finally, Porto by the Tiber, near today's Fiumicino Airport, guarded the lower river and guaranteed Rome's access to the sea.

While these locations helped protect the Roman district's territory, the feudal allegiances of many Roman barons on the border with the Regno of Naples and the very porousness of the district's borders in the face of these feudal loyalties argued against these fortresses' use to preserve the integrity of any "territorial" state. Almost all are today on tertiary routes, no longer of obvious commercial or military value; and while some of their original strategic impact dated back to the defense of the Byzantine duchy of Rome, their possession really demonstrates how fourteenth-century strategy was conceived in personal terms: in forwarding or thwarting the designs of families and their local power. First and foremost, their possession now meant the existence of Roman garrisons in the center of the lands held by the Colonna, the Anguillara, the di Vico, and the Orsini.

With the defeat and submission of Janni di Vico, Cola's internal reform of Rome and his external foreign policy seem to have succeeded. He had rallied the Romans against the power of formerly untouchable barons and had brought the free communes of neighboring Lazio, Umbria, and Tuscany into a working military and political alliance. Yet much of his external success was largely the result of the common threat posed by di Vico's expansionist policies. In this regard Giovanni Villani also reports that Cola used the occasion of the Roman Synod and the attendance of the ambassadors of the free communes to arrest and hang the "lord of Corneto, who had robbed the countryside around Rome." This must have been the Manfredo named by the Anonimo romano as one of Cola's allies in the campaign against the prefect. The tribune's turning against formerly useful tyrants must have sent ample warning to the barons: they now came to realize that Cola's policy of divide and conquer would eventually eliminate them one by one.

On July 8, 1347, Cola had written to Clement VI that "two alone assumed the spirit of rebellion." The first, Janni di Vico, had been subdued; but the second, the count of Fondi, was a more resourceful opponent, with many more friends than the prefect had. On July 27, even before di Vico had surrendered the Rocca di Respampani, Cola had decided to move against the count of Fondi,[4] as he informed Clement VI:

Unless he comes obedient to the commands of the Holy Roman Church, of Your Holiness, the Roman people and myself before the end of six days, from that point I will hold him a defiant rebel against the Roman people and shall deprive him of both his military honors and his county; and I have disposed to proceed against him with the army, after I myself have assumed his military honors in the name of God. To this end on behalf of the honor of the nourishing City, I shall move forward this August 1, hoping—indeed holding it certain—that with the help and merciful accompaniment of God, I shall have in the field 1,500 knights ready for action along with those who have been granted to me by the cities of Tuscany for three months; as well as 500 Genoese crossbowmen and an infinite number of other infantry. Trusting in God and in Your Holiness I do not doubt that I shall trample him completely under foot, and that he shall never rise again. (28, BBCR 2.3:109, ll. 81–94)

Cola's words were alarming. Nicola, count of Fondi, was the grand-nephew of Pope Boniface VIII. One of the "newer" Roman families, the Caetani had a long association with the southern reaches of Lazio known as the Marittima, the coastal and low-lying areas between the mountains and the ancient port of Gaeta, from which they may have derived their name. Fondi itself is on the via Appia (see map 2), on the plain between the Monti Ausoni and Monti Aurunci, at the inland apex of a rich agricultural triangle of wheat, olive and vineyard, figs and lemons, almost equidistant between Terracina and Gaeta. In 1140 its ruling Aquila family took the title of counts of Fondi; and in 1226 the county of Fondi submitted to the crown of Naples. In 1299 it passed to the nephew of Boniface VIII, Roffredo Caetani, the husband of Giovanna, the last of the Aquila family.

Thus Fondi and its county, while within the bounds of the district of Rome and therefore subject to the papacy, could — should the need arise — also claim to be a fief of the kings of Naples by a century-old association. Such ambiguity of loyalty again demonstrates the porous nature of boundaries between the newly emerging states of the fourteenth century. As Cola would tell Emperor Charles IV in 1350, and as Villani confirms, Nicola Caetani had been a notorious rebel against the crown of Naples, twice defeating royal armies sent against him. He was also a traitor to Rome: through his connivance Terracina fell to the Genoese fleet in 1346, while at Itri, in September of that year, he and his allies completely destroyed a Neapolitan army sent against him by Queen Giovanna. Straddling the border as he did, the count of Fondi could thus shift allegiances and hostilities almost at will and therefore posed as great a threat to Rome as had Janni di Vico.

On August 20, 1347, Cola informed the pope that he had chosen the primary rival of the Caetani in southern Lazio, Giovanni Colonna, the grandson of Stefano il Vecchio, as his captain for the Campagna. Giovanni, the eldest son of Stefanuccio, had attended Cola's Lateran lecture on the *lex de imperio Vespasiani,* and it was he who greeted his grandfather Stefano at Palestrina after il Vecchio's flight from Rome following Cola's revolution. He was a charismatic and handsome young man. In his letter to Cardinal Giovanni Colonna, Petrarch had named him the most enjoyable of his hosts in Rome and Palestrina. Young Giovanni quickly became a political force. On April 13, 1344, he was named senator along with Giordano Orsini; and after Cola's revolution he was among the first of the barons, along with his father, Stefanuccio, to come to a political accommodation with the *buono stato* by swearing the oath of allegiance on the Campidoglio.

Colonna's scorched-earth policies against the Caetani added to the centuries-long abandonment of the Campagna and the climatic traumas that

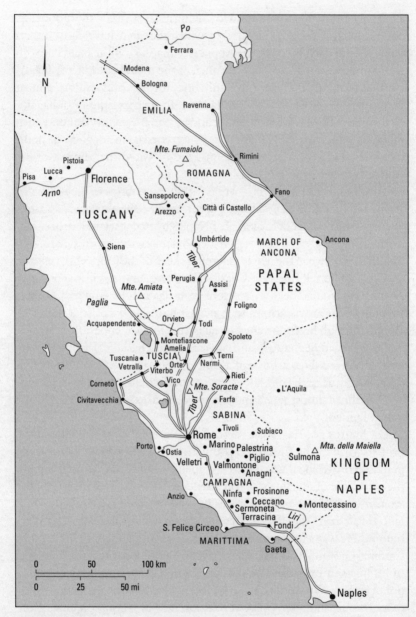

MAP 2. The Papal States and region in the fourteenth century.
Copyright Italica Press.

were effecting almost all of Europe by the late 1340s. Cola informed the pope: "Since in these regions there has begun to spread some, modest, famine, I have applied and am applying whatever remedies are possible and have made arrangements to have grain and other supplies imported from parts of Sicily. And I have caused to be brought back into cultivation parts of the district of Rome that had long lain uncultivated" (35, BBCR 2.3:131, ll. 60–64).

Despite his attempts to revive the greatness of Rome's ancient military, Cola and the Roman army suffered the same inconsistencies as any medieval levy. Troops provided by allies were consigned for only set periods, to set areas of operation and set pay; and Cola seems to have done much haggling with Rome's allies over these issues.[5] As early as August 5, at the height of his Roman Synod, when his government's prestige was at its apex and the ambassadors of the Italian communes crammed the city, the tribune had written to the *signoria* of Florence to request military help to proceed against the count of Fondi, who was at Gaeta "an enemy of the church, of Queen Giovanna, and of Rome," declaring that Caetani is "surrounded and shut in there. Either he will come to our summons or he will be trampled under foot forever." But the Florentine ambassadors had replied that their troops were not to go beyond the boundaries of the district of Rome, according to orders of the Florentine government. Cola therefore argued that since the count of Fondi was a Roman citizen—and enemy—and since Gaeta was within Rome's *dominium,* his request was valid. On August 6, 1347, in a postscript to his letter to Todi, Cola made the same argument for the Gaeta campaign, and as late as August 20, he reiterates this point to the *signoria* of Florence, stressing the role of Rome as the "queen of the world." But again, on August 27, Cola complains to the *signoria* that its soldiers had refused to serve against the count, saying that they had orders from Florence: "Nor have we been able, with prayers and exhortations, to drive as far as Sermoneta, which has not only been part of the District, but which continues to be well within it [about seventy kilometers miles north of Lazio's southern boundary]" (36, BBCR 2.3:132, ll. 17–20).

Despite the allies' unwillingness to help, however, Cola and the Roman army prevailed against Caetani, as he informs the Florentines in a postscript to this letter of August 27:

We reveal to you another joy: yesterday [August 26], when our Roman forces met in battle the forces of the said traitor at the foot of [the cliff of] Sermoneta, his people quickly showed their backs and climbed the mountain, so that the glorious victory brought many captives into our power and one of their banners into our hands. The banner was dragged along ignominiously through the army and then through the City. (ll. 47–52)

The battle must have been fought near the present site of Latina Scala; the town of Sermoneta itself lies 257 meters above the sheer mountainside east of the plain crossed by the via Appia. The terror among Caetani's troops must have been great, to force them up those cliffs. Thus by August 26 Cola had defeated Nicola Caetani as well; and the effects of his victory were definitive: on September 1 all the settlements of the Sabina and of the Patrimony (thus of the eastern and northern sections of Lazio, including the eastern bank of the Tiber up to Rieti, and the western bank as far as Bolsena) voluntarily submitted to Rome's government, as Cola says to an unnamed cardinal in Avignon, "to rid themselves of their tyrannical governments."

Janni di Vico had been defeated by July 22; Cola had had a resounding success with his Roman Synod of July 31 to August 15; and he then proceeded to defeat Nicola Caetani in the battle of Sermoneta on August 26. But no sooner had Nicola Caetani surrendered Gaeta and submitted than his younger stepbrother, Giovanni, took over what was quickly becoming a hydra-headed rebellion. On September 17 Cola wrote to Rainaldo Orsini in Avignon that he had dispatched Roman troops to reinforce Giovanni Colonna, but by October 11 he reported to Clement VI that the Caetani were besieging Colonna at Frosinone.

Taming the barons had become one of the chief goals of the *buono stato*.[6] The policy grew not only from Cola's sense of government but also from the very constitution of Rome. Both a surviving fragment of the *Statuta urbis* of 1305, which revived legislation dating back to Brancaleone in the 1250s, and then a chapter of the statutes that revived and revised them in 1363 clearly stated the Roman commune's opposition to the barons. It lists them by name: Colonna, Orsini, Sant'Eustachio, Ginnazzano, Normanni, Savelli, Poli, Capocci, and Caetani. By 1305 there already existed a register, kept by the Camera Urbis, naming the chief members among the urban and rural barony, to record the *iuramentum,* the barons' oaths of obedience to city governments sworn on the Holy Sacrament throughout the peninsula. The Roman barons were also to swear not to harbor any murderers, thieves, or bandits in their *domus* or *fortilizie,* their *castre* or loggie, on pain of a fine of 1,000 silver marks. Public *infamia* would greet those who defied the statute; a senator and captain-general were to hold an inquisition on the barons' compliance three months after their oaths.

Cola's actions thus fall within the long tradition of Roman, and other Italian, communal legislation. In this regard Cola also acted as the agent of the pope, whose chief public policy had always been the pacification of the barons to guarantee the safe return of the papacy to Rome. Nor had Cola ever indicated that the policies of the *buono stato* would be any different. The tribune's goal had always been to bring the barons into obedience to the *buono stato* through a series of oaths publicly performed, witnessed, and legitimized. The fact that most of the barons had not attended the Roman Synod must, therefore, have put Rienzo and his government on guard, as had the plot discovered against the tribune's life. Cola himself had privately disclosed this conspiracy to the pope, but the *Chronicon Estense* independently confirmed it:

In the same month of August the Colonna, Orsini, Savelli and other nobles of the City of Rome were not happy with the rule of the aforesaid Roman tribune; and they plotted together to escape from his lordship. They plotted with an assassin, who was supposed to kill him. But all this came to the attention of the tribune who had the agent captured and flogged. He confessed that he planned to kill him at the command of the aforesaid [barons]. The tribune then sent for them and interrogated them about this, and they confessed that it was true. (RIS 15.3: 154)

The immediate cause for the crisis, however, was characteristically reported by the Anonimo romano as a personality clash: an insult given to Cola by Stefano il Vecchio. It happened at the dinner party held on the Capitoline on September 14. The elder Colonna approached Rienzo in the middle of the festivities, touched the rich materials of the tribune's robes, and then—using the familiar *tu* form reserved for family, servants, and children—told him loudly enough for others to hear, "For you, tribune, it would be more appropriate to wear the honest clothes of a poor old man than these pompous things." The words ring true to what we know of Stefano il Vecchio: fearless, arrogant, and more than capable of combining a mockery of the tribune's high ideals of justice with an insulting allusion to his plebeian origins.

On September 17 Cola wrote to the papal notary, Rainaldo Orsini, on the outcome of that dinner party:[7]

We have conducted courteously to our prison on the Capitoline—not restraining them in the least—several of the barons of the City who were regarded with a certain suspicion by us and the Roman people and who were taken into our custody:

Lord Stefano Colonna [il Vecchio], Lord Rainaldo Orsini, Count Bertoldo, Giordano, Cola, and Orso of Lord Jacopo de Filiis Ursi [Orsini] and Giovanni Colonna. After purging any scruples of our growing suspicion from our conscience, in order that they might be reconciled not only with us, but also with God, we employed the following stratagem to cause them to be confessed most devoutly:

On the fifteenth of September, as many as there were, we sent that many friars and chosen religious to the prison. They were ignorant of our pure intention and they believed that we were ready to employ the harshest severity on the barons. Just as we had ordered them, the clerics said to these barons: "The Lord Tribune intends to sentence you to death." Meanwhile the parliament bell kept tolling loudly and continuously. The barons were terrified and believed that they were in danger of imminent death. Not expecting any outcome but death, they tearfully made their confessions.

As we had prearranged, at the assembly to which the entire Roman people had come at our invitation and request, we not only forgave these barons in their absence in this public parliament, indeed we also had them heaped with praise and offices. And so, with the benevolence of the peaceable people already bestowed on them, we caused them to come before the entire people, who unanimously forgave them of whatever and in whatever way they were obliged to restore or to make amends to them. And by our will and the will of the entire people, we gave to these barons consecrated rings, honors and offices. . . .

Then with pure and spontaneous hearts they swore to the Roman Church, to the Roman people, and at our command against anyone who might want to disturb the peaceful condition of the City. Then on the 17th day of this September the aforesaid barons, again aroused by their confessors and inspired by the flame of the Holy Spirit, again made their confessions and afterward, solemnly celebrating the Mass of the Holy Spirit at the altar on the Capitoline, . . . they reverently asked for the Eucharist. . . .

And by the grace of the Holy Spirit they were so joined to us and with the Roman people that—as far as could be seen—for the preservation of the *buono stato* of the City they were always in concord with us and with the Roman people in a love that is not false. . . . (40, BBCR 2.3:145–47, ll. 11–69)

None of Cola's "tricks" were unusual in a premodern political context; such stratagems were to become key elements in Machiavelli's advice; and stratagem over force was considered a virtue of the wise ruler who wished to avoid too much bloodshed or confrontation. But Cola also seems to have been forcing the arrogant barons to undergo the peace and reconciliation ceremony that—according to Cola's letter of August 1350 to the archbishop of Prague—eighteen hundred other Romans had already undergone voluntarily, an enormous proportion of Rome's population of less than thirty thousand: at least one in every sixteen persons. Everyone in Rome probably knew someone who had undergone the ritual; everyone had certainly heard of someone else. It also means that over the two hundred days of Cola's rule in 1347, eight to ten people would have been reconciled at four or five lengthy ceremonies a day, ceremonies similar to those described by the Anonimo romano and the notarial records of Antonio de Scambiis. Like that in many Italian communes from the twelfth century on, this ceremony was quite public and involved a complex, psychologically and spiritually moving liturgy that became a central and continuous part of Rome's new civic life for years to come. As in many other Italian cities, a certain degree of compulsion to make peace was also taken as a normal part of the process. Cola's claim that he was attempting to "trick" the barons into just such an act of public penitence and reconciliation therefore has the ring of truth. If his claims did not, it would have been the height of self-destruction to have lied to the papal notary Rainaldo Orsini in Avignon when so many of Rome's citizens could have affirmed the contrary.

The Anonimo romano notes that Cola then decked out the Capitoline with red and white silk bunting. "This he did to symbolize blood." But Cola's biographer again misperceives the evidence; for in Cola's symbolic world, red and white were the colors of the apocalyptic angel, the figure of justice. The Anonimo romano does collaborate all other points of Cola's account but adds the psychologically rich details that locate his work so directly and firmly on the soil of Rome:

When the barons heard this news [of their execution] along with the pealing of the bell, they became so frozen with fear that they couldn't speak. Most of them humbled themselves and did penance and took communion. Messer Ranallo delli Orsini and another baron, because they had eaten fresh figs earlier in the morning, could not take communion. Messer Stefano [il Vecchio] della Colonna refused to confess or take communion. He said that he was not prepared and had not yet arranged his affairs. (AR, XVIII, ll. 1431–40, Porta, 190–91)

The Anonimo romano's account seems to have been informed by the barons' point of view here: he relates their psychological state and their perception of events from their prison on the upper floor of the Senators' Palace and is not privy to the "trick" unfolding downstairs in the palace or the information Cola revealed in his letters. Thus he relates that Cola was dissuaded from executing them: "some Roman citizens, weighing carefully the judgment that the tribune planned to make, restrained him with sweet and flattering words." The parliament that Cola held would certainly have contained an announcement of his judgment against the barons for treason; the Roman people's almost certain agreement with this; provision for leading citizens to argue on behalf of mercy; and then, perhaps, a chance for the barons to plead their own defense, a scene reported by the *Chronicon Estense.* The Anonimo romano corroborates Cola's account of the barons' public appearance:

It was the third hour. All the barons, sad, like condemned men, went down to the audience hall. They stood before the people. The tribune, changed in his purpose, ascended the platform and made a beautiful speech. It was based on the Paternoster: "Forgive us our trespasses." Then he pardoned the barons and he said that they wished to be of service to the people and make peace with the people. One by one they bowed their heads to the people. (AR, XVIII, ll. 1445–54, Porta, 191)

Cola then restored their offices to them, gave each of them a fur-trimmed robe and banner, dined with them, and rode through Rome with them as a sign of this reconciliation. The Anonimo romano is clear in his choice of words: the Italian here for "make peace," *pacificaoli,* implies not the peace of a treaty, a *treugam,* but a religious, Christian meaning: peace as reconciliation. Thus, Cola's words about unanimity, concord, and mercy make it clear that his intention from this entire episode was a public ceremony of peace and reconciliation fully in keeping with contemporary Italian practice. But it was also inconsistent with the barons' perception of themselves as leaders of Rome's social and military hierarchy. Many had served the *buono stato* well and appeared ready, after Stefano's lead, to accept the new state of affairs under the tribune. There were also signs, however, that they did not share the joy of the majority of Rome's citizens with this *buono stato,* as their absence from the Roman Synod indicates. Their sudden arrest, the public ceremony of reconciliation, and their consequent release could only add to their sense of betrayal and humiliation.

But there was also a considerable body of public opinion that wanted them permanently removed from the scene. The Anonimo romano declares that "this deed [of forgiveness] greatly displeased the 'discreet men' of Rome," that is, the *bovattieri* and *cavallerotti,* the middle class and traders who had been Cola's supporters in the *buono stato.* The comment reveals an enormous sea change in the balance of power then going on beneath the surface of events: the shift away from the old feudal aristocracy and toward the new merchant class in Rome that, while slow in arriving, was firmly taking place by the 1340s. These *descreti* wanted an end to the troublesome barons. Cola had promised this to them, but not in a way, it seems, that they had envisioned; for their *buon governo,* with its strict codes of communal justice, was not really the same as Cola's *buono stato,* which built upon the commune of medieval Italy but strove for something new and different: to make the *buono stato* in the image of the apocalyptic new age of peace, justice, and reconciliation. And it was this aspect that such a bourgeois as Cochetus de Chotiis misses, and that the Anonimo romano so admirably sees, describes in great detail, but ultimately fails to understand.

Among the intellectual supporters of the *buono stato,* Petrarch also criticized Cola for his leniency, relying more on the abstract inspirations of classical history and the secular practice of contemporary princes than on the Gospel models that Cola was attempting to insert into Rome's civil fabric. Petrarch urged the extermination of the barons as traitors, and did so in terms evocative of the grand deeds of the early Roman republic. The poet's moral certainties appear to have lent to the growing atmosphere of confrontation. We know from a now lost letter that Petrarch wrote from Vaucluse in late 1352 that sometime around September 1347 he had written to Cola, either urging him to execute the barons or bemoaning the fact that he had let them go. *Familiari* 13.6 recalls it:

He used to style himself "severe and clement." To tell the truth, he should have decided to put into practice only the clemency of this title and not the severity that was quite necessary because of the republic's disease. I say if he had determined to show only mercy to the traitors of their country in sparing their lives, he should at least have deprived them of all means of doing harm, and especially he should have driven them from their frowning strongholds. In this way those who had previously been enemies of Rome would have become her citizens. At any rate, those who had been a source of constant fear would have become an object of contempt. (CRCR, 130–38, at 132)

But now there was no going back. Cola had already suspected Stefanuccio's son, Giovanni Colonna, of plotting his assassination, as he told an anonymous friend in Avignon in his letter of July 15; now, by the end of September, the enmity of the barons was clear. Cola informed the pope of their growing rebellion in a letter of October 11:

Yes it is true that your rectors of the Campagna and the Patrimony are attempting to strike at me and the Roman people; and this has made it necessary for us to ally with the Hungarians against our wills. For the count of the Campagna [Giovanni Colonna] has recently allied himself with Giovanni Caetani against the Roman people, from whose jaws he was saved by my aid and that of the Roman people. He now holds in prison those Romans who were delivering supplies to our army during the rebellion of the count of Fondi. Look how he repays me for the service he has received! And he and the rector of the Patrimony [Giordano

Orsini] have made an alliance with the tyrants to disturb the *status* of your most faithful Roman people. It is best to remain silent on the kinds of things they have perpetrated on their powerless and impoverished subjects. They have become not cultivators of justice but extorters of money. . . .

And we hold all of the Roman *[castre* and *rocche]* without the violence by which Lord Cardinal [Giovanni] Colonna holds his, despite the appearances of the legal instruments of his fictitious titles of sale. For there are none or few *rocche* in the Campagna—just as in the province of Rome—that have not been caught in the net of the aforesaid Lord Cardinal by such "purchases." (43, BBCR 2.3:168–70, ll. 169–214)

As a skilled notary who had worked for years within the City Chamber, Cola had direct access to many of the records of land purchases within Rome's jurisdiction. Now he was ready to question the legitimacy of one of the most powerful men in Christendom and of the system by which Rome's barons had acquired their vast rural estates.[8]

Outright rebellion was slow in materializing. In the weeks following their release on September 17, the barons "did not gather their forces," the Anonimo romano notes, but quietly went about fortifying their castles and strongholds, laying in supplies, arms, and men, and refurbishing their defenses. The Orsini concentrated their forces at Marino, the town in the Alban Hills, across Lago Albano from both Albano and Castel Gandolfo, off the via Appia about twenty kilometers outside the Porta San Giovanni. They were led by the brothers Rainaldo and Giordano, the sons of Orsello. Rainaldo had been among those arrested by Cola on September 17, but his brother Giordano does not appear named among them.

Rienzo seems to have been unaware that the barons were preparing for war. He apparently trusted that his mutual oath of reconciliation with them was still in effect, or so he tells the Florentines in his letter of November 9, after the rebellion had begun.[9] When their preparations were finally discovered, an edict was issued "demanding that the rebels return to Rome." The response of the Orsini, however, was to attack Cola's messenger and thus to begin their revolt. They began making daily forays from Marino into the countryside along the via Appia, plundering everything they could lay their hands on. Meanwhile, discontent and "rancor" grew within the city.

Cola still held out the possibility of bringing the rebels to heel through his own reputation and their fear of Roman justice. A second messenger was dispatched; when this, too, had no effect, he took the extreme step of commissioning a *pittura infamante:* "He commanded that Messer

Ranallo and Messer Giordano be painted in front of the Palace of the Campidoglio, like knights, but with their heads turned upside-down and their feet in the air" (AR, XVIII, ll. 1493–96, Porta, 192–93).

It was the final act of condemnation by the commune: to portray two of its chief citizens in *infamia*, traitors and criminals, hung in effigy, would mean the commune's eventual condemnation of them to death, the confiscation of their properties, and—if the practice of communal justice held true against the justice of Cola's *buono stato*—the destruction and leveling of their *fortilizie* within the city. The severity and finality of their public condemnation and symbolic execution were received by the Orsini with all the fury that the *pittura infamante* intended. Giordano stepped up his raids, coming in one attack as far as the Porta San Giovanni, signaling that the Orsini now controlled all the territory between Marino and Rome. He carried off not only goods and livestock but also men, women, and children. Rainaldo brought the campaign into the Patrimony, crossing the Tiber, probably at the bridgehead of the via Flaminia near Magliano Sabina. Here the target was Nepi, a town originally part of the Matildine lands that passed to the papacy in the eleventh century. It lies between the via Cassia and via Flaminia, about fifteen kilometers southeast of Lago di Vico. The Anonimo romano describes the devastating raids in a series of brief, vivid sentences, some no more than two words long in the Italian: "He entered the territory of the city of Nepi, and rode here and there burning and plundering. He burned the farmsteads. He burned the castle, the houses, and the people in them. Nor did he feel disgust with himself when he burned alive a noble lady, an aged widow, in a tower" (AR, XVIII, ll. 1500–1505, Porta, 193).

Finally, the Romans decided to move against the Orsini; and then, the Anonimo romano reports, "their perverse mind blamed the Colonna." With public opinion now behind him, Cola once again raised the levy. It was an impressive force: twenty thousand infantry and eight hundred cavalry, according to the Anonimo romano. If these figures are correct, Cola must have raised troops not only within the walls of Rome, with its population of 30,000, but also in the city's district, from the free communes allied with him, and from the military aid provided by the king of Hungary. The army marched out of Rome in the last days of October, no later than November 1 or 2. It was midautumn, and the grape harvest was under way in the Alban Hills around Marino. The town rises atop a spur of pepperino marble on the northern and exterior slope of one of the many extinct volcanic craters, now lake basins, that make up the Colli and remain covered with thick stands of Mediterranean oak.

The Roman army encamped at Machantrevola, "a valley under a long forest."

But October and November in Lazio is the season of the Tramontana. There, out in the high hills and deep forests of scrub oak, Rome's army camped and waited to begin hostilities, its camp buffeted by the high winds and rains from the north. "Finally, after about eight days, they devastated everything around the castle of Marino. They depopulated its whole area. They cut down vines, trees; they burned mills; they leveled the noble forest untouched up to that time. They wasted everything. For years that castle was not so strong nor so great" (AR, XVIII, ll. 1520–25, Porta, 193–94).

The Anonimo romano was not being especially critical here. Before the age of artillery and gunpowder, this was medieval warfare at its most routine: few pitched battles, long sieges, scorched earth, the plunder of whatever goods and livestock, plantings and harvests an army could get its hands on. Less frequently castles and other strongly defended centers were attacked outright, but only after elaborate preparations had been made.

Marino had an excellent defensive position. With the cone and lake to the town's back, and steep, rolling hills interrupting access from the south and east, an army would find open assault difficult. The city itself was defended by a castle, much of which is still visible on the northern stretch of wall adjacent to the Porta Romana. At the top of the town stood the *rocca* of the Orsini, later of the Colonna, which today retains two of its rounded towers facing the Piazza della Repubblica. In addition, Marino had been well prepared, as the Anonimo romano recounts, with "arrows, lances, men, provisions, walls, timbers, and wine." The Orsini had made sure that the town was also siege-worthy: they had already "renovated the moat and put a strong palisade of double wood around it." Thus attackers would have to first fill in the moat under the ready eye and constant attack of archers and the ballista deployed from the town, castle walls, and towers. Then they would have to attack and scale the wooden stockade, here a double-perimeter wall; and then—after the outworks had been taken and destroyed—attack first the castle and then the *rocca* and once again face the hail of arrows, lances, stones, and most likely the pitch, oil, and burning bales hurled down on them.

But the Roman army was large and bent on finally crushing all the barons. "All Rome was there," the Anonimo romano recounts as if describing a sporting event. The Orsini would have to rely on their own planning and military skill, but not on these alone. Politics played a part, too. For the Orsini and the Colonna knew that, despite their atrocities, they could probably rely on their contacts in Avignon to check the power of Rome and its tribune. Cola realized this as well; he knew he was acting, in name at least, as the agent of the pope but that he had mighty enemies in the Curia, including Cardinal Giovanni Colonna.

The Romans had completed their devastation of the district around Marino and were preparing their assault when disturbing news came from Rome. "In those days, a cardinal, a papal legate, came unexpectedly to Rome," the Anonimo romano writes. The cardinal-legate was Bertrand de Déaulx, to whom Clement VI had written on October 12, informing him that he would lead the papal campaign against the tribune. Bertrand commanded Cola back to Rome with the entire army.[10] The tribune had delayed answering as long as he could. This was not the first summons he had received from the Vatican palace, where the legate had taken up residence. He must now obey or risk being deposed. He, the Romans, the Orsini, and their allies all knew that he must obey. Giovanni Villani reports what Cola probably already knew: that the legate was providing covert aid to the rebellion, interpreting his mandate from Clement VI as broadly as the pope had intended.

But Cola used the summons to his advantage. He broke camp and began his withdrawal down the slopes. His retreat must have been a great relief to the Orsini and their garrisons, for they appear to have relaxed their defenses. The army suddenly wheeled and attacked the *casteluzza*, "not far from Marino," and overwhelmed its defenses at once. The fortress was captured and leveled. Without interruption the Roman force then swerved on the *rocca* and its "round tower," deploying siege engines that it had previously constructed. The Anonimo romano remarks, "You have never seen such clever devices." The siege began again in earnest but could not be completed before Cola himself had to return to Rome. He therefore destroyed the neighboring mill and called off the campaign, withdrawing the entire army, but not before a final insult, fully in character with medieval warfare and with Italian notions of high gesture. He took two dogs, named them Rainaldo and Giordano, and christened them the "canine cavaliers." He then drowned them in the millstream (AR, XVIII, ll. 1542–44, Porta, 194).

It must have taken the army about two days to return to Rome, and Cola no doubt remained with the host. The soldiers' mood was grim by the time they reached the city. On the day after the army's return, early in the morning, a large force of cavalry and many foot marched across the *abitato* toward the Vatican, through the district controlled by the Orsini. Now, as Cola and his Romans reached the Ponte Sant'Angelo, the streets were lined not with cheering crowds but with soldiers; and the soldiers under the tribune's command began to carry out something that Cola and the members of his *buono stato* had told the people no one in Rome would ever do again. In front of the fifth-century church of San Celso, now a baroque structure on the modern via del Banco di Santo Spirito, they turned to the Orsini *case-torri* that rose up on the banks of the Tiber and began to tear down the towers, one by one. The work was quick: many eager hands made it so. Cola then, with his escort, crossed the Ponte Sant'Angelo fully armed and arrived at the Vatican palace to answer the legate's summons.

There, awaiting them, was Cardinal de Déaulx. Though known as the best diplomat in the College of Cardinals through long years of papal service, when chosen by Clement VI as his legate to Naples he had panicked at the first show of resolve from the young Queen Giovanna and fled to the monastery of S. Severino, and then silently left the city, much to the pope's consternation. Now at the Vatican, in the papal audience hall, the cardinal sat awaiting the papal underling. Bertrand's mission was simple: to bring the papal rector, the self-styled "tribune," to heel, to remind him of his duty to the pope, to strip him of his lofty titles, and then to gradually restore the status quo. But the tribune had other ideas about how things should go in the city he now governed:

He went with his knights to St. Peter's, entered the sacristy, and put on the imperial state Dalmatic over his armor. The emperors wore this Dalmatic at their coronations. It is a rich garment, all decorated with little pearls. Wearing this garment over his armor like a Caesar, Cola entered the papal palace, with trumpets blaring. Cola appeared before the legate, his scepter in his hand, his crown on his head. Terrifying, fantastic he looked. When he had come before the legate, the tribune spoke and said, "You have summoned us. What is your pleasure to command?" The legate began, "We possess certain information from our Lord the Pope." When the tribune heard this, he raised his voice and said, "What 'information' is this?" When the legate heard this reproachful reply, he stopped short and fell silent. The tribune turned his back [and walked out]. (AR, XVIII, ll. 1548–66, Porta, 194–95)

Realizing that the tribune had his own "information" about Bertrand's alliance with the barons—a fact well enough known for it to be reported by the *Chronicon Estense*—the legate fled to the safety of Montefiascone, just east of Lago di Bolsena, residence of the rector of the Patrimony. Cola realized that the legate's summons had been a ploy to prevent the fall of Marino; yet it was one he had to obey. He, like Cardinal Bertrand, had acted out the next scene in the pope's play, costumes and all. On November 9 Cola wrote to Florence requesting aid for his continuing campaign at Marino. "We have left the vines and forests devastated up to their walls. Except for the fact that we had removed our army at the request of the legate," Cola tells the Florentines, "the castle of Marino itself would be occupied by us now." But the legate had checked the tribune despite his act of defiance. The Orsini, the Colonna, and their allies remained unconquered.

By mid-November the rebellion had grown even stronger. The Anonimo romano reports that "there was great muttering through the city," though whether this was spontaneous among the people and Cola's former supporters or fed by both papal and baronial agents he does not say, nor does he seem capable of analyzing the papal role in these events. Whether the Anonimo romano was actually a Colonna sympathizer is also hard to determine. But with the revolt in Marino still not crushed, the Colonna now appeared emboldened enough to move on their own.[11] They prepared a large force at their chief stronghold, Palestrina: seven hundred cavalry and four thousand infantry, according to the Anonimo romano. Whatever the real number, it was a force about three times that of the levy based on the *rioni* that Cola had instituted, and a clear sign of the vast power in men and resources for making war that this one baronial family wielded. The Colonna must have felt great confidence, knowing that the Roman army, however feared and victorious, remained preoccupied with Marino and was being kept inactive by the legate and the onset of winter.

The Colonna strategists decided to avoid dissipating their feudal levy in a campaign of scorched earth and raid, such as the Orsini had been following, and thus to maintain the tenuous attendance and loyalty of their feudatories. They also gambled that one swift attack was preferable to the rebellions already attempted by Janni di Vico and the Caetani. Deception could work to their advantage, and therefore they sent messages to Rome to the effect that they desired to return to their homes inside the city and were requesting that the gates be opened to them upon their return from the countryside. But there were further elements to their plot: they had been dealing secretly with the *cavallerotti* within Rome, the "plebeian knights" who had seen their prospects for enrichment under the *buono stato* quickly melt away in a long and drawn-out campaign against the nobles in the countryside. "Many barons were in on the plot with them," the Anonimo romano also reveals.

The Anonimo romano's account of the next few days is problematic and contains several internal contradictions. On the one hand, he recounts how Cola met the news of the Colonna preparations with great fear: "He began to behave like a sick madman; he neither ate nor slept." On the other hand, he recounts the tribune's masterful control of the situation. Cola had received news of the preparations and around November 18, a Sunday, held a public assembly to prepare the city for the coming battle and to encourage the people to action. Here again we see an example of the Anonimo romano's literary portrayal of Cola's inner life, probably derived from classical models, and the public record of the tribune's actions, which appear quite different from the psychological portrait constructed after Rienzo's death. Publicly the tribune roused the Romans, recounting a favorable dream he had had the night before—which contradicts the "sleepless night" motif already used by the Anonimo romano. Even if both constructs are correct—the private fear and the public confidence—the biographer thus presents the classic portrait of the public statesman who did not allow private misgivings to show.

Another assembly took place on the following evening, of the nineteenth, the day before the battle, and the Anonimo romano constructs two parallel and simultaneous narratives: one inside Rome's walls, the other outside, among the barons in the countryside. Before dawn on November 20, Cola had the alarm bell sounded and the people assembled. Everything about the behavior of the tribune again gives the lie to the Anonimo romano's picture of a "sick madman." He delivered a "well-ordered" speech on the perfidy of the Colonna and their disgrace of Boniface VIII and the church; and he condemned them as perjurers and betrayers of the Roman people. The tribune also told the people that Boniface had appeared to him in a dream and had promised the Colonnas' defeat. Cola then made the most of this association, offering a chalice and a pallium to the chapel of Boniface in St. Peter's.

Cola's intelligence agents were also at work outside the walls. He tells the people that the Colonna and their allies "have come and made camp four miles from the city in a place called the Monument." This is the enormous pyramidal tomb on the east side of the via Appia, near the present *casale* of Sta. Maria Nuova, just after the fifth milestone, on the edge of the ruins of the Villa of the Quintili. The Monument was something of a natural wonder in the Middle Ages and remains so today: its base of marble-faced brick gradually eroded to form what appears to be an immense stem or trunk of a brick tree formed by the pyramid above. Yet a natural image is not really right for the Monument, for it is a pyramid whose base is narrower than its body: it is an unnatural structure, an apt symbol for the conspirators to have chosen for their rendezvous. Here amid the ruins of villa, tomb, and medieval turrets, all rising out of the damp mists of the ancient burial road, the Colonna made their camp. The grim irony was not lost on Cola, as he told the Romans: "And this is a true sign that not only will they be defeated, but they will also be killed and buried in that Monument."

After he had said all this, Cola had the trumpets, cymbals, and kettle drums sounded and put the battalions in order and named battalion captains, and gave the watchword: "Knights of the Holy Spirit." When this was done, calmly, noise-lessly, with the legions of infantry and cavalry set in order, they went to the Porta San Lorenzo, which went by the name Porta Tiburtina. (AR, XVIII, ll. 1599–1610, Porta, 196)

Why the Porta Tiburtina, if the Colonna had encamped on the via Appia, south of the Porta Appia? Here we must skip ahead of the Anonimo romano's narrative inside the city and move to simultaneous events outside the walls. In the middle of the night, "around midnight," the Colonna had suddenly broken camp and moved their army across the hilly countryside, broken by numerous streambeds and slopes, to what they may have considered a better terrain for maneuvering their forces. An attack on the Porta Appia and the salient that it thrust south around the area of the Baths of Caracalla would necessarily require them to divide their forces and to attack immense walls that lay upon moderate but still consider-able rises, from within whose natural bastion, however, the defenders could concentrate their own forces at will. On the other hand, the front afforded by the walls of the Porta Tiburtina and Porta Prenestina stretched straight across the eastern slope of the Esquiline and allowed some room for maneuver. Below the walls, and along the via Tiburtina, the hill sloped gently down into a fairly broad valley, the Campo Verano, where troops could be ordered more rationally—if need be. But the Colonna were dis-counting the need, for they were working in concert with traitors within the walls who had promised to open the gates to them. Once they were inside, the open expanse of the Esquiline could facilitate a broad attack on whatever forces the Romans under Rienzo might muster in a field far more conducive to a quick cavalry charge. And so they used the cover of night to march around the southeastern corner of the city past the turn-ing of the Aurelian Wall east of the Anfiteatro Castrense and Sta. Croce in Gerusalemme.

At the center of the plain, across which now stretch the University of Rome and the cemetery of the Campo Verano, there rises a small hillock. Here, ever since the fourth century, there had stood one of Rome's most important basilicas, that of San Lorenzo fuori le Mura. Although sited outside the walls, the church was one of the major pilgrimage goals of the city, and it grew rich on pious donations. A sprawling monastic complex had grown up amid the pleasant wooded hillside next to it. Here Stefano il Vecchio had rested on his flight from Rome in May; and it was here that the Colonna army now decided to muster and plan its assault. The campaign had started out vengefully: the Colonna had followed the Orsini's example and had badly damaged the monastery of Grottaferrata, just a few miles north of Marino. Now, as Cola would later tell the Florentines, they swept down upon San Lorenzo, and despite the family having numerous sons named after Santo Stefano, the first martyr and co-patron of the basilica, they proceeded to ransack the complex.

Inside the monastery the leaders planned their tactics for the next morning. They included Stefanuccio (Stefano il Vecchio's son), Giovanni Colonna (Stefanuccio's son), Pietro de Agapito (the former provost of Marseilles), and Giordano Orsini di Marino. Others had joined them: Pietro Colonna, known as Sciaretta, the nephew of Stefano il Vecchio and the son of the Sciarra Colonna who had led the raid against Boniface VIII at Anagni; Cola di Buccio de Vraccia or Braccia, one of the robber barons of the mountains around Rieti who had fled the territory of Rome once Cola had defeated Janni di Vico; and others. They took whatever rest they could before the morning of the battle. But the mood of the troops matched the cold and vengeful season: that night the army was buffeted by rainstorms and chill winds. The low-lying plain outside the gate had turned into a mud-clogged and water-soaked field; and the season was not treating the barons well:

Stefanuccio had been stricken with a stomach flu and trembled like a leaf. Pietro de Agapito, being a bit of a worrier, dreamt that he saw his wife a widow who was weeping and tearing at herself. Fearing such a dream, he wanted to leave the host. He didn't want to see himself in a rout. They were also hearing the alarm bell ring. They knew the people were both very enraged and emboldened. (AR, XVIII, ll. 1643–51, Porta, 197–98)

Inside the walls, all was ready: Cola had reminded the army of the depredations of the Colonna and the threat to the *buono stato*, the troops were well provisioned and motivated, and they had been reinforced not only by Rome's allies among the free communes of Lazio and Tuscany but also by several hundred cavalry provided by Lewis of Hungary in exchange for Cola's alliance against Queen Giovanna. The alliance had been sealed in October, according to Villani, to the tumultuous approval of the people of Rome. In addition, several of the barons whom Cola had arrested and then reconciled and freed had accepted his act of mercy and remained loyal to the *buono stato,* even against their own allies and relatives: Giordano Orsini del Monte and Cola Orsini del Castel Sant'Angelo, along with many of the Orsini of the Ponte Sant'Angelo and Campo dei Fiori, the chancellor Malabranca and his son Matteo, as well as Roberto, the son of Bertoldo Orsini, "and many others." But some whose aid was offered were rebuffed.

Cola had received reports that Janni di Vico was involved in the conspiracy to throw open the gates of the city and to attack the citizen army from inside. He and his son Francesco had arrived to the tribune's call with one hundred knights of his own and fifteen "lesser nobles of Tuscany," along with their retinues, as well as "five hundred loads of grain for provisions, as a prefect ought to do." But once safely inside Rome, according to the Anonimo romano, Janni was invited to dinner on the Capitoline with his retinue; there, as they sat, he, his son, and their allies were disarmed, arrested, and thrown into the Capitoline prison. Their weapons and horses were distributed to the Romans. But the arrest must have caused some uproar: Cola was forced to hold a public meeting and there to lay out his evidence of the plot against the city. "Do not be amazed," he told the assembly, "that I am holding the Prefect in prison: he came here to stab the Roman people in the back and to destroy them." The Anonimo romano gives some indications that a widespread plot was indeed in the making; and the *Chronicon Estense* bears this out with only some differences of detail.

As morning broke amid the pealing of the Capitoline bell, Stefanuccio Colonna made his first gambit: riding out from the rebel camp, he approached the Porta San Lorenzo (fig. 23) mounted on his palfrey, accompanied by a single squire. As he neared the gate, he called out to the guard on duty—by name—to open the gate, declaring that he was a Roman citizen and had come to return home and to aid the *buono stato.* But that is where things began to go seriously wrong. For the Romans had gotten wind of the plot, and the guard in charge of the gate that day had unexpectedly been changed. Instead of a friend of the Colonna, one of Cola's supporters, Paolo Bussa, "who had a reputation as a good crossbowman," called back to Stefanuccio Colonna: "The guard you're calling isn't here. The guards have been changed. I've come here now with my companions. There's no way you can get in here; the gate is sealed tight. Don't you know how furious the people are at you for disturbing the *buono stato?* Don't you hear the bell? I'm begging you, for God's sake, get yourself out of here. You don't want to be in such trouble" (AR, XVIII, ll. 1660–69, Porta, 198). And to show the Colonna that their plot had been uncovered, and that no one inside the city was going to open up the gates to them that day, Paolo took the keys to the gate—which locked and opened from the inside—and hurled them down into a muddy puddle in front of Stefanuccio.

That was the end of it. The barons had not come, like a real Roman army, with siege engines, engineers, timbers, scaling ladders, trebuchets, or anything else to launch an assault against the still mighty Aurelian Wall, much less to launch a lengthy siege. Rome's walls stretched out for nearly twenty kilometers, and five thousand men could barely cover one sector of its perimeter. Now surprise, betrayal, and all had been lost. Stefanuccio returned to the rest of the barons waiting for him at San Lorenzo. There was now no honorable choice but to break camp and return home. But at the very least a show of force could be made: a taunt and a challenge to the Romans cowering behind their walls and gates; a demonstration that these were true nobles and chivalrous knights. So they agreed: they would form their battalions, unfurl their standards, sound their trumpets and drums, and declare their defiance. Three companies were formed: the order of the day was that all would parade before the walls and then turn right, along the via Tiburtina, toward Tivoli and Palestrina. Under no circumstances would anyone break ranks and attack the walls. The penalty for doing so was the loss of a foot. Petruccio Frangipane, son of one of Rome's most ancient and noble families, led the procession of horse and foot. He had been arrested by Cola weeks before and was now burning for revenge. First one company passed the walls, reached the gate, sounded its trumpets, and departed. Then the second did the same.

The third, led by Giovanni—Janni—Colonna and including most of the leaders of the conspiracy, now began its pass. Janni and seven of his companions were riding a little ahead of the main battalion when suddenly, and amid great confusion and alarm, the massive doors began to open to the sounds of hammers, hatchets, and pikes. Finally, their friends inside the city had reached the walls and were taking their part in the plot. Janni wheeled his horse and charged the gate, confident that he and his company could enter the narrow crack now opening in the walls, secure the gate, and allow the rest of the barons' army to pour into the city. Giovanni Villani reports that the Colonna shattered the gate and entered Rome with about five hundred cavalry, a figure also used by both the *Chronicon Estense* and the Paduan notary Antonio di Giovanni Zuparo, who reported "the news of the City" in an entry for November 20, 1347.

These sources reckon the infantry at between eight hundred and one thousand. But the Anonimo romano, who appears to have been on the scene, insists that it was not the conspirators who were tearing down the gate but the Roman army itself, locked inside after Paolo had tossed out the key, intent on taking up the insult and the challenge offered by the barons.

Janni quickly took up his shield and, with a lance at his side, spurred on his war horse. Arrayed like a true baron, running hard, he did not hold back; he entered the city gate. My, what great fear he inspired in the people! Then all the chivalry of Rome turned to flee from him. In the same way all the people turned and fled, for the space of almost half a cross-bow shot. Despite all this, Janni Colonna was not followed by his dear friends; and so he remained there, alone, as if he had been called to judgment. (AR, XVIII, ll. 1702–12, Porta, 199–200)

And like the day of judgment, like the stillness before the apocalyptic trumpet, silence surrounded the young Colonna, mounted there on his warhorse. The scattered Romans now realized that their enemy was alone and in their hands. As they turned upon the baron, his horse started and ran off into a "grotto"—probably the depression made by a niche inside the wall—next to the gate, throwing its rider into the mud-filled pool left by the recent rains. The Romans now gathered around the pit as the nobleman laboriously rose to his feet under the weight of the mud and his own battle armor. The Anonimo romano's description of what happened next gives the feeling of an eyewitness account:

Realizing his misfortune, Janni asked mercy from the people and begged them in God's name not to despoil him of his armor. What more is there to say? There he was stripped, and wounded three times, he died. Fonneruglia de Treio was the first man to strike him. Janni Colonna was a young man of great energy; his beard had not even begun yet to grow. The fame of his virtue and glory resounded through every land. He lay naked, supine, stabbed, dead, on top of a little mound against the city wall, inside the gate. His hair was covered with mud. He could scarcely be recognized. (AR, XVIII, ll. 1717–28, Porta, 200)

Soon after the rains stopped, the sky began to clear, and the foggy weather turned serene and happy. It was then that Janni's father, Stefanuccio, realized that his son and his companions were not with the main party. Seeing the tumult at the gate, now the father spurred his horse and entered the city just in time to see "his son lying on the ground, in the midst of a crowd of people who were killing him, between the pit and the pool of water." His first reaction was revulsion and panic. He wheeled around and fled outside the gate; but then "his love for this son conquered him. He did not speak a word; again he turned and entered the gate to see if he could possibly rescue his son." Realizing now that it was too late, Stefanuccio again turned to flee, but he, too, had fallen into the trap. A stone hurled from the gate above struck his shoulders and the back of his horse; then came the lances from all sides—into him and into his horse— his horse bucked and Stefanuccio, too, was dismounted; and soon he too lay naked and dead just outside the gate. "Between his nose and his eyes," just where a dagger might penetrate a knight's raised visor, "he had a wound so terrible that it looked like the cleft of a wolf's jaws. His son Janni had only two wounds, one in the groin and one in the chest" (ll. 1759–62).

And then the onslaught began: it was the third hour (midmorning), according to Antonio di Giovanni Zuparo. Like the terrible slaughter of the French chivalry by the English at the rain-soaked field of Crécy in Normandy two years before, the battle at Porta San Lorenzo became more of a rout than a battle. Hemmed in between the walls and the slope at San Lorenzo, hampered by the mud and the press of their own numbers, and with no room to maneuver their heavy warhorses, the barons were helpless against the counterattack from the Roman cavalry and infantry streaming out of the gate and from the archers and ballista that rained down on them from the walls. The Romans were led by Cola Orsini and Giordano Orsini del Monte. All discipline disappeared among the Colonna forces, and every man fought for himself: amid the groves around San Lorenzo and the vineyards along the slopes of the Esquiline, the slaughter raged on. Pietro de Agapito Colonna, provost of Marseilles and senator of Rome, had taken up arms that morning for the first time in his life: family loyalty had forced him to give up a successful church career to marry and thus return his life and property to the Colonna; and family loyalty had brought him before the walls of Rome that day. Thrown from his horse in the middle of the melee, he attempted to flee on foot but slipped and fell on the wet ground. There, in a vineyard near the abbey, the Roman infantry caught up with him. "He was bald and aged, he prayed in God's name that they pardon him. His prayers were useless; first they took his money, then they disarmed him, and then they took his life. He lay in the vineyard, naked and dead, bald, fat: he did not look like a man of war."

The rest of the barons' army melted away in terror, leaving their weapons scattered across the field as they fled. "They did not look back; not one of them struck a blow. Messer Giordano Orsini [di Marino] whipped up his horse and did not stop until he reached Marino." Soon about a dozen of Rome's leading barons lay dead, their bodies strewn amid the groves and gardens around the gate. There also lay Janni Colonna, Pietro da Agapito's brother, two other Colonna, "their bastards, valiant in arms," according to Villani, as well as Cola Pali di Molara, Giordano degli Aretini, Cola Farfaro, Polo di Libano, "and many other gentlemen of Rome, Orvieto, and other towns near Rome, friends of the dead men mentioned above." The *Chronicon Estense* adds to the list Buccio de Gagigariis, the two lords of Luyano, Cola Ballo de Gavi, and eighty of their companions. Among the "seriously wounded" he counts the same Cola Pali di Molara, Buccio de Gesso, Giordano Orsini da Marino himself, Cola de Buço de Branço, Cino Caetani (brother of the count of Fondi), and Camillo, a bastard son of Stefano Colonna. Countless others had also been slaughtered, but true to medieval narrative, the sources mention only the "important" people. Many more were captured by the Romans, who threw the most prominent of them into prison on the Capitoline.

The Orsini allies of the *buono stato* distinguished themselves in the battle: Villani names Cola Orsini and Giordano del Monte as leaders of the forces of Rome against their relatives of the Marino branch, and the *Chronicon Estense* confirms this but adds that the third division was led by Cola himself. According to this source—and confirmed by Zuparo—it was the tribune who ordered the gates opened and who personally led two bands of knights against the barons, blocking the road into the city with his cavalry charge and pressing the barons back. When the gates were opened, the *Chronicon Estense* continues, Janni Colonna and his companion Cenesto Theotonico (a German mercenary?) made straight at the Roman tribune, cut their way through his company, and actually seized Cola's standard and cast it and the dove atop it to the ground. The Anonimo romano also reports the incident, but he adds another of his disparaging, and strangely interior, descriptions: "It's true that the standard of the tribune did fall to the ground. Jolted, the tribune stood for a time with his eyes raised to heaven. If he said anything it was this: 'Ah, God, have you betrayed me?'" (AR, XVIII, ll. 1786–90, Porta, 202).

As the bodies of the barons lay on display for all Rome to pass and gaze upon, "until the ninth hour," Cola reassembled the army. Amid the blare of silver trumpets, wearing his crown of silver and olive branches, he lead a triumphal procession across the *disabitato,* up to the Capitoline and Sta. Maria Aracoeli, which in the middle of November was now serving as Rome's public assembly space. There, according to the *Chronicon Estense,* he made a speech thanking his troops and the entire Roman people. But then, according to the Anonimo romano, the tribune laid down his scepter and his crown before the image of the Black Madonna that is still preserved in the sacristy of the church and never bore them or raised his banner again. Telling the assembled Romans that he wanted to return his sword to its sheath, he wiped his bloody blade on his own clothing and declared, "I have cut off an ear from the head that neither the pope nor the emperor could touch."[12]

What does the Anonimo romano intend with this terse description? Certainly not tumultuous triumph, not the proud processions and display that had symbolized Cola's rebirth of peace and concord under the *buono stato*. The tribune's remarks themselves seem overburdened by a deep and bitter irony, coupled as they are with his abandoning the symbols of military rule and triumph. The reader can almost conclude that Rienzo had returned from the battlefield with a deep sense of disgust and failure. True, he had triumphed over the barons and crushed yet another rebellion, but at what price? Where now were his dreams of peace and reconciliation, of social harmony, and the revival of ancient Rome that would usher in the New Age? He had arrested the barons only to force them to make peace with the Romans and then released them as the agents of the united commune: now they lay naked and dead, their wounds a gaping mockery of the dreams of ancient glory with which Petrarch—in the safety of far-off Avignon—had filled the Romans' minds. How could, and would, the knight of the Holy Spirit now reconcile the dead with the living, the blood-soaked field of battle with the sacred ground around the first martyr's tomb?

Later that day, Cola wrote the government and people of Florence to inform them of his victory and to provide the official version of events leading up to it. He begins by quoting the *Exultemus* from Psalm 117: "This is the day which the Lord hath made: let us be glad and rejoice therein" (24). It is a day in which "the common people and the just may rejoice together and in which every one of the tyrants may weep and melt away." The conspirators had violently attempted to afflict Rome's good and peaceful people and to subject them to the yoke of tyranny, "declaring that they would rather first expose themselves to the dangers of death than suffer being under our rule for more than six months. And so it is true," the tribune writes, "that from Pentecost day, on which we assumed the rule of the City, to today, the day of our victory, a span of six months has elapsed."

Cola then draws a parallel between the victory at Porta San Lorenzo and Judith's execution of Holofrenes (Judith 13), the general-in-chief of the armies of Assyria sent to conquer Judaea and its capital, Jerusalem. Judith, a pious and beautiful widow who had long completed her period of mourning, put off her widows weeds and donned the bright and beautiful "clothes of joy" (10:3) that she used to wear for her husband, her perfumes, and her jewelry "and made herself beautiful enough to beguile the eye of any man who saw her" (10:5). After making her way to Holofrenes' camp, charming him and all his men, and gaining his confidence and his bedroom—all the while maintaining her virtue—she slew the drunken general in his bed, slicing off his head. Judith then returned to the Israelites with the general's head, giving them heart to march out against the Assyrian camp. The death of their general caused panic among the enemy ranks. "The rout was complete, with one accord they fled along every track across the plain or through the mountains" (15:2). Judith and her women companions returned to Jerusalem in triumph, then "she and her companions put on wreaths of olive" (15:13) and led the procession through the city. "When this was over, everyone returned home" (16:21). "Never again during the lifetime of Judith, nor indeed for a long time after her death, did anyone trouble the Israelites" (16:25).

For Cola, this historical concordance now served as the typos for his delivery of the New Jerusalem from the tyrants of his own age. Like Judith, Cola had decided to use his personal charms and his charisma to insinuate his way into Rome's circles of power in order to save his city. The description of Judith exchanging her widow's weeds for the bright, beautiful clothes she used to wear for her husband had been echoed in the words of the Apocalypse (21:2) and by Cola himself in his first letter to the Romans from Avignon, in which he compares Rome to the widow risen from her long mourning.

But there, amid the triumph of Rome's weakest, there was enacted, ironically among its most powerful, a moving pietà of mourning widows and sisters that must have reminded the Anonimo romano of paintings he had seen by Giotto and Simone Martini. The bodies of the Colonna dead—Stefanuccio, Giovanni, and Pietro—were brought in solemn procession to the same church of Sta. Maria in Aracoeli, to the chapel of the Colonna family. "The countesses came with a multitude of women, tearing their hair, to wail over and mourn their dead." But the tribune refused to allow the obsequies at the Aracoeli and declared that "if they provoke me any further I shall have these three cursed corpses thrown into the pit of the hanged men, since they are perjurers and do not deserve to be buried." And so, as the "lover of the world" turned a bitter eye and cold heart upon his fallen enemies, the Colonna women had the bodies of their slain men carried secretly to their convent of San Silvestro in Capite. "And there they were buried by the nuns without lamentation." The widows of Rome's most powerful family, now reduced to acting out the experience of its most common, mourned silently, like the very image of Rome Cola once had painted on the Capitoline, and contemplated the destruction of their clan, and feared the unchecked revenge of the people of Rome.

While many of the leading barons had been slaughtered, many more had been captured and now languished in Rome's prison atop the Capitoline. They made up a long list, the birds of prey whom "the dove of our simplicity" had shut up: Giovanni Guictitii, Lotio de Tulfa Nova, Janni di Vico and his son Francesco, Manuzio and Berardo of Orvieto, Petruccio di Cola dei Celgarii of the lords of Farneto, his brother Puzio, Nicolo Cataluzio of Bisentio on Lago di Vico, Jannutio called the Slav, Francesco Marcuzio, Giovanni Ser Gilii of Viterbo, Cecchino de Alviano, his brother Stefano, Sciarra (Colonna?) of Tuscanella, Malatesta of Rocca Vetii, Monaldo Leoncelli of Orvieto, and Cola Forca Petolo. Yet Cola's letter does not exult in the victory. Instead, he tells the Florentines that he still seeks to treat the conquered with mercy.

After repeating his account of the vision of Boniface VIII, Cola then also claims that other patron saints had aided him and the Romans in their victory: St. Martin, the son of a tribune, had also taken revenge for the rebels' attacks on pilgrims on November 11, his feast day. In one of those pious puns so popular among medieval writers, Cola also notes that St. Columban, whose feast day was November 23, had come to the aid of Cola's own standard, that of the dove, the Latin *columba*.

Stefano il Vecchio had not taken part in the battle, but the news must have reached him at Palestrina within hours: his son, his grandson, and his eldest brother's son now lay dead, their bodies mutilated. Stefano was an old man who had by now seen his eldest brother and his younger brothers, Cardinal Pietro and Sciarra, die long before him; and then his son Agapito, the bishop of Luni; and his young and brilliant son Giacomo, the bishop of Lombez. But now his closest son, and then his *eldest* son, lay dead; and he must have sunk into a dark despair and cursed the day he had ever met young Rienzo and invited him into his home, cursed the role he had played in the life of Rome and perhaps even as head of his own clan. In his letter to Florence of November 20 declaring Rome's victory, Cola describes Stefano il Vecchio in the way only poetic understanding can achieve: "old, unhappy, living on, and half-dead."

Soon the news would also reach Avignon and the ears of Stefano's oldest surviving son, Cardinal Giovanni, that the Colonna family had been destroyed. Petrarch, the cardinal's protégé and longtime friend, now had the bitter task of conveying his condolences to his dear patron and to the Colonna family in Rome because of acts that he himself had long pressed the Romans to take.[13] Petrarch never gave his condolences to Cardinal Giovanni in person: he had already left Avignon for Italy on November 20, the very day of the battle of Porta San Lorenzo. But then in September, probably of 1348, soon after the death of Cardinal Giovanni, Petrarch did write to Stefano il Vecchio to express his grief and condolences over the cardinal's passing. Petrarch let out his sorrow for all the deaths that Stefano had had to endure: his five brothers, his wife, seven of his sons, and Giovanni, his grandson. After praising Stefano's character, life, and achievements on behalf of Rome, Petrarch reminded the old man of that conversation they had had, many long years before, in 1337, as they strolled together through Rome. It was then that Stefano had told Petrarch that he felt he would have the bad fortune to outlive all his sons. When Petrarch's messenger returned to Parma, he informed the poet that Stefano had been so deeply moved by his letter that the proud old man had finally allowed himself to give vent to his long, unspoken, grief; he wept uncontrollably for so long that the messenger thought he would never recover. Finally, Stefano il Vecchio Colonna finished reading Petrarch's letter, dried his tears, and declared that he would never weep again.

CHAPTER 11

Abdication and Exile

I'm going to tell you how the Tribune fell from his lordship.
The morning after the battle all the Roman knights were called
out, the ones he called the "Holy Militia," and he said to them,
"I want to give you a double payback. Come with me." No one
knew what he planned to do. With trumpets blaring, he went
to the place where the battle had taken place. He took with him
one of his sons, Lorienzo. In the place where Stefanuccio had
died a puddle of water still stood. When they arrived, Cola had
his son dismount, and he sprinkled over him some water from
the puddle, which was mixed with Stefanuccio's blood, and he
said, "You will be Knight of the Victory." All the others were
amazed at this, in fact stunned. He ordered the constables of
the cavalry to dub his son with the flat of their swords. After
this was done, he returned to the Campidoglio and said, "Go
on your way. What we have done was common work. We all
have to be Romans. For us as well as you it's expected that we
fight for our country." The knights were deeply disturbed at
hearing this. From then on they no longer wanted to bear arms.

Anonimo romano, XVIII, ll. 1888–1908, Porta, 206

Opera comune, "common work," was what Cola had called the victory over
the barons at Porta San Lorenzo, hardly something to be proud of for
those who had been there. Cola's actions had shocked and disturbed the
loyal knights of Rome: no great celebration, no double pay, *paca doppia*
as the Anonimo romano records Cola's words.[1] This may, indeed, have
sounded like what Cola had said; but this master of language could, in-

stead, have intended the pun of a *pacca doppia,* "double slap." Such punning was common among Italy's preachers and public speakers; Bernardino da Siena would make it a highly charged art in the next century. Whatever his words, Cola's harsh and bitter repudiation of battlefield triumph had grown out of his realization that his dreams of peace and reconciliation now lay dead with the Colonna and the common men who had followed them into battle. Cola's mockery of his own ceremonial knighting in Constantine's baptismal font by anointing his son with the blood-soaked water of Stefanuccio's death thus inverted another of the fearful symmetries that infused the life of the Italian communes: eye for eye, house for house, son for son. Giovanni Villani, who received reports of events in Florence, writes that Cola made a grand festivity of the victory on the day after, November 21, staging a great procession of all the clergy of Rome to Sta. Maria Maggiore, the site of his own coronation; and then, on the third day, took his militia to the battlefield to dub his son Lorienzo.

Then, hastily returning to the Capitoline, he provided the knights with the second part of their *pacca:* a summary dismissal, a belittling of their joint victory, and a reminder that public duty, not private gain, was to be expected of all members of the *buono stato.* Cola had cruelly robbed the knightly class of their greatest incentives: the booty of war, but even more important for a class ethos based on self-conscious and external signs of status and valor, the praise and glory that come from military prowess and victory on the battlefield. Cola may well have realized that his "victory" went far deeper than the destruction of the barons' military objectives: it had destroyed their best and brightest, but it had also humiliated both the vanquished and the victors.

To the world at large the tribune announced the victory over the barons as a great triumph. Villani reports that he sent an envoy to Perugia, Siena, and his own Florence, "richly dressed" and bearing the olive branch as a sign of victory. Yet Rienzo, too, had been vanquished at the summit of his career. The Colonna had forced him to rend the social fabric of the New Jerusalem in ways that he was not prepared to do: justice and reconciliation of enemies, yes; peacekeeping, yes; but the wanton destruction and mindless slaughter that the Colonna had brought upon their own heads must have filled him with a deep disgust.

Historians have taken the Anonimo romano's lead in attributing Cola's rapid shift of mind and mood to a deep character flaw bordering on psychosis; and by the time of the battle of Porta San Lorenzo, Cola had certainly come to a crisis, but a crisis more political and public than psychological and private. Sometime shortly before the battle he had realized that the barons' audacity had had one and only one source: the active participation of the papal legate in a conspiracy aimed at toppling him and restoring the senatorship. Cola by then knew for certain that the pope and the Curia were directing his overthrow on an active and daily basis. Villani later reported the conspiracy as if it were common knowledge.

The campaign had begun almost immediately after Cola's Roman Synod and his coronation as tribune.[2] On August 21 Clement VI had written to his legate Bertrand de Déaulx, giving him full authority to rein in the tribune and to use whatever means at his disposal to strip him of his titles and his ambitions: "You may diligently strive to provide a remedy in due season, for every possible avenue must be closed to the dangers and the evils that can arise." The letters of Petrarch and Cochetus de Chotiis confirm that independent reports, rumor, and innuendo had begun to flow steadily from Rome to Avignon. On August 20, 1347, Cola wrote the pope to counter such rumors. But the papal response had been set in motion even before the letter reached Avignon. In early September Petrarch wrote Cola one of his unaddressed letters, the *Sine nomine* 2, recounting an attack on a Roman envoy just outside Avignon that had probably taken place on September 1:

Your Excellency's courier, who has recently experienced cruel treatment, will bear witness to you of the kindness and the mercy, yes, of the justice that you may expect in these quarters. A new species of barbarity that a youth, unescorted, unsuspecting, and entirely innocent of all blame, should have been set upon like an enemy! His ambassador's wand, which they should have respected and feared — if anything is considered sacred in their eyes — and likewise his letter case, which was filled with most important and grateful dispatches, were both plied about his innocent head until they broke to pieces. The letters themselves were torn and scattered to the winds, although they might have softened hearts of stone. This is hospitality! This is charity! Your messenger was seized at the River Durance. There he was tortured and scourged and forbidden to enter the city. Now, his features covered with gore, he casts himself at your feet and delivers his message of threats and blows and lashes. (CRCR, 73–77 at 73; Zacour, 35–42)

This violation of diplomatic immunity was not an isolated incident. The papal court had already turned against Cola and his *buono stato*. Several days later, probably sometime between September 2 and September 8, Petrarch wrote Cola his *Sine nomine* 3 to inform him of a recent debate in a papal consistory. Its subject was the proposition:

Whether or not it would make for the happiness of the world at large if the City of Rome and Italy should be united and should enjoy peace and harmony. After countless arguments had been exchanged, however, the one considered the wisest among them closed the discussion with this venomous statement: "That such an outcome would by no means be advantageous!" And this decision, to tell the truth, was received with great applause and with general approbation. (CRCR, 84–86 at 85; Zacour, 42–44)

Petrarch's news struck a hard blow: years later, in a letter of August 1350 to the archbishop of Prague, Cola would repeat Petrarch's account, adding that "our lord the supreme pontiff, owing to the insinuations of wicked men and his own lack of charity, regarded this union with such great suspicion." Cola received Petrarch's news of the attack upon the Roman envoy on September 16 and the next day wrote an angry letter to the papal notary Rainaldo Orsini, recounting the attack almost verbatim from Petrarch's letter, informing Orsini that a formal embassy would be dispatched to protest the action. In the meantime, Cola and the Roman people

do not intend to trouble ourselves about keeping many representatives at the papal court. God and the truth, to whom all hearts lie open, will judge between us and our detractors. We are fully aware, indeed, that as a reward for our good works we are assailed in Avignon undeservedly and, yes, in a way displeasing to God. . . .

The reverence due to our lord and master the pope subdues and checks the righteous indignation of my soul, great though it be. Otherwise, in defense of our courier, we should take legal action against the ruler, the governing body, and the people of the city of Avignon.

With a struggle we yield to the reverence due to our lord and master the pope, hoping that such evils may be corrected by an edict of His Holiness so that they may not recur in the future. However, we reserve for the deliberation of our own parliament the question of taking said legal action. (40, BBCR 2.3:149–50, ll. 128–47)

By September 14, however, Cola had moved against the barons, arresting them and forcing them into the ceremony of reconciliation atop the Capitoline. News of the event raced to Avignon, and sometime between October 4 and 9 the pope wrote to the Roman tribune, telling him that he had not heard of any crime of which the barons were guilty, declaring that "we believe that they are truly without blame," and requesting that Cola restore them to liberty, "out of reverence for Us and the Apostolic See." While the tone of the letter retained its civility, Clement had already sent several secret letters and instructions designed to undermine Rienzo's government.[3] On September 12 he had written to Raymond de Chameyrac, former papal vicar in the city, ordering him to prevent and block any of Cola's actions "in prejudice to the Roman Church," and failing that to inform the pope of these actions without delay. By September 19 Clement informed his legate Bertrand de Déaulx that he had received a copy of Cola's letter of September 1 sent to an unnamed cardinal in Avignon. He tells Bertrand that he must act quickly to prevent the dangers that are sure to stem from Cola's actions. On the same day, the pope wrote to Pietro de Pinu, the vice-rector of the Patrimony, ordering him to prevent Cola's and Rome's occupation of any *terre, rocche,* and *fortilizie* in the Patrimony and to strengthen and guard them against the Romans. Clement further advises Pietro to exchange aid with the other rectors of the Papal States. Cardinal Bertrand de Déaulx is to coordinate all their efforts against Rienzo.

On October 5 the pope wrote to Petrarch's friend Lellius, Lello di Pietro dei Stefaneschi dei Cosecchi (Tosetti).[4] Given the fluid spelling of family names in the fourteenth century, he even may have been related somehow to papal notary Rainaldo Orsini's Roman informant, Cochetus de Chotiis. Lello, a master of the palace guard in Avignon but the son of a venerable Roman family, an ally of the Colonna, and a syndic of the city, had been summoned by the government of Rome to render account of his term of public office. Clement not only declared Cola's summons null and void but also absolved the nobleman from obeying the summons. Before concluding, Clement bluntly threatened Lello that answering the summons would cause him to lose both the graces of the pope and his position in the papal court. Lello caved in to the pope's demands, and we soon find him repeating rumors of Cola's misgovernment to his friend Petrarch. Only later, after he had expressed his growing doubts to Cola, did Petrarch learn that Lello had deliberately misled him.

Years later, in his letter of August 15, 1350, to the archbishop of Prague, Cola would recall that almost as soon as he had assumed the tribunate, Cardinal Giovanni Colonna had also begun a campaign of slander against him, urging the house of Colonna to rebellion. Cola therefore decided to confront these unsubstantiated charges in a town meeting. On September 29, 1347, the feast of St. Michael the Archangel, at the church of Sant'Angelo in Pescheria—of which Giovanni Colonna was the titular cardinal—in the presence of the entire people and after readings from the Apocalypse (1:1–15, 5:1, 8:3, and 12:7), the tribune declared that if the cardinal had been moved out of zeal of his love for the people, and if he believed Cola to be a schismatic and possessed by unclean spirits, then God would punish Rienzo; but if Colonna were tormenting him out of family loyalty, then God would provide justice by the hand of St. Michael. The massacre of the Porta San Lorenzo proved the justice of these words, Cola later claimed. Caught up in the fury of his desperation on hearing the news of the battle, the cardinal smashed his own head against a wall and soon afterward died of a brain fistula. Cola's story had more poetry than fact behind it: Colonna actually died about a year later and under other circumstances, as we shall see.

The pope's obsession with Rome and its tribune only increased as the fall progressed. On October 7 and 9 Clement VI wrote to the Thirteen Good Men, the leaders of the city's *rioni,* claiming that he had heard no reason for the arrest of the barons and that he believed them to be without fault, and therefore urging the Thirteen to ask Cola to release them. On October 7 Clement dispatched the first of three letters to Legate Bertrand. This informed Bertrand that Cola had usurped his titles and had illegally occupied the lands of the church. It therefore instructed the legate to absolve all the Roman people, its barons, and its citizens, collectively and individually, from any "promises, pacts, conventions or obligations" that they had entered into under oath to Cola himself or to any corporate bodies within the city or its territories. But loyalty to the popular leader was strong, and Clement therefore accompanied this letter with another, broadening Bertrand's legatory powers within Rome and its district. Finally the pope armed his legate with authority to deprive "a certain Nicolas di Rienzo, a Roman citizen, who called himself Tribune," of the office of rector. After recounting Cola's acts of subversion of the papal government of the city, Clement then authorized Bertrand to select "worthy senators" to take over Rome's government. The pope concludes by granting his legate full powers to declare interdict, suspension, and excommunication against anyone who opposed his actions.

Cola must already have had wind of the pope's final actions, for on October 11 he wrote to Clement in Avignon in a bid to defend himself. But the tone of the letter is no longer that of a faithful agent attempting to reconcile the demands of his lord with the realities of the Roman scene. The wagging tongues in Rome and Avignon had portrayed Cola as an irreverent heretic defiling the sacred Christian symbol of Constantine's bath, daring to assume the titles and crowns of the tribune. If before Cola had subtly used Scripture to chide the pope over salt taxes and the true meaning of the salt of the earth, he is now unapologetic in his defense and engages the pope and his Curia on a deeper theological level that calls into question the very nature of Christian symbols and the meaning of the sacramental system:

Inasmuch as it pleases your holiness that I be dismissed and removed from this administration, considering holy and just whatever is a pleasure and a favor to Your Holiness, I am ready to give up the administration, disposed never to go contrary to your best wishes. And to this end it is not necessary to fatigue the Curia and deafen the whole world with legal proceedings; for your one least courier would have and will suffice when it shall please you. . . .

Since the reformation of the City demanded more elegant provision than the other cities of the world, [Rome's enemies] strive incessantly in many and various ways to assail my innocence. If I did receive the bath of knighthood in the basin in which Constantine was baptized, for which I am blamed, why should what was allowed a pagan in cleansing himself of leprosy not be allowed to a Christian cleansing the City and the world of leprosy? And why is a stone, which stands in a temple that one can and ought to enter, more holy than the temple that confers sanctity to the stone? Why is a man with a contrite heart, who is allowed to take the body of Christ for his salvation, not permitted to enter a stone font which, through disuse, was held of no account? It seemed to those who find fault with this act that the entrance was made without devotion, that the font was more noble than the very body of our Lord, Jesus Christ. I think this not only a sin to think and believe, but consider it the thought of an infidel! And if I am said to have added names to myself and amplified my titles, and to have assumed various crowns of leaves, what pertinence does it have to the Faith to have renewed the ancient Roman names of offices with ancient rites? . . . (43, BBCR 2.3:162–64, ll. 54–84; DKPSP, 226–31; CRCR, 91)

Cola makes it clear that he is working within a framework of historical type and fulfillment, of prefiguration and realization, of ancient precedent and modern enactment. He tells the pope that the monuments of ancient Rome—Constantine's baptismal font, his arch, and the inscriptions and sculpture upon it—have provided the inspiration for Cola's revival of the city and its ancient government.

The pope waited another week before writing again to Rome, even before he could have received Cola's response to the charges being circulated against him. On October 12, the day after Rienzo's letter was sent from Rome, Clement wrote the tribune a reassuring letter, informing him of Legate Bertrand's mission and requesting Cola's "discretion" and his "useful promotion" of his and the nuncio's mission in Rome. The brief letter, filled with the language of "urging" and "grace," was, however, sent on the very same day as Clement's next, secret, missive to Bertrand de Déaulx. The lengthy letter immediately picks up on the themes of the pope's rightful title to the government of Rome and of Cola's usurpation of these titles and of church lands. Clement writes not to inform his legate of these claims and charges but to plan the destabilization of the tribune's *buono stato.*[5]

The first stage was to be one of propaganda and rumor. Bertrand is instructed to spread "things that it shall seem to your prudence ought to

ABDICATION AND EXILE   237

be said." These include the pope's and Curia's ongoing and constant love of the city and its people, Rienzo's turning the Roman people against the church, his dismissal of the vicar Raymond de Chameyrac, his crowning himself tribune, and his profanation of Constantine's font, "filthy with the contagion of his vices." On a practical level Clement instructs the legate to prevent Cola's further "usurpation" of church lands but, even more important, to stop the evolving alliance of Rome and Lewis of Hungary against the pope's vassal, Giovanna of Naples, and to counter Cola's summons to the emperor and electors of Germany and his claims for the sovereignty of Rome and its people.

The cardinal-legate is to work on two levels: on the first he is to extract promises from Cola that he will renounce his titles and return to full obedience to the legate and the pope. He is to do this publicly before citizens of Rome. Cola is to be held in check by a public threat of excommunication, which he will automatically incur if he acts against the limits imposed by Cardinal Bertrand. But then there was the secret, private instruction that Clement wove into the fabric of his letter. These instructions assumed that Cola would not abide the legate's threats: "We think and believe very probably that his promises will have little strength." The legate is, therefore, despite any public promises of compliance extracted from Rienzo—and thus after his public humiliation—to proceed to "deprive him of the office of rector, which was granted to him by us, as well as of every title usurped by him or granted to him—though only in fact—by the said people."

Bertrand is further instructed to conspire to restore the senatorship: "Strive to make provision for the City and people with senators, with the people, or with others, just as a careful consideration of time and circumstance in the affair seem expedient."[6] Working under the assumption that Rienzo will not abide by the legate's public instructions—even assuming that he would respond to his summons—Clement instructs Bertrand to "not hesitate to commence proceedings against him." The pope has already laid out the basis for possible charges against Rienzo. He therefore next commands Bertrand to "see whether you find in him cause for a charge of heresy or of aid to heretics, and in that case do not fail to proceed against him as a heretic." "After a decent interval" Bertrand is to warn the Roman people, with threat of grave punishment, "that they abstain from offering or exhibiting any obedience, counsel, aid and favor to Nicholas, and that they not presume to participate with him in anything" under threat of interdict. The legate is to absolve the barons and all other Romans from the bond (religio) of any oaths taken to the said Nicholas

or the Roman people and from all "pacts, promises, obligations and conventions. . . . We are writing down nothing concerning the above clearly
or explicitly, but we are entrusting everything to your profound circum-
spection and prudence."

But Clement could not conceal some of his true motives for wanting
Cola out of the way: "We are appointing to the rule and government of
the Patrimony of St. Peter in Tuscany our beloved son, the nobleman and
knight Guiscard de Combron, our nephew." He informs Bertrand that
he will also provide him with mercenaries, both horse and foot, "as many
as you think sufficient" to oppose Cola, along with funds for their support. Bertrand is to annul any bonds of fealty to Cola in the Sabina and
other lands of the church so that no one will answer his summons, pay
the hearth tax, the salt tax, or other sales taxes, so that commerce and trade
cease, none of Cola's officials are received or admitted—and are actively
expelled—none of his followers are elected to any office public or private,
and on the contrary face retribution spiritual and temporal. Clement then
tells Bertrand that to pry the loyalty of the people away from their tribune he is to manage the food supply so that complaints about shortages
start to spread and the people will rise up against Cola. Simultaneously,
throughout Rome's thirteen *rioni,* the legate is to begin distributing
money and food to sway public opinion away from Rienzo. The legate is
constantly to monitor the popular mood and to report it to the pope.

Pope Clement has already sent Cardinal Bertrand other secret instructions, "which you are to use as you shall recognize most effectively."
His letters are in duplicate: one in which Cola is excommunicated; and,
as we have already seen, "in the other we greet him as if he still stood
among the company of the faithful." Bertrand is to employ either as the
time and place seems expedient. He is also to present or have presented
sealed papal letters to the barons of the City and certain communes of
Tuscany intended to draw them to the legate's side. "This should be done
quickly, lest they are prevented from a union, confederation or league."
The spiritual proceedings against Cola will provide the expedient ground-
work for the cardinal-legate to work against him on a political level.

The strategy is thus complete and set into motion. Yet even then, Pope
Clement could still not be certain that he could pry the Romans away from
their tribune. He therefore instructs Bertrand to administer the coup de
grace if necessary:

Finally, we think that the letters authorizing the fiftieth-year Jubilee [for 1350]
should be held back for the time being rather than being issued, since we do not

know whether the aforesaid people will withdraw from that intractable man or whether they will follow him in his errors. But if, in abandoning him to his errors, they become disposed toward and return to the devotion and obedience of Ourselves and the Church, as they are bound to do, we shall quickly dispatch letters of that import and follow them freely with pleasing favors and paternal affection in these and other matters. (Theiner 182, 2:186; DKPSP, 235, ll. 9–21)

It would take some time to set all the pieces into place: contacts with the barons were already bearing some fruits; their rebellion was growing more bold by the day; they acted under the unspoken protection of the legate. Food shortages were growing, rumors and false accusations were spreading, and "murmurings" were racing throughout the *rioni*. The grist for the rumor mill was all prearranged: Cola had defiled the sacred font of Constantine; he had demonstrated his arrogance and madness in crowning himself tribune; word had it that he had aided and abetted heretics within and around the city; he was probably a heretic himself. The Anonimo romano accurately reflects the climate of rumor and scandal coursing through Rome even if he could not know their cause: "People began to hate the tribune; they spoke ill of him and said he was very arrogant. He began to behave wickedly and to abandon his honest dress; he dressed in clothing like that of an Asian tyrant." The tribune began taking forced loans from the wealthy; but apparently no one could verify these stories because, as the Anonimo romano reported, "he imposed silence upon them."

The legate and tribune spent the next few weeks waiting and testing one another, sounding out public opinion among all segments of Rome's population, Bertrand spreading, and Cola countering, rumors. Yet the people's loyalty and Cola's coalition held fast, fast enough to rally the Romans and to stage a major campaign against the Orsini at the heart of their power: Marino. By mid-November nothing had moved the tribune, who had become even stronger. In fact, as Clement tells Bertrand in a letter of November 12, he fears Cola's diplomacy will ensure the loyalty of Perugia, Siena, Florence, and other free communes, as well as the alliance of Lewis of Hungary.

On November 13 Clement therefore wrote to Bertrand de Déaulx to protest Cola's war against Rainaldo and Giordano Orsini, his destruction of their *domus* within the city, and the siege of Marino. He instructed the legate to attempt to rein in Rienzo and to bring about a peace treaty between him and the barons without delay. Failing that, Bertrand is to work to raise an army against Rienzo. The Orsini of Marino, the pope tells him, are the nephews of the late and dearly remembered Cardinal Napoleone Orsini, who had shown friendship to Clement when he was still a young man just beginning his church career. On the same day Clement wrote to his own nephew Guiscard de Combron, ordering him, in conjunction with Legate Bertrand, to lend the Orsini whatever military aid he could. The pope sent the same instructions to the other rectors of the Papal States. On the same day Clement wrote Rainaldo and Giordano Orsini declaring his support in their struggle against Cola and promising the aid of Bertrand de Déaulx and his rectors.

On November 29, 1347, Petrarch wrote to Cola from Genoa (*Fam.* VII.7) to report the rumors and bad news coming from Rome. It is not certain that the news of the battle of Porta San Lorenzo had yet reached Genoa: at that time of the year, travel would have been slow and difficult. But the battle is not the subject of the letter. Petrarch is full of admonition for the tribune and of reproachful credence in the rumors spreading from the city:

Do not suppose that I am writing like this merely by chance, or that I am complaining without just cause. Letters from my friends have followed me since I left the Curia. In these letters reports of your doings have reached me that are far different from the earlier reports. I hear that you no longer, as formerly, love the whole people but only its worst element; that it is only these whom you humor, for whom you show any consideration, and whose support you seek. . . .

It is possible, however, that what I am saying is false. I wish it were so! Never shall I be more gladly proven wrong. The writer of that letter ranks high in my estimation; but I detect significant traces of an ill-will with which I have become familiar through many incidents. I scarcely know whether such envy is due to his noble birth or his eager courage. Therefore, though my grief urges me to write further, I shall check the impulse, a thing, I assure you, that would be impossible if I did not cheer my fallen spirits by refusing to believe the unwelcome news. (CRCR, 99–101 at 100–101)

Petrarch's informant was Lello de Pietro dei Stefaneschi, the young nobleman and syndic whom the pope had ordered to defy the tribune. Clement must also have provided additional incentives for him to help turn Petrarch's heart and mind against Cola and thus to deprive him of one of his most effective spokesmen. Petrarch's letter, coming at so late a date, also offers good evidence that the papal policy was working well: even those, like Petrarch, privy to the workings of the Curia in Avignon and close to the barons in Rome were still in the dark about the legate's covert campaign to subvert the *buono stato*.

But by the time Petrarch had written, the battle of Porta San Lorenzo had already taken place: the Colonna and their allies had been destroyed, and the tribune had emerged triumphant. By the first week of December there was no choice for Clement and Bertrand but to carry out the last of their measures against Cola. The Anonimo romano reports that after the battle of Porta San Lorenzo, Cola grew "ruddy and fleshy" and turned into a tyrant; yet a span of only two weeks had passed, enough for the legate's rumor mill to grind its meal but hardly long enough for the physical and psychic changes attributed to the tribune. But on December 3, 1347, in a letter to the Roman people, the pope, through his legate, issued the condemnation and excommunication of Cola di Rienzo.[7] Expressing his great solicitude and pastoral care that "daily wears us out," Clement informs the Roman people of the dangers that Rienzo has brought to them and to their country. Clement then rehearses the long and familiar list of Cola's crimes, to which he adds Cola's involvement with the affairs of Naples and his alliance with Lewis of Hungary.

But legal and political crimes were not enough. Clement speaks to the Romans in a language that matches Cola's. Quoting the apocalyptic message of 2 Thessalonians, the pope names Rienzo "the precursor of Antichrist, the man of sin revealed to the Gentiles, the son of perdition, who opposes and is exalted above all that is called God, or that is worshipped, so that he sits in the temple of God and gives himself out as if he were God" (2:3–5). Cola is "full of every fraud and every falseness, the son of the devil, the enemy of justice, a monstrous beast, the names of blasphemy are written upon his head." Clement has now pulled out all the stops, for he has equated Cola with the great beast from the sea "with seven heads and ten horns" in Apocalypse 13:1, the Antichrist himself. Cola is beyond the healing medicine of the church and its legate. He must now be toppled, and like the beast and false prophet "cast alive into the pool of fire that burns with brimstone" (Apoc. 19:20), confined, and most important of all for this most eloquent of papal enemies, "shut up."

Wherefore we warn, demand, and urge you all considerately; we exhort you with wholesome and paternal counsel to meditate carefully over the things that have been done and many others that can occur to your prudent consideration. Desist from all support, counsel, aid, and favor of this Nicholas, and leave to his errors him whose iniquity crawls like a serpent, spreads like an ulcer, and infects like poison. Shun him as a sick beast that contaminates the whole flock with its disease. Persist in reverence and obedience to the Church, receive its admonitions humbly in your usual manner, and fulfill them effectively. (Theiner 185, 2:189; BBCR 2.4:99–106; DKPSP, 236–37)

Under threat of interdict and eventual excommunication for any who defied the papal order and actively rallied to Cola, the Roman people had

been left powerless, open to the mercy of their and Cola's enemies.[8]
Should they defy the papal order, not only would Clement cancel the upcoming Jubilee, but Rome would fall under those most dreadful of punishments: suspension, the prohibition imposed on a cleric from exercising the functions of his office; excommunication of individuals; and finally
interdict, the suspension of all the sacraments—baptism, confession, the
Eucharist, holy matrimony, the last rites, burials on sacred ground—all
hope of salvation and grace removed from the city and community as a
whole. For individuals this meant the horror of facing death without
benefit of clergy, in a state of sin, simply for living within Rome's bounds.
As Richard Trexler has demonstrated, these venerable spiritual weapons
were far from powerless in the fourteenth century and were reserved by
the papacy for use when all else failed. Interdict was an especially potent
weapon against Rome, for it was specifically designed to prevent foreigners
from traveling to or remaining in a city, and it thus struck at the very foundations of Rome's spiritual and economic wealth: its pilgrims, courtiers,
and diplomats. Not even travel or flight could lift the interdict from a commune's citizens. Interdict also encouraged subjects to rebel against their
lords, who more often than not faced individual excommunication. Such
a package of spiritual sanctions had proven highly effective against Venice
in 1311, for example, and would have a significant impact on Florence in
1376, despite that city's continued defiance in the War of the Eight Saints.
Writing on this situation in Florence, Trexler notes that standard papal
tactics accompanying interdict included "the charge of suspicion of
heresy . . . [and] that of harming bishops and cardinals. But the foster-
ing of sedition in church lands was the most self-evident and notorious
of crimes. Certainly any one of these charges would have been sufficient
for an angry pope."

For loyal allies of the Roman tribune, these sanctions would thus mean
the Inquisition, trial for heresy, the confiscation of property and goods,
charges leveled against friends and family, prison, torture, even death and
condemnation to hell for all eternity. One could always defy the pope and
his legates: many had in the past. But at what cost? The memory of Arnold
of Brescia still lingered in Romans' hearts, as did that of the many Spiritual Franciscans hunted down, imprisoned, and burned at the stake. Rome
itself had been torn apart by years of bloody strife between the allies of
pope or emperor locked in endless wars. Had not the emperor himself,
Frederick II, been excommunicated? Had not his grandsons defied the
pope for the throne of Naples? And had not the pope raised a bloody army
from France under Charles of Anjou to destroy the Hohenstaufen, either

slaying them in battle or humiliating them by public execution in Naples's marketplace? Even Rome's antipope, Pietro da Corbara, had finally been forced to abdicate and undergo a humiliating penance and life imprisonment in the papal palace in Avignon. What would the Romans do now, as the barons lurked outside the walls like wolves, salivating for revenge, and thirsting for the blood of the tribune and his allies? What would the tribune do to save himself and his *buono stato*?

The answer was quick in coming. On December 2 Cola wrote a circular letter to the communes of the Sabina (48, BBCR 2.3:186–87). He may have written others to other towns within the province of Rome that have not survived. In it, he informs the Sabines that he is recalling from office Iannocto Herrici, the Roman podesta appointed for the region, as part of the demands placed on him by the papal legate. Cola is complying, he informs his supporters, in order to ensure concord and to avoid violence and breaches of the peace. Always mindful of the livelihood of his supporters, Cola asks that the towns involved make provisions to pay Iannocto the salary due him for his time of public service. But before he does, he makes one of the brilliant biblical associations that spoke so much more than Cola was willing or able to say. He quotes the Gospel of John, telling the people of the Sabine hills, "Do not let your hearts be troubled, or be afraid." Cola knew that he had no need to spell out the whole passage from which he quoted:

These things I have spoken to you while yet dwelling with you. But the Advocate, the Holy Spirit, whom the Father will send in my name, he will teach you all things, and bring to your mind whatever I have said to you. Peace I leave with you, my peace I give to you; not as the world gives do I give to you. Do not let your heart be troubled, or be afraid. You have heard me say to you, "I go away and am coming to you." (John 14:27)

Cola trusted that his readers would not press any comparison to Jesus but would pick up on the essence of the message: he would soon be gone; so it must be if true peace, reconciliation, and the honor of the Roman people were to survive; but he promised to return. Gone are the grand titles of Cola's previous letters, they had all been stripped away by the legate. But he did keep one, despite Cardinal Bertrand's pressures: he signed it "Tribunus Augustus." It is the last surviving letter Cola sent from Rome under his *buono stato*. The Anonimo romano then picks up the tale. The next day "the cardinal-legate, who was mentioned above, cursed him and judged him a heretic. Then he plotted with the lords, Luca Saviello and Sciaretta della Colonna, and gave them all his support. Then the streets were blockaded; the administrators of the neighboring towns brought no grain to Rome, every day a new tumult rose up."

Clement VI's letter to Bertrand de Déaulx dated December 3, 1347, provides all the details of the plot. The pope tells the legate that he agrees with Bertrand's plans to hire mercenaries to take back papal territories from Cola. He tells him to hire "not only 400 or 500, but more, if necessary, as you will." Clement will provide Bertrand with 7,000 florins, which the treasurer of the Patrimony has at his disposal; another 4,000 will come from Ponzio de Pereto, the archdeacon of Vendôme, and another 6,500 from Pietro Vitalis, the chancellor of the church of Lucca in Tuscany and apostolic nuncio. All this money—to the sum of 17,500 florins—is to be placed on deposit with certain merchants of the Apostolic Camera. Pope Clement is also ordering Guillelmo, bishop of Cassino, and Ponzio de Pereto to make all their liquid funds available to Bertrand. "And don't worry about the money," the pope tells the legate, "for certainly, if the work requires more, the Lord willing, we will send it to you quickly. And we leave it up to you how and where it will be spent."

The pope then orders Bertrand to aid Rainaldo and Giordano Orsini and the Colonna against Cola; but if there are negotiations for peace, Clement advises Bertrand that he has already written to Cola's Orsini allies (on December 1, threatening them with excommunication if they continue to aid Cola), and both Orso and Nicolo have replied that Cola will acquiesce to the legate's demands. At the same time, the pope orders the lifting of the excommunication against Luca Savelli, Sciarra Colonna, and others for their adherence to Janni di Vico and tells the legate that he intends to bring the count of Fondi, Nicola Caetani, back into the favor of the church. The pope then introduces still another element designed to discredit the tribune: two Germans, named Theoderic and Albert, have appeared to bring charges of necromancy against Cola di Rienzo, apparently at the urging of Cardinal Giovanni Colonna.

But the pope's instructions to his legate in Rome were not all about toppling the Roman tribune. Other matters long festering in Rome had to be attended to, as Bertrand had informed his master. These included the urgently needed repairs to the city's major basilicas and pilgrimage churches, especially the Lateran and St. Peter's. Clement's answer here is indifferent: no specific provision can now be made in money or workmen, but the legate is free to do what he likes. On the same day, December 3, Clement VI also wrote to the cities of Italy concerning their alliance with Cola: Florence, Perugia, Siena, Narni, Pisa, Viterbo, Gubbio, Arezzo, Spoleto, Rieti, Foligno, Orvieto, and Pistoia are told that they are now to aid the legate against the tribune; while the people of Rome are given the reasons for Cola's excommunication. The stage had been set and the characters named and given their lines. Pope and legate now sat and waited for the last act to begin.[9]

Cola di Rienzo had become deeply intricated in the politics of the kingdom of Naples because Rome's strategic location and its internal politics had made it necessary; yet these politics finally came back to overwhelm him. The same porousness of the boundaries of the Regno and the Papal States in Lazio that made it easy for the Roman nobility to hold fiefs in, and divide their loyalties between, Rome and Naples also made for the same lawlessness on Rome's southern borders that fostered the careers of the brothers Nicola and Janni Caetani and of numerous other adventurers. Among these was Janni Pippino, count of Minervino, count palatine of Altamura, and lord of Bari in Apulia, on Italy's heel. Pippino's depredations had earned him the enmity of King Robert the Wise, who had him arrested and imprisoned. But according to the Anonimo romano, King Andrew, Giovanna's consort, had freed Pippino, and the paladin had fled the Regno for the relative safety of the Papal States, where he soon developed a reputation for his "robberies and violence" around Terracina. By the late fall Pippino had taken up residence where he was sure he could enjoy the friendship and alliance of some of the major barons of Rome and its district, the Colonna most importantly. Villani tells us that "the said count arrived in Rome with 150 cavalry with the aid of the captain of the Patrimony [by then the pope's nephew], and through the operation of the pope's legate." Meanwhile, Giordano Orsini continued his raids from Marino; but the tribune could do little without the express approval of the legate. As Villani says so succinctly, "In the beginning the Church favored the Tribune, and then . . . it did the opposite."

We have a remarkable record of the next seven days in December, provided by the *Chronicon Estense*, who appears well informed and reliable on both events and personalities. The chronicle's observations read like a modern diplomatic dispatch from a country about to face the trauma of a coup d'état. They convey the atmosphere of distrust and high tension that the papal destabilization had caused:

On Friday the seventh of the month, the lord tribune called the council together and introduced in the council the Thirty-Eight *sapientes* [senior advisers], proposing to them that among the number of the said Thirty-Eight there were two traitors, of whom one was Jacobello Ganelluçio. Then a certain Folcheto, a blood relative of the said Jacobello, rose to his feet in order to substantiate that Jacobello was not a traitor, and challenged any accusers, in any fashion, to combat. Then the Councilors of the people expelled those Thirty-Eight, causing them harm and hurt. In response to all this the majority of the citizens rushed to arms in support of the said tribune.

On December tenth the lord tribune of Rome called the council together in the presence of the vicar of the lord pope. At the meeting he made strong excuses for the aforesaid behavior of the Roman people; and he offered to resign his tribunal office and to rule always according to the wishes and pleasure of the lord pope and to observe the articles of agreement that the lord cardinal had brought to him on behalf of the lord pope. The people then asked to hear these articles. But the tribune excused himself, saying that there was not enough time left that day for a complete reading. Upon which the people responded, "Whatever the tribune accepts could not, nor would not, be to the detriment of the Roman people." Then the vicar of the said pope returned to the hospice of Saint Peter [in the Vatican Borgo].

On the morning of December eleventh the vicar of the lord pope left the city of Rome and entered Montefiascone and there he set up residence, so indicating that he intended to proceed against the tribune and the Roman people. Because of this the Roman people turned against the lord pope and his vicar.

On Wednesday, December twelfth the aforesaid tribune had the prefect [Janni di Vico] and his son [Francesco] released from the jails; and they dined with the tribune with joyful expressions. That night, he had them shut back in jail. On the next day he had them taken out again, and for the entire day they held discussions; and on the same day a peace was concluded between the said prefect and Giordano Orsini del Monte at the urging and efforts of the lord tribune. As a warranty [of the agreement Francesco,] the son of the prefect, accepted as his wife the daughter of the said Giordano and on the same day the prefect was released completely. Nevertheless his son, along with sixteen other men, was detained in the prisons. Furthermore, it was said that the aforesaid vicar was saying that he would attempt to stir up scandal among the Romans so that they would pick up their swords against one another. Because of this the people were turned vehemently against the vicar and they looked forward to the arrival of the king of Hungary.

On Thursday, December thirteenth, at nightfall the foreign mercenaries of the lord tribune rode to the castle of Marino and seized beasts and other goods, and when they had been brought to Rome the tribune had the horses and arms of the prefect restored to him.

On Saturday, the fifteenth of the month, a notice was found above the doorway of Sant'Angelo [in Pescheria]. It was written by Luca Savelli exhorting his friends to appear before him personally within four days. This came to the attention of the tribune, and he ordered his marshal to tear up the said notice and to replace it with another announcement to this effect: "We, Nicolas, knight and rector for our lord the Pope, order Luca Savelli to appear before us within three days." He showed Savelli that he knew nothing of his own summons and [warned him] that if this order were not fulfilled he could expect no mercy from the tribune. Because of this notice several men were detained by the said tribune's marshal. As a result of his capture of these men the marshal was insulted by the count of Vico and his brother; and thereupon the tribune had cited the count palatine [Janni Pippino of Altamura] the brother of the aforesaid men, who was at that time collecting forces to go to Apulia [to fight in the invasion of Naples].

Giordano Orsini del Monte then wanted to join the mercenaries headed for Apulia; and he received from the aforesaid count 100 gold florins for their mutual enterprise so that he could pay whatever other mercenaries he could find. But Giordano saw that the count [palatine] was gathering other forces and he feared that the count was tricking him, and he therefore ordered him detained, as we said above, and he looked for reasons to place him in the tribune's hands. But the count [palatine] learned of his intentions and he immediately returned to his *domus* in the *contrada* San Paolo and had the alarm bell rung. Then the tribune did the same; and then the uproar spread throughout the city. (RSI 15.3:157–58)

The *Chronicon Estense*'s chronology agrees with the other sources, most notably the Anonimo romano. On December 14, 1347, Luca Savelli began the uprising by posting a manifesto on the doors of Sant'Angelo in Pescheria, just as Cola himself had done on Pentecost day. This was the cue for the paladin of Altamura, who had established himself in the safety of the Colonna *contrada* of SS. Apostoli, at the base of the Corso and below the Capitoline. The trouble began when that most dreaded Roman symbol of hatred and civil war—a barricade—was thrown up "under the arch of San Salvatore in Pesoli," now the church of S. Stanislao dei Polacchi. It was the ideal place to challenge the tribune: right at the edge of his own *contrada,* that of Sant'Angelo in Pescheria—and within direct eyesight of the palace on the Capitoline.

Emboldened, the count palatine, "along with the neighbors and friends of the Colonna," according to Villani, had the bell of the church rung to rally the Colonna forces in the *contrada,* both horse and foot. Soon a full-scale uprising had begun amid shouts of "'Long live the Colonna! Death to the tribune and his followers!' At this uproar barricades went up in every *contrada* of the city, each one with its own forces, each guarding its own *contrada*." The Anonimo romano picks up details from his side of the barricades: "All night and all day the bell of Sant'Angelo in Pescheria sounded the alarm. It was rung by a Jew." A curious detail, yet a revealing one. The Jews were one of the major groups in the *rione* Sant'Angelo in Pescheria. Cola had grown up among them, and several times during his career he appears to have shown them fair enough dealing so that Jews from Perugia came to Rome seeking justice from him during the Roman Synod. The Jews of Rome formed a class of petty bourgeois, protected by papal regulation but, as in most of Europe, exploited by the local barons whenever possible. For many reasons it was therefore more than plausible that the Anonimo romano's story is correct; but the most convincing argument for its truthfulness is the saddest. Only a Jew would dare enter the campanile tower of Sant'Angelo that day on behalf of the tribune: no Christian in the city could defy the legate's threat of interdict or excommunication to aid him. And then the Anonimo romano completes the picture: "No one gathered to break down the barricade."

Rome must have offered a surreal scene that night and into the next morning: amid the erection of barricades, the pealing of alarm bells from the Colonna district, from Sant'Angelo, and then from the Campidoglio, the shouts of armed bands again reverberated down the dark, undulating streets of the *abitato,* a scene of chaos and anarchy punctuated by the quick movement of torches and shadows that had so horrified Cola and his fellow Romans for years. The devil-like image of *Mal Governo* had again raised his horns above the city, and with him all the dogs of war, bloodshed, and hatred were about to be unleashed. On what was probably the night of December 14–15, "the tribune immediately sent a detachment of cavalry to the barricade. While he fought there, a [German] constable named Scarpetta was killed by a lance. The tribune learned that Scarpetta was dead, and that the people were not gathering at his alarm, although the bell of Sant'Angelo in Pescheria was ringing." The *Chronicon Estense* adds that "then the tribune mounted the Capitoline where he remained until the fourth hour of the night with five bands of knights." Villani continues the account: "The Colonna approached the Campidoglio, but the Tribune was not backed up, as he should have been, neither by the Orsini, nor by the people."

What the Anonimo romano reports next has been at the core of the legend of Cola di Rienzo for the next six hundred years:

He breathed quickly and trembled; he wept; he did not know what to do. With his heart jolted and stricken he didn't have the strength of a little boy. He spoke with great difficulty. He imagined that agents were placed against him in the midst of the City. This was not the case, because no rebel had appeared. There was no one who raised himself against the people; Cola simply trembled. He believed he was about to be killed. What more can I say? (AR, XVIII, ll. 1958–66, Porta, 208)

Beginning with this passage from the Anonimo romano, historians have tended to emphasize the interior, psychological, and character issues involved in Cola's response, largely ignoring the religious and political nature of the crisis that ensued. As Rome dissolved into its old familiar

warring camps of fortress, faction, and party, each for himself and everyone against the other, Cola was faced with a terrible choice: he could attempt again to attack the Colonna behind their barricades, or he could
stand firm upon the Capitoline with his trusted troops until his loyalists
gathered courage and rallied to the tocsin. He could then begin, *contrada*
by *contrada, rione* by *rione,* to win back the city; tearing down the barricades and the fortresses, defeating their defenders, sending Roman against
Roman, spilling the blood of dozens, hundreds of friends and enemies in
fighting that would bring back the civil wars of the 1330s and recall the
bloody factional strife sparked by the descents upon Rome of the emperors
Henry VII and Lewis of Bavaria. But Cola and his allies—as well as his
enemies—had seen and caused enough bloodshed in these past few
weeks to last a lifetime.

Cola could hold out for just this result; and so he could see the seven
months of the *buono stato,* its work of justice and peace, of reconciliation,
security, and prosperity go up in smoke and ashes, all in order to save
himself and preserve his power. The *buono stato* had been born without
violence, and if it had used force to preserve security and to pursue justice, it had done so for the common good with the legitimate tools available to the medieval commune. Should Cola now destroy the fragile civil
society that he had worked so hard to rebuild? He had said repeatedly
that the *buono stato* had not been about him or his personal ambitions,
but about the salvation and renewal of the queen of cities, the image of
Jerusalem itself. He had protested to the pope time and again that the
least word from him or his legate would suffice to have him step down
from power.

Cola himself would reveal this repugnance for further bloodshed several years later, in August 1350, in a letter to the archbishop of Prague. No
sooner had he enjoyed the triumph of his crowning as tribune, he recalls,
than one night a chaplain confided to him the unnerving prophecies of a
friar named Guglielmo. Cola's triumph also marked his fall, Guglielmo
foretold, for the tribune had risen to power without effort and without
bloodshed; but just as surely as the friar prophesied Cola's bloody victory over the Colonna, he also foretold how God would test him in defeat. For the next twelve nights, the dove that usually sang atop the Senators' Palace was replaced by a screeching owl whose cries so disturbed
Cola's sleep with the guilt of his bloodletting that he finally decided to
assemble the clergy and people of Rome in the Aracoeli and there publicly lay down the insignia of his office. Nevertheless, Cola stressed that
he had no intention of leaving Rome without first providing it with a

"popular government" securely in the hands of his supporters. But in the midst of these arrangements, the paladin of Altamura rose up in revolt.

And now there was another factor in the momentous decision Cola faced. He knew, and every Roman knew, that as soon as one person lifted a hand to come to his aid, the legate would hurl his interdict against the entire city and excommunication against its citizens. Pope Clement and Cardinal Bertrand had also made it clear that they would cancel the Jubilee of 1350 and the rebirth that this would bring to Rome. Everything— the return of the papacy to its home, the wealth and prestige that would accrue to the city, the vast new spiritual riches that would flow from its churches and monasteries—all would be lost. Rienzo knew that if he chose to fight, he would have allies. He already had troops supplied by King Lewis of Hungary; others, loyal Romans, would come to him. He also knew that should he cower before the legate, he would be labeled a weakling and a traitor by many who, like his old friend Petrarch, had warned him of the mockery and derision that would await him. Had not Dante himself placed that great Spiritual man, Pope Celestine V, in the vestibule of hell, solely for his act of resignation, his *gran rifiuto*?[10]

But Cola also knew that there was a long history and tradition of courageous and powerful men and women who at the peak of their power had resigned their offices and stepped down and chosen a self-imposed humiliation in the service of a higher good. Pope Celestine himself was still widely revered by many, lay and cleric alike, for his purity and sanctity: Had not the Colonna themselves waged a civil war against Pope Boniface to protect Celestine's memory? Did not the Poor Hermits whom Celestine had founded still live the poor Gospel life in their hermitages in and around Rome? And then even more recently, in the neighboring kingdom of Naples, had not Prince Philip, the heir and regent of Majorca, resigned his kingdom to enter a Franciscan community in the Castel Nuovo? Had not Queen Sancia, Philip's sister and the wife of King Robert, given up the regency of the kingdom to retire to a Clariss convent? Had not Robert's own brother, St. Louis of Toulouse, renounced claims to kingdoms and high church office to assume the humble robes of a Franciscan? Louis had announced his decision right here, atop the Capitoline, inside the church of the Aracoeli, before the assembled nobility of Rome, Provence, and the kingdom of Naples. There had been many lesser examples of princes, barons, and knights both in Naples and elsewhere throughout Italy and Christendom who in recent years had turned their backs on the power of the world to seek a higher realm and a greater good. Here, too, in Rome, the blessed Venturino, rising to the peak of fame and spiritual power, realized that his very presence posed a grave threat to Rome and to the church. He had then quietly left the city.

Dante himself had to absorb and slowly learn the bitter lessons of humiliation and exile that so infuse the spiritual pilgrimage that forms the central motif of his *Divine Comedy.* At his coronation ceremony Cola had once used the text of Dante that spoke so eloquently of the dichotomy between the poet and the prince and the two worlds that they inhabit. Cola understood deeply the conflict between the *vita activa,* the life of action and command, and the *vita contemplativa,* the life of the prophet, the artist, and the intellectual. He knew that the two were most often irreconcilable, and that the honest demands of one life must cancel out the requirements of the other. The revolt of the paladin of Altamura "could easily have been prevented," Cola wrote the archbishop of Prague, "but lest I stain myself with even more blood, I left the palace, and after a solemn parliament, even though inside me I was unwilling and in mourning, I assigned the palace to the people and to my vicars." And so Cola di Rienzo made his decision and, on the morning of December 15, he emerged from the palace on the Capitoline. According to the Anonimo romano,

Weeping and sighing, the tribune made a speech to the people who happened to be there, and he said that he had ruled well and that, because of envy, people were not content with him. "Now in the seventh month I step down from my position of command." After he spoke these words, he began to weep, then he mounted his horse. The silver trumpets sounded, and with the imperial insignia and accompanied by armed men, "he descended triumphantly" and rode to the Castel Sant'Angelo. There he remained closed in and hidden away. (AR, XVIII, ll. 1968–77, Porta, 208–9)

But before Cola had reached the castle, as he rode slowly through the *abitato* from the Campidoglio to the Borgo, he and the Romans played out one final public ritual, a grand procession. "When the Tribune descended from his greatness, those who were with him also wept. The miserable people wept as well," the Anonimo romano recalls. One can well imagine the scene as Cola proceeded along the via Papalis, its narrow width lined with Romans who, under pain of interdict, could do nothing to help him, but who had turned out to give the tribune their farewells. The Romans played their part well: such public mourning was long an accepted, and expected, part of civic life. The Orsini could not actively take up arms on the tribune's behalf, but they had offered him refuge at their stronghold in Castel Sant'Angelo, a part of the compromise worked out with the legate behind the scenes. Meanwhile, Cola's wife, Livia, left her official residence, the Lalli Palace, dressed as a Clariss nun. We do not know whether she had assumed the dress as a disguise, intent on rejoining her husband and family after they were safely out of the city, or like so many ladies, grand and small, as a sign of penance and abnegation.

Cola's official apartment was broken into almost at once, a "ritual of violence" that was a common event following the death or downfall of a medieval ruler. His papers, official correspondence, and insignia of state were thoroughly trashed. But then an uneasy calm came over the city. The Romans seem to have perceived this abdication as an essentially religious act: they understood that on the political plane they and Cola had no choice; but they also appreciated the symbolism of the abdication as an act of spiritual abnegation on behalf of the peace that Cola had long sought for Rome and its people. For two days Stefano il Vecchio kept the barons outside the walls. The Anonimo romano reports that they did so out of fear, and this may have been one of their reasons for staying away; but the *Chronicon Estense* offers evidence that fits the mood more closely: "On Monday, December 17th, Lord Stefano Colonna arrived in Rome, and he immediately had it proclaimed throughout the City that no one ought to presume or to dare break the peace previously made between so many by the lord tribune Cola di Rienzo; since the said Nicolo had brought peace among many; and great evil and scandal would follow otherwise" (RIS 15.3:158). Thus the barons' absence came from the same deep sense of respect, if not for Cola personally, then for the feelings of the Roman people, whom they knew had been deprived of a leader, and a leader who had made his departure such an outpouring of public sympathy. Cola had defeated the barons in battle repeatedly—in siege, in the open field, even in the disastrous melee of the Porta San Lorenzo—and men of war could learn to respect a man who had beaten them time and again. What's more, while Cola had shown his temper that day in the Aracoeli against the women of the Colonna clan, he had taken no revenge against the defenseless family.

Thus Stefano il Vecchio may have come to the very same realization that Cola had reached immediately after the battle of Porta San Lorenzo: that enough blood had been shed, that enough sons, brothers, and husbands had been lost, that enough households in Rome had been left bereaved by hatred and violence. If Cola had meted out harsh justice, he had shunned revenge; and Stefano Colonna took the lesson to heart. In the days after the barons returned to the city, Cola's family was left in peace; and none of the supporters of the *buono stato* were hunted down; in fact many still held high government positions years later.

But that was until the return of the cardinal-legate. Bertrand de Déaulx had trembled in his seat at the Vatican palace and had fallen silent before the tribune. Now, with his enemy safely toppled, he could finally raise his voice: "The cardinal-legate entered Rome [from Montefiascone] and started proceedings against the tribune; he damned the majority of his actions, and said that he was a heretic." Having revoked all the acts and decisions of the *buono stato,* Cardinal Bertrand quickly reestablished the senatorship, naming Bertoldo Orsini and Luca Savelli Rome's new rulers on behalf of the pope.

The Anonimo romano states outright that the new senators "ruled weakly." But they did do the legate's bidding, and among their first actions was one of those exquisite gestures of public revenge so common in the Italian city-state. Cola, now an outlaw and a heretic, was also the object of public *infamia.* They therefore ordered his portrait, dressed as a knight, to be painted on the walls of the Senators' Palace, but upside down, like the hanged man of the tarot. The Anonimo romano notes that they also painted Cecco Mancini, Cola's in-law, notary, and chancellor, and Cola's nephew Conte, who subsequently surrendered to the new government the castle of Civitavecchia.

So the tribune's exile began.[11] As he wrote years later, "I exchanged the laurel leaves of my tribune's crown for the forest leaves of the wanderer and the pilgrim." Sometime early in 1348, possibly as early as January after the legate had published his final excommunication, Rienzo left the Castel Sant'Angelo and was escorted secretly out of the city. But before he left Rome, Cola commissioned one final apocalyptic painting, in the piazza of Castel Sant'Angelo, on the wall of Sta. Maria Maddalena, a church that no longer exists. It showed "an angel in armor, with the arms of Rome, holding a cross in his hand; above the cross was a dove. The angel was trampling the asp and the basilisk, the lion and the dragon, under his feet." The visual sources for his painting and its message would have been clear to the Romans. In the manuscript of the *Liber Ystoriarum Romanorum* that the Savelli owned in Rome, the Ecclesia Romana stands triumphant over just these four beasts. Cola's painting also took its place in a long tradition of St. Michael slaying the dragon while acting as the protector of the city. The tribune thus identified himself with the apocalyptic angel Michael, the "captain of the heavenly host" who crushes the serpent in Apocalypse 12:7–9. But as soon as the painting was completed, "the fools of Rome" threw mud on it to show their contempt. "One evening Cola di Rienzo came in secret, unrecognized, to see the picture before his departure. He saw it and realized the fools had dishonored it. He then ordered a lamp to be burnt before it for one year." It seems that Cola continued to have protection and support within Rome for some time; and he expected his supporters to remain in power on one level or another for at least that year.

Cola's movements after his night flight from Rome are difficult to reconstruct. According to the Sienese chronicler Agnolo di Tura del Graso, he left the city "on December 13 with a small company and went to Civitavecchia, where he stayed a few days and then returned to Rome, believing that he could reassume the lordship of the City, but he was unable, and so he remained in the Castel Sant'Angelo until the king of Hungary arrived [in Naples on January 22], and then he went to Naples." As Giovanni Villani records, "He left the Campidoglio incognito and entered Castel Sant'Angelo. There he lived secretly until the arrival of the king of Hungary in Naples, and some say that he traveled there incognito by sea in a boat" (*Cronica* XII.105, p. 282).

Agnolo di Tura repeatedly misreports events in Rome, for example, confusing the revolt of the count of Fondi with the battle of Porta San Lorenzo and stating that Cola entered Castel Sant'Angelo after his flight from Rome. But Cola's nephew was still castellan of Civitavecchia, and it would have made some sense for him to seek refuge there. In addition, that city was on the coast; and the sea offered a relatively safe and fast route to Naples. In August 1350 Cola also told Charles IV that he had spent some time on the island of Ponza in the Gulf of Gaeta, where he met a hermit member of the Colonna family. If his story is true, it would confirm that he reached Naples by sea. Cola was not above seeking out a powerful ally and the safety of a kingdom long known for its protection of dissidents and papal enemies. Queen Giovanna had fled Naples on January 15, 1348; Lewis of Hungary reached Aversa, thirteen kilometers northwest of Naples, on January 17 and crowned himself king of Naples on January 27. The most likely reconstruction of events is that Cola must have remained in the Castel Sant'Angelo for about a month before departing for the Regno, where his ally and new protector now reigned. He might well have fled to Civitavecchia and, on his nephew Conte's deposition from its rule, finally decided to travel to Naples by sea and thus avoid passing through the territory of his enemies, the Colonna and Caetani.

Cola's presence in Naples is confirmed in a letter from Clement VI to Bertrand de Déaulx dated May 7, 1348, in which he informs his legate of political events relating to the Regno and commands Bertrand to warn Lewis of Hungary not to aid or abet Rienzo, "excommunicated and strongly suspected of heresy . . . who is reported to be residing in the city of Naples for some time." Cola also had the sympathy of the archbishop of Naples, Giovanni Orsini, to whom Clement wrote on January 13, 1349, gingerly cautioning his powerful colleague to avoid Rienzo's heretical errors and to aid in his capture. But, in fact, Cola remained in Naples for only a short time. By June 1349 he had returned to the area around Rome, for on June 12, 1349, Clement VI wrote from Avignon to Rome, ordering Legate Annibaldo de Ceccano to proceed against Rienzo. If Cola had reached Naples by the winter of 1348 and found King Lewis enthroned there, what had happened subsequently that forced him to flee to the mountains around Rome? One explanation would be his fear that Lewis of Hungary might reverse long-standing royal policy under King Robert and Queen Sancia and turn his refugee over to the Inquisition. Another reason might, as Villani reports, be what forced King Lewis himself to flee the city that spring: the arrival of the Black Death.[12]

Few events in the history of the world have equaled the great plague of 1348, a disaster matched only by World Wars I and II in terms of its destruction and long-term impact. According to the fourteenth-century historian Gilles li Muisis, the plague first came aboard some ships leaving the besieged Genoese trading outpost of Caffa, the modern Feodosia on the Black Sea coast of the Crimea. From there, and probably in the normal course of east-west trade that was then so highly developed in the Mediterranean, the plague followed the shipping lanes and quickly touched port first in Constantinople. By December 1347 it had reached Sicily, Corsica and Sardinia, and then Marseilles. By January 1348 it was at Genoa. By the time Genoese authorities realized what was upon them, it was too late: quarantines and forced expulsions could not contain the plague from spreading inland from Liguria. By February it had entered the port of Pisa, and from there it spread rapidly through Tuscany to Florence and throughout the spring and summer beyond there into central and northern Italy. It traveled along the Adriatic at almost the same speed, hitting Venice in January 1348. The spread of the disease was well documented, its extent radiating out from its first centers with horrific speed and thoroughness. Few regions were spared. The effect on the society and the mentality of the fourteenth century was staggering. The classic account of the disaster comes from the pen of Petrarch's young literary follower and friend, Giovanni Boccaccio, whose *Decameron* is framed by the horrors of the plague in Florence.

The Black Death had reached Avignon by February 1348. The plague killed off many in the city, including Cardinal Giovanni Colonna (July 3, 1348), Petrarch's beloved Laura, and many more of the friends whom Petrarch was to mourn in letters written from then on. Pope Clement set a brave example to the city, remaining in residence in his palace for as long as possible, performing public liturgies and processions to placate divine wrath, and protecting the city's and Europe's Jews from the pogroms that fell upon them for their supposed role in the disaster.

The overall effect of the Black Death on Europe's population was staggering. A contemporary report provided to the pope calculated the total number of dead throughout the world at precisely 42,836,486, of which 1,244,434 died in Germany alone. While the figures cannot be taken as statistics in any sense of the word, medieval accountants certainly could add up their numbers, and the numbers reported to the pope corroborate the sense of enormous loss conveyed by Boccaccio and other medieval witnesses. The current consensus among historians now gives credence to an average 47 to 48 percent mortality across Europe.

Cola may well have been in Naples when the Black Death hit the city around May 1348. According to the *Chronicon Estense,* the plague killed sixty-three thousand out of a population of about one hundred thousand. Like King Lewis, Cola left Naples and probably sought the relative safety of the mountainous area east and north of Rome, where the Inquisition was to locate him in June 1349.

There is some evidence that Rome itself was also stricken. Popular legend records that the grand stairway leading from the foot of the Capitoline to Sta. Maria in Aracoeli, and begun in October 1348 according to the inscription placed just to the left of the church's central portal, was built to commemorate the city's salvation from the plague. But scholars today are fairly certain that the stairway was conceived and planned in preparation for the Jubilee of 1350, the only major public work undertaken in Rome since the death of Boniface VIII in 1303. As such its inspiration may have derived, as some say, from Cola himself during his tribunate. Construction was supervised by Lorenzo Simeoni Andreotti, and its high cost—5,000 florins—was financed by funds collected from processionals mounted to avoid the Black Death.

The plague was felt by many to be among the most potent signs of the Last Days that had been prophesied increasingly by preachers and writers throughout the fourteenth century. Were not the four horsemen of Apocalypse 6 War, Famine, Plague, and then Death itself? Nor did the Romans and the Italians escape other signs of the final days. Just as the

Black Death had begun its juggernaut through Europe, on January 25, 1348, a devastating earthquake struck Villach in Austria. Then, in September 1349, series of quakes struck central and southern Italy, destroying buildings, towns, and cities.[13] On June 11, 1351, Petrarch wrote from Piacenza to his friend Socrates (*Fam.* II.7) describing the earthquakes of 1349. He reports the heavy damage to many of Rome's monuments, including the Torre dei Conti, San Paolo fuori le Mura, and the Lateran. His words reflect the apocalyptic mood of the times:

But look—you may still be ignorant of this, perhaps—Rome herself was so violently shaken by the strange trembling that nothing similar to it had ever been known there in the two thousand years and more since the City's founding. . . .

I feel deep concern for the highest welfare of the republic, and sad forebodings make me tremble not so much for Rome as for the whole of Italy. I fear not so much the convulsions of Nature as the upheavals of men's minds. I am terrified by many things but above all by that ancient prophecy uttered so long before the City was founded and inserted not in any minor writings but in the Sacred Scriptures themselves. Though I was then entirely absorbed in secular literature and not familiar with the Scriptures, I confess that when I first read it [Num. 24:24] I shuddered, and the blood in my heart grew cold and chilled. . . .

Some may hold that this prophecy has long since been fulfilled in the fall of the Roman Empire; but I trust that this recent trembling of the City does not portend a second overthrow of peace and liberty. (CRCR, 122–24)

Petrarch's impressions of the destruction grew even worse after he had actually visited Rome as a pilgrim during the Jubilee of 1350:

The houses are overthrown, the walls come to the ground, the temples fall, the sanctuaries perish, the laws are trodden underfoot. The Lateran lies on the ground, and the mother of all the churches stands without a roof and exposed to wind and rain. The holy dwellings of St. Peter and St. Paul totter, and what was lately the temple of the Apostles is a shapeless heap of ruins to excite pity in hearts of stone. (*Fam.* IX.13)

The Torre delle Milizie had also collapsed, losing half of its height, while the citizens of Rome abandoned their brick, stone, and timber structures to live in tents for several weeks after the initial quakes. According to Matteo Villani, the earthquake toppled the campanile of San Paolo fuori le Mura and part of its loggie, probably the atrium arcades.

Petrarch, the man of ancient learning and reason, had harshly criticized the Spiritual Franciscans at the court of Naples for their apocalyptic reaction to the earthquake there on November 25, 1343. Now, in the wake of plague, earthquake, and the wholesale death of friends and loved ones, even he could give some credence, however reluctantly, to the deeply religious understanding—even apocalyptic expectation—of these catastrophes.

With the fall of their tribune and the world cataclysms of the Black Death, the Romans now began to share this apocalyptic expectation. In 1349 William of Blofield, an English Carmelite, reported Joachite prophecies then widespread throughout the city:

That Antichrist is now six years old and is a very handsome boy, one most learned in every field of knowledge, so much so that there is no one now alive who can equal him. They are also preaching that there is another boy born twelve years ago beyond the land of the Tartars who has been brought up in the Christian faith. It is he who will destroy the perfidy of the Saracens. He is the greatest of the Christians but he will quickly end his empire upon the coming of Antichrist. These prophets also say about the present pope, among other things, that he will have a violent end. They also say that after the death of this pope, there will be so many more revolutions in the world than there have been in any other age. But after this there will rise up another pope, a good and just one, and he will create cardinals who fear the Lord, and there will be the greatest peace during this age. And after him there will not be another pope; but Antichrist will come and will reveal himself. (HBD, no. 54, pp. 154–55)

• • •

In a letter to Emperor Charles IV written no later than mid-July 1350, the toppled tribune picks up his own story at the point of his abdication:

I was not compelled by man, but inspired by God. In public parliament before the people I freely and solemnly laid down the tribune's crown and the scepter of justice. With the people in tears, I departed and "remained in solitude, awaiting him who would save me from faintheartedness and from the tempest" [Ps. 54:8–9]. In the garb of poverty and in prayer I stayed with the hermits of the Apennines in the kingdom of Naples. (49, BBCR 2.3:192–93, ll. 30–36)

After leaving Naples, Cola headed for the remote mountain recesses of the Abruzzi region in the north of the kingdom.[14] According to the Anonimo romano, Cola spent his exile in fear of the Roman barons, wandering "like a Fraticello, lying low all around the mountains of Maiella with the hermits and penitents." Pietro Angeleri da Morrone, Pope Celestine V, had been a hermit in the Montagna del Morrone, a spur of the Montagna della Maiella, just north and east of Sulmona. The Badia Morronese still stands on the barren slopes that rise abruptly from the valley, within eyesight of the main road north from Sulmona to L'Aquila. To this day the Montagna della Maiella is dotted with tiny hermitages and caves—S. Antonio, S. Michele, S. Germano, Sto. Spirito, and S. Nicolao are only a few. But one must first climb into its forbidding mass to reach them. On the lower, hidden slopes, between the rocky outcroppings and along the shoulders formed by the high, snow-clad ridges, lie small Alpine meadows and thick stands of beech, oak, and pine interspersed by small streams and brooks. Across the meadows, within sight and almost within hailing distance of one another, stand shepherd huts, constructed of stone and wood, their small kitchen gardens bounded by low stone walls.

Here many of the excommunicated Spiritual Franciscans, now the "Fraticelli," had retreated after the death of Angelo Clareno in 1337. Many of Clareno's companions and followers thus escaped the Inquisition and were able to remain true to their strict adherence to Franciscan poverty and Joachite prophecy. Cola's exile, though bitter, thus afforded him a ready-made community, a large degree of protection, and freedom to move along the borders of the Papal States and to enter and leave at will.

As Cola told Archbishop Ernst von Pardubitz in his *Libellus* of August 1350, soon after he had settled in among the hermits of Maiella, he decided, or was encouraged, to return to Roman territory. Cola entered the Papal States taking the route north and east by way of L'Aquila, past the Rocca and Castello di Corno. Just a few miles south of Antrodoco, on the western slopes of the Cimita di Castello, above the via Salaria and the Velino, perches the Orsini fortress of Castel Sant'Angelo. Here he met Francesco Orsini, probably of the Soriano branch of the family, and Nicola Orsini, Francesco's nephew who in 1347 had been the tribune's commander for the campaign against Janni di Vico. Cola decided to accompany the papal notary Francesco Orsini toward Rome. But he soon learned that Francesco had "made plans to present me to the pope against my will . . . [and then] Nicola Orsini, his nephew, induced by bad advice, made arrangements to sell me out, for a money ransom, to Lord Rainaldo Orsini, my chief enemy." Cola's capture had been planned on the highest levels. In his letter to Bertrand de Déaulx dated May 9, 1348, Clement VI revealed his knowledge of the plot to capture the tribune: Rienzo would be invited to join the Orsini in Rome on the pretext of aiding the peace negotiations between the Orsini and Janni di Vico. On the same day Clement wrote to Francesco declaring that Cola was a dangerous enemy of the church and intimating that he should be arrested and "annihilated." The next day the pope again wrote his legate, warning Bertrand to be on his guard against the Roman people's rising up to Cola's cause once more.

Cola was seized and held in the Castel Sant'Angelo in the Vatican Borgo until Rainaldo Orsini could come to Rome to fetch and murder him. But shortly afterward, as Cola later wrote, on the feast of Michael the Archangel, September 29, 1348, Francesco and Nicola Orsini suddenly and simultaneously both dropped dead without uttering a sound. Cola says that he walked free by the grace of the archangel. Here Rienzo again uses his great associative skills to reveal the cause of his release. For it was St. Michael who had appeared atop "their very Castel Sant'Angelo" to save the Roman people from the great plague of 590 during the procession around the city led by Pope Gregory the Great. His jailers killed by the plague, Rienzo emerged from the Castel Sant'Angelo without hindrance; and the capture of Rainaldo Orsini by Janni Caetani "on the same day" allowed Cola to return to the Abruzzi.

And so, freed by the Lord, I remained in my hermitage until the lord archbishop of Naples [Giovanni Orsini] wrote to me. During my days in power he was my friend and the representative of the party of the barons of the kingdom of Naples during the negotiations entrusted to me over the civil war afflicting that kingdom. I don't know how he knew that I was in that hermitage, but he wrote that he had received letters from Our Lord Pope [49, BBCR 2.4:131–32] authorizing him to carry out negotiations for my complete reconciliation, because, as he asserted, I was of use to the pope in the March of Ancona.

I, however, believed this great father and friend, nor did I expect that he hid a twitching scorpion's tail. In good faith I got myself ready for my reconciliation with the pope. But as soon as I had gotten on the road, messengers reported back to me that the lord archbishop had fallen straight into the hands of Lord Louis [of Taranto], the husband of Queen Giovanna of Naples. And, since the archbishop was then suspected [of having a hand in] the invasion of the city of Naples by [Lewis] the king of Hungary, he was stripped of his treasure and came close to losing his life.

After I had therefore returned to my hermitage, I received letters from one of [Archbishop Giovanni's] intimates who sympathized with me more than others did, to the effect that the negotiations that were being undertaken by the lord archbishop of Naples at the request of the legate were a fraud. And so struck, I was tossed this way and that and I almost sank, but the Lord kept me afloat and also vindicated me. (57, BBCR 2.3:265–66, ll. 901–19)

Pope Clement had been making plans for the Jubilee almost since the Romans' mission to Avignon in 1343.[15] His reasons were varied and good. The benefits to the city of Rome and its district included the security, peace, and justice that the *buono stato* eventually secured; the increase in revenues and prestige to the city and its chief shrines; the renewal of spiritual and religious life in what was still, after all, the capital of Christendom; and, in a sense, a spiritual down payment on the papacy's promise that it would eventually return to its proper see, once Rome and its warring barons had been brought back to peace and harmony. Though Pope Clement had used the threat of withdrawing the Jubilee as one of his chief weapons to cow the Romans into submission and to force them to reject their tribune, he was, after all, the city's bishop and deeply concerned for its spiritual well-being. The disasters of the years since Cola's over-throw—the Black Death, the great earthquake, the arrival of the Flagel-lants with their millennial expectations and local outpourings of hatred against the Jews, the ongoing war between England and France and the devastation caused by their unemployed mercenary bands during peri-ods of truce, the widespread famines and renewed violence throughout Italy, but especially around Rome and in its district—all these made the fulfillment of the pope's promise for the Jubilee of prime importance. Many, in addition, gave serious belief to the widespread prophecies that the year 1350 would, more or less, signal the beginning of the final days, the ending of the period of tribulation, and the beginning of the New Age. Rome must have its Jubilee, and the pope and his legate would give it to them. Clement himself could not make it to Rome that year, he in-formed his fellow Christians, because the French and English war was tak-ing up all his concerns and required his residence in Avignon, close to the theater of action. He therefore appointed two cardinals, Gui du Boulogne and Annibaldo de Ceccano, as his legates.

Like that of 1300, the Jubilee of 1350 attracted hundreds of thousands of pilgrims, but this time to a depressed and strife-ridden city. Despite Rome's shrunken population, which some historians have estimated at as low as seventeen thousand, the number of pilgrims descending upon the city seems to have matched that of 1300. Giovanni's brother and con-tinuator, Matteo Villani, writes:

The multitude of Christians who went to Rome was impossible to count; but ac-cording to the estimate of those who were residing in the City, on Christmas day and the solemn days around it, and in the period from Lent to Easter, there were continually in Rome between 1,000,000 and 1,200,000 pilgrims. Then, between the Ascension and Pentecost, there were more than 900,000 packing the streets day and night, it is reported. With the arrival of summer, and the extraordinary heat, there began to be a shortage of workers for the harvest. But this did not mean that there were fewer pilgrims. On any given day there were continually no fewer than 200,000 foreign visitors. (*Cronica* I.lviii, ll. 34–46, Porta, 109–10)

The *Tertia Vita* of Clement VI agrees: "There was such a multitude that one of the pilgrims, a reliable man, told me that every day of that year 5,000 pilgrims could be counted entering and leaving Rome."

Prices inflated immediately for the Jubilee, as they had in 1300. Pilgrims arriving in Rome met a time of scarcity, high prices, and ill-feeling on both sides. Matteo Villani laments the high costs of hotels in the city; and Buccio di Ranallo of L'Aquila reported that he had spent between six and thirteen denarii a night for lodging in May 1350. The 1350 Jubilee, in fact, had made the pilgrim trade so lucrative that Matteo Villani reported that "the Romans were all turned into inn-keepers, giving their houses to pilgrims and their horses" (ll. 46–51).

The Jubilee attracted the faithful from all over Christendom, including Petrarch himself and Birgitta of Sweden, the great mystic, reformer, and critic of papal corruption. The indulgences earned by Birgitta and Petrarch, like those of the hundreds of thousands of other pilgrims, had been much easier to obtain after Cardinal Annibaldo had issued new rules governing the number of times these *romei* needed to visit Rome's principal churches to obtain the plenary indulgence: thirty times for Romans, fifteen for Italians, ten times for the *ultramontanes,* that is, those coming from Provence and other regions bordering the Alps, and only five times for those coming from regions even farther off: England, Germany, remote parts of Spain or northern France, eastern Europe, or Scandinavia. But what many saw as the cardinal's cavalier attitude toward the liberties of the Roman people and toward the livelihoods of its innkeepers, taverners, souvenir sellers, money changers, and others began to earn him the enmity of most of the city's population, an enmity that soon erupted into open hostility.

We have already met Cardinal Annibaldo several times, first at Avignon as the host of the opulent reception given for the newly elected Clement VI in 1343.[16] His riches and extravagance—based on the many benefices showered upon him by admiring popes—were well known to contemporaries, including Petrarch, and made the butt of much ridicule. After a rapid rise through church ranks, aided by his "high culture and the maturity of his counsels," Annibaldo was made archbishop of Naples in 1326, cardinal-priest of San Lorenzo in Lucina in 1327, and then cardinal-bishop of Tusculum in 1333. Named papal legate to arrange a truce between England and France in 1342, he was a trusted member of the Curia; and as one of the only surviving Italian cardinals under Clement VI, his opinions and connections in Italy carried much weight in Avignon. Annibaldo knew Rome, its personalities, and its politics. He was an uncle of that Martino de Porto who had seized the Marseilles galley and whom Cola had executed in 1347, and he had many relatives and political connections within Rome and the Campagna. He was thus an ideal candidate to replace Cardinal Bertrand de Déaulx, who had competently handled the deposition of Cola di Rienzo and thus acquitted himself of the pope's displeasure for his previous failures in Naples and Rome. Clement rewarded Bertrand with the title cardinal-bishop of Sabina on November 1348, and on November 17, 1348, Bertrand left Rome for Avignon, where he died on October 21, 1355.

The Anonimo romano reveals Annibaldo's character in four piercing phrases: "First, he was a Campanian; second, he had a squint; third, he was very pompous and full of vainglory; as for the fourth, I prefer to remain silent" (AR, XXIII, ll. 29–32, Porta, 212). Annibaldo's mission was a difficult one. Not only had he to organize and then supervise the Jubilee, ensuring that the hundreds of thousands of pilgrims arriving in Rome that year were housed, fed, safely conducted to Rome's great churches, and returned homeward without incident; but he also had to see to the repair and maintenance of Rome's religious monuments—many, like the Lateran, badly damaged in the earthquake of 1349. Moreover, he had to root out the abuses that had crept into the life of the church there during the papal absence. In addition to his spiritual duties, the cardinal had to guarantee that the city's administration, left in shambles by Cola's overthrow, received much-needed reform. The economy had also collapsed. On March 23, 1348, Clement VI had written to Bertrand de Déaulx on a number of issues, one of them being a shipment to the legate of 10,000 florins for him to distribute to the Roman people "in alms." But although the pope tells Bertrand that he should entrust these funds to bankers, he acknowledges that "we can scarcely and with great difficulty find enough bankers left."

But there was another reason for Annibaldo's appointment. As Clement specified in his letter to the cardinal on November 30, 1348, he was to continue the vigilance that his predecessor, Bertrand, had maintained against the church's great enemy, Cola di Rienzo. Annibaldo was to vigorously prevent any alliances and leagues that Cola might form and to move with interdiction, suspension, and excommunication against him and any who aid or abet him. In addition, the pope warned, Cola had many "allies and agents, making secret arrangements, and designing crafty machinations." Annibaldo set about his reforms with great energy: "He punished penitentiaries; he deposed and imprisoned them. He created knights; he bestowed dignities and offices," according to the Anonimo romano. Pope Clement was also impressed, and on June 6, 1349, he wrote to Annibaldo to commend him for the return of civic concord and peace among all citizens and to impress upon him that the restored government of the senators was the best way to ensure the "reformation of the collapsed condition [*status*] of the City." But the pope remained fixated on Rienzo. In the same letter he called on both Annibaldo and Cardinal Gui de Boulogne, also then in Rome, to do all they could to capture "that son of Belial." On June 12 the pope wrote again, pressing Annibaldo to move against Cola.

Tensions were already roiling beneath the city's streets when a minor incident touched off a crisis reported by the Anonimo romano. Some curious Romans had come to the Borgo to see the camel that people said the legate housed in his stables near St. Peter's. After the crowd around the animal became too aggressive, one of the cardinal's officials made threats and ordered the crowds to disperse. Rocks were hurled, barriers were torn down, and soon the streets were pouring out Romans from the Borgo and the area around St. Peter's and the Portico, "fully equipped with steel armor, bucklers, breastplates, shields, and bows. There was a great battle at the Palace. The gate was barred; the noise was terrible: rocks flew; javelins and lances were thrown like hailstones. It looked as if they wanted to sack the fortress." Annibaldo may have rested assured that the tribune had been deposed and exiled; but he had not counted on the Romans themselves retaining the militia spirit—and weapons—that had made them invincible against all comers.

When Annibaldo saw what was happening,

he was amazed and afraid. He stood above on the balcony. He watched everything going on below. He didn't understand why it was happening. He pressed his hand to his face and said, "What does all this mean? What have I done? Why do you disgrace me like this? Are these the inducements you Romans offer the Holy Father to come to Rome? The pope would not be lord in this land, not even an archpriest would! I can't believe I came here to waste my time. These Romans combine the basest poverty with the highest arrogance!" (AR, XXIII, ll. 56–66, Porta, 213–14)

Finally, the commander of the hospital of Santo Spirito, Janni de Lucca, rushed to the scene and quieted the Romans. The crowds dispersed, but Annibaldo's troubles were just beginning. One day shortly thereafter, probably at the end of May 1350, after celebrating Mass at St. Peter's, the cardinal led a procession toward St. Paul's to gain his own pilgrimage indulgence. The entourage pressed slowly through the narrow streets between St. Peter's and the hospital of Santo Spirito on its way to the Ponte Sant'Angelo and the via Papalis. As it passed the church of San Lorenzo de Piscibus, or Lorenzino, whose deconsecrated apse still faces the Borgo Santo Spirito, "suddenly two javelins came flying through the window-grating of a little house next to San Lorenzo." One missed and continued across the street, but one hit and pierced the cardinal's hat. The stunned procession stopped dead; bodyguards fanned out to catch the attackers. The Anonimo romano's report reads like a police blotter: as the cardinal's entourage shouted, "Catch him! Catch him!"

they ran into the house from which the javelins had come. It had a back door; through that door the attackers, having dropped their javelins, had escaped; they mingled with the great crowd that was there for the Jubilee absolution and were not recognized. No one was found in the house; two javelins were found. The house was torn down. *The just man takes the place of the sinner:* the priest [of San Lorenzo?] was seized and put to the torture; but he did not tell who those assassins were. (AR, XXIII, ll. 89–114, Porta, 214–15)

Upon his hasty return to the papal palace, the legate seethed for revenge and ordered a manhunt for the criminals. He was certain that only Cola di Rienzo could be behind the assassination plot. After consulting with Pope Clement, Annibaldo therefore again publicly issued the excommunications against the fallen tribune, using the opportunity to annul all his acts that Bertrand de Déaulx had not already reversed; he also issued condemnations against all of Cola's followers: removing whatever supporters of the *buono stato* remained in power in Rome from their offices and dignities, "denying them fire and water," that is, forcing them into exile. The cardinal-legate's reaction may not have been extreme. In his letter of March 23, 1348, Pope Clement had told Bertrand de Déaulx that papal notary Francesco Orsini had been informed that Cola was headed back to Rome from Naples to regroup his forces and that he must take great pains to capture him. In August 1350 Cola wrote to the archbishop of Prague that his supporters within the city had collected funds to finance his return and the armed expulsion of the senators. Cola's brother had been entrusted with the treasure, however, and he had absconded with the money, thus ending the plot. On June 10, 1350, Clement VI had written to Annibaldo acknowledging reports of widespread talk in Rome of once again raising Cola to power.

Henceforth, Annibaldo went around Rome like a military governor in a conquered city. He "always wore a steel helmet under his hat and a strong breastplate under his cloak." Shortly after the attempt on his life, according to the Anonimo romano, Annibaldo met with one of his colleagues who happened to be in the city, "the cardinal of San Giovanni Crisogono" in Trastevere. The advice of the Frenchman—probably Cardinal Gui de Boulogne—reveals the deep suspicion and hatred of Rome that most of the Avignon Curia had developed by that time. "Anyone who wants to reform Rome will have to lay waste to the whole thing and then build it up again from scratch," the prince of the church reportedly told him.

By July Annibaldo had had enough of Rome, its Jubilee, and its people. On the pope's approval, he turned the management of the city over to Ponzio de Pereto, now bishop of Orvieto, and quit Rome to take on another diplomatic mission to Naples, where he hoped to repair some of the damage done by the disastrous war between Lewis of Hungary and Queen Giovanna and by the ensuing anarchy in the Regno. Annibaldo's route, probably the via Casalina, brought him through the Roman Campagna to Ceccano, his hometown, and then south toward Monte Cassino, before entering the Regno. South of San Germano, just past Aquino and north of the via Casalina within site of Monte Cassino, at the villa of San Giorgio, the cardinal suddenly took sick. Like many medieval reports, the Anonimo romano blamed the illness on a bad mixture of foods and too much local wine. "He was one of the good drinkers of the Church of God." Upon the advice of his attendant physicians, Matteo da Viterbo and Caetano da Parma, he took more food as an antidote, went up to bed, and died the night of July 17. The news probably took about two weeks to reach Avignon; and already in a letter to Emperor Charles IV dated August 17, Pope Clement refers to the cardinal as "of good memory." Some contemporaries reported that the cardinal had been poisoned.

An autopsy—still uncommon in the fourteenth century—was performed: the cardinal's fat belly was discovered to be filled with clear wax. He was anointed with aloe and his body conveyed back to Rome, dressed like the poor Franciscan that he was. But by the time the body had reached St. Peter's, something terrible seems to have happened. One of the cardinal's two nephews suddenly died, then the whole household was taken ill: "The whole household died; not a man escaped. Some died in the Campania; some in Rome, some in Viterbo. Messer Janni Caetani, the other nephew, died in Santo Spirito in Rome. There wasn't a dog left pissing against the wall." The cardinal's body arrived at St. Peter's "without company, without mourning, without clergy; the tomb of his chapel was opened without ceremony. There he was thrown in, not laid in. And he was thrown in so that he fell on his face, and so on his face he remained."

Now, at the height of the Jubilee, pilgrims had come from all over Europe, some, like Birgitta, from as far away as Scandinavia; and with them in the overcrowded conditions and high, dry heat of the Roman summer came the Black Death. But unlike the bubonic plague, whose arrival and visible marks were well known to all by now, this outbreak might have been the septicemic, killing people by the score within days. Heat and dryness foster its spread even more quickly than dampness. Great men tossed unceremoniously, without mourners, into their expensive graves, not "a dog left pissing against the wall," recall all too chillingly Boccaccio's eyewitness account of the plague in Florence.

With the cardinal's death, yet another of Cola's enemies had been removed. But following the attempt on Cardinal Annibaldo's life, Cola's supporters had been excommunicated, stripped of their offices and their power to help him. He was unsafe anywhere in Rome. He therefore returned to his mountain hermitage. Shortly afterward he was again found out, but this time by someone with very different motives.[17] As he told Emperor Charles IV in July 1350:

When I had led a strict life there for thirty months [until about June 1350], a brother named Angelo of Monte Volcano arrived who, it is said, was a hermit whom many hermits revered. He greeted me by my own name, at which I was quite stupefied, because I had hidden my real name from the others. He told me that I had wasted enough time on myself in this deserted spot, and that from that point on I ought to labor more for the world than for my own comfort. He opened up to me that a divine revelation had informed him that I was staying there, adding that God was preparing the universal reform already foretold by many of the Spirituals, especially because of the prayers and insistence of the Glorious Virgin. God had sent the great plague and the earthquake because of the multitude of sins, and he threatened another more serious flagellation because of unreformed pastors and peoples. He had intended to punish the people and the Church and whip them terribly with these scourges before the coming of St. Francis, but at the insistence of Dominic and Francis, who, as he asserted, had held up the then collapsing Church of God by preaching in the spirit of Enoch and Elijah, the judgment of God was put off until the present time. (49, BBCR 2.3:193–94, ll. 35–56)

Fra Angelo found Cola di Rienzo already living incognito among these hermits, and he identified him as the fallen tribune by what Cola assumed were prophetic powers. Although Angelo seems to have deepened Cola's understanding of the Joachite tradition and its prophecies, Rienzo was already influenced by apocalyptic thought from the time of his first letter to Rome from Avignon in 1343; and the Joachite nature of this thought had matured over the years and was revealed throughout his months as tribune. The fact that he chose the Poor Hermits' remote mountain retreats without much hesitation is a good indication that he already had contacts with them. The Anonimo romano indicates that Cola assumed the identity of a Fraticello from the time that he first arrived among the Hermits. They no doubt knew who Cola was, but they probably agreed to protect him under some pseudonym, much as the abbot of Subiaco had done for Angelo Clareno throughout the 1320s until the Inquisition found the Spiritual leader and ordered his arrest. But while gold and riches are as dust and air to spiritual friars and isolated hermits, gossip can be like manna, milk and honey combined, and otherwise virtuous men often gobble it up greedily. So news of Cola's presence almost certainly reached Fra Angelo after no long while. Angelo sought him out because he knew that Cola already shared the Hermits' most cherished beliefs and realized that Rienzo would soon be a divine agent of the Last Days.

Fra Angelo had rebuked Cola and told him to ignore his own comfort and to seek the world's good. Cola therefore decided to test fate and to become an agent of history, rather than its victim. If events would not fall into his hands, he must spur on events himself. Cola di Rienzo would travel north, across the Alps, once again. But this time he would go not west to Avignon, to the seat of the corrupt pope and Curia, but east to Prague, the capital of Charles IV of Luxemburg, the king of the Romans, the first prince of the Germans, the man Cola knew would be the Emperor of the Last Days.

CHAPTER 12

Last World Emperor
and Angel Pope

Finally he went to Bohemia, to the Emperor Charles, . . . and
found him in a city named Prague.
                          Anonimo romano, XXVII, ll. 23–26, Porta, 237–38

Stirred by Fra Angelo to take up his role in the Last Days, and weary of
his long years of hiding from Rome's barons and their plots to destroy
him, in June 1350 Cola di Rienzo decided that his fate lay with the Roman emperor in his far-off capital. Accompanied by a small group of loyal
retainers, perhaps disguised as somewhat lax Franciscans on horseback,
or perhaps as pilgrims returning home from the Jubilee in Rome, Cola
would have covered nearly 1,050 kilometers by the time he had journeyed
from the Montagna della Maiella to the capital of Bohemia.[1] Cola probably could not have made more than fifty to sixty-five kilometers a day
on the plains of Emilia-Romagna, in the Po valley, and across the Bohemian plain. The rest of his journey involved crossing the passes of the
Apennines and then the high pass of the Brenner, a slow series of ascents
and descents where he could not have made more than fifteen to twenty-
five kilometers a day. Overall his journey would have taken about five to
six weeks. Especially in the Alps, through the Tyrol, the Inn and Danube
valleys, and beyond the Bavarian forests into Bohemia, Cola's path would
have led him through thickly wooded, mountainous, and difficult terrain.
In 1356 Petrarch made the journey from Milan to Prague to secure the al-

liance of Charles IV for the Visconti. He later wrote to his traveling companion, Sagremor de Pommiers, describing the danger he felt every stage of the way: "We covered many miles a day through German forests, attended by a band of armed men—footmen with their bows ready, riders with their swords drawn—doubtful even of our own guides, and in great danger from roving robbers. . . . There were many of us, and that fact gave us some comfort, though it did not avert danger" (*Fam.* X.1, quoted in Wilkins, 152). And so, Cola probably arrived in Prague no earlier than mid-July 1350; this fits well with the date of Cola's first surviving letters to Emperor Charles IV, which he wrote there in late July.[2]

In 1306 the last of the Premyslid dynasty of Bohemia, King Václav (Wenceslas) III, died without an heir. Yet his younger sister Elizabeth survived, and she was soon married to the heir of one of the German empire's most promising families: John of Luxemburg, son of Emperor Henry VII. John himself had a European reputation for his debonair manner, his generosity, and his chivalric heroism; but his private life was something quite different. He and his wife, Elizabeth, quarreled violently and were estranged quickly. John suspected and accused his queen of gross infidelity. When their first son, Wenceslas, was born in 1316, he was taken from Elizabeth's care almost immediately and held a virtual prisoner in a darkened room for two months during a particularly bitter winter. King John never seemed overly fond of his wife's son, and he would remain jealous of the young man for the rest of his life, several times giving credence to gossip that his son was plotting to usurp him. When this Wenceslas was seven years old, King John, whose cultural and political world were decidedly French, took him to Paris to the court of Charles IV and renamed him in honor of the French king. John exiled his queen to a castle outside Prague.

Though the move was a family tragedy, it was a great boon to the Luxemburg dynasty and the kingdom of Bohemia; for the young Charles was raised at the French court. He was educated in Paris and married to Blanche (d. 1348), the sister of Charles IV's successor, Philip VI, the first Valois king. Charles of Moravia quickly adopted the French court style, a suave elegance that relied on nuance, diplomatic adroitness, and a clear sense of dynastic and national self-interest. He also developed the cultured and shrewd personality that would later mark his reign as king of Bohemia and Holy Roman Emperor. A highly educated man who studied theology and quoted Scripture in his writings, he also was proficient in French, German, Latin, and later in Italian and Czech.

As ruler of the Tyrol, John of Bohemia had become deeply involved in the politics of northern Italy in the early 1330s; but he preferred to remain in the French orbit and named Charles his chief agent in Italy. In his autobiography Charles would later recount the endless military campaigns, sieges, battles, plots, ambushes, adventures on the high seas, captures, and narrow escapes that filled his Italian years. In October 1333, however, Charles was named margrave of Bohemia and his father's regent for that kingdom. Upon his return home, Charles found that his mother had died a virtual prisoner and that the kingdom had fallen into anarchy. As Charles later wrote in his autobiography, "Justice only in part prevailed in the kingdom, for the barons were often tyrannous and did not fear the king as they should have done. And the kingdom was thus divided" (Hillenbrand, *Vita Caroli Quarti*, c. 8).

After quickly restoring royal castles, prerogatives, and other rights, reestablishing order, and quelling the rebellious barons, Charles invited his wife, Blanche, to join him in Prague and then began the long and successful campaign to rebuild the kingdom on an autonomous, prosperous, and just footing that would earn him the title "Father of Bohemia." Whereas his father, John, had used his eastern lands as a pawnshop to finance his chivalric deeds in France and the Low Countries, Charles turned to the needs of Bohemia: paying off John's enormous debts, reforming taxation and refilling the depleted treasury, purifying the realm's coinage and standardizing weights and measures, revamping and modernizing the legal system, encouraging trade, and importing new agricultural products, including the grape vine. In a series of military campaigns to the north, east, and west, he eventually annexed lower Lusatia and the portions of Silesia that John had not already taken, acquired the mark of Brandenburg, established Bohemian dominion over parts of Poland, and in the west rounded out the holdings of Luxemburg and annexed Brabant.

As emperor, Charles would also remake the history of the Holy Roman Empire, which had not really been a unified state since the twelfth century. The imperial house could no longer, as the Ottonians, Salians, and Hohenstaufen before had, attempt to dominate the empire and its princes in the mold of an ancient emperor or even a contemporary king. Bowing to reality, in 1356 Charles would issue the Golden Bull whose thirty-one chapters recognized the power and rights of the imperial princes in electing the emperor. The resulting seven "electors" and their seven territorial states would henceforth become the chief powers of the empire. Equally important, Charles heeded the new currents of political theory and neglected to request papal approval of his imperial election. Charles's genius established the precedent for a recognized constitutional process of imperial succession that would remain the fundamental law of the German lands until Napoleon swept it away in 1806 with the creation of the Confederation of the Rhine.

Charles's greatest work in the 1330s and 1340s was his re-creation of Prague itself. While the oldest sections of the city had contained about 50 hectares, by 1348 Prague had expanded to between 200 and 250 hectares in area and had reached a population of about 30,000. Another of Charles's great achievements, seen by him as very much part of the re-creation of his kingdom, was the formation in 1344 of Prague as the seat of an archbishopric that would take Bohemia out from under the control of Mainz in Germany. As soon as his archbishopric had been created, Charles began construction of a new cathedral of St. Vitus in the citadel, as well as the new palace for himself in the wooded mountains south of Prague. Here at Karlstejn, built between 1348 and 1367, Charles combined the functions of a new fortress with those of imperial palace and artistic center that fused an overall French Gothic aesthetic with the new Italian style.

By 1338 Charles had founded the College of All Saints in the Hradcany Castle at Prague; but in 1348 he went one great step further and induced Pope Clement VI to authorize the creation of the Charles University in Prague. Charles himself shared much of the intellectual fervor that he encouraged in his kingdom. In addition to his French and Italian artists, he attracted many other Italians to his court, including Angelo of Florence, who established the first botanical garden in any of the "German" lands. In 1351 Charles began a correspondence with Petrarch that would last for the next two decades and result in Petrarch's invitation to Prague in 1356 and the ongoing—and frank—exchange between the two men on literature, politics, and the revival of the Roman Empire. Both Charles's friend Ernst van Pardubic, the first archbishop of Prague, and his chancellor, Johann von Neumarkt, were among the new humanists of the fourteenth century, men who combined a love of letters with the desire to reform political life. Ernst was a man of some learning. He also became a correspondent of Petrarch and was a patron of the arts, commissioning Italian painters heavily inspired by the Sienese school of Simone Martini. Immediately upon his appointment as archbishop, Ernst threw himself into the task of reforming the Czech church, curbing the excesses of corrupt clergy and lax monastic establishments.

Unlike King John, Charles concentrated his energies on building up his Bohemian state and seldom ventured on foreign expeditions. In chapter 14 of his autobiography he recalled that in 1338 he accompanied his father to Avignon. There Charles met an old friend from Paris, Pierre Roger, who had been abbot of Fécamp and his teacher at the royal court. Once in conversation Pierre had predicted that Charles would become emperor; while he replied to Roger that he would become pope. As Pope Clement VI, Pierre would later repay Charles's friendship with great dividends. The Luxemburgs had long urged the pope to depose their enemy, Emperor Lewis of Bavaria, and in 1346 the growing hostility of the German barons to the Bavarian and his seizure of the Tyrol all coincided to persuade the pope to agree to Lewis's deposition. In July the German electors chose Charles as king of the Romans, emperor in all but one vital aspect: his crowning by the pope or his representative at St. Peter's in Rome. Lewis clung to his throne, however, and another of Germany's long and disastrous civil wars had begun. Lewis was clearly gaining the upper hand when he was killed in an accident in October 1347. Free of the responsibility of kingdoms and empires, King John could now devote himself to what he did best: knight errantry. The early stages of the Hundred Years' War between England and France offered the perfect opportunity; and on August 26, 1346, John was slain by the English under Edward III, along with his retainers and the best of the French nobility, at the battle of Crécy.

And so by 1346 Charles of Moravia had become king of Bohemia, king of the Romans, and Emperor Charles IV. From that point on he would rarely pick up his sword again, and when he did, it would be only after the greatest deliberation. Though considered shrewd, calculating, and businesslike by some, the man whom Cola met in Prague was worthy of the Roman tribune and apocalyptic leader.[3] In the preface to his autobiography Charles reveals a deeply spiritual thinker whose life is guided not only by the words of Scripture but also by vision and miracle, by the spiritual discernment between the *carnalia*—the world of visible, tangible, and temporary things—and the *spiritualia,* the *archana* described by St. Paul as the hidden, eternal truths that lie beneath and beyond the appearances of things.

Charles, like many of his contemporaries, also believed in the power and truth of visions, and he relates several in his autobiography. Chapters 11 to 13 of his autobiography also appear to be transcriptions of sermons that the king gave before his court. In his second sermon Charles notes that after all the peoples of the world have been taught the Christian faith, the events of the Apocalypse will come to pass. Like Robert of Naples, another "sermonizing monarch," Charles shared the prevailing Joachite expectations of the age: that the mysteries of the Last Days about to be revealed are being prepared by the poor in spirit and fostered by those who pursue justice.

As in the Joachite prophecies that dominated much of the thinking of the court of Naples and found their physical manifestations in such complex and symbolic buildings as Sta. Chiara at Naples, Charles's mystical writings find a physical manifestation in the creation of a physical "tabernacle": the structural plan and the frescoes commissioned by him for the imperial palace at Karlstejn. Construction was based on a three-level plan. On the lowest, a series of historical and genealogical paintings reflects the earthly foundations of Charles's rule. On the next, the palace is dominated by the Chapel of the Virgin Mary and an apocalyptic fresco cycle. To underscore the parallel between the imperial seat and the New Jerusalem, the highest, third, level houses the Chapel of the Holy Cross, the depository of Charles's greatest collection of relics from the Crucifixion: the nails and sponge, thorns from Christ's crown, and splinters of the True Cross. From the lowest level to this chapel, the "pilgrim" ascends nearly 750 feet through various stairs, halls, and passages, reflecting in flesh, blood, and stone the mystical ascent of those who understand and unravel the secrets of revelation.

The Chapel of the Virgin Mary contains a series of scenes depicting Charles giving and receiving relics. Here his court painters employed several techniques borrowed from contemporary Italian painting, and also used in Clement VI's new papal palace, most notably the use of trompe l'oeil to create deep illusionist spaces and mysterious perspectives for the colonnaded arcades that support the main scenes (fig. 24). These arcades begin at the plane of the viewer and then recede into shadow and darkness, creating an almost endless series of visual paths and passages that penetrate the hidden spaces beyond and lead the viewer's gaze upward through the darkness. In this they replicate the look and feel of a Romanesque crypt supporting a church nave above, their mysterious divine space visually symbolizing the realm of *archana* and *invisibilia* that lie beneath, and support, the visible forms of public piety and worship that the emperor enacts above.

Even more important than the visual symbolism of the scene's frames are the actual scenes being depicted. For here Charles is seen exchanging relics with two monarchs: Charles V of France (on the left, symbolizing the West) and Peter, king of Cyprus and Jerusalem (symbolizing the East). The final scene on the right shows Charles about to lay down his crown upon the altar of Jerusalem, thus fulfilling the prophecy of the Last World Emperor, who would reunite West and East, travel to the Holy Land, and there defeat the enemies of Christ, retake Jerusalem, and then lay down his crown to issue in the age of peace and justice just before the coming of Antichrist and the Last Days.

Given this understanding, the peculiar—and unique—decoration of the chapel of the Holy Cross (1357–67) makes sense: its jewel-encrusted walls and gold ornament are not a throwback to a primitive decorative motif joined rather incongruously to the new Italianate frescoes but corporealize the New Jerusalem, for "the foundations of the wall of the city were adorned with all manner of precious stones" (Apoc. 21:19). Above these foundation walls Master Theoderic painted a series of apostles, evangelists, canonized popes, bishops, and abbots—the inhabitants of the heavenly city—while off to one of the sides a choir loft gave the space the fitting harmonies of the New Jerusalem. Capping the entire scheme were the culminating events of the Apocalypse: the heavenly Jerusalem, the Lamb and the Twenty-four Elders, and the Apocalyptic Christ in majesty surrounded by the hierarchies of angels. He holds the book with the seven seals and is surrounded by the seven candlesticks and seven stars.

The Karlstejn frescoes reveal something more mundane about Charles that is just as important: they contain several of the many portraits of the emperor commissioned in painting and stone during his reign. Here, in stark contrast to the debonair, clean-shaven, and worldly look of King Charles V of France, for example, Charles himself, though courtly in gesture and demeanor, is cloaked in the long robe and high round crown of empire. His extended features, marked by a prominent aquiline nose, thick brows, and intense, deep-set eyes, are largely hidden by the mustache and lengthy beard that the emperor wore through most of his life. They give him less the look of a contemporary king of the Gothic international style, much less that of the ancient Roman tribune conveyed by Cola's classicizing portrait relief (see fig. 11) than that of an eastern monk or Byzantine icon wrapped in mystery and intense spiritual power. In August 1350, in Prague, the deposed Roman tribune would come face-to-face with this reigning Roman emperor.

The Anonimo romano records that Cola arrived at the court of Prague on August 1, 1350, and then had an audience with the emperor.[4] He presents Cola's speech to Charles IV and seems to have had access if not to the speech itself, then certainly to Cola's letters from Prague that contained the very same speaking points. It is likely that Cola had his major themes prepared well ahead of his arrival, and his letters either could have been drawn up from the notes for his address or could have constituted the raw material for the address itself. The Anonimo romano's reconstruction succinctly follows the rules of the *ars arengandi,* moving briefly and rapidly from salutation to exordium to exposition, to petition, to a conclusion that the *Anonimo* seems to have made even shorter for dramatic effect:

Most serene prince, to whom is granted the glory of all the world.

I am that Cola whom God granted the power to govern Rome and its district in peace, justice, and liberty. I held the obedience of Tuscany and Campagna and the Marittima; I reined in the arrogance of the barons and purged many injustices. I am a worm, a frail man, a weed like all the others. I used to carry in my hand the rod of iron, which in my humility I have converted into a rod of wood because God wished to castigate me.

The barons are pursuing me; they seek my life. Because of envy and because of pride they have driven me from my dominium. They refuse to be punished.

I am of your lineage; I am a bastard son of the Emperor Henry the valiant. To you I flee; to your wings I run, under whose shade and shield a man ought to be safe. I believe that I am safe. I believe that you will defend me. You will not let me die at the hands of tyrants; you will not let me drown in the lake of injustice. And this is as it should be, since you are emperor. Your sword ought to cut down the tyrants.

I have seen the prophecy of Fra Angelo of Montecielo in the Montagna della Maiella, and he said that the eagle will kill the crows. (AR, XXVII, ll. 31–54, Porta, 238)

Just as he had charmed Pope Clement VI in Avignon in 1343, so now, too, the tribune won over the emperor: "After Cola had spoken Charles stretched forth his hand and received him graciously, saying that he need have no doubts about anything." But the Anonimo romano was not on the scene and depended on much later reports. Here again the *Chronicon Estense* appears to have both sources that are more complete and details that are so psychologically right that one suspects an eyewitness report lay behind his account:

In August 1350 in Germany in the city of Prague a stranger entered the house of a Florentine spice merchant and said to him that he should announce to the Lord Charles, elected as emperor on behalf of the Roman church, that this man wished to speak with the emperor secretly in his chamber to tell him some useful tidings. The emperor sent for him to appear before him. The stranger entered the emperor's chamber; and he began to narrate his story to him, saying that in Mongibello there lived a hermit, named Fra Angelo, who had chosen two ambassadors, of whom he sent one to the Lord Pope in Avignon; "but the other he sent to you, Lord Emperor; and I am one of those ambassadors." The emperor told him that he should explain his words. The stranger spoke in this way: "Know,

Lord Emperor, that the aforesaid Fra Angelo announces to you that until now the Father and the Son have reigned; but now power is taken from them and handed over to the Holy Spirit, and the Spirit is to reign in the future." The emperor, hearing that this man was separating the Father and the Son from the Holy Spirit, said to him, "Are you who I think you are?" And the stranger replied, "Who do you think I am?" The emperor responded: "I think that you are the Tribune of Rome." The man responded, "Truly I am he who was Tribune and Lord of Rome." Then the emperor said, "Wait here a little while until I return."

Leaving the room, he sent for the archbishop of Prague and the archbishop of Trier and for two other bishops and the ambassadors of the king of Caria and of the king of Scotland, and for other learned men, and he led them before the tribune. The emperor said to him, "Repeat what you have said." The tribune then repeated what he had said and added that the other ambassador would say similar things to the lord pope. And when he had said these things the lord pope would have him burned; and on the third day he would rise again by the virtue of the Holy Spirit. Because of this the people of Avignon would rush to arms and burst into the papal palace and slay the pope along with all his cardinals. Then another pope—an Italian—would be elected, who would remove the curia from Avignon and return it to the City of Rome. "Then the pope will send for you, Emperor, and for me; and we are supposed to be united with the lord pope in the said City; and there he will crown you with the golden crown of the kingdom of Sicily, of Calabria, Apulia, Terra Laboris, the Abruzzi and other lands. But he will crown me with a crown of silver and he will make me king of Rome and of all Italy; and thus we will be one with the lord pope."

Hearing all this the archbishops and the others said to the lord emperor, "Lord, we've heard enough; we'll leave now." And they all left the room. Then the emperor said to them, "What does this look like to you?" They said to him, "Have him put what he's said in writing for you." And this was done. Then they sent off the writing, closed and sealed with the emperor's seal, to the lord pope.

The tribune then said that he wanted to give his two sons as surety for what he had said; and that the emperor could have them both hung if this tribune had not been set up as lord of the City of Rome before the end of two months. At that point the emperor had him put under house arrest until the arrival of the lord pope's reply. (RIS 15.3:150)

Charles IV realized that this was the very man who had summoned him, along with Lewis the Bavarian and the German electors, to come to Rome to be judged by the Roman people. He also knew that Cola was a condemned and hunted heretic, an accused usurper of the pope's titles and rights in Rome, and the sworn enemy of many of the barons whose support Charles would need if and when he decided to descend to Rome for his imperial coronation. Yet there seemed much that the two men had in common: they were both reformers to the core; both men had taken a state torn by baronial strife, by the destruction of public laws and institutions, by a collapse of economic and urban life, and had almost overnight, and "by the grace of God" as Charles wrote in his autobiography, revived and reformed the realms granted to them by the Holy Spirit. Cola had also studied deeply and well the art of ancient statecraft; he understood the thinking of the ancients and of contemporaries on the status and the claims of the Roman emperors. He was also a man to whom had been revealed the deep *archana* of the Holy Spirit concerning the role of the emperor, the pope, and the Roman Empire in the Last Days that Charles himself understood would soon approach. The emperor's ability to recognize Rienzo from the tribune's use of the Joachite schema of the three ages of Father, Son, and Holy Spirit also points to Cola's widespread reputation as a Joachite thinker before his disappearance in December 1347.

Finally, aside from Cola's great personal charm and the moral authority that his tribunate and then his years among the hermits of the Maiella had given him, Cola's elaborate story about his illegitimate birth as the son of Emperor Henry VII, and thus as Charles's own natural uncle, may well have done what Cola intended it to do. On one level it was a symbolic exposition of Cola's role as the son of empire: the political orphan who sought and found legitimization in the arms of the empire and the reformed church. But on the other hand, Cola may well have heard of, understood, and deeply empathized with the profound sadness and emotional orphanage of Charles's youth. In all this the emperor may have found much to ponder; and he would naturally be led to take pity on this ingenious man, this superb leader and thinker, now "a worm," left without home and family, with nothing but his wits, his few close friends, and his dreams of Roman glory.

Charles would have to inform the pope of the tribune's arrival at Prague; but for now he took Rienzo into his court as Cola took on a public role in Prague. "His fluent tongue amazed those Germans, Bohemians and Slavs; he stupefied everyone." At the same time, Charles was aware that Avignon would soon be demanding the imprisonment and trial of this accused heretic. This may explain why the Anonimo romano adds that Cola "disputed with the masters in theology," probably of Charles University, for Cola had come to Prague not only with dreams of the Roman past but also with very clear and urgent visions of the Joachite future. Despite this, "he was not imprisoned but detained honorably under some guards. Ample food and wine were given to him."

At first, that is. In the initial days and weeks after his arrival, Cola enjoyed the freedom of Prague and direct access to the emperor and his chancellor, Johann von Neumarkt, a good stylist and an admirer of the Latin classics. Charles relied strongly on Cola's knowledge of imperial traditions, Roman history, and the contemporary situation in Italy; and he retained him as one of his advisers, at least unofficially, as late as the spring of 1351. In February 1351 Petrarch had written to the emperor from Padua, inviting him to come to Italy to receive his imperial crown and to bring unity and peace to the peninsula. Soon after that Charles replied to the poet laureate. Unknown to Petrarch, however, the emperor's letter was written by Cola di Rienzo; and in it Cola takes up, one by one, Petrarch's reasons for the emperor's visit.[5]

Rienzo acknowledges the serious condition of Rome and uses his familiar image of the sinking ship, which Petrarch himself had often employed. But who now is equal to the ancients in their accomplishments? The emperor today cannot equal what the ancient Romans had done at the cost of so much blood. The empire, as Augustus once said, "is a monster." How much more true is this now that the empire has moved north to the Germans? Such an endeavor as an imperial journey to Rome and the subduing of Italy needs much planning, and it cannot be undertaken without causing great confusion, Cola's silver pen asserts. Such a military expedition should be undertaken only as a last resort, and nothing should be undertaken that will lead ultimately to the detriment of Caesar. This letter reached Petrarch only in November 1353, and on November 23 (*Fam.* XVIII.1) Petrarch responded, refuting the emperor's arguments one by one: times have not changed, it was Tiberius and not Augustus who said that the "empire is a monster," and finally the sword is the only remedy left: all others have been tried. As in 1351, so in 1353: Charles IV was not convinced. Throughout the exchange Petrarch never seems to have realized that it was his old friend Cola who had refused the call for imperial intervention.

It may also be during this period that Cola wrote his commentary on Dante's *De monarchia*.[6] Dante's *On World Government* was probably completed between 1310 and 1313 in connection with the Italian journey of Emperor Henry VII in 1312–13. Long known from two manuscripts, one from Hungary and one from Prague itself, the unsigned commentary was composed sometime between April 1343 and December 1352. As such it is the earliest surviving commentary on Dante's political treatise. From internal evidence, stylistic analysis, a study of its classical and Patristic sources, its language, and the author's remarkable knowledge of Roman history (most especially Livy), his quotation, probably from memory, of several key sections of the *Mirabilia Urbis Romae,* and his detailed knowledge of the topography of Rome and Lazio, historians are nearly certain that Cola was its author. In addition, many of the key passages and themes of the commentary, the meditations of the author not directly linked to Dante's work, are repeated in Cola's own letters during his Bohemian period. Given this evidence and the shift in Cola's fortunes and his style after the fall of 1350, it seems likely that the *Commentary* derives from this first period of great expectations and high imperial hopes. Cola would have been attracted to the work not only because of his admiration for the great poet but also because Dante's experience of exile and expectations for Italian renewal held a spiritual and a political attraction that were both compelling and closely akin to Cola's own.

Cola's letters to Emperor Charles IV and to Chancellor Johann von Neumarkt, and their responses, cover the brief period from late July, soon after Cola's arrival, to late August 1350, by which time Charles had decided to hand Cola over to the archbishop of Prague.[7] This correspondence offers a unique view of the political nature of apocalyptic expectations, not just in Rome but throughout fourteenth-century Europe, and it raises the question of whether Cola's synthesis of Roman revival, communal *buon governo,* and apocalyptic expectation could have flourished on any other than Rome's native soil. On the other hand, Cola's new enthusiasm for the emperor was not a cynical change of loyalty. Cola's age was exhausted by the outworn ideologies of the Guelph-Ghibelline struggle. While Dante and Marsiglio of Padua were just introducing the modern notion of the secular state, pope and emperor remained twin powers — the two swords — seen working for the salvation and protection of Christendom. As Napoleone Orsini had told John XXII, in Rome no one was seriously either Guelph or Ghibelline, but each looked out for his friends and family regardless of outmoded labels.

In addition, many fourteenth-century humanists, like Petrarch or Barbato da Sulmona, equally sang the praises of republics or empires: for hierarchy was always posited to exist, and lordships of one type or another — *dominium* — could easily coexist in republican Venice or Florence, tyrannical Milan, or royal Naples. Allegiance or defiance were really matters not of ideology but of the practical matters of local customs, liberties, and privileges once granted and long defended. There were, of course, exceptions and more solidly defined political divisions, but as Petrarch's ever-changing loyalties show, it would be as wrong to portray him as a fierce adherent to republican government as it would to dismiss him as a pen hired by tyrants. Nor did medieval monarchs make any sharp differentiation among whom they chose to ally with or support. City-states,

tyrants, condottieri, other princes and kings, all were seen to coexist with
the same ultimate sources of authority and power: from God and the powers devolved from, or granted by, God. Finally, and even granting Cola's
instinct for self-preservation and promotion, like Petrarch, he consistently
sought aid for the cause dearest to him: the revival of Rome and then of
Italy, from whatever source would offer it. One can therefore accept his
statements at face value: he sought not wealth or personal power and was
willing to give his life for the vision of the reformed city, the image of the
New Jerusalem.

In his first two letters to Emperor Charles, from late July 1350, Cola offered a medley of Joachite prophecies of Angel Pope and Last World Emperor. Central to these prophecies were the books that Cola had seen while
among the Poor Hermits of the Abruzzi: the *Oracles of Cyril,* Joachim of
Fiore's supposed commentary on them, and the prophecies of Merlin concerning the Last Days, a manuscript of which Cola brought with him to
Prague. According to the *Chronicle* of Francis of Prague, once in the imperial city, Cola had also discovered a manuscript book containing the
Joachite prophecies of the Franciscan Jean de Roquetaillade.

In the present days, a great schism will arise, pitting the true people of
Christ against the pseudopope and his minions. The pseudopope, though
not specifically identified, is the Antichrist who will persecute the true elect
until the arrival of a simple and holy man, like Celestine V. This saintly, angelic pope will then dispose of the wealth and earthly power of the church
and revive the simple Gospel life of Christ and his first disciples. Cola therefore informs Charles of his role as the Last World Emperor who would
collaborate with the Angel Pope to return to Rome during the Jubilee year.
Cola's own mission is to prepare for the emperor's peaceful return, without the bloodshed that had marked previous imperial journeys to Rome.

Like Abraham sacrificing Isaac, Cola offers his own son as a guarantee of his good faith. Such pledges were standard practice among Europe's
feudal classes, even among the highest kings and emperors. Upon the defeat and capture of Charles II of Naples by the Aragonese in 1283, for example, Charles gave up all three of his sons to a house arrest near Montser-
rat in Catalonia to guarantee his own freedom and return to Naples. The
young Charles IV was repeatedly captured during his campaigns in Italy;
and when he managed his escapes, he invariably left his wife and children
in his enemies' hands. The laws of chivalry demanded that they be returned
and happily reunited with him, as they were on every occasion, as were
the sons of Charles II to Naples.

Rienzo tells Charles that he is to the emperor as John the Baptist is to Christ. Cola presses his attempt to win over the emperor by using a Joachite structure of historical parallels in succeeding ages. To the emperor's claim that Rome could not be revived without some miracle, Cola replies that Charles can revive the empire just as Francis of Assisi had revived the church. As Francis was to the pope, so Cola is to the emperor, thus completing another Joachite concordance. Although Cola claims to have received his thinking from Fra Angelo, he actually seems to have borrowed much from the political works of William of Ockham, Marsiglio of Padua, and more immediately from Dante's own *De monarchia*. The theory of the two swords of empire and church actually prevents Peter from wielding the secular sword; thus the basis of the Papal States and their temporal government is illegitimate. Cola asserts that to say this is not to seek discord but to have the secular and spiritual toil in their proper places in peace for the salvation of all. The church's place is in poverty.

In all this Cola claims that he is making clear obscure things that have been hidden. In his synthesis of mystical understanding and imperial political theory, he could thus not have failed to win over the interest of an emperor as deeply immersed in the language of *archana* and *invisibilia* as in the keen nuance of political realities. Cola also appeals to the emperor's practical sense of government and financial reform. He repeats to Charles that Rienzo is perceived as a man of the people and is most qualified to retake both Rome and Italy for the empire. He only awaits the imperial nod to proceed. It is best to do this before the current term of the senators (July–December 1350) expires to prevent the loss of 100,000 florins in income from the salt tax, from other *gabelle,* and from the Jubilee now under way in Rome.

But if Charles IV shared Cola's predilection for spiritual *archana,* he was quite aware that as emperor he was also the chief defender of the Christian faith and that he was harboring an infamous heretic within his palace walls. At the end of July Charles therefore responded to Cola's pleas and claims. The emperor immediately brings Cola up short with two Gospel precepts: "Love thy neighbor as thyself" (Matt. 22:37–40), and "It is not for you to know the times or the moments" (Acts 1:7). As in the sermons embedded in his autobiography, Charles shows a clear and immediate understanding of Scripture, exploring the meaning of the *archana* and the *mysteria,* warning Cola that the prophecies, even those supported by a series of Old Testament figures including Jonah and Saul, are not so easily reckoned. Many people have a high opinion of themselves, but such people will be made low. Charles then bluntly tells Cola that his understanding of the prophecies is incorrect, and that only God can judge the pope. He warns Cola to beware of the teachings of the hermit Angelo.

Informing Cola that he will not judge his story of his imperial birth as the son of Henry VII, and that whatever the truth of it, all men are worthy of love if they first love God, he reveals his appreciation of the core of Cola's tale: the tribune's attempt to reach the emperor on a human, emotional level. Finally, Charles rebukes Cola by telling him that even if, as he reports, all Rome and Italy will condemn the emperor for imprisoning Cola, Charles must fear God's judgment more than the opinions of men and must do his duty. He concludes by again warning Cola to dismiss his fantasies of earthly glory that have led him to defy God. He advises the former tribune instead to take on *spiritual* weapons: the helmet of salvation and the shield of faith described by St. Paul in Ephesians 6:16.

The emperor's letter may have been intended to smooth the way for the sense of betrayal that Cola would soon feel. After months of papal entreaties and then demands that the emperor hand Cola di Rienzo over to the Inquisition, Charles seemed more and more inclined to cooperate with the pope. The emperor therefore decided to send his guest to the archbishop of Prague for an inquisition before surrendering him to papal agents. Cola was, however, given an opportunity to defend himself publicly before this happened. The text of his defense takes the form of a letter (57) to Archbishop Ernst dated sometime before August 15, 1350, entitled "The True Little Book *(Libellus)* of the Tribune against Schisms and Errors, Written to the Archbishop of Prague."[8]

The "little book" offers a concise summary both of Cola's thinking and of the apocalyptic expectations of the time and merits close examination. It also presents a remarkable treatise on the growing tyranny of signorial Italy that had filled the vacuum left by the absence of the papacy in Avignon, as well as on the illegitimacy of papal claims to wield the secular sword. The reason for this illegitimacy, Cola tells the archbishop, is the fact that the true church is based on poverty and humility, not on power. The tribune begins by explaining to the archbishop that his letter is a response to the charges of heresy and to the *infamia* that Cola has suffered as a result. He then immediately launches an attack on the Avignon papacy that reveals a sound knowledge of current reformist and Spiritual ecclesiology: that the church is an *ecclesia,* that is, "a union of the faithful, faithfully gathered into one body, which is Christ." Thus the pope is and ought to be the shepherd, the pastor and the vicar of Christ. But the pontiff has abandoned his sheep, and scandal and schism have arisen from

Avignon. On a personal level Cola can testify that he and his own family have suffered like scattered sheep, suffering oppressions and tribulations at the hands of tyrants and wolves, despite the fact that he has adhered to the "pure, true and full doctrine" of the church. Echoing Petrarch's own anonymous criticisms of the Avignon papacy, Cola goes on to say that this pope acts more like the hireling than the real shepherd or like Peter fleeing Rome only to meet Jesus returning to the city, "to be crucified again."

Here Cola provides the first of many references to his own return to Rome. The comparison is not specifically to Jesus but to Cola's own willingness to return to Rome to suffer on behalf of its people and the cause of Roman greatness. In Rome itself the faithful, like sheep, have been abandoned to the wolves: the Orsini, Colonna, and other barons continue their depredations under the title of "senators." But they are really public thieves who live as *infami*, robbing church treasures. Upon appeal, however, the pope and his court seem to prefer the destruction of the sheep rather than to hear his flock summon him back to Rome. This refusal has had disastrous consequences: "the massacre of the people, attacks upon and slaughter of pilgrims, the desolation of the cities of Italy, schism and division, the stripping of monasteries, hospitals and holy places." Guelph and Ghibelline, Cola writes, are only empty slogans used by both sides as pretexts. Party division and the excommunication of one side against the other has resulted only in the damming of everyone. What is worse, former imperial lands have now come under the nominal lordship of the church and have fallen under the real control of one party or another while the papacy allies itself with and legitimizes the rule of such tyrants as Luchino Visconti. Throughout Italy papal rectors and podestas all do the same, usurping legitimate authority with the acquiescence of the popes themselves.

But the papacy has done even worse: its active meddling in the affairs of the kingdom of Naples has produced the martyrdom of King Andrew; and war and evil now reign throughout the kingdom as the mercenary Great Company runs rampant. While in the Regno Cola himself witnessed the brutality of the band under the condottiere Werner, duke of Ürslingen, "who raped and dragged off with them more than fifty nuns, married women, matrons and virgins, along with their professional whores." But Werner now enjoys the favor of the pope! Cola then asks the archbishop if the same wave of destruction is about to sweep Germany. If the pope has his way, Cola warns, the emperor will never be crowned in Rome without great bloodshed. Yet Christ forbade temporal power to the spiritual realm when he commanded Peter to lay down his sword.

Cola, on the other hand, is the ideal candidate to fulfill the imperial mission in Italy, and he is ready to die in the attempt. Who has done more for the Roman church? Who has done more to restore civil society in Rome? Yet his efforts met only with detraction and jealously that eventually won over the pope. Furthermore, Cola's summons to Lewis and Charles to Rome for the Pentecost synod of 1348 was issued only to encourage similar acts of submission among the tyrants of Italy and to goad them to liberate their subject peoples. Cola's own difficulties are a test from God: "I reprove and train those whom I love" (Apoc. 3:19). Cola then employs one of the great topoi in the theory of dissent that had been created by the Spiritual Franciscans in their struggle with the papacy: the church is more than simply the hierarchy and its pronouncements, and the remaining faithful can work for reform even in the face of official hostility.

Following the Spirituals' radical ecclesiology, Cola tells the archbishop that the worldly sword must be wrested from the popes and that Cola himself will not rest until this has been achieved. No one else appears working toward this end, and therefore he must do it. If Octavius was adopted by Caesar, why not now Cola by Caesar to accomplish this task? Then, paraphrasing one of the most potent images used by Angelo Clareno, that of Christ expelled by the Synagogue of his own day as a heretic and dissenter, he sees himself equally expelled from the Synagogue by Herod, Pilate, and Pharaoh, "my name defamed, until I repair the Synagogue by accomplishing my task." Indeed, the pope ought to fulfill the wishes of Christ who prohibited the sword to Peter: the power of the papacy is to save, not to slay, the people. He ought to follow the example of the martyrs and remain in peace and holiness, not in warlike furor. Like pseudoprophets, the hierarchy cries out, "'Peace, Peace,' and there is no peace" (Jer. 6:15) while they abandon the flock and seek the quiet of Avignon. If there were true zealots for reform in the Curia, the church would not now be sleeping. But the church has lost its former zeal; in sheep's clothing the wolves "plunder everything," and those who wish to reform it are shut out by the keepers of the keys.

God has exiled Cola only for a while but will then "renew" him. Cola had assumed his tribunate at age thirty-three, at the same age that Christ had taken up his mission; and his rise and fall have been prophesied through the Holy Spirit. If Cola rose to the tribunate on May 19 and abdicated on December 15, so he was certain that by September 14, 1350, he would return to Rome and to "my resurrection" to restore liberty and concord. But all this must be done secretly. Cola cannot show himself to be Caesar's agent but a common man, a man of the people. He comes to his task after his years of weeping and solitude under the banner of Christ, not of Guelph or Ghibelline. *Doctus sum in scolis adversitatis,* "I am educated in the school of hard knocks," he tells the archbishop. He is not the shepherd but the sheepdog that can turn not only against the wolves but also against the bad shepherd who allies with the wolves. By Pentecost 1351 Cola promises the emperor a united Italy (except for Sicily, Sardinia, Corsica, and Provence to the Rhone). If Cola does not accomplish this, then Caesar can have his head, but he is confident because God will aid him as he did David and Judith.

Cola then asks the rhetorical question that he knew would form a basis for his inquisition: How are we to believe that Fra Angelo's prophecies to Cola are from God and not from the devil? The answer is simple: good works will stem from them, peace in the world and love in the church. It shall all be accomplished without bloodshed, but with peace and security; and so finally Cola will find a legitimate home and mother in the church, not like his previous birth as illegitimate son of the emperor, hidden in a tavern. So, too, the popes will return to their legitimate bride, Rome, and away from the taverns of Avignon. But the pope and his Curia hate Cola and have rejoiced more at his capture than over that of Turks or Saracens. Cola concludes his letter with a lengthy exposition of the *Oracles of Cyril* and demonstrates how he is the object of many of them: his youth, his son Lorienzo, his imprisonment, his absence from Rome as a penance for his vanity, the fate of his family, the character and role of the pope. But his memory of the prophecies is now sketchy, Cola tells the archbishop, and he would need to see the full text once again to give its prophecies a full interpretation.

In a letter (58) to Charles IV from Prague in late August 1350, Cola repeats these Joachite themes and tells the emperor that they now labor at the end of the sixth *aetas;* the sixth angel has placed the tuba to his lips, and its terrible sound will soon be heard. Cola himself would not have fully believed the *Oracles of Cyril,* he tells Charles, if he had not personally seen the papal Curia in Avignon, Pope Clement's nepotism, the enriching of his young *paparelli,* and the pope's and the Curia's extravagant spending, rich buildings, the use of armed force, and the presence of merchants in the Temple. To support the evidence of his own experience, Cola may also have used "The Prophecy of Abbot Joachim about the Kingdom of Bohemia," which begins, "in the sixth period of this age." This has survived in several manuscripts, two from Prague.

The Romans took seven years to conquer all of Italy, but Cola will accomplish the same in seven months. To do so, Cola again asks to be released in time to be sent back to Italy before the end of the term of the current senators. The emperor would thus provide the greatest possible praise to God: to bring peace and universal conversion to the world without bloodshed, to end schism, and to bring reconciliation. Rome will then become the New Jerusalem. Cola has sown the seeds that the emperor will reap. The acceptable time is at hand. Emperor Charles must now open his eyes and awaken from his sleep.

We do not have a response to Cola's treatise, and Cola was soon sent to the archbishop's prison to await his inquisition. By late August Rienzo had written to Ernst von Pardubic, asking to be released. But instead of agreeing, Ernst wrote back laying out the basis of Cola's inquisition, detailing its major charges. These included, first, Cola's audacity in assuming such titles as "Candidate of the Holy Spirit"; second, Cola's claims that his works were inspired by the Holy Spirit; third, his declarations that the Romans and Italians can elect the emperor; and, fourth, Cola's reliance not on Scripture but on such prophecies as Cyril and Methodius, which are apocryphal and dangerous. Ernst has read these prophecies, and while he agrees that they can be useful as invectives against vices, he does not believe that Cola does enough to explain them in this light. And although Cola's propositions and ideas might come from God, and they appear admirable to Ernst, they can be twisted to serve the machinations of certain men. Ernst tells Cola that he is "not satisfied" by his response.

Sometime in late August or early September 1350, Cola replied to the archbishop's charges. The directness of the accusations had plainly had its effect, for already Cola has changed his title from Tribunus Augustus to *vester servulus,* "your humble servant." Cola immediately admits to his arrogance and claims that God is now punishing him for that. But he does protest that Ernst's charges that he claimed that the Romans could elect the emperor are imprecise; and at the insistence of Legate Bertrand, Cola had annulled it.

Despite his protests of innocence, by September 1350 Cola had been moved to the archiepiscopal prison at Raudnitz, on the Elbe River about forty kilometers north of Prague.[9] From his remote cell Cola writes to Archbishop Ernst with a far more detailed rebuttal to the charges against him. Cola begins by addressing the issue of his being the *"candidatus Spiritus Sancti,"* discussing the notion of election, agency, and divine providence. At the same time Cola stands by statements he has made on the imperial election: "I say what I said, and although I may have also excited people with letters, this was done craftily against crafty people," including the Italian tyrants invited to the Roman Synod. Cola admits that he has always been susceptible to prophecies of the Last Coming: unlike the wise prelate, he is a simple man. But Cola has always worked to spread peace, justice, and freedom in Rome. He is therefore ready to die for love of the people, and he has done more out of love than Caesar has done out of terror.

Cola does not understand what Ernst means by "not satisfied," and he declares that the archbishop is tempting God's judgment by asserting that "if God found me acceptable, I would exit my prison, or would have never entered it." What of God's prophets in Jerusalem, who were not only ensnared but killed, Cola asks indignantly. He then charges that Ernst's actions are not for divine, but for very human, reward. The tribune impugns the motives of the spiritual arm, noting that Lombardy is teeming with tyrants who attack the church, but that the governing councils of these very tyrants are full of bishops. The time of darkness and apocalyptic retribution is coming, he warns.

Cola was to remain imprisoned at Raudnitz for the duration of his inquisition. Sometime during 1351, from his prison cell, he wrote a lengthy letter to Cardinal Gui de Boulogne.[10] Gui was the son of Robert VII, count of Auvergne, and of Marie of Flanders, and thus related to Philip VI of France and to the house of Luxemburg and so also to Charles IV, to whom he was a close friend. His niece, Jeanne d'Auvergne, was married to the future French king, John, son of Philip VI, on September 26, 1349. Gui became archbishop of Lyons in 1340, and cardinal-priest of Sta. Cecilia in 1342. In January 1349 Clement VI appointed him ambassador plenipotentiary to Lewis of Hungary; and he traveled there to settle Lewis's dispute with Giovanna over Naples. In 1350 he was sent to Italy to supervise activities during the Jubilee and met Petrarch in Padua in February 1350. The two had been friends since their days together in Avignon; and Petrarch accompanied Gui's entourage on the trip back west to France. Petrarch describes Gui as "of an agile mind, ready of speech and jovial."

In the wake of the Jubilee, the anarchy in Rome returned. In 1351, therefore, Clement VI appointed a commission of four cardinals to reform the government of the city. Gui was appointed along with Bertrand de Déaulx, Guglielmo Curti, and Niccola Capocci, a member of one of Rome's most distinguished families. Gui, who seems to have been sympathetic to Rome's plight and its attempts at reform, immediately solicited Petrarch's opinions for the commission. Petrarch therefore composed two lengthy letters defending the communal rights and liberties of the Romans (*Fam.* XI.16–17). In 1351, when it was thought Charles IV would go to Italy, Gui de Boulogne was selected to travel to Italy to meet him, and it was suggested that he should take Petrarch and Pierre d'Auvergne along with him.

Since Gui de Boulogne was somewhat sympathetic to Cola and the Romans and was also a friend of Petrarch, Cola wasted no time in returning to his themes: the terrible condition of Rome under the barons. What greater anguish than to know that the misery of the blameless people remains unmitigated? As the people suffer in the jaws of wolves, their wounds fester; and an impious rector subjects a pious people. Yet this is not a special plea for himself; for Cola admits that the people, Roman citizens, can rule themselves better than can Cola di Rienzo. Thus his actions are not a sign of arrogance or appropriation of others' rights and duties. In fact, all his actions throughout his rule followed the papal plan. Cola, long exposed naked in the Roman council, alone carried the pope's voice when all others had failed. Little wonder, then, that Cola now weeps for the city, abandoned and lamentable, and for her people. Cola declares that he remains a partisan: of peace and justice. Why, then, should his vision for a just Roman society be branded as ambition? Yet, despite Cola's innocence and suffering, the pope grows daily more angry with him.

All Christian sources agree on the renewal of Rome, as do the pagan writers: there is no need to believe in the Apocalypse to believe in this Roman revival. Cicero, Ptolemy of Alexandria, and Macrobius all spoke of the great coming of justice in history. According to Virgil, the golden age will return: *Iam redet et virgo, redeunt Saturnia regna,* "Now at last the Virgin returns, and the reign of Saturn comes back." Even the Bible and the church fathers so teach. But Cola is condemned for such reading, and like Boethius, he finds himself in chains, while his accusers abandon the fathers of the church and waste their time reading the fables of Lancelot and Tristan.

As he had from the beginning of his imprisonment, Cola continues to request that he be transferred to Avignon to appear before the Curia. He knows that powerful forces there are arrayed against him and the Roman people. But, Cola tells Gui, he trusts in the *Magnificat,* Mary's hymn of liberation,

that the Church will liberate the poor, the man alone and defenseless in defying all the tyrants rather than the one sung in the Roman proverb: "The man who wants to enter paradise, should adore the barons." . . . In fact, it is never read in Sacred Scripture that the Lord heeds the voice of the powerful and the forceful. No. He heeds the voice of the afflicted and the poor, the voice of the people cry-ing out, the voice of those who beg on the people's behalf. Indeed, with all the swords of his Word the Lord in his wrath will smash kings and princes into pieces, and he will depose and torment barons, he will strike down the robust and the strong to aid his suffering peoples. (70, BBCR 2.3:402–3, ll. 407–23)

Now in chains, Cola declares that he will take his chances to answer the charges leveled against him by the barons and his other enemies. He is ready to go to Avignon, and after his examination to be either executed or sent as a penitent to Jerusalem.

Cola's years in Bohemia produced his most elevated and mystical apocalyptic writings. But his days and nights at Prague and Raudnitz were marked by a long endurance and expectation of another, far more earthly fate. Very soon after Emperor Charles IV had decided that he could no longer prevent Cola's arrest at the hands of papal agents, he decided to entrust his guest—now his prisoner—to his friend and collaborator, Archbishop Ernst of Prague. Though a sophisticated and cultured man ready to cooperate fully with his lord in the revitalization of kingdom and empire, Ernst was also a devout and zealous church reformer. As the first archbishop appointed for Prague, he was no doubt eager to prove the viability of the post and of his tenure in it. He therefore took the pope's command seriously: Cola di Rienzo was a notorious and dangerous heretic who must be imprisoned, examined, and then sent off to Avignon for trial and possible punishment.

Aside from his dreams of imperial revival and apocalyptic renewal, Cola's Bohemian letters also reflect his deeply human concerns during the period: not only for his own physical well-being and that of his companions but also for those whom he had left behind in Italy: his wife, children and extended family, and for his friends and supporters back in Rome now exposed to the vengeance of the barons and the likelihood that the *buono stato* would never survive his abdication.[11] Cola maintained contact with the Romans but must have felt that the normal channels of communication to his political supporters would be too dangerous for the safety of all involved. He therefore relied on a series of letters to his friend, the abbot of the Benedictine monastery of Sant'Alessio on the Aventine. Had Cola known the abbots of Sant'Alessio since his youth among the wharves and fisheries of the Ripa? Or had the legend of Alexius, the patrician youth turned wandering hermit—an unrecognized stranger even within his own family—resonated with Cola at a later time? Themes of illegitimacy and sudden discovery of great character and lineage surrounded the tribune throughout his life. Cola's second letter to Charles IV from Prague in late July uses the Alexius theme quite effectively.

Cola's first letter to the abbot of Sant'Alessio is one of consolation under tribulation and trial, but these tribulations are political ones. He comforts the towns of Tuscany, whose *populares* have been afflicted by the senators, "because they have attempted to vindicate the liberty of the people." They and others in Italy look forward to Cola's future life and to his "resurrection." Meanwhile, God delays his return in order to punish him. Probably in an attempt to cover his tracks, the tribune asks the abbot of Sant'Alessio that he tell Nicolo of the monastery of Sant'Eufemia that *he,* in turn, signal Cola's father-in-law (Francesco Mancini?) to bring his son—presumably Lorienzo—to Bohemia by any road he can. Cola concludes the letter with a reference to "all my companions," among them the chancellor of Rome. "I could write many words of comfort, especially to the consuls and to the people; but it is better to remain silent." And he asks the abbot to comfort all those who are now in doubt. In another letter written in Prague sometime later in 1350, Cola writes the chancellor of Rome to comfort the nobles and *populares* in Rome and the merchants of Tuscany who have doubts about his presence in Bohemia, informing them that he is working "for the peace and the *status* of all Tuscany and Italy" and "for the peace and salvation of everyone." Cola advises the Tuscan Guelphs to doubt neither the emperor nor his impartiality.

Cola writes to the abbot again in August 1350, sending news of himself and his companions, declaring that the rumors that have reached Rome about their ill-treatment in Bohemia are false: they are fine and hope to be freed happily soon. Cola does warn, however, that he can say no more, lest his enemies hear some news and are forewarned of his return. Even if this return is delayed, this is God's will. Cola has received news that the senators have begun to take recriminations against his supporters; but he encourages the abbot, saying that upon his return the tyrants will come to heel.

Cola again asks that Fra Nicolo of Sant'Eufemia contact his father-in-law concerning his son, and that he free him just at the proper time. What Cola means here is unclear. Is his son to help prepare for this return to Rome, or does Cola wants his son released to be sent—unknowingly— as a hostage to the emperor? In any case, it seems probable that Lorienzo was in safekeeping at Sant'Eufemia, a monastery in Albano in the Alban hills that belonged to Sant'Alessio in Rome.

There had, apparently, been widespread rumors about the fate of Cola, his family, and his companions. In his letter to Archbishop Ernst of August 15, 1350, Cola had already noted that his sister and mother-in-law "have been held captive by the barons of this world in a certain monastery. I do not know what has happened to my wife." That same month, in his answer to Charles IV's rebuttal, Cola also wrote to the emperor that he was still willing to offer his son as a hostage of his good intentions:

I still believe, despite the rumors about my capture, that both he and all my relatives are all living securely in Rome as long as I live. They would already have been killed by the barons in revenge for their own relatives killed in the wars of the Tribune. But the barons would never presume to offend them, even if they crossed right before their eyes, fearing my return by the date I have already set. And as God and the world can see, I have left nothing in the world to inherit, nor do I seek any kingdom except that of God. Not only have I abandoned honors but I am horrified just by the memory of the ones I sought. I have not only rejected the world and the riches of the world, but also my own wife, whom at her own request I wished to dedicate to a monastery of the heavenly lord. And I have dedicated myself to the Order of Jerusalem, and today I would accept it most willingly, if I were able. (58, BBCR 2.3:319, ll. 760–74)

In these letters Cola first began to display publicly the grave doubts and anguish that would beset him over the next months: the long years of wandering and then imprisonment were beginning to have their effect. Cola tells the archbishop that the *Oracles of Cyril* had spoken very clearly about his own life. Thus Cyril had already prophesied the theft of the funds that Cola had amassed to effect his return to Rome and to topple the senators, and that it was his own brother Francesco who would steal the money. Cyril had also foretold that Cola would be confined to a cell that was more "like a hollow, indeed like a cave, what is called a *stupba* in your language" (57, BBCR 2.3:268, ll. 959–65). Cola also knew that his cave would be "tricameral," for the three chains that now bind him divide his cave into three distinct chambers. Cola also therefore had every reason to believe something else that the prophecies made clear: that he would soon be dead.

In his letter to Archbishop Ernst, Cola first made public the condition that he claims to have had "for seven years and four months," that is, since April 1343: the *morbus sincopi,* "which makes a man's heart tremble" (57, BBCR 2.3:269, ll. 978–84), what had often been referred to in English as the "falling disease" and which has since become associated with epilepsy.[12] It is a strange revelation and might bear all the marks of self-service, given Cola's desperate situation. But his later letters refer to it several times more. Should we, with this information, revise our readings of Cola's radically changed moods, his sudden inaction, his trembling and apparent inability to communicate, followed by just as sudden returns to lucidity and high energy? How closely do the Anonimo romano's descriptions, borrowed as they might be from classical sources, follow the symptoms of a partial or an absence seizure once referred to as "petit mal"? Cola sometimes described his condition as a heart ailment that would cause him to collapse. This may fit the symptoms of tonic-clonic seizures; and his reference to his heart and to his stomach problems probably followed medieval science, the diagnosis of his physician, or his own reading in classical scientific sources. The conditions were well known to medieval physicians. The *tremor cordis* was discussed at length by Cola's contemporary the Genoese physician Galvano de Levanto, as was the falling disease *(caducus)*. Sections of the *Breviarium practicae medicinae,* widely attributed to the most famous late-medieval physician, Arnald of Villanova (c.1240–1311) cover the topics *De syncopi cardiaca passione et tremore cordis* (On the cardiac disease syncopis and heart tremor) and *De epilepsia.* Arnald described the conditions as follows:

Syncopis and *exolutio* and *lipothymia* signify the same condition: they are synonyms. . . . It happens sometimes because of overwork, especially in those who are affected by liver or stomach trouble [which Cola did have]. Syncopis also results from passion of the spirit, as for example, from too much joy, sadness, or fear. . . . Infected air, when it is drawn in through the mouth and suddenly reaches the heart, can also induce syncopis. . . .

The symptoms of syncopis are the following: the patient suddenly falls to the floor or his bed, as if dead or deprived of his senses. If you place your hand next to his heart, [you will detect] a great state of anxiety, rapid breathing, fast pulse, and emission of heat. . . .

This disease might also [arise] from some humor concentrated in a chamber of the heart, which if heated brings on a heart tremor, heat, thirst, quick pulse, and great difficulty in breathing. If this humor is made cold, there follows heart tremor, weak pulse, depression, and sluggishness without thirst. (BBCR 2.5:314–15 n. 7)

Epilepsy is an occlusion of the chief ventricles of the brain, with loss of sensation and motion; or, epilepsy is a non-continuous spasm of the whole body. The disease takes its rise from different causes. . . . There are three species of epilepsy according to the threefold diversity of places in which the cause itself is contained. The first species is properly called epilepsy. It comes from a defect of the brain. . . . Of this type, the infallible sign is that victims suddenly fall, emit a great foam, and do not speak. . . . There is a second type called analepsy. This comes from matter existing in the stomach. . . . There is a third type, called catalepsy, which comes from matter contained in the extremities. . . . (von Storch and von Storch, 253–54)

In his *Lilium medicinae* (1305), Bernard of Gordon also discusses the causes and effects of epilepsy, both violent and moderate paroxysms.

Sometimes a patient "did not need a support, but there came to him a dizziness in the head, and blindness in the eyes, and he himself recited the Hail Mary, and before he had finished it, the paroxysm had passed off, and he spat once and the whole thing passed off." Some patients remembered nothing of their seizures, "and there are some who remember and are ashamed" (Eadie and Bladin, 30–31).

The *Breviarium*'s treatment for syncopis suggested "a potion composed of good, crystal-clear wine combined with the best quality, fragrant rose water. For nothing comforts a man's heart more than wine drunk in moderation." Its prescriptions for epilepsy enjoined a vast array of herbs, ground bones, and potions, sometimes mixed with wine and honey. Given the difficulty of clearly diagnosing epilepsy, even for modern experts, any conclusions should be treated with caution. Rienzo preferred never to make his condition public knowledge. Yet some, like the Anonimo romano or his sources, noticed clear changes in Cola's behavior.

As the days of summer faded into fall and the onset of the northern winter, Cola and his companions began to lose hope. In a postscript (58, BBCR 2.3:331–32, ll. 981–89) to his letter to Charles IV written in August, Cola had already rather poignantly asked the emperor to help his servants and companions, who were near death from lack of food and water. The tribune asks the emperor that following the ancient custom of the Jubilee, he see fit to release them from their imprisonment. Cola alone, and not his innocent companions, needs to suffer for his sins. By October or November 1350 Cola writes to the archbishop from Raudnitz protesting the harsh conditions of his own imprisonment. He tells him that ever since the onset of his illness, even in Italy, where the climate is far more temperate, and even in the summer, he has always needed a fire. How much more, therefore, in those frigid northern places of wandering? And this is not only for the warmth but also for the strength and comfort the fiery air provides for his heart. And so he asks for fire not only during the night but also during the day, which he will pay for at his expense. "Lest some day, after I fall, and no one comes to help me, I will not get up again" (67, BBCR 2.3:368, ll. 1–15).

Cola then also asks for help for his companions, lest they die of the cold, that either the archbishop frees them or, again at Cola's expense, someone provide them with warm clothing (ll. 17–22). He asks Ernst once more that, if his letters have not been sent, to please have them either sent or returned to him. Finally, Cola takes the offensive, warning the archbishop that "the Spirit of the Lord takes on many forms, sometimes gently and he dare not judge anyone, and sometimes terribly, taking revenge on nations and finding ever new ways of torment. Nowadays the second mode is far more necessary than the first" (ll. 23–30).

Cola's physical suffering, the uncertainties of his situation, and his constant psychological struggle to maintain his dignity and hope seem to have had their effect not only on his physical health but also on another of his chief possessions: his Latinity.[13] Cola's style undergoes a marked change during his years in Bohemia. From the relatively simple syntax and *cursus* of his public and political letters, Cola's letters in Prague take on a new complex structure, with a new vocabulary drawn from the language of inner turmoil, emotion, and spiritual self-examination, borrowed generously from his prophetic readings in Merlin, Cyril, and other pseudo-Joachite tracts. This also seems to parallel his more complex personal situation: no longer in control of events, dependent on the favor and goodwill of his hosts and captors, intent upon convincing the emperor of his apocalyptic role, and the imperial court of Cola's own place in the events of the Last Days. Yet at the same time, wary of betraying himself to his inquisitors, Cola uses a language and sentence structure that often seem deliberately complex and vague, his earlier straightforward declaratives couched now in conditionals, in past imperfects, his modifiers uncertain, his antecedents often ambiguous.

Perhaps much of this stylistic change reflects the hardships of his imprisonment in Prague and Raudnitz and the gradual deterioration of his health. On the other hand, this may be the result of his one apparent relief in all the months of his captivity. From as early as August 1350 Cola had begun to correspond with the imperial notary and chancellor Johann von Neumarkt. A lifelong friend and supporter of Emperor Charles, Johann was chancellor from 1352 to 1374, with only a brief interruption in 1364–65, and served as bishop of Leitomischl (1353–64) and then of Olmütz (1364–80). He was a patron of the new arts in Bohemia, especially of the book, importing the Italian painting and decorative styles and creating a new Bohemian style in such manuscripts as the *Liber viaticus* of c. 1360. Johann was also a correspondent of Petrarch and on one occasion at least requested a copy of his *De remediis utriusque fortunae*. Cola's correspondence with Johann, whom he calls "beloved friend" soon after his arrival in Prague, rarely touches upon his fate or that of Rome or the empire. The two men focus, instead, on Latin style and rhetorical devices that seem to push Cola's predicament into the background. Johann only rarely issues advice amid the discussion of Latin poetry and prose, praising Cola's Latin *vox* but warning him to conform to the emperor's will. Here again, Cola's language and style have undergone a profound change, replacing apocalyptic imagery and prophecy with tropes of springtime flowers, bees, and nectar. The dispersal of shadows and the coming of fresh spring are still there, but even this language of renewal has moved away from Cola's religious and civic world into that of literature and poetry. Whatever the reason for his change in style—a reflection of personal mood, a calculated effort to project a nonpolitical image, or simply the stylistic influence of Johann von Neumarkt and perhaps of Petrarch—it seems that as Rienzo's clear and optimistic vision of the political and religious future begins to fade, so too does the clarity and easy strength of his civic Latin style.

By September 1350 Cola had revealed to the archbishop that he was now in the habit of inflicting a regular Sunday flagellation upon himself to repent for his sins. How long Cola had been undertaking the "Discipline"—as the practice of the Flagellants was called—is uncertain. He might have adopted it among the Poor Hermits of the Maiella during his first years of exile; but then again, the impact on Rome of Fra Venturino's pilgrimage in 1335 and the constant example of the confraternities on urban life may have convinced him of the merits of the Discipline from an early age. Whenever he began, his practice seems to have shocked even his captor and could not have helped his physical condition.

By September 28, 1350, in fact, only about a month into his harsh confinement, Cola di Rienzo began to feel that hope for his release and return to Rome during the Jubilee was dwindling, as he wrote to Fra Michele of Monte Sant'Angelo. Whether Michele was a friar at Monte Gargano on the Adriatic coast of Apulia, where the Archangel Michael was said to have appeared, or at a convent in or near Rome is uncertain. From the context of the letter it seems more likely that he was among Cola's contacts in the city. Cola tells Michele that while he was on the Montagna della Maiella he had begun to open the closed and unknown tablets of God when a satanic brother—Fra Angelo de Monte Vulcano—led him astray, and his understanding was clouded and given a carnal interpretation. But now he is undergoing penitence and is willing, with a certain Frater Andreas and others, to travel among the infidels and suffer martyrdom, if necessary, for the name of Christ. In this Cola seems to have the model of Venturino before him: similarly held by the Inquisition, freed, and then sent off on a "pilgrimage" to the East.

Cola then describes his former life among the Spirituals as one without works: his was merely an intellectual appreciation of those true religious who have been forced to flee into their forest hermitages. In this it seems that he is not repudiating his Joachite influences or friends but emphasizing his own inability to live up to their Gospel lives. Cola then demonstrates his continuing fascination with Joachite concordances between the First and Second Ages:

What was more acceptable to the athletes of the early church, is considered more irksome in these last days. Therefore it is not surprising if after Babylon has been destroyed, the New Jerusalem is expected by Spirituals and those sojourning in the shadows. [Cf. Ps. 106:10.] For perhaps David would not have been chosen if Saul had not hesitated. The Church would not have risen if the Synagogue had not offended. (64, BBCR 2.3:359, ll. 54–59)

Cola protests that he is judged not for his work on behalf of peace and justice but for his belief in prophecy. Like the Spirituals, he declares that he is ready to suffer, even if unjustly. Yet the time of consolation is coming, and Cola describes its arrival in apocalyptic imagery.

Despite his apocalyptic expectations, toward the end of this letter his language reveals that Cola is beginning to lose hope for his earthly situation, and he writes a lengthy series of instructions to Fra Michele that read like a last will and testament.[14] Cola's chief concern is for his son. He hopes that Lorenzo will be kept chaste and humble and will be competently instructed in doctrine and protected from the dangers of the world. One of these dangers was a lactate intolerance: "And, since his stomach is the same as mine, warn him not to take milk often." Cola then asks Michele to inform his father's brother that he should sell all his personal belongings: his books, his arms, and the other effects of his life in Rome. He should then give the proceeds of the sale to the Holy Sepulcher in Jerusalem; but if the Muslims do not allow the transfer of the funds, then half should go to the clergy and half to Christians still in the Holy Land. Cola's wife, Livia, who has already adopted the religious habit, should become a Clariss nun along with their two daughters and her sister. But Fra Michele is to keep all this a secret. Cola then writes a postscript, which he asks Michele to show to his son. In it he asks for prayers for peace in the Holy Land, and grants sixty florins for the support of poor pilgrims. If he should die before the end of the Jubilee year, then the Roman consuls and the people should choose a successor to him. But should he live, Cola pledges to resign ten days after the conclusion of the Jubilee, and he asks that this information be passed on to the Roman chancellor (64, BBCR 2.3:362–65, ll. 113–75).

On that same day, September 28, 1350, Cola wrote a private letter to Lorenzo. He begins by asking his son to remember their patron saints in Rome: Sant'Alessio, of course, Iohannes Calybite (of the hut), and the seven sons of Symphorosa, early Roman martyrs. He choices are poignant reflections on his own situation and his own youth growing up in and around the Arenula and the Ripa. Alessio was the impoverished and unrecognized heir of Rome. Iohannes Calybite was a hermit saint whose relics rested in the church at the center of the Tiber Island (see fig. 2, right) and whose story is remarkably like that of Sant'Alessio. Symphorosa and her sons had been martyred under Hadrian for their defense of the Christian faith. Their relics had rested at Tivoli, but in Cola's day they had been transferred to the church of Sant'Angelo in Pescheria. Cola thus entrusts his son to the spiritual patrons of his Roman neighborhood just as he might commend him to the powerful and influential men of the *rione*.

He advises Lorienzo to remain constant amid change and to live with patience and in poverty, and he concludes:

> But just as you remember these saints, do not think of me or any of your household; for I—wherever I am—am well, since I am with God in His mercy. And since he is your suitable father-mentor, who shows you the way of God in all things, look now, I give Fra Michele to you as a real father. In all things you should obey his judgments more than my own. Because of spies, keep your real name and news sent to you hidden! So now, I am writing to Fra Michele. His actions proceed from my desires. The Blessed of the Blessed give you eternal blessing! (65, BBCR 2.3:366–67)

Abdication and condemnation, exile and wandering, the dashed dream of imperial revival under Charles IV, prison and deprivation, poor health, constant anxiety, and finally the loss of all hope for himself, his companions, and his family seem to have brought the visionary to the end of his long path. A voluntary appearance in Avignon, a speedy judgment before his enemies, exile to the Holy Land just like the chastened Venturino da Bergamo, even death itself were now preferable to this state of inaction and despair. In his letter to Gui de Boulogne, Cola once again offers to join the Knights Hospitallers of Jerusalem and for his wife to enter a convent. As it is now, his sons and daughters and the members of his extended family are wandering about without security, in poverty. Will it ever happen again, Cola asks, that he will be able to live in safety and happiness among his fellow citizens? Will he ever again be able to settle down to a normal life?

And yet, as Rienzo himself had so often written and spurred others to think, out of the deepest darkness and despair, out of the most terrible tribulations the light must come again, hope be reborn, and divine grace return. And so it was. Shortly after his letter to Gui de Boulogne in 1351, probably by February, Cola was released from his cell and given the freedom of the kingdom. Sometime after that he voluntarily agreed to go and face his accusers in Avignon.

Ever since Cola's first flight from Rome in early 1348, Clement VI had been writing to Charles IV to enlist his aid in hunting down and destroying the fallen tribune.[15] In a letter dated Avignon, February 5, 1348, Clement immediately informs the emperor of Cola's "subversion" of Rome, naming him "pernicious and plague-bearing." The pope reviews the events of the past seven months, recalling how Cola had been his *familiaris,* and how Clement had treated him with "the zeal of a father's love." But Cola has betrayed this trust by his unwarranted assumption of titles, his expulsion of Vicar Raymond, his usurpation of church and imperial rights, and his call on electors to justify Charles's own election. Even after paternal warning and calls to repent and reform from Bertrand de Déaulx, Cola continued in his contemptuous ways beyond the pope's patience. Therefore, Clement recalls, he ordered his legate to proceed against Cola, and "he lost his tribunal insignia and in ignominy has been expelled from the aforesaid City." The legate had deprived him of his office, "and he has formally declared him to be suspect of the crime of heresy." At that point Cola had just gone into hiding, and despite Clement's best efforts to enlist barons, legates, bishops, and inquisitors to track down and capture the tribune, all had failed. But then Cola had shown up at Prague, right in the emperor's own hands. Almost as soon as Cola arrived, Clement VI began sending a series of letters to Charles requesting that he surrender the tribune to papal agents.

In a letter dated August 17, 1350, Clement immediately comes to the point, naming "Nicholas Rienzi, Roman citizen, that raging son of Belial, that father of iniquity, pernicious and noxious," who deserved to be condemned as a heretic by both papal legates Bertrand and Annibaldo, "of good memory." The pope tells Charles that it is a miracle that Cola has now fallen into his hands, and he asks Charles and Archbishop Ernst that they order Cola detained. On August 17 Clement enjoined Ernst to send Cola to him, and on the next day he wrote again to warn the archbishop to guard the tribune carefully. But whatever Cola's sense of failure to win the sympathies of the imperial court, both Charles and Ernst appear to have resisted papal pressure, for Clement reports that Ernst has written back asking the pope to send detailed articles of the accusations. Therefore, Clement is writing to Charles to use his influence on Ernst, lest Cola use his fraudulent crafts to win back his freedom.

But over six months later the heretical tribune was still not Clement's. Instead, Charles IV had sent an embassy to Avignon to discuss the matter with the pope. Clement therefore writes the emperor on February 1, 1351, to report that he has received the embassy of Archbishop Ernst and Duke Nikolas von Troppau bearing the emperor's letters. Clement reiterates that he has written many letters to Charles requesting that "that pestilential man Nicholas Rienzi, Roman citizen, who fell into your hands miraculously by divine power," be sent off to Avignon. Still the emperor and his archbishop had not surrendered their prisoner. They apparently presented the pope with fairly firm arguments for their lack of action, perhaps even questioning the legal basis of Cola's condemnation.

On February 24/25, 1351, Clement VI therefore wrote to all the archbishops and bishops of Germany and Bohemia, warning against the infection of the healthy flock by one diseased sheep. He then proceeded carefully to lay out the legal and procedural basis for Cola's condemnation. Cola di Rienzo is a pertinacious and unrepentant heretic. He was legally and properly excommunicated and publicly condemned as a heretic in a parliament at Montefiascone before the prelates, nobles, and syndics of the cities and other lands of the province of the Patrimony of St. Peter in Tuscany. Cola refused to appear, and in his absence he had been condemned as contumacious. Clement then reveals some surprising news: that "Cola is said to be in hiding in your territories." Therefore, to protect the simple faithful, Clement orders the bishops and archbishops to have read in their dioceses on Sundays and feast days the public condemnation of Cola as a heretic whenever people assemble for divine services or for sermons. From the pope's references to Cola's presence in the empire and his access to the German and Bohemian faithful, it seems likely that by the beginning of 1351 he had been released from prison and had some limited freedom of the realm.

Finally, on March 24, 1352, Clement separately informed the emperor and the archbishop that he had dispatched Roger de Moulinneuf, his master of the guards, Giovanni, bishop of Spoleto, and Hugue de Charlus, members of the pope's *familia,* to personally take charge of Cola di Rienzo and conduct him back to Avignon. But Clement's letter seems to confirm the tribune's freedom of movement among the people and his apparent popularity with them: Clement asks Ernst to deliver Cola to papal agents "without causing any disturbance."

Cola's last dated letter from Bohemia comes from Raudnitz sometime in 1351. Clement's final request for Cola's transfer to Avignon was written on March 24, 1352, and therefore must have reached Prague by the end of April 1352, shortly after which Cola began his journey to the papal court.[16] This could have happened as late as July, which is when Matthias von Neuenburg dates it in his *Chronicle,* but this seems too late, and thirty days to cross this distance to Avignon improbably short. Cola's progress from Prague to Avignon bears out the fact that he had freely traveled around the empire and had made many friends over the course of the previous year. The Anonimo romano describes the journey as a triumphal procession:

During the journey that he made through all the lands [of the empire], people rose up, crowds gathered amid the stir, they followed behind him. They held him back, they said that they wanted to save him from the hands of the pope. They did not want him to go. To everyone he replied, "I am going voluntarily. I am not forced." He thanked them, and so he passed from city to city. Solemn honors were paid to him along the way. When the people saw him, they marveled, and they accompanied him. (AR, XXVII, ll. 73–81, Porta, 239)

The trip up the Danube valley to the headwaters of the Rhone and thence to Avignon could have taken Cola about six to eight weeks, probably closer to the shorter limit. The Anonimo romano states that Cola reached Avignon on his favorite date: August 1.

Petrarch was on the scene at the time, and he describes Cola's arrival in a lengthy letter to Francesco Nelli (*Fam.* XIII.6) that is remarkable for its calculated attempt to distance himself from the fallen tribune and for his repudiation of Cola's well-known Joachite beliefs:

There recently came to the Curia or, rather, he did not come but was led here a prisoner, Cola di Rienzo, formerly the widely feared tribune of Rome, today the most wretched of men. He has now touched the very lowest depths of misfortune; for, though he is extremely miserable, I do not know whether he is to be pitied by any means. He might have died a glorious death on the Capitol; but he has submitted to the chains first of a Bohemian, and then of a Limousin—to his everlasting disgrace and in mockery of the Roman name and republic.

The constant praise and exhortations that so busily engaged my pen are, perhaps, better known than I should like at present. . . . Several letters that I wrote to him survive, letters that even today I am not displeased to have written. I am not used to predicting the future. I wish that he, too, had not been addicted to prophecy! . . . Though my desire to destroy them should be great, I am now powerless. They have gone out into the world and are no longer subject to my control.

But to resume my story. Rienzo entered the Curia, humbled and despised, . . . the unhappy man proceeded on his way, hemmed in on this side and that by two guards, while the rabble eagerly rushed forward to gaze on the face of the man whose illustrious name they had only heard of. He was being sent to the Roman pontiff by the king of the Romans! Strange traffic indeed. . . .

Upon his arrival, then, the supreme pontiff immediately appointed three princes of the church to try his case, with instructions to discover the most suitable punishment for the man who desired the freedom of the republic. . . . He came, but not in chains. This alone was missing from his public disgrace; as for the rest, he was so carefully guarded that there was no hope of escape. As soon as he reached the city gate, the poor unfortunate inquired whether I was in attendance at the Curia, perhaps hoping that I might be of some assistance to him—which, to my knowledge, I can not be—or else simply because he was reminded of an old friendship formerly contracted in that city. Now, therefore, the life of that man, in whose hands the safety and the welfare of so many nations rested, hangs on the nod of strangers. His life and his name are both at stake. Do not be surprised at the outcome; men are now wavering in their opinions; and you will be sure to hear one of two sentences: either that he has been deprived of all legal rights, or that he has been condemned to death. . . .

Now at last listen to what first prompted me to write, and you will have good cause for laughter after the sad recital that has preceded. While the trial is in this unsettled state, I learn from the letters of friends that one hope of safety still remains—the rumor that has spread abroad that Rienzo is a most famous poet! Consequently it seems an act of sacrilege to do violence to a man so worthy and dedicated to so sacred a study! . . .

What shall I say of this strange rumor? I heartily rejoice. I consider it a cause for endless congratulation that the Muses are held so much in honor even today. . . . I do not begrudge him that the rumor of his being a poet should bring him salvation in his hour of extreme need and when the trial has assumed such a doubtful aspect.

If you were to ask me my private opinion, however, I should answer that Cola di Rienzo is a very fluent speaker, possessing great convincing powers and a decided vein for oratory. As a writer he is pleasing and elegant. His diction, though not extensive, is charming and brilliant. I suppose he has read all the poets, at least all those who are generally known. But he is no more a poet for that reason than he would be a weaver for robing himself with a mantle woven by another's hands. The mere production of verses is not sufficient to merit the composer the name of poet. (CRCR, 130–35)

The Anonimo romano tells a more succinct, less cagey version of the same story:

Cola arrived at Avignon and spoke before the pope. He asserted that he was not a Patarine [antipapal heretic], nor had he incurred the sentence of Cardinal Don Bruno [Bertrand de Déaulx, cardinal of Embrun] against him. He wanted to stand trial. At these words the pope remained silent. Cola was shut up in a high and wide tower. A chain held one of his legs. The chain was attached to the vault of the tower. There Cola stayed dressed in middling clothes. He had books enough: his Titus Livy, his histories of Rome, the Bible, and enough other books. He never stopped studying. He had ample nourishment from the pope's sideboard, which he gave him for God's sake. (AR, XXVII, ll. 82–93, Porta, 239–40)

Much had changed in Avignon since Cola was last there in the early 1340s. The city had been ravaged by the Black Death, and many of its former luminaries were now dead, including Petrarch's Laura and Cardinal Giovanni Colonna. In the spring of 1348, Queen Giovanna of Naples, fleeing from the invasion of Lewis of Bavaria, had sought refuge and support from Pope Clement there. During her stay she had finally decided on an expedient to raise cash to support her struggle against the Hungarians: as Angevin lord of Avignon, she would sell the city to the pope. On June 9, 1348, she exchanged the papal city for 80,000 florins. In conjunction with the bargain, on November 1, 1348, Emperor Charles IV renounced his imperial titles to Avignon as the ancient king of Burgundy. While the Avignonese protested both the sale and renunciation, they were already a minority within their own city, and their voices meant very little. The pope became temporal lord over Avignon. The population of the city had also changed: the Black Death had reduced it by up to 50 percent, and entire households had been wiped out with their properties left empty; there was much more room for the survivors to create larger and more comfortable housing; and by now more and more of the College of Cardinals, the members of their *livrées,* and those who served them and the pope were decidedly French, many from Clement's own Limousin. In its arts, culture, and manners the city had long lost any real Italian influence, other than that of its merchants and financiers.

We have no transcript of the meeting of Pope Clement and Cola di Rienzo. Nor do we know where it took place. Many years had passed, almost a decade since they had first met in the papal palace. Clement was too sophisticated a man to have rejoiced outwardly when the fallen tribune was brought into his presence. The pope may well have been shocked at Cola's changed appearance. The Roman had probably been out of the Raudnitz dungeon for about a year and had used the time to travel freely through Bohemia and Bavaria. Some traces of good health may have returned, but he would still have been nearing forty, probably already sporting a beard in the German style, suffering from his "falling sickness," and grown flabby and soft from prison food and lack of physical activity. And his fears for the safety of his own person, his friends, and his family— never mind his bitter disappointment over the fate of Rome—would have shown on his brow and in his eyes, and perhaps even in the facility of his tongue. Could Clement have rejoiced to have seen his former *familiaris* so shipwrecked? Still, the Roman was a dangerous enemy of the church and must be dealt with firmly. But the pope's only recorded response was silence.

Cola was led from the pope and taken to the other end of the palace, tradition says to the Tour de Trouillas, for the duration of his trial.[17] The tower rose nearly fifty-three meters high, housed much of the garrison, and served as the palace's northern bastion. Above the ground-floor storage rooms rose two floors—large, central rooms supported by a single column, much like a Cistercian chapter house. The Chamber of the Sergeant at Arms occupied the entire third level; below that was the Tower Room, and here, to its tall central column, Cola di Rienzo was chained. Pope Clement was taking no chances that his prisoner, so eagerly awaited all these years, would ever regain his freedom. But, as the Anonimo romano reports, his confinement was not harsh, nothing like the prison at Raudnitz; and here in Avignon the climate was pleasant, much like that of Italy, some thought even better through much of the year. The room itself was spacious: nearly fifteen meters square and about eight high, lit by three large windows recessed into the tower walls: two to the east overlooking Clement VI's gardens, and one to the north.

Cola was treated well and attended by fellow Italians. The first reference to him in the papal expense books comes from August 14, 1352, with the purchase for the tribune of what seems to be a luxurious bed, worth twenty-four florins, by Stefano Priozi. Then, on October 21, 1352, Cola's prison warden, Michele di Pistoia, a sergeant at arms, is recorded as having made further purchases on his behalf. So the time passed, the three unnamed cardinals appointed to look into Rienzo's orthodoxy began to meet as Cola sat with his Livy, his Bible, and his other books, planning his legal strategy, perhaps meeting with friends and supporters, awaiting vindication before his judges. We will probably never know whether Cola knew the presence of, or had any contact with, another famous prisoner then being held in the papal palace. Jean de Roquetaillade had been brought to Avignon in 1349 to stand trial for his own Joachite views and was detained there until 1356, during which time he wrote several treatises on prophecy, including his famous *Vade mecum in tribulatione*.[18] While Cola makes no mention of the Franciscan, Jean de Roquetaillade certainly knew of Cola; and in his later *Liber ostensor* he evoked the person and the work of the tribune several times and summed up much of what was then currently known about him.

Meanwhile, Petrarch reported to Nelli that word of Cola's return and of his imaginative, even poetic, genius had begun to circulate through Avignon. It looked as if the tribune might again escape his fate. Sometime in the fall of 1352, perhaps in October, Petrarch wrote another of his unsigned letters, his *Sine nomine* 4, to the Roman people. By now Cola's growing stature had attracted the poet laureate's renewed loyalty; and we find Petrarch describing the opening of the trial, decrying the tribune's imprisonment, and calling for the revival of Rome's ancient greatness:

Illustrious people, no longer be ignorant of the charges preferred against him who was once your head and ruler but who is now—shall I say your fellow citizen or exile? You will hear facts that may or may not be known to you but that will surely fill you with wonder and indignation. He is accused not of neglecting, but of defending, the cause of liberty. He is pronounced guilty not for having deserted, but for having mounted the Capitol. This, finally, is the chief charge against him, a crime to be atoned for on the scaffold: that he has had the presumption to affirm that even today the Roman Empire is at Rome and at the disposal of the people of Rome. . . .

Your wretched fellow citizen does not deny having made such assertions and continues to adhere to his previous statements. This is the terrible crime for which his life now hangs in the balance. He adds—and I believe that he speaks the truth— that he reached these conclusions only after consulting many wise men; and he demands that counsel and the opportunity to present his defense be given to him. This is denied him: and unless divine mercy and your good will intercede on his behalf, it is all over. Innocent and without counsel, he will surely be condemned. A great many feel pity for him. Truly, there is hardly one who does not, except those for whom it would be proper to pity and to pardon the sins of others and not to envy them their virtues.

In this city there is no lack of prominent jurists who maintain that, according to civil law, this maxim of the illustrious prisoner could be proved in the clearest way. There is no lack of others who say that, were they permitted to speak freely, they could add many reliable examples from the pages of history that would corroborate that same maxim. But no one dares murmur a syllable now, except in a remote corner, or in the darkness, or in fear. I myself, who am writing to you, should not refuse, perhaps, to die for the truth, if my death would seem to be of any advantage to the City. Yet I too remain silent, nor do I affix my name to this letter, supposing that the style will be sufficient to reveal the writer. I add only this: that it is a Roman citizen who addresses you. (CRCR, 150–56)

Cola, meanwhile, had decided on a defense strategy that might just use the real motives of his accusers to his own advantage. As Petrarch had hinted—and Cola himself had often stated—it was not doctrinal heresy for which he had been condemned: prophecy had little to do with the wrath that the pope and the Curia now poured down upon him. Almost everyone at the time seems to have accepted the validity of the coming Apocalypse and only differed as to the form of interpretation that one assigned to certain texts, dates, and the identification of certain figures vaguely indicated in the prophecies. No, it was not prophecy but the fact that Cola had so eloquently and convincingly summoned up the ancient life of Rome as capital of the world and had dared to summon pope and emperor to the city where they belonged. Cola may well have figured that if he could focus the trial on these issues, he might be able to defend himself competently and gain the sympathy and cooperation of many secret allies in and outside Avignon.

Nor was this a cynical calculation or a renunciation of his deeply held Joachite beliefs. He was, as he would himself say, no theologian. Like most of his contemporaries, he believed in the authority of the church and its hierarchy and was willing to be corrected, if truly he were in error, over matters of doctrine and interpretation. To his genuine sense of penitence, which we have already seen at work in Bohemia, Cola must also have added the shrewd calculations of the Roman politician. What loss to him to renounce prophets and books whose words were obscure, "multiform," as he called them, and who might indeed have been liable to error and misinterpretation? If he followed the advice of the emperor and of Archbishop Ernst, of Petrarch and probably of many other friends and supporters, he would take a respite from "prophecy" and would focus his vision instead on what everyone agreed was his genius: the revival and reform of Rome. Cola therefore set out to reconcile himself with the church on matters of doctrine. By so doing, he pulled the rug out from under his accusers and became in effect a political prisoner to whose cause, now freed from the stigma of heresy, his many supporters could rally. Petrarch himself had pinpointed another aspect of Rienzo's transformation: for in Cola's reputation as a "poet" he had achieved—as Ronald Witt has underscored—an essential shift in late medieval perceptions of modes of being, away from the life of the orator, of rhetoric and the "active" life, and toward that of the poet, of grammar and the "contemplative." If Cola's statements convinced his judges that his prophetic speculations were not deeply held beliefs but imaginative constructions in the mode of Petrarch and other poets, so much the better for him and his reform message.

Sometime in the fall of 1352 Cola therefore wrote to Archbishop Ernst of Prague, repudiating his earlier embrace of the teachings and prophecies of Fra Angelo on the Montagna della Maiella: "That satanic angel, who in the shape of a man made me drunk and alienated me with his [forbidden] fruits in the forest, not long ago appeared quite different in his

comments, but he fled before I recognized him. . . . And truly, he did se-
duce many, so that he might accomplish what he had planned" (73, BBCR
2.3:416, ll. 17–21). Late in 1352 or early in 1353, Cola wrote from his cell to
an unnamed Roman prelate then in Avignon (74, BBCR 2.3:419–20). He
declared ignorance of doctrine, his general lack of higher learning, and
his readiness to be corrected on church teachings.

In that letter, in one to Venetian doge Andrea Dandolo dated September 1353, and in other scattered texts, Cola also referred to his poetry.
He might actually have composed a lengthy poetic epic on the kingdom
of Bohemia for Charles IV. It is also likely that Cola's rhetorical use of the
rhythmed and rhymed *cursus velox* in his letter writing may have con-
tributed to his reputation; and Cola's correspondence with Johann von
Neumarkt remained focused on such stylistics throughout this period.
Sometime in 1353 the imperial chancellor wrote to Cola from Prague.
Again, his theme was letters and classical style. Praising Cola, Johann
joined the chorus now lionizing the tribune for his literary accomplishments: "Your letters are very able, mine very feeble. Yours are like stars
radiating a shining splendor, mine like the glitter of a dying ember. Yours
preside like masterful dogma on a bishop's throne, mine like student essays on a wooden stool" (BBCR 2.3:425, ll. 35–38). Cola's powerful allies
now had clear ground for coming to his defense. But the tribune's recan-
tations, his legal strategies, and the growing movement for his release
paled in comparison to the great event of the year: on December 6, 1352,
at the age of sixty-two, Pope Clement VI suddenly died. Although the
pope had suffered many years from gravel of the urinary tract, his death
was actually caused by the rupture of an internal growth. Almost immediately the Avignon rumor mill began turning out what purported to be
eyewitness accounts of the sexually dissolute life that had finally done in
the worldly pontiff. Matteo Villani, Matthias von Neuenburg, and the
monk of Melsa helped spread the tales. But most vicious were the remarks
by Petrarch, who claims himself to have seen what he describes. Whatever the personal truth, a recent encyclopedist of the papacy, Richard P.
McBrien, places Clement among the worst of the successors to St. Peter.
Pope Clement was buried in Avignon's cathedral, but his body was soon
moved north to the Benedictine abbey of St.-Robert in La Chaise-Dieu,
about twenty-five kilometers northeast of Le Puy, where he was once abbot and where he had desired to be buried. In 1562 the Huguenots dese-
crated his tomb and burned and scattered his remains.[19]

CHAPTER 13

Apocalypse in Rome

Cola's deeds were examined and he was found to be a faithful
Christian. And so the process and the sentence of Don Bruno
and the Cardinal of Ceccano were revoked, and he was absolved.
He came into the pope's good graces and was set free.

Anonimo romano, XXVII, ll. 93–97, Porta, 240

Upon the death of Clement VI on December 6, 1352, the elaborate ma-
chine established for electing popes went into motion; and by December
18, 1352, Clement's successor had been chosen by the College of Cardinals. Étienne Aubert, the cardinal-bishop of Ostia, was crowned Pope Innocent VI on December 30, 1352, by Cardinal Gaillard de la Mothe, the
senior cardinal-deacon.[1] Born in Les Mont, Beyssac (Corrèze), in 1282,
Étienne studied law at the University of Toulouse and received his licen-
tiate in 1321, when he entered the French royal civil service. By 1329 he
had both earned a doctorate in law and become lieutenant seneschal of
Toulouse and Albi. By 1330 he had risen to chief judge of Toulouse and
in 1336 was appointed clerk to the Great Chamber of the French Parliament. Étienne served the royal court well on a series of diplomatic missions in 1337 and 1338, and by January 1338 he had been named bishop of
Noyon. On October 11, 1340, he became bishop of Clermont in the Auvergne, and in September 1342 cardinal-priest of SS. Giovanni e Paolo.
In June 1348 Étienne was appointed grand penitentiary, a post reserved
for only the most respected jurists. In February 1352 Clement VI named
his compatriot cardinal-bishop of Ostia and Velletri.

Unlike the worldly Clement, Innocent was an austere and a deeply reform-minded man. Already seventy years old in 1352, Étienne was in poor health at the time of his election and was thus seen as a transitional figure, a caretaker on the papal throne who would reign briefly but provide a needed contrast to the extravagance and worldliness of his predecessor. As a condition of his election Innocent had signed an agreement with his fellow cardinals that the College of Cardinals as a whole was superior to any pope; but upon his elevation Innocent immediately revoked the understanding, thus signaling that he intended to reign as a powerful and independent monarch.

His ten-year pontificate bore out his first papal act. Innocent reformed most of Clement's abuses, cutting back papal expenses and reducing Avignon's court and bureaucracy, simplifying ceremonial and the extravagant lifestyle of the papal *familia,* and demanding that the College of Cardinals do the same. Innocent pressed for the same overhaul of church appointments and doctrine that he had applied to morals. He thoroughly reformed the Dominicans and the Hospitallers and expanded the universities of both Toulouse and of Bologna, while he not only reinvigorated but actually intensified the church's persecution of the Fraticelli, the hereticized Spiritual Franciscans.

Innocent reversed another of Clement's major policies: that of relative military inactivity. While Clement had inherited a treasury of 1.5 million florins from Benedict XII, he left Innocent VI with a mere 35,000 florins, having spent lavishly on papal buildings, court ceremony, and rewards to relatives and fellow Limousins. Where Clement had devoted only about 21 percent of papal revenues on war expenditures, Innocent was to spend upwards of 66 percent, most of this on the reconquest of the Papal States in Italy. In this, however, Innocent was motivated by the same reform impulse that spurred his other activities: only by reconquering the states could the papacy ever hope to squelch the anarchic violence of the barons and the new petty tyrants of central Italy and thus ensure a safe return to Rome. Italy became a chief priority of Innocent's papacy; and this, combined with Clement's death, removed all impediments to a fair hearing for the prisoner in the Trouillas Tower.

These changes coincided with Cola's legal strategy to seek forgiveness and reconciliation for his misunderstanding of apocalyptic prophecy. Innocent was thus able to begin proceedings on a new basis; he allowed testimony from many sources sympathetic to the former tribune, including—according to one of Innocent's own letters—the appeal that the Roman people had finally made at Petrarch's urging. The Anonimo romano reports that Cola received a fair hearing; his deeds were examined and his orthodoxy upheld.

But it was not Cola's ultimate orthodoxy or Innocent's personality alone that produced his exoneration. The situation in Rome was particularly troubling to the new pope and was one in which he thought Cola might prove especially useful.[2] The years following Rienzo's abdication had seen a succession of ineffectual senators drawn from the baronial clans, the Black Death, the Jubilee of 1350, the huge influx of pilgrims into the city, and the Romans' open hostility to legate Annibaldo de Ceccano. By the end of 1350 Rome had once again devolved into anarchy: roaming bands of armed retainers were now swelled by unemployed mercenaries; kidnappings, rapes, and murders multiplied inside and outside the walls.

On December 26, 1351, however, the Romans staged another bloodless revolution, and at St. John Lateran they chose Giovanni Cerroni, a *popolano,* as rector and head of government, later bringing him to the Capitoline and acclaiming him senator and captain. On May 22, 1352, Clement VI wrote from Avignon confirming Cerroni in his office for another six months and providing him with a stipend of 14,000 florins. But the new senator and captain did not long survive; and in September 1352, after the failure of a campaign against Janni di Vico, Cerroni resigned. He fled to the Abruzzi; but in a perverse variation of Cola's abdication he absconded with most of the public treasury. At just about that time, in October 1352, Petrarch wrote to the Romans, urging them to act on behalf of Cola di Rienzo; and it was at that point that they apparently did intervene for the former tribune.

Soon after Pope Clement's death, however, disorder broke out again. Without the approval of the new pope, two barons seized the senatorship: Bertoldo Orsini and Stefaniello Colonna, the grandson of Stefano il Vecchio. Bertoldo and Stefaniello claimed to have been "elected to the *regimen* of the City by the Roman people, at the pleasure of our Lord Pope, by the decree and authority of the Sacred Senate." On February 16, 1353, on a Saturday in Lent, according to the Anonimo romano, at the height of a famine that was then affecting all of Italy, "a call suddenly arose in the market of Rome" on the Capitoline just outside the Senators' Palace. "The people! The people!" the cry rang across the hill. A huge crowd now gathered and began stoning and pillaging the palace, making off with whatever they could find, especially the barons' horses. At the sound of the tumult Bertoldo Orsini, now a middle-aged man, armed himself and mounted his horse, charging down the palace ramp. But the hail of stones and the press of the crowd forced him off his horse. There at the palace, below the image of Our Lady, he was stoned to death by the angry crowd, "throwing rocks on his head as on St. Stephen." Since he had seized power without papal approval, as the Anonimo romano recounts, "the count passed from this life excommunicated. He did not say a single word. He was left there dead, and everyone went home." But his colleague Stefaniello, still a youth, took another tack. The Colonna baron slid down a rope from the upper floor of the palace and slinked out a postern gate disguised as a workman. He quickly fled the city for his fortress at Palestrina. The Anonimo romano's explanation for the Romans' action was brutally simple. It was well known that the senators had been cornering the market on grain and shipping it *out* of Rome for their own profit. "Hungry people do not know how to fear; they do not wait for someone to say, 'Do this.' This is a fact about famine that has toppled many powerful men." He concludes the episode: "Behold a marvel! Once it was known that the senator had been stoned to death, the famine suddenly ceased throughout the country, and the price of grain became reasonable" (AR, XXVI, ll. 52–54, Porta, 221–22).

But no sooner had the pair been toppled than they were replaced by close relatives: Giovanni Orsini and Pietro Sciarra Colonna, who took office in March 1353. Finally on September 14, 1353, the people again overthrew the senators and elected Francesco Baroncelli, another *popolano,* as "second tribune and august consul." Baroncelli had been among Cola's earliest supporters and had been part of the delegation to Florence in July 1347. Before expelling them from the city, however, the Romans dragged Orsini and Colonna before Baroncelli's house in an act of public humiliation. All this seems to have been set in motion by the news of Cola's impending release. As the tribune told Archbishop Ernst of Prague, he had already written to the Romans promising to return before September 14, 1350, and he had told them to elect Baroncelli if he could not keep his pledge. Baroncelli was a talented orator and respected citizen of the *buono stato* and soon began following Cola di Rienzo in more than just title, reaching out to Rome's neighbors, attempting to form a renewed alliance. Several letters survive between Baroncelli and Florence. But the pope could not have known of this election when on September 15, 1353, he wrote to Hugo Harpaion, the apostolic internuncio in Rome:

After carefully seeking a remedy for this evil [of Rome's decline], we have caused our beloved son, the noble Cola di Rienzo, a Roman knight, to be absolved from all the penalties and the judgments by which he had been overwhelmed; and, if God grant it, we shall quickly send him as a free man to the City, hoping that he may have gained understanding from his troubles; that, having utterly renounced the unjust and perverse endeavors of the malicious, he will sanely oppose his former fantastic innovations, drawing on his own activity and shrewdness, which is indeed great, and also on that of the inhabitants and of the many nobles of the said City who desire to live a quiet life and to enhance the general welfare; hoping, finally, that, with the assistance and the favor of God, he will resist the absorbing greed and the lawless, injurious desires of certain leaders. (CRCR, 168–69; Theiner 257, 2:255–56; BBCR 2.4:172–74)

The next day Innocent wrote to the Roman people to announce his decision to free Cola and send him to Rome as its newly appointed senator to "curb [the barons'] criminal appetite with the bit of justice and so that, having stifled all hatred and rancor, he will, with the favor of God and with our aid, cause you and your compatriots to enjoy the prayed-for quiet and peace." Innocent's references to Cola as "knight" thus swept away all the charges and suspicions of heresy associated with his dubbing, coronation, and ceremonial bath in Constantine's fountain. Cola's arguments to Clement in his letter of October 11, 1347, thus were found to be sound doctrine and even sounder politics for both the ex-tribune and the new pope.[3]

And so Cola di Rienzo emerged from the Trouillas Tower a free man, even if, as Innocent told the Romans, "weakened by the inconveniences of his prison chamber—which, however, was quite respectable and within the walls of the palace." On September 24, 1353, Pope Innocent granted him 200 florins in traveling expenses to return to Italy and catch up with the new legate for the Papal States, Cardinal Gil Albornoz, who had already arrived in Italy to pave the way for the pope's return to Rome.[4]

After Cola di Rienzo no other name so dominates the history of Rome and central Italy in the mid–fourteenth century as that of the great cardinal-soldier. Called Gilio Conchese di Spagna by the Anonimo romano, Albornoz was born Gil Alvarez Carillo Albornoz into a family of the lower nobility in Cuença in New Castile around 1290. Gil entered holy orders and probably studied canon law at the University of Toulouse, where he may well have been a student of Étienne Aubert, the future Innocent VI. The young man's talent and drive were apparent immediately, and by 1335 Albornoz was serving as a member of the royal council at the court of King Alfonso XI of Castile. By 1338 he had been named archbishop of Toledo, royal councilor, primate of all Spain, and papal legate. As such Albornoz participated actively in the later phases of the Spanish Reconquista, crusading to eliminate the remaining Muslim states to the southern borders of Castile. He played a major role in the battles of Tarifa and Rio Salado in 1340, at Algeciras in 1344, and at Gibraltar in 1349–50.

Albornoz also maintained a vital place in the diplomatic and legal affairs of the kingdom. He acted as royal ambassador to France and Avignon in 1345; and in 1348, at the command of the king, he drew up the Constitutions of Alcala, a new code of law that set out to standardize and reform the diverse laws, customs, and privileges of the many towns of Castile and to unify their older codes with the new regulations governing the recently conquered Muslim lands. It was an enormous undertaking, combining a keen knowledge of law with a sense of equity and justice in weighing so many diverse traditions and historically determined local laws and customs. Albornoz's accomplishment was a milestone of medieval legislation.

In 1350, however, with the succession to the throne of Pedro the Cruel, Albornoz's relations with the crown cooled. In that year he resigned his post as archbishop of Toledo and primate, left Castile, and moved to Avignon. Over the years many members of his family also withdrew from royal service to follow him. On December 15, 1350, Clement VI named Albornoz cardinal-priest of San Clemente, and from that time on the Spaniard became a major force within the College of Cardinals. With Clement's death Innocent VI named Albornoz grand penitentiary. But the new pope soon realized that the Spaniard would be the ideal candidate to carry out his plans for the reconquest of the Papal States. On June 30, 1353, Innocent named Albornoz his legate plenipotentiary for all of Italy, excluding the Regno of Naples and Sicily, and his vicar-general for the Papal States.

The cardinal-legate's mission was to be as much spiritual as temporal; but unlike his predecessors as papal vicars in the lands of St. Peter, Albornoz was to bring to bear on the anarchy of the papal lands his long years of experience as both military commander and master of bureaucracy and legislation. In so doing he was ideally suited to use the combination of diplomacy, physical force, excommunication, forgiveness, reconciliation, and legislation needed to destroy the many petty tyrants of the Romagna and the Marches, to win over the struggling and divided communes, to gain the loyalty of barons and officials, and to hunt down and bring to justice brigands, outlaws, and heretics.

Albornoz left Avignon with his entourage, including many of his faithful family lieutenants, on August 13, 1353. His mission took him east through Provence and across the Alps and the Lombard plain, where he arrived at Milan on September 14. After consulting with its archbishop, Giovanni Visconti, one of Italy's most feared tyrants, Albornoz then made his way south via Florence, Siena, and Perugia. After assembling a small army made up of troops from allied Guelph cities, his own retainers, and local mercenaries, he entered the Papal States on November 20, 1353, and soon made his headquarters at Montefiascone, the capital of the rector of the Patrimony. The only towns he then held were Montefiascone, Aquapendente, and Bolsena, all on the extreme northern fringe of the Patrimony. All the others remained in the hands of Janni di Vico. Cola's attempt to destroy the prefect of the city had failed largely because of Clement VI's intervention, and Janni was now prefect of Viterbo and lord of Terni, Amelia, Narni, Norchia, Orvieto, Marta, and Canino in the Patrimony and by then once again of Tarquinia, Vetralla, Tuscania, and the Rocca di Respampani. He also controlled Civitavecchia, Rieti, Todi, Marsicano, Ficulle, and Cetona and was in the process of absorbing Perugia. It was reported that di Vico had eyes on Rome itself and that—if he took the city—he would soon declare himself king over central Italy.

The Anonimo romano records that the legate could well have declared a crusade against the prefect; but the history of papal crusades against Ghibellines and other enemies in Italy had so turned the Italians against the notion of the holy war that Albornoz decided to pursue the more expedient strategy of forming a military alliance with the League of Tuscany. In this he was repeating the strategy Rienzo had pursued in 1347. The League was now a formidable force; and it had already proven its worth by thwarting the advance of the Great Company of mercenaries through central Italy. Now, therefore, Albornoz was able to draw troops, supplies, and funding from Florence, Siena, and Perugia. True again to Cola's first strategy, they were soon joined by the Roman militia itself, dispatched by Francesco Baroncelli, who was reviving Cola's foreign policy and sending diplomatic feelers to Florence and other cities.

Cola left Avignon sometime after September 24, 1353, and sped south to catch up with Albornoz.[5] The journey must have been arduous: the tribune had spent the last year in prison, well fed but inactive and confined. And haste was needed to cross the hills of Provence and then the high Alps. He traced Albornoz's own quick route and probably caught up with the papal army at Montefiascone in early November. There plans were already in the works for the reconquest of the Patrimony, and Janni di Vico was to be the legate's first target.

As in 1347, so in 1353: Albornoz's strategy, like Cola's, would be to divide di Vico's territories by securing the route south from Tuscany toward Rome. Tuscania, Vetralla, and the territory in between, including the Rocca di Respampani, were to be the first cockpit. But Cardinal Albornoz had a weapon that Cola could not wield. On September 15, 1353, In-

nocent VI had published Clement VI's condemnation and excommunication of Janni di Vico, and on December 17 Albornoz declared him a contumacious enemy of the church. The way was clear to strip him of his lands,
strongholds, titles, and rights. Tuscania was the first city to fall, in March
1354, in large part through Rienzo's widely reported military exploits.
Then, in the late spring of 1354, Viterbo submitted, again largely through
the work of the Roman militia and of Rienzo, whose presence back in
Italy so close to Rome was now the great topic of hope and conversation.
Cola had already energized the Romans:

Not only in the host, but also in Montefiascone, he had so many invitations from
the Romans that it is amazing to tell. Every Roman bowed down to him. Visitors pressed him. A great line of *popolani* stretched out behind him. Everyone was
astonished, even the legate, who began to understand the requests of the citizens
of Rome. They all considered Cola a marvel. It seemed amazing to them that he
had emerged unharmed from the hands of so many powerful men. In the devastation of Viterbo, as was narrated above, the Romans were there. When the host
returned, a great party of Romans gathered to see Cola di Rienzo; *popolani,* with
great tongues and hearts, greater offers, little follow-through. They would say,
"Return to your Rome. Cure it of its great infirmity. Be its lord. We will give you
aid, favor, and strength. Have no doubts. You were never so missed or loved as
you are now." This puff the Roman *popolani* poured on him; they didn't provide
him with a penny. (AR, XXVII, ll. 111–29, Porta, 240–41)

Nor, it seems, did Cardinal Albornoz. Innocent had written to his legate
instructing him to name Cola senator and to support his reentry into
Rome to replace Francesco Baroncelli, who had recently fulfilled his term;
but Albornoz decided to prevent Cola from moving beyond Perugia and
appointed instead Guido Giordano de' Patrizi dell'Isola, a member of an
old baronial family whom Cola had appointed podesta for Arezzo in 1347.
The legate's choice may shed some light on his motives, for it seems
Rome's barons were already wary of Cola's return and were probably lobbying the legate to prevent, or at least delay, Cola's mission. Albornoz
had still been in Avignon when Cola had been led to the Trouillas Tower
a suspected heretic. The cardinal had studied canon law at the University
of Toulouse, and he had devoted himself to the never-ending crusade
against the infidel. There were many reasons for Albornoz to dislike and
distrust this strange Roman. Albornoz therefore decided to maintain Cola
in his entourage, and he provided him with a salary large enough for him
to live comfortably and honorably as a knight, but not enough for him to
further his plans or the pope's mission.

In the meantime, the cardinal's war of conquest was going well. By

April 1354 Albornoz had retaken Corneto. Orvieto, besieged by the cardinal's army, finally surrendered on June 9, and on June 24 its people agreed to submit to papal overlordship for the duration of Innocent's lifetime, even though the city was not even officially part of papal possessions. On June 5, 1354, Janni di Vico had formally submitted to the papal legate. As part of his agreement with the rebellious prefect, Albornoz followed the precedent already set by Rienzo: upon his complete submission, di Vico was first allowed to live as a free citizen of Viterbo, rather than its lord and tyrant; he was paid 16,000 florins to surrender Vetralla to the papacy. But word of the cardinal's lenient terms reached Avignon, and Pope Innocent shot off an angry letter to Albornoz expressing his outrage that so vile a man as Janni di Vico should have been rewarded for his resistance. The legate, already uncomfortable with di Vico's presence in Viterbo, rescinded the original agreement, and in compensation for his loss of Viterban citizenship, di Vico was again made lord of Corneto for twelve years. Albornoz was also forced to return Vetralla to the prefect, whose influence over the area would remain in force despite his official deposition. To this day the arms of di Vico still appear upon the facade of Viterbo's Palazzo dei Priori, and his memory is still honored at Vetralla.

But the cardinal's policy of clemency toward his defeated enemies had its desired effect, as he plainly told the pope. In the wake of di Vico's submission, dozens of petty tyrants from all over the Patrimony came flocking to make a similar arrangement with the legate. Spello, Amelia, and Gubbio had submitted to him by July; Narni by October; and Rieti by November. By the end of the year, when the duchy of Spoleto agreed to the cardinal's terms, the church was in effective control of all the lands of St. Peter from the sea at Corneto to the upper reaches of Umbria. By 1355 Albornoz was moving against the lords of the March of Ancona; and by 1357 he had reconquered the Romagna. In December 1356 Albornoz was named cardinal-bishop of Sta. Sabina; and on April 27, 1357, at the parliament that he had summoned at Fano in the March of Ancona, Albornoz issued a new code of laws that would apply without exception to all the lands of the church in Italy. These "Ordinances," or Egidian Constitutions, were to become the basis of the new papal monarchy of the Renaissance and would survive even the revision of the Napoleonic era as the basic laws of the Papal States until their dissolution in 1870.

The impact of Cola and his Roman government and the fear of a recurrence of other regimes, such as that of Janni di Vico or of the lords of the Romagna, are apparent in Albornoz's legislation. Many elements that

Cola had pursued—the prohibition of the party labels "Guelph" and "Ghibelline," for example—demonstrate that these were policies either that Cola was consciously pursuing on behalf of the papacy or that were generally viewed as just and right. But then there are the ordinances that prevented a recurrence of a government like Cola's: a ban on further elections and assemblies, on the rise of local political favorites, on the creation or usurpation of titles, on any subjects of the popes electing or inviting in the emperor or any other king or power to rival the papacy. Despite his temporary recall to Avignon at the connivance of Archbishop Visconti of Milan, who feared losing his influence on the Romagna, Albornoz was to remain the lord of the Papal States until 1367. On August 23 of that year Gil Albornoz died at Buonriposo, just a few miles outside Viterbo. There the cardinal was waiting for the final journey of Pope Urban V, who had recently entered Viterbo from Avignon and was hesitating to make the final journey to Rome.

Albornoz had triumphed. But at what cost? The "Reformer and Conservator of the Peace and Pacificator General in the Patrimony of St. Peter" brought nearly two decades of constant war to central Italy, pitched battles and sieges, thousands killed and wounded, and the costly and onerous construction of the *rocche* that today still dominate so many towns of central Italy from Assisi to Subiaco. Albornoz brought the spirit of the Reconquista to Italy; and even after he had restored territories and cities to the papacy, he retained the forms of government of the tyrants he toppled and nullified many of the more democratic reforms of the remaining free communes. The wars cost the church an enormous amount in coin as well. Between August 1353 and August 1357, for the first stage of his reconquest, Albornoz obtained 560,000 florins from the papal treasury. By the late 1350s his expenses amounted to about 40,000 florins a month, largely for the recruitment and maintenance of soldiers. In 1354 the cardinal employed 30 "banners" with 600 horsemen, in 1355 the number had risen to 50 banners with 1,000 horse, and the following year to 100 banners with 2,000 horse. While negligible compared with the expenses of the great new kingdoms of Christendom now engaged in the Hundred Years' War—Edward III had spent £300,000 sterling or about 2 million florins for his Flemish campaigns of 1338–39 alone—the amount was staggering for any one of Italy's city-states, as it was for the church.

Even more staggering, however, was the impact of the most important element of military strategy in the mid–fourteenth century—in Italy and in France—the rise of the mercenary Great Companies and the men who led them, the condottieri.[6] The word itself derives from the Italian *condotta,* or contract, for the men who arranged and led the hiring of the great bands of mercenaries were first and foremost entrepreneurs, and their special service was the rental of armies.

The use of mercenaries had ancient roots; and in Italy the long-standing and common practice of city-states hiring foreign podestas to ensure civil justice and administration soon carried over into the military sphere. By the fourteenth century, as the old urban militias found their tactics and weaponry outmoded, and while urban and commercial concerns made many citizens unwilling to serve, the communes turned more and more to professional soldiers to fill their defense needs, appointing captains-general to act as their military podesta. The professional soldiers who would hire out themselves and their retinues thus came to be known as contract soldiers, or condottieri.

A *condotta* with a city or prince would stipulate every aspect of their arrangement: the types of campaign required—defensive or offensive (more expensive)—the types of troops, their mix, their weapons, and their terms of service and pay. Because most soldiers were professionals, their engagements, at least among themselves, tended to minimize bloodletting and great acts of heroism. Surrender and ransom were frequent occurrences and a fight to the death a rarity—if the condottieri could help it. But such rules did not exclude great pitched battles and the constant atrocities committed by these armed bands against defenseless rural populations and conquered cities.

The most famous of the mercenary bands of the early fourteenth century was the Great Company first led by Duke Werner of Ürslingen, near Rottweil in the Black Forest. Cola's "Guarnerio," Werner flew on his emblem the words "I am Duke Werner, leader of the Great Company, the enemy of God, of pity, and of mercy." The Great Company first appeared in Tuscany in 1342, working for Pisa in its war against Florence. By that time the troop consisted of three thousand *barbute,* the Italian name for the soldiers helmeted and heavily armed in the German style.

From the start the Great Company was organized, financed, governed, and judged like a traveling city-state. It dealt with the Italian city-states as equals, sending ambassadors, negotiators, procurers, and orators to settle alliances, seal contracts, and extract favorable terms. Its constituent bands were constantly accompanied by their followers: by representatives of major Italian banking houses, who accepted their deposits of payments and booty and issued interest; by merchants who set up traveling markets to sell its plundered movables; and by a host of women: prostitutes, kidnapped nuns and young women—as Cola had seen with his own eyes.

By the end of 1342 Werner and his company began the first of their great treks through central Italy, extorting enormous protection payments from various city-states in Tuscany and the Romagna. Never strong or well equipped enough with siege machinery to take or starve a walled city, they specialized in burning, pillaging, and ravaging isolated villages, convents, and monasteries, stripping fields and orchards and carrying off harvests and women, leaving destruction and starvation in their path. For a while the company found work with Astorge de Durfort, Pope Clement's relative and papal rector in the Romagna, providing him with 1,150 horse and 400 foot; but it was not until the invasion of the kingdom of Naples by Lewis of Hungary that the Great Company really came into its own.

In 1347 Lewis hired Werner and his band for the invasion of the Regno. There they unleashed the full fury of their superior arms and tactics on Giovanna's forces and against the defenseless countryside. They were soon joined by many of Lewis's Hungarian troops: light cavalry armed with bows and throwing lances who relied on swift maneuver rather than the full impact of a heavy cavalry charge. Among the new contingents were two leaders who would become famous throughout Italy: Conrad of Landau and Fra Morreale. Together the three contingents formed the largest mercenary troop that had ever appeared in Italy. Sometime in late January or early February 1348, the Great Company entered the Papal States and began its march on Rome. Along the way it stopped at Anagni. But the people of the commune decided to resist, executing Werner's "legates" as common criminals. In reprisal Werner stormed the papal city, set it to the torch, and massacred its civilian population. The rest of the Roman district fared better as the militia of Rome foiled his surprise attack on the city. By late February Werner had decided to move against the smaller towns of southern Tuscany, but as Agnolo di Tura del Graso reports, Florence, Siena, Perugia, and Arezzo formed a league with the pope's cooperation and mounted three thousand cavalry to counter him. This League of Tuscany was able to block his path, and Werner eventually passed back into the Regno.

By 1349 the Great Company was no longer in Lewis's employ; but it remained as busy as ever and in that year defeated Giovanna's army at Meleto, collecting booty and ransoms from the victory reportedly worth 500,000 florins. It was the ransom of a kingdom, and Werner decided that he had done about all he could in the Regno. The leaders therefore split their forces, Werner heading for central and northern Italy, and Conrad and Morreale turning back south. By 1351 King Lewis had made peace with Queen Giovanna, and Werner finally decided that business opportunities in Italy were drying up. He therefore retired back to his native Swabia and died in his bed, a wealthy and respected man, in 1354.

Werner's place in the Great Company was quickly taken by his former companion, Fra Morreale. Montreal d'Albarno had been a Knight Hospitaller in Provence until he was ejected from the order for reasons unknown. He soon found his way to Italy. After being elected by the members of the company, he took over Werner's contracts with King Lewis and in partnership with Conrad of Landau made his headquarters at Aversa, about thirteen kilometers northwest of Naples. When Giovanna finally managed to expel the company from the Regno, they traveled north into the Papal States. By that time their numbers had grown to about ten thousand soldiers: seven thousand men-at-arms and about three thousand crossbowmen and other contingents, as well as about 20,000 camp followers, a total larger than the population of Rome at the time. While the company theoretically boasted 234 leaders whose names and seals had to be affixed to their various *condotte*, Morreale was the company's undisputed commander. According to the Anonimo romano, Morreale had made a career of devastation: "He burned and robbed the towns, he held the men for ransom and carried off the women—those who were attractive." By 1353 Morreale and the Great Company were circling central Italy and extorting money from its great cities: 16,000 florins from Pisa, 16,000 from Siena, 28,000 from Florence (25,000 for Morreale and 3,000 for his constables), and 50,000 from Rimini. Along the way Morreale stopped to invest 60,000 florins of the proceeds with his Venetian bankers; and this came nowhere close to exhausting the war chest that the company kept with it under the care of its treasurers. Its accountants could also expect enormous receivables from the papacy for the company's role in aiding Cardinal Albornoz in the reconquest of the Papal States and from its alliance with the league formed by Padua, Ferrara, and Mantua against Giovanni Visconti, archbishop of Milan.

And so in the spring of 1354, amid the pleas of the Romans for him to revive his *buono stato,* and after Cardinal Albornoz had refused his and the pope's requests for funding for the expedition, Rienzo launched yet another plan to return to Rome.[7] Cola had been spending much time in Perugia, visiting the city from his lodging with the cardinal's army in Montefiascone. He had attempted several times to persuade Perugia's city council to approve funding for his expedition. On September 16, 1353, Innocent VI had written to the council of Perugia, acknowledging their efforts on behalf of Cola's liberation and recommending him as the city's podesta to end its long and bloody factional strife. According to the Anonimo romano, however, "from the commune of Perugia Cola could not get a penny of Cortona." But on March 26, 1354, Innocent VI again wrote to the Perugians, agreeing with their recommendation that Cola be restored to power in Rome. On the same day the pope wrote Albornoz, informing him of this correspondence and ordering the legate to see to Cola's restoration. The way was now clear for the former tribune, now senator, to reclaim his place. But he still lacked the means.

Cola soon heard that two of Fra Morreale's brothers, both Provençals, a doctor of laws named Messer Arimbaldo de Narba and a knight of Narbonne named Brettone, were staying at an inn in Perugia. Morreale had set them up there to watch over the Great Company's deposits with the city's merchant bankers. Rienzo found them at their lodgings and invited them to dinner. Soon he was recounting his visions of ancient Roman glory and Old Testament heroes, quoting his Livy and his Bible. In the inn's common room the taverner's son spellbound everyone with his tales. As the spring evenings passed and Cola wove his magic web of word and image, Messer Arimbaldo fell irretrievably under the spell of Rome. "As the wine warmed, his soul would climb on high. The dreamer pleased the dreamer," the Anonimo romano remarks. Soon Arimbaldo and Cola were inseparable. The mercenary never left the tribune's side, walking with him, sharing his meals, sharing his bed. "They planned to do great deeds, to raise up Rome and return it to its pristine glory." But there was one catch, Cola confided to his new companions, and that was money. "Without soldiers it could not be done." Three thousand florins would do the trick, but where to find it? Without hesitation Arimbaldo pledged not 3,000 but 4,000 florins from the Great Company's treasury in Perugia. In return Cola promised to make the doctor of laws a Roman citizen and a great, honored captain (AR, XXVII, ll. 174–98, Porta, 242–43).

But before the transaction was completed, Arimbaldo decided to write to Morreale to inform him of his decision; and here—if we can believe that the Anonimo romano actually saw the correspondence—he revealed his true mercenary's heart:

Honored brother.

I've won more in one day than you have in your whole lifetime. I've just bought the lordship of Rome, which is promised to me by Messer Nicola de Rienzi, knight, tribune, who is visited [here] by the Romans and summoned by the people.

I believe that the plan will not fail. I am sure that with the help of your talent my *stato* will not fall through. We need money to prime the pump. Whenever it pleases you, brother, I'll take four thousand florins from our account and go to Rome with a powerful army. (AR, XXVII, 204–14, Porta, 243–44)

If there were any doubt that Arimbaldo saw before him the opportunity that had been denied the Great Company all these years—to actually seize the papal capital and to take its Christian treasures for ransom, with Cola di Rienzo himself as the company's front man—Morreale's response quickly dispelled it:

I've thought over and over about the job you're planning. What you're planning to carry off is a big, important piece of work. In my heart I can't come to think you'll carry it off. My mind won't get a grip on it. My good sense tells me no. But go ahead: do it, and do it well. First of all watch that the 4000 florins aren't lost. If you run into anything funny, write me. I'll come with help—with 1000, 2000 men—as many as you need; and I'll do some magnificent things. Don't have any doubts. You and your brother love and honor one another. Don't make a peep about this. (AR, XXVII, ll. 214–28, Porta, 244)

Cola realized that he was playing a dangerous game: he had already written to the archbishop of Prague in his *True Little Book* of August 15, 1350, condemning the rapacity of this very Great Company; but he had been made immobile, a glittering trophy of the cardinal-legate from Spain, and now he intended to spring yet another trap. "When Messer Arimbaldo received this letter, he was very happy," the Anonimo romano relates. "He and the tribune prepared themselves for the journey."

In Perugia, now again a papal possession, were 250 mercenaries recently released from service by the Malatesta of Rimini, sworn enemies of the popes. But they were good soldiers looking for work; and so negotiations between Cola and the band began while open debate continued among the Germans. They were aware of the dangers: "the Romans are bad people, proud and arrogant," one said; they are vile and impoverished, another added; the barons hate Cola and will oppose his government, a third warned. But in the end the band decided to sign on with Cola and Arimbaldo, at least until they had secured the rule of Rome. "Germans, when they first come down from Germany, are simple, pure and guileless. After they have worked among the Italians, they become astute masters: vicious and skilled in every evil." Finally Cola had an audience with the cardinal-legate and received Albornoz's approval and his appointment as senator. He now had funding and a band of knights on whom he could rely; and to these he added a company of Perugians, "good men," and about one hundred Tuscan infantry as personal retainers. The new senator assumed that this time his seizure of power would not be peaceful, and he was prepared for resistance.

One thing was certain about the Rome that now awaited its restored tribune. During the seven years of Cola's absence the high purpose and concord that he had achieved during his rule had all but disappeared. Cola had originally risen to power after decades of baronial civil war, and the flight of the papacy from its own see had left the city bereft of unity, peace, and prosperity. The failure of this leadership—both temporal and spiritual—had, however, inspired the newly emerging classes of Roman merchants, businessmen, and intellectuals to look elsewhere for models of civil life and for leaders who could implement their dreams of reform and revival. Cola's appearance on the scene fit the man perfectly with the time: he was no isolated hero but a leader who emerged out of a strong and self-conscious movement that thrust him forward as spokesman and formulator of a new paradigm of political life—one that we would later associate with civic humanism and Renaissance concepts of reform and rebirth. This reform movement—of the Thirteen Good Men, of the *uomini discreti*, of the *buono stato*—had already formed the kernel of that same political synthesis that Cola would so eloquently embody: the reform of the civil society in the *buon governo*, the revival of Roman imperial greatness, and the expectation of the new apocalyptic age of justice, peace, and enlightenment. These found their highest expression in the vivid symbolic complex of the Jubilee of 1350. Here in one grand world event the pope would return to his see; the emperor would come to Rome and Italy to bring peace and unity to all the assembled peoples of Christendom; the city of Rome itself would be restored to peace, justice, and prosperity. A new age would begin.

But the actual events of Cola's rise and then the collapse of the *buono stato* shattered these hopes. And they shattered them not so much because one leader had risen and fallen but because of the form of his fall: at the hands of the pope in alliance with the barons. Cola's excommunication, the threat of interdict upon the city, and looming cancellation of the Jubilee could not appear but a deliberate disregard for the hopes and lives of the people of Rome. The reaction of the Romans to the Legate Annibaldo de Ceccano is dramatic testimony to their bitter sense of betrayal. What followed in the wake of Cola's departure—earthquake, plague, famine, and further depopulation, coupled with the renewal of baronial corruption and civil strife—also bred a deep revulsion to any thought of rebuilding civil society with the players who were still on the board. Papacy, barons, and legates now took their place among the meaningless display and titles of rule. Tribune, senator, rector, parliament were all seen as mockeries of their Roman past and masks for unbridled power and wealth.

But so, too, among Rome's ruling class: both those who opposed the *buono stato* and those who had joined in its defense. The barons were by now in the deep crisis of the fourteenth century: their base in the district of Rome quickly eroding as depopulation and economic collapse accompanied plague and famine, and as the new merchant classes of *bovattieri* found their opportunity to move capital earned through commerce and trade into the countryside, gobbling up vast new estates from the ruined fortunes of the barons and their vassals. Though fought with as much venom as before, civil war only hastened the collapse of old wealth and power both in the countryside and in the city; while the refuse of Europe's disastrous new wars—the mercenary companies—had by now added both terror and a new level of viciousness to war that gave even Rome's barons pause.

Cola's rise and fall had left the great baronial families of Rome with nothing but the graves of their fathers, brothers, and cousins; and their new papal titles gave them little but the hatred of the people and the indifference of the pope in far-off Avignon. If Stefano il Vecchio's sense of patriotic duty had masked his own dynastic ambition and interests, it still did so within the context of some public service; but even the sacrifices of a Stefano il Vecchio (d. 1349) had been mocked and discarded by the events of the decade. Close upon the horizon now, in Perugia, in Montefiascone, and in Viterbo, throughout the district of Rome and the Papal States, Cardinal Albornoz was already demonstrating how empty the barons' titles of rectors, senators, and podesta were: convenient flatteries while the popes lacked the power and wealth to do anything about them. But now, with papal money and soldiers, they were merely obstacles to a new papal monarchy, and they would be crushed ruthlessly.

Roman society in the 1350s thus lived devoid of great myths and without a clear vision of civil society, unable to heal any of its divisions in order to formulate meaningful reform strategies, and thus also incapable of finding enduring leaders to embody its ideals. The return of the ex-tribune had been carefully planned by Cola and his remaining supporters for years, and it was enthusiastically embraced as rumor of his survival became a reality; but such enthusiasm had no deep roots among any broad segment of Roman society, which had learned in the intervening seven years to watch out only for itself and to mock the slogans and the pronouncements of politicians of whatever label: pope, archbishop, legate, baron, senator, or tribune. Tangible results—in new wealth and security, devoid of vision and ideology—were now the only viable currency in Rome as Cola di Rienzo began his triumphal procession from Perugia to the Porta Sant'Angelo.

Rienzo reached the city at Monte Mario, the northern pilgrim's first sight of Rome. Cola must have chosen the road especially for this: for no one was more conscious than he that he was now the long-traveling pilgrim, finally reaching the goal of his arduous journey. There at Monte Mario the Roman people came out to meet him, as they had greeted so many emperors and conquering heroes in centuries past, with an elaborate ceremony, "with branches of olive in their hands as a sign of victory and peace. The people welcomed him joyfully, as if he were Scipio Africanus. Triumphal arches were built. He entered the Porta Sant'Angelo" (AR, XXVII, ll. 293–98, Porta, 246). The date was August 1, 1354.

Cola's last public act in Rome had been to commission an apocalyptic painting in the Piazza Sant'Angelo in the winter of 1348 before going into his long exile. Near there today the via Cola di Rienzo begins on its way to cross the Tiber to end in the Piazza del Popolo. There at the gate Cola now summoned the Archangel Michael as his special protector. And then, just as symbolically, now "resurrected," Cola decided to reverse the route of his last procession in Rome, turning disgrace into new triumph by marching from St. Peter's to the Capitoline. The procession again recalled the glories of the *buono stato*, as gold and silver ornaments and new triumphal arches marked the route. According to the Anonimo romano, the welcome drew a huge crowd: "It seemed that all Rome was turned out in joy. Great was the people's happiness and favor" (ll. 298–303). Cola's choice of the date for his return, August 1, was not random either, for it recalled both his previous title, Tribunus Augustus, and the beginning of his last great triumph in Rome, the Roman Synod of 1347; and it came at the beginning of the month when Romans celebrated the dawning of the Christian age by commemorating Emperor Augustus's vision of the Christ child on the Aracoeli.

Just as his abdication had begun at the Capitoline with a speech to the people, so now Cola's triumphal return was to begin with a great oration. Just as King Nebuchadnezzar, toppled in his pride and humbled by God, had wandered in exile for seven years, so now Cola tells the people that he has been returned to office and has assumed the senatorship not out of any virtue of his own but through God's mercy and the voice of the pope. Just as Cola had himself been raised up, so now he intended to "raise up and reform the government of Rome." Cola's use of the story of Nebuchadnezzar was a brilliant allegory of exile and return; and for the Spiritual Franciscans and for any in the audience who knew the full story of Daniel 4, it was clear that the apocalyptic New Jerusalem had returned. Nebuchadnezzar, the king of Babylon, was subject to great and troubling dreams and visions. Of all his councilors, only the Jewish exile Daniel had the grace to interpret them correctly. The king once dreamt:

I saw a tree in the middle of the world; it was very tall. The tree grew taller and stronger, until it reached the sky and it could be seen from the very ends of the earth. Its foliage was beautiful, its fruit abundant, in it was food for all. For the wild animals it provided shade, the birds of heaven nested in its branches, all living creatures found their food in it. (Dan. 4:7–9)

But then, the king related, an angel passed overhead and shouted, "Cut the tree down, lop off its branches, strip off its leaves, throw away its fruit, . . . But leave the stump with its roots in the ground, bound with hoops of iron and bronze." The angel commanded that it be left to live like all the other beasts, subject to the rain and storms, losing its human heart, for seven years (vv. 10–13). Daniel easily interpreted the dream (vv. 16–24): the tree was Nebuchadnezzar himself; toppled from his throne by God's will, he would be "driven from human society." "You will make your home with the wild animals" for seven years; and, Daniel tells the king, "your kingdom will be kept for you until you come to understand that Heaven rules all."

Nebuchadnezzar "was drenched by the dew of heaven; his hair grew like an eagle's feathers and his nails became like a bird's talons" (v. 30). But after seven years Nebuchadnezzar was restored to his reason, his kingdom, and his glory. The image of the great king reduced to a wandering beast is a frightening one and would inspire one of William Blake's most vivid works. And so, too, the Romans must have been frightened by Cola's comparison to the king of Babylon as he stood there, himself strangely transformed by nearly seven years of exile and deprivation, bearded like some apocalyptic king of tapestries and paintings, and like the German mercenaries who now surrounded him.

It was all there once again: the revival of empire after a long decline, the apocalyptic expectation of the New Age. Cola himself declared that "he wanted every man to prepare himself for the *buono stato*" that was to come. He then kept the first of his promises: he appointed Messer Brettone and Arimbaldo de Narba his captains of war "and gave them the banner of Rome." Then, just as in times past, the Romans held a great festival on the Campidoglio in his honor. Now the great drama had begun, one that would be played out just as the Anonimo romano intended to construct it, as a great passion play: "The Romans held a great festival for him, as the Jews did for Christ, when he entered Jerusalem riding on an ass [Matt. 21:1–11]. They honored him, spreading before him carpets and olive branches, singing, *Benedictus, qui venit*" (ll. 315–19).

But among the onlookers at Cola's triumph, even as he entered the city, his enemies were already plotting his destruction. "The barons were all watching carefully to see what would happen." And the first indication—at least in the Anonimo romano's reconstruction of the drama—was not long in coming. When the festival on the Campidoglio was over, all the Romans left the scene and returned home. "They left him alone with his disciples in the piazza; there was no one who offered him a little dinner." Just so Jesus had left the crowds and companions and walked back to Bethany to spend the night (Matt. 21:17).

As soon as the festival was over, Rome returned to normal, and Cola again took up the serious business of government. The very next day he met with ambassadors from the district of Rome and set out his policies, sending out envoys and ambassadors to the surrounding towns and cities, "describing his fortunate return." One of these letters survives. On August 5, 1354, Cola addressed the government and the people of Florence. The Lord has saved him from the shadows and brought him into the light, pulled him from the perils of the raging sea and restored him to his former glories. For now Cola realizes that it is the Lord "who wounds and heals, who kills and brings back to life, who leads into hell and back again." Cola next expresses his reverence for the sacrosanct Mother Church, "our most holy Lord Pope," "the most reverend lord legate," and the Sacred College of Cardinals in "word, work, heart and soul."

Rienzo again pledges himself and his government *(regimen)* to bring back for Rome's people and its pilgrims "good days and the awaited time of justice, liberty and peace." Cola realizes that there are some who oppose him, but he promises not to "render evil for evil and to observe justice for all with an evenly balanced scale, so that our judgments may always come forth from God's countenance [Ps. 16:2] with justice and not neglect equity and clemency." Cola informs the Florentines of this joyful news, since he knows them to be "faithful friends of the Church and of us and most fervent lovers of our honor and of the peaceful condition *[status]* of the Roman republic." The letter was sealed on the Capitoline with Cola's own privy seal. On August 22, about as quickly as the news could reach Florence, the city fathers absorb and interpret the news, and a proper diplomatic letter dispatched, the Florentines replied to "Lord Nicola, illustrious Senator of the Mother City. . . . Magnificent and most beloved friend." The letter is a brief but very warm congratulations for Cola's miraculous restoration and a fervent prayer that his fame and honor will now grow and that he may sweetly revive "the *status* of the City's ancient liberty and peace."

Word of Cola's restoration was also quick to reach Avignon. Rienzo dispatched his envoys as usual; and these reached the papal city in about two weeks at the earliest. Others within Rome had probably also sent messengers to Avignon and to Cardinal Albornoz in Montefiascone. The news was welcome to Pope Innocent, who after some deliberation acted to confirm Cola's assumption of power. On September 9 he wrote to Albornoz with some sound political advice designed to overcome the legate's opposition to Cola's appointment and to instruct him to extend Rienzo's senatorial term by six months: "[My decision], my son, is as sane as it appears. The opinion of many and the deliberation of certain of our brothers whom we have consulted praises it: that you confirm and extend the offices conferred by you on our beloved son, the man Nicholas di Rienzo, Roman knight" (Theiner 273, 2:267). This is necessary, Innocent reminds Albornoz, because people in Rome are already saying that the short term of Cola's appointment will mean that the barons will be more willing to defy him, and that Cola himself will be less willing to pursue justice forcefully—they realizing that his power will soon end, he fearing retribution once he again becomes a private citizen. Innocent advises Albornoz that the barons will weigh the fact that Rienzo rules by the will of the pope and of his legate. Cola himself realizes this and will therefore become far more moderate, so that "in our times the City may rejoice in peace, may have joy in concord, and may have the benefit of liberty."

Two days later, Innocent wrote to Rienzo from Villeneuve, affirming Cola's title of knight and adding that of senator. Innocent's letter, an exhortation to just and moderate rule, is replete with references to Cola's past titles. Without explicitly saying so—but specifically telling Cola to "piece together for yourself and with your own eyes all this and many other things out of the little that we write"—Innocent signals Rienzo that he is legitimizing his previous actions and titles. He enumerates these: *clemens et severus,* the protector of orphans, the defender of the weak and the poor. Innocent hopes that Cola will win the good regard of all the groups enumerated by Jesus in the Sermon on the Mount: the just, those suffering, the destitute, the humble, and the gentle.

Rienzo had obtained what he had been campaigning for since his abdication: the authority and the power to return to Rome to accomplish
his mission. But now his power came not from the emperor, from whom
he had pressed for it for so long and at such great risk, but from the papacy itself, again confirming what Cola had worked so hard to deny: that
it was the pope who was Rome's actual temporal lord, and not the Roman people or the emperor. In exchanging the title of tribune for that of
senator, Cola adopted both the name that he had taught the Romans to
hate so deeply and the position of the ancient elite against that of the
popular leader. Yet Cola's career in Rome had, after all, started with a papal commission, and he had accepted it willingly and had fully cooperated
with Pope Clement's plan. Now he had returned to the height of power,
once again as a papal lieutenant, and at the urging of the people of Rome
themselves. Did it really matter whether he bore the title of tribune or
senator, if the reformation and renewal of the city were to be his goals?
It was clear that the Roman people knew who Cola was: they continually—
at least through the ears and mouth of the Anonimo romano—referred
to him as their "tribune," and Cola left off immediately where he had
begun, with great new hopes for the *buono stato*. Still, it was one thing to
rule on behalf of the pope but through the will of the assembled people,
and quite another to rule the people, however willing, as the pope's rector.

Despite the ambiguities of his new position, in early September 1354
Cola wrote to Emperor Charles IV. He praises imperial rule over Italy
and exhorts the emperor to make his long-promised journey to Rome to
receive his crown so that the Italian people, who have long lived blindly,
without the clear light of imperial glory, may now rejoice that Caesar has
shone forth like a true light to the whole city. "For your coming forth is
as the morning rising, fair as the moon, bright as the sun, terrible as an
army set in array" (Cant. 6:9). The emperor will bring to Rome the "tran-
quil and peaceful reformation of the world and especially the happy *status* of the City of Rome." The emperor's return will also put an end to the
"war, famine, plague and ruin" that have afflicted the city in his absence.
Cola's words recall the Four Horsemen of the Apocalypse; and if he could
summon up apocalyptic visions of destruction, so, too, could he call up
its imagery of the New Jerusalem. Just as he had urged Pope Clement
more than a decade ago, so now Cola exhorts Emperor Charles to come
to join his spouse, the city of Rome, the Holy Jerusalem, to end its bitter vexations and bring remedy and healing. The Romans are ready to obey
the emperor's commands, Cola writes, and to see the emperor and Holy
Mother Church once again joined in the bonds of union.

Reform, brightness, light, renewal: Rienzo's letter reverberates with all the themes that he and Charles had traded during the tribune's Prague years, in a language well known to each, the basic themes of the newly emerging concept of the Renaissance. It is the last genuine letter from Cola's pen that has survived. The tribune's mission to Prague in 1350 and his long years of lobbying for the emperor to return to Italy had paid off. By the early fall Charles would have received Cola's letter and the news that the tribune—now papal senator—had returned to Rome, just as he had promised, and was now preparing the way for Charles's long-delayed journey to the empire's true capital and his coronation. Charles decided immediately that the time was right. If he were to delay, it would be late fall; and the Alpine passes would already be filling with snow. The emperor's expedition set out on September 26, 1354, and reached Italy on October 13, with enough time to reach Rome and for Cola to complete all the preparations for this monumental event.

Meanwhile, much had to be accomplished in Rome, and the pattern of Rienzo's second reign soon began to match closely that of his first. Cola realized that he could not long stay in power bolstered only by the *cavalieri e masnadieri a soldo*—the mercenary horse and foot, as Villani put it—who had secured his return to the city in August. The Anonimo romano noted that Cola had been accompanied by "infantrymen on this side and that. It seemed clear that Cola wanted to rule by tyranny." Long removed from his fellow citizens and far too long among foreigners and military camps, Cola had mistakenly felt that his entry into Rome would be hard-won; and the triumphal entry that greeted him had probably taken even him by surprise. He therefore set out immediately to counteract the quickly growing sense that he had returned not a liberator but another tyrant. And the rumors were already spreading. Matteo Villani confirms that the barons opposed his new *tribunato* from the start.

According to the Anonimo romano, Cola therefore repeated the measures of his last tribunate: he summoned the barons to the Campidoglio to offer fealty to the revived *buono stato*. Again, this was a standard procedure in all of Italy's communes; but who actually came to swear obedience is uncertain. The Anonimo romano records only that former senator Stefaniello Colonna refused the oath and hastily retreated to his fortress at Palestrina.[8] Cola sent two ambassadors to enforce compliance. But when the knights Buccio de Giubileo and Janni Cafariello arrived there, the young Colonna had the Roman envoys seized, and he tossed one into a dark dungeon, pulling one of his teeth and fining him 400 florins.

Unlike his dead brother, uncles, and grandfather, Stefaniello wasted no time. Like most of Rome's barons, by the 1350s he had begun supplementing his own feudal retainers and tenants with mercenaries. Hungarian mounted archers from the Great Company may well have made up the majority of the contingents, for the Anonimo romano tells us that the very next day "he overran the fields of Rome with his archers and brigands; he led off all the cattle." It seems as if everyone in Rome sensed that events were quickly repeating themselves, like the overlapping visions of the Apocalypse. As soon as word reached Rome, Cola's response came just as swiftly. Without any assembly of the people or muster of militia, he took up the chase. "The tribune rode out of the City with a few servants; he passed through the gate alone. The soldiers followed him, some armed, some not, as time permitted." They raced through the Porta Maggiore and up the via Prenestina directly to Palestrina, for Cola had seen enough of the new mercenary tactics to understand the value of speed and surprise. But the Romans' search through the forests and wastelands of the high country around Palestrina was in vain: the Colonna forces had now adopted brigand tactics and were hiding with their loot "in the wood called Pantano," a hamlet about twenty-two kilometers outside Rome, just south of the via Prenestina and the ruins of ancient Gabii. During the night they evaded the Roman search party and made their way upland to Palestrina.

That evening Cola and his troops reached Tivoli, where the senator set up his temporary headquarters and began planning the campaign against the Colonna, sending word to Rome and to the cities of its district subject to its summons. There he once again set out his standards: the azure banner with the apocalyptic seven silver stars and golden sun, along with the arms of Rome: the SPQR. Soon the regular Roman militia arrived, "with many banners, bagpipes, and trumpets," along with the German mercenaries under their commanders Brettone and Arimbaldo. They were quickly supplemented by contingents from Velletri, in the Campagna just south and east of the Colli Albani, from the communes of Campagna and the Montagna northeast of Rome, and by the feudal levies of the abbey of Farfa, one of the largest landholders in Rome and its district.

But trouble arrived early as well. Writing years after the event, the Anonimo romano attempted to cast a gloomy spell over the preparations: "A hard fact: [Cola's] standard wasn't as shining bright as it was before; it stood there sad, flaccid; it did not wave proudly in the wind" (AR, XXVII, ll. 395–96, Porta, 249). Almost as soon as they arrived, the German mercenaries and their constables demanded money for their service.

After delaying as long as he could, Cola realized that he would have to satisfy the mercenaries or risk either their departure and the collapse of the army or the looting and massacre of Tivoli. He therefore did what many humanists ever since have done: he appealed to history to both stir consciences and raise money. In ancient Rome, he told his inseparable shadows Brettone and Arimbaldo, the republic had faced a similar crisis and the need to pay its soldiers. But the ancient consul brought together the "barons" of the city and told them, "We who hold offices and dignities should be the first to give what we can, out of good will." From the donations of the patricians the army was paid. The mercenary captains appeared duly impressed by the high idealism of the ancients—and interested enough in keeping the army away from now defenseless Rome—and gave Cola 500 florins each, which Cola then used to pay the mercenaries. But the commune of Tivoli itself came up with the money to pay the militia.

With the Romans and the mercenaries now behind him, Cola addressed the people of Tivoli at the Piazza San Lorenzo, outside the duomo. After reviewing his own exile and wandering, Cola recounted his years with Emperor Charles and then revealed to the Romans that the emperor now planned to come to Rome, just as Cola had promised. Cola now had the pope's favor as well, despite the efforts of the Colonna to destroy him. It was therefore up to the Roman people to smash Stefaniello and these enemies of the people. His speech succeeded; the next day the militia of Tivoli joined the muster of the allied forces at a place called Castiglione di Santa Prassede on the route to Palestrina.

The siege of Palestrina was a difficult one; while the Romans soon succeeded in encircling the city from the plain and began destroying the fields all around its district, the city itself stands at 479 meters above sea level and rises steeply up the bowl of the southern face of the Monti Prenestini, culminating in the palace of the Colonna itself, the former sanctuary of Fortuna Primigenia. While the Romans and their allies camped below and blocked access to the plain, the Colonna continued to supply their fortress from the steep mountainside above, probably through the narrow gate that still bears the Colonna crest at the west end of the actual sanctuary. As he watched the supply trains constantly arriving and departing from the citadel, Rienzo realized that the Romans' former unity of purpose was now gone; and, according to the Anonimo romano, he began to regret that he had not followed up his victory at the Porta San Lorenzo in 1347.

Then, just as suddenly as Cola had been forced to call off the siege of

Marino seven years before, he now ordered the army to retreat from Palestrina. But new times had brought new reasons. For one, the militias of Tivoli and of Velletri had come to blows; and that of Velletri had decided to go over to the side of Palestrina. It was a common enough occurrence among Italy's competing city-states: territorial rivalry and a constantly shifting sense of self-interest, especially in the crisis years of the midcentury, made long-term alliances uncertain at best. Cola might have been able to use his considerable persuasive skills to heal the rift, however, if it had not been for the arrival of serious news from Rome. This time, however, it was not the arrival of the papal legate who had summoned the tribune to the Vatican palace but something far more ominous. Fra Morreale was making his way to Rome.

Fra Morreale was, according to almost everyone's estimate, a gangster. Like many gangsters, he did not treat the women in his life with much gentleness or respect. One of the mercenary captain's "maids," who "had suffered many insults and outrages at the hands of her master," had escaped from his camp and made her way to Rome to seek out the tribune. Upon his hasty return to the city, Cola interviewed the woman and confirmed what he had probably known all along: that Morreale now planned to enter Rome, murder him, and set himself up as lord. The timing could not have been better; with Cola and the militia tied up at Palestrina, Morreale would have entered an undefended city. His companions Brettone and Arimbaldo had probably summoned him from his temporary headquarters at Città di Castello, the border town of the Papal States on the upper Tiber valley in Umbria, where he left the Great Company under the command of Conrad of Landau and Hannekin Bongarten. Brettone and Arimbaldo themselves would then either have turned their highly skilled and professional forces upon the unsuspecting Roman militia and cut them to pieces or made off in the night to join their brother in the city.

And so Fra Morreale entered Rome, presumably to collect on Cola's debt to him. But once inside the gates, according to the Anonimo romano, he was immediately arrested and brought to the prison on the Capitoline.[9] There he joined both Brettone and Arimbaldo, whom Cola had already ordered seized. Morreale's first thoughts were for the woman: How much had she told the tribune? "He was very much afraid that she would be the ruin of him." But a condottiere's life was full of captures, prisons, ransoms, and releases; and so Morreale was soon pacing his cell, calculating how many florins it would take for Cola to open his prison doors. The three men worked out a plan. Morreale would, of course, be set free to secure the ransom money, leaving Brettone and Arimbaldo as security: "Let one or two of us stay here. Let me go. I'll come back with ten thousand, twenty thousand florins for him . . . as much money and as many men as he pleases. Let's do it, for God's sake!" (AR, XXVII, ll. 503–5b, Porta, 253).

But Fra Morreale's luck had run its course. He was put to the torture, confessed his crimes and consoled his brothers, heard Mass the next morning, and was led to the block at the palace, Rome's traditional place of execution, up the stairway of the Lion, before the image of the Madonna. After making a defiant speech to the Romans, boasting of his military prowess and conquests, Fra Morreale was beheaded and then buried by the Franciscans in the Aracoeli. Cola's justice had been swift, and it had shocked the people. But had the senator delayed, Morreale may have shared the fate of his brother Arimbaldo; for an express letter soon came from Cardinal Albornoz ordering Rienzo to release the condottiere. Good mercenaries were simply too hard for a devout churchman to find; and Arimbaldo was sent off to the pope's vicar. Brettone remained in chains in the Capitoline prison. But Cola realized that his actions against a brave and renowned soldier smacked of treachery; and he therefore assembled and addressed the people. This is what he said:

Gentlemen, do not be disturbed at the death of this man, who was the worst man in the world. He robbed cities and castles; he killed and captured men and women: he took two thousand women captive. And this time he came here to upset our *stato,* not to raise it up again. He sought to make himself lord without restraint. He wanted to do us a favor: He planned to depopulate the Campagna and the land of Rome, and the rest of Italy.

But with God's favor we'll bring our troubles to a happy ending. But for now let's do as a grain thresher does: he throws the chaff and empty husks to the wind, he keeps the rest for himself. So we have condemned this false man. His money, horses and arms we shall take to wage our struggle. (AR, XXVII, ll. 103b-118b, Porta, 256–57)

Cola's speech calmed the Romans both because it spoke to Morreale's true record and revealed that his money—as was often the case in communal justice—was now going to serve the city and because another fact was then well known. Although Cola took much of the money Morreale brought into Rome to pay the militia, he was unable to take it all, for most of it had already been stolen by Messer Janni di Castiello; "the barons of Rome considered him a traitor, because he did not keep faith with his friend" (ll. 125b-127b). The Anonimo romano's cryptic remark is a non se-

APOCALYPSE IN ROME 335

quitur unless the reader makes one assumption: that the "friend" was none other than Morreale, and that Janni di Castiello had been Morreale's agent within the city, his contact with the barons, and his conduit for the funds with which he planned to win over Cola's enemies to his own banner. Upon the discovery of Fra Morreale's plot, however, Janni di Castiello had abandoned his paymaster, fled Rome, and left the barons without the funds they needed to hire men and buy arms.

The campaign against the Colonna continued. To replace the fallen condottieri Brettone and Arimbaldo, Cola now appointed as captain of the people "the wise and experienced warrior" Liccardo Imprennente degli Annibaldi, the lord of Monte Compatri in the Alban Hills, just east of Frascati. Liccardo was a member of one of Rome's most respected families, the successors to the Frangipane in the Forum area and the virtual lords of the Colosseum, their principal fortress in the city. While the Annibaldi's star had been eclipsed by the rise of the Caetani, to whom they had ceded the Torre delle Milizie and sold Sermoneta and Ninfa, they remained an "old" family in fourteenth-century Rome. Cola's choice was a good one both politically and militarily; and Liccardo soon proved his worth, vigorously pursuing the campaign against Palestrina and putting the Colonna on the defensive throughout the Campagna. Even the Hungarian mercenaries, now a familiar presence among Rome's troops, praised Annibaldi for his leadership.

By the end of September 1354, all was going well in Rome, but the senator knew that the situation could not last.[10] The funds that he had seized from Fra Morreale had gone immediately to the militia and to the remnants of the mercenaries who still served with Liccardo Annibaldi. While the Colonna might be on the defensive, the rest of the barons were growing increasingly hostile, and Cardinal Albornoz was again showing the opposition to Cola that had delayed his entry to Rome for months. The legate knew that the barons were allied against Cola and that the Colonna were in open revolt, ravaging the countryside and murdering Romans. But not a penny was forthcoming from his treasury. Arimbaldo was now back at Perugia, or even at Montefiascone with Albornoz and probably already plotting his revenge and the rescue of his brother Brettone from prison on the Capitoline. Cola also realized that Rome was no longer the city that he had left behind in 1347. It had profited somewhat from the Jubilee, true, but it had also suffered immensely: from the plague, the earthquake, and the continued civil war. Its population may well, in fact, have by then reached its all-time low for the Middle Ages, about seventeen thousand. This drastic depopulation well explains both the commune's and the barons' new need to rely more and more on mercenaries for their military actions.

But the mercenaries demanded pay; the Roman militia itself could not serve without their just wages; and the Roman countryside no longer provided even a fraction of the income that had once streamed into the coffers of the *buono stato*. Whatever communes and rural *terre* and *castre* that were still free from the barons' civil wars now owed obedience to the papal vicar: all of the Patrimony, the Sabina, and lands of lower Umbria had fallen under the tight grip of Albornoz. Cola's first steps had been to drastically reduce his government's spending by cutting his personal and domestic expenses. While this might seem a pittance for a modern government, for a medieval ruler the magnificence of his table and of his personal appearance was a true sign of his power and of his realm's wealth. So, too, was the munificence he lavished upon his retainers, his guests, and visiting dignitaries. It was the surest sign of the power and importance of Pope Clement VI, for example; and if his court life had nearly bankrupted the papal treasury, it still made Avignon the most important city in Christendom.

Yet even spending cuts could not make up for the huge deficit that the new war was creating. Cola therefore had no choice but to rely upon a device that most of the communes of mid- and late-fourteenth-century Italy had found more and more essential: the *gabelle* and the monopoly on salt. The various *gabelle* available to Italian city-states—sales taxes, customs duties, and exchange taxes—had all moved from extraordinary levies to regular taxes and important components of government revenues. There had been much opposition to the taxes, especially to those sales and use taxes that most affected working people; but despite the protests, shutdowns, demonstrations, and riots, people eventually became used to them. And so Cola imposed new *gabelle* on wine "and other commodities." That on wine amounted to six denarii per cartload.

The other great source of income available to the Roman government, and a monopoly of the Italian government even into the twentieth century, was the salt supply. Since antiquity the *campo salino*, or salt flats, at Ostia had provided a major source of income for Rome. The via Salaria, the "Salt Road," had in fact been built by the ancient Romans to bring this coveted salt into the hills of Sabina. From the beginning of the Middle Ages, salt had provided a major source of papal income, and it was a part of the papal regalia that formed a central point of contention in the struggle between the popes and the commune. While the papacy eventually acknowledged that the salt monopoly belonged to the "Roman people," Clement VI had been obsessed by retaining papal rights to the Ostia flats, and as late as 1353 Innocent VI had vigorously protested the seizure of the public works by Senators Stefaniello Colonna and Bertoldo Orsini and their privatization to a small circle of merchants. The potential income from the salt monopoly was enormous, for the government could not only regulate the price of salt but also stipulate how much salt each household of the district of Rome was required to purchase, thus in effect tying a necessity of life and agricultural industry to the financial needs of the commune. Despite the repeated claim by modern historians that it was this tax that finally broke the backs of the Romans, the Anonimo romano is clear: "The Romans put up with it in order to have a government."

As late as September 16, Cola retained the support and consensus of the Roman people. On that date he held a public parliament in front of the Senators' Palace to confirm the privileges of the hospital of Sto. Spirito in Sassia. Because of the hospital's service to the poor during the great famine of 1347, and because of the brothers' armed resistance to the depredations of the barons during Rienzo's absence, Cola, with the approval of the Roman people, exempted the hospital from all taxes and levies, including that on salt. When asked for their assent, the Romans replied, acclaiming it in alta voce, *"Placet, Placet, volumus, volumus!"* "It's good, it's good. We agree, we agree!" Well choreographed, but hardly the response of a resentful and treacherous people.

Throughout September Cola focused on the affairs of state from atop the Capitoline, sending dispatches to Liccardo at his base near Palestrina, directing operations, and devising every means possible to support the war effort.

Such a man had never been seen. He alone bore the cares of the Romans. He would see more standing on the Campidoglio than his officials did at their posts. He was always fund-raising, he was always writing to his officials. He would give them the method and the tactics to do things quickly: how to close the passes through which [the enemy] were taking the offensive, how to capture men and spies. He would never let up. (AR, XXVII, 144b-151b, Porta, 258)

Yet while Cola's attention remained focused on the theater of war, forces both within and outside the city were moving against him, and after so many plots and betrayals Cola could not be sure who his real enemies were. After long years of exile, narrow escapes, and betrayals, and after the past year among Albornoz's camps and campaigns, he was now used to acting quickly and apparently without consensus or consultation.

The Anonimo romano reports that in the City Chamber Cola had so intimidated the councilors that no one dared oppose him; "they feared the Tribune like a demon. In the council chamber he got everything he wanted; no councilor contradicted him" (ll. 179b-181b). Even practices once hailed as true signs of democracy under the first *buono stato* were now seen as acts of tyranny. Cola's levy of the city militia—fifty infantrymen from each *rione* to be ready at the sound of the Campidoglio bell, a standard feature of most urban democracies in Italy—was now construed as a sure sign of oppression.

The sources agree that the crisis to Cola's government came from within. A venerable and highly respected citizen of Rome, Pandolfuccio di Guido di Pandolfo de' Franchi, who had served as Rome's chief ambassador to Florence in the embassy of July 1347, began a public campaign of speeches and other actions designed to take the reins of power from the ex-tribune. "He was a noble man who wanted to be lord of the people," the Anonimo romano writes. "He had the power to move the people through his authority and through his eloquence," Villani adds. What faction Pandolfo represented is unclear: Colonna or Orsini, barons or *bovattieri,* Cardinal Albornoz or the agents of the condottiere Arimbaldo. Apparently Cola himself was not certain. But he decided to act. Without prior warning or consultation with his council, he had Pandolfo arrested and then summarily executed by beheading, probably below the statue of the Lion on the Capitoline. Though there is good reason to assume that Pandolfo might indeed have been the respected mouthpiece for a larger conspiracy among the barons to overthrow the government, the sources make no such connections; and the act shocked every element of Roman society. But the senator did not stop there. Cola began ordering the arrest of "one man after another" and then releasing them once ransoms were paid into the public treasury. "The murmuring sounded quietly through Rome." Finally, and for no apparent reason that the sources will ever reveal, Cola summarily dismissed his captain of war, Liccardo Annibaldi, and the war against the Colonna ground to a halt.

Historians have ever since attempted to make sense of this string of events. Writing years later, the Anonimo romano combined his personal memories, reports from other witnesses, and the standard ancient portrayals of depraved Roman emperors to create the image of a man completely changed after his return to Rome:[11]

He used to be sober, temperate, and abstinent. Now he became an intemperate drinker, he used wine in great amounts. At every hour he would make confections and drink. He observed neither order nor time. He would mix Greco with Faiano, and Malvasia with Ribolla. He was quite ready to drink at any hour. It was a horrible thing to see how much he would drink. He drank too much. He would say that he had gotten used to it in prison. He also became immensely fat. He had a round belly, triumphal like an ancient abbot's. His skin shone all over like a peacock's; ruddy; long beard. His facial expression would suddenly change, suddenly his eyes would become inflamed. His mind and opinions would change like fire. He had clear eyes, little by little they would become red as blood. . . .

At the same moment laughing, he would weep; and letting out tears and sighs he would laugh, so varied and mobile was his wandering will. Now he would weep, and now he would enjoy himself. (AR, XXVII, ll. 335–51, Porta, 247–48; ll. 181b-184b, Porta, 259)

We have already seen how even *before* the battle of Porta San Lorenzo the Anonimo romano had portrayed Cola as moody and wildly temperamental. Just before his first abdication, his biographer had described him as an Asian tyrant. Yet at the same time he portrayed him as fully under control, rational and the master of the situation, deftly ordering his battalions and exhorting them to valor in the best Roman tradition. So, too, after Cola's return, the Anonimo romano portrays the senator in one paragraph as hardworking, budget-conscious, rationally planning the city's finances—and winning the people's approval—energetically, carefully, and unceasingly overseeing military operations while all others thought of their own self-interest; while in the next Cola is tyrannical and self-indulgent. The knight who distinguished himself in battle at Tuscania and Viterbo just months before is now like an "Asian abbot" with a triumphal belly, weeping and striking out against the Romans like a mad tyrant. Caligula, Tiberius, and Nero all come to mind. Was the rumor mill once again in full operation in Rome in 1354 as it had been in 1347? Had the Anonimo romano actually observed Cola's behavior, or was he merely repeating rumors and stale reports?

It does seem as if Cola had changed, at least in the eyes of his Romans. Long years of wandering and deprivation, of prison, poor diet, and inactivity had no doubt changed him physically. He had returned to Rome with a beard, looking more like a German emperor or captain of war than an ancient Roman tribune. And if we draw anything from the silence of the sources, he had come back to Rome without his family. Livia, Lorienzo, and Cola's other children, nieces, and nephews had now disappeared into the safety of convents or remote hermitages, or had suffered even worse fates. He had seen his father-in-law and his own brother betray him. Cola was also suffering from the chronic illness that he described to Charles IV as the falling sickness. If this were epilepsy, it might explain the sudden onsets of almost demonic behavior of a generalized seizure: the high tension and anxiety, the weeping, the violent body movements, the myoclonic seizures that would look like rages. In Cola's thinking at least, they also matched the diagnosis for *syncopis* in Arnald of Villanova, the best-known medical authority of the time. Such a condition and the prescribed medication might also explain Cola's drinking, his constant mixing of grape varieties, and his new reliance on confections and drink, very close to the wine and sweet rose-water regimen prescribed by Arnald.

But all such analyses of a man dead for 650 years must ultimately prove futile, just as futile as psychiatric approaches to interpreting Cola's recorded behavior as indications of a bipolar personality. Here, in the final analysis, the insights of the deconstructionists must bear some weight: that the text before us reveals not a true image of a human being but a literary construction indebted as much to the Anonimo romano's classical and contemporary sources as to eyewitness accounts and the reports of hearsay and deliberately manufactured rumors and slanders. The Anonimo romano's image of Cola divided the tribune's life into two distinct spheres: that of the private individual, subject to hideous character flaws, and that of the public official whose acts are consistently exemplary, courageous, and inspiring. The Anonimo romano thus interwove his narrative with two genres: the *gesta,* the public acts and deeds of a historical figure or legendary hero, and the *vita,* the private biography full of personal details, telling external signs—such as style of clothing, body type and shape, gesture and word—that reveal inner character, virtues, and vices. One cannot approach such history writing with the idea that the writer is presenting a full and complete picture of the man. Never in the Anonimo romano's account are Cola's public actions interrupted or disturbed by his private character. Even during the battle of Porta San Lorenzo, the Anonimo romano reveals to us Cola's inner anxieties and his conflict between duty and fear, but the battle itself is fought without reference to this: the Romans are victorious, Cola leads them throughout. He does not collapse in fear, demoralize his forces, and thus forfeit the victory. Thus we are left to explain public events through the public records, neither through modern medical or psychological analysis nor through the moral categories of the medieval biographer.

By the end of September 1354 Cola di Rienzo seems to have had victory within his grasp, but forces within Rome—apparently those of the barons allied with external forces, the condottieri or the cardinal-legate himself—had so turned the city against its new senator that Cola's very real political blunders had left him no room for maneuver. Just as in December 1347, he now found himself confronted by a growing rebellion outside the city and a conspiracy within. Villani records that it was the Colonna, along with Luca Savelli, Cola's enemy since 1347, who hatched the plot. The execution of Pandolfo de Guido had alienated all political groups in Rome and convinced the barons that they would have to forgo the sham of a political campaign. They would have to move directly against the tribune.[12]

Once again the rebellion started in the Colonna district of the city, this time not near San Marco but farther up in Trevi, near the Column of Antoninus. The account in the Anonimo romano (AR, XXVII, ll. 195b–376b, Porta, 259–65) is one of the most exiting in all historical literature. Early on the morning of October 8, 1354, Cola was rising from bed in the palace on the Campidoglio. He had just washed his face when he heard a tumult rising from below the hill off to the northeast, from Trevi. A lone voice had begun the cry, *"Viva il popolo!"* The cry soon grew into a chant and began spreading down the via Lata—the Corso—toward the Capitoline. There it was joined by shouting from the banks of the Tiber, from the *rioni* of Sant'Angelo and the Ripa. Soon the cries of the angry Romans were unmistakable, and they were moving toward the Capitoline. As they came together, the crowds—now men, women, and children—were met by many young men who had enlisted in the tribune's own militia. But then the shout was suddenly changed: "Death to the traitor Cola di Rienzo! Death!" and the crowd charged up the Capitoline and surrounded the palace, throwing rocks, shouting again and again, "Death to the traitor who made the tax! Death!"

The Senators' Palace (see fig. 6) had been reinforced several times over the course of the century, its lovely lower loggie filled in with stonework and planks, its doors protected by a long, arched ramp, its perimeter fortified with the high stockade that Cola himself had built from the planks of the barons' *fortilizie*. Its lofty bell tower was ever ready to sound the tocsin to rally the militia of the *rioni* at a moment's notice to come to the defense of the government. But the bell did not ring. Not a sound came from the palace. At the first sounds of uproar, perhaps in fact even before the signal for the riot to begin, the entire palace staff—notaries, judges, servants—"and everyone else had worked hard to save their skins." Cola was left alone except for three companions, one of whom was his own kinsman Locciolo Pellicciaro, probably a furrier for whom the senator had found work at city hall. Rienzo emerged onto the palace's loggia to address the Romans below.

Both the Anonimo romano and another unnamed member of his or Petrarch's circle recorded Cola's speech. At first Cola decided to use reason: he told the crowd that he was also for the people, his soldiers were enlisted men, not the tools of a tyrant, and the letter of the pope, written on September 11 confirming Cola's office as senator, had just arrived. All that was left was for Cola to read the confirmation of his papal appointment to the City Council. But according to papal correspondence, the pope had also written Albornoz on September 9 with the same news and had instructed him to extend Cola's appointment, which usually meant by at least six months. If Cola had not yet announced the pope's appointment, Albornoz therefore was the only other man in Italy with the official news; and he had gotten it a few days before, probably by the first days of October. Whether by intent or inadvertence, the news had also reached the barons, and after a few days of organizing they were now ready to make sure that the papal order never went into effect.

Cola realized that the crowd outside was bent on his destruction. He therefore donned full battle armor, grabbed the glorious crimson banner of the people of Rome, with the letters "SPQR" emblazoned in gold upon it, and emerged onto the balcony of the upper hall, alone. Villani and the Anonimo romano are in agreement on what happened next: Cola stretched out his hand to call for silence so that he could address the crowd below. But the people—or at least some in that crowd, afraid that his voice and his genius as an orator would calm the people and bring them back to reason—tried to prevent him from speaking. He was met with a hail of rocks, arrows, and javelins that rained upon the balcony so thickly that the tribune could no longer stand outside. Meanwhile, others in the crowd had rushed the palace gates with burning torches and had set the palisades on fire.

As Cola motioned for silence, a javelin pierced his hand. Wounded and bleeding now, Cola reacted with a gesture that was to impress contemporaries with his courage: he dropped his sword and instead picked up the banner of Rome and its people. He stretched it out between his two hands, mixing his own blood with the crimson of the banner, and gestured to the people as if to say, "You refuse to let me speak. Look! I am a citizen and a plebeian just like you. If you kill me, you kill yourselves, who are Romans!" But it was too late. Cola decided that he would have to leave the balcony and the upper hall of the palace: not only because of the hail of javelins, arrows, and rocks but also because Messer Bret-

tone, the condottiere, was being held there. If the upper hall did not collapse in flames first, the man whom Cola had hoodwinked repeatedly
would very likely break out of his cell and slay him with his own hands.
He therefore took the expedient that Senator Stefaniello Colonna had used
the year before. He stripped the cloths from the banqueting table, tied
them into a rope, and lowered himself into the cortile between the rear
of the palace and the ancient Tabularium, at that time the Cancelleria and
prison.

By that time the palace was engulfed in fire: the upper hall had already
collapsed in flames, and the stairs to the piazza had caved in. But the destruction had saved him from the crowds outside: their entry was now
barred, and since the day was getting on to evening, there was some chance
that the people would have vented their anger and slowly dispersed, especially if Cola's supporters in the Arenula below could summon up their
courage and charge the hill. But a strange thing happened. Cola's own
kinsman, Locciolo, who had remained in the palace, continued to urge
the people on, gesturing and shouting to them that Cola was trapped inside the building. And so the crowds remained outside, calling for the tribune's death.

The palace was in flames, and the prisoners in the Cancelleria prison
were about to break out. Cola hesitated in the cortile. According to the
Anonimo romano—who by his own account could not have been inside
the palace—the tribune wavered between two choices: to don his armor
and take up his sword to die like a true Roman, or to cast it off and attempt his escape, just as Senator Colonna had, disguised as a workman.
Many a hero, even Caesar and Emperor Charles IV, had chosen guile and
escape to return to fight another day. Cola had even humbled himself publicly seven years ago to do the same. The palace was collapsing all around
him. His fellow Romans were now setting fire to the first gate with "wood,
oil and pitch. The gate was burning, the roof of the loggia was blazing;
the second gate was burning and the roof and the timbers were falling
piece by piece. The noise was horrible."

Cola cast off his battle armor, quickly cut off his beard, and blackened
his face with some of the charcoal that filled the place. He found a filthy
old cloak that belonged to one of the palace porters. Covering himself
with the man's blanket, he raced through the flames and down to the gates:
"He passed the first gate, which was burning; he passed the stairway and
the roof tower, which was collapsing; he passed the last gate freely." He
was now outside in the fresh fall evening, free from the palace and the
flames. Still disguised, Cola easily mingled with the excited, distracted

crowd. But the best orator of his day could not resist what he did best. Turning to the people and reverting to his native Romanesco dialect, he urged on the Romans, *"Suso, suso a gliu tradetore!"*, "Up, up to the traitor!" But as he gestured, someone in the crowd who was paying more attention to the speaker than to the palace noticed something curious. As Cola turned and passed out of the last gate, this man barred his path; and then his suspicions were confirmed. He recognized the tribune. "Wait a minute, where are you going?" he said. The man then stripped the peasant's feather cap from Cola's head and held up his arms to confirm up close what he had noticed flickering against the flames: the tribune's splendid golden bracelets.

Cola had now been discovered, and there was nothing left to do. He therefore cast off the rest of his disguise to reveal himself to the Romans. People in the crowd later remembered every detail of that evening. There Cola stood in a loose jacket of green silk, trimmed in gold, with blue stockings, "like barons wear." He was taken by the arms and led before the palace to the Place of the Lion: there in 1347 Cola had had beheaded Martino del Porto. Just weeks before in 1354 Cola had executed Fra Morreale, and then, days later, Pandalfuccio de' Pandolfi. There, as in the Apocalypse before that great last trumpet announcing the Second Coming, "a great silence fell." Cola stood at the place of execution for almost an hour. No one dared touch the famous tribune, the liberator of the people, the man who had escaped every danger and every plot against his life, who had raised himself back to power as if from the dead. Cola himself stood motionless, his arms folded over his chest, looking across the silent cloud of witnesses, hidden in the fading light, their faces glowing against the crackling flames of the burning palace.

Finally a man—everyone remembered who it was, Cecco dello Viecchio—came forward out of the huddled mob. Who knows what decision, what memory of insult or revenge, what promise of reward had spurred him on. He held a dagger in his hand. He approached the tribune and thrust his blade into Cola's gut. "He was the first." The act freed a frenzy of bloodlust in the mob, as first one and then another of Rome's citizens approached the tribune. One, Laurentio de Treio, a notary just like Cola, took a sword and split his skull. Then one man after another approached; some were even brave enough to press their blades into the bleeding body. But Cola had died at once, and the Anonimo romano reports, "He felt no pain." Someone else then came and tied his feet together with a rope. Cola's body was cast to the ground, and then began the hideous spectacle of the ritual desecration of his corpse. The crowd dragged the body down the slope of the Capitoline, piercing him with their swords and knives as he passed along the dirt path, his clothing and then his skin peeling off behind him. It was a long way that Cola di Rienzo had to travel that night: all the way to the Piazza San Marcello, up the via Lata, today's Corso, to the heart of the Colonna district. By the time the crowd reached the church, they were making merry with their catch: the tribune's body had been stabbed so many times that it "looked like a sieve." His head, already split by the first sword, oozing his brains, had melted along the Corso, and by the time the mob had hoisted up his body, feet first, it no longer had a head.

The Anonimo romano describes the scene in the ritualistic language of execution long familiar to the Italian communes. As his body hung there, bleeding, skinless, "his guts dangled from his belly. He was horribly fat. He was white as bloody milk. He was so fat that he looked like a giant buffalo or cow in a slaughterhouse." This is the stylized language frequently used to describe the executed man: a repudiation of his humanity that objectifies the victim to justify the horror of the execution. So, too, the chief agents of the duke of Athens executed in Florence in 1343; so, too, Pietro Colonna trapped and murdered by the Romans at the battle of San Lorenzo gate; so, too, even Cardinal Annibaldo de Ceccano: their bodies were fat and unnatural, like animals at the slaughter, bloated, cut open, objects of scorn and contempt.

The body of the tribune and senator of Rome hung tied, upside down, outside the church of San Marcello for two days and one night as the boys of the *contrada* used it as a target for their rocks. Finally, at the command of Jugurta and Sciaretta Colonna, the body was cut down and dragged off to the Mausoleum of Augustus, not far from the piazza on the bank of the Tiber. Here was performed the final act of mockery of their fallen enemy. The spot had been chosen with full malice aforethought. For the tomb of Augustus, once used as a fortress by the Colonna, was long known to be associated with the first emperor and with Cola's symbol of the transformation of ancient Rome from the pagan to the Christian era. So here, in mockery of his dreams of ancient glory, the Colonna chose to burn the body of the Tribunus Augustus. But they would not do so themselves. For this task they would choose that special group of outsiders whom Cola seemed to have favored during his tribunate, among whom he had grown up, who would by their unwilling participation add to the mockery of the event and reinforce the fact that no true Christian would even touch the body. The Colonna ordered the Jews of Rome to gather up the stinking carcass, lay it upon its pile of thistles, and burn it into ashes. "So the corpse was burnt and reduced to powder; not a speck was left." The ashes were then collected and, like those of Arnold of Brescia, who was hung and burned by the emperor Frederick Barbarossa so long ago, they were tossed unceremoniously into the Tiber, lest by any chance followers gather up the stray remains and make them the object of veneration or political memory.

But the old medieval models no longer applied; and holy memory long tied to physical relics was already giving way to a modern sense of fame that Cola himself had helped to create. A document survived, either a letter or a sermon composed by a writer in Cola's or Petrarch's circle, mourning the tribune's death and declaring that Rome had now, finally, itself become the fallen Babylon of the Apocalypse. On October 15 Pope Innocent VI reacted to the news of Rienzo's death and ordered Cardinal Albornoz to find and bring to justice his assassins, no matter what their age, sex, or social station—whether clerical or lay. On November 21 the thirteen *rioni* elected a new government: the Thirteen Good Men would now maintain the remnants of Cola's *buono stato*. But Albornoz had other ideas for Rome. Cola's assassins were never brought to justice, even though the Anonimo romano pointedly records the names of several; and in February 1355 the cardinal-legate effectively dissolved the popular regime and appointed instead Orso Andrea Orsini and Giovanni Tebaldi of Sant'Eustachio as senators. Rome returned to the baronial system that had been in place when Cola first went to Avignon in 1343.

In the spring of 1355 Charles IV finally completed his preparations in Lombardy and descended on Rome.[13] He had probably heard the news of Cola's death sometime in the winter of 1354 or early 1355; but the plans for his coronation were set. And so he made the journey with a small army; and on April 5, 1355, he was crowned in St. Peter's by the papal vicar of the city and immediately retreated north with his Germans. His brief adventure earned him the great contempt of Petrarch, who had hoped that the return of the emperor would be a decisive event for Italian politics and history, just as Dante had hoped when Henry VII had come in 1312. But Charles was no last world emperor, and his arrival in Rome ushered in no golden age of peace or justice. Charles died famous and successful in 1378. Petrarch himself was to go on to serve tyrants and republics, to speak the truth to emperors and popes, and would live to become the greatest writer then known to Europe: an inspiration for an entire new generation of humanists who would soon see him as the father of the Renaissance. And for years afterward he would, occasionally, reminisce about his former friend Cola di Rienzo and about the dream of bringing ancient Rome to life once again. Petrarch died in his home in Arquà near Ravenna on July 19, 1374.

Later in 1355, Janni Pippino, paladin of Altamura, the man who had started the riots that had deposed Cola in December 1347, was captured in his hometown in Apulia. He had been a notorious brigand from the reign of King Robert the Wise and then chief of a Great Company during the anarchy set off by the invasion of Lewis of Hungary; and he had finally been captured by the crown. Instead of being beheaded, like a true nobleman, "he was hanged by the gullet. . . . His head was crowned with a paper miter." On it was written, "Messer Janni Pipino, knight of Altamura, Paladin, the count of Minervino, lord of Bari, liberator of Rome."

But in the spring of 1355 none of this mattered to Cola di Rienzo, whose ashes now mingled with the deep waters of the Tiber as it races westward around the Campo Marzio and embraces the *abitato*. It descends past the banks of the Borgo, past St. Peter's, the hospital of Sto. Spirito, and the castles of the Orsini. It curves east now toward the Island of the Tiber. It sweeps along past the mills and docks and washes the shore along the banks of the Pescheria, by Sant'Angelo and, farther along, past Trastevere and its docks, past the Ripa and the shadow of the Aventine. And so the ashes of Cola di Rienzo mingled with the granite and lime of the high mountain passes of the Alpi di Luna, with the muds and clays of farms in Umbria, with the sandy wastes of the Campagna. And Cola's dreams then joined those of so many Romans ancient and more modern, illustrious and obscure, out past Ostia to the mouths of the Tiber, to Fiumicino and the Island of the Dead, and then on, finally, to the broad sea itself.

Notes

Introduction

1. For the most recently proposed identity of the Anonimo romano see Giuseppe Billanovich, "Come nacque un capolavoro." For a brief overview of the author and his background see also Seibt, 21–32.

2. We will discuss Seibt's interpretations at various points in these notes.

3. See Horowitz; Kershaw, 599–600 nn. 118–35.

4. For a good summary of Kristeller's thinking here, see Monfasani, 1161–63. Prof. Kristeller himself raised his objections to Burdach—and to the issue of Cola di Rienzo's possible Joachite sources—several times to me personally during my years as a doctoral student at Columbia University. By the 1960s Kristeller had begun stressing Cola's professional role as a notary, and thus as a rhetorician, to explain his impact on the early Renaissance.

Chapter 1. Birth, Youth, and Society

1. For the topography of fourteenth-century Rome, the closest contemporary description was written shortly after 1345 by Giovanni Cavallini dei Cerronis: *Polistoria*, VIII.5, 7, 11, in VCT, 4:11–54; and newly edited in Laureys. The grand corpus of medieval and Renaissance descriptions of Rome, including the Mirabilian tradition, has been collected in Valentini and Zucchetti, *Codice topografico;* and later collected in D'Onofrio 1 and 2. Visual sources include Egger, *Codex Escurialensis;* Egger and Hülsen, *Die römischen Skizzenbücher;* Frutaz, *Le piante di Roma;* Lanciani, *Forma Urbis Romae;* Ulrichs, *Codex Urbis;* and, most recently, Sassoli, *Roma Veduta,* esp. 1–78.

On Lazio and the region of Rome see D'Onofrio, *Il Tevere;* Small, "District"; Tomassetti, *La campagna romana;* rev. ed., Chiumenti and Bilancia. Of utmost importance is Toubert, *Les structures.*

2. The best English-language secondary work on medieval Rome's monuments and topography remains Krautheimer, *Rome.* Of less value in English is Hetherington, *Medieval Rome,* whose judgments on the Roman society and people behind the monuments often tend to be colored by modern prejudices. See also Armellini, *Le Chiese di Roma;* Armellini and Cecchelli, *Le Chiese di Roma dal secolo iv al xix;* Cecchilli, *La vita di Roma del Medioevo,* vol. 1: *Le arti minori e il costume;* Hülsen, *Le chiese.* Good modern guides to Roman neighborhoods and monuments include Macadam, *Blue Guide: Rome;* Masson, *Companion Guide;* Touring Club Italiano, *Roma e dintorni.* Despite his late-nineteenth-century approach and political passions, Gregorovius remains the best in-depth narrative history. Volume 6 covers the fourteenth century, including the life and career of Cola di Rienzo. A one-volume abridgment was edited by Morrison as *Rome and Medieval Culture.* On Cola see pp. 269–307.

Many of medieval Rome's monuments have now been studied in detail. For those directly pertinent to the city during Rienzo's life see Amadei, *Le torri di Roma;* Asso, "Monte Giordano"; Cecchelli, "Il Campidoglio"; Cusanno, *Le fortificazioni medioevali;* idem, "Il complesso fortificato"; and idem, *Turris Comitum;* Gnoli, *Topografia e toponomastica;* Passagli, "Urbanizzazione e topografia"; Pietrangeli, "Il palazzo Senatorio"; Pressouyre, *Rome au fil du temps;* Rodocanachi, *Le Capitole;* and Tomassetti, "Torri di Roma."

3. On the city's population see Pardi, "La populazione"; Russell, *Population;* idem, *Medieval Regions,* 51–52, 99–100, 163–64; and Tomassetti, "Del sale e focatico." On comparative sizes of cities see Benevolo, 176–77; Epstein, 212–14.

4. The primary sources for Cola's origins and youth include Agnolo di Tura del Grasso, *Cronaca Senese,* RIS 15.6:577–79; AR, XVIII, ll. 1–7, Porta, 143; Wright, 31; Bishop's Priest of Butrinto Nicola, *Relatio,* Baluze 3:491–561, esp. 531–41, for Henry VII's coronation journey; Clement VI, Speech in Consistory (Avignon, November 17, 1348), BBCR 2.5:33–36; Cola di Rienzo, Letter 36, to the City of Florence (Rome August 27, 1347), BBCR 2.3:133; Letter 43, to Clement VI (Rome October 11, 1347), BBCR 2.3:165–66; Letter 50, to Emperor Charles IV (Prague, late July 1350), BBCR 2.3:198–213; Letter 57, to the archbishop of Prague (no later than August 15, 1350), BBCR 2.3:231–78; Ildebrandino Conti, bishop of Padua, Letter to his vicar Leonardo de S. Sepulcro (Valmontone, July 29/30, 1347), BBCR 2.5:1–15. On Ildebrandino Conti's Joachite leanings see now Maria Chiara Billanovich, "Un lettore trecentesco." Ildebrandino was a correspondent of Petrarch, who confided to the bishop some of his most damning criticisms of the Avignon papacy. See *Sine nomine* 8, Zacour 66–69.

5. On Cola's neighborhood see Bevilacqua, *Il Monte dei Cenci;* Campajola, "Il Ghetto di Roma"; Milano, *Il Ghetto di Roma;* Pietrangeli, *Guide Rionali di Roma. Rione XI: S. Angelo;* Proia and Romano, *Il rione S. Angelo.*

For the *rioni* in general and their political, social, and religious structures see

Duchesne, "Les régions de Rome"; Hubert, "Rioni"; Ilari, "Appunti"; Passagli, "Geografia parrocchiale"; Re, "Le regioni." See also Pietrangeli and others, *Guide Rionali*. For the clerical life of the city see Fabre, Duchesne, and Mollat, *Le Liber censuum*.

6. Little evidence exists on the Roman "hospitality industry" before the Renaissance. But a contextualization from both earlier and later periods, as well as materials from other cities, including Siena, Florence, and Venice, helps round out fragmentary sources. For documents see Gatti, *Statuti dei Mercanti;* Palermo, *Il porto;* Sartini, *Statuti;* Schiaparelli, "Alcuni documenti"; Schiaperelli and Re, "Maestri di Strada." A *pars* of the Venetian Senate dated October 13, 1347, for example, clearly indicates the importance of taverns to the economy of that city and the various social status of their proprietors. See Kohl, *Records,* K1174.

On premodern travel and accommodation see Casson, *Travel.* Cowell, *At Play in the Tavern,* while literary in its approach to the tavern in French medieval culture, offers useful insights into the intellectual and social freedoms afforded by the urban tavern and inn. See also Gnoli, *Alberghi ed osterie;* Labarge, *Medieval Travellers;* Mossa and Baldassari, *La vita economica,* 15–21; Pecchiai, "I segni"; Peyer, *Viaggiare;* Romani, *Pellegrini;* Tuliani, *Osti.* See now Modigliani, "Taverne," for the most recent research, with surveys of taverns (mostly Quattrocento), and typical plans.

7. For the sources of Rome's economic and social life see Bartolini, "Documenti inediti"; Gatti, *Statuti dei Mercanti;* also D'Onofrio 2:9–38; Re, *Statuti;* Rota, "Il codice degli 'statuta Urbis'"; Scaccia-Scarafoni, "L'antico statuto"; Schiaparelli, "Alcuni documenti"; Schiaparelli and Re, "Maestri di Strada." For Rome's notarial sources see chapter 2, notes 4–5.

On Rome's medieval social and economic infrastructures see above all Brentano, 1–70; Hubert, *Rome aux XIIIe et XIVe siècles;* Hubert, *Espace urbain;* and Modigliani, *Mercati,* for the markets on the Campidoglio, at Sant'Angelo in Pescheria, and elsewhere in the city. Less useful but comprehensive is Mossa and Baldassari, *La vita economica.*

8. We have little evidence for Cola's youth and family, aside from the few cryptic remarks in the AR, in Cola's own letters, and the stray comments of his clerical critics. Much of what we present is therefore again based upon the contextualization of his life on fourteenth-century Italian structures. Good discussions of late medieval Italian families and children include Broise and Maire-Vigueur, "Strutture famigliari"; Haas, *Renaissance Man;* Herlihy, *Women;* Herlihy and Klapisch-Zuber, *Tuscans;* Larner, *Italy,* 59–78; Origo, *Merchant,* 188–279; and Ross, "Middle-Class Child." Kelley, *Renaissance Humanism,* 11, calls Cola "the son of a Neapolitan tavernkeeper."

9. Nothing is known of Cola's stay and life in Anagni. But it is impossible for him not to have been influenced by the social and artistic structures of the city. See Carbonetti and Vendittelli, "Anagni"; Hugenholtz, "The Anagni Frescoes"; Marchetti Longhi, "Anagni"; Matthiae, *Pittura romana;* Parlato and Romano, *Italia romanica,* 305–25; Ravasi, *La cripta;* Sibilia, *La città dei papi;* Smith, "Anagni," provides an excellent description and analysis of the fresco cycles.

Chapter 2. Education, Profession, and Family

1. For Cola's education see AR, XVIII, ll. 7–22, Porta, 143; Wright, 31. We can assume that this education, though apparently better than that of most members of his profession, followed the normative course of Italian schooling for the fourteenth century. For this see Black, "Humanism and Education"; Gehl, *Moral Art;* Grendler, *Schooling;* Huntsman, "Grammar"; Hyde, "Commune, University, and Society"; Murphy, *Rhetoric;* Reynolds, *Medieval Reading;* Thorndike, "Elementary and Secondary Education"; Wagner, *Seven Liberal Arts.* Witt, *Footsteps,* has now reevaluated and synthesized the last generation of work on the origins of humanism and has thoroughly examined the origins of the movement in both Italian rhetorical and grammatical education of the later Middle Ages. See esp. pp. 1–80.

2. On the *ars dictaminis* see also Banker, *"Ars dictaminis";* Witt, "Boncampagno"; idem, "Brunetto Latini"; and idem, "Medieval 'Ars Dictaminis.'" For a good review of the development of oratory in the fourteenth century see McManamon; and now Witt, *Footsteps,* 1–22 et passim.

3. For the university of Rome see Renazzi, *Storia;* Valentini, "Lo 'Studium Urbis' durante il secolo xiv."

4. For Cola's training and career as a notary see Barraclough, *Public Notaries;* Brentano, "Notarial Cartularies"; Brentano, 25–34, 40–45 et passim; Boüard, "Les notaries de Rome"; Faulhaber, *"Summa dictaminis";* Larner, 176–79, 221–24; and especially Toubert, *Les structures* 1:97–129.

On the social and cultural impact of the notarial profession on early Renaissance Italy, Paul Oskar Kristeller's view that early Renaissance humanism is in large part the product of the late medieval rhetorical tradition has been central to all contemporary interpretations. His views that Rienzo's training in the notarial arts were in large part responsible for his appreciations of classical literature and his views of reform and renewal have been expressed both privately and in such writings as *Renaissance Thought,* 12–19; idem, *Renaissance Thought II,* 233–45. This interpretation has most recently been forcefully restated and reevaluated in Witt, *Footsteps,* esp. 1–5. Monfasani, 1161–63, has recently reiterated Kristeller's eventual turning away from Burdach and Piur's thesis of the origins of the Renaissance in the North. See also Lombardo, "Nobili, mercanti e popoli minuti"; Miglio, "Gli atti privati"; and Petrucci, "I documenti privati."

On the regulation of the notarial profession in Rome see Re, *Statuti,* Bk. I.cc. XXXII–XLVII (pp. 21–34), CXIII–CXV (74–76), CXIX (77); Bk. 2, LXVI (117), c. CLXXIV (180); Bk. 3.c. XVII (209), XX (211), XLII (225), XLIV (226), XLVIII–LXVII (229–35).

5. The use of notarial documents as sources for Cola's life and career would seem the logical starting point to any study. They begin to appear in Italy with regularity from the twelfth century; but these documents, the "protocol books," have largely been destroyed for the earlier Middle Ages in Rome and only begin to appear with any regularity in December 1347. From that point on they become increasingly numerous and reliable as documentation, but only steadily for the 1370s on. The classic introduction to the issues remains Brentano, 40–42 and

notes. The best review of the Roman evidence is Lori Sanfilippo, "I protocolli notarile." See also Corbo, "Relazione descrittiva," for Rome; Calleri, *L'arte dei giudici,* for Florence; and Cherubino, "Dal libro di ricordi," for Siena.

Many of the protocol books of Roman notaries noted by Brentano have now been edited. Among these are Lori Sanfilippo, *Lorenzo Staglia (1372);* idem, *Pietro di Nicola Astalli (1368);* Mosti, *Iohannes Nicolai Pauli;* idem, *Anthonius Goioli Petri Scopte;* idem, *Francesco di Stefano de Caputgallis.*

6. On Cola's family and married life, we have a good deal of often-contradictory evidence scattered throughout his own letters and in other sources. These include AR, XVIII, ll. 1017–28, Porta, 177; Wright, 63, ll. 1115–18, Porta 180; Wright 66; ll. 1977–78, Porta, 209; Wright 93; *Chronicon Estense,* RIS 15.3:460; Cola di Rienzo, Letter 18, to some friends in Avignon (Rome, July 15, 1347), BBCR 2.3:53–59; Letter 36, to the city of Florence (Rome, August 27, 1347), BBCR 2.3:133; Letter 43, to Clement VI (Rome, October 11, 1347), BBCR 2.3:165–66; Letter 50, to Emperor Charles IV (Prague, late July 1350), BBCR 2.3:198–213; Letter 57, to the archbishop of Prague (before August 15, 1350), BBCR 2.3:231–78; Letter 64, to Fra Michele of Monte Sant' Angelo (Raudnitz, Bohemia, September 28, 1350), BBCR 2.3:363; Letter 70, to Cardinal Gui de Boulogne (Raudnitz, 1351), BBCR 2.3:377–405.

Marriage and gender information here is extrapolated in large part from the Florentine *castato* of 1427. See Herlihy and Klapisch-Zuber, *Tuscans.*

Chapter 3. Reviving Antiquity

1. On the general idea of reform and renewal in Western culture see Kristeller, *Renaissance Thought,* 70–91; Ladner, *Idea of Reform,* 9–48; and Panofsky, esp. 1–41. For Petrarch's notions of decline and revival, including that of a "middle" age, see *Fam.* XX.8 and Mommsen, "Petrarch's Conception."

2. On Rome as the symbol of cultural and spiritual revival see Master Gregorius, *Marvels of Rome,* 18–19, 36; *Mirabilia Urbis Romae,* in D'Onofrio 1:46–100; and *Marvels of Rome,* Gardiner, 3–4, 29–30; Benson, "Political 'Renovatio'"; Bloch, "New Fascination"; Brentano, 66–90; Costa-Zalessow, "Personification"; Davis, *Dante;* idem, "Il buono tempo antico"; Graf, *Roma;* Krautheimer, *Rome,* 144–228, 271–310; Miglio, "'Et rerum facta'"; Ross, "Study"; and Settis, "Continuità." For the notion of *axis mundi* and its foundational importance see Eliade, *Sacred and Profane,* esp. 20–65; and idem, *Cosmos and History,* esp. 1–17.

3. On Rome as the symbol of the political revival of antiquity see the Romans' own sense of their historical role in the Statutes of 1363, Re, *Statuti* II.191, 188. Important studies include Davis, "Ptolemy"; idem, "Roman Patriotism"; Dupré Theseider, *Roma dal Comune;* Frugoni, "L'antichità"; Maire-Vigueur, "Capital"; Petrucci, "I documenti privati"; and *Public Lettering,* 1–15; Erler, *Lupa;* Gregorovius 4.2:449–545, 656–59; Marchioli, "L'Epigrafia"; Miglio, "Roma"; Salimei, *Senatori;* Saxl, "Capitol"; idem, "Classical Inscription"; and Schimmelpfennig and Schmugge, *Rom.*

4. On the revival of Rome as the spiritual capital of Christendom and the heir of the Christian empire of Constantine, see *The [Forged] Donation of Constantine*, Barry, ed. The Roman bishops, communes and barons expressed this revival in many ways, but most especially in the visual arts and architecture. For the "fashion of antiquity" see, above all, Krautheimer, passim. See also De Caprio, "La cultura romana"; Esch, "Spolien"; Greenhalgh, *"Ipsa ruina docet"*; idem, "Iconografia antica"; Kemp, "Stefaneschi-Altar"; Kinney, "Mirabilia"; idem, "Rape or Restitution"; and idem, "Sta. Maria in Trastevere"; Kitzinger, "The Arts"; Köhren-Jansen, *Giottos Navicella;* Paravicini Bagliani, "Bonifacio VIII"; Paeseler, "Giottos Navicella"; Rice, *Altars and Altarpieces,* 252–56; Romano, *"Regio dissimilitudinis'"; Settimana di storia dell'arte medievale Roma anno 1300;* and Urban, "Die Kirchenbaukunst." The best brief summary of the revival of ancient public lettering in Rome is Petrucci, *Public Lettering,* esp. 1–15. For the treasures at the Lateran see Kessler and Zacharias, *Rome 1300,* 9–37.

5. On Petrarch and the cultural revival associated with him, especially concerning Rome, see his *Collatio laureationis; Fam.* II.14, PLFM, 113; IV.6, 192; IV.7–8, 193–96; Marcello "Recenti studi"; Blanc, "La construction d'une utopie néo-urbaine"; Dotti, "Il primo libro delle 'Senili'"; Feo, "L'epistola"; Kölmel, "Petrarca"; Macek, "Pétrarch"; Mazzocco, "Petrarca"; idem, "Antiquarianism"; Musumarra, "Petrarca e Roma"; Petrucci, *La scittura;* Toppani, "Petrarca"; Wilkins, 8–52; and now Witt, *Footsteps,* 230–91, esp. 276–91. Summit, "Topography," has recently argued, convincingly, that Petrarch's concept of Roman antiquity merged both classical and Christian identities and owed much to the Mirabilian tradition.

Chapter 4. The Popes at Avignon

1. On Cola's life after his return from Anagni see AR, XVIII, ll. 21–45, Porta, 143–44; Wright, 31–32; and CRCR, 1–9.

2. On the history of Avignon see *Avignon au temps de Pétrarque: 1304–1374;* Becriaux, *Avignon;* Brun, *Avignon;* Gagnière, *Histoire d'Avignon;* Moulinas, *Avignon;* and Origo, 3–34.

3. On the Avignon papacy see Darbois, *Quand les papes;* Guillemain, *La cour;* idem, *Les papes;* Mollat, *Popes;* Renouard, *Avignon Papacy;* and Vicaire, *La papauté.*

4. On Clement VI see Jugie, "Clement VI"; Mollat, *Popes,* 37–43; and Wood, *Clement VI.*

5. On papal patronage, architecture, and cultural life see the titles cited in notes 2 and 3 and Giacomo Stefaneschi's Ceremonial in *De Rome en Avignon;* Castelnuovo, *Un pittore italiano;* Contamine, "Peasant Hut"; Delle Ville, *Mathèo de Viterbo;* Fausto, *La Construzione;* Gagnière, *Palace;* Girard, *L'aventure gothique;* Laclotte, *L'Ecole d'Avignon;* Roques, *Les peintures murales;* Schwarz, 144–61; and Vingtain, *Avignon.*

6. On the theoretical underpinnings of Clement VI's reign see Wood, 1–78 et passim.

7. On Cardinal Giovanni Colonna, the Colonna family, and their vast interests in Avignon and Rome, see Paravicini Bagliani, "Colonna, Giacomo," DBI 27:311–14; idem, "Colonna, Giovanni," DBI 27:333–37; Rehberg, "Familien"; idem, *Die Kanoniker,* which demonstrates both the Colonnas' deep penetration of the canonries of both Sta. Maria Maggiore and the Lateran, and their key role in Avignon as agents for church offices for Roman and other Italian families. See also idem, *Kirche,* esp. 37–78, 161–223, 436–506; Waley, "Colonna, Pietro," DBI 27:399–402. See also Foote's review of Rehberg, *Die Kanoniker.* Rollo-Koster, "Amongst Brothers," also stresses the role of religious confraternities for both social and political networks among Italian merchants and other laity.

8. On Cola's mission to Avignon see Amargier, "Pétrarque"; Barone, "Il potere pontificio"; Filippini, "Cola di Rienzo"; Kölmel, "Petrarca"; Macek, "Pétrarch"; and Wilkins, 32–44.

Dante had set the tone for the literary attacks on the papal exile from Rome. See his Letter V, "Now Is the Acceptable Time;" Letter VII, to the Italian cardinals, both in Coogan, *Babylon,* 25–27. Martinez, "Lament," traces these literary critiques of Avignon as Babylon back to the biblical tradition of Lamentations.

9. Pope Clement's response to the Roman embassy, which contains the basis of Cola's own address, can be found in Schmidinger, "Die Antwort Clemens' VI." Independent, if brief, accounts of the Roman embassy also appear in the six *Vitae* of Clement VI. See esp. 1 (Baluze 1:245), which repeats Clement's *"desidero enim videre vos"* theme; 3, by Jean la Porte d'Annonay (Baluze 1:278–79); 4 (Baluze 1:290); 5, with the text of the Jubilee bull (Baluze 1:298–303); 6 (Baluze 1:304–5). The *Vitae,* for understandable reasons, show some confusion as to which embassy Clement granted the Jubilee. Schmidinger, 329–37, indicates that it was Cola's delegation that finally won it. For a good overview of public oratory through the fourteenth century see McManamon. For the development of diplomatic form during the period see Mattingly, 23–28.

10. For Cola's letters to the Romans on his mission see Letter 1, to the Roman People (Avignon, January 28, 1343), BBCR 2.3:1–4; Letter 2, to the Senate and People of Rome (Avignon, January 28–31, 1343), BBCR 2.3:4–8.

11. On Cola's life in the papal *familia* see AR, XVIII ll. 29–41, Porta 144; Wright 32.

12. On Cola's relationship with Petrarch during this period see Petrarch's *Sine nomine* 7 (Avignon, 1343), BBCR 2.3:9–11; Zacour, 64–66; CRCR, 1–8. Zacour's arguments for rejecting Cola as the letter's recipient have no firm basis in external context or internal reference. In fact, the unabashed enthusiasm for the revival of the republic and the almost apocalyptic expectations placed upon it more fit a period before Cola's 1347 revolution than after it. Zacour offers no good reason to identify the recipient as one of the four cardinals charged with reforming the city's government in 1351. Petrarch's contacts with the commission of cardinals were never anonymous; in fact, the poet seemed to relish the chance to offer *public* advice to well-placed churchmen at that point. See also chapter 12, note 10.

13. On Clement VI's relationship with the Roman barons concerning Rienzo see Letter to the Senators of Rome (Villeneuve, August 9, 1343), Theiner 130, 2:119.

14. For Cola's palace politics after Petrarch's departure, see Letter 4, to Cle-

ment VI (April 13, 1344), BBCR 2.3:12. Mattingly, 61–62, notes that "resident diplomatic agents" were first documented in the 1340s. For the Colonna role in sending Petrarch to Naples see Wilkins, 39.

15. On Clement's endorsement of Cola's role in his Roman policy, see Letter to Cola di Rienzo (Avignon, April 13, 1344), Theiner, 139, 2:141; BBCR 2.3:13–14; Letter to Cola di Rienzo (Avignon, June 17, 1344), Theiner 140, 2:141–42; BBCR 2.3:15–16.

Chapter 5. Cola and the Barons

1. On the state of anarchy in fourteenth-century Rome see AR, XVIII, ll. 45–64, 203–13, 291–308, Porta, 144–45, 150, 153; Wright, 32–33, 37, 40–41. Contemporary political writers had much to say on the matter. See, for example, Bartolo da Sassoferrato, "De Guelphis et Ghibelinis," Emerton, 255–84; and Quaglione, 129–46; idem, "De regimine civitatis," Quaglione, 147–70; idem, "De tyranno," Quaglione, 171–213; and Emerton, 117–54; and Ptolemy of Lucca, *On the Government of Rulers*, Blyhte, trans. For papal attempts to resolve the apparently endless factional conflict, see Coste, "Les lettres collectives"; and Benedict XII, Letter to the barons of Rome (Avignon, March 18, 1336), in CRCR, 27. For one baron's excuse for such strife, see Petrarch, Letter to Stefano il Vecchio (*Fam.* VIII.1), PLFM, 391–92. Cola's own characterization of the barons as "tyrants" is borne out by contemporary practice. See Seibt, 115–18.

Useful secondary studies include Bowsky, "Medieval Citizenship"; Davis, "Ptolemy of Lucca"; idem, "Roman Patriotism"; Dean, "Marriage"; Hyde, "Contemporary Views," esp. 298, for Bartolo's contribution; Polecritti, *Preaching Peace*, 125–80; Riesenberg, "Civism."

2. On Rome's baronial families see Brentano, 171–209; idem, "Violence"; Carocci, *Baroni;* idem, "Baroni"; Larner, *Italy,* 83–105; Maire-Vigueur, "Capital"; idem, "Classe dominante."

3. On individual families see Bevilacqua, *Il Monte dei Cenci;* Brentano, passim; Klapisch-Zuber, "Kinship and Politics"; Krautheimer, *Rome,* 150–58, 295–320; Rehberg, "Familien"; idem, *Kanoniker;* and idem, *Kirche.* Excellent prosopographical profiles of Rome's leading barons now appear in the DBI. See bibliography for entries by Paravicini Bagliani and Waley, among others.

4. On the barons' *fortilizie* within the city see Asso, "Monte Giordano"; Brentano, 25–46, 102–5 et passim; and Krautheimer, *Rome,* 8–20, 295–309 et passim; Carocci, "Baroni in città," 140–49, 164–79; Cusanno, *Le fortificazioni;* idem, "Il complesso fortificato"; idem, "Turris Comitum"; and Katermaa-Ottela, "Le casetorri."

5. On the barons' holdings in the countryside see Carocci, *Baroni,* 69–98, 140–52, 184–245; and idem, "Baroni," 161–62; Ermini, "La libertà comunale"; Falco, "I comuni della Campagna"; Partner, *Lands,* 327–29 et passim; Tomassetti, "Documenti feudali."

6. On the barons' family structures and ties, see Brentano, 173–209 et passim; Carocci, *Baroni di Roma,* 151–80; idem, "Baroni in città," 155–60.

7. On the barons' political alliances and allegiances see the reports from the Aragonese ambassador in Finke, *Acta Aragonensia,* 1:286–87, 302–3, 307, quoted in Brentano, 116–17.

8. On the barons' social ethos and their role within the fabric of Roman society, see Brentano, 127–36, 173–209, et passim; Carocci, "Baroni in città," 152–54; idem, "La celebrazione aristocratica"; idem, "Una nobiltà bipartita"; Maire-Vigueur, "Capital économique," 223–24.

9. On the official government of Rome see Rota, "Il codice"; Salimei, *Senatori;* Barone, "Il potere"; Boüard, *Le régime;* Brentano, 91–136; Dupré Theseider, *Roma dal Comune;* Esch, "Dal Medioevo"; Gregorovius 4.2:456–62, 496–99.

10. For Cola's role in the City Chamber see Clement VI, Letter to Cola di Rienzo. (Avignon, June 17, 1344), Theiner 140, 2:141–42; AR, XVIII, ll. 52–64, Porta, 144–45; Wright, 32–33; ll. 203–11, Porta, 150, Wright, 37; Cola di Rienzo, Approval of the Statues of the Merchants by Orso Orsini (March 28, 1346), BBCR 2.4:43; Gatti, *Statuti,* 80; Letter 57 to the archbishop of Prague (August 1350), BBCR 2.3:258, ll. 726–33.

Chapter 6. Preparing for the Apocalypse

1. On Cola's Navicella painting on the Campidoglio, see AR, XVIII, ll. 64–249, Porta 147–51; Wright, 33–38. On Cola's visual program see Schwarz, "Images," 66–74; Sonnay, "La politique."

2. On the use of visual images in the fourteenth-century Italian communes, see Antoine, *"Ad perpetuam memoriam";* Belting, "Langage et réalité"; idem, "New Role"; Belting and Blume, *Malerei;* Benocci, "Le figurazioni"; Frugoni, *Distant City,* esp. 118–88; idem, "L'iconografia"; Romano, "'Regio dissimilitudinis'"; Schwarz, 136–213; Wieruszowski, "Art"; and Wollesen, "'Ut poesis pictura?'"

3. On Lorenzetti's "Good and Bad Government" see Greenstein, "The Vision of Peace"; Rowley, *Ambrogio Lorenzetti,* 1:99–142; Rubenstein, "Political Ideas"; Schwarz, 121–35; Skinner, "Ambrogio Lorenzetti"; Starn, *Ambrogio Lorenzetti;* and discussion for chapter 8 below.

4. On the *pittura infamante* see Edgerton, *Pictures,* 22–89; Ortalli, "Pingatur in Palatio";" and Zorzi, "Rituali."

5. For analysis of Cola's "Navicella" painting, its antecedents, and its imagery, see also Convenevolo da Prato, *Regia Carmina;* Kemp, "Stefaneschi-Altar"; Kessler and Zacharias, 216–28; Köhren-Jansen, *Giottos Navicella;* Paeseler, "Giottos Navicella"; Paravicini Bagliani, "Bonifacio VIII"; Rice, *Altars and Altarpieces,* 252–56; Schneller, *Medieval Model Books;* and Schwarz, 94–135. Witt, *Footsteps,* 234–35, discusses Petrarch's relationship with Convenevolo. For animal symbolism see Porta, "La symbolique."

6. On Cola's Lateran lecture on the *lex de imperio Vespasiani,* see AR, XVIII, ll. 133–203, Porta, 147–50; Wright, 35–37. For the assemblage of potent symbols of Rome collected at the Lateran, see Master Gregory 19–21, 36; Marvels, D'Onofrio 1:62–63; and Gardiner, 19–21. For useful interpretations see Frugoni, "L'antichità," 3–72. See especially 14–16, 53–54 for the *lex Vespasiani;* Kessler and Zacharias,

9–37; Krautheimer, *Rome,* 191–93, 322–26; Petrucci, *Public Lettering,* 1–15; Schwarz, 74–76.

7. There is a lively literature of interpretation on Cola's understanding and use of the *lex de imperio Vespasiani.* See Antoine, 604–11; Benes, "Cola di Rienzo"; Cantarelli, "La *lex de imperio Vespasiani*"; Collins, "Cola di Rienzo"; Greenhalgh, "*Ipsa ruina docet,*" 161–63; Juhar, "Der Romgedanke"; Seibt, 148–53; Sordi, "Cola di Rienzo." On the actual bronze tablet of the *lex,* see Collins, 168 n. 18; Crawford, *Roman Statutes* 1:549–53; Gordon, *Roman Epigraphy,* 121–23, and his figure 46.

8. The term "civic religion" is now used sparingly when discussing late medieval Italian spirituality. Nevertheless, the impact of the commune on religious practice and of religious motivation for the duties of Italian communal government remained strong through the fourteenth century. See, for example, Brentano, 137–69, 211–88; Golinelli, *Città e culto;* Guidoni, "La cultura urbanistica"; Vauchez, "Comparsa e affermazione"; idem, *Laity;* idem, "Patronage"; idem, "Penitenti"; idem, *Religion civique;* Webb, *Patrons and Defenders.* For a useful discussion of current interpretations of "civic religion," see Peterson, "Out of the Margins," esp. 851–54.

Much of this interface between the civic and the religious spheres was the work of the lay confraternities. This aspect of medieval spirituality has received an enormous amount of study in recent years. Among the more useful works are Banker, *Death;* Eisenbichler, *Crossing;* Esposito, "Le 'confraternite' del Gonfalone"; Little and Buzzetti, *Liberty;* and *Le mouvement confraternel.*

9. On the Jubilee and pilgrimage to Rome, so much has been written in the last decade, and to Rome over the last century, that only a small sampling of material is offered here. Much more is known and discussed about the Jubilee of 1300, but the primary sources, especially the discussions by Giovanni Villani, XII, and Matteo Villani I.xxxi, lviii, indicate that the two events shared much in common.

See Birch, *Pilgrimage,* with extensive recent bibliography; Brezzi, "Holy Years"; idem, "La realtà politica"; idem, *Storia;* Cilento, "Sulla tradizione"; De Angelis, *Il Giubileo;* idem, *L'ospedale;* Dickson, "Crowd"; Fagiolo and Madonna, *Roma 1300–1875,* esp. 210–29, 314–17; Fedele, "Il Giubileo del 1350"; Foreville, "Jubilé"; Arsenio Frugoni, "Il Giubileo"; Giuliano, "Roma 1300"; Kessler and Zacharias, *Rome 1300;* Llewellyn, *Rome in the Dark Ages,* 173–98; Manselli, "La religiosità giubilare del 1300"; Millefiorini, "Il Giubileo del 1300"; Paglia, "Dalle 'peregrinationes maiores'"; Romani, *Pellegrini e viaggiatori; Settimana di storia dell'arte medievale Roma anno 1300;* Stickler, *Il Giubileo di Bonifacio VIII;* Thiery, "Comunicazione e immagine."

10. The literature on the apocalyptic tradition in the West as well as in Italy and its impact on fourteenth-century Italian thought is enormous. One cannot avoid the influence of Norman Cohn, *The Pursuit of the Millennium,* which fixed the association of apocalypse with violence and social upheaval. More sober analyses include the essays included in AMA; Aurell, "Prophétie et messianisme politique"; Emmerson, "The Apocalypse in Medieval Culture"; Emmerson and Herzman, *Apocalyptic Imagination;* Garin, "L'altesa dell'età nuova e la Renova-

tio"; Klein, "The Apocalypse in Medieval Art"; Lerner, "Medieval Return"; McGinn, "John's Apocalypse"; Schwarz, 178–88. The essays in Bynum and Freedman, *Last Things,* provide useful summations of the current status of research. Convenient collections of documents include McGinn, *Apocalyptic Spirituality;* idem, *Visions of the End.*

Emmerson, *Antichrist;* McGinn, *Antichrist,* esp. 1–56 and 157–77; and Wright, *Art and Antichrist,* provide good discussions of the textual and iconographic identifications and understandings of the apocalyptic figure of Antichrist in the later Middle Ages.

11. For Joachim of Fiore and his influence see his *Enchiridion super Apocalypsim;* idem, *Liber de Concordia novi ac veteris testamenti;* and *Il Libro delle Figure;* Lee, Reeves, and Silano, *Western Mediterranean Prophesy.*

The study of Joachim and his influence is an immense and almost prophetically contested field. Useful studies for our purposes include Bloomfield; Daniel, "Double Procession"; idem, "Exodus and Exile"; idem, "Joachim of Fiore"; Fonseca, "Continuità e diversità"; McGinn, *Calabrian Abbot;* idem, "New Bibliography," in *Visions,* 371–73; Moynihan; Reeves, *Influence of Prophesy;* idem, *Prophetic Future;* Reeves and Hirsch-Reich, *Figurae.*

12. On the Spiritual Franciscans and their influence, see Angelo Clareno, Letter 28 [29], to Philip of Majorca (Subiaco, December 29, 1330), as cited. Important studies of direct political influence include Baron, "Franciscan Poverty"; and Becker, "Heresy in Medieval and Renaissance Florence." More spiritual readings include Burr, "Mendicant Readings"; idem, *Olivi's Peaceable Kingdom;* Campagnola, *Chi Erano gli Spirituali?;* Cazenave, "La vision eschatologique"; Douie, *Fraticelli;* Duprè-Theseider, "L'attesa escatologica"; Leff, *Heresy* 1:49–255; Manselli, *Da Gioacchino;* McGinn, "Pastor Angelicus"; Messini, "Profitismo e profezie"; Musto, "Franciscan Joachimism"; idem, "Queen Sancia"; Potestà; Vauchez, "Les théologiens"; and von Auw, *Angelo Clareno.* Burr, *Spiritual Franciscans,* offers the latest word on the field. Giangreco, "Miles," attempts to analyze Cola's Joachimism and concludes that a case can be made for it from before his exile in December 1347; and it only became stronger during his stay with the Fraticelli. While Giangreco uses both the Anonimo romano and Cola's correspondence, the basic framework for his interpretation relies directly on materials and conclusions that I had already laid out in my 1986 edition of *Petrarch: The Revolution of Cola di Rienzo.* Giangreco citations of the historiography from the 1930s on, and his remarks on Cola's early Joachimism on pages 85–87, for example, follow those of my 1986 edition closely and at times paraphrase my own findings on page 171 n. 3, which Giangreco attributes—incorrectly—to Cosenza's original 1913 edition.

13. For the Spiritual and Joachite influence in and around Rome, see Angelo Clareno, Letters (Musto ed. Roman, von Auw Arabic) I (1), II (2), VI (6), XV (15), XVII (17), XXXIII (34), L (51). For studies see D'Alatri, "Fraticellismo"; Mosti, "L'eresia"; Rusconi, "Spirituali"; Sensi, "Dossier sui Clareni"; and von Auw, *Epistolae,* liv–lix.

14. On the "peaceful apocalypse" and religious movements for peace and justice in late medieval Italy, see the Great Alleluia of 1233 and the Flagellants of 1260,

in Musto, *Catholic Peacemakers* 1:539–55; Venturino da Bergamo, Anonymous Legend and Testimony before the papal inquisition, in Musto, *Catholic Peacemakers* 1:556–66; Giovanni Villani, *Cronica,* VIII.36, pp. 77–79; X.55, pp. 139–45.

See also Clementi, *Il Beato Venturino;* Corsi, "La 'crociata'"; Gennaro, "Venturino da Bergamo"; idem, "Venturino spirituale"; Henderson, "Flagellant Movement"; idem, *Piety and Charity;* Larner, *Italy,* 228–55; Meersseman, "Disciplinati"; Morghen, "Raniero Fasani"; Miglio, "Gli ideali"; Peretto, *Movimenti;* Rusconi, "L'Italia senza papa."

15. For the widespread Joachite influence on literature as demonstrated through such figures as Dante and Petrarch, see Petrarch, *Sine nomine* 18, in Zacour, 108–17; Herzman, "Dante"; Kaske, "The Seven *Status Ecclesie*"; and now Ciccia, *Dante;* and Papka, "Limits." Petrarch's *Sine nomine* letters are, of course, the mother lode of references to Avignon as Babylon. See, for example, Zacour 23–26, and letters 8–10, Zacour, 66–73; 14, Zacour, 84–90; 17–19, Zacour, 96–121.

16. On Rome as Babylon, see Emmerson, "Apocalypse," 313–18; *Mirabilia Urbis Romae,* D'Onofrio 1:55; Gardiner, *Marvels* II.1, pp. 17–18; Jacobus de Voragine, *Golden Legend* 1:62–71 at 70–71. On Olivi, see Burr, "Mendicant Readings," 96–97. For the Reformation use of these themes, see Chastel, 49–90.

17. On Cola's apocalyptic painting at Sant'Angelo in Pescheria, see AR, XVIII, ll. 213–49, Porta, 150–51; Wright, 37–38; Hugenholtz, "Anagni Frescoes"; Schwarz, 77–80, 178–231; Smith, "Anagni."

Chapter 7. Pentecost

1. For Cola's appeal to the *buono stato* see AR, XVIII, ll. 249–55, Porta, 151; Wright, 38; ll. 291–308, Porta, 153; Wright, 40; Thomas Aquinas, *Summa Theologica* Q.90, art. 2, Q.96, art. 4, D'Entrèves, ed., 104–5, 110–11.

Useful studies include Boüard, *Le régime politique;* Collina, "Cola di Rienzo"; Arsenio Frugoni, "Cola di Rienzo 'tribunus sompniator.'" The corporate nature of the *buono stato* shared much in common with the lay confraternities. See chapter 6, note 8, and Henderson, *Piety and Charity,* 16–18.

2. For the visual background see Belting, "Langage et réalité," 491–511; Rowley, *Ambrogio Lorenzetti* 1:99–142; Schwarz, 26–47; Sonnay, "La politique artistique"; and chapter 6, note 3. For medieval and early modern examples of the jointer and floor planes, both almost three feet long and used for smoothing joints and edges, see Mercer, 107–8, and figures 101–2. For the two-handed frame and pit saws, used for finishing boards from raw timber, see Mercer, 22–23, 152–53, and figures 21–24, 142. Page 24, figure 24 presents a drawn detail of a fresco from c. 1350, by "Cristofano" Buffalmacco in the Campo Santo, Pisa, of just such a saw being worked by two carpenters.

3. For the social groups that made up Cola's *buono stato,* and his appeal to each, see AR, XVIII, ll. 256–90, Porta, 151–53; Wright, 39; Ildebrandino Conti, archbishop of Padua, Letter to his vicar Leonardo de S. Sepulcro (Valmontone, July 29/30, 1347), BBCR 2.5:1–15; Giovanni Villani, *Cronica,* XII.90, pp. 276–77.

For important studies see Gennaro, "Mercanti e bovattieri"; Macek, "Les racines sociales"; Miglio, "Gruppi sociali." For the baronial families in power at the time of the revolution, see Salimei, *Senatori e statuti,* 109–17.

4. On Stefano Colonna see Petrarch, "The Triumph of Fame" II, Wilkins, *Triumphs,* 85; Rehberg, *Machte und Kirche,* 37–42, 79–82; Waley, "Colonna, Stefano, il Vecchio," DBI 27:433–37.

5. For the Pentecost revolution see AR, XVIII, ll. 308–45, Porta, 153–54; Wright, 40–41; Cola di Rienzo, Letter 7, to Viterbo (May 24, 1347), BBCR 2.3:16–27, ll. 94–96, 114–20; Letter 50, to Emperor Charles IV (Prague, July 1350), BBCR 2.3:204, ll. 201–8; *Chronicon Estense,* RIS 15.3:148–49; Giovanni Villani, XII.90.

6. The remarks of Rosenstock-Huessy on the revolutionary sense of creating a new age are apropos here. See *Driving Power,* 3–32. For possible visual underpinnings to Cola's tribunate see Schwarz, 26–30; Seibt, 209–11.

7. On Petrarch's inspiration of these events see his Letter to Cola di Rienzo (June 24–27, 1347), *Variae* 48 (Hortatoria), BBCR 2.3:63–81; CRCR, 9–24 at 17; and Macek, "Pétrarch et Cola di Rienzo."

Chapter 8. The *Buono Stato*

1. For the ordinances of the *buono stato* read atop the Capitoline, see AR, XVIII, ll. 339–710, Porta, 154–67; Wright, 41–53. On the legal and administrative basis of the *buono stato* in contemporary practice see Bartolo da Sassoferrato, "De Guelphis et Ghibelinis," Quaglione, 129–46; idem, "De regimine civitatis," Quaglione, 147–70; and idem, "De tyranno," Quaglione, 171–213.

2. For a useful and thoughtful discussion of the distinction between the imperial powers identified by Cola in the *lex de imperio Vespasiani* and his own communal authority, see Collins, 173–80. Wood, *Clement VI,* 82–84, relying largely on Cola's *Libellus,* written under duress in prison in 1350, and on secondhand accounts by Cola's enemies, asserts that Cola's "actions betokened his own imperial ambitions."

3. For background on the Roman militia see Egidi, *Intorno all'esercito;* Gasparri, *I milites cittadini*; Gregorovius 2:176–80, 422–25, 438–39. For the Ordinances of Justice of 1295 in Florence, see Kohl, "Ordinances."

4. On the definition of the late ancient and medieval district of Rome and its revenues, see Otto IV, emperor, Document defining the Roman District (June 8, 1201), BBCR 2.5:331.

Gregorovius 1:508–10; 2:209–13, 448–61, still offers the most concise description of what the Romans, Byzantines, and popes meant by the "duchy" and "district" of Rome. Valuable studies include De la Roncière, "Indirect Taxes or 'Gabelles'"; Llewellyn, 141–72; Pardi, "La populazione"; Partner, *Lands,* 420–40; Small, "District of Rome"; Tomassetti, "Del sale e focatico"; Toubert, *Les structures;* Waley, *Italian City-Republics,* 56–109, 147–63.

5. The conceptual origins of Cola's *buono stato* lie in many sources, including contemporary political practice and theory and religious notions of unfolding ages.

On medieval meanings of *status* see Du Cange, *Glossarium* 6:363–65. For religious connotations of *status* see Daniel, "Joachim of Fiore"; Arsenio Frugoni, "Cola di Rienzo 'tribunus sompniator'"; Ladner, *Idea of Reform*, 226–31. The *bonus status* of Rome was a term used frequently enough by Clement VI, as, for example, in his letter to Cola of August 9, 1343, Theiner 130, 2:119. Ullmann, *Growth of Papal Government*, 451–57; idem, *History of Political Thought*, 169–79, 214–19; idem, *Principles of Government*, 87, 215–97, discusses "state" in this context. Skinner, *Foundations* 2:352–58, traces the development of the concept and warns (2:352) against using the term for medieval contexts. For the Spirituals see chapter 6, note 12; for Dante, see chapter 6, note 15; for Robert of Anjou's usage, see Musto, "Franciscan Joachimism," esp. 461–73, 484–86.

6. For its communal uses see Giovanni Villani, *Chronica* XII.90, pp. 276–83. A search of Kohl, *Records,* returns ninety-six documents dated between February 1336 and April 1397 in which *bonus status* or a variant refers to the prosperous or peaceful condition of the Venetian empire and its holdings.

7. For the visual representations of the *buon comune,* see Chiara Frugoni, *Distant City,* 118–88; De Matteis, *"La teologia politica";* Rowley, *Ambrogio Lorenzetti* 1:99–142; Sonnay, "La politique artistique"; Starn, *Ambrogio Lorenzetti,* 25–36; and chapter 6, note 3.

8. For Petrarch's concordances of secular history, see *Variae* 48, *Epistola Hortatoria,* CRCR, 9–36; Feo, "L'epistola come mezzo di propaganda"; Mommsen, "Petrarch's Conception." See also Davis, *"Il buon tempo antico."* For a good brief review of Petrarch's views of the state and its ends in peace and justice, see Kohl's introduction to Petrarch, "How a Ruler Ought to Govern His State," 25–34.

9. For the events following the Pentecost revolution, see AR, XVIII ll. 335–478, Porta, 154–59; Wright, 41–45; Cola di Rienzo, Letter 8, to the Cities and Princes of Italy (June 7, 1347), BBCR 2.3:17–27; Letter 14, to the Viceroy of Sicily (July 1, 1347), BBCR 2.3:37–41; Letter 15, to Clement VI (July 8, 1347), BBCR 2.3:41–49; Giovanni Villani, *Chronica* XII.90, pp. 276–83.

10. For the Colonna see Paravicini Bagliani, "Colonna, Stefano, il Giovane," DBI 27:437–38; idem, "Colonna, Stefano" [Stefanello], DBI 27:438–40; Waley, "Colonna, Stefano, il Vecchio," DBI 27:433–37.

11. The Anonimo romano digresses from the narrative flow of events to devote an entire section of his work to the theme of justice and the use of force in the *buono stato*. See AR, XVIII, ll. 478–738, Porta, 159–68; Wright, 46–54; Petrarch, *Variae* 48 *(Hortatoria),* CRCR, 17–18. For a parallel see Siena, *Constitutio* of 1232–1338; AS, 23, f. 477.

12. Useful studies on communal justice include Bowsky, "The *Buon Governo* of Siena"; idem, "Medieval Citizenship"; idem, "The Medieval Commune"; Brezzi, *Roma e l'impero;* Chambers and Dean, *Clean Hands,* esp. 14–18, 260–62; Chojnacki, "Crime, Punishment"; Chiara Frugoni, *Distant City,* 118–88; Mellinkoff, "Riding Backwards"; Zorzi, "Rituali." For a brief discussion of confraternities of justice see Falvey, esp. 33–34. Merback, 17–21, 126–57 et passim, cautions that "rituals of punishment" in the later Middle Ages also held deep resonances of the sufferings of Jesus and cannot be wholly explained by either

bodily metaphors or deep structures of retribution. His notes on pp. 320–24 provide a good review of previous scholarship. Gragnolati, esp. 92–94, examines the work of Bonvesin de la Riva and observes a similar resonance in bodily suffering to Christ's own passion and the "cleansing power of blood" (97).

13. On the Marseilles galley see Clement VI, Letter to Senate and People of Rome (February 1, 1347), BBCR 2.5:123–24; idem, Letters to Raymond of Orvieto, to Senate, and to Stefano Colonna and Nicola Orsini (April 27, 1347), BBCR 2.5:124–26.

14. On Cola's reform of the commercial laws see his approval of statutes of the Arte della Lana (June 27, 1347), BBCR 2.4:44; idem, approval of Statutes of the Merchants (September 2, 1347), BBCR 2.4:44–45. See also his adjudication of a dispute involving the nuns of SS. Cosmas and Damiano in Trastevere (November 1347), BBCR 2.4:50–55.

15. If Cola's *buono stato* was based on communal justice, so too was it founded on medieval Christian ideas of peacemaking and reconciliation. See AR, XVIII, ll. 479–99, Porta, 159–60; Wright, 46–47; archive of S. Angelo in Pescheria, Protocol of de Scambiis, vol. an. 1368, c. 97, in Fedele, "Una composizione di pace," 468–69; Rota, "Il codice degli 'statuta Urbis,'" *Statuta Urbis* of 1363, II.20–21. For the biblical origins see Musto, *Catholic Peacemakers* 1:1–81.

See discussions in Fedele, "Un giudicato di Cola di Rienzo"; Koch et al., "Ritual Reconciliation"; Miglio, "Gli ideali di pace"; Polecritti, *Preaching Peace,* 84–124; Sassetti, "Giacomo della Merca paciere"; Waley, "A Blood-Feud"; and Weissman, "Cults," 211. Najemy's distinction between "corporate" and "consensus" politics offers some insight into Cola's attempts to rise above purely communal, guild-based structures of power.

Chapter 9. Cola and the World

1. For Cola's diplomacy and views of Rome's place in the world, see AR, XVIII, ll. 523–37, 1029–1178; Porta, 160–62, 177–82; Wright, 47–48, 63–68; Cola di Rienzo, Letter 7 to Viterbo (May 24, 1347), BBCR 2.3:17–27, col. 1; Letter 8, to the Cities and Princes of Italy (June 7, 1347), BBCR 2.3:17–27, col. 2; Letter 9, to Guido Gonzaga (June 11, 1347), BBCR 2.3:28; Letter 11, to Florence (late June 1347), BBCR 2.3:30; Letter 14, to the Viceroy of Sicily (July 1, 1347), BBCR, 2.3:38–39.

2. On Cola's diplomatic corps see AR, XVIII, ll. 544–65; Porta, 161–62; Wright, 48; Francesco Baroncelli, Speech to the Florentines (July 1347), BBCR 2.4:7–14; Pandolfuccio di Guido di Pandolfo de' Franchi, Speech to the Florentine government (July 2, 1347), BBCR 2.4:5–7; idem, Speech to the Florentine government (July 3, 1347), BBCR 2.4:15. On the Baroncelli family see Rehberg, "Familien," 154–57; idem, *Die Kanoniker,* 389–99, 449–50.

On diplomacy in Italy during this period see Ganshof, *Middle Ages,* 218–54, and esp. 248 for his negative views on Rienzo, quoted in the introduction. See also Mariani, "Cola di Rienzo nel giudizio"; Mattingly, 1–70; Miglio, "Il progetto politico"; Mollat, *Popes,* 173–87; Waley, *Italian City-Republics,* 110–38.

3. For various responses to Cola's declaration of the *buono stato,* see Agnolo di Tura del Graso, *Cronaca Senese,* RIS 15.6:551–52; Terracina, Document dated September 27, 1347, BBCR 2.5:20–22; Todi, Letter to Rome and Cola di Rienzo (August 17, 1347), Gabrielli, 242–43; BBCR 2.4:30–31; Giovanni Villani, *Cronica* XII.90, pp. 277–78; DKPSP, 212–13; XII.104, pp. 278–79; DKPSP, 213–14.

4. For the response of Italy's intellectuals, see Barbato da Sulmona, *Romana respublica urbi Rome,* in Weiss, "Barbato da Sulmona," 13–22; Petrarch, Letter to Cola and the Roman People, *Variae 48, Hortatoria* (June 24–27, 1347), BBCR 2.3: 63–81; CRCR, 10–14; Letter to Cola, *Variae* 38 (July 24–26, 1347), CRCR, 39–43; to Cola (August 21–25, 1347), *Sine nomine* 2 (August–September 1347), CRCR, 69–83; Zacour, 35–42; *Sine nomine* 3 (September 2–8, 1347), CRCR, 84–87; Zacour, 42–44. See also Feo, "L'epistola"; Wilkins, 63–73.

5. The impact of the Kingdom of Naples on Roman and Italian politics in general during this period is as unstudied as it is fundamental. But see De Frede, "Da Carlo I d'Angio à Giovanna I"; Mollat, *Popes,* 173–87; Musto, "An Introduction to Neapolitan History," esp. xxxviii–xliv; idem, "Franciscan Joachimism"; idem, "Queen Sancia."

6. On Rome as a new center of diplomacy see AR, XVIII, ll. 1028–1178, Porta, 177–82; Wright, 63–68. The Anonimo romano's story of Rome's prestige, even in Muslim lands, is borne out by Cola in his Letter 50 to Charles IV (Prague, late July 1350). See BBCR 2.3:207–8, ll. 298–313. For prophecies of the overthrow of Islam in the Last Days, see McGinn, *Visions,* 149–57. Studies include Bigalli; and Daniel, "Apocalyptic Conversion."

7. On Cola's diplomacy with Avignon and his lord Pope Clement VI, see Cola's Letter 15, to Clement VI (July 8, 1347), BBCR 2.3:47; Letter 18, to a friend in Avignon (July 15, 1347), BBCR 2.3:53–59; DKPSP, 193–96; Letter 25, to Petrarch (July 28, 1347), BBCR 2.3:85–86; CRCR, 37–38.

8. On Clement's growing unease with Cola's *buono stato* see Clement VI, Letters to Raymond of Orvieto and Cola di Rienzo (Avignon, June 27, 1347), BBCR 2.3:31–36; to Cola (Avignon, July 14, 1347), BBCR 2.3:52.

9. On Cola's Roman Synod see AR, XVIII, ll. 1030–1378, Porta, 177–89; Wright, 64–74; *Chronica Mutinense,* 135–36; Cola's Letter 16, to Mantua, Florence, Lucca (July 9, 1347), BBCR 2.3:50–51; DKPSP, 192–93; Letter 19, to Florence (July 19, 1347), BBCR 2.3:59–60; Letter 21, to Florence (July 22, 1347), BBCR 2.3:61–62. See also Miglio, "Il progetto politico di Cola di Rienzo."

10. On the symbolic meanings of Cola's pageantry, see *Mirabilia* 17, D'Onofrio 1:70; *Marvels,* II.6, 26–28; Bertelli, 62–96, who also sees Dante and the St. Francis Master in Assisi as important examples in this tradition; Frugoni, *Distant City,* 136–37; Newbigin, *"Cene";* Schwarz, "Images and Illusions," 28–39; Seibt, 155–215; Trexler, "Ritual Behavior"; Weissman, "Cults," esp. 210–11; Wollesen, "'Ut poesis pictura?'" esp. 197–210 and figure 7, p. 194. Seibt, borrowing much from the long tradition of German interpretations of Italian history, places far too much emphasis on Cola's personal imperial ambitions. In this he concurs with Wood. See chapter 8, note 2.

11. On Cola's coinage see Papencordt. See also figure 22.

12. On Cola's knighting and ritual bath see AR, XVIII, ll. 1228–1380, Porta, 184–89; Wright, 69–74; Cochetus de Chotiis, Letter to an Orsini (August 2, 1347), Papencordt, item 9, pp. xvii–xix; BBCR 2.4:21–26; Jacobus de Voragine, *The Golden Legend* 12, 1:63–65; Giovanni Villani, *Cronica* XII.90, pp. 277–78; DKPSP, 213–14.

13. On the Decree on the Sovereignty of the Roman People and the diplomatic furor that ensued, see AR, XVIII, ll. 1307–40, Porta, 186–88; Wright 72–73, *Chronicon Estense*, RIS 15.3:151–53; Cola di Rienzo, Letter 27, On the Sovereignty of the Roman People (August 1, 1347), BBCR 2.3:100–106; DKPSP, 205–6; Raymond of Orvieto, Letter to Clement VI (August 1, 1347), Papencordt, xvi–xvii; BBCR 2.4:19–21.

Again, Seibt, 137–40, 148–50, 163–69, 178–90 et passim, makes too much of Cola's personal imperial ambitions here. Collins, 173–75, 182–83, places this act in its proper perspective. See also chapter 8, notes 1–3, and Vinay, "Cola di Rienzo."

14. On Cola's coronation see anonymous Cod. Torinese c. 182 A, in Gabrielli, 245–47; BBCR 2.4:36–38; DKPSP 214–16; Cavallini, *Polistoria*, VIII.2; Letter of an unknown author, perhaps Cochetus (August 18, 1347), Papencordt, xx; BBCR 2.4:32–35; Vatican, Cod. arch. Vat. c. 3 A, in Gabrielli, 247; Letter 35, to Clement VI (August 20, 1347), BBCR 2.3:128–31. See also Arsenio Frugoni, "Cola di Rienzo"; Seibt, 171–73, 210–15; Schwarz, 24–35.

15. On Cola's plans for the imperial election on Pentecost day, June 8, 1348, see AR, XVIII, ll. 1373–80, Porta, 189; Wright, 74; Seibt, 169–70; and Wood, 43–47, 78–95, who tends to agree that Cola sought to usurp papal prerogatives over Rome's imperial rule. For Venetian legislation see Kohl, *Records*, K1469.

16. On reactions to Cola's coronation and Roman Synod see Clement VI, Letters to Raymond of Orvieto and Cola (August 17, 1347), BBCR 2.3:120–22; Letter to Bertrand de Déaulx (August 21, 1347), CRCR, 69–71, DKPSP, 216–17; Cola di Rienzo, Letter 28, to Clement VI (July 27 and August 5, 1347), BBCR 2.3:106–16; Letter 29, to Florence (August 5, 1347), BBCR 2.3:117–18; Letter 30, to Todi (August 6, 1347), BBCR 2.3:119–20; Letter 35, to Clement VI (August, 20, 1347), BBCR 2.3:128–31; Lucca, Letter to Cola di Rienzo and Rome (June 23, 1347), BBCR 2.3: 29; Petrarch, *Variae* 40, CRCR, 44–52; *Variae* 42 (August 22–31, 1347), CRCR, 53–57; Eclogue 5, "The Shepherd's Affection" (August 22–31, 1347), BBCR 2.3: 87–99; CRCR, 57–68.

Chapter 10. War with the Barons

1. For estimates of the Roman district's population and income potential, see Pardi, "La populazione"; and Tomassetti, "Del sale e focatico." There are countless books published on warfare in the Middle Ages. Two recent and useful titles are France, *Western Warfare*; and Keen, *Medieval Warfare*.

2. For an account of the causes of the war see AR, XVIII, ll. 738–1026, Porta, 168–77, ll. 1380–1790, Porta, 189–202; Wright, 54–63, 74–87.

3. For the campaign against Janni di Vico see AR, XVIII, ll. 767–823, Porta, 169–71; Wright, 55–57; *Chronicon Estense*, RIS 15.3:150–55; Clement VI, Letter to

Andrea Orsini (August 1, 1346), Theiner 149, 2:151; Cochetus de Chotiis, Letter to Rainaldo Orsini (August 2, 1347), Papencordt, item 9, xvii–xix; Cola di Rienzo, Letter 15, to Clement VI (July 8, 1347), BBCR 2.3:44–48; Letter 18, to an unknown friend in Avignon (July 15, 1347), BBCR 2.3:55–56, ll. 63–83; Negotiations between Cola and Janni di Vico (July 16, 1347), Papencordt, item 5, v–vi; Letter 28, to Clement VI (July 27–August 5, 1347), BBCR 2.3:106–16.

Useful studies include Calisse, "I Prefetti di Vico"; Carocci, *Baroni di Roma*, 86–87, 120–22; Cecchelli, *Vita di Roma*, 1:1093–98; De Cesaris, "I Prefetti di Vico," esp. 7, for his "politica di attesa"; France, *Western Warfare*, 107–27; TCI, *Lazio*, "Blera," and region, 234–42; "Tarquinia (Corneto)," 167–83; "Tuscania," 305–19; "Vetralla," 242–47; "Viterbo," 248–75. Giangreco, "Miles," 80 n. 9, citing Wright, 20, claims that Janni di Vico was a Joachite sympathizer, although neither writer cites a source for this.

4. For the revolt of Nicola, count of Fondi, see AR, XVIII, ll. 993–1010, Porta, 176–77; Wright, 62; Cola di Rienzo, Letter 35, to Clement VI (August, 20, 1347), BBCR 2.3:128–31; Letter 37, to an unnamed cardinal in Rome (September 1, 1347), BBCR 2.3:134; Letter 40, to Rainaldo Orsini (September 17, 1347), BBCR 2.3:144–45; Letter 43, to Clement VI (October 11, 1347), BBCR 2.3:158–72; Giovanni Villani, *Cronica* XII.105, 279–81.

For secondary works see Ermini, "La libertà comunale"; Falco, "I comuni della Campagna"; Faraglia, "Barbato da Sulmona"; Martini, "Caetani, Giacomo," DBI 16:172–74; idem, "Caetani, Nicola," DBI 16:193–95; Paravicini Bagliani, "Colonna, Giovanni" [son of Stefano il Giovane], DBI 27:338–39; TCI, *Lazio*, "Fondi," 719–24; "Gaeta," 733–48; "Ninfa," 687–89; "San Felice Circeo," 771–76; "Sermoneta," 690–93.

5. On Cola's attempts to win and keep military alliances with the free communes of central Italy, see Letter 19, to Florence (July 19, 1347), BBCR 2.3:59–60; Letter 21, to Florence (July 22, 1347), BBCR 2.3:61–62; Letter 29, Postscript, to Florence (August 5, 1347), BBCR 2.3:118; Letter 30, to Todi, Postscript (August 6, 1347), BBCR 2.3:120; Letter 33, to Florence (August 20, 1347), BBCR 2.3:123; Letter 36, to Florence (August 27, 1347), BBCR 2.3:132–33.

6. On Cola's use of communal legislation to curb the barons, see AR, XVIII, ll. 749–67, Porta, 168–69; Wright, 55; Cola di Rienzo, Letter 50, to Emperor Charles IV (Prague, July 1350), BBCR 2.3:207, ll. 271–83; Rota, "I codici degli statuta Urbis," 149, 158–65. Oaths of obedience from its colonial and administrative nobility were long part of Venice's policy, for example. Kohl, *Records,* headnotes 11 documents between May 1340 and February 1347 (K362, 584, 620, 677, 688, 797, 816, 1377, 2865, 3917, 3918) requiring such oaths of fealty. Florence required such oaths in the Ordinances of Justice of July 1295, excerpted and trans. in Kohl, "Ordinances," 139–42.

7. For Cola's arrest of the barons and its aftermath, see AR, XVIII, ll. 1380–1465, Porta, 189–92; Wright, 74–77; *Chronicon Estense*, RIS 15.3:154; Cola di Rienzo, Letter 40 (September 14, 1347), BBCR 2.3:145–47, ll. 11–69. For Petrarch's criticisms of Cola's ultimate clemency see *Fam.* XIII.6, to Francesco, Prior of the Holy Apostles (Vaucluse, August 10, 1352), CRCR, 130–38.

8. Cola's accusations against Cardinal Giovanni Colonna are well borne out by modern research. See Rehberg, *Kirche und Machte,* 120–29 et passim; and idem, *Die Kanoniker,* which demonstrates the patterns of patronage and office acquisition that flowed through the Colonna in Avignon.

9. On the revolt of the Orsini see AR, XVIII, ll. 1465–1527, Porta, 192–94; Wright, 77–79; Clement VI, Letter to Cola (Avignon, October 12, 1347), BBCR 2.3:173; Cola di Rienzo, Letter 43 (October 11, 1347), BBCR 2.3:168–70, ll. 169–214.

For the Marino campaign see TCI, *Roma e Dintorni,* "Marino," 718–21; Tomassetti, *Campagna Romana,* 4:196–97, 236, 259.

10. On Bertrand's summons to Cola see AR, XVIII, ll., 1527–67, Porta, 194–95; Wright, 79–80; Partner, "Bertrand de Deux," DBI 9:642–44.

11. On the revolt of the Colonna and the battle of Porta San Lorenzo, see AR, XVIII, ll., 1567–1790, Porta, 195–202; Wright, 80–87; *Chronicon Estense,* RIS 15.3:155–56; Antonio di Giovanni Zuparo, "De novis Urbis," BBCR 2.5:24.

For some of the chief actors see Paravicini Bagliani, "Colonna, Giacomo" [son of Stefano il Vecchio], DBI 27:316–18; idem, "Colonna, Giovanni" [son of Stefano il Vecchio], DBI 27:333–37; idem, "Colonna, Stefano, il Giovane," DBI 27:437–38; idem, "Colonna, Stefano" [Stefanello], DBI 27:438–40.

12. For the aftermath of the Roman victory see AR, XVIII, ll., 1790–1888, Porta, 202–6; Wright, 87–90; Clement VI, letters of consolation to Stefano il Vecchio and other members of the Colonna family (Avignon, January 27, 1348), CLC 1578–80, 3:3.208; Cola di Rienzo, Letter 45, to Florence (November 9, 1347), BBCR 2.3:174–75; Letter 46, to the cities and princes of Italy (November 20, 1347), BBCR 2.3:175–81; Petrarch, *Fam.* VII.13, to Giovanni Colonna (November–December 1347), PLFM, 367–72.

13. For Petrarch's letter to Stefano see *Fam.* VIII.1, to Stefano il Vecchio Colonna (September 8, 1348/9), PLFM, 386–95. For Stefano's reaction to Petrarch's letter see Wilkins, 78–79. McClure, 37–38, discusses this in the context of Petrarch's overall art of consolation. In this context, Martinez's link of the image of the widowed Rome to the tradition of lamentations takes on added weight.

Chapter 11. Abdication and Exile

1. On Cola's negative reaction to his massacre of the Colonna see AR, XVIII, ll. 1888–1908, Porta, 206; Wright, 90–91.

2. On the diplomatic break between Avignon and Rome see Clement VI, Letter to Matteo de Viterbo (August 17, 1347), BBCR 2.4:28–29; Letters to rectors of the Papal States (August 17, 1347), BBCR 2.4:29–30; Letter to Bertrand de Déaulx (August 21, 1347), BBCR 2.4:38–41; Cola di Rienzo, Letter 35, to Clement VI (August 20, 1347), BBCR 2.3:128–31; DKPSP, 217–20; Letters to Bertrand de Déaulx (September 15, 1347), BBCR 2.4:55–57; Letter 40, to Rainaldo Orsini (September 17, 1347), BBCR 2.3:147–51; CRCR 72–73; DKPSP, 220–22; Letter 57, to Ernst von Pardubitz, archbishop of Prague (before August 15, 1350), BBCR 2.3:

241–42, 263–66; CRCR, 86–87; Petrarch, *Sine nomine* 2 (August–September, 1347), CRCR, 73–77; Zacour, 35–42; *Sine nomine* 3 (September 2–8, 1347), CRCR, 84–87; Zacour, 42–44. Mattingly, 39–44, surveys what was expected of diplomatic immunities and privileges.

3. For Clement's alliance with the barons see Clement VI, Letter to Raymond of Orvieto (September 12, 1347), BBCR 2.4:49–50; Letter to Bertrand de Déaulx (September 19, 1347), BBCR 2.4:60; Letter to Pietro de Pinu, vice-rector of the Patrimony of St. Peter in Tuscia (September 19, 1347), BBCR 2.4:61–62; Letter to Cola (October 4, 1347), Theiner 177, 2:181; BBCR 2.3:157; Letter to Cola (Avignon, October 6, 9, 1347), BBCR 2.3:157; Cola di Rienzo, Letter 57, to Ernst von Pardubitz, archbishop of Prague (before August 15, 1350), BBCR 2.3: 241–42, 263–66.

4. For the pope's manipulation of Lello Petri Stefani de Tosettis see Clement VI, Letter to Lello Petri Stefani de Tosettis (October 5, 1347), Theiner 178, 2:181; CRCR, 104; to Lello Petri Stefani de Tosettis (October 7, 1347), BBCR 2.4:62–64; Petrarch, *Fam.* VII.7 (Genoa, November 29, 1347), CRCR, 88–104.

On Lello and the Tosetti and their ties to the Colonna, see Rehberg, "Familien," 79:131–39, idem, *Die Kanoniker,* 282–84, 382–84, 445; idem, *Kirche und Macht,* 481–82; CRCR, 103–4 n. 35; on the contrada de Tosectis or Tosectorum in the regione Columne, see Bartolini, "Documenti inediti," 225; on the *arcus Antonini prope columpnam eius, ubi modo est turris de Tosectis,* see Valentini, *Codice topografici* 3:185.

5. On Clement's campaign to destabilize the *buono stato,* see Clement VI, Letter to the Thirteen Good Men of Rome (October 7 and 9, 1347), BBCR 2.4:64–65; Letters to Bertrand de Déaulx (October 7, 1347), Theiner 180, 2:183–83; Letters to Bertrand de Déaulx (October 9, 1347), BBCR 2.4:65–78; Letter to Cola (Avignon, October 12, 1347), BBCR 2.3:173; to Bertrand de Déaulx (Avignon, October 12, 1347), Theiner 182, 2:183–86; DKPSP, 231–35; Cola di Rienzo, Letter 43, to Clement VI (October 11, 1347), BBCR 2.3:158–72, DKPSP, 226–31; CRCR, 91; Petrarch, *Fam.* VII.7 to Cola (Genoa, November 29, 1347), CRCR, 99–101.

6. On papal diplomacy with the barons see Clement VI, Letter to the Roman Barons (October 7, 1347), Theiner 179, 2:181–82; to Bertrand de Déaulx (October 15, 1347), BBCR 2.4:78–79; to Bertrand de Déaulx (November 3, 1347), BBCR 2.4:79–80; to Bertrand de Déaulx (November 12, 1347), BBCR 2.4:81–84; to Bertrand de Déaulx (November 13, 1347), BBCR 2.4:84–85; Theiner, 184, 2:187; to Guiscard de Combron, rector of the Patrimony (November 13, 1347), copies to the other rectors of the Papal States, BBCR 2.4:85–86; to Rainaldo and Giordano Orsini (November 13, 1347), BBCR 2.4:86–87; to Giordano Orsini, son of Poncello (December 1, 1347), BBCR 2.4:89–91.

7. On Clement's condemnation and excommunication of Cola di Rienzo, see AR, XVIII, ll. 1932–38, Porta, 207; Wright, 91; see Clement VI, Letter to the Roman People (December 3, 1347), BBCR 2.4:99–106; Theiner 185, 2:187–89; DKPSP, 235–37; *Constitutiones* MGH, 376, 8:419–22; to the cities of Italy: copies to Florence, Perugia, Siena, Narni, Pisa, Viterbo, Gubbio, Arezzo, Spoleto, Rieti, Foligno, Orvieto, and Pistoia (December 3, 1347), BBCR 2.4:96–98; to

Bertrand de Déaulx (December 3, 1347), BBCR 2.4:91–96; Cola di Rienzo, Letter 48, to a city in Sabina (December 2, 1347), BBCR 2.3:186–87.

8. On the potent weapons of suspension, interdict, and excommunication, see Trexler, *Spiritual Power,* esp. 1–15. The quotation is from p. 15. On the excommunication of Frederick II and papal substitution of Charles of Anjou, see De Frede, 5–31. On the image of Antichrist in Thessalonians and Apocalypse 13, see Emmerson, *Antichrist,* 21–23; and Wright, *Art and Antichrist,* 3–7.

9. On the political and moral crisis of Cola's abdication, see AR, XVIII, ll. 1908–92, Porta, 206–9; Wright, 91–93; *Chronicon Estense,* RIS 15.3:157–58, 167; Cola di Rienzo, Letter 57 to the archbishop of Prague (August 1350), BBCR 2.3: 251–53, ll. 518–601; Giovanni Villani, *Cronica* XII.105, pp. 281–82.

10. Long before Cola's abdication Dante had condemned Celestine for abandoning his responsibilities to the reform and renewal of the Christian life. See Inferno III.58–60. For Petrarch's criticisms of Cola see *Fam.* VII.7, CRCR, 99–104.

On rituals of violence surrounding the collapse of medieval rule, see Bertelli, 39–61, 231–52. Cola had many contemporary examples of voluntary abdications, including Pope Celestine V, Saint Louis of Toulouse, Queen Sancia of Majorca of Naples, her brother Prince Philip of Majorca, Delphine of Pumichel, and Elzéar of Sabran. For Celestine see Herde, *Cölestin V;* on Louis of Toulouse, see Pasztor, "Per la storia"; Toynbee, *St. Louis of Toulouse.* On Sancia, see Musto, "Franciscan Joachimism," esp. 454–56; idem, "Sancia." On Philip of Majorca see Musto, "Franciscan Joachimism," esp. 435 and n. 64; 447–53; idem, "Sancia," esp. 182–83, 195–97. On Delphine and Elzéar see Vauchez, "Two Laypersons."

11. On Cola's flight to Naples and exile see Agnolo di Tura del Graso, *Cronaca Senese,* RIS 15.6:552–53; Clement VI, Letter to Bertrand de Déaulx (May 7, 1348), BBCR 2.4:119–20; to Francesco Orsini (May 7, 1348), CLC 1637, 3.3:217; to Giovanni [Orsini], archbishop of Naples (January 13, 1349), BBCR 2.4:131–32; to Annibaldo de Ceccano (June 6, 1349), CLC 2011, 3.3:274; to Annibaldo de Ceccano (June 12, 1349), BBCR 2.4:136; Theiner 192, 2:197; CLC 2013, 3.3:274; Cola di Rienzo, Letter 58 to Charles IV (July 1350), BBCR 2.3:309 ll. 593–601; Giovanni Villani, *Cronica* XII. 105, p. 282. On Petrarch's concerns over the Hungarian invasion, see *Fam.* VII.1, to Barbato da Sulmona, PLFM, 331–33.

Dykmans, "Cardinal Annibal," 258, had also concluded that it was the Black Death that freed Cola from the Castel Sant'Angelo. On the emerging theme of exile in the Renaissance see Shaw, *Politics of Exile;* and Starn, *Contrary Commonwealth,* esp. 60–74, 121–47.

12. Among the most useful sources for the Black Death are Agnolo di Tura del Grasso, *Cronaca Senese,* RIS 15.6:552–53; Giovanni Boccaccio, *The Decameron,* Prologue; Gilles li Muisis, *Chronicle,* in HBD, no. 6a, p. 46; Petrarch, *Fam.* VIII.7–8 to "Socrates," PLFM, 415–21; and Matteo Villani, *Cronica* I.1–5. For the plague in Avignon see Clement VI, Letter ordering protection of Jews (*Sicut Judeis,* July 5, 1348), HBD, no. 73, pp. 221–22; Ludwig van Kempen or Beeringen, Petrarch's "Socrates," Letter of April 27, 1348, in Gagnière, *Histoire d'Avignon,* 260–61. For Ludwig, see Rehberg, *Kirche und Machte,* 496–97; Wilkins, 9, 76–77 et passim.

For useful studies see Cohn, *Cult of Remembrance;* Lerner, "The Black Death";

McNeill, *Plagues and Peoples,* 159–87, 324–33; Zeigler, *Black Death,* esp. 40–62, 64–67. Cohn, "Black Death," vigorously challenges the consensus.

13. On the earthquake and plague in Rome see AR, XXIII, ll. 150–227, Porta, 216–19; Wright, 101–3; Clement VI, Speech in Consistory (November 17, 1348), BBCR 2.5:33–36, which seems to refer to it; *Continuatio Novimontensis* (Neuberg in Austria), in HBD, no. 9, p. 59; Petrarch, *Fam.* II.7, to "Socrates" (Piacenza, June 11, 1351), PLFM 2:99–101; CRCR, 122–23; IX.13 (1350); Matteo Villani, *Cronica,* I.xlvii, Porta, 86–87; William of Blofield, OFM of Norwich, "Rumors in Rome in 1349," in HBD, no. 54, pp. 154–55; translated from Lerner, "Eschatological Mentalities," 552. Petrarch had criticized the Neapolitan Joachites for their apocalyptic interpretations of the earthquake of 1343 in *Fam.* V.3. See Wilkins, 41–42. On the apocalyptic associations of earthquake and plague in the 1340s, see now the excellent study by Smoller.

14. For Cola's stay on the Montagna della Maiella see AR, XXVII, ll. 1–23, Porta, 237; Wright, 125; Clement VI, Letter to Bertrand de Déaulx (May 9, 1348), BBCR 2.4:121–23; to papal notary Francesco Orsini (May 7, 1348), BBCR 2.4:123–24; CLC 1637, 3.3:217; to Bertrand de Déaulx (May 10, 1348), BBCR 2.4:124–25; Cola di Rienzo, Letter 49, to Charles IV (July 1350), BBCR 2.3:192–93; Letter 57, to Archbishop Ernst von Pardubitz (August 1350), BBCR 2.3: 231–78; esp. 264–66, ll. 880–919.

For the Fraticelli in and around Rome see chapter 6, note 13.

15. For the Jubilee of 1350 see AR, XXIII, ll. 1–150, Porta, 211–16; Wright, 97–101; Matteo Villani, *Cronica* I.xxxi, Porta, 57–58; I.xlviii, Porta, 108–11; *Tertia Vita* of Clement VI, Baluze 1:288.

Studies include works cited for chapter 6, note 9. See also Brezzi, *Anni santi,* 40–50; Fedele, "Il Giubileo del 1350"; Manselli, "Religiosità giubilare," 730; Rusconi, "Italia senza papa."

16. For Annibaldo de Ceccano and his Jubilee mission, see renewal of excommunication of Cola di Rienzo, BBCR 2.5:246–47; Letter to Clement VI (June 10, 1350), BBCR 2.5:366–67; AR, XXIII, ll. 1–227, Porta, 211–19; Wright, 97–103; Clement VI, Letter to Bertrand de Déaulx (March 23, 1348), BBCR 2.4:116–19; Letter to Annibaldo de Ceccano (November 30, 1348), CLC 1827, 3.3:245; BBCR 2.4:126–30; to Annibaldo de Ceccano (June 6, 1349), CLC 2011, 3.3:274; BBCR 2.4:133–35; to Annibaldo de Ceccano (June 12, 1349), CLC 2013, 3.3:274; BBCR, 2.4:136; to Annibaldo de Ceccano (June 10, 1350), CLC 2218, 3.3:309; BBCR, 2.4:137; to Annibaldo de Ceccano (June 11, 1350) on the assassination attempt against him, CLC 2219, 3.3:309; to Charles IV (Avignon, August 17, 1350), CLC 2284, 3.3:318; Theiner 200, 2:201, BBCR 2.4:138–39; Petrarch, *Fam.* VI.1, to Annibaldo de Ceccano, PLFM, 281–89. On Annibaldo's poisoning see, for example, *Vita Prima* of Clement VI, Baluze 1:254 and note at 2:401. Dykmans, "Cardinal Annibal," 267–77, thinks the rumors plausible.

Other studies include Dykmans, "Le cardinal Annibal de Ceccano et la vision béatifique"; Guillemain, "Caetani, Annibaldo (Annibale)." On autopsies and dissection in general, see Siraisi, 86–97.

17. For Cola's decision to leave Maiella see AR, XXVII, ll. 23–4, Porta, 237–38;

Wright, 125–26; Cola di Rienzo, Letter 49 to Charles IV (July 1350), BBCR 2.3:193–94, ll. 35–56. Dykmans, "Cardinal Annibal," 259, speculates that Annibaldo may have discovered Cola's hiding place, thus hastening his departure for Bohemia.

Chapter 12. Last World Emperor and Angel Pope

1. For Cola's journey to Bohemia see AR, XVIII, ll. 1995–97, XXVII, ll. 23–26, Porta, 209, 238; Wright, 93, 125–26; Petrarch, *Fam.* X.1, in Wilkins, 152.

2. On Emperor Charles IV, Bohemia and Prague see Charles IV, *Acta Karoli IV;* idem, *Vita Karoli Quarti,* in Jarrett, *Emperor Charles IV,* 33–68; idem, *Vita Caroli quarti* in Hillenbrand; Froissart, *Chronicles,* 41–49; Jarrett, *Emperor Charles IV;* Martindale, *Gothic Art,* 221–38; Russell, *Medieval Regions,* 99–100.

3. On Charles' mystical and apocalyptic thought as manifested at Karlstejn, see Dvoráková, *Gothic Mural Painting,* 41–70, esp. 51–65, color plates VI, VIII-X, XV, XVII-XVIII, illus. 62–85, 138–63, 176–83; Klaniczay, "The Cult of the Dynastic Saints"; Martindale, *Gothic Art,* 230–31. In *Art and Propaganda,* Iva Rosario examines the same evidence for Karlstejn and derives decidedly less assured conclusions. For parallels to Angevin spirituality in both word and art see Bruzelius, "Queen Sancia"; Musto, "Franciscan Joachimism," esp. 419–22, 456–86; idem, "Sancia," 192–94, 202–14.

4. For Cola at Charles IV's court see AR, XXVII, ll. 26–64, Porta, 238–39; Wright, 125–27; *Chronicon Estense,* RIS 15.3:150; Cola di Rienzo, Letter 50, to Charles IV (Prague, July 1350), BBCR 2.3:198–213, esp. ll. 103–67. See also Ludvíkovsky, "List Karla IV, Colovi di Rinzo"; Weider, "Cola di Rienzo."

5. For Petrarch's correspondence with Charles/Cola see Charles IV, Letter to Francesco Petrarch (February 1351), BBCR 2.3:406–410; Petrarch, *Fam.* X.1. See Bayley, "Petrarch, Charles IV"; Wilkins, 97–98.

6. For Cola's Commentary on Dante's *De monarchia* see Dante, *Monarchia,* Kay, ed.; idem, *On World Government,* Bigongiari, ed.; Cola di Rienzo, *Commentary,* in Ricci, "Il commento."

7. Cola's correspondence with Charles IV contain the richest statements of his Franciscan Joachimism and his beliefs in the prophesies of the emperor of the last days and the angelic pope. See Charles IV, Letter to Cola di Rienzo (Prague, July 1350), BBCR 2.3:214–19; Cola di Rienzo, Letter 49, to Emperor Charles IV (Prague, July, 1350), BBCR 2.3:191–97; McGinn, *Visions of the End,* 241–43; Letter 50, to Charles IV (Prague, July 1350), BBCR 2.3:198–213; Letter 58, to Charles IV (late August 1350), BBCR 2.3:279–332; McGinn, *Visions of the End,* 243–44; Francis of Prague, *Cronica,* 452–53; "Oraculum Angelicum Cyrilli," Piur, ed., 221–343.

For secondary studies see McGinn, "Angel Pope"; idem, *"Pastor Angelicus";* Reeves, *Influence of Prophesy,* 307–19, 395–462, 522–23; Lee, Reeves, Silano, *Western Mediterranean Prophesy,* 13–14, 75–88.

8. For Cola's correspondence with Archbishop Ernst see Cola di Rienzo, Letter 57, "The True Little Book," to Archbishop Ernst of Prague (Prague, before

August 15, 1350), BBCR 2.3:231–78; Letter 60, to Archbishop Ernst of Prague (Prague, late August 1350), BBCR 2.3:334–36; Letter 62, to Archbishop Ernst of Prague (Prague, late August-early September 1350), BBCR 2.3:339–41; Ernst of Prague, Reply to Cola di Rienzo (late August 1350), BBCR 2.3:337–39.

9. For Cola's inquisition at Raudnitz, see Cola di Rienzo, Letter 63, to Archbishop Ernst of Prague (Raudnitz, September 1350), BBCR 2.3:342–54; Letter 66, to Archbishop Ernst of Prague (Raudnitz, September 28, 1350), BBCR 2.3:367; Letter 67, to Archbishop Ernst of Prague (Raudnitz, October-November 1350), BBCR 2.3:368–69.

10. For Gui de Boulogne, see Cola di Rienzo, Letter 70, to Cardinal Gui de Boulogne (Raudnitz, 1351), BBCR 2.3:377–405.

Eubel 1:18 identifies Gui as the cardinal of Sta. Cecilia; but Gui also seems to have been associated with S. Giovanni in Crisogono and thus was probably the cardinal who confided to a frustrated Annibaldo de Ceccano that Rome would have to be torn down before it could be reformed. For Gui's presence in Rome in 1350, see AR, XXIII, ll. 144–50, Porta, 216; Wright 101; and Dykmans, "Cardinal Annibal," 262. For Gui's friendship with Petrarch see *Fam.* XI.16–17, CRCR, 107–25; and Wilkins, 88–89, 119–27 et passim.

11. For Cola's ties to Rome and his family during his inquisition and imprisonment see his Letter 52, to the abbot of Sant'Alessio in Rome (Prague, August 1350), BBCR 2.3:220–22; Letter 53, to the chancellor of Rome (Prague, August, 1350), BBCR 2.3:222; Letter 59, to the abbot of Sant'Alessio in Rome (late August, 1350), BBCR 2.3:333–34; Letter 64, to Fra Michele of Monte S. Angelo (Raudnitz, September 28, 1350), BBCR 2.3:356–65; Letter 65, to his son (Raudnitz, September 28, 1350), BBCR 2.3:366–67.

12. On the possibility of Cola's epilepsy see the descriptions in AR, XVIII, ll. 1580–83, XXVII, ll. 333–51; ll. 177b-184b, Porta, 195, 247–48, 258–59; Wright 81, 136, 147; Cola di Rienzo, Letter 67 to Archbishop Ernst of Prague (Raudnitz, October-November 1350), BBCR 2.3:368, ll. 1–15; Arnald of Villanova (attributed), *Breviarium practicae medicinae,* section on syncopis cited in BBCR 2.5:314–15 n. 7; section on epilepsy in von Storch and Storch, in a translation from the Pavia 1482 edition, p. 40. A *Translatio libri Galieni De rigore et tremore et iectigatione et spasmo* is also attributed to Arnald.

On Arnald's connections between the health of the body and apocalyptic thought see Backman. On the medieval practice of diagnosis by pulse and touch, see Siraisi, 125–28. On the medieval study, and understanding, of complexion and its changes, see Siraisi, 101–4. For background on the "falling sickness" and epilepsy, see Eadie and Bladin, 3–12; National Society for Epilepsy, "Epileptic Seizures"; Patrick, "Epilepsy FAQ"; Temkin; Zeigler, *Medicine and Religion,* 99, 118 et passim.

13. On Cola's Latinity see his Letter 54, to Johann von Neumarkt (Prague, August 1350), BBCR 2.3:223–25; Letter 56, to Johann von Neumarkt (Prague, August 1350), BBCR 2.3:228–30; Letter 68, to Johann von Neumarkt (Raudnitz May 1351), BBCR 2.3:370–72; Johann von Neumarkt, reply to Cola di Rienzo (August 1350), BBCR 2.3:226–27; to Cola di Rienzo (Prague, Spring 1351), BBCR 2.3:372–76.

For studies see Burdach, *Vom Mittelalter* 2.1:108–9; Ricci, "Commento," 676. Cola's style in the 1340s was in not humanist but did show an elegance within the Italian notarial form. Ronald G. Witt has suggested that Cola's change of style in Bohemia toward the more elegant Latin noted by Johann von Neumarkt might reflect some influence of Petrarch. On a deeper level, Witt's contrast (*Footsteps*, 11–12) between the "rhetorician-orator" and the "grammarian-poet"—and between the *vita activa* and *contemplativa* these modes represent—may offer some insights into contemporaries' perception of Cola abandoning politics in favor of "poetry."

14. On Cola's renunciation of prophecy and his "will" see Letter 64, to Fra Michele of Monte S. Angelo (Raudnitz, September 28, 1350), BBCR 2.3:356–65; Letter 65, to his son (Raudnitz, September 28, 1350), BBCR 2.3:366–67.

15. For Clement VI's attempts to capture Cola after his abdication see Clement VI, Letter to Charles IV (December 7, 1347), MGH, *Constitutiones* 390, 8:433–35; CLC 1545, 3.3:203; to Charles IV (Avignon, February 5, 1348), Theiner 187, 2:190–91; BBCR 2.4:111–15; MGH, *Constitutiones* 517, 8:531–33; CLC 1588, 3.3:209; to Charles IV (Avignon, August 17, 1350), Theiner 200, 2:201; BBCR 2.4:138–39; CLC 2284, 3.3:318; to Ernst of Prague (August 17, 1350), BBCR 2.4:139–40; CLC 2285, 3.3:318; to Ernst of Prague (August 18, 1350), BBCR 2.4:140–41; to Charles IV (Avignon, February 1, 1351), Theiner 204, 2:206–7; BBCR 2.4:142–43; to the archbishops and bishops of Germany and Bohemia (February 25, 1351), BBCR 2.4:143–46; to the bishop of Orvieto and the Thirteen Good Men of Rome (Avignon, November, 23, 1351), Theiner 215, 2:220–21; to the bishops of Germany and Bohemia (Avignon, Feb. 24, 1352), Theiner 217, 2:221–22; to Ernst of Prague (Villeneuve, March 24, 1352), BBCR 2.4:146–47; to Charles IV (Villeneuve, March 24, 1352), Theiner 218, 2:222; BBCR 2.4:147; CLC 2599, 2601, 3.3:366.

16. For Cola's return to Avignon and fame as a poet, see AR, XXVII, ll. 64–99, Porta, 239–40; Wright, 127–28; Cola di Rienzo, Letter 73, to Archbishop Ernst of Prague (Avignon, Fall 1352), BBCR 2.3:415–19; Letter 74, to a unnamed Roman prelate in Avignon (Avignon, late 1352 or early 1353), BBCR 2.3:419–20; Letter 75, to Andrea Dandolo, the doge of Venice (Avignon, September 1353), BBCR 2.3:421–22; Johann von Neumarkt, Letter to Cola di Rienzo (Prague 1353), BBCR 2.3:423–25; Petrarch, *Fam.* XIII.6, CRCR, 130–48; *Sine nomine* 4, CRCR, 149–60. See also note 13.

17. For Cola's imprisonment and the political maneuverings around it, see Colombe, "Nicolas Rienzi"; Faucon, "Note sur la détention"; Wilkins, 115–27; Zacour, *Petrarch and Talleyrand;* idem, *Talleyrand*. On the Tour de Trouillas, see Vingtain, 166–69.

18. On John of Roquetaillade see Bignami-Odier, *Etudes;* Jacob; McGinn, *Visions,* 230–33; Reeves, *Influence,* 320–25. For his imprisonment in Avignon during Cola's own detention there see Lerner, "Medieval Return," 67–68; and Maire-Vigueur, "Cola di Rienzo et Jean de Roquetaillade."

19. For the final judgments on Clement VI see McBride, 240–42; Mollat, *Popes,* 42–43 and notes. For Clement VI's tomb see Morganstern.

Chapter 13. Apocalypse in Rome

1. On the election of Innocent VI and Cola's release see AR, XXVII, ll. 93–99, Porta, 240; Wright, 128. See also Guillemain, *La Cour Pontificale,* 332–35; Jugie, "Innocent VI," DHP, 886–88; Mollat, *Popes,* 44–51, 125–43; Renouard, *Avignon Papacy,* 49–53.

2. On Rome without Cola see AR, XVIII, ll. 1486–93; XXVI, ll. 1–55; Porta, 209, 220–22; Wright 93, 107–8; Clement VI, Letter to the Romans (17 May 1352), authorizing Thirteen Good Men to elect Giovanni de Cerronibus, CLC 2636, 3.3:371; Letter to the Romans (22 May 1352), confirming de Cerronibus in office, CLC 2640, 3.3:373; Francesco Baroncelli, Speech to Florentines (July 1347), BBCR 2.4:7–14; Letter to Florence (29 September 1353), Papencordt, lxxxviii–lxxxix; Response of Florence (12 October 1353), Papencordt, lxxxix-c. See Matteo Villani, *Cronica* III.lxxviii, Porta 419–20 for Baroncelli's government.

On Rome's rulers see Salimei, *Senatori e statuti,* 116–24. On the Cerroni and their ties to the Colonna, see Rehberg, "Familien" 78:68–74. For the Baroncelli and their Colonna affiliation see Rehberg, *Die Kanoniker,* 398–99, 449–50.

3. On Innocent's policy toward Rome and Cola see Innocent VI, Letter to Hugo Harpaion, apostolic internuncio (September 15, 1353); BBCR 2.4:172–74; to the Roman people, (September 16, 1353), Theiner 257, 2:255–56; BBCR 2.4:175–76; both in CRCR, 168–71; to Perugia (September 16, 1353), BBCR 2.4:177–78; to Stefano bishop of Castro and preceptor of the Hospital of Sto. Spirito in Sassia (September 20, 1353), BBCR 2.4:179; to Gil Albornoz (September 23, 1353), BBCR 2.4:180–81; to Cola di Rienzo (September 24, 1353), CRCR, 171 and 176 n. 13.

4. On Gil Albornoz see Albornoz, *Egidian Constitutions,* in *The Medieval Town,* Mundy and Reisenberg; idem, *Egidian Constitutions,* in Emerton, ed.; idem, *Die Constitutiones Sanctae Matris Ecclesiae;* AR, XXVI, ll. 56–482, Porta, 222–36; Wright, 109–21; Battelli, "Le raccolte documentarie"; Glénison, and Mollat, *L'Administration;* Matteo Villani, books III and IV, passim. See Fedele, "Una composizione di pace," 466–71; and Rota, "Il codice degli 'statuta,'" 158–62, for the Statutes of 1363 and the survival of the *buono stato's* legislation into the era of Albornoz.

For studies see Beneyto Perez, *El Cardenal Albornoz;* idem, *El Cardenal Albornoz: hombre de iglesia;* Colliva, *Il Cardinale Albornoz;* Dupré Theseider, "Albornoz, Egidio de," DBI 2:45–53; idem, "Egidio de Albornoz"; Erler, *Aegidius Albornoz;* Mollat, *Popes,* 125–60.

5. For Cola's campaigns with Albornoz see AR, XXVII, ll. 98–147, Porta, 240–41; Wright, 128–30; Matteo Villani, *Cronica,* I.cix; IV.ix–x, Porta 1:466.

6. For the mercenaries and Fra Morreale, see Agnolo di Tura del Graso, *Cronaca Senese,* RIS 15.6:554; AR, XXVII, ll. 147–287, Porta, 241–46; Wright, 130–34; Cola di Rienzo, *True Little Book* of August 15, 1350, Letter 57, BBCR 2.3:238–39, ll. 186–213; Letter 58 to Charles IV (August 1350), BBCR 2.3:324, ll. 882–891; Matteo Villani, *Cronica,* I.cviii, IV.xvi, Porta 1:464–65, 494–95.

On the condottieri see Caferro, *Mercenary Companies,* esp. 1–14; Deiss, *Cap-*

tains of Fortune; Mallett, "Mercenaries"; idem, *Mercenaries* (still probably the best treatment); and Trease, *Condottieri.*

7. For Cola's return to Rome, see Albornoz, Letter to Innocent VI (August 5, 1354), Papencordt, xc; BBCR 2.4:183–84; AR, XXVII, ll. 287–351, Porta, 246–48; Wright, 134–36; Cola di Rienzo, Letter 77, to Florence (August 5, 1354), BBCR 2.3:426–28; Letter 80, to Charles IV (September 1354), BBCR 2.3:430–32; (spurious) letters to Giannino di Guccio (September 18, 1354), BBCR 2.3:444–45; Florence, Letter to Cola di Rienzo (August 22, 1354), BBCR 2.3:428; Innocent VI, Letter to Perugia (March 26, 1354), BBCR 2.4:181–82; to Gil Albornoz (March 26, 1354), BBCR 2.4:182; to Gil Albornoz (Villeneuve, September 9, 1354), Theiner 273, 2:267; BBCR 2.4:185–86; to Cola di Rienzo (Villeneuve, September 11, 1354), Theiner 274, 2:267.

8. On the 1354 revolt of the barons, see AR, XXVII, ll. 351–500, Porta, 248–53, Wright, 136–41.

9. On Fra Morreale's capture and execution, see AR, XXVII, ll. 500–101b, Porta, 253–56, Wright, 141–44. Porta's edition shows a lacuna in the group A of his sources here. See also Matteo Villani, IV.xxiii, Porta 1:504–78.

On the Annibaldi in the 14th century and their ties to the Colonna, see DBI 3:340–52; Rehberg "Familien" 78:21–22; idem, *Die Kanoniker,* 217–29.

10. On Cola's administrative and tax policies in 1354, see AR, XXVII, ll. 101b–195b, Porta, 256–59; Wright 145–47; Cola di Rienzo, license to the chapter of St. Peter's to extract salt from Ostia (August 1, 1347), BBCR 2.4:40–41; confirmation of privileges of Sto. Spirito in Sassia (September 16, 1354), BBCR 2.4:186–88. See also Tomassetti, "Del sale e focatico."

11. For Cola's changed character in the Anonimo romano's literary devices see Seibt, 38–107. For the possibility of Rienzo's epilepsy, see chapter 12, note 12.

12. For Cola's overthrow and death see the description by an anonymous adherent of the *buono stato* in BBCR 2.4:208–18; AR, XXVII, ll. 195b-423b, Porta, 259–67; Wright 147–54; Cola di Rienzo, speech to the Romans from the Senators' Palace, BBCR 2.4:204–7; Innocent VI, Letter to Gil Albornoz (October 15, 1354), BBCR 2.4:218–19; to Gil Albornoz (November 8, 1354) Theiner 276, 2:273; Matteo Villani, *Cronica,* IV.xxvi, Porta 1:509–11. On Janni Pippino's death see AR, XVII, ll. 2003–30, Porta, 209–10; Wright, 94.

See also Bertelli, 231–52, esp. 235–39; Cecchelli, "Il Campidoglio"; Partner, *Lands of St. Peter,* 335–48; Wilkins, 249–51; Zorzi, "Rituali di violenza," 395–96, 425. Ganshof, *Middle Ages,* 248 asserts, in the face of this evidence: "Later the pope intervened, his legate, Cardinal Albornoz, re-established legitimate authority. . . ."

13. For Charles IV's coronation journey to Rome see Matteo Villani, *Cronica* IV.xcii, V.ii, Porta 1:605–6, 608–10.

Bibliography

Primary Sources

Agnolo di Tura del Grasso. *Cronaca Senese*. RIS 15.6:577–79.

Albornoz, Gil. *L'Administration des Etats de l'Eglise au xive siècle. Correspondance des légats et vicaires-généraux. Gil Albornoz et Androin de la Roche (1353–67)*. Ed. Jean Glénison and Guillaume Mollat. Bibliotheque des Ecoles françaises d'Athènes et de Rome. Ser. 1.203. Paris: E. de Bocard, 1964.

——. *Die Constitutiones Sanctae Matris Ecclesiae des Kardinals Aegidius Abornoz von 1337*. Ed. Wolfgang Weber. Aalen: Scientia Verlag, 1982.

——. *Egidian Constitutions*. "Selections from the Ordinances of Cardinal Albornoz, as Published at the Parliament of Fano, April–May 1357." In *Humanism and Tyranny: Studies in the Italian Trecento,* edited by Ephraim Emerton, 215–51. Cambridge, Mass.: Harvard University Press, 1925. Reprint, New York: Peter Smith, 1964.

——. *Egidian Constitutions*. In *The Medieval Town*, edited by John Hine Mundy and Peter Reisenberg, 167–71. New York: Van Nostrand, 1958.

——. Letter to Innocent VI (August 5, 1354). Papencordt, xc; BBCR 2.4:183–84.

——. "Le raccolte documentarie del card. Albornoz sulla pacificazione delle terre della Chiesa." In *El Cardenal Albornoz y el Colegio de España*, edited by G. Battelli, 1:521–67. Bologna: Colegio de España, 1972.

Alighieri, Dante. Letter V, "Now Is the Acceptable Time." Letter VII, to the Italian cardinals. In *Babylon on the Rhone: A Translation of Letters by Dante, Petrarch and Catherine of Siena on the Avignon Papacy*, edited and translated by Robert Coogan, 25–27. Potomac, Md.: Studia Humanitatis, 1983.

——. *Monarchia*. Ed. and trans. Richard Kay. Toronto: PIMS, 1998.

——. *On World Government (De monarchia)*. Ed. Dino Bigongiari. Trans. Herbert W. Schneider. Indianapolis: Bobbs-Merrill, 1957.

Annibaldo de Ceccano. Renews excommunication of Cola di Rienzo, BBCR 2.5:246–47; letter to Clement VI (June 10, 1350), BBCR 2.5:366–67.

Anonimo romano. *Cronica, Vita di Cola di Rienzo.* Ed. Ettone Mazzali. Milan: Rizzoli, 1991.

——. *Cronica, Vita di Cola di Rienzo.* Electronic editions at:
http://digilander.iol.it/bepi/cronica/cronica.html
http://www.liberliber.it/biblioteca/c/cronica_vita_di_cola_di_rienzo
http://www.ncl.ac.uk/ostia/atexts/cola.htm
http://victorian.fortunecity.com/duchamp/451/cronica.html

——. *The Life of Cola di Rienzo.* Ed. and trans. John Wright. Toronto: Pontifical Institute, 1975.

——. *La vita di Cola di Rienzo.* Ed. Alberto Maria Ghisalberti. Rome: L. S. Olschki, 1928.

——. *La vita di Cola di Rienzo.* Ed. F. Cusin. Florence: Sansoni, 1943.

——. *La vita di Cola di Rienzo.* Ed. A. Frugoni. Florence: Le Monnier, 1957.

——. *Vita di Cola di Rienzo. Cronica.* Ed. Giuseppe Porta. Milan: Adelphi, 1979.

——. *La vita di Cola di Rienzo, tribuno del popolo romano, scritta da incerto autore nel secolo decimo quatro.* Ed. Zeferino Re. Forlì: Bordandini, 1828.

——. *Vita Nicolai Laurentii (sive di Cola di Rienzo), Tribuni Romanorum.* Ed. Ludovico Antonio Muratori. Trans. Petrus Hercules Gherardius. *Antiquitates Italiae Medii Aevi* 3. Milan, 1740.

Anonymous adherent of *Buono Stato.* Description of Cola's death. BBCR 2.4:208–18.

Aquinas, Thomas. *Summa Theologica* Q.90, art. 2, Q.96, art. 4. In *Aquinas: Selected Political Writings* edited by A. P. D'Entrèves and translated by J. G. Dawson, 104–5, 110–11. Oxford: Basil Blackwell, 1948.

Arnald of Villanova (attributed). *Breviarium practicae medicinae.* In BBCR 2.5:316–17.

——. *Breviarium practicae medicinae.* In von Storch and von Storch.

——. *Translatio libri Galieni De rigore et tremore et iectigatione et spasmo.* Vol. 16 of *Arnaldi de Villanova opera medica omnia.* Granada-Barcelona: Seminarium Historiae Medicae Granatensis, 2000.

Bacco, Enrico. *Naples: An Early Guide.* Ed. and trans. Eileen Gardiner, with introductions by Ronald G. Musto and Caroline Bruzelius. New York: Italica Press, 1991.

Baluze, Etienne. *Vitae paparum avenionensium, hoc est Historia pontificum romanorum qui in Gallia sederunt ab anno Christi MCCCV usque ad annum MCCCXCIV.* Vols. 1–4. Ed. Guillaume Mollat. Paris: Letouzey et Ané, 1914–22.

Barbato da Sulmona. *Romana respublica urbi Rome.* In Weiss, "Barbato da Sulmona," 13–22.

Baroncelli, Francesco. Speech to Florentines (July 1347), BBCR 2.4:7–14; letter to Florence (September 29, 1353), Papencordt, lxxxviii–lxxxix; response of Florence (October 12, 1353), Papencordt, lxxxix–c.

Bartolini, F. "Documenti inediti dei 'Magistri aedificiorum Urbis' (secoli XIII e XIV)." ASRSP 60 (1937): 191–230.

Bartolo da Sassoferrato. "De Guelphis et Ghibelinis." In *Humanism and Tyranny* edited and translated by Ephraim Emerton, 255–84. Gloucester, Mass.: Peter Smith, 1964.

———. "De Guelphis et Ghibelinis." In *Politica e dirito nel Trecento italiano,* edited by Diego Quaglione, 129–46. Florence: Olschki, 1983.

———. "De regimine civitatis." In *Politica e dirito nel Trecento italiano,* edited by Diego Quaglione, 147–70. Florence: Olschki, 1983.

———. "Tractatus de Tyrannia." In *Humanism and Tyranny,* edited and translated by Ephraim Emerton, 117–54. Gloucester, Mass.: Peter Smith, 1964.

———. "De tyranno." In *Politica e dirito nel Trecento italiano,* edited by Diego Quaglione, 171–213. Florence: Olschki, 1983.

Benedict XII. Letter to the barons of Rome (Avignon, March 18, 1336). CRCR, 27.

Benes of Weitmil. *Cronica Ecclesiae Pragensis.* In *Fontes Rerum Bohemicarum,* edited by J. Emler, 4:459–548. Prague: FRB, 1884.

Bishop's Priest of Butrinto Nicola. *Relatio de itinere italico Henrici VII imperatoris.* In Baluze 3:491–561.

Boccaccio, Giovanni. *The Decameron.* Prologue.

Caciorgna, Maria Teresa, ed. *Le pergamene di Sezze.* Codice Diplomatico di Roma e della Regione Romana 5. 2 vols. Rome: Società Romana di Storia Patria, 1989.

Castagnoli, Ferdinando, Carlo Cecchelli, Gustavo Giovannoni, and Mario Zocca, eds. *Topografia e urbanistica di Roma antica.* Storia di Roma 22. Bologna: Istituto di Studi Romani, 1958.

Catalog of Turin. In Giorgio Falco, "Il Catalogo di Torino delle chiese, degli ospedali, dei monasteri di Roma nel sec. xiv." ASRSP 32 (1909): 411–43; VCT 3:291–318.

Cavallini, Giovanni dei Cerronis. *Polistoria de virtituibus et dotibus Romanorum.* VCT 4:11–54.

———. Ioannis Caballini de Cerronibus. *Polistoria de virtituibus et dotibus Romanorum.* Ed. Marc Laureys. Bibliotheca scriptorum Graecorum et Romanorum Teubneriana. Stuttgart-Leipzig: B. G. Teubner, 1995.

Charles IV. *Acta Karoli IV imperatoris inedita. Ein beitrag zu den urkunden kaiser Karls IV.* Ed. Franz Zimmermann. Innsbruck: Wagner, 1891.

———. Letter to Cola di Rienzo (Prague, July 1350), BBCR 2.3:214–19; Letter to Francesco Petrarch (February 1351), BBCR 2.3:406–10.

———. *Vita Caroli quarti. Die Autobiographie Karls IV.* Ed. and trans. Eugen Hillenbrand. Stuttgart: Fleischauer & Spohn, 1979.

———. *Vita Karoli Quarti.* In Bede Jarrett, *The Emperor Charles IV,* 33–68. New York: Sheed and Ward, 1935.

Chronicon Estense. RIS 15.3:148–49.

Chronicon Mutinense. RIS 15.3:551–637.

Clareno, Angelo. "The Letters of Angelo Clareno." Ed. Ronald G. Musto. 2 vols. Ph.D. diss. New York: Columbia University, 1977.

———. "The Letters of Angelo Clareno." Ed. Lydia von Auw. *Angeli Clareni Epistolae.* Rome: Istituto Storico Italiano per il Medio Evo, 1980.

Clement VI. Letter to Bertrand de Déaulx (August 21, 1347). CRCR, 69–71; DKPSP, 216–17.

———. Letters, in Theiner and BBCR.

———. Letters on Cola di Rienzo. In *Monumenta Germaniae historica . . . . Legum sectio IV, Constitutiones et acta publica imperatorum et regum, 1345–1348.* Vol. 8, pt. 1–3. Ed. Karl Zeumer and Richard Salomon. Hanover: Impensis Bibliopolii Hahniani, 1910–1926.

———. *Lettres closes, patentes et curiales intéressant les pays autres que la France (1342–1352)*. Bibliotheque des Ecoles françaises d'Athenes et de Rome. Ser. 3.3 Ed. Eugène Déprez and Guillaume Mollat. Paris: A. Fontemoing, 1901, 1960–61.

———. Speech in Consistory (Avignon, November 17, 1348). BBCR 2.5:33–36.

———. Speech to the Roman Ambassadors (January 27, 1343). In Heinrich Schmidinger, "Die Antwort Clemens' VI. an die Gesandschaft der Stadt Rom vom Jahre 1343." In *Miscellanea in onore di Monsignor Martino Giusti*, 2:323–65. Vatican City: BAV, 1978.

Cochetus de Chotiis. Letter of an unknown author, perhaps Cochetis (August 18, 1347). Papencordt, xx; BBCR 2.4:32–35.

———. Letter to Rainaldo Orsini (August 2, 1347). Papencordt, item 9, xvii–xix; BBCR 2.4:21–26.

Cola di Rienzo. Approval of the Statues of the Merchants by Orso Orsini (March 28, 1346). BBCR 2.4:43; Gatti, *Statuti dei Mercanti*, 80.

———. "Il commento di Cola di Rienzo alla *Monarchia* di Dante." Ed. Pier Giorgio Ricci. *Studi Medievali*, 3d ser., 6.2 (1965): 665–708.

———. *Epistolae*. In BBCR and Papencordt.

———. *Epistolario di Cola di Rienzo*. Ed. Annibale Gabrielli. Istituto storico italiano per il medio evo. Fonti per la storia d'Italia 6. Rome: Forzani e Compagnia, 1890.

———. Letters. English translations in CRCR.

———. Letters. English translations in DKPSP.

———. Letters 49 and 58. In Bernard McGinn ed. & trans. *Visions of the End: Apocalyptic Traditions in the Middle Ages,* edited and translated by Bernard McGinn, 239–44. Records of Civilization 96. 2d rev. ed., New York: Columbia University Press, 1998.

Colonna, Giovanni. *Margherita Colonna. Le due vite scritte dal fratello Giovanni Colonna Senatore di Roma e da Stefania monaca di S. Silvestro in Capite.* Lateranum, n.s., 1–2. Rome: Lateranum, 1935.

Constantine, The [Forged] Donation of. In *Readings in Church History*. Ed. Colman J. Barry, OSB, 1:239. Westminster, Md.: Newman Press, 1966.

Conti, Ildebrandino, archbishop of Padua. Letter to his vicar Leonardo de S. Sepulcro (Valmontone July 29/30, 1347). BBCR 2.5:1–15.

Continuatio Novimontensis (Neuberg in s. Austria). In HBD, no. 9, p. 59.

Convenevolo da Prato. *Regia Carmina dedicata a Roberto d'Angiò, re di Sicilia e di Gerusalemme.* Ed. Cesare Grassi. Prato and Milan: Gruppo Bibliofili Pratesi & Silvana, 1982.

Coste, Jean Paul. "Les lettres collectives des papes d'Avignon à la noblesse romaine." In *Le fonctionnement administratif de la papauté d'Avignon. Aux origines de l'état moderne,* 151–70. Collection de l'Ecole française de Rome 138. Rome: EFR, 1990.

Crawford, M. H. *Roman Statutes*. 2 vols. London: Universty of London Institute of Classical Studies, 1996.

Cyril the Carmelite. "Oraculum Angelicum Cyrilli." Edited by Paul Piur. In *Vom Mittelalter zur Reformation* 2.4:221–343. Berlin: Weidmann, 1912.

Donato di Neri and Neri di Donato di Neri. *Cronaca Senese.* RIS 15.6:577–79.

D'Onofrio, Cesare, ed. *Visitiamo Roma mille anni fa. La città dei Mirabilia.* Rome: Romana Società Editrice, 1988.

——. *Visitiamo Roma nel Quattrocento. La città degli Umanisti.* Rome: Romana Società Editrice, 1989.

Egger, Hermann, ed. *Codex Escurialensis: Ein Skizzenbuch aus der Werkstatt Domenico Ghirlandaios.* Sonderschriften 4. 2 vols. Vienna: Österreichisches Archäologisches Institut, 1905–6.

Egger, Hermann, and C. Hülsen, eds. *Die römischen Skizzenbücher von M. van Heemskerck im Königlichen Kupferstichkabinett zu Berlin.* Berlin: J. Bard, 1913.

Ernst of Prague. Reply to Cola di Rienzo (late August 1350). BBCR 2.3:337–39.

Fabre, P., L. Duchesne, and G. Mollat, eds. *Le Liber censuum de l'Eglise romaine.* 3 vols. Paris, 1889–1952.

Finke, Heinrich. *Acta Aragonensia.* 3 vols. Berlin: W. Rothchild, 1908–33.

Florence. Letter to Cola di Rienzo (August 22, 1354). BBCR 2.3:428.

Francis of Prague. *Cronica.* In *Fontes Rerum Bohemicarum,* edited by J. Emler, 4:347–456. Prague: N F. Palackého, 1884.

Froissart, Jean. *Chronicles of England, France and Spain.* Ed. H. P. Dunster. New York: Dutton, 1961.

Frutaz, Amato Pietro. *Le piante di Roma.* Rome: Istituto di Studi Romani, 1962.

Gatti, Giuseppe, ed. *Statuti dei Mercanti di Roma.* Rome: F. Cuggiani, 1885; D'Onofrio 2:9–38.

Gilles li Muisis. *Chronicle.* In HBD, no. 6a, p. 46.

Gnoli, Umberto. *Topografia e toponomastica di Roma medioevale e moderna.* Rome: Staderini, 1939.

Gordon, Arthur E., ed. *Illustrated Introduction to Roman Epigraphy.* Berkeley and London: University of California Press, 1983.

Great Alleluia of 1233 and the Flagellants of 1260. In *Catholic Peacemakers: A Documentary History,* edited and translated by Ronald G. Musto, 1:539–55. New York: Garland, 1993.

Gregorius, Master. *The Marvels of Rome.* Ed. and trans. John Osborne. Toronto: Pontifical Institute, 1987.

Innocent VI. English translation of selected letters in CRCR.

——. Letters in BBCR and Theiner.

Jacobus de Voragine. *The Golden Legend: Readings on the Saints.* Trans. William Granger Ryan. 2 vols. Princeton, N.J.: Princeton University Press, 1993.

Joachim of Fiore. *Enchiridion super Apocalypsim.* Ed. Edward Kilian Burger. Toronto Studies and Texts 78. Toronto: Pontifical Institute, 1986.

——. *Liber de Concordia novi ac veteris testamenti.* Transactions of the American Philosophical Society 73.8. Ed. E. Randolf Daniel. Philadelphia: APS, 1983.

——. *Il Libro delle Figure dell' Abate Gioachino da Fiore.* Ed. L. Tondelli, M. Reeves, and B. Hirsch-Reich. 2d ed. 2 vols. Turin: Società Editrice, 1954.

Johann von Neumarkt. Reply to Cola di Rienzo (August 1350), BBCR 2.3:226–27;

to Cola di Rienzo (Prague, spring 1351), BBCR 2.3:372–76; to Cola di Rienzo (Prague 1353), BBCR 2.3:423–25.

Kohl, Benjamin G., trans. "The Ordinances of Justice of Florence, 1295." In *Major Problems in the History of the Italian Renaissance,* edited by Benjamin G. Kohl and Alison Andrews Smith, 139–42. Lexington, Mass.: D. C. Heath, 1995.

——, ed. *The Records of the Venetian Senate on Disk, 1335–1400.* CD-ROM. New York: Italica Press, 2001.

Kohl, Benjamin, and Ronald G. Witt, eds. *The Earthly Republic: Italian Humanists on Government and Society.* Manchester: Manchester University Press, 1978.

Lanciani, Rodolfo. *Forma Urbis Romae.* Milan: U. Hoepli, 1893–1901.

Lori Sanfilippo, Isa. *Il protocollo notarile di Lorenzo Staglia (1372).* Codice diplomatico di Roma e della Regione romana 3. Rome: Società Romana di Storia Patria, 1986.

——. *Il protocollo notarile di Pietro di Nicola Astalli (1368).* Codice diplomatico di Roma e della Regione romana 6. Rome: Società Romana di Storia Patria, 1989.

Lucca. Letter to Cola di Rienzo and Rome (June 23, 1347). BBCR 2.3:29.

Ludwig van Kempen or Beeringen. Letter of April 27, 1348. In Gagnière, *Histoire d'Avignon,* 260–61.

Machiavelli, Niccolò. *History of Florence and of the Affairs of Italy.* New York: Harper and Row, 1960.

McGinn, Bernard, ed. *Apocalyptic Spirituality.* New York: Paulist Press, 1979.

——. *Visions of the End: Apocalyptic Traditions in the Middle Ages.* Records of Civilization 96. 2d rev. ed. New York: Columbia University Press, 1998.

Mirabilia Urbis Romae. In D'Onofrio 1:46–100.

——. *The Marvels of Rome. Mirabilia Urbis Romae.* Ed. and trans. Francis Morgan Nichols. 2d ed. Ed. Eileen Gardiner. New York: Italica Press, 1986.

Mosti, Renzo, ed. *I Protocolli di 'Iohannes Nicolai Pauli.' Un notaio romano del '300.* Collection de l'Ecole française de Rome 63. Rome: EFR, 1982.

——. *Il Protocollo notarile di 'Anthonius Goioli Petri Scopte (1365).* Rome: R. Mosti, 1991.

——. *Un notaio romano del Trecento: I protocolli di Francesco di Stefano de Caputgallis (1374–86).* Rome: Viella, 1994.

Musto, Ronald G., ed. *Catholic Peacemakers. A Documentary History.* 2 vols. in 3. New York: Garland, 1993–96.

Otto IV, emperor. Document defining the Roman District (June 8, 1201). BBCR 2.5:331.

Palermo, Luciano. *Il porto di Roma nel xiv e xv secolo: Strutture socio-economiche e statuti.* Fonti e studi per la storia economica e sociale di Roma e dello Stato Pontificio nel tardo Medioevo 2. Rome: Centro di ricerca, 1979.

Pandolfuccio di Guido di Pandolfo de' Franchi. Speech to the Florentine government (July 2, 1347), BBCR 2.4:5–7; speech to the Florentine government (July 3, 1347), BBCR 2.4:15.

Petrarca, Francesco. *Collatio laureationis.* In *Opere Latine di Francesco Petrarca,* edited by Antonietta Bufano, 1265ff. Turin: UTET, 1975.

——. Eclogue 5, "The Shepherd's Affection" (August 22–31, 1347), BBCR 2.3:

87–99; CRCR, 57–68; *Sine nomine* 2 (August–September 1347), CRCR, 69–83; Zacour, 35–42; *Sine nomine* 3 (September 2–8, 1347), CRCR, 84–87; Zacour, 42–44.

——. *Familiares.* English translation in CRCR.

——. *Familiares.* English translation in PLFM.

——. "How a Ruler Ought to Govern His State." In *The Earthly Republic: Italian Humanists on Government and Society,* edited by Benjamin G. Kohl and Ronald G. Witt, 25–78. Manchester: Manchester University Press, 1978.

——. *Sine nomine.* English trans. in CRCR.

——. *Sine nomine.* English trans. in Zacour.

——. *The Sonnets of Petrarch.* Ed. Thomas G. Bergin, 18–19. New York: Heritage Press, 1966.

——. "The Triumph of Fame." In *The Triumphs of Petrarch,* edited and translated by Ernest H. Wilkins, 85. Chicago: University of Chicago Press, 1962.

——. *Variae.* English translation in CRCR.

——. *Variae 48, Hortaroria* (June 24–27, 1347). BBCR 2.3:63–81.

Pressouyre, Sylvia. *Rome au fil du temps. Atlas historique d'urbanisme et d'architecture.* Boulogne: J. Cuenot, 1973.

Ptolemy of Lucca. *On the Government of Rulers. De regimine principum.* Trans. James M. Blyhte. Philadelphia: University of Pennsylvania Press, 1997.

Raymond of Orvieto. Letter to Clement VI (August 1, 1347). Papencordt, xvi–xvii; BBCR 2.4:19–21.

Re, Camillo, ed. *Statuti della città di Roma.* Rome: Tipografia della Pace, 1880.

Rota, A. "Il codice degli 'statuta Urbis' del 1305 e i caratteri politici della sua riforma." ASRSP 70 (1947): 147–62.

Salimei, A. *Senatori e statuti di Roma nel Medio Evo. I senatori, cronologia e bibliografia dal 1144 al 1447.* Rome: Biblioteca d'arte editrice, 1935.

Sartini, F. *Statuti dell'Arte degli Albergatori della città e contado di Firenze (1324–1342).* Florence: L. S. Olschki, 1967.

Sassoli, Mario Gori. *Roma Veduta: Disegni e stampe panoramiche della città dal XV al XIX secolo.* Rome: Artemide, 2000.

Schiaparelli, L. "Alcuni documenti sui 'Magistri aedificiorum urbis' (secoli xiii e xiv)." ASRSP 25 (1902): 5–60.

Schiaparelli, L., and E. Re. "Maestri di Strada." ASRSP 43 (1920): 5–102.

Stefaneschi, Giacomo. *De coronatione.* In *Le Cérémonial papal de la fin du Moyen Age à la Renaissance.* Vol. 2. Ed. Marc Dykmans. Brussels and Rome: Institut historique belge de Rome, 1981.

Terracina. Document dated September 27, 1347. BBCR 2.5:20–22.

Todi. Letter to Rome and Cola di Rienzo (August 17, 1347). Gabrielli, 242–43; BBCR 2.4:30–31.

Tomassetti, G. "Documenti feudali della provincia di Roma nel medio evo." *Studi e documenti di storia e diritto* 19 (1898): 291–320.

Ulrichs, L. C., ed. *Codex Urbis Romae Topographicus.* Würzburg: Stahel, 1871.

Venturino da Bergamo. Anonymous legend, and testimony before the papal inquisition. In Musto, *Catholic Peacemakers,* 1:556–66.

Villani, Giovanni. *Cronica, con le continuazioni di Matteo e Filippo.* Turin: Einaudi, 1979.

————. English translation in DKPSP, 212–13; XII.104, pp. 278–79; DKPSP, 213–14.

Villani, Matteo. *Cronica, con le continuazioni di Filippo Villani.* Ed. Giussepe Porta. 2 vols. Parma: Fondazione Pietro Bembo, 1995.

————. http://www.unizh.ch/rose/decameron/seminario/VI_10/chantal/villani .htm.

von Storch, Edna P., and Theo. J. C. von Storch, M.D. "Arnold of Villanova on Epilepsy." Trans. Adrian P. English, O.P. *Annals of Medical History,* n.s., 10 (1938): 251–60.

William of Blofield, OFM of Norwich. "Rumors in Rome in 1349." In HBD, no. 54, pp. 154–55; translated from Lerner, "Eschatological Mentalities," 552.

Zuparo, Antonio di Giovanni. "De novis Urbis." BBCR 2.5:24.

Secondary Works

Amadei, Emma. *Le torri di Roma.* Rome: U. Sofia-Moretti, 1969.

Amargier, Paul. "Pétrarque et ses amis au temps de la verte feuillée." In *La papauté d'Avignon,* edited by Marie-Humbert Vicaire, 127–40.

Anselmi, Gian Mario. "La Cronica dell'Anonimo romano." BISIMEAM 91 (1984): 423–40.

————. "Il tempo della storia e quello della vita nella *Cronica* dell' Anonimo romano." *Studi e problemi di critica testuale* 21 (October 1980): 181–94.

Antoine, Jean-Philippe. "*Ad perpetuam memoriam.* Les nouvelles fonctions de l'image peinte en Italie, 1250–1400." *Mélanges de l'Ecole française de Rome. Moyen Age et Temps Modernes* 100.2 (1988): 541–615.

Armellini, Mariano. *Le Chiese di Roma dal secolo iv al xix.* Rome, 1891.

Armellini, Mariano, and C. Cecchelli. *Le Chiese di Roma dal secolo iv al xix.* Rome: Tipografia Vaticana, 1982.

Asso, M. F. P. "Monte Giordano." *Quaderni dell' Istituto di Storia dell'Architettura* 1 (1953): 12–15, and figs. 19–20.

Aurell, Martin. "Prophétie et messianisme politique." TPPO 317–61.

Aurigemma, Marcello. "Recenti studi sul Petrarca." *Cultura e scuola* 23.92 (1984): 7–14.

Avignon au temps de Pétrarque: 1304–1374. Avignon: Archives de Vaucluse, 1974.

Backman, Clifford R. "Arnau of Vilanova and the Body at the End of the World." BFLT, 140–55.

Banker, James R. "The *Ars dictaminis* and Rhetorical Textbooks at the Bolognese University in the Fourteenth Century." *Medievalia et Humanistica,* n.s., 5 (1974): 153–68.

————. *Death in the Community: Memorialization and Confraternities in an Italian Commune in the Late Middle Ages.* Athens: University of Georgia Press, 1988.

Baron, Hans. "Franciscan Poverty and Civic Wealth as Factors in the Rise of Humanistic Thought." *Speculum* 13 (1938): 1–37.

Barone, Giulia. "I francescani a Roma." *Storia della Città* 9 (1978): 33–35.

———. "Il potere pontificio e la città di Roma tra xiii e xiv secolo." In *Dal Patrimonio di S. Pietro allo Stato Pontificio. La Marca nel contesto del potere temporale,* edited by Enrico Menesto, 91–104. Ascoli Piceno: Commune di Ascoli Piceno, 1991.

Barr, Cyrilla. "From *Devozione* to *Rappresentazione:* Dramatic Elements in the Holy Week *Laude* of Assisi." In Eisenbichler, 11–32.

Barraclough, Geoffrey. *Public Notaries and the Papal Curia.* London: Macmillan, 1934.

Bartolini, F. "Documenti inediti dei 'Magistri aedificiorum Urbis' (secoli xiii e xiv)." ASRSP 60 (1937): 191–230.

Barzini, Luigi. "Cola di Rienzo or the Obsession of Antiquity." In *The Italians,* 117–32. New York: Atheneum, 1986.

Bayley, C. C. "Petrarch, Charles IV and the 'Renovatio imperii.'" *Speculum* 17 (1942): 323–41.

Becker, Marvin B. "Heresy in Medieval and Renaissance Florence. A Comment." *Past and Present* 62 (1974): 153–61.

Becriaux, Henri. *Avignon, son histoire, ses monuments.* 2d ed. Avignon: Aubanel, 1971.

Belincourt, Marjorie A. "The Relationship of Some Fourteenth-Century Commentaries on Valerius Maximus." *Mediaeval Studies* 34 (1972): 361–87.

Belting, Hans. "Langage et réalité dans la peinture monumentale publique en Italie au Trecento." In *Artistes, Artisans et Production artistique au Moyen Age,* 491–511. Actes du Colloque internationale de Rennes, 1983. Vol. 3. Ed. Xavier Barral i Altet. Paris: Picard, 1990.

Belting, Hans, and Dieter Blume, eds. *Malerei und Stadtkultur in der Dantezeit.* Munich: Hirmer, 1989.

Benes, Carrie E. "Cola di Rienzo and the *Lex Regia.*" *Viator* 30 (1999): 231–51.

Benevolo, Leonardo. *Storia della città.* Vol. 2, *La città medievale.* Bari: Laterza, 1993.

Beneyto Perez, Juan. *El Cardenal Albornoz: Canciller de Castilla y caudillo de Italia.* Madrid: Espasa-Calpe, 1950.

———. *El Cardenal Albornoz: Hombre de iglesia y de estado en Castilla y en Italia.* Madrid: Fundación Universitaria Española, 1986.

Benocci, C. "Le figurazioni di Roma nel xiv secolo." *Storia della Città* 23 (1982): 63–74.

Benson, Robert. "Political 'Renovatio': Two Models from Roman Antiquity." In Benson and Constable, *Renaissance and Renewal,* 339–86.

Benson, Robert, and Giles Constable, eds. *Renaissance and Renewal in the Twelfth Century.* Oxford: Oxford University Press, 1982.

Bertelli, Sergio. *The King's Body: Sacred Rituals of Power in Medieval and Early Modern Europe.* Trans. R. Burr Litchfield. State College: Pennsylvania State University Press, 2001.

Bevilacqua, M. *Il Monte dei Cenci. Una famiglia romana e il suo insediamento urbano tra medioevo ed età barocca.* Rome: Gangemi, 1988.

Bigalli, Davide. *I Tartari e l'Apocalisse: Ricerche sull'escatologia in Adamo Marsh e Ruggero Bacone.* Florence: La Nuova Italia, 1971.

Bignami-Odier, Jeanne. *Etudes sur Jean de Roquetaillade.* Paris: Vrin, 1952.

Billanovich, Giuseppe. "Come nacque un capolavoro: La 'cronica' del non più Anonimo Romano." *Rendiconti dell'Accademia Nazionale dei Lincei,* n.s., 9.6 (1995): 195–211.

Billanovich, Maria Chiara. "Un lettore trecentesco della *Concordia* di Gioacchino da Fiore: Il vescovo Ildebrandino Conti e le sue postille." *Florensia* 12 (1998): 53–115.

Birch, Debra J. *Pilgrimage to Rome in the Middle Ages: Continuity and Change.* Studies in the History of Medieval Religion 13. Rochester, N.Y.: Boydell Press, 1998.

Black, Robert. *Humanism and Education in Medieval and Renaissance Italy.* New York: Cambridge University Press, 2001.

Blanc, Pierre. "La construction d'une utopie néo-urbaine: Rome dans la pensée, l'action et l'oeuvre de Pétrarque de 1333 à 1342." In *Jérusalem, Rome, Constantinople: L'Image et le mythe de la ville au Moyen Age,* 149–68. Culture et civilisation médiévales 5. Ed. Daniel Poirion. Paris: University of Paris, 1986.

Bloch, Herbert. "The New Fascination with Ancient Rome." In Benson and Constable, *Renaissance and Renewal,* 616–36.

Blomquist, Thomas W., and Maureen F. Mazzaoui, eds. *The Other Tuscany: Essays in the History of Lucca, Pisa, and Siena during the Thirteenth, Fourteenth, and Fifteenth Centuries.* Studies in Medieval Culture 34. Kalamazoo, Mich.: Medieval Institute, 1994.

Bloomfield, Morton W. "Joachim of Fiore: A Critical Survey of His Canon, Teachings, Sources, Biography and Influence." *Traditio* 13 (1957): 249–311.

Bolgar, R. R. *The Classical Heritage and Its Beneficiaries.* Cambridge: Cambridge University Press, 1977.

Bornstein, Daniel. *The Bianchi of 1399: Popular Devotion in Late Medieval Italy.* Ithaca, N.Y.: Cornell University Press, 1993.

Boüard, Alain de. "Les notaires de Rome au Moyen âge." *Ecole française de Rome. Mélanges d'archéologie et d'histoire* 31 (1911): 291–307.

———. *Le régime politique et les institutions de Rome au Moyen-Age, 1252–1347.* Bibliothèque des Ecoles françaises d'Athènes et de Rome 118. Paris: E. de Boccard for EFR, 1920.

Bowen, James. *A History of Western Education.* Vol. 2, *Civilization of Europe, Sixth to Sixteenth Centuries.* New York: St. Martin's, 1981.

Bowsky, William M. "The *Buon Governo* of Siena (1287–1355): A Medieval Italian Oligarchy." *Speculum* 37 (1962): 368–81.

———. "Medieval Citizenship: The Individual and the State in the Commune of Siena, 1287–1355." *Studies in Medieval and Renaissance History* 4 (1967): 195–243.

———. "The Medieval Commune and Internal Violence: Police Power and Public Safety in Siena 1287–1355." *American Historical Review* 73 (1967): 1–17.

Brentano, Robert. "Notarial Cartularies and Religious Personality: Rome, Rieti, and Bishop Thomas of Secinario (1339–1341)." BLSSH, 169–83.

———. *Rome before Avignon: A Social History of Thirteenth-Century Rome.* New York: Basic Books, 1974.

———. "Violence, Disorder, and Order in Thirteenth-Century Rome," In Martinez, *Violence and Disorder,* 308–30.

Brezzi, Paolo. "Holy Years in the Economic Life of the City of Rome." *Journal of the European Economic Society* 4 (1975): 673–90.

———. "La realtà politica e sociale di Roma all'Alba del secolo xiv." RRA, 719–25.

———. *Roma e l'impero medioevale.* Storia di Roma 10. Bologna: Istituto di Studi Romani, 1947.

———. *Storia degli Anni Santi: Da Bonifacio VIII ai giorni nostri.* Milan: Mursia, 1975.

Broise, H., and Jean-Claude Maire-Vigueur. "Strutture famigliari, spazio domestico e architettura civile a Roma alla fine del Medioevo." In *Storia dell'arte Italiana.* Vol. 5, *Momenti di Architettura,* edited by Giulio Bollati and Paolo Fossati, 99–160. Turin: G. Einaudi, 1983.

Brun, Robert. *Avignon au temps des papes: Les monuments, les artistes, la société.* Paris: A. Colin, 1928.

Bruzelius, Caroline. "Queen Sancia of Mallorca and the Convent Church of Sta. Chiara in Naples." *Memoirs of the American Academy in Rome* 40 (1995): 69–100.

Bulwer-Lytton, Edward. *Rienzo: The Last of the Roman Tribunes.* Leipzig: Bernhard Tauchnitz, 1842.

Burr, David. "Mendicant Readings of the Apocalypse." AMA, 89–102.

———. *Olivi's Peaceable Kingdom: A Reading of the Apocalypse Commentary.* Philadelphia: University of Pennsylvania Press, 1993.

———. *The Spiritual Franciscans: From Protest to Persecution in the Century after St. Francis.* University Park: Pennsylvania State University Press, 2001.

Bynum, Caroline Walker, and Paul Freedman, eds. *Last Things: Death and the Apocalypse in the Middle Ages.* Philadelphia: University of Pennsylvania Press, 2000.

Byron, Lord George Gordon. *Childe Harold's Pilgrimage.* Philadelphia: Moes Thomas, 1812.

Caferro, William. *Mercenary Companies and the Decline of Siena.* Baltimore: Johns Hopkins University Press, 1998.

Calisse, Carlo. "I Prefetti di Vico." ASRSP 10 (1887): 1–136, 353–594.

Calleri, S. *L'arte dei giudici e notai di Firenze nell'età comunale e nel suo statuto del 1344.* Milan: Giuffrè, 1966.

Campagnola, Stanislao da, ed. *Chi Erano gli Spirituali?* Assisi: Società Internazionale di Studi Francescani, 1976.

Campajola, Viviana. "Il Ghetto di Roma." *Quaderni dell' Istituto di Storia dell'Architettura* 67–70. Rome: Università di Roma, Istituto di Storia di Architettura (1965): 67–84.

Cantarelli, L. "La *lex de imperio Vespasiani.*" *Commissione Archeologica Comunale di Roma. Bullettino* 18 (1890): 194–208, 235–46.

Carbonetti, Cristina, and M. Vendittelli. "Anagni." In *Lazio medievale: Ricerca topografica su 33 abitati delle antiche diocesi . . . ,* edited by Isa Belli Barsali and Cristina Carbonetti, 71–105. Rome: Multigrafica, 1980.

Carettoni, Gianfilippo. "Il foro romano nel medioevo e nel rinascimento." *Studi Romani* 11 (1963): 406–16.

———. "Il Palatino nel medioevo." *Studi Romani* 9 (1961): 508–18.

Carocci, Sandro. *Baroni di Roma: Dominazioni signorili e lignaggi aristocratici nel duecento e nel primo trecento.* Istituto storico italiano per il Medio Evo, Nuovi studi storici 23/Collection Ecole française de Rome 181. Rome: ISIME and EFR, 1993.

———. "Baroni in città: Considerazioni sull' insediamento e i diritti urbani della grande nobiltà." In Hubert, *Rome aux XIIIe et XIVe siècles,* 137–73.

———. "La celebrazione aristocratica nello Stato della Chiesa." CFP, 345–67.

———. "Una nobiltà bipartita. Rappresentazioni sociali e lignaggi preeminenti a Roma nel Duecento e nella prima metà del Trecento." BISIMEAM 95 (1989): 71–122.

Casson, Lionel. *Travel in the Ancient World.* Baltimore: Johns Hopkins University Press, 1994.

Castellani, Arrigo. "Note di lettura: La 'Cronica' d'Anonimo romano." *Studi linguistici italiani* 13 (1987): 66–84.

Castellani, Giuseppe. "I *Fragmenti Romanae Historiae:* Studio preparatorio alla nuova edizione di essi." ASRSP 43 (1920): 113–56.

Castelnuovo, Enrico. *Un pittore italiano alla corte di Avignone: Matteo Giovanetti e la pittura in Provenza nel secolo xiv.* Turin: Einaudi, 1962.

Cazenave, Annie. "La vision eschatologique des spirituels franciscains autour de leur condemnation." In *The Use and Abuse of Eschatology in the Middle Ages.* Mediaevalia Lovanensia. Ser. 1, Studia 15. Ed. Werner Verbeke, Daniel Verhelst, and Andries Welkenhuysen, 393–403. Louvain: Louvain University Press, 1988.

Cecchelli, Carlo. "Il Campidoglio nel medioevo." ASRSP 67 (1944): 209–32.

———. *La vita di Roma del Medioevo.* Vol. 1, *Le arti minori e il costume.* Rome: Fratelli Palombo, 1951.

Chambers, David S., and Trevor Dean. *Clean Hands and Rough Justice: An Investigating Magistrate in Renaissance Italy.* Ann Arbor: University of Michigan Press, 1997.

Chastel, André. *The Sack of Rome, 1527.* Trans. Beth Archer. Princeton, N.J.: Princeton University Press, 1983.

Cherubino, Giovanni. "Dal libro di ricordi di un notaio senese del trecento." In *Signori, Contadini, Borghesi. Ricerche sulla società italiana del basso medioevo,* 395–415. Florence: La Nuova Italia, 1974.

Chojnacki, Stanley. "Crime, Punishment and the Trecento Venetian State." In Martinez, *Violence,* 184–228.

Ciccia, Carmelo. *Dante e Gioacchino da Fiore.* Cosenza: L. Pellegrini, 1997.

Cilento, Nicola. "Sulla tradizione della *Salvatio Romae:* La magica tutela della città medievale." In RRA, 695–703.

Clementi, Giuseppe. *Il Beato Venturino da Bergamo dell'Ordine di Predicatori (1304–1346).* Storia e Documenti. Rome: Libreria Salesiana, 1904.

Cohn, Norman. *The Pursuit of the Millennium.* New York: Harper and Row, 1961.

Cohn, Samuel K., Jr. "The Black Death: End of a Paradigm." *American Historical Review* 107 (2002): 703–38.

——. *The Cult of Remembrance and the Black Death: Six Renaissance Cities in Central Italy*. Baltimore: Johns Hopkins University Press, 1992.

Collins, Amanda. "Cola di Rienzo, the Lateran Basilica, and the *Lex de imperio* of Vespasian." *Mediaeval Studies* 60 (1998): 159–83.

Colliva, P. *Il Cardinale Albornoz. Lo Stato della Chiesa. Le Constitutiones Aegidianae*. Bologna: Real Colegio de España, 1977.

Colombe, Dr. "Nicolas Rienzi au palais des papes d'Avignon." *Mémoires de l'Académie de Vaucluse,* ser. 2, 11 (1911): 323–44.

Contamine, Philippe. "Peasant Hut to Papal Palace: The Fourteenth and Fifteenth Centuries." In *A History of Private Life*. Vol. 2, *Revelations of the Medieval World,* edited by Georges Duby, translated by Arthur Goldhammer, 425–505. Cambridge, Mass.: Harvard University Press, 1988.

Contini, Gianfranco. "Invito a un capolavoro." *Letteratura* 4.4 (1940): 3–14.

Corbo, Anna Maria. "Relazione descrittiva degli archivi notarili Romani dei secoli xiv–xv nell'Archivio di Stato e nell'Archivio Capitolino." BLSSH, 49–67.

Corsi, Dinora. "La 'crociata' di Venturino da Bergamo nella crisi spirituale di metà Trecento." *Archivio Storico Italiano* 147.4 (1989): 697–747.

Costa-Zalessow, Natalia. "The Personification of Italy from Dante through the Trecento." *Italica* 68.4 (1991): 316–31.

Cowell, Andrew. *At Play in the Tavern: Signs, Coins, and Bodies in the Middle Ages*. Ann Arbor: University of Michigan Press, 1999.

Cusanno, Anna Maria. "Il complesso fortificato 'delle Milizie' a Magnanapoli." *Bollettino d'arte* 55–56 (1989): 91–108.

——. *Le fortificazioni medioevali a Roma. La Torre dei Conti e la Torre delle Milizie*. Assessorato alla Cultura 42. Rome: Comune di Roma, 1991.

——. "*Turris Comitum:* Vicende storiche ed ipotesi sulla 'Torre della Città.'" *L'Urbe* 5–6 (1988): 20–38.

D'Alatri, Mariano. "Fraticellismo ed inquisizione nell'Italia centrale." *Picenum Seraphicum* 11 (1974): 289–314.

D'Annunzio, Gabriele. *Vite di uomini illustri et di uomini oscuri: La vita di Cola di Rienzo*. Milan: Fratelli Treves, 1913.

Daniel, E. Randolph. "Apocalyptic Conversion: The Joachite Alternative to the Crusades." *Traditio* 25 (1969): 127–54.

——. "The Double Procession of the Holy Spirit in Joachim of Fiore's Understanding of History." *Speculum* 55 (1980): 469–83.

——. "Exodus and Exile: Joachim of Fiore's Apocalyptic Scenario." BFLT, 124–39.

——. "Joachim of Fiore: Patterns of History in the Apocalypse." AMA, 72–88.

Darbois, Roland. *Quand les papes regnaient en Avignon*. Paris: Fayard, 1981.

Dardano, Maurizio. "L'articolazione e il confine della frase nella 'Cronica' di Anonimo romano." In *Italia Linguistica: Idee, Storia, Strutture,* edited by Federica Albani Leoni, 203–22. Bologna: Il Mulino, 1983.

Davis, Charles T. "*Il buono tempo antico* (The Good Old Time)." In *Dante's Italy and Other Essays,* 71–93. Philadelphia: University of Pennsylvania Press, 1984.

——. *Dante and the Idea of Rome*. Oxford: Clarendon, 1957.

——. "Ptolemy of Lucca and the Roman Republic." In *Dante's Italy and Other Essays*, 254–89. Philadelphia: University of Pennsylvania Press, 1984.

——. "Roman Patriotism and Republican Propaganda: Ptolemy of Lucca and Pope Nicholas III." In *Dante's Italy and Other Essays*, 224–53. Philadelphia: University of Pennsylvania Press, 1984.

De Angelis, Pietro. *Il Giubileo dell'anno 1350 e l'Ospedale di Santo Spirito in Saxia*. Rome: De Angelis, 1949.

——. *L'ospedale di S. Spirito in Saxia e le sue filiali nel mondo*. 2 vols. Rome: Pietro de Angelis, 1958.

De Caprio, V. "La cultura romana nel periodo avignonese 1305–1377." In *Letteratura Italiana. Storia e Geografia*, edited by Roberto Antonelli, Angelo Cicchetti, and Giorgio Inglese, 495–505. Turin: Einaudi, 1987.

De Cesaris, Mario. "I Prefetti di Vico." In *Comune di Vetralla. Quaderni della Cultura* 1 (1993): 3–17.

De Frede, C. "Da Carlo I d'Angio à Giovanna I (1263–1382)." In *Storia di Napoli*, 3:1–333. Naples: Società editrice storia di Napoli, 1969.

De la Roncière, Charles M. "Indirect Taxes or 'Gabelles' at Florence in the Fourteenth Century: The Evolution of Tariffs and Problems of Collection." In *Florentine Studies: Politics and Society in Renaissance Florence*, edited by Nicolai Rubinstein, 140–92. Evanston, Ill.: Northwestern University Press, 1968.

De Matteis, M. C. *"La teologia politica comunale" di Remigio de Girolami*. Bologna: Patron, 1977.

Dean, Trevor. "Marriage and Mutilation: Vendetta in Late Medieval Italy." *Past and Present* 157 (1997): 3–36.

Deiss, Joseph Jay. *Captains of Fortune: Profiles of Six Italian Condottieri*. London: Gollancz, 1966.

Delle Ville, P. *Mathèo de Viterbo Pictor Pape*. Turin: Gribaudo, 1995.

Dickson, Gary. "The Crowd at the Feet of Pope Boniface VIII: Pilgrimage, Crusade and the First Roman Jubilee (1300)." *Journal of Medieval History* 25 (1999): 279–307.

D'Onofrio, Cesare. *Il Tevere e Roma*. Rome: U. Bozzi, 1970.

Dotti, Ugo. "Il primo libro delle 'Senili' di Francesco Petrarca." *Giornale storico della letteratura italiana* 169 (1992): 228–39.

Douie, Decima. *The Nature and the Effect of the Heresy of the Fraticelli*. Manchester: University of Manchester Press, 1932.

Du Cange, Charles Du Fresne. *Glossarium mediae et infimae latinitatis*. 7 vols. Paris: F. Didot Frères, 1840–50.

du Cerceau, Jean Antoine. *Conjuration de Nicholas Gabrini, dit de Rienzi, Tyran de Rome, en 1347*. Paris, 1733. English translation, *The Life and Times of Rienzi*. Philadelphia: E. L. Carey and A. Hart, 1836.

Duchesne, L. "Les régions de Rome au Moyen Age." In *Scripta Minora. Etudes de topographie romaine et de géographie ecclésiastique*, 91–114. Collection de l'Ecole française de Rome 13. Rome: EFR, 1973.

Dupré Theseider, Eugenio. "Albornoz, Egidio de." DBI 2:45–53.

———. "L'attesa escatologica durante il periodo avignonese." In *L'Attesa dell'età nuova nella spiritualità della fine del medioevo*, 65–126. Convegni del Centro di Studi sulla Spiritualità Medievale. Todi: CSSM, 1962.

———. "Egidio de Albornoz e la riconquista dello Stato della Chiesa." In *El Cardenal Albornoz y el Colegio de España*, 1:433–59. Bologna: Colegio de España, 1972.

———. *Roma dal Comune di populo alla Signoria pontificia (1252–1377)*. Storia di Roma 11. Bologna: Istituto di Studi Romani & L. Cappelli, 1952.

Dvoráková, Vlasta, Josef Krása, Anezka Merhautová, and Karen Stejskal. *Gothic Mural Painting in Bohemia and Moravia, 1300–1378*. New York: Oxford University Press, 1964.

Dykmans, Marc. "Le Cardinal Annibal de Ceccano (c.1282–1350). Etude biographique et testament de 17 Juin 1348." *Bulletin de l'Institut Historique Belge de Rome* 48 (1973): 145–315.

———. "Le cardinal Annibal de Ceccano et la vision béatifique." *Gregorianum* 50 (1969): 343–82.

———. "Colonna, Agapito" [son of Giacomo della Sciarra]. DBI 27:256–60.

Eadie, Mervyn J., and Peter F. Bladin. *A Disease Once Sacred: A History of the Medical Understanding of Epilepsy*. Eastleigh, UK: John Libbey, 2001.

Edgerton, Samuel, Jr. *Pictures and Punishment: Art and Criminal Prosecution during the Florentine Renaissance*. Ithaca, N.Y.: Cornell University Press, 1985.

Egidi, Pietro. *Intorno all'esercito del Comune di Roma nella prima metà del secolo xiv*. Viterbo: Società Agnesotti, 1897.

Eisenbichler, Konrad, ed. *Crossing the Boundaries: Christian Piety and the Arts in Italian Medieval and Renaissance Confraternities*. Kalamazoo, Mich.: Medieval Institute, 1990.

Eliade, Mircea. *Cosmos and History: The Myth of the Eternal Return*. New York: Harper and Row, 1959.

———. *The Sacred and the Profane: The Nature of Religion*. New York: Harper and Row, 1961.

Emmerson, Richard K. *Antichrist in the Middle Ages: A Study of Medieval Apocalypticism, Art, and Literature*. Seattle: University of Washington Press, 1981.

———. "The Apocalypse in Medieval Culture." AMA, 293–332.

Emmerson, Richard K., and Ronald B. Herzman. *The Apocalyptic Imagination in Medieval Literature*. Philadelphia: University of Pennsylania Press, 1992.

Epstein, Steven A. *Genoa and the Genoese, 958–1528*. Chapel Hill: University of North Carolina Press, 1996.

Erler, Adalbert. *Aegidius Albornoz als Gesetzgeber des Kirchenstaates*. Berlin: E. Schmidt, 1970.

———. *Lupa, Lex und Reiterstandbild im mittelalterlichen Rom: Eine rechgeschichtliche Studie*. Wiesbaden: F. Steiner, 1972.

Ermini, G. "La libertà comunale nello Stato della Chiesa. Da Innocenzo III all'Albornoz (1198–1367)." ASRSP 49 (1926): 5–126.

Esch, Arnold. "Dal Medioevo al Rinascimento: Uomini a Roma dal 1350 al 1450." ASRSP, 3d ser., 25 (1971): 1–10.

———. "Spolien." *Archiv für Kulturgeschichte* 51 (1969): 1–64.

Esposito, Aliano A. "Le 'confraternite' del Gonfalone (secoli xiv–xv)." In *Le confraternite romane: Esperienza religiosa, società, committenza artistica Ricerche per la storia religiosa di Roma,* edited by Luigi Fiorani, 5:91–136. Rome: Storia e letteratura, 1984.

———. "Un inventario di beni in Roma dell'Ospedale di S. Spirito in Sassia (1322)." ASRSP 99 (1976): 71–115.

Eubel, Konrad. *Hierarchia Catholica Medii Aevi.* Regensburg: Monastic Library, 1913–14.

Fagiolo, Marcello, and Maria Luisa Madonna, eds. *Roma 1300–1875: L'Arte degli anni santi.* Milan: Mondadori, 1984.

Falco, Giorgio. "I comuni della Campagna e della Marittima nel medio evo. III. Il declinare delle autonomie comunali (sec. xiv)." ASRSP 49 (1926): 127–302.

Falvey, Kathleen. "Early Italian Dramatic Traditions and Comforting Rituals: Some Initial Consideratons." In Eisenbichler, 33–55.

Faraglia, N. F. "Barbato da Sulmona e gli uomini illustri della corte di Roberto d'Angiò." *Archivio Storico Italiano,* 5th ser., 3 (1889): 313–60.

Faucon, Maurice. "Note sur la détention de Rienzi à Avignon." *Ecole française de Rome. Mélanges d'archéologie et d'histoire* 7 (1887): 53–58.

Faulhaber, Charles B. "The *Summa dictaminis* of Guido Faba." In *Medieval Eloquence: Studies in the Theory and Practice of Medieval Rhetoric,* edited by James J. Murphy, 85–111. Berkeley and Los Angeles: University of California Press, 1978.

Fausto, Piola Caselli. *La Construzione del Palazzo dei Papi di Avignone (1316–1367).* Milan: A. Guffrè, 1981.

Fedele, Pietro. "Una composizione di pace fra privati." ASRSP 26 (1903): 466–71.

———. "Il Giubileo del 1350." *Roma* 11 (1933): 193–212.

———. "Un giudicato di Cola di Rienzo fra il monastero di S. Cosimato e gli Stefaneschi." ASRSP 26 (1903): 437–51.

Felici, Lucio "'La Vita di Cola di Rienzo' nella tradizione chronachistica romana." *Studi romani* 25.3 (1977): 325–43.

Feo, Michele. "L'epistola come mezzo di propaganda politica in Francesco Petrarca." CFP, 203–26.

Ferri, G. "La 'Romana Fraternitas.'" ASRSP 26 (1903): 453–66.

Filippini, Francesco. "Cola di Rienzo e la Curia Avignonese." *Studi Storici* 10 (1901): 241–87; 11 (1902): 3–35.

Fleischer, Victor. *Rienzo: The Rise and Fall of a Dictator.* London: Aigion Press, 1948.

Folena, Gianfranco. "Varia Fortuna del Romanesco." *Lingua Nostra* 52.1 (1991): 7–10.

Fonseca, Cosimo Damiano. "Continuità e diversità nel profetismo gioachimita tra quattrocento e cinquecento." In *Il profetismo gioachimita tra quattrocento e cinquecento,* 11–14. Atti del III Congresso internazionale di studi gioachimiti. Ed. Gian Luca Potestà. Genoa: Marietti, 1991.

Foote, David. "Review of Andreas Rehberg, *Die Kanoniker von S. Giovanni in Laterano und S. Maria Maggiore.*" *Catholic Historical Review* 87 (2001): 733–35.

Foreville, R. "Jubilé." *Dictionnaire de Spiritualité* 7 (1974): 1478–87.

France, John. *Western Warfare in the Age of the Crusades, 1000–1300*. Ithaca, N.Y.: Cornell University Press, 1999.

Frugoni, Arsenio. "Cola di Rienzo 'tribunus sompniator.'" In *Incontri nel Rinascimento*, 9–23. Brescia: La Scuola, 1954.

——. "Il Giubileo di Bonifacio VIII." BISIMEAM 62 (1950): 1–121.

Frugoni, Chiara. "L'antichità: Dai 'Mirabilia' alla propaganda politica." In *Memoria dell'antico nell'arte italiana*. Vol. 1, *L'uso dei classici*, edited by Salvatore Settis, 3–72. Biblioteca di Storia dell'Arte. Turin: Einaudi, 1984.

——. *A Distant City: Images of Urban Experience in the Medieval World*. Trans. William McCuaig. Princeton, N.J.: Princeton University Press, 1991.

——. "L'iconografia e la vita religiosa nei secoli xiii-xiv." In *Storia dell'Italia religiosa*. Vol. 1, *L'antichità e il medioevo*, edited by André Vauchez, 485–504. Rome: Laterza, 1993.

Gagnière, Sylvain. *Histoire d'Avignon*. Aix-en-Provence: Edisud, 1979.

——. *The Palace of the Popes at Avignon*. Paris: Caisse nationale des monumnets historiques, 1965.

Ganshof, François L. *The Middle Ages (Histoire des relations internationales*. Vol. 1, *Le Moyen Age.)* Trans. Remy Inglis Hall. New York: Harper and Row, 1970.

Garin, Eugenio. "L'altesa dell'età nuova e la *Renovatio*." In *L'età nuova. Ricerche di storia della cultura dal xii al xvi secolo*, 81–104. Napoli: Morano, 1969.

Garms, J., and B. Ward-Perkins, eds. *Mittelalterlichen Grabmäler in Rom und Latium vom 13. bis zum 15. Jahrhundert*. Vol. 1, *Die Grabplatten und Tafeln*. Rome: Österreichen Kulturinstituts in Rom, 1981.

Gasparri, Stefano. *I milites cittadini: Studi sulla cavalleria in Italia*. Nuovi studi storici 19. Rome: Istituto Palazzo Barberini, 1992.

Gehl, Paul F. *A Moral Art: Grammar, Society, and Culture in Trecento Florence*. Ithaca, N.Y.: Cornell University Press, 1993.

Gennaro, Clara. "Mercanti e bovattieri nella Roma della seconda metà del Trecento." BISIMEAM 78 (1967): 155–203.

——. "Venturino da Bergamo e la peregrinatio romana del 1335." In *Studi sul medioevo offerti a Raffaelo Morghen*, 1:375–406. Rome: ISIMEAM, 1974.

——. "Venturino spirituale." *Rivista di Storia e Letteratura Religiosa* 23.3 (1987): 434–66.

Giangreco, Thomas C. "*Miles Spiritus Sancti:* The Apocalyptic Dimension of Cola di Rienzo's Reform Ideology." In *Reform and Renewal in the Middle Ages and the Renaissance: Studies in Honor of Louis Pascoe, SJ*, edited by Thomas M. Izbicki and Christopher M. Bellitto, 75–92. Leiden: E. J. Brill, 2000.

——. "Reform, Renewal and Renaissance: The Thought of Cola di Rienzo in Its Historical Context." Ph.D. diss., Fordham University, 1997.

Gibbon, Edward. *The Decline and Fall of the Roman Empire*. New York: Modern Library, 1954.

Girard, Alain. *L'aventure gothique entre Pont-Saint-Esprit et Avignon du XIIIe au XIVe siècle: Genèse des formes et du sens de l'art gothique dans la basse vallée du Rhône*. Aix-en-Provence: Edisud, 1996.

Giuliano, Antonio. "Roma 1300." *Xenia* 4 (1982): 15–22.

Gnoli, Umberto. *Alberghi ed osterie di Roma nella Rinascenza*. Spoleto: C. Moneta, 1935.

Golinelli, Paolo. *Città e culto dei santi nel medioevo italiano*. Biblioteca di Storia Urbana Medievale. 2d ed., rev. Bologna: CLUEB, 1996.

Graf, Arturo. *Roma nella memoria e nelle immaginazione del medio evo*. Turin: Loescher, 1882–83.

Gragnolati, Manuele. "From Decay to Splendor: Body and Pain in Bonvesin de la Riva's *Book of the Three Scriptures*." BFLT, 83–97.

Greenhalgh, Michael. "Iconografia antica e sue trasformazioni durante il Medioevo." In *Memoria dell'antico nell'arte italiana*. Vol. 2, *I generi e i temi ritrovati*, edited by Salvatore Settis, 153–97. Turin: Einaudi, 1985.

——. *"Ipsa ruina docet:* L'uso dell'Antico nel Medioevo." In *Memoria dell'Antico nell'arte italiana*. Vol. 1, *L'uso dei classici*, edited by Salvatore Settis, 113–67. Turin: Einaudi, 1984.

Greenstein, Jack M. "The Vision of Peace: Meaning and Representation in Ambrogio Lorenzetti's *Sala della Pace* Cityscapes." *Art History* 2.4 (1988): 492–510.

Gregorovius, Ferdinand A. *History of the City of Rome in the Middle Ages*. Trans. Annie Hamilton. 8 vols. in 13. London: G. Bell and Sons, 1903–12. Reprint, New York: AMS, 1967. Reprint and CD-ROM, New York: Italica Press, 2000–.

Grendler, Paul F. *Schooling in Renaissance Italy: Literacy and Learning, 1300–1600*. Baltimore: Johns Hopkins University Press, 1989.

Grierson, Philip, and Lucia Travaini. *Medieval European Coinage*. Vol. 14.3, *South Italy, Sicily, Sardinia*. Cambridge: Cambridge University Press, 1998.

Guidoni, Enrico. "La cultura urbanistica a Roma e nell'Italia centrale tra Due e Trecento." In RRA, 689–94.

Guilleman, Bernard. "Caetani, Annibaldo." DBI 16:111–15.

——. *La cour pontificale d'Avignon, 1309–1376: Étude d'une société*. Bibliothèque des Ecoles françaises d'Athènes et de Rome. [Ser. 1] Fasc. 201. Paris: E. de Boccard, 1962.

——. *Les papes d'Avignon, 1309–1376*. Paris: Cerf, 1998.

Haas, Louis. *The Renaissance Man and His Children: Childbirth and Early Childhood in Florence, 1300–1600*. New York: St. Martin's, 1997.

Haskins, Charles Homer. *The Renaissance of the Twelfth Century*. Cleveland: World, 1966.

Henderson, John. "The Flagellant Movement and Flagellant Confraternities in Central Italy, 1260–1400." *Studies in Church History* 15 (1978): 147–60.

——. *Piety and Charity in Late Medieval Florence*. New York: Clarendon, 1994.

Herde, Peter. *Cölestin V (1294). (Peter von Murrone). Der Engelpapst*. Stuttgart: Päpste und Papsttum, 1981.

Herlihy, David. *Women, Family and Society in Medieval Europe: Historical Essays, 1978–1991*. Ed. Anthony Molho. Providence, R.I., and Oxford: Berghahn Books, 1995.

Herlihy, David, and Christiane Klapisch-Zuber. *The Tuscans and Their Families: A Study of the Florentine Castato of 1427*. New Haven, Conn.: Yale University Press, 1985.

Herzman, Ronald B. "Dante and the Apocalypse." In AMA, 398–413.

Hetherington, Paul. *Medieval Rome.* New York: St. Martin's, 1994.

Horowitz, Joseph. "The Specter of Hitler in the Music of Wagner." *New York Times,* November 8, 1998. 2:1, 38.

Hubert, Étienne. "Un censier des biens romains du monastère S. Silvestro in Capite (1333–1334)." In *Materiali per la storia dei patrimoni immobiliari urbani a Roma nel Medioevo: Due censuali di beni del secolo xiv.* ASRSP 111 (1988): 75–160.

———. *Espace urbain et habitat à Rome du Xe siècle à la fin du XIIIe siècle.* Collection de l'Ecole française de Rome 135. Rome: EFR, 1990.

———. "Rioni." In Philippe Boutry and Philippe Levillain, eds. *Dictionnaire historique de la Papauté,* 1459–60. Paris: Fayard, 1994.

———, ed. *Rome aux XIIIe et XIVe siècles.* Collection de l'Ecole française de Rome 170. Rome: EFR, 1993.

Hugenholtz, F. W. "The Anagni Frescoes: A Manifesto. An Historical Investigation." *Medelingen van het Nederlands Institut te Romens* 6 (1979): 139–72.

Hülsen, Christian. *Le chiese di Roma nel Medio Evo: Cataloghi ed appunti.* Florence: Olschki, 1927.

Huntsman, Jeffrey. "Grammar." In *The Seven Liberal Arts in the Middle Ages,* edited by David L. Wagner, 58–95. Bloomington: Indiana University Press, 1983.

Hyde, J. K. "Commune, University, and Society in Early Medieval Bologna." In *Universities in Politics: Case Studies from the Late Middle Ages and Early Modern Period,* edited by John W. Baldwin and Richard A. Goldthwaite, 17–46. Baltimore: Johns Hopkins University Press, 1972.

———. "Contemporary Views on Faction and Civil Strife in Thirteenth- and Fourteenth-Century Italy." In Martinez, *Violence,* 273–307.

Ilari, A. "Appunti di topografia romana: Le regioni diaconali." *Rivista Diocesana di Roma* 3–4 (1966): 1–15.

———. "La 'Romana Fraternitas' al tempo di Papa Giovanni XXII." *Bollettino del clero romano* 40 (1959): 423–30.

Jacob, Ernest F. "John of Roquetaillade." In *Essays in Later Medieval History,* 175–94. New York: Barnes and Noble, 1968.

Jarrett, Bede. *The Emperor Charles IV.* New York: Sheed and Ward, 1935.

Jugie, Pierre. "Clement VI." DHP, 369–72.

———. "Innocent VI." DHP, 886–88.

Juhar, M.-B. "Der Romgedanke bei Cola di Rienzo." Ph.D. diss., Christian Albrechts-Universität, 1977.

Kaske, Robert E. "The Seven *Status Ecclesie* in *Purgatorio* XXXII and XXXIII." In *Dante, Petrarch, Boccaccio: Studies in the Italian Trecento in Honor of Charles S. Singleton.* MARTS 22. Ed. Aldo S. Bernardo and Anthony L. Pellegrini, 89–113. Binghamton: State University of New York Press, 1983.

Katermaa-Ottela, Aino. "Le casetorri medievali in Roma." *Opuscula Instituti Romani Finlandiae. Commentationes humanarum litterarum* 67.1 (1981): 41–55.

Keen, Maurice, ed. *Medieval Warfare: A History.* New York: Oxford University Press, 1999.

Kelley, Donald R. *Renaissance Humanism*. Boston: Twayne, 1991.

Kemp, Wolfgang. "Zum Programm von Stefaneschi-Altar und Navicella." *Zeitschrift für Kunstgeschichte* 30 (1967): 309–20.

Kershaw, Ian. *Hitler, 1896–1936: Hubris*. New York: Norton, 1999.

Kessler, Herbert L., and Johanna Zacharias. *Rome 1300: On the Path of the Pilgrim*. New Haven, Conn.: Yale University Press, 2000.

Kinney, Dale. "*Mirabilia urbis Romae*." In *The Classics in the Middle Ages*, edited by Aldo S. Bernardo and Saul Levin, 207–21. Binghamton, N.Y.: MARTS, 1990.

———. "Rape or Restitution of the Past? Interpreting *Spolia*." In *The Art of Interpreting*, edited by Susan C. Scott, 57–67. University Park: Pennsylvania State University Press, 1995.

———. "Sta. Maria in Trastevere, from Its Founding to the Year 1215." Ph.D. diss., New York University, Institute of Fine Arts, 1975.

Kitzinger, Ernst. "The Arts as Aspects of a Renaissance: Rome and Italy." In Benson and Constable, *Renaissance and Renewal in the Twelfth Century*, 637–70.

Klaniczay, Gábor. "The Cult of the Dynastic Saints in Central Europe: Fourteenth-Century Angevins and Luxemburgs." In *The Uses of Supernatural Power: The Transformation of Popular Religion in Medieval and Early-Modern Europe*, translated by Karen Margolis, 111–28. Princeton, N.J.: Princeton University Press, 1990.

Klapisch-Zuber, Christiane. "Kinship and Politics in Fourteenth-Century Florence." In *The Family in Italy from Antiquity to the Present*, edited by David I. Kertzer and Richard P. Saller, 208–28. New Haven, Conn.: Yale University Press, 1991.

Klein, Peter K. "The Apocalypse in Medieval Art." AMA, 159–99.

Koch, Klaus-Friedrick, Sonya Altorki, Andrew Arno, and Letitia Hickson. "Ritual Reconciliation and the Obviation of Grievances: A Comparative Study in the Ethnography of Law." *Ethnology* 16.3 (1977): 269–83.

Kohl, Benjamin G. *Padua under the Carrara, 1318–1405*. Baltimore: Johns Hopkins University Press, 1998.

Köhren-Jansen, Helmtrud. *Giottos Navicella: Bildtradition, Deitung, Rezeptionsgeschichte*. Römische Studien der Bibliotheca Hertziana 8. Worms: Wernersche Verlagsgesellschaft, 1993.

Kölmel, Von Wilhelm. "Petrarca und das Reich. Zum historisch-politischen Aspekt der 'studia humanitatis.'" *Historisches Jahrbuch* 90 (1970): 1–30.

Krautheimer, Richard, et al. *Corpus Basilicorum Christianorum Romae*. 5 vols. Vatican City: BAV 1937–77.

———. *Rome: Profile of a City, 312–1308*. Princeton, N.J.: Princeton University Press, 1980.

Kristeller, Paul Oskar. *Renaissance Thought: The Classic, Scholastic and Humanist Strains*. New York: Harper and Row, 1961.

———. *Renaissance Thought II*. New York: Harper and Row, 1965. Revised edition, *Renaissance Thought and the Arts*. Princeton, N.J.: Princeton University Press, 1990.

Labarge, Margaret Wade. *Medieval Travellers: The Rich and the Restless*. London: Hamish Hamilton, 1982.

Laclotte, Michel. *L'Ecole d'Avignon*. Paris: Flammarion, 1960.

Ladner, Gerhart B. *The Idea of Reform: Its Impact on Christian Thought and Action in the Age of the Fathers*. New York: Harper and Row, 1967.

Lambert, Malcolm D. *Medieval Heresy: Popular Movements from the Gregorian Reform to the Reformation*. 2d ed. Oxford: Basil Blackwell, 1992.

Lanciani, Rodolfo. *The Destruction of Ancient Rome: A Sketch of the History of the Monuments*. New York: Macmillan, 1899.

——. *Wanderings in the Roman Campagna*. London: Constable, 1909.

Larner, John. *Italy in the Age of Dante and Petrarch, 1216–1380*. London: Longman, 1980.

Lee, Harold, Marjorie Reeves, and Giulio Silano. *Western Mediterranean Prophecy: The School of Joachim of Fiore and the Fourteenth-Century Breviloquium*. Studies and Texts 88. Toronto: Pontifical Institute, 1989.

Leff, Gordon. *Heresy in the Middle Ages*. Vol. 1. New York: Barnes and Noble, 1967.

Lerner, Robert E. "The Black Death and Western European Eschatological Mentalities." *American Historical Review* 86 (1981): 533–52.

——. "The Medieval Return to the Thousand-Year Sabbath." AMA, 51–71.

Little, Lester K., and Sandro Buzzetti, eds. *Liberty, Charity, Fraternity: Lay Religious Confraternities at Bergamo in the Age of the Commune*. Smith College Studies in History 51. Northampton, Mass.: Smith College, 1988.

Llewellyn, Peter. *Rome in the Dark Ages*. London: Constable, 1993.

Lombardo, Maria Luisa. "Nobili, mercanti e popoli minuti negli atti dei notai Romani del xiv e xv secolo." BLSSH, 291–310.

Lori Sanfilippo, Isa. "I protocolli notarili romani del Trecento." ASRSP 110 (1987): 99–150.

Ludvíkovsky, Jaroslav. "List Karla IV. Colovi di Rinzo do vézení." *Studia Minora Facultatis Philosophicae Universitatis Brunensis*, series E, 24 (1981): 117–21.

Macadam, Alta. *Blue Guide: Rome*. 6th ed. New York: Norton, 1998.

Macek, Josef. "Pétrarch et Cola di Rienzo." *Historica* 8 (1965): 5–51.

——. "Les racines sociales de l'insurrection de Cola di Rienzo." *Historica* 6 (1963): 45–107.

Maire-Vigueur, Jean-Claude. "Capital économique et capital symbolique. Les contradictions de la société romaine à la fin du Moyen Age." BLSSII, 213–24.

——. "Classe dominante et classes dirigeantes à Rome à la fin du Moyen Age." *Storia della città* 1 (1976): 4–26.

——. "Cola di Rienzo." DBI 26:662–75.

——. "Cola di Rienzo et Jean de Roquetaillade ou la rencontre de l'imaginaire." TPPO, 381–89.

Mallett, Michael E. "Mercenaries." In Keen, 209–30.

——. *Mercenaries and Their Masters*. Totowa, N.J.: Rowman and Littlefield, 1974.

Manselli, Raoul. *Da Gioacchino da Fiore a Cristoforo Colombo: Studi sul francescanesimo spirituale, sull'ecclesiologia e sull'escatologismo bassomedievali*. Ed. Paolo Vian. Rome: Istituto Storico Italiano per Il Medioevo, 1997.

——. "La religiosità giubilare del 1300: Proposte di un'interpretazione." In RRA, 727–30.

Marchetti Longhi, G. "Anagni di Bonifacio VIII." *Bollettino dell'Istituto di storia e arte del Lazio meridionale* 3 (1965): 167–206.

Marchioli, Nicoletta Giovè. "L'Epigrafia comunale cittadina." In *Le forme della propaganda politica nel Due e nel Trecento,* 263–86. Collection de l'Ecole francaise de Rome 201. Ed. Paolo Cammarosano. Rome: EFR, 1994.

Mariani, Marisa. "Cola di Rienzo nel giudizio dei contemporanei fiorentini." *Studi Romani* 8 (1960): 647–66.

Maroni-Lumbriso, Matizia, and A. Martini. *Le confraternitate romane nelle loro chiese.* Rome: Fondazione Marco Besso, 1963.

Martindale, Andrew. *Gothic Art: From the Twelfth to the Fifteenth Century.* New York: Praeger, 1967.

Martinez, Lauro, ed. *Violence and Disorder in Italian Cities, 1200–1500.* Berkeley and Los Angeles: University of California Press, 1972.

Martinez, Ronald. "Lament and Lamentations in the *Purgatorio* and the Case of Dante's Statius." *Dante Studies* 115 (1997): 45–88.

Martini, P. Supino. "Caetani, Giacomo." DBI 16:172–74.

———. "Caetani, Giovanni." DBI 16:178–79.

———. "Caetani, Nicola." DBI 16:193–95.

Masson, Georgina. *The Companion Guide to Rome.* Englewood Cliffs, N.J.: Prentice-Hall, 1983.

Matthiae, Guglielmo. *Pittura romana del Medioevo.* Ed. F. Gandolfo. Rome: Palombi, 1988.

Mattingly, Garrett. *Renaissance Diplomacy.* Baltimore: Penguin Books, 1964.

Mazzei, Francesco. *Cola di Rienzo: La fantastica vita e l'orribile morte del tribuno del popolo romano.* Milan: Rusconi, 1980.

Mazzocco, Angelo. "The Antiquarianism of Francesco Petrarca." *Journal of Medieval and Renaissance Studies* 7 (1977): 203–24.

———. "Petrarca, Poggio and Biondo: Humanism's Foremost Interpreters of Roman Ruins." In *Francis Petrarch: Six Centuries Later: A Symposium,* edited by Aldo Scaglione, 354–64. Chapel Hill: University of North Carolina Press, 1975.

Mazzotta, Giuseppe. *The Worlds of Petrarch.* Durham, N.C.: Duke University Press, 1994.

McBrien, Richard P. *Lives of the Popes: The Pontiffs from St. Peter to John Paul II.* San Francisco: HarperCollins, 1997.

McClure, George W. *Sorrow and Consolation in Italian Humanism.* Princeton, N.J.: Princeton University Press, 1991.

McGinn, Bernard. "Angel Pope and Papal Antichrist." *Church History* 47.2 (1978): 155–73.

———. *Antichrist: Two Thousand Years of the Human Fascination with Evil.* San Francisco: Harper, 1994.

———. *Apocalyptic Spirituality.* New York: Paulist Press, 1979.

———. *The Calabrian Abbot: Joachim of Fiore in the History of Western Thought.* New York: Macmillan, 1985.

———. "Introduction: John's Apocalypse and the Apocalyptic Mentality." AMA, 3–19.

————. "Pastor Angelicus: Apocalyptic Myth and Political Hope in the Fourteenth Century." In *Santi e santità nel secolo xiv,* 219–51. Atti del xv convegno internazionale. Perugia: Centro di Studi Francescani, 1989.

McManamon, John M. "Innovation in Early Humanist Rhetoric: The Oratory of Pier Paolo Vergerio the Elder." *Rinascimento* 22 (1982): 3–32.

McNeill, William H. *Plagues and Peoples.* New York: History Book Club, 1993.

Meersseman, Giles G., O.P. "Disciplinati e Penitenti nel Duecento." In *Il movimento dei Disciplinati nel settimo centenario del suo inizio.* Disputazione di storia patria per l'Umbria 1. Lodovico Scaramucci, ed. Perugia: DSPU, 1962.

Melczer, William. "Cola di Rienzo and Petrarch's Political Solitude." *Explorations in Renaissance Culture* 2 (1975): 1–13.

Mellinkoff, Ruth. "Riding Backwards: Theme of Humiliation and Symbol of Evil." *Viator* 4 (1973): 153–77.

Merback, Mitchell B. *The Thief, the Cross, and the Wheel: Pain and the Spectacle of Punishment in Medieval and Renaissance Europe.* Chicago: University of Chicago Press, 1999.

Mercer, Henry C. *Ancient Carpenters' Tools.* 3d ed. Doylestown, Pa.: Bucks County Historical Society, 1951.

Messini, A. "Profitismo e profezie ritmiche italiana d'ispirazione Gioachimito-Francescana nei secoli xiii, xiv e xv." *Miscellanea Francescana* 37 (1937): 39–54.

Miglio, Massimo. "Colonna, Landolfo" [son of Landolfo, b. c. 1250]. DBI 27:349–52.

————. "'Et rerum facta est pulcherrima Roma.' Attualità della tradizione e proposte di innovazione." In *Aspetti culturali della società italiana nel periodo del papato avignonese,* 311–69. Convegni del Centro di Studi sulla Spiritualità Medievale 19. Todi: CSSM, 1981.

————. "Gli atti privati come contributo alla conoscenza delle condizioni culturali di Roma nei secoli xiv–xv." BLSSH, 225–37.

————. "Gli ideali di pace e di giustizia in Roma a metà del Trecento." In *La pace nel pensiero, nella politica, negli ideali del Trecento,* 175–97. Convegni del Centro di Studi sulla Spiritualità Medievale 15. Todi: CSSM, 1975.

————. "Gruppi sociali e azione politica nella Roma di Cola di Rienzo." *Studi Romani* 23.4 (1975): 442–61.

————. "Il progetto politico di Cola di Rienzo ed i comuni dell'Italia centrale." *Bollettino dell' Istituto Storico Artistico Orvietano* 39 (1988): 55–64.

————. "Roma dopo Avignone: La rinacità politica dell'antico." In *Memoria dell'antico nell'arte italiana.* Vol. 1, *L'uso dei classici,* edited by Salvatore Settis, 73–111. Turin: Einaudi, 1984.

Miglio, Massimo, A. Modigliami, and I. Ait, et al. *Taverne, locande e stufe a Roma nel Rinascimento.* Rome: Roma nel Rinascimento, 1999.

Milano, Attilio. *Il Ghetto di Roma.* Rome: Staderini, 1964.

Millefiorini, Pietro. "Il Giubileo del 1300. Storia e storiografia." *La Civiltà Cattolica* 150.4 (1999): 333–46.

Mitford, Miss Mary Russell. *Rienzi.* In *The Dramatic Works of Mary Russell Mitford.* London: Huest and Blackett, 1854.

Modigliani, Anna. *Mercati, botteghe e spazi di commercio a Roma tra medioevo ed età moderna.* Rome: Roma nel Rinascimento, 1998.

———. "Taverne e hosterie a Roma nel tardo medioevo: Tipologia, uso degli spazi, arredo e distribuzione nella città." In *Taverne, locande e stufe a Roma nel Rinascimento,* edited by Massimo Miglio et al., 19–45. Rome: Roma nel Rinascimento, 1999.

Mollat, Guillaume. *The Popes at Avignon, 1305–1378.* London: Thomas Nelson and Sons, 1963.

Mollat, Michel, and Philippe Wolff. *The Popular Revolutions of the Late Middle Ages.* London: George Allen and Unwin, 1973.

Mommsen, Theodor E. "Petrarch and the Sala Virorum Illustrium in Padua." *Art Bulletin* 34 (1952): 95–116.

———. "Petrarch's Conception of the 'Dark Ages.'" In *Medieval and Renaissance Studies,* edited by Eugene F. Rice Jr., 106–26. Ithaca, N.Y.: Cornell University Press, 1966.

Monachino, Vincenzo, et al. *La Carità Cristiana in Roma.* Bologna: Cappelli, 1968.

Monfasani, John. "Toward the Genesis of the Kristeller Thesis of Renaissance Humanism: Four Bibliographical Notes." *Renaissance Quarterly* 53.4 (2000): 1156–68.

Morganstern, Anne McGee. "Art and Ceremony in Papal Avignon: A Prescription for the Tomb of Clement VI." *Gesta* 40 (2001): 61–77.

Morghen, Raffaello. *Cola di Rienzo.* Ed. L. Gatto. 2 vols. Rome: Ateneo, 1956.

———. "Raniero Fasani e il movimento dei disciplinati del 1260." In *Il movimento dei Disciplinati nel settimo centenario del suo inizio,* edited by Lodovico Scaramucci, 29–42. Perguia: Disputazione di storia patria per l'Umbria, 1962.

Morrison, Karl F., ed. *Rome and Medieval Culture.* Chicago: University of Chicago Press, 1971. Abridged edition of Gregorovius.

Mossa, Giovanni, and Maurizio Baldassari. *La vita economica di Roma nel medioevo.* Rome: Liber, 1971.

Mosti, Renzo. "L'eresia dei Fraticelli nei Territorii de Tivoli." *Società Tiburtina di Storia e d'Arte. Atti e Memoriale* 38 (1965): 41–110.

Moulinas, René. *Avignon.* Marguerittes: Equinoxe, 1990.

Le mouvement confraternel au Moyen-Age: France, Italie, Suisse. Collection de l'Ecole française de Rome 97. Geneva: Librarie Droz, 1987.

Moynihan, Robert. "The Development of the 'Pseudo-Joachim' Commentary 'Super Hieremiam': New Evidence." *Mélanges de l'Ecole française de Rome. Moyen Age et Temps Modernes* 98.1 (1986): 109–42.

Murphy, James J. *Rhetoric in the Middle Ages: A History of Rhetorical Theory from Augustine to the Renaissance.* Berkeley and Los Angeles: University of California Press, 1974.

Musto, Ronald G. "Franciscan Joachimism at the Court of Naples, 1309–1345: A New Appraisal." *Archivum Franciscanum Historicum* 90 (1997): 419–86.

———. "An Introduction to Neapolitan History." In Bacco, *Naples,* xix–lxii.

———. "Queen Sancia of Naples (1286–1345) and the Spiritual Franciscans." In

Women of the Medieval World, edited by Julus Kirshner and Suzanne F. Wemple, 179–214. Oxford: Basil Blackwell, 1985.

Musumarra, Carmelo. "Petrarca e Roma." *Critica Letteraria* 18.1 (1990): 155–67.

Najemy, John M. *Corporatism and Consensus in Florentine Electoral Politics, 1280–1400.* Chapel Hill: University of North Carolina Press, 1982.

National Society for Epilepsy. "Epileptic Seizures." http://bay.erg.ion.bpmf.ac.uk /NSEhome/seizures.html.

Newbigin, Nerida. "*Cene* and *Cenacoli* in the Ascension and Pentecost Companies of Fifteenth-Century Florence." In Eisenbichler, 90–107.

Origo, Iris. *The Merchant of Prato: Francesco di Marco Datini, 1335–1410.* Foreword by Barbara Tuchman. Boston: Godine, 1986.

——. *Tribune of Rome: A Biography of Cola di Rienzo.* London: Hogarth Press, 1938.

Ortalli, G. "Pingatur in Palatio." In *La pittura infamanate nei secoli xiii–xiv,* edited by G. Ortalli, 43–48. Rome: Jouvence, 1979.

Paeseler, W. "Giottos Navicella und ihr spätantikes Vorbild." *Römisches Jahrbuch für Kunstgeschichte* 5 (1941): 49–162.

Paglia, Vincenzo. "Dalle 'peregrinationes maiores' all'istituzione dell'anno santo." *Ricerche di Storia Sociale e Religiosa* 26 (1996): 217–30.

Panofsky, Irwin. *Renaissance and Renascences in Western Art.* New York: Harper and Row, 1972.

Papencordt, Felix. *Cola di Rienzo und sein Zeit.* Appendices. Hamburg: A. Perthes, 1841.

Papka, Claudia Rattazzi. "The Limits of Apocalypse: Eschatology, Epistemology, and Textuality in the *Commedia* and *Piers Plowman.*" BFLT, 233–56.

Paravicini Bagliani, Agostino. "Bonifacio VIII, l'affresco di Giotto e i processi contro i nemici della Chiesa. Postilla al giubileo del 1300." *Mélanges de l'Ecole française de Rome. Moyen Age* 112 (2000): 459–83.

——. "Colonna, Agapito" [b. c.1260]. DBI 27:253–56.

——. "Colonna, Giacomo" [son of Stefano il Vecchio]. DBI 27:316–18.

——. "Colonna, Giovanni" [son of Stefano il Giovane]. DBI 27:338–39.

——. "Colonna, Giovanni" [son of Stefano il Vecchio]. DBI 27:333–37.

——. "Colonna, Stefano, il Giovane." DBI 27:437–38.

——. "Colonna, Stefano" [Stefanello]. DBI 27:438–40.

Pardi, G. "La populazione del distretto di Roma sui primordi del Quattrocento." ASPSP 49 (1926): 331–54.

Parlato, Enrico, and Serena Romano. *Italia romanica: Roma e il Lazio.* Milan: Jaca Book, 1992.

Partner, Peter. "Bertrand de Deux." DBI 9:642–44.

——. *The Lands of St. Peter: The Papal State in the Middle Ages and Early Renaissance.* London: Methuen, 1972.

Passagli, Susanna. "Geografia parrocchiale e circoscrizioni territoriali nei secoli XII–XIV: Istituzioni e realtà quotidiana." In Hubert, *Rome aux XIIIe et XIVe siècles,* 43–86.

——. "Urbanizzazione e topografia a Roma nell'area dei Fori imperiali tra xiv e xvi secolo." *Mélanges de l'Ecole française de Rome. Moyen Age* 101 (1989): 273–325.

Pasztor, Edith. *Per la storia di San Ludovico d'Angio (1274–1297)*. Rome: ISIME, 1955.

Patrick, Andrew, ed. "Epilepsy FAQ: Frequently Asked Questions about Epilepsy." http://debra.dgbt.doc.ca/~andrew/epilepsy/FAQ.html#basic.

Pecchiai, P. "I segni sulle case di Roma nel medio evo." *Archivi d'Italia e rassegna internazionale degli archivi* 18 (1951): 227–51; 19 (1952): 25–48.

Peretto, E. *Movimenti spirituali laicali del medioevo. Fra ortodossia ed eresia*. La Spiritualità Cristiana. Storia e testi 8. Rome: Studium, 1985.

Peterson, David S. "Out of the Margins: Religion and the Church in Renaissance Italy." *Renaissance Quarterly* 53.3 (2000): 835–79.

Petrucci, Armando. "I documenti privati come fonte per lo studio dell'alfabetismo e della cultura scritta." BLSSH, 251–66.

——. *Public Lettering: Script, Power, and Culture*. Trans. Linda Lappin. Chicago: University of Chicago Press, 1993.

——. *La scittura di Francesco Petrarca*. Studi e Testi 248. Rome: Biblioteca Apostolica Vaticana, 1967.

Peyer, H. C. *Von der Gastfreundschaft zum Gasthaus: Studien zur Gastlichkeit im Mittelalter*. Hannover: Hahnsche, 1987. Italian edition, *Viaggiare nel Medioevo. Dall'hospitalità alla locanda*. Bari: Laterza, 1997.

Pietrangeli, Carlo. *Guide Rionali di Roma. Rione XI: S. Angelo*. Rome: Palombi, 1967.

——. "Il palazzo Senatorio nel Medioevo." *Capitolium* 35 (1960): 3–19.

Piur, Paul. *Cola di Rienzo*. Vienna: L. W. Seidel, 1931.

Polecritti, Cynthia L. *Preaching Peace in Renaissance Italy: Bernardino of Siena and His Audience*. Washington, D.C.: Catholic University of America Press, 2000.

Porta, Arturo Francesco della. *Cola di Rienzo: Dramma in 4 Atti*. Milan: Ceschinu, 1932.

Porta, Giuseppe. "La Lingua della 'Cronica' di Anonimo romano." In *Il romanesco ieri e oggi*, edited by Tullio de Mauro, 13–26. Rome: Bulzoni, 1989.

——. "Un nuovo manoscritto della 'Cronica' di Anonimo romano." *Studi Medievali*, 3d ser., 25.1 (1984): 445–48.

——. "La symbolique des animaux dans les chroniques italiennes du XIVe siècle." *Reinardus* 9 (1996): 135–43.

Potestà, Gian Luca. *Angelo Clareno. Dai poveri eremiti ai fraticelli*. Rome: Istituto Storico Italiano per il Medioevo, 1990.

Pozzi, Mario. "Appunti sulla 'Cronica' di Anonimo romano." *Giornale storico della Letteratura Italiana* 99 (1982): 481–504.

Preston, H. W., and L. Dodge. "Cola di Rienzo." *Atlantic Monthly,* January 1893, 62–78.

Proia, A., and P. Romano. *Il rione S. Angelo*. Rome: Guide Rionali, 1935.

Rashdall, Hastings. *The Universities of Europe in the Middle Ages*. Vol. 2, *Italy-Spain-France-Germany-Scotland*. 9th ed. Ed. F. M. Powicke and A. B. Emden. Oxford: Clarendon, 1936.

Ravasi, Gianfranco. *La cripta della cattedrale di Anagni*. Anagni: Cathedral, 1995.

Re, C. "Le regioni di Roma nel Medio Evo." *Studi e documenti di storia e diritto* 10 (1889): 349–81.

Reale, Ugo. *Cola di Rienzo: La straordinario vita del tribuno che sogno riportare Roma all'antico valore* . . . Rome: Newton Compton, 1991.

Reeves, Marjorie. *The Influence of Prophecy in the Later Middle Ages: A Study in Joachimism.* Oxford: Oxford University Press, 1969.

———. *Joachim of Fiore and the Prophetic Future.* London: SPCK, 1976.

Reeves, Marjorie, and Beatrice Hirsch-Reich. *The Figurae of Joachim of Fiore.* Oxford: Clarendon, 1972.

Rehberg, Andreas. "Familien aus Rom und die Colonna auf dem kurialen Pfründermarkt (1278–1348/78)." *Quellen und Forschungen aus italienischen Archiven und Bibliotheken* 78 (1998): 1–122; 79 (1999): 99–214.

———. *Die Kanoniker von S. Giovanni in Laterano und S. Maria Maggiore im 14. Jahrhundert: Eine Prosopographie.* Tübingen: Max Niemeyer, 1999.

———. *Kirche und Machte im römischen Trecento: Die Colonna und ihre Klientel auf dem kurialen Pfründenmarkt (1278–1378).* Bibliothek des Deutschen Historischen Instituts in Rom 88. Tübingen: Max Niemeyer, 1999.

Renazzi, Filippo Maria. *Storia dell'Università degli Studi di Roma.* 4 vols. Rome, 1803–6.

Renouard, Yves. *The Avignon Papacy: The Popes in Exile, 1305–1403.* New York: Barnes and Noble, 1994.

Reynolds, Suzanne. *Medieval Reading: Grammar, Rhetoric and the Classical Text.* Cambridge: Cambridge University Press, 1996.

Rice, Louise. *The Altars and Altarpieces of the New St. Peter's: Outfitting the Basilica, 1621–1666.* New York: Cambridge University Press, 1997.

Riesenberg, Peter. "Civism and Roman Law in Fourteenth-Century Italian Society." In *Economy, Society and Government in Medieval Italy,* edited by David Herlihy, Robert S. Lopez, and Vsevolod Slessarev, 237–54. Kent, Ohio: Kent State University Press, 1969.

Rodocanachi, Emmanuel. *Le Capitole romain antique et moderne.* Paris: Hachette, 1904.

———. *Cola di Rienzo.* Paris: A. Lahure, 1888.

Rollo-Koster, Joëlle. "Amongst Brothers: Italians' Networks in Papal Avignon (1360s–80s)." *Medieval Prosopography* 21 (2000): 153–89.

Romani, Mario. *Pellegrini e viaggiatori nell' economia di Roma dal xiv al xvii secolo.* Milan: Vita e pensiero, 1948.

Romano, Serena. "'*Regio dissimilitudinis*': Immagine e parole nella Roma di Cola di Rienzo." In *Bilan et perspectives des études médiévales en Europe,* edited by Jacqueline Hamesse, 329–56. Louvain: Federation Internationale des Institutes d'Etudes Médiévales, 1995.

Roques, Marguerite. *Les peintures murales du Sud-Est de la France (XIIIe–XVIe siècle).* Paris: A. & J. Picard, 1961.

Rosario, Iva. *Art and Propaganda: Charles IV of Bohemia 1346–1378.* Rochester, N.Y.: Boydell Press, 2000.

Rosenstock-Huessy, Eugen. *The Driving Power of Western Civilizaton: The Christian Revolution of the Middle Ages.* Boston: Beacon Press, 1950.

Ross, James Bruce. "The Middle-Class Child in Urban Italy, Fourteenth to Early

Sixteenth Century." In *The History of Childhood,* edited by Lloyd de Mause, 183–228. New York: Psychohistory Press, 1974.

———. "A Study of Twelfth-Century Interest in the Antiquities of Rome." In *Medieval and Historiographic Essays in Honor of James Westfall Thompson,* edited by James Lea Cate and Eugene N. Anderson, 302–21. Chicago: University of Chicago Press, 1938.

Rota, A. "Il codice degli 'statuta Urbis' del 1305 e i caratteri politici della sua riforma." ASRSP 70 (1947): 147–62.

Rowley, George. *Ambrogio Lorenzetti.* 2 vols. Princeton, N.J.: Princeton University Press, 1958.

Rubenstein, Nicolai. "Political Ideas in Sienese Art: The Frescoes by Ambrogio Lorenzetti and Taddeo di Bartolo in the Palazzo Pubblico." *Journal of the Warburg and Courtauld Institutes* 21 (1958): 179–207.

Rusconi, Roberto. "L'Italia senza papa: L'età avignonese e il Grande Scisma d'Occidente." In *Storia dell'Italia religiosa.* Vol. 1, *L'antichità e il medioevo,* edited by André Vauchez, 427–54. Rome: Laterza, 1993.

———. "Spirituali e Fraticelli dell'Italia Centro-orientale." *Picenum Seraphicum* 11 (1974): 7–447.

Russell, Josiah Cox. *Late Ancient and Medieval Population.* Transactions of the American Philosophical Society 43.3. Philadelphia: APS, 1958.

———. *Medieval Regions and Their Cities.* Bloomington: University of Indiana Press, 1972.

Salimei, A. *Senatori e statuti di Roma nel Medio Evo. I senatori, cronologia e bibliografia dal 1144 al 1447.* Rome: Biblioteca d'arte editrice, 1935.

Sanfilippo, Mario. "Dell' Anonimo e della sua e altrui nobilità." *Quaderni medievali* 9 (1980): 121–28.

Sassetti, Angelo Sachetti. "Giacomo della Merca paciere a Rieti." *Archivum Franciscanum Historicum* 50 (1957): 75–82.

Saxl, Fritz. "The Capitol during the Renaissance: A Symbol of the Imperial Idea." In *Lectures,* 200–214. London: Warburg Institute, 1957.

———. "The Classical Inscription in Renaissance Art and Politics." *Journal of the Warburg and Courtauld Institutes* 4 (1940–41): 19–46.

Scaccia-Scarafoni, C. "L'antico statuto del 'Magistri Stratarum.'" ASRSP 50 (1927): 239–308.

Schiaparelli, L. "Alcuni documenti sui 'Magistri aedificiorum urbis' (secoli xiii e xiv)." ASRSP 25 (1902): 5–60.

Schiaparelli, L., and E. Re. "Maestri di Strada." ASRSP 43 (1920): 5–102.

Schimmelpfennig, Bernhard, and Ludwig Schmugge, eds. *Rom im hohen Mittelalter: Studien zu den Romvorstellungen und zur Rompolitik vom 10. bis zum 12. Jahrhundert.* Sigmaringen: Jan Thorbecke Verlag, 1992.

Schmid, Peter. "Rienzo, Cola Di (Nicola di Lorenzo)." *Biographisch-Bibliographisches Kirchenlexikon* 8 (1994): 329–34. http://www.bautz.de/bbkl/r/rienzo_c.shtml.

Schneller, Robert W. *A Survey of Medieval Model Books.* Haarlem: E. F. Bohn, 1963.

Schwarz, Amy. "Images and Illusions of Power in Trecento Art: Cola di Rienzo and the Ancient Roman Republic." Ph.D. diss., State University of New York at Binghamton, 1994.

Seibt, Gustav. *Anonimo romano. Scrivere la storia alle soglie del Rinascimento.* Rome: Viella, 2000. Revised edition, translated by Cristina Colotto and Roberto Delle Donne of *Anonimo romano. Geschichtsschreibung in Rom an der Schwelle zut Renaissance.* Stuttgart: Klett-Cotta, 1992.

Sensi, Mario. "Dossier sui Clareni della Valle Spoletana." *Bibliotheca Franciscana* 1974.

Settimana di storia dell'arte medievale. *Roma anno 1300.* Rome: Bretschneider, 1983.

Settis, Salvatore. "Continuità, distanza, conoscenza. Tre usi dell'antico." In *Memoria dell'antico nell'arte italiana.* Vol. 3, *Dalla tradizione all'archeologia,* edited by Salvatore Settis, 373–486. Biblioteca di Storia dell'Arte. Turin: Einaudi, 1986.

Shaw, Christine. *The Politics of Exile in Renaissance Italy.* Cambridge: Cambridge University Press, 2000.

Sibilia, Salvatore. *La città dei papi.* Rome: Fratelli Palombi, 1939.

Siraisi, Nancy G. *Medieval and Early Renaissance Medicine: An Introduction to Knowledge and Practice.* Chicago: University of Chicago Press, 1990.

Skinner, Quentin. "Ambrogio Lorenzetti: The Artist as Political Philosopher." In Belting and Blume, *Malerei und Stadtkultur in der Dantezeit,* 85–103.

———. *The Foundations of Modern Political Thought.* 2 vols. Cambridge: Cambridge University Press, 1978.

Small, Carola M. "The District of Rome in the Early Fourteenth Century, 1300 to 1347." *Canadian Journal of History/Annales Canadiennes d'Histoire* 16 (1981): 193–213.

Smith, M. Q. "Anagni: An Example of Medieval Typological Decoration." *Papers of the British School at Rome,* n.s. 20 (1965): 1–47.

Smoller, Laura A. "Of Earthquakes, Hail, Frogs, and Geography: Plague and the Investigation of the Apocalypse in the Later Middle Ages." BFLT, 156–87.

Sonnay, Philippe. "La politique artistique de Cola di Rienzo (1313–1354)." *Revue de l'art* 55 (1982): 35–43.

Sordi, Marta. "Cola di Rienzo e le clausole mancanti della 'lex de imperio Vespasiani." In *Studi in onore di Edoardo Volterra,* 2:303–11. Milan: A. Giuffre 1971.

Starn, Randolph. *Ambrogio Lorenzetti: The Palazzo Pubblico, Siena.* New York: George Braziller, 1994.

———. *Contrary Commonwealth: The Theme of Exile in Medieval and Renaissance Italy.* Berkeley and Los Angeles: University of California Press, 1982.

Stickler, A. M. *Il Giubileo di Bonifacio VIII. Aspetti giuridici-pastorali.* Quaderni della Fondazione Camillo Caetani 2. Rome: Fondazione Camillo Caetani, 1977.

Summit, Jennifer. "Topography as Historiography: Petrarch, Chaucer, and the Making of Medieval Rome." *Journal of Medieval and Early Modern Studies* 30 (2000): 211–46.

Surdich, F. "Colonna, Giovanni" [son of Bartolomeo di Giovanni, of Gallicano]. DBI 27:337–38.

Tanturli, Giuliano. "La Cronica di Anonimo romano." *Paragone* 31 (October 1980): 84–93.

Tartaro, Achille. *La letteratura civile e religiosa del Trecento.* Bari: Laterza, 1972.

Temkin, Owsei. *The Falling Sickness: A History of Epilepsy from the Greeks to the Beginnings of Modern Neurology.* Baltimore: Johns Hopkins University Press, 1971.

Thiery, Antonio. "Comunicazione e immagine nella Roma del Giubileo dal concretismo di Francesco d'Assisi al realismo di Giotto." In RRA, 543–51.

Thorndike, Lynn. "Elementary and Secondary Education in the Middle Ages." *Speculum* 15 (1940): 400–408.

Tomassetti, Francesco. "Del sale e focatico del comune di Roma nel medio evo." ASRSP 20 (1897): 313–68.

———. "Torri di Roma." *Capitolium* 1 (1925): 266–77.

Tomassetti, Giuseppe. *La campagna romana antica, medievale, e moderna.* 7 vols. Vols. 5–7, L. Chiumenti and F. Bilanci, eds. Florence: L. S. Olschki, 1979–80.

Toppani, I. "Petrarca, Cola di Rienzo e il mito di Roma." *Atti dell'Istituto Veneto di Scienze, Lettere ed Arti (1976–77)* 85 (1977): 155–72.

Toubert, Pierre. *Les structures du Latium médiéval. Le Latium méridional et la Sabina du IXe a la fin du XIIe siècle.* Bibliotèque des Ecoles françaises d'Athènes et de Rome, fasc. 221. Rome: EFR, 1973.

Touring Club Italiano. *Lazio.* 4th ed. Milan: TCI, 1981.

———. *Roma e dintorni.* 7th ed. Milan: TCI, 1977.

Toynbee, Margaret R. *St. Louis of Toulouse and the Process of Canonization in the Fourteenth Century.* Manchester: Manchester University Press, 1929.

Trease, Geoffrey. *The Condottieri: Soldiers of Fortune.* New York: Holt, Rinehart and Winston, 1971.

Trexler, Richard. "Ritual Behavior in Renaissance Florence: The Setting." *Medievalia et Humanistica,* n.s., 4 (1973): 125–44.

———. *The Spiritual Power: Republican Florence under Interdict.* Leiden: J. Brill, 1974.

Trifone, Pietro. "Aspetti dello stile nominale nella *Cronica* trecentesca di Anonimo romano." *Studi linguistici italiani* 12 (1986): 217–39.

Tuliani, Maurizio. *Osti, avventori e melandrini: Alberghi, locande e taverne a Siena e nel suo contado tra Trecento e Quattrocento.* Siena: Protagon, 1994.

Ullmann, Walter. *The Growth of Papal Government in the Middle Ages.* 3d ed. London: Methuen, 1970, 451–57.

———. *A History of Political Thought in the Middle Ages.* Baltimore: Penguin Books, 1968.

———. *Principles of Government and Politics in the Middle Ages.* London: Methuen, 1961.

Urban, G. "Die Kirchenbaukunst des Quattrocento in Rom." *Römisches Jahrbuch für Kunstgeschichte* 9–10 (1961–62): 73–287.

Valentini, R. "Lo 'Studium Urbis' durante il secolo xiv." ASRSP 67 (1944): 371–89.

Vauchez, André. "Comparsa e affermazione di una religiosità laica (xii secolo-inizio xiv secolo)." In *Storia dell'Italia religiosa.* Vol. 1, *L'Antichità e il medioevo,* 397–425. Rome and Bari: Laterza, 1993.

———. *The Laity in the Middle Ages: Religious Beliefs and Devotional Practices.* Ed. Daniel E. Bornstein. Trans. Margery J. Schneider. Notre Dame, Ind.: University of Notre Dame Press, 1993.

———. "Patronage des saints et religion civique dans l'Italie communale." In *Les laïcs au Moyen Age,* 169–86. Paris: Editions du Cerf, 1987.

———. "Penitenti laici e terziari in Italia nei secoli xiii e xiv." In *Ordini mendicanti e società italiana, xiii–xiv secolo,* 206–20. Milan: A. Mondadori, 1990.

———. "Les théologiens face aux prophéties à l'époque des papes d'Avignon et du Grand Schisme." TPPO, 577–88.

———. "Two Laypersons in Search of Perfection: Elzár of Sabran and Delphine of Pumichel." In *The Laity in the Middle Ages,* 73–82.

———, ed. *Religion civique à l'Epoque médiévale et moderne. Chrétienté et Islam.* Actes de colloque Nanterre 1993. Collection de l'Ecole française de Rome 213. Rome: EFR, 1995.

Vicaire, Marie-Humbert, ed. *La papauté d'Avignon et en Languedoc 1316–1342.* Cahiers de Fanjeaux 26. Toulouse: Privat, 1991.

Vinay, G. "Cola di Rienzo e la crisi dell'universalismo medievale." *Convivium* 2 (1948): 96–107.

Vingtain, Dominique. *Avignon. Le palais des Papes.* St. Léger Vauban: Zodiaque, 1998.

von Auw, Lydia. *Angelo Clareno et les Spirituels Italiens.* Uomini e Dottrine 25. Rome: Storia e letteratura, 1979.

Wagner, David L., ed. *The Seven Liberal Arts in the Middle Ages.* Bloomington: Indiana University Press, 1983.

Wagner, Richard. *Rienzi: Der Letzte der Tribunen.* Premier, Dresden, October 20, 1842.

Waley, Daniel "A Blood-Feud with a Happy Ending: Siena, 1285–1304." In *City and Countryside in Late Medieval and Renaissance Italy: Essays Presented to Philip Jones,* edited by Trevor Dean and Chris Wickham, 45–53. London: Hambledon Press, 1990.

———. "Colonna, Giacomo" [b. c.1250]. DBI 27:311–14.

———. "Colonna, Giacomo, detto Sciarra" [b. c.1250]. DBI 27:314–16.

———. "Colonna, Giovanni" [b. c.1235]. DBI 27:331–33.

———. "Colonna, Pietro" [son of Giovanni di Oddone, b. c.1260]. DBI 27:399–402.

———. "Colonna, Stefano, il Vecchio." DBI 27:433–37.

———. *The Italian City-Republics.* New York: McGraw-Hill, 1978.

Webb, Diana. *Patrons and Defenders: The Saints in the Italian City-State.* International Library of Historical Studies 4. New York: St. Martin's, 1996.

Weider, J. "Cola di Rienzo." In *Karl IV. und sein Kreis Lebensbilder zur Geschichte der bömischen Länder* 3. Ed. F. Seibt. Munich: Oldenbourg, 1978.

Weiss, Roberto. "Barbato da Sulmona, il Petrarca e la rivoluzione di Cola di Rienzo." In *Studi petrarcheschi,* edited by Carlo Calcaterra, 13–22. Bologna: Minerva, 1950.

Weissman, Ronald F. E. "Cults and Contexts: In Search of the Renaissance Confraternity." In Eisenbichler, 201–20.

Wieruszowski, H. "Art and the Commune in the Time of Dante." *Speculum* 19 (1944): 14–33.

Wilkins, Ernest Hatch. *Life of Petrarch.* Chicago: University of Chicago Press, 1963.

Witt, Ronald. "Boncampagno and the Defense of Rhetoric." *Journal of Medieval and Renaissance Studies* 16.1 (1986): 1–31.

——. "Brunetto Latini and the Italian Tradition of *Ars dictaminis.*" *Stanford Italian Review* 3 (1983): 5–24.

——. *In the Footsteps of the Ancients: The Origins of Humanism from Lovato to Bruni.* Studies in Medieval and Reformation Thought 74. Leiden: Brill, 2000.

——. "Medieval 'Ars Dictaminis' and the Beginnings of Humanism: A New Construction of the Problem." *Renaissance Quarterly* 35 (1982): 1–35.

Wollesen, Jens. T. "'Ut poesis pictura?' Problems of Images and Texts in the Early Trecento." In *Petrarch's Triumphs: Allegory and Spectacle,* edited by Konrad Eisenbichler and Amilcare A. Iannucci, 183–210. University of Toronto Italian Studies 4. Ottawa: Dovehouse Editions, 1990.

Wood, Diana. *Clement VI: The Pontificate and Ideas of an Avignon Pope.* Cambridge: Cambridge University Press, 1989.

Wright, Rosemary Muir. *Art and Antichrist in Medieval Europe.* Manchester: Manchester University Press, 1995.

Zacour, Norman P. "Petrarch and Talleyrand." *Speculum* 31 (1956): 683–703.

——. *Talleyrand, the Cardinal of Perigord (1301–1364).* Transactions of the American Philosophical Society, n.s., 50:7 Philadelphia: APS, 1960.

Zeigler, Joseph. *Medicine and Religion c. 1300: The Case of Arnau of Vilanova.* New York: Oxford: Clarendon, 1998.

Zeigler, Philip. *The Black Death.* Harmondsworth: Penguin Books, 1975.

Zeller, Jacques S. *Les tribuns et les révolutions en Italie.* Paris: Didier, 1874.

Zorzi, Andrea. "Rituali di violenza, cerimoniali penali, rappresentazioni della giustizia nelle città italiane centro-settentrionali (secoli xiii–xv)." In CFP, 395–425.

Index

Charlemagne, 25, 46

Charles, duke of Durazzo, 166, 167, 168

Charles Martel, heir of Giovanna I, 167

Charles Martel, king of Hungary, 166

Charles of Anjou, 77, 242

Charles of Calabria, 79, 166

Charles of Moravia. *See* Charles IV, emperor

Charles the Bald, 145

Charles V, emperor, 51

Charles V, of France, 274, 275

Charles IV, emperor, 1, 27, 43, 115, 268, 269, 288; in Burdach's thought, 12; and Clement VI, 273, 278, 283, 300, 303; and Cola, 43, 139, 276–77, 282, 290; and Cola's summons to Rome, 181, 186, 285; coronation in Rome, 273, 277, 289, 329, 330, 346; and dislike of war, 273; and Hungary, 168; and Italy, 270, 271, 281; letters to Cola, 282; letters to Petrarch, 272; and Lewis of Bavaria, 273; and papacy, 271; and Petrarch, 272, 279; portraits and appearance of, 275; and Prague, 272; thought and reputation of, 270–75, 277–78, 282–83

Charles IV, of France, 270

Charles II of Naples, 166, 281

Charlus, Hugue de, 300

chiliasm, 119

chivalric romances, 179, 289

Chotiis, Cochetus de, 211; on Cola, 178, 183, 185, 232; relation to Cosecchi (Tosetti), 234; on Roman diplomacy, 162; on Roman Synod, 184, 188–89; on Vetralla campaign, 199, 201

Christ, 51; of Apocalypse, 48, 119, 127, 275; and papal powers, 66, 71; child, 49; child of *ara coeli,* 325; in Joachite concordances, 282, 285; miracles of, 117; Mystical Body of, 283; in salvation history, 46, 47; in Spiritual ecclesiology, 61, 87, 128, 236, 284, 285; temptations of, 117; victory over paganism, 125

Chronicon Estense, 44; on barons' arrest, 210; on barons' plot against Cola, 207, 216, 221; on Black Death, 256; on Cola in Prague, 276–77; on Cola's coronation, 185; on fall of *buono stato,* 245–48, 252; on Janni di Vico, 201; on Pentecost revolution, 141; on Porta S.

Lorenzo, 222, 225; on Roman Synod, 184

Chronicon Mutinense, 176

church fathers, 62, 74

Cicero, 62; in Anonimo romano, 3; on ballots, 187; in Clement VI, 62; in Cola, 34; *De inventione,* 37; *De republica,* 148; in medieval curriculum, 37; in Petrarch, 53; as prophet, 289; on *status,* 148

Cimabue, 49

Cimita di Castello, 259

Ciociaria, 201

Città di Castello, 333

civic religion, 116, 145, 153

Civitavecchia, 195, 201, 253, 254, 314

Clareno, Angelo, 88, 121, 122, 124, 259, 268, 285

Clariss Order, 252, 297

Clement V, 60, 61, 87, 137, 138

Clement IV, 77

Clement VI, 43, 160, 308; and Albornoz, 313; and barons, 233, 244, 323; and Black Death, 256; career, 61, 240; character and personality, 61–62, 65–66, 81, 190, 303, 307; and Charles IV, 273; and Cola's knighting, 179; on Cola's origins, 27; and Commission on Rome's reform, 288; court and ceremonial, 62–63, 73, 262, 336; crusade plans, 72; death of, 307–8; *desidero videre vos,* 72; and destabilization of *buono stato,* 232–33, 236; and di Vico, 196, 314–15; election and coronation, 61, 138, 262; excommunicates Cola, 241; expenditures, 309; and Giovanna I, 168; intellectual interests, 62, 65; and Jews, 256; and Jubilee of 1350, 71–72, 171–72, 191, 238, 242, 250, 260–61, 323; and Marseilles galley, 156; and mercenaries, 238, 239, 244, 319; and Naples, 77, 79, 167–68, 191; New Palace, 62, 65, 274; papal rule of Rome, 72, 75–77, 80, 82, 168, 171, 207, 236; papal supremacy, 66–67, 72; patronage of arts, 62, 65; plans Cola's capture, 259–60, 283, 299–300; plans Cola's downfall, 190–92, 215, 235; policy toward Rome, 66, 67, 74, 83, 135, 170, 179, 189, 329; posthumous reputation, 307; and Orsini, 195, 239, 240; and repairs to Roman churches,

Palazzo del Podestà (Bargello), 107; Pazzi conspirators, 155; and Petrarch, 54; *pitture infamanti,* 108, 109; population, c.1340, 25, 146; and Roman Synod, 183; Venturino da Bergamo, OP, 123; War of the Eight Saints, 242

focatico. See taxes: hearth *(focatico)*

Foligno, 161, 244

Fondi, 203. *See also* Caetani: Nicola, count of Fondi

Fonti per la storia d'Italia, 10

Forlì, 162

Formello, 195

Fortifiocca, Tomaso, 4, 103

Foucault, Michel, 154

Fragmenta Historiae romanae, 16

France, 1, 72, 136; diplomacy with Rome, 169; Hundred Years' War, 161, 261, 273; and Jubilee of 1350, 262; papal travels in, 60; Parliament of Paris, 308

Francesco: Cola's brother, 292; Livia's father, 42

Francesco da Firenze, 65

Franchi, Pandolfuccio di Guido di Pandolfo de', 164, 338, 341, 344

Franciscan Order, 48; Conventuals, 121; Joachimism, 121, 148, 259; of Rome, 334; Spirituals, 20, 61, 87, 121–22, 124, 138, 242, 257, 259, 283, 285, 297, 309

Francis of Assisi, 108, 113, 121, 128, 267, 282

Francis of Prague, 281

Frangipane family, 50, 85, 335; Petruccio, 222

Frascati, 335

Fraticelli, 258, 309. *See also* Franciscan Order: Spirituals

Frederick I, emperor, 48

Frederick II, emperor, 49, 110, 242

Frederick II, of Sicily, 149

French Revolution, 8

fresco. *See* painting

Froissart, Jean, 62

Frosinone, 206

Frugoni, A., 16

funerals. *See* ritual: funeral

gabelle. See taxes: *gabelle*

Gabii, 331

Gabrielli, Annibale, 10, 12

Gaeta, 161, 164, 165, 203, 205–6, 254

Gagigariis, Buccio de, 225

Galvano de Levanto, 293

Ganelluçio, Folcheto, 245; Jacobello, 245

Gano, Cristofano di, 44

Ganshof, François, *The Middle Ages: A History of International Relations,* 16

Garibaldi, Giuseppe, 9

Gatti, 196

Gavignano, 93

Genoa, 25, 202, 203, 240, 255

George, St., 139

German empire, 270; and Black Death, 256; claims to Provence, 60; elections and electors, 160, 176, 177, 181, 186–88, 237, 271, 273, 276–77, 287–88, 299, 317; emperor of, 1, 187; and Jubilee of 1350, 262; and Revolution of 1848, 8

Gesso, Buccio de, 225

Ghibelline Party, 96, 280, 314, 317

Ghiselberti, A. M., 16, 19

Giacomo, Maestro, 35

Giacomo, prior of S. Spirito in Sassia, 185, 186

Giangreco, Thomas, 20, 359n12

Gianni, ambassador of di Vico, 200

Gibbon, Edward, 8; *History of the Decline and Fall of the Roman Empire,* 5–6

Gilio Conchese di Spagna. *See* Albornoz, Giles

Ginnazzano, 206

Giotto di Bodone, 49, 110, 125; influence of, 65, 227; in Naples, 107, 108; Navicella mosaic, 49, 110–12, 117; in Rome, 110; Scrovegni (Arena) Chapel, 153; St. Peter's altarpiece, 110

Giovanetti, Matteo, 65

Giovanna I of Naples, 43, 79, 245, 266, 319; accession, 77, 79, 166; and Andrew of Hungary, 79, 167, 168; and Angevin coup, 167; and Caetani, 203, 205; and Clement VI, 167; flight from Naples, 254; and Great Company, 319; and Lewis of Hungary, 320; and Louis of Taranto, 260; and papacy, 167, 216; produces heir, 167; receives Golden Rose at Avignon, 64; and Roman diplomacy, 162, 168, 220; sells Avignon to papacy, 303; sexual rumors around, 167

Giovanni, bishop of Spoleto, 300

Giovanni da Lucca, 65

Giovanni d'Arezzo, 65

Giovanni de Randazzo, 149, 153

Giovanni Ser Gilii, 228

Compositor: Integrated Composition Systems, Inc.
Text: 10/13 Galliard
Display: Galliard
Printer and binder: Friesen Corporation